Lecture Notes in Computer Science 14801

Founding Editors

Gerhard Goos, Germany
Juris Hartmanis, USA

Editorial Board Members

Elisa Bertino, USA
Wen Gao, China

Bernhard Steffen, Germany
Moti Yung, USA

Advanced Research in Computing and Software Science
Subline of Lecture Notes in Computer Science

Subline Series Editors

Giorgio Ausiello, *University of Rome 'La Sapienza', Italy*
Vladimiro Sassone, *University of Southampton, UK*

Subline Advisory Board

Susanne Albers, *TU Munich, Germany*
Benjamin C. Pierce, *University of Pennsylvania, USA*
Bernhard Steffen, *University of Dortmund, Germany*
Deng Xiaotie, *Peking University, Beijing, China*
Jeannette M. Wing, *Microsoft Research, Redmond, WA, USA*

More information about this series at https://link.springer.com/bookseries/558

Jesus Carretero · Sameer Shende ·
Javier Garcia-Blas · Ivona Brandic ·
Katzalin Olcoz · Martin Schreiber
Editors

Euro-Par 2024: Parallel Processing

30th European Conference on Parallel and Distributed Processing
Madrid, Spain, August 26–30, 2024
Proceedings, Part I

Editors
Jesus Carretero
University Carlos III of Madrid
Madrid, Madrid, Spain

Javier Garcia-Blas
University Carlos III of Madrid
Madrid, Spain

Katzalin Olcoz
Universidad Complutense de Madrid
Madrid, Spain

Sameer Shende
University of Oregon
Eugene, OR, USA

Ivona Brandic
TU Wien
Vienna, Austria

Martin Schreiber
Université Grenoble Alpes
Saint Martin d'Hères, France

ISSN 0302-9743 ISSN 1611-3349 (electronic)
Lecture Notes in Computer Science
ISBN 978-3-031-69576-6 ISBN 978-3-031-69577-3 (eBook)
https://doi.org/10.1007/978-3-031-69577-3

© The Editor(s) (if applicable) and The Author(s), under exclusive license to Springer Nature Switzerland AG 2024

Chapter "Efficient Code Region Characterization Through Automatic Performance Counters Reduction Using Machine Learning Techniques" is licensed under the terms of the Creative Commons Attribution 4.0 International License (http://creativecommons.org/licenses/by/4.0/). For further details see license information in the chapter.

This work is subject to copyright. All rights are solely and exclusively licensed by the Publisher, whether the whole or part of the material is concerned, specifically the rights of translation, reprinting, reuse of illustrations, recitation, broadcasting, reproduction on microfilms or in any other physical way, and transmission or information storage and retrieval, electronic adaptation, computer software, or by similar or dissimilar methodology now known or hereafter developed.

The use of general descriptive names, registered names, trademarks, service marks, etc. in this publication does not imply, even in the absence of a specific statement, that such names are exempt from the relevant protective laws and regulations and therefore free for general use.

The publisher, the authors and the editors are safe to assume that the advice and information in this book are believed to be true and accurate at the date of publication. Neither the publisher nor the authors or the editors give a warranty, expressed or implied, with respect to the material contained herein or for any errors or omissions that may have been made. The publisher remains neutral with regard to jurisdictional claims in published maps and institutional affiliations.

This Springer imprint is published by the registered company Springer Nature Switzerland AG
The registered company address is: Gewerbestrasse 11, 6330 Cham, Switzerland

If disposing of this product, please recycle the paper.

Preface

This book constitutes one of the three volumes of the proceedings of the 30th International Conference on Parallel and Distributed Computing, Euro-Par 2024, held in Madrid, Spain, in August 2024. The 30th edition of Euro-Par was organized by the Department of Computer Science and Engineering at the University Carlos III of Madrid. Euro-Par is the prime European conference covering all aspects of parallel and distributed processing, ranging from theory to practice, from small to the largest parallel and distributed systems and infrastructures, from fundamental computational problems to full-fledged applications, from architecture, compiler, language and interface design and implementation, to tools, support infrastructures, and application performance aspects.

For over 25 years, Euro-Par has consistently brought together researchers in parallel and distributed computing. Founded by pioneers as a merger of the three thematically related European conference series PARLE and CONPAR-VAPP, Euro-Par started with the aim to create the main annual scientific event on parallel and distributed computing in Europe and to be the primary choice of professionals for the presentation of their latest results. Since its inception, Euro-Par has covered all aspects of parallel and distributed computing, ranging from theory to practice, scaling from the smallest to the largest parallel and distributed systems, from fundamental computational problems and models to full-fledged applications, from architecture and interface design and implementation to tools, infrastructures and applications. Over time, Euro-Par has forged a community that follows the latest developments in the field while bringing together a broad and diverse audience, supporting young researchers and promoting networking across borders. Previous conference editions took place in Stockholm, Lyon, Passau, Southampton, Toulouse, Munich, Manchester, Paderborn, Klagenfurt, Pisa, Lisbon, Dresden, Rennes, Las Palmas, Delft, Ischia, Bordeaux, Rhodes, Aachen, Porto, Vienna, Grenoble, Santiago de Compostela, Turin, Göttingen, Warsaw, Lisbon, Glasgow, and Limassol.

Euro-Par's unique organization into topics provides an excellent forum for focused technical discussion, as well as interaction with a large, broad and diverse audience. See https://2024.euro-par.org/ for more info. Euro-Par 2024 accepted papers in the following 6 tracks:

- Programming, Compilers and Performance
- Scheduling, Resource Management, Cloud, Edge Computing and Workflows
- Architectures and Accelerators
- Data Analytics, AI and Computational Science
- Theory and Algorithms
- Multidisciplinary, Domain-Specific and Applied Parallel and Distributed Computing

A total of 309 full papers were submitted by authors from 52 different countries. The number of submitted papers, the range of topics, and the requirement to obtain high-quality reviews mandated careful selection using a large pool of experts. The chairs along with 144 members of the program committee produced a total of 1236 single-blind reviews, an average of about 4 reviews per paper. The accepted papers were selected in a two-phase process. Following initial discussion, each track proposed sets of papers for acceptance, further discussion or rejection. The papers from all tracks were reviewed and discussed in an online selection meeting on April 2024. The outcome was to select 88 papers to be presented at the conference and published in these proceedings, a 29% acceptance rate. Six of the accepted papers were selected to be presented in a plenary session and compete for the Euro-Par 2024 best paper award, which was generously sponsored by Springer. The six papers were:

1. Milo Lurati, Stijn Heldens, Alessio Sclocco, Ben van Werkhoven. Bringing Autotuning to HIP: Analysis of Tuning Impact and Difficulty on AMD and Nvidia GPUs.
2. Olivier Beaumont, Rémi Bouzel, Lionel Eyraud-Dubois, Esragul Korkmaz, Laercio Pilla, Alexandre Van Kempen. A 1.25(1+e)-Approximation Algorithm for Scheduling with Rejection Costs Proportional to Processing Times.
3. Hamidreza Ramezanikebrya, Matei Ripeanu. (Re)assessing PiM Effectiveness for Sequence Alignment.
4. Thorsten Wittkopp, Philipp Wiesner, Odej Kao. LogRCA: Log-Based Root Cause Analysis for Distributed Services.
5. Kåre von Geijer, Philippas Tsigas. How to Relax Instantly: Elastic Relaxation of Concurrent Data Structures.
6. Richard Angersbach, Sebastian Kuckuk, Harald Köstler. Code Generation for Octree-Based Multigrid Solvers with Fused Higher-Order Interpolation and Communication.

To increase reproducibility of the research appearing at Euro-Par, the conference encourages authors to submit artifacts, such as source code, data sets and reproducibility instructions. In the notification of acceptance authors were encouraged to submit artifacts for evaluation. A total of 17 artifacts were submitted in support of accepted papers and evaluated by the Artifact Evaluation Committee (AEC). The AEC successfully reproduced results for 14 artifacts. These papers are marked in the proceedings by a special stamp and the artifacts are available online in the Zenodo repository (https://zenodo.org/communities/europar_2024). Selected artifacts will also be published in a Euro-Par special issue of the Journal of Open Source Software.

In addition to the technical program, we had the pleasure of hosting three distinguished keynote talks by:

- Mateo Valero, Barcelona Supercomputing Center, Spain
- Franck Capello. Argonne Labs, USA
- Ilkay Altintas, San Diego Supercomputing Center, USA

Euro-Par 2024 started with two days of workshops, a tutorial and a PhD symposium, and was followed by three days dedicated to the main conference sessions. A poster and demo session ran alongside the main conference. Silvina Caino and Demetris

Zeinalipour coordinated the workshops as workshop co-chairs. Ester Martín and Leonel Sousa coordinated the PhD Symposium. David E. Singh and Thaleia Doudall coordinated the poster and demo session. A selection of the papers presented at the workshops are published in separate Springer LNCS volumes. Contributions presented at the PhD symposium and the poster session are also published in the same volume.

In 2024 edition, the proceedings of the conference are printed in three volumes: LNCS 14801, LNCS 14802 and LNCS 14803. This volume, LNCS 14801, includes papers related to tracks:

- Programming, Compilers and Performance
- Scheduling, Resource Management, Cloud, Edge Computing and Workflows

We would like to thank the authors, chairs, PC members, and reviewers for contributing to the success of Euro-Par 2024. Similarly, we would like to extend our appreciation to the Euro-Par Steering Committee for its support.

August 2024

Jesus Carretero
Sameer Shende
Javier Garcia-Blas
Ivona Brandic
Katzalin Olcoz
Martin Schreiber

Organization

General Chairs

Jesus Carretero	University Carlos III of Madrid, Spain
Sameer Shende	University of Oregon, USA

Program Chairs

Javier Garcia-Blas	University Carlos III of Madrid, Spain
Ivona Brandic	TU Wien, Austria

Workshop Chairs

Silvina Caino-Lores	Inria, France
Demetris Zeinalipour	University of Cyprus, Cyprus

PhD Symposium Chairs

Leonel Sousa	INESC-ID, IST, Universidade de Lisboa, Portugal
Gracia Ester Martín Garzón	University of Almeria, Spain

Posters and Demos Chairs

David E. Singh	University Carlos III of Madrid, Spain
Thaleia Dimitra Doudali	IMDEA Software Institute, Spain

Publicity Chairs

Diego R. Llanos	University of Valladolid, Spain
Siddhartha Jana	INTEL, USA
Maciej Cytowski	Pawsey Supercomputing Research Centre, Australia
Carlos Jaime Barrios	Universidad de Santander, Colombia

Industrial Chairs

Krzysztof Rzadca	University of Warsaw, Poland
Jesus Escudero Sahuquillo	University of Castilla-La Mancha, Spain

Women in HPC Chairs

Marta Garcia-Gasulla	Barcelona Supercomputing Center, Spain
Sarah Neuwirth	Johannes Gutenberg University Mainz, Germany

Publication Chairs

Katzalin Olcoz   Universidad Complutense de Madrid, Spain
Martin Schreiber   University of Grenoble Alpes/Inria, France

Local Chair

Felix Garcia-Carballeira   University Carlos III of Madrid, Spain

Finance Chair

Javier Fernandez Muñoz   University Carlos III of Madrid, Spain

Web Chairs

Alejandro Calderon   University Carlos III of Madrid, Spain
Alberto Cascajo   University Carlos III of Madrid, Spain

Steering Committee

Fernando Silva (SC Chair)   University of Porto, Portugal
Dora Blanco Heras   University of Santiago de Compostela, Spain
  (Vice-chair)
Christos Kaklamanis   Computer Technology Institute, Greece
Demetris Zeinalipour   University of Cyprus, Cyprus
  (Workshops Chair)
Ewa Deelman   University of South California, USA
Felix Wolf (Web Chair)   Technical University of Darmstadt, Germany
Francisco Fernández Rivera   University of Santiago de Compostela, Spain
George Papadopoulos   University of Cyprus, Cyprus
Henk Sips (Finances Chair)   Delft University of Technology, Netherlands
Ivona Brandić   Technical University of Wien, Austria
Jesus Carretero   University Carlos III, Madrid, Spain
Krzysztof Rzadca   University of Warsaw, Poland
  (Industrial Session
  Co-chair)
Leonel Sousa (PhD   University of Lisbon, Portugal
  Symposium Co-chair)
Maciej Malawski   AGH University of Science and Technology, Poland
  (Publicity Co-chair)
Marco Aldinucci   University of Turin, Italy
  (EU Strategy Chair)
Massimo Torquati   University of Pisa, Italy
  (Artifacts Co-chair)
Phil Trinder   University of Glasgow, UK
Ramin Yahyapour   GWDG, Germany

Rosa M. Badia   Barcelona Supercomputing Center, Spain
Tomàs Margalef   University Autonoma of Barcelona, Spain
Wolfgang Nagel   Dresden University of Technology, Germany

Honorary Members

Christian Lengauer   University of Passau, Germany
Luc Bougé   ENS Rennes, France
Ron Perrott   Oxford e-Research Centre, UK
Karl Dieter Reinartz   University of Erlangen-Nürnberg, Germany

Scientific Organization

Track 1: Programming, Compilers and Performance

Chairs
Stefano Markidis   KTH Royal Institute of Technology, Sweden
Cristina Silvano   Politecnico di Milano, Italy

Program Committee
Michela Becchi   North Carolina State University, USA
Siegfried Benkner   University of Vienna, Austria
Jean-Baptiste Besnard   Paratools, France
Walter Binder   University of Lugano, Switzerland
Bruno Bodin   University of Edinburgh, UK
Joao Cardoso   University of Porto, Portugal
Paul Carpenter   Barcelona Supercomputing Center, Spain
Jeronimo Castrillon   TU Dresden, Germany
Brad Chamberlain   Hewlett Packard Enterprise, USA
Serena Curzel   Politecnico di Milano, Italy
Tom Deakin   University of Bristol, UK
Bernhard Egger   Seoul National University, South Korea
R. Govindarajan   Indian Institute of Science, India
Giulia Guidi   Cornell University, USA
Georg Hager   Erlangen Regional Computing Center, Germany
Abhinav Jangda   Microsoft Research, USA
Seyong Lee   Oak Ridge National Laboratory, USA
Lucas Mello Schnorr   UFRGS, Brazil
Ivy Peng   KTH Royal Institute of Technology, USA
Istvan Reguly   Pázmány Péter Catholic University, Hungary
Bernhard Scholz   University of Sydney, Australia
Giuseppe Tagliavini   University of Bologna, Italy
Nathan Tallent   Pacific Northwest National Laboratory, USA
Miwako Tsuji   RIKEN R-CCS, Japan
Antonino Tumeo   Pacific Northwest National Laboratory, USA
Didem Unat   Koç University, USA
Hans Vandierendonck   Queen's University Belfast, UK

Ana Lucia Varbanescu	University of Amsterdam, Netherlands
Veronica Vergara Larrea	Oak Ridge National Laboratory, USA
Sotirios Xydis	National Technical University of Athens, Greece

Track 2. Scheduling, Resource Management, Cloud, Edge Computing, and Workflows

Chairs

Luiz Fernando Bittencour	University of Campinas, Brazil
Anne Benoit	ENS Lyon, France

Program Committee

Marco Aldinucci	University of Turin, Italy
Atakan Aral	University of Vienna, Austria
Luciana Arantes	Sorbonne University, France
Danilo Ardagna	Politecnico di Milano, Italy
Marcos Assuncao	ETS Montreal, Canada
Muhammad Ajmal Azad	Birmingham City University England, UK
Olivier Beaumont	Inria, France
Rob Bisseling	Utrecht University, Netherlands
Edson Borin	University of Campinas, Brazil
Francisco Brasileiro	UFCG, Brazil
Rodrigo N. Calheiros	Western Sydney University, Australia
Valeria Cardellini	University of Roma "Tor Vergata", Italy
Harold Castro	Universidad de Los Andes, Colombia
Antonio Celesti	Department of MIFT, University of Messina, Italy
Daniel Cordeiro	University of São Paulo, Brazil
Anthony Danalis	University of Tennessee, USA
Marios Dikaiakos	University of Cyprus, Cyprus
Ciprian Dobre	Politehnica Bucharest, Romania
Pierre-Francois Dutot	Université Grenoble Alpes, France
Rafael Ferreira da Silva	Oak Ridge National Laboratory, USA
Felix Freitag	Universitat Politècnica de Catalunya, Spain
Alfredo Goldman	University of São Paulo, Brazil
Carlos Guerrero	Universitat de les Illes Balears, Spain
Sascha Hunold	Faculty of Informatics, TU Wien, Austria
Nectarios Koziris	National Technical University of Athens, Greece
Johannes Langguth	Simula Research Laboratory, Norway
Marco Lapegna	University of Naples Federico II, Italy
Laurent Lefevre	Inria, France
Jiajia Li	NCSU, USA
Maciej Malawski	AGH University of Science and Technology, Poland
Anirban Mandal	Renaissance Computing Institute, USA
Zoltan Mann	University of Amsterdam, Netherlands
Loris Marchal	CNRS, France
Alba Cristina M. A. Melo	University of Brasilia (UnB), Brazil

Dimitrios Nikolopoulos	Virginia Tech, USA
Katzalin Olcoz	Universidad Complutense de Madrid, Spain
Carla Osthoff Barros	National Laboratory for Scientific Computing LNCC, Brazil
Guillaume Pallez	Inria, France
Nikela Papadopoulou	University of Glasgow, UK
Fanny Pascual	Sorbonne Université, France
Radu Prodan	University of Klagenfurt, Austria
Veronika Rehn-Sonigo	FEMTO-ST, France
Jason Riedy	AMD, USA
Silvio Rizzi	Argonne National Laboratory, USA
Krzysztof Rzadca	University of Warsaw, Poland
Uwe Schwiegelshohn	TU Dortmund University, Germany
Oliver Sinnen	University of Auckland, New Zealand
Jacopo Soldani	University of Pisa, Italy
Dante Sánchez-Gallegos	Universidad Carlos III de Madrid, Spain
Javid Taheri	Karlstad University, Sweden
Andrei Tchernykh	CICESE Research Center, Mexico
Carlos A. Varela	Rensselaer Polytechnic Institute, USA
Massimo Villari	University of Messina, Italy
Frédéric Vivien	Inria, France
Vladimir Vlassov	KTH Royal Institute of Technology, Sweden
Ramin Yahyapour	GWDG - University of Göttingen, Germany
Taylan Özden	Technical University of Darmstadt, Germany

Artifacts Evaluation

Chairs

Massimo Torquati	University of Pisa, Italy
Francisco D. Igual	Universidad Complutense de Madrid, Spain

Artifacts Evaluation Committee

Valerio Besozzi	University of Pisa, Italy
Adrián Castelló	Universitat Politècnica de València, Spain
Luis M. Costero	Universidad Complutense de Madrid, Spain
Daniele De Sensi	Sapienza University of Rome, Italy
Manuel F. Dolz	Universitat Jaume I de Castelló, Spain
Javier Garcia Blas	University Carlos III of Madrid, Spain
Carlos García	Universidad Complutense de Madrid, Spain
Giulio Malenza	University of Turin, Italy
Iker Martín Álvarez	Universitat Jaume I de Castelló, Spain
Panagiotis Mpakos	NTUA Athens, Greece
Javier Fernandez Muñoz	University Carlos III of Madrid, Spain

Ricardo Nobre   INESC-ID, Instituto Superior Técnico, Universidade de
                     Lisboa, Portugal
Alberto Ottimo   University of Pisa, Italy
Nicolò Tonci   University of Pisa, Italy

Sponsors

Contents – Part I

Programming, Compilers and Performance

FlexiGran: Flexible Granularity Locking in Hierarchies 3
  Anju Mongandampulath Akathoott and Rupesh Nasre

Efficient Code Region Characterization Through Automatic Performance
Counters Reduction Using Machine Learning Techniques 18
  *Suren Harutyunyan, Eduardo César, Anna Sikora, Jiří Filipovič,
  Akash Dutta, Ali Jannesari, and Jordi Alcaraz*

ESIMD GPU Implementations of Deep Learning Sparse Matrix Kernels 33
  Mohammad Zubair and Christoph Bauinger

Deconstructing HPL-MxP Benchmark: A Numerical Perspective 47
  Greg Henry, Eric Petit, Alexander Lyashevsky, and Peter Caday

ImageMap: Enabling Efficient Mapping from Image Processing DSL
to CGRA 61
  Bizhao Shi, Tuo Dai, Sunan Zou, Xinming Wei, and Guojie Luo

Predicting GPU Kernel's Performance on Upcoming Architectures 77
  *Lucas Van Lanker, Hugo Taboada, Elisabeth Brunet,
  and François Trahay*

Bringing Auto-Tuning to HIP: Analysis of Tuning Impact and Difficulty
on AMD and Nvidia GPUs 91
  Milo Lurati, Stijn Heldens, Alessio Sclocco, and Ben van Werkhoven

A Mechanism to Generate Interception Based Tools for HPC Libraries 107
  Bengisu Elis, David Boehme, Olga Pearce, and Martin Schulz

OMPGPT: A Generative Pre-trained Transformer Model for OpenMP 121
  *Le Chen, Arijit Bhattacharjee, Nesreen Ahmed, Niranjan Hasabnis,
  Gal Oren, Vy Vo, and Ali Jannesari*

**Scheduling, Resource Management, Cloud, Edge Computing,
and Workflows**

Scheduling Distributed I/O Resources in HPC Systems 137
  Alexis Bandet, Francieli Boito, and Guillaume Pallez

Light-Weight Prediction for Improving Energy Consumption in HPC
Platforms.. 152
    *Danilo Carastan-Santos, Georges Da Costa, Millian Poquet,
Patricia Stolf, and Denis Trystram*

EKRM: Efficient Key-Value Retrieval Method to Reduce Data Lookup
Overhead for Redis... 166
    *Yiming Yao, Xiaolin Wang, Diyu Zhou, Liujia Li, Jianyu Wu, Liren Zhu,
Zhenlin Wang, and Yingwei Luo*

Automated Data Management and Learning-Based Scheduling for
Ray-Based Hybrid HPC-Cloud Systems............................ 180
    *Tingkai Liu, Huili Tao, Yicheng Lu, Zhongbo Zhu, Marquita Ellis,
Sara Kokkila-Schumacher, and Volodymyr Kindratenko*

Solving the Restricted Assignment Problem to Schedule Multi-get
Requests in Key-Value Stores.................................. 195
    Louis-Claude Canon, Anthony Dugois, and Loris Marchal

PriCE: Privacy-Preserving and Cost-Effective Scheduling for Parallelizing
the Large Medical Image Processing Workflow over Hybrid Clouds 210
    *Yuandou Wang, Neel Kanwal, Kjersti Engan, Chunming Rong,
Paola Grosso, and Zhiming Zhao*

A $1.25(1 + \epsilon)$-Approximation Algorithm for Scheduling with Rejection
Costs Proportional to Processing Times 225
    *Olivier Beaumont, Rémi Bouzel, Lionel Eyraud-Dubois,
Esragul Korkmaz, Laercio Pilla, and Alexandre Van Kempen*

DProbe: Profiling and Predicting Multi-tenant Deep Learning Workloads
for GPU Resource Scaling 239
    *Zechun Zhou, Jingwei Sun, Hengquan Mei, Peng Sun,
and Guangzhong Sun*

sAirflow: Adopting Serverless in a Legacy Workflow Scheduler........... 254
    Filip Mikina, Pawel Zuk, and Krzysztof Rzadca

Hurry: Dynamic Collaborative Framework For Low-Orbit
Mega-Constellation Data Downloading 269
    *Handong Luo, Wenhao Liu, Qi Zhang, Ziheng Yang, Quanwei Lin,
Wenjun Zhu, Kun Qiu, Zhe Chen, and Yue Gao*

Optimizing Service Replication and Placement for IoT Applications in Fog
Computing Systems... 283
    Farah Ait-Salaht, Maher Rebai, and Nora Izri

Deadline-Driven Enhancements and Response Time Analysis of ROS2
Multi-threaded Executors 298
    Zhengda Wu, Yixiao Feng, Mingtai Lv, Sining Yang, and Bo Zhang

Efficient Coupling Streaming AI and Ensemble Simulations on HPC
Clusters 313
    *Jiazhi Jiang, Hongbin Zhang, Deyin Liu, Jiangsu Du, Xiaojiao Yao,
    Jinhui Wei, Pin Chen, Dan Huang, and Yutong Lu*

Context-Aware Runtime Type Prediction for Heterogeneous Microservices ... 329
    Yibing Lin, Binbin Feng, and Zhijun Ding

Makespan Minimization for Scheduling on Heterogeneous Platforms
with Precedence Constraints 343
    Vincent Fagnon, Giorgio Lucarelli, and Christophe Rapine

Node Bundle Scheduling: An Ultra-low Latency Traffic Scheduling
Algorithm for TAS-Based Time-Sensitive Networks 357
    Qian Yang, Xuyan Jiang, Wei Quan, Rulin Liu, and Zhigang Sun

Towards High-performance Transactions via Hierarchical Blockchain
Sharding 373
    *Haibo Tang, Huan Zhang, Zhenyu Zhang, Zhao Zhang, Cheqing Jin,
    and Aoying Zhou*

Resource-Aware Heterogeneous Federated Learning with Specialized
Local Models 389
    Sixing Yu, J. Pablo Muñoz, and Ali Jannesari

Author Index 405

Contents – Part II

Architectures and Accelerators

Efficient RNIC Cache Side-Channel Attack Detection Through
DPU-Driven Architecture 3
   Yunkun Liao, Jingya Wu, Wenyan Lu, Xiaowei Li, and Guihai Yan

Parallel Writing of Nested Data in Columnar Formats 18
   Jonas Hahnfeld, Jakob Blomer, and Thorsten Kollegger

FakeGuard: Novel Architecture Support for Deepfake Detection Networks 32
   Xingbin Wang, Dan Meng, Rui Hou, and Yan Wang

Exploring Processor Micro-architectures Optimised for BLAS3
Micro-kernels 47
   Stepan Nassyr and Dirk Pleiter

Fault Tolerant in the Expand Ad-Hoc Parallel File System 62
   *Dario Muñoz-Muñoz, Felix Garcia-Carballeira,
   Diego Camarmas-Alonso, Alejandro Calderon-Mateos,
   and Jesus Carretero*

ImSPU: Implicit Sharing of Computation Resources Between Vector
and Scalar Processing Units 77
   *Hongbing Tan, Xiaowei He, Guichu Sun, Liquan Xiao, Yuanhu Cheng,
   Jing Zhang, Zhong Zheng, Quan Deng, Bingcai Sui, Yongwen Wang,
   and Libo Huang*

ADE-HGNN: Accelerating HGNNs Through Attention Disparity
Exploitation 91
   *Dengke Han, Meng Wu, Runzhen Xue, Mingyu Yan, Xiaochun Ye,
   and Dongrui Fan*

Watt: A Write-Optimized RRAM-Based Accelerator for Attention 107
   *Xuan Zhang, Zhuoran Song, Xing Li, Zhezhi He, Naifeng Jing, Li Jiang,
   and Xiaoyao Liang*

Optimizing Communication for Latency Sensitive HPC Applications on up
to 48 FPGAs Using ACCL 121
   *Marius Meyer, Tobias Kenter, Lucian Petrica, Kenneth O'Brien,
   Michaela Blott, and Christian Plessl*

A Folded Computation-in-Memory Accelerator for Fast Polynomial
Multiplication in BIKE 137
   Chuhui Wang, Zewen Ye, Haibin Shen, and Kejie Huang

(re)Assessing PiM Effectiveness for Sequence Alignment................ 152
   Hamidreza Ramezanikebrya and Matei Ripeanu

MEPAD: A Memory-Efficient Parallelized Direct Convolution Algorithm
for Deep Neural Networks 167
   Leandro Fiorin and Cristina Silvano

A High-Performance Collective I/O Framework Leveraging Node-Local
Persistent Memory 182
   Keegan Sanchez, Alex Gavin, Suren Byna, Kesheng Wu,
   and Xuechen Zhang

PCTC: Hardware and Software Co-design for Pruned Capsule Networks on
Tensor Cores 196
   Mohammad Hafezan, Reza Jahadi, and Ehsan Atoofian

Harnessing Data Movement Strategies to Optimize Performance-Energy
Efficiency of Oil & Gas Simulations in HPC 211
   Pedro Rigon, Brenda Schussler, Alexandre Sardinha, Pedro M. Silva,
   Fábio Oliveira, Alexandre Carissimi, Jairo Panetta, Filippo Spiga,
   Arthur Lorenzon, and Philippe O. A. Navaux

Compact Parallel Hash Tables on the GPU........................... 226
   Steef Hegeman, Daan Wöltgens, Anton Wijs, and Alfons Laarman

Hybrid Congestion Control for BXI-Based Interconnection Networks 242
   Gabriel Gomez-Lopez, Miguel Sánchez de la Rosa,
   Jesús Escudero-Sahuquillo, Pedro J. Garcia, Francisco J. Quiles,
   and Pierre-Axel Lagadec

Data Analytics, AI and Computational Science

Athena: Add More Intelligence to RMT-Based Network Data Plane
with Low-Bit Quantization.. 259
   Yunkun Liao, Hanyue Lin, Jingya Wu, Wenyan Lu, Huawei Li,
   Xiaowei Li, and Guihai Yan

Lightweight Byzantine-Robust and Privacy-Preserving Federated Learning.... 274
   Zhi Lu, Songfeng Lu, Yongquan Cui, Junjun Wu, Hewang Nie, Jue Xiao,
   and Zepu Yi

CSIMD: Cross-Search Algorithm with Improved Multi-dimensional
Dichotomy for Micro-Batch-Based Pipeline Parallel Training in DNN 288
    *Guangyao Zhou, Haocheng Lan, Yuanlun Xie, Wenhong Tian,
Jiahong Qian, and Teng Su*

Disttack: Graph Adversarial Attacks Toward Distributed GNN Training 302
    *Yuxiang Zhang, Xin Liu, Meng Wu, Wei Yan, Mingyu Yan, Xiaochun Ye,
and Dongrui Fan*

WActiGrad: Structured Pruning for Efficient Finetuning and Inference
of Large Language Models on AI Accelerators 317
    *Krishna Teja Chitty-Venkata, Varuni Katti Sastry, Murali Emani,
Venkatram Vishwanath, Sanjif Shanmugavelu, and Sylvia Howland*

VeriChroma: Ownership Verification for Federated Models via RGB
Filters 332
    Hewang Nie, Songfeng Lu, Mu Wang, Jue Xiao, Zhi Lu, and Zepu Yi

GDL-GNN: Applying GPU Dataloading of Large Datasets for Graph
Neural Network Inference 346
    Haoran Dang, Meng Wu, Mingyu Yan, Xiaochun Ye, and Dongrui Fan

LogRCA: Log-Based Root Cause Analysis for Distributed Services 362
    Thorsten Wittkopp, Philipp Wiesner, and Odej Kao

Inference with Transformer Encoders on ARM and RISC-V Multicore
Processors 377
    *Héctor Martínez, Francisco D. Igual, Rafael Rodríguez-Sánchez,
Sandra Catalán, Adrián Castelló, and Enrique S. Quintana-Ortí*

FedGG: Leveraging Generative Adversarial Networks and Gradient
Smoothing for Privacy Protection in Federated Learning 393
    *Jiguang Lv, Shuchun Xu, Xiaodong Zhan, Tao Liu, Dapeng Man,
and Wu Yang*

Improving Generalization and Personalization in Long-Tailed Federated
Learning via Classifier Retraining 408
    Yuhang Li, Tong Liu, Wenfeng Shen, Yangguang Cui, and Weijia Lu

Quartet: A Holistic Hybrid Parallel Framework for Training Large
Language Models 424
    *Weigang Zhang, Biyu Zhou, Xing Wu, Chaochen Gao, Zhibing Liu,
Xuehai Tang, Ruixuan Li, Jizhong Han, and Songlin Hu*

PEANUTS: A Persistent Memory-Based Network Unilateral Transfer
System for Enhanced MPI-IO Data Transfer........................ 439
  Kohei Hiraga and Osamu Tatebe

FLUK: Protecting Federated Learning Against Malicious Clients
for Internet of Vehicles 454
  *Mengde Zhu, Wanyi Ning, Qi Qi, Jingyu Wang, Zirui Zhuang,
  Haifeng Sun, Jun Huang, and Jianxin Liao*

Optimizing Federated Learning Using Remote Embeddings for Graph
Neural Networks... 470
  Pranjal Naman and Yogesh Simmhan

Asymmetric Coded Distributed Computation for Resilient Prediction
Serving Systems... 485
  Lin Wang, Yuchong Hu, Yuxue Liu, Renzhi Xiao, and Dan Feng

Author Index 501

Contents – Part III

Theory and Algorithms

Accelerated Block-Sparsity-Aware Matrix Reordering for Leveraging
Tensor Cores in Sparse Matrix-Multivector Multiplication 3
    Eunji Lee, Yoonsang Han, and Gordon Euhyun Moon

Reduced-Precision and Reduced-Exponent Formats for Accelerating
Adaptive Precision Sparse Matrix–Vector Product 17
    *Stef Graillat, Fabienne Jézéquel, Theo Mary, Roméo Molina,
and Daichi Mukunoki*

Mixed Precision Randomized Low-Rank Approximation with GPU Tensor
Cores. 31
    *Marc Baboulin, Simplice Donfack, Oguz Kaya, Theo Mary,
and Matthieu Robeyns*

Boolean Matrix Multiplication for Highly Clustered Data on the
Congested Clique 45
    Andrzej Lingas

Minimizing I/O in Toom-Cook Algorithms. 59
    Roy Nissim, Oded Schwartz, and Yuval Spiizer

GPU-Accelerated BFS for Dynamic Networks 74
    Filippo Ziche, Nicola Bombieri, Federico Busato, and Rosalba Giugno

QClique: Optimizing Performance and Accuracy in Maximum
Weighted Clique. 88
    *Qasim Abbas, Mohsen Koohi Esfahani, Ian Overton, and Hans
Vandierendonck*

A Fast Wait-Free Solution to Read-Reclaim Races in Reference Counting 103
    *Ivo Gabe de Wolff, Daniel Anderson, Gabriele K. Keller,
and Aleksei Seletskiy*

How to Relax Instantly: Elastic Relaxation of Concurrent Data Structures 119
    Kåre von Geijer and Philippas Tsigas

ALZI: An Improved Parallel Algorithm for Finding Connected
Components in Large Graphs.................................... 134
  Sharon Boddu and Maleq Khan

**Multidisciplinary, Domain-Specific and Applied Parallel
and Distributed Computing**

TaroRTL: Accelerating RTL Simulation Using Coroutine-Based
Heterogeneous Task Graph Scheduling 151
  Dian-Lun Lin, Umit Ogras, Joshua San Miguel, and Tsung-Wei Huang

Combining Compression and Prefetching to Improve Checkpointing
for Inverse Seismic Problems in GPUs............................ 167
  *Thiago Maltempi, Sandro Rigo, Marcio Pereira, Hervé Yviquel,
  Jessé Costa, and Guido Araujo*

Accelerating Large-Scale Sparse LU Factorization for RF Circuit
Simulation.. 182
  *Guofeng Feng, Hongyu Wang, Zhuoqiang Guo, Mingzhen Li,
  Tong Zhao, Zhou Jin, Weile Jia, Guangming Tan, and Ninghui Sun*

A Joint Approach to Local Updating and Gradient Compression
for Efficient Asynchronous Federated Learning................... 196
  *Jiajun Song, Jiajun Luo, Rongwei Lu, Shuzhao Xie, Bin Chen,
  and Zhi Wang*

Accelerating Stencil Computation with Fully Homomorphic Encryption
Using GPU 212
  Xianlong Zhou, Pei Li, Jiageng Chen, and Shixiong Yao

GPU Cache System for COMPSs: A Task-Based Distributed Computing
Framework... 225
  *Cristian Cătălin Tatu, Javier Conejero, Fernando Vázquez-Novoa,
  and Rosa M. Badia*

Code Generation for Octree-Based Multigrid Solvers with Fused Higher-
Order Interpolation and Communication........................... 240
  Richard Angersbach, Sebastian Kuckuk, and Harald Köstler

Distributed Simulation for Digital Twins of Large-Scale Real-World
DiffServ-Based Networks... 255
  *Zhuoyao Huang, Nan Zhang, Jingran Shen, Georgios Diamantopoulos,
  Zhengchang Hua, Nikos Tziritas, and Georgios Theodoropoulos*

On the Use of GPU Computing for Accelerating EEG Preprocessing......... 270
   F. Romero, M. Lupión, N.C. Cruz, L.F. Romero, and P.M. Ortigosa

Pipe-AGCM: A Fine-Grain Pipelining Scheme for Optimizing the Parallel
Atmospheric General Circulation Model............................. 283
   *Dazheng Liu, Xiaoli Ren, Jianping Wu, Wenjuan Liu, Juan Zhao,
and Shaoliang Peng*

A Framework for Automated Parallel Execution of Scientific Multi-
workflow Applications in the Cloud with Work Stealing 298
   *Helena S. I. L. Silva, Maria C. S. Castro, Fabricio A. B. Silva,
and Alba C. M. A. Melo*

DF* PageRank: Incrementally Expanding Approaches for Updating
PageRank on Dynamic Graphs...................................... 312
   Subhajit Sahu, Kishore Kothapalli, Hemalatha Eedi, and Sathya Peri

Cloud-Native GPU-Enabled Architecture for Parallel Video Encoding 327
   *Andoni Salcedo-Navarro, Raúl Peña-Ortiz, José M. Claver,
Miguel Garcia-Pineda, and Juan Gutiérrez-Aguado*

AdapCK: Optimizing I/O for Checkpointing on Large-Scale High
Performance Computing Systems 342
   Jie Jia, Yi Liu, Yanke Liu, Yifan Chen, and Fang Lin

Efficient SpMV for Graph Matrices Through Vectoring and Caching......... 356
   YuAng Chen and Jeffery Xu Yu

VLASPH: Smoothed Particle Hydrodynamics on VLA SIMD Architectures... 371
   *Xiaokang Fan, Zhen Ge, Sifan Long, Tao Tang, Chun Huang, Lin Peng,
and Canqun Yang*

Investigating Portability in Chapel for Tree-Based Optimization on GPU-
Powered Clusters 386
   *Tiago Carneiro, Engin Kayraklioglu, Guillaume Helbecque,
and Nouredine Melab*

MPR: An MPI Framework for Distributed Self-adaptive Stream Processing ... 400
   *Júnior Löff, Dalvan Griebler, Luiz Gustavo Fernandes,
and Walter Binder*

Author Index 415

Programming, Compilers and Performance

FlexiGran: Flexible Granularity Locking in Hierarchies

Anju Mongandampulath Akathoott[✉] [iD] and Rupesh Nasre [iD]

Indian Institute of Technology Madras, Chennai, India
{cs16d019,rupesh}@cse.iitm.ac.in

Abstract. Locking continues to be a primary technique used to achieve thread synchronization. Especially in the case of rooted hierarchies, semantic locking can be achieved with physical locks at various granularity levels. Such a multi-granularity locking (MGL) provides interesting trade-off between the locking cost and the size of the locked sub-hierarchy. At one extreme, fine-grained locking precisely locks the nodes of interest, but incurs a high locking cost. In contrast, a coarse-grained lock may lock the root of the hierarchy minimizing the locking cost, but locking many more nodes than required. Existing approaches to MGL (i) do not work well with non-tree hierarchies such as DAGs, (ii) disallow structural updates to the hierarchy, (iii) do not support the co-existence of fine-grained and coarse-grained locks, or (iv) are rigid towards their underlying memory usage. In this work, we propose a versatile technique named FLEXIGRAN, which does not have any of these issues. It allows co-existence of hierarchical and fine-grained locks in an arbitrarily shaped hierarchy which can undergo structural alterations at run time, while allowing a user to control its memory usage by adding optional approximations. We illustrate the effectiveness of FLEXIGRAN using STMBench7, and compare it empirically with two recent locking techniques, DomLock and HiFi. On a static hierarchy with more than 1 million nodes, FLEXIGRAN shows an improvement in throughput of around 159% and 374% on an average, compared to HiFi and DomLock respectively.

Keywords: Hierarchical data structures · Fine-grained/Hierarchical locking · Synchronization · Concurrency · Dominators

1 Introduction

It is common for structured as well as semi-structured databases to represent the underlying data in a hierarchical fashion. It enables the database management system to operate at various levels for the same data item with the hope of improved performance. A rooted hierarchy is characterized by a *containment* relationship – a node *contains* all of its descendant nodes. Many structured [12] as well as semi-structured [3] databases exploit the containment relationship in constructing their responses to queries. Varying the levels in the hierarchy at

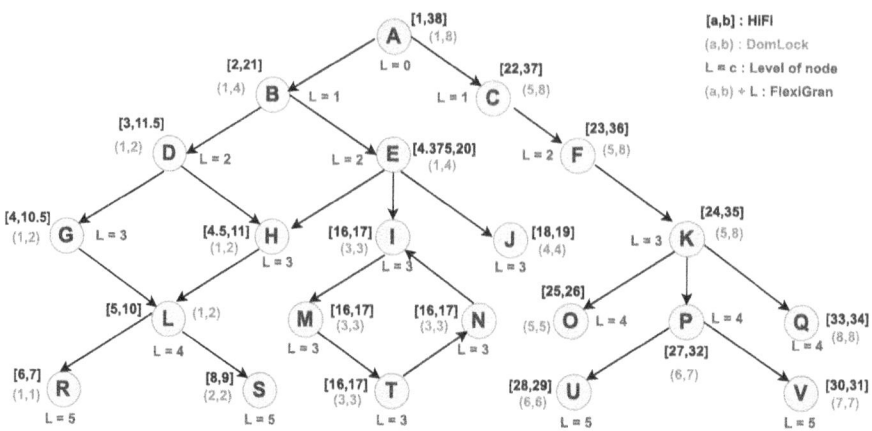

Fig. 1. Example hierarchy demonstrating the working of DomLock, HiFi and FLEXI-GRAN

which locks are taken can lead to a trade-off between the locking cost (number of nodes locked) and the locking precision (extra nodes locked over the nodes of interest), affecting performance.

Locking can be done at different granularity levels. Coarse- and fine-grained locking are the extreme cases. Multi-granularity locking (MGL) lies in the middle, where locking a node semantically locks the whole sub-hierarchy rooted at that node. Intention locking (IL) [5] was the first MGL technique that was successfully adapted in databases [13]. A recent technique named DomLock [7] gave higher performance than IL with its ability to avoid long traversals and multi-path locking in checking overlaps of sub-hierarchies. HiFi [4], built on similar lines, supported hierarchical and fine-grained locks in hierarchies.

These existing methods have certain limitations. For instance, IL is inefficient for DAGs and large lock requests. DomLock does not permit co-existence of hierarchical and fine-grained locks. HiFi does permit it, but does not support structural update operations. Our proposal FLEXIGRAN addresses these shortcomings and enables flexible locking for hierarchies.

This work makes the following contributions.

- We propose FLEXIGRAN, a flexible granularity locking technique for hierarchies. In particular, it supports co-existence of fine-grained and hierarchical locks, permits concurrent structural updates to the hierarchy.
- FLEXIGRAN uses a memory-efficient bit representation and allows grouping nodes to further reduce the memory usage. Such a grouping trades-off precision for memory usage and throughput.
- We empirically evaluate FLEXIGRAN and compare its performance against recent hierarchical locking techniques DomLock and HiFi using the STM-Bench7 benchmark.[1]

---

[1] Additional experiments can be found here.

2 Background and Motivation

Two extreme ways of locking are fine-grained and coarse-grained. Fine-grained locking involves a thread taking a separate lock on each node. It is well-suited if a thread wants to work on only a few nodes at a time. In contrast, when the number of nodes to be locked by a thread at a time is large, acquiring fine-grained locks on each of the nodes becomes expensive. In such scenarios, if the underlying data is stored in a hierarchy, hierarchical locking is more suitable. It is a specific type of MGL where *explicitly* locking a node x translates to *implicitly* locking all the nodes in the sub-hierarchy rooted at x. Using MGL protocol can make the locking cost remain constant irrespective of the number of nodes to be locked. In extreme cases, MGL degeneralizes to fine-grained and coarse-grained locking. One of the key challenges in MGL is to identify if a new hierarchical lock request is in conflict with an existing one (and if yes, the thread should block or sleep). Identifying overlaps is not straightforward, since MGL locks the sub-hierarchy only implicitly.

2.1 DomLock and HiFi

DomLock [7] is a relatively recent hierarchical locking technique which avoids the drawbacks of IL by taking explicit locks only on the dominator nodes (semantically) of the subsets of nodes to be locked. It exploits the idea of numeric intervals to assign special ranges to the nodes in the hierarchy. The numbers are assigned such that the interval of a node subsumes the intervals of all of its descendants. Each interval is of the form (a, d) where a and d are positive numbers. The interval (a, d) subsumes (b, c) if and only if $a \leq b$ and $c \leq d$. Capturing all the subsumptions in a hierarchy using such intervals helps in quickly identifying overlaps across sub-hierarchies by simply comparing the interval attributes alone, without requiring to traverse the graph. Figure 1 shows an example of DomLock's interval assignment.

DomLock reduces the costly traversal, works seamlessly with non-tree hierarchies, and is significantly faster than IL due to its quick overlap check using intervals. On the other hand, DomLock does not support the co-existence of hierarchical and fine-grained locks. Thus, even when a thread wants to lock a single node (fine-grained lock) somewhere close to the root, DomLock ends up locking the whole sub-hierarchy rooted at that node (due to its only-hierarchical-locks-supported feature), reducing concurrency considerably. Another technique, HiFi [4], was proposed to overcome this limitation. The core of supporting co-existence of hierarchical and fine-grained locks lies in implementing the compatibility protocol shown in Table 1. (Clearly, conflicts arise only when at least one of the requests considered is a write.) HiFi is able to assess the ancestor-descendant relationships based on three invariants: (i) interval of each node is unique, (ii) interval of a parent strictly subsumes the intervals of all its descendants, and (iii) intervals of two nodes partially overlap if they have a common descendant. To assign intervals that satisfy all of these invariants, HiFi performs two DFS passes on the graph in the preprocessing stage. In the first DFS, nodes

Table 1. Compatibility matrix showing the protocol for the co-existence of hierarchical and fine-grained locks in a system. F: Fine-grained, H: Hierarchical, R: Read, W: Write, ✓: Yes, lock can be granted, X: No, lock cannot be granted

	\multicolumn{4}{c}{Lock already taken by another thread on}					
		Ancestor				Descendant		
New locking request	FR	FW	HR	HW	FR	FW	HR	HW
FR	✓	✓	✓	X	✓	✓	✓	✓
FW	✓	✓	X	X	✓	✓	✓	✓
HR	✓	✓	✓	X	✓	X	✓	X
HW	✓	✓	X	X	X	X	X	X

are assigned intervals of the form (pre, post), where pre and post are the pre-visit and post-visit numbers respectively of the nodes from the DFS. Since these initial intervals may not satisfy all the invariants required for non-tree structures, HiFi performs a second DFS – in this pass, it propagates and readjusts the intervals (so as to satisfy all the invariants) in bottom-up order. To illustrate the working of these intervals, consider our running example from Fig. 1. HiFi allows a fine-grained lock on C [22, 37] and a hierarchical lock on K [24, 35] simultaneously, as C is interpreted as K's ancestor. Similarly, locking K [24, 35] hierarchically and U [28, 29] in fine-grained mode simultaneously are not permitted, as U is identified as a descendant of K from the subsumption of U's interval by K's interval. Simultaneous hierarchical locks on G [4, 10.5] and H [4.5, 11] are not permitted as their intervals overlap in the number line, suggesting their overlap in the hierarchy.

IL, DomLock, and HiFi have certain limitations. IL is inefficient for DAGs and large lock requests. DomLock supports dynamic operations (structural updates to the hierarchy), but does not support the co-existence of hierarchical and fine-grained locks. In contrast, HiFi supports the co-existence of hierarchical and fine-grained operations, but does not support any kind of dynamic operations. Also, in the preprocessing phase, HiFi performs two sequential DFS traversals back to back. Though this is a one time step, our quantitative analysis suggests that it is costly on large hierarchies. None of these methods allows strategic grouping of nodes to reduce memory usage for large hierarchies. Our flexible proposal FLEXIGRAN extends DomLock to support the co-existence of hierarchical and fine-grained locks in a hierarchy that can undergo structural modifications at run time. We reduce the preprocessing cost by performing a single DFS in that stage. We also exploit fast bitwise operations to enhance FLEXIGRAN's performance.

3 Flexible Granularity Locking

The key intent behind FLEXIGRAN is to enable efficient co-existence of hierarchical and fine-grained locking in a dynamic hierarchy. To support such a co-existence, the locking protocol must follow the compatibility rules shown in

Table 1. Here, the correct identification of ancestor-descendant relationships is crucial. DomLock may face issues here, as the intervals of the nodes need not be unique. For example, in Fig. 1, the nodes C and K have the same interval (5, 8) in DomLock, though C is an ancestor of K. In HiFi, this problem does not occur, as each node's interval is unique.

Our proposal FLEXIGRAN utilizes the single-DFS-based intervals as in DomLock itself. To help assess the ancestor-descendant relationship, we make use of the level at which the nodes lie in the hierarchy. The root node's level is taken as 0. All the nodes in a cycle have the same level value, as there is no ancestor-descendant relationship among them. For any other node, the maximum number of edges traversed to reach that node from the root is taken as its level value. If two nodes have the same interval in FLEXIGRAN, and if their levels are different, the node with the smaller level value is the ancestor of the other node. For example, nodes C and K have the same interval (5, 8) in FLEXIGRAN, but the level value of C is 1 whereas that of K is 3, implying that C is an ancestor of K.

Similar to DomLock, a lock pool maintains the bookkeeping of the already acquired locks. Whenever a thread makes a new locking request, it examines the entries by the other threads in the pool to see if there is any overlap with an already acquired lock, as per the protocol in Table 1. If there is no conflict, the thread is allowed to proceed and execute the critical section code. Otherwise, the thread waits until the conflicts dissolve after a while. FLEXIGRAN improvises on DomLock's lock pool implementation using fast bitsets.

A Fast Lock Pool Using Bit-Level Data: We implement the lock pool using a vector of bitsets, deviating from DomLock's way of keeping track of the intervals by recording the numbers, as they are. Each thread has its own slot in the lock pool, where the entry is a sequence of bits. If there are n leaf nodes in the hierarchy, we fix each entry in the pool to be a sequence of m bits, where $m \leq n$. (We take $m = n$ for ease of explanation of the technique; but in the experiments, the value of m is chosen to be $< n$, aiming maximum performance benefits.) Each bit sequence is initialized to zeros in all the bit positions. A thread marks the range it wants to lock by setting the corresponding bits in its slot to 1. For example, consider a scenario with two threads T1 and T2, wherein T1's lock request is {K} and T2's lock request is {U, V} both in hierarchical mode. T1 wants to lock the sub-hierarchy rooted at K with interval (5, 8). Assuming it goes first, T1 sets the bits from position 5 to position 8 of the bit sequence in $pool[1]$. Thread T2 finds that it should lock node P in the hierarchical mode with range (6, 7) to ensure locking of nodes {U, V}. Note that identification of the dominator node does not require any traversal; it requires only the computation of the tightest interval that subsumes the intervals of all the nodes to be locked. Thus, T2 sets the bits corresponding to P's interval (6, 7) in the bit sequence at $pool[2]$. After this, T2 goes over the entries in the pool to check for possible overlaps. A simple bitwise AND operation of the entries $pool[1]$ and $pool[2]$ produces a bit sequence which has 1 at positions 6 and 7. This indicates an overlapping lock request. For correctness, T2 is made to wait until this conflict goes away (that

Algorithm 1. FLEXLOCK(*from, to, myTid, mode, gran, level*)

1: *mutex.acquire();*
2: *seqNum[myTid]* ← *++globalSequenceNumber*
3: *lockMode[myTid]* ← *mode*
4: *lockGranularity[myTid]* ← *gran*
5: *levelLocked[myTid]* ← *level*
6: *lockState[myTid].lockRange(from, to)*
7: *mutex.release()*
8: **for** each entry $i \neq myTid$ in the pool **do**
9:    **while** *doRangesOverlap(myTid, i)* && *seqNum[i] < mySeqNum* **do**
10:      **continue;**
11: **return;**

is, until T1 is done). In a different scenario, if T2 tries to lock the range (1, 2) instead, the bitwise AND of *pool*[1] and *pool*[2] produces a zero bit sequence, which declares no overlap between these requests. For locking an internal node in fine-grained mode as well, the bitset-range covering its interval will be set to 1, but since we look at the additional attribute *granularity*, the combined information tells us that only one node is locked. In brief, FLEXIGRAN employs fast bit operations, and keeps track of the levels of nodes and granularities of lock requests that make it capable of supporting the coexistence of hierarchical and fine-grained locks, a feature not supported by DomLock.

3.1 Checking for Overlaps

Whenever a thread requests for a lock, it performs the steps mentioned in Algorithm 1. To avoid taking a global mutex lock for the complete process of overlap check, we employ sequence numbers and set priorities to threads (lower sequence number indicates higher priority). The technique is built on the lines of the *Bakery algorithm* [9,10]. A global variable *globalSequenceNumber* is initialized to zero before threads start raising lock requests. When a thread enters the procedure described in Algorithm 1, it first acquires the mutex, increments *globalSequenceNumber*, and writes the incremented sequence number to its slot in the array *seqNum* (Line 2). Similarly, the thread writes its lock mode (read/write), lock granularity (hierarchical/fine-grained) and the level of the node it wants to lock (which is an integer ≥ 0) in its own slots in the respective arrays (Lines 3–5). In the next step, the thread sets all the bits in the range [from, to] of the bit sequence in its slot in the lock pool (Line 6). At this stage, the thread unlocks the mutex (Line 7). Then, the thread loops over each entry in the lock pool (Line 8) to see if there is an overlap. If yes, the thread compares its sequence number with that of the other thread. If the other thread has a lower sequence number (which means higher priority), the requesting thread waits until the conflict goes away (Line 10). It proceeds to look for conflicts with the remaining entries in the pool, when the currently conflicting thread finishes its critical section and resets all the bits in its slot in the lock pool. Once no conflict is identified with

Algorithm 2. DORANGESOVERLAP(*T1, T2*): LMLockMode LM-LockMode, LG-LockGranularity, LL-LevelLocked

1: **if** *LM[T1]* = READ and *LM[T2]* = READ **then**
2:    **return** false;
3: **if** *pool[T1]* & *pool[T2]* ≠ 0 **then**
4:    **if** *LG[T1]* and *LG[T2]* are both HIERARCHICAL **then**
5:      **return** true;
6:    **if** *LG[T1]* is FINE-GRAINED **then**
7:      **if** *LG[T2]* is FINE-GRAINED **then**
8:        **if** *pool[T1]* ⊕ *pool[T2]* is 0 and *LL[T1]* = *LL[T2]* **then**
9:          **return** true;
10:      **else**
11:        **if** *nodeLockedByT2*.isAncestorOf*(nodeReqstdByT1)* **then**
12:          **return** true;
13:    **else**
14:      **if** *nodeLockedByT2*.isDescendantOf*(nodeReqstdByT1)* **then**
15:        **return** true;
16: **return** false;

any higher priority thread, the thread proceeds to execute the critical section (Line 11). Coming out of the conflict check procedure is equivalent to acquiring an implicit lock. The time to obtain a lock in FLEXIGRAN varies across lock requests based on the number and types of concurrent requests, and the critical section sizes associated with various requests in the system. If there is a conflict, only the highest priority thread among the conflicting ones comes out of the blocking wait in Algorithm 1. Such a locking scheme will be practically better suited for longer critical sections.

The detailed steps of checking for an overlap between two threads is given in Algorithm 2. Here the first parameter (*T1*) is the id of the thread making the new lock request and the second one (*T2*) is that of the thread with which we want to check for a possible conflict. If both the requests are of read mode, then the algorithm returns false, as there is no conflict (Line 2). If the bitwise AND operation of the lock pool entries of the two threads results in a non-zero value (Line 3), there *may* be an overlapped request, and further checks are necessary to decide if there is an actual overlap. If the locking granularities of both the threads are *hierarchical*, then it is a true overlap (Even if the two sub-hierarchies overlap at only a single node, locks can not be granted on both simultaneously.) and the algorithm returns true (Line 5). If both the threads ask for fine-grained locks (Lines 6–7), the new request can be granted if the requested nodes are different. If the nodes are the same, the bit sequences corresponding to them in the lock pool will be exactly the same; but its converse does not hold. An example can be easily seen in Fig. 1 – There are three different nodes C, F, and K with the same interval (5, 8). So, to distinguish such nodes, we additionally consider their level values. In the example, the nodes C, F, and K have level values 1, 2 and 3, respectively. FLEXIGRAN first performs an *XOR* operation of the bit sequences to check if the requested nodes are the same. If yes, the level values are compared additionally. If they also match, the algorithm returns true, indicating an overlap (Line 9). If the new request is fine-grained and the other one is hierarchical, control reaches the else block at Line 10. In this case, only if the hierarchical lock is on an ancestor of the node to be locked in fine-grained mode, the lock is not granted (Line 12).

If the new request is for a hierarchical lock, the control reaches Line 13. At this point, it is guaranteed that the conflicting request is for a fine-grained lock (The case of both the requests being hierarchical is handled at Line 5). Here, the hierarchical lock has to be rejected only if the fine-grained lock is on a descendant node of the node to be locked in hierarchical mode (Line 15). If none of these conditions are met, there is no overlap and the algorithm returns false (Line 16), suggesting the requested lock can be granted.

Once a thread finishes working on the critical section, it resets all the bits in its bitset, the corresponding mode, granularity and level attributes to indicate that the node is not locked any more.

Ancestor-descendant Relationships: When the bit sequences of two threads produce a non-zero value on bitwise AND, we need to further check the ancestor-descendant relationships between the nodes involved if one of the requests is fine-grained. Let us consider two nodes N_1 and N_2. Assume that the first and the last 1's in node N_2's bit sequence are at positions b_1 and b_2 respectively. If N_1 has a 1 at both a position $< b_1$ and a position $> b_2$ in its bit sequence, N_1 is an ancestor of N_2 (Example: $N_1 = $ E, $N_2 = $ I in Fig. 1). On the other hand, if all 1's in N_1's bit sequence are at positions between $> b_1$ and $< b_2$, then N_1 is a descendant of N_2 (Example: $N_1 = $ P and $N_2 = $ K in Fig. 1). Even in cases where either N_1's first 1 is at b_1 or last 1 is at b_2, but not both, the arguments hold, if the other end point satisfies the corresponding criterion (Example: A is an ancestor of B in Fig. 1. The first 1's in both A and B are at the same position, but the last one of A is at position 8, which is > 4, the position of the last 1 in B). If N_1 has its first and last 1 at exactly the bit positions b_1 and b_2 respectively, we look at their level values to make a judgement (Example: Though the nodes C and F have their first and last 1's in the bit sequences exactly at the same positions, C is an ancestor of F in Fig. 1, as C's level is 1 and F's level is 2).

Algorithm 3. FLEXUNLOCK($myTid$)

1: $lockState[myTid].resetAllBits()$;
2: $lockMode[myTid] \leftarrow $ NOT_LOCKED;
3: $lockGranularity[myTid] \leftarrow $ NOT_LOCKED;
4: $levelLocked[myTid] \leftarrow -1$;
5: $seqNum[myTid] \leftarrow $ INT_MAX;

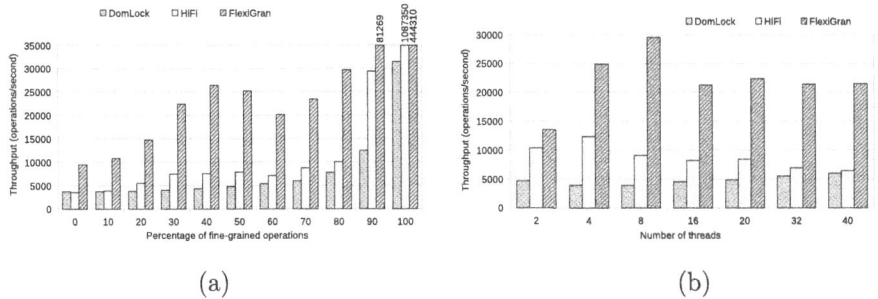

Fig. 2. Effect of (a) varying the percentage of fine-grained operations and (b) the number of threads

3.2 FLEXIGRAN with Dynamic Hierarchies

A salient feature of FLEXIGRAN is that it supports dynamically changing hierarchies. Under the premise that hierarchy's root does not change, FLEXIGRAN supports arbitrary addition and deletion of edges at run-time. To add an edge (N_1, N_2), note that it suffices to take a hierarchical exclusive lock on a dominator of N_1 and N_2. DomLock uses this idea and updates intervals of the nodes (since N_2's interval should now be subsumed in N_1's interval). However, the exclusive lock on the dominator results in reduced concurrency. FLEXIGRAN improvises on DomLock by taking fine-grained write locks on N_1 and N_2. This allows simultaneous hierarchical locks on the descendants of N_1 and N_2, and fine-grained locks on any ancestor or descendant of N_1 and N_2, which improves concurrency. When an edge is added from N_1 to N_2, the intervals of the ancestors of N_1 (at most up to the dominator of N_1 and N_2) may need to be expanded. Since N_1 and N_2 are locked in fine-grained mode, no ancestor of N_1 will be locked in hierarchical mode, until the lock on N_1 is released. So, it is sufficient to take fine-grained locks on the ancestors for updating intervals. For deletion of an edge (N_1, N_2), taking a fine-grained write lock on N_1 is sufficient.

3.3 Space-Time Trade-offs with Bitsets

A key advantage of using bitsets is that they allow us to trade-off space for performance. Thus, FLEXIGRAN can permit us to use fewer bits than the number of nodes, and their indexing helps insert controlled approximation into the overlap check. On one hand, this can increase false positives, by declaring lock requests to be overlapping when they are not. This can reduce concurrency since the thread would unnecessarily wait for the falsely-conflicting thread to unlock its nodes. On the other hand, reducing the number of bits improves cache-efficiency, reduces the number of bits to be ANDed, and leads to improved performance. In our experiments, we observed that the benefits outweigh the demerits when controlled approximations are added.

4 Experimental Evaluation

We compare FLEXIGRAN against DomLock and HiFi. We implemented FLEXI-GRAN as part of STMBench7 [6], a well known benchmark for parallel hierarchical applications. All our experiments were run on an Intel Xeon CPU E5-2640 v4 server with 20 cores (10 * dual socket) clocked at 2.4GHz and 64GB memory. It runs CentOS Linux release 7.5.1804 (Core) 64-bit operating system, and has hyperthreading enabled. We study the effect of various parameters, and use the following configuration values as defaults: the configurable hierarchy has 1.2 million nodes, 20 threads run in parallel, the critical section is medium in size ($14\mu s$), 50% of the operations are fine-grained and the remaining are hierarchical operations, lock request size is 50 nodes for hierarchical type requests (a fine-grained request locks a single node). We report throughput (number of operations per second) as output by STMBench7. Each experiment reports the average values from 10 runs.

4.1 Varying Fine-Grained Operation Percentage

One of the contributions of FLEXIGRAN is co-existence of hierarchical and fine-grained operations. In this experiment, we vary the percentage of fine-grained lock requests from 0 to 100 in steps of 10. Figure 2(a) compares the performances of DomLock, HiFi, and FLEXIGRAN. The X-axis value of 0 represents the case of all the requests being hierarchical in nature, while that of 100 indicates only fine-grained requests. As expected, DomLock's performance is poor as it locks nodes in hierarchical mode even for fine-grained operations, significantly reducing concurrency. On an average, FLEXIGRAN performs 165% better than HiFi in this experiment. We further observe that except for the case of 100% fine-grained requests, FLEXIGRAN outperforms HiFi (as well as DomLock) considerably. If the requests are completely fine-grained in nature, HiFi performs better than FLEXIGRAN. This corner case happens because HiFi needs only comparison of intervals whereas FLEXIGRAN needs additional checking of the level values to resolve conflicts. The impact of the additional processing time is visible towards the right end of the plot, as threads spend less time in the critical section.

4.2 Varying the Number of Threads

Figure 2(b) compares the throughput of FLEXIGRAN against that of DomLock and HiFi as we vary the number of parallel threads (from 2 to 40) working on an STMBench7 hierarchy with 1.2 million nodes. We omit the single-threaded execution as there is no locking involved. 50% of the lock requests are fine-grained, and the critical section is of medium size. Both FLEXIGRAN and HiFi consistently outperform DomLock. In all the cases, FLEXIGRAN outperforms both HiFi and DomLock by huge margins. FLEXIGRAN shows a performance improvement of 159% and 374% on an average, over HiFi and DomLock respectively. We also observe that beyond 8 threads, FLEXIGRAN's performance reduces slightly as the NUMA (Non-Uniform Memory Access) effects come into picture when threads are run on cores spread across different sockets.

4.3 Varying the Distribution of Locked Nodes and Hierarchy Size

In hierarchical requests, a thread requests for a number of nodes, whose dominator is identified and locked by the thread. The nodes in such a request can follow any distribution. In this experiment, we group the nodes in the graph to a number of buckets and each thread randomly picks a bucket and then chooses nodes for its hierarchical request from that bucket alone. The X axis shows the number of such buckets (varied from 1 to 6000). If the number of buckets is 1, it implies the nodes are picked randomly from anywhere in the graph and hence, the chances of the dominators being close to the root are higher. This experiment was run with 20 threads, on a graph with 6000 nodes in the composite part level (the lowest level at which dominators can be present when each lock request contains a number of nodes). The hierarchical requests in STMBench7 contain a group of atomic parts and their dominator can be present anywhere from composite levels up till the root node. When there are many buckets to choose from, the dominators will be relatively away from the root, leading to less overlap among requests from multiple threads, leading to better throughput. This impact is very high when the number of buckets is 6000, which is also the number of composite parts in the graph, as each thread tries to lock atomic parts

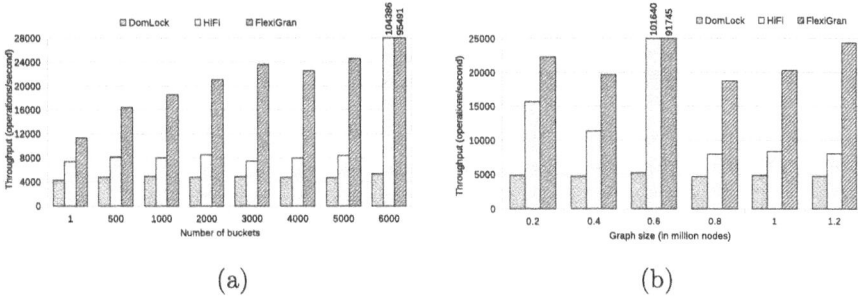

Fig. 3. Effect of varying (a) the distribution of nodes locked in hierarchical requests and (b) the graph size

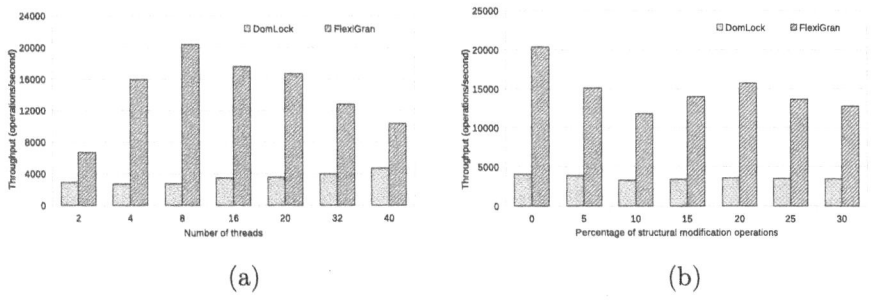

Fig. 4. Effect of varying (a) the number of threads and (b) the percentage of structural modifications in a dynamic hierarchy

that lie in the sub-hierarchy rooted at a single composite part, leading to almost no overlap and thus maximum performance. It is to be noted that the composite parts do not have any direct interconnections among themselves; they can be connected via common parent at assembly levels. If a bucket has more than one composite part, the dominator of nodes from this bucket will be at higher levels (assemblies) in the hierarchy. In this experiment (Fig. 3(a)) as well, DomLock's performance is quite poor compared to that of FLEXIGRAN and HiFi. At 6000 buckets, there is no overlap across requests and HiFi turns out to be very fast in checking for overlaps using its intervals alone, performing slightly better than FLEXIGRAN. Except for this extreme case, FLEXIGRAN outperforms HiFi consistently and considerably.

In Fig. 3(b), the X axis shows the number of nodes in the hierarchy (from 0.2 million to 1.2 million). The configuration uses 3000 buckets for the threads to pick nodes for hierarchical locking. As expected, DomLock's performance is low for all the hierarchy sizes considered. FLEXIGRAN outperforms HiFi for almost all the hierarchies, except for the one with 0.6 million nodes. Here the performances of both the techniques shoot up. This hierarchy has 3000 composite parts, leading to each composite part falling to a separate bucket (each thread picks the nodes for its hierarchical requests from one of these buckets). Since the composite parts are not interconnected, there will be almost no overlap among the requests, leading to very high throughput values.

4.4 Structural Modification Operations

In this subsection, we discuss two experiments on a dynamic hierarchy: varying the number of threads and varying the percentage of structural updates. To conduct these experiments, we enable the edge addition and deletion operations of STMBench7. In the first experiment, out of all the operations, 10% of the operations are dynamic, that is, they change the hierarchy structure. 50% of all the operations are fine-grained. Figure 4(a) compares the performances of FLEXIGRAN and DomLock in this context (HiFi does not support structural modifications) as we vary the number of parallel threads from 2 to 40. On an average, FLEXIGRAN performs 338% better than DomLock. We observe that, FLEXIGRAN outperforms DomLock consistently. FLEXIGRAN's performance improves up to 8 threads and then slowly declines. This indicates the higher overhead of using bit-vectors with higher amount of parallelism. In contrast, DomLock's performance consistently improves with the number of threads, indicating a better scaling behavior with only intervals. To understand this better, we show the effect of varying the percentage of dynamic updates in the hierarchy in Fig. 4(b). In this experiment, we use 20 parallel threads and 50% fine-grained operations, and vary the number of dynamic updates from 0 to 30% (the remaining operations perform locking but do not change the hierarchy structure). As expected, the performance of both the techniques slightly reduces with increased number of dynamic updates, but FLEXIGRAN outperforms DomLock with a large margin throughout.

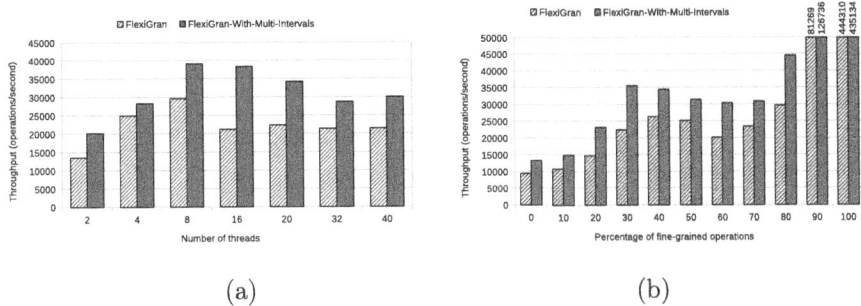

Fig. 5. Effect of varying (a) the number of threads and (b) the percentage of fine-grained operations in FLEXIGRAN with multiple intervals

4.5 False Subsumptions in FLEXIGRAN

Being interval-based locking techniques, FLEXIGRAN as well as DomLock are vulnerable to false subsumptions that can lead to unnecessary lock rejections, and thus reduced throughput. Additionally, using shorter bitsets can also contribute to false subsumptions. To reduce the negative effects of false subsumptions, multiple intervals per node proposed in MID [1] can be used. We studied the impact of applying an additional set of intervals in FLEXIGRAN. Figure 5(a) shows that when we vary the number of threads, FLEXIGRAN with two sets of intervals performs 43% better on an average, compared to FLEXIGRAN with a single set of intervals as we increase the number of threads from 2 to 40. In this experiment, 50% of the lock requests were fine-grained in nature. Most of the false subsumptions arising out of the remaining 50% of hierarchical lock requests get nullified by the second set of intervals, leading to good improvement in performance. Figure 5(b) shows that whenever hierarchical requests are present, using multiple intervals per node helps improve the throughput. The number of intervals per node can be increased for achieving higher precision, but at the cost of some additional overheads to maintain those intervals.

5 Related Work

A fully coarse-gained lock is seldom an optimal locking choice in databases [14, 15]. If all the transactions request locking small parts of the database, picked randomly, fine-grained locking is a performance-friendly option. If most transactions try to lock large chunks of the database, coarser grained locks are preferred. Unrau et al. [16] proposed using either coarse-grained mode (for shorter critical sections), or fine-grained mode (for larger duration), but not both at the same time.

Multi-Granularity Locking (MGL) techniques lock data at sub-hierarchy levels. At the extreme cases, MGL becomes fine-grained or coarse-grained locking. FLEXIGRAN, DomLock, HiFi, and IL (Intention Locks) are all MGL techniques.

IL [5] was pioneered to be the practically adapted MGL implementation for many database applications, but it requires traversals for overlap checks and sometimes multi-path locking in DAGs. Liu and Zhang's [11] fine-grained locking technique for hierarchies is based on IL. Hierarchical versions of concurrency control algorithms other than IL are also popular in database applications [2].

DomLock [7] is a relatively recent MGL technique for hierarchies which avoids the drawbacks of IL. With its numeric intervals, it is able to check for overlaps without traversing the graph, and without the need for explicitly locking multiple paths. NumLock [8] is an improvisation on DomLock. Across various locking options, locking cost and degree of concurrency varies considerably. NumLock generates a few pareto-optimal MGL options using a greedy algorithm and then analyses and reports the optimal one among them. HiFi [4] is another technique which was built on top of DomLock, to enable hierarchical and fine-grained locks together, but it works only on static hierarchies. FLEXIGRAN overcomes the limitations of both DomLock and HiFi, exploits fast bitwise operations, and is flexible with adding approximations to the bit-sequence based representation. We compare FLEXIGRAN with DomLock and HiFi.

6 Conclusion

We proposed a new locking technique named FLEXIGRAN, which allows flexible granularity locking in hierarchies by supporting co-existence of fine-grained and hierarchical locks. We used fast bitwise operations to enhance the performance of FLEXIGRAN and demonstrated its effectiveness using hierarchies from STM-Bench7. We also showed that adding approximations help FLEXIGRAN reduce its memory requirement, without hurting performance. While maximizing performance in static hierarchies, FLEXIGRAN also offers extensibility to hierarchies that undergo structural modifications. We compared the performance of our technique with that of DomLock and HiFi. While noting that FLEXIGRAN always surpasses DomLock, we also identified a couple of extreme scenarios in which HiFi performs better than FLEXIGRAN. We also studied the performance of FLEXIGRAN on an XML hierarchy. In the present form, when approximations are added, the performance remains good, as the bitwise operations finish faster on smaller inputs; but it is definitely leading to unnecessary locking of extra nodes. Reducing such unnecessary locking would be an interesting future work. Choosing the optimal number of bits to be used per lock pool entry and automatically choosing the percentage of fine-grained operations based on the resource availability also requires additional research. We believe that the core ideas of FLEXIGRAN can be applied to many core systems if the hierarchy and the meta data are maintained on the GPU. Also, it can be implemented in other languages that support mutex locks, bit manipulations, etc.

Acknowledgments. We thank the reviewers for providing valuable feedback and Dr. Martin Burtscher for supporting the travel.

Disclosure of Interests. The authors declare that there is no competing interest.

References

1. Anju, M.A., Nasre, R.: Multi-interval DomLock: toward improving concurrency in hierarchies. ACM Trans. Parallel Comput. **9**(3), 1–27 (2022). https://doi.org/10.1145/3543543
2. Carey, M.J.: Granularity hierarchies in concurrency control. In: Proceedings of the 2nd ACM SIGACT-SIGMOD Symposium on Principles of Database Systems, pp. 156–165. PODS 1983, ACM, NY, USA (1983). https://doi.org/10.1145/588058.588079
3. Eswaran, K.P., Gray, J.N., Lorie, R.A., Traiger, I.L.: The notions of consistency and predicate locks in a database system. Commun. ACM **19**(11), 624–633 (1976)
4. Ganesh, K., Kalikar, S., Nasre, R.: Multi-granularity locking in hierarchies with synergistic hierarchical and fine-grained locks. In: European Conference on Parallel Processing, pp. 546–559 (2018)
5. Gray, J.N., Lorie, R.A., Putzolu, G.R.: Granularity of locks in a shared data base. In: Proceedings of the 1st International Conference on Very Large Data Bases, pp. 428–451. ACM, New York, NY, USA (1975)
6. Guerraoui, R., Kapalka, M., Vitek, J.: STMBench7: a benchmark for software transactional memory. In: Proceedings of the 2nd ACM SIGOPS/EuroSys European Conference on Computer Systems 2007, pp. 315–324. ACM, New York, NY, USA (2007)
7. Kalikar, S., Nasre, R.: DomLock: a new multi-granularity locking technique for hierarchies. ACM Trans. Parallel Comput. (TOPC) **4**(2), 1–29 (2017)
8. Kalikar, S., Nasre, R.: NumLock: towards optimal multi-granularity locking in hierarchies. In: Proceedings of the 47th International Conference on Parallel Processing, pp. 1–10. ACM, New York, NY, USA (2018)
9. Lamport, L.: A new solution of Dijkstra's concurrent programming problem. Commun. ACM **17**(8), 453–455 (1974). https://doi.org/10.1145/361082.361093
10. Lamport, L.: A new solution of Dijkstra's concurrent programming problem, pp. 171–178. Association for Computing Machinery, New York, NY, USA (2019). https://doi.org/10.1145/3335772.3335782
11. Liu, P., Zhang, C.: Unleashing concurrency for irregular data structures. In: Proceedings of the 36th International Conference on Software Engineering, pp. 480–490. Association for Computing Machinery, New York, NY, USA (2014)
12. Lomet, D., Mokbel, M.F.: Locking key ranges with unbundled transaction services. Proc. VLDB Endow. **2**(1), 265–276 (2009). https://doi.org/10.14778/1687627.1687658 https://doi.org/10.14778/1687627.1687658
13. Microsoft: SQL Server 2019 (2021). https://www.microsoft.com/en-in/sql-server/sql-server-2019. Accessed 01 Sep 2021
14. Ries, D.R., Stonebraker, M.: Effects of locking granularity in a database management system. ACM Trans. Database Syst. (TODS) **2**(3), 233–246 (1977)
15. Ries, D.R., Stonebraker, M.R.: Locking granularity revisited. ACM Trans. Database Syst. (TODS) **4**(2), 210–227 (1979)
16. Unrau, R.C., Krieger, O., Gamsa, B., Stumm, M.: Experiences with locking in a NUMA multiprocessor operating system kernel. In: Proceedings of OSDI, pp. 11–es (1994)

Efficient Code Region Characterization Through Automatic Performance Counters Reduction Using Machine Learning Techniques

Suren Harutyunyan[1]([✉]), Eduardo César[1], Anna Sikora[1],
Jiří Filipovič[2], Akash Dutta[3], Ali Jannesari[3], and Jordi Alcaraz[4]

[1] Universitat Autònoma de Barcelona, Bellaterra, Spain
{suren.harutyunyan,eduardo.cesar,anna.sikora}@uab.cat
[2] Masaryk University, Brno, Czech Republic
fila@ics.muni.cz
[3] Iowa State University, Ames, IA, USA
{adutta,jannesar}@iastate.edu
[4] University of Oregon, Eugene, OR, USA
jordia@uoregon.edu

Abstract. Leveraging hardware performance counters provides valuable insights into system resource utilization, aiding performance analysis and tuning for parallel applications. The available counters vary with architecture and are collected at execution time. Their abundance and the limited number of registers for measurement make gathering laborious and costly. Efficient characterization of parallel regions necessitates a dimension reduction strategy. While recent efforts have focused on manually reducing the number of counters for specific architectures, this paper introduces a novel approach: an automatic dimension reduction technique for efficiently characterizing parallel code regions across diverse architectures. The methodology is based on Machine Learning ensembles because of their precision and ability at capturing different relationships between the input features and the target variables. Evaluation results show that ensembles can successfully reduce the number of hardware performance counters that characterize a code region. We validate our approach on CPUs using a comprehensive dataset of OpenMP regions, showing that any region can be accurately characterized by 8 relevant hardware performance counters. In addition, we also apply the proposed methodology on GPUs using a reduced set of kernels, demonstrating its effectiveness across various hardware configurations and workloads.

Keywords: Performance Counters · Automatic Dimension Reduction · Machine Learning Ensembles · Parallel Region Classification

---

This work was supported by the Ministerio de Ciencia e Innovación MCIN AEI/10.13039/501100011033 under contract PID2020-113614RB-C21, by the Catalan government under contract 2021 SGR 00574, and by the Ministry of Education, Youth and Sports from the Large Infrastructures for Research, Experimental Development and Innovations project "e-Infrastructure CZ - LM2023054.

© The Author(s) 2024
J. Carretero et al. (Eds.): Euro-Par 2024, LNCS 14801, pp. 18–32, 2024.
https://doi.org/10.1007/978-3-031-69577-3_2

1 Introduction

Modern HPC systems present challenges for performance analysis and tuning of parallel applications. Automated analysis during runtime contributes to this complexity, since it must be performed efficiently in a landscape of heterogeneous architectures.

Gathering relevant metrics, especially at the processor level, is crucial for effective behaviour and performance analysis. Hardware performance counters (HwPCs) are a set of special-purpose registers that store metrics about the use of system resources and hardware related activities. These metrics provide valuable insights and can be used for low-level performance analysis or tuning.

Several works [1,8,9,18] propose leveraging HwPCs' to identify and characterize parallel regions during runtime. However, each processor exposes a large number of HwPCs, which cannot be read simultaneously.

Two primary methods are used for collecting HwPC metrics: i) executing an application multiple times to gather accurate measurements at a high cost, ii) a less costly single execution that multiplexes the limited number of registers among performance monitoring events at the cost of precision. These problems underscore the importance of reducing the number of HwPCs used to characterize and classify a code region to achieve higher precision, reduce overhead, and enable a more efficient dynamic tuning process.

Recently, Alcaraz et al. [1] introduced a method that helped characterize a parallel code region using a reduced list of HwPCs. The methodology was effective if the original set of HwPCs and the number of code regions were not too big, because it requires human intervention. This manual intervention is necessary to check and discard redundant HwPCs.

In this work, we propose an automated technique that can accurately characterize parallel code regions. The methodology focuses on Machine Learning ensembles that can automatically identify, rank, and obtain a reduced list of HwPCs independently of the number of available counters and regions. The proposed approach is architecture agnostic and works equally well for both CPUs and GPUs. To prove its effectiveness, this ensemble methodology is tested with an exhaustive database with a large number of kernels on CPUs, and on 2 different GPU architectures with medium sized databases. Results show that ensembles models produce a reduced set of HwPCs that accurately characterizes OpenMP and CUDA parallel code regions.

This paper is organized as follows. Section 2 presents the motivation of this work. Section 3 introduces the rationale behind ensembles, the techniques used in the proposed methodology, and how these are evaluated. Section 4 describes the main contribution of this paper: the ensemble methodology for automatic ranking and reduction of HwPCs. Section 5 shows the evaluation of the methodology on different architectures. Section 6 presents relevant related work. Finally, Sect. 7 concludes the work and discusses its future directions.

2 Motivation

Alcaraz et al. in [1] presented a methodology, based on Principal Component Analysis (PCA) and correlation analysis, for reducing the number of HwPCs needed for characterizing OpenMP parallel regions. Principal Component Analysis was used to visualize the different kernels and verify whether they can be classified visually. It can also be applied to discover relationships among HwPCs weights in each principal component, where similar weights potentially point out redundancies. In addition, if the PCA resulting from excluding a set of HwPCs remained similar to the previous PCA and there is minimal impact on the explained variance with fewer dimensions, the reduction can be deemed valid.

Finally, correlation analysis was used to reduce HwPCs. These were discarded if the correlation value between two, or more, counters was very high and could be logically explained. Very high correlation points to the possibility of counters explaining similar information. The methodology was tested on a dataset created by executing the STREAM benchmark [12], which consists of 4 different code patterns. The different execution configurations consisted of various problem sizes, compilation flags, etc.

This reduction method has some serious limitations. It involves the user intervention, and is effective when the number of HwPCs and code regions is small. As the number of HwPCs and tested configurations can be extremely large, applying the same methodology can become unwieldy. To overcome these limitations, we choose to leverage Machine Learning techniques because they have demonstrated unparalleled efficacy and precision in tackling tasks necessitating the analysis of extensive datasets.

3 Supervised Machine Learning Algorithms

In this section, a theoretical description of the concepts that are used in the presented research is provided.

The methodology designed for automatically identifying the set of relevant HwPCs consists of an ensemble of supervised models presented in Table 1. A ML ensemble is a general meta approach that combines different models trained simultaneously on the same dataset. The models are trained to operate jointly to produce better performance results than any individual model on its own because of the following reasons [17]:

1. **Reduce bias and variance:** Multiple models in an ensemble can complement each other and help reduce the bias and variance of the overall model. This can result in more accurate predictions.
2. **Combine different approaches:** Ensembles combine different approaches or models that may have different strengths and weaknesses. This can help overcome the limitations of individual models and lead to better overall performance.
3. **Robustness:** ML ensembles can still perform well even if some of the individual models are not performing well.

Table 1. Models and metrics used for classification

Algorithms	Metric
Logistic Model with Elastic Net	Accuracy
Random Forest	
XGBoost	
TabNet	

4. **Diversity:** ML ensembles incorporate a range of different models which make them more generalizable and better able to handle a variety of inputs.

Overall, ML ensembles represent a powerful instrument for enhancing predictive efficacy, including classification accuracy, and attaining superior results across diverse application domains. For the present work the models discussed below were selected based on their precision and their ability at capturing different relationships between the input features and the target variables. Additionally, other factors such as the training cost were considered.

Logistic Model with Elastic Net is a combination of the Logistic Model [7] with Elastic Net [23], which integrates both L1 (Lasso, or Least Absolute Shrinkage Selector Operator Regression) [19] and L2 (Ridge) [10] regularizations. This combination offers advantages in managing multicollinearity among predictors, mitigating overfitting, and facilitating feature selection. The model is computationally efficient and effective in scenarios where there exists clear class separation and simple relationships between features and target variables.

Random Forest [4] is a flexible meta-estimator that can be used for both regression and classification. It is based on Bagging (Bootstrap Aggregation), it is resilient to outliers, and is most effective for datasets with a small to medium number of features. It is mainly used to capture the nonlinear relationships between them. This approach first fits in parallel a number of decision trees on various random sub-samples of the dataset, called Bootstrap Samples (or bags). Second, it produces the output by averaging (Aggregating) the individual outputs, thus improving the predictive accuracy and controlling over-fitting.

XGBoost (Extreme Gradient Boosting) [6] is a fast and scalable implementation of gradient-boosted trees. It reduces the tree search space via information given by the distribution of the features. This approach can be used for both regression and classification, handling a wide range of data sizes. It is effective on datasets with imbalanced class distributions. It is based on Boosting, an iterative technique that sequentially builds models, assesses their errors, and assigns higher weights to incorrectly predicted values to improve the next models. Since each new model aims to rectify the errors of the previous one, the result is a model with the highest accuracy.

TabNet [3] is a Deep Neural Network designed for tabular data capable of performing both classification and regression tasks. It is especially effective in scenarios where the dataset has a large number of features with complex relationships to the target variable. It employs a learner that resembles decision tree-based models, aiming to achieve interpretability and sparse feature selection. TabNet performs both output mapping and feature selection, making it a powerful tool for analyzing and understanding complex tabular datasets.

Accuracy has been used as the metric to score the component models of the ensemble. It measures the proportion of correctly classified instances among all instances, indicating the closeness of the model's predictions to the ground truth value. It is commonly used because of its simplicity and intuitive interpretation, making it easy to understand.

The following is the formulation of the accuracy score in the case of a binary classification:

$$\text{Binary Classification Accuracy} = \frac{TP + TN}{TP + TN + FP + FN}, \quad (1)$$

where TP denotes the True Positives, FP are the False Positives, TN are the True Negatives, and FN are the False Negatives.

Conversely, in the case of multiclass classification, the accuracy score is the fraction of correct classifications and is formulated as follows:

$$\text{Multiclass Classification Accuracy} = \frac{\text{Correct Classifications}}{\text{All Classifications}} \quad (2)$$

After the ensemble is trained, during the inference phase, each model generates its own classification prediction. The final class is determined through a majority vote mechanism, where the most predicted class is the final label. This serves to mitigate the individual variance of the predictions, thereby enhancing the robustness of the results.

4 Performance Counters Reduction Using ML Ensembles

In this section we describe the proposed HwPC reduction methodology presented on Fig. 1. Given a database containing values of HwPCs for various code regions, the methodology reduces the number of HwPCs to a minimal set capable of accurately characterizing and classifying any code region. This minimal set is established through the scoring and ranking of HwPCs using a Machine Learning ensemble. Step 1 is composed of a training and validation of an ensemble of classifier models. The models analyze the relationship between the code regions and a set of HwPCs. After training/validation, Step 2 is used to extract the importance of each HwPC for each model. Step 3 reduces the ranked HwPCs to the minimal set that characterize a code region.

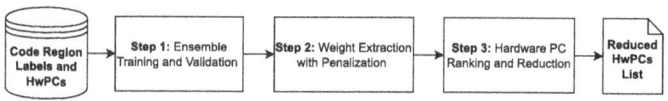

Fig. 1. Performance counters reduction with model ensembles.

Code Regions Labels and HwPCs. First, we provide a brief description of the data sources and the input for the methodology. For each code region, data has been collected on execution time, tuning parameters, and HwPCs' values. As we are looking for the most important HwPCs that characterize code regions, new datasets that only include the code region label and HwPCs' values are generated. These datasets are pre-processed for deleting features with 0 variance.

Step 1: Ensemble Training and Validation. Figure 2 shows Step 1 (ensemble training and validation) components. The methods included for the classification task are Logistic Regression with Elastic Net, Random Forest, XGBoost, and TabNet. As discussed in Sect. 3, each model has a different set of strengths and captures different relationships between the input features and the target variable. Altogether, they capture linear and non-linear relationships that may arise between code regions and HwPCs. For example, Logistic Regression focuses on linear relationships, while XGBoost focuses on non-linear ones.

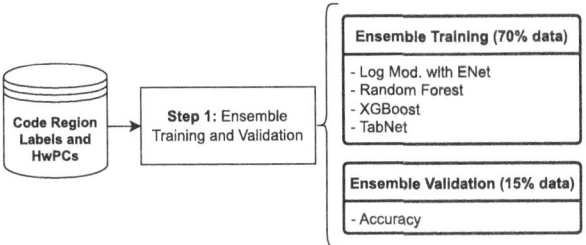

Fig. 2. Step 1: Ensemble training and validation.

Additionally, each different model is more effective for datasets of different sizes and class distributions. Random Forest and XGBoost excel on large datasets with large numbers of features and samples. On the other hand, TabNet offers the advantage of a competent classifier when the labeled data is limited. This is paramount since the collected kernel execution data can differ not only on the number of features (HwPCs) but also on the number of available tuning configurations/parameters, and samples. Thus a combination can leverage the strengths of each model and improve overall performance.

The data is split into 70% for training, 15% for validation, and 15% for testing. After training, the models are validated using the accuracy metric. It is used to determine the most performant models, and is later used to form the weights given to the predictions of each model.

Step 2: Weight Extraction with Penalization. Once the training is complete, the models assign scores to the HwPCs, which represent the relative importance of each feature in making the prediction. These scores are normalized from 0.0 to 1.0. The scores are computed as follows:

1. **Logistic Model with Elastic Net**: The importance of features is determined by the magnitude of the coefficients learned during model training. A higher absolute magnitude of the coefficient indicates greater importance of the corresponding HwPC in influencing the predicted outcome.
2. **Random Forest**: Random Forest: Feature importance is determined by the average decrease in impurity, measured by either Gini impurity or entropy, caused by each HwPC when used to split the data across all decision trees within the forest. HwPCs that consistently result in larger reductions in impurity across multiple trees are assigned higher importance scores.
3. **XGBoost**: Feature importance is determined by the average gain of each feature when employed to split the data across all decision trees within the ensemble. Gain is defined as the improvement in model performance achieved by splitting the data based on a particular HwPC, typically measured by the reduction in loss. HwPCs with higher average gain across all trees are considered more influential in the model.
4. **TabNet**: TabNet: Feature importance scores are determined by the contribution of each feature to the final decision made by the neural network architecture. The model utilizes an attention mechanism to dynamically weigh the importance of each HwPC at every decision step within the network.

To combine the different scores across the models we use a weighted average that assigns higher weights to the more accurate models. The weights are determined by accuracy of the models during the validation process. In this way, models with higher accuracy have more influence in the HwPC's score. Accuracy directly reflects the performance of each model, making models with higher accuracy generally more reliable and capable of producing better predictions.

Let $HwPC = \{h_0, h_1, ..., h_{N-1}\}$ be a set of N HwPCs. The ith HwPC has a set of corresponding model scores or coefficients $\{c_{i_0}, c_{i_1}, c_{i_2}, c_{i_3}\}$. There is also a set of discount factor weights extracted during the validation of the ensemble $\{w_0, w_1, w_2, w_3\}$. The weighted average of the ith HwPC's score is calculated with Expression 3, where j denotes the model in the ensemble.

$$W_i = \frac{\sum_{j=1}^{4} c_{i_j} w_j}{\sum_{j=1}^{4} w_j}, \tag{3}$$

Figure 3 illustrates the weight extraction process. Each model has a weight (accuracy) associated to its predictions and assigns a score to each HwPC. The final score is the weighted average of the scores of the HwPCs.

Step 3: Hardware Performance Counter Ranking and Reduction. Once the weighted average of the scores for each HwPC is calculated, it is used to arrange the list of HwPCs in descending order.

From this ordered list, we apply Algorithm 1 to determine the minimal set of HwPCs capable of characterizing the parallel regions in the dataset. Firstly, we calculate the reference line shown in Fig. 4b, which passes through points (0,0) and (N-1, accuracyN-1). This line extends from the point with the lowest

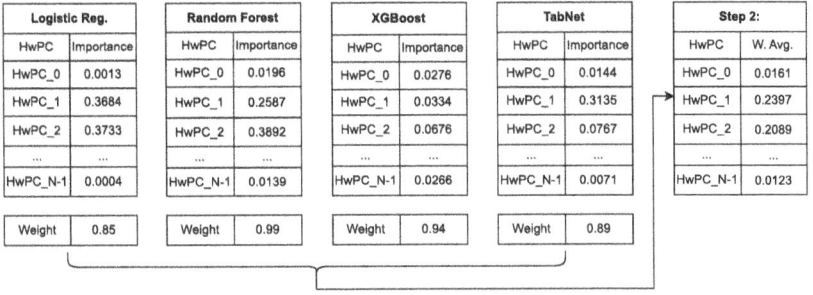

Fig. 3. Step 2: HwPC importance per model and weighted average.

Algorithm 1. HwPCs Reduction

Input: List H of N HwPCs ordered by rank
Output: Reduced list of K HwPCs
/* The reference line is the one going from the accuracy using 0 HwPCs
(0) and the accuracy using all HwPCs (already computed in Step 1) */
1: Compute straight line L between $(0,0)$ and $(N-1, Accuracy_{N-1})$
2: $K \leftarrow 1$
3: $OldDiff \leftarrow 0$ // The accuracy with 0 HwPCs
4: Obtain sub-array S_1 of first HwPC from H
5: Train and validate an Ensemble using S_1
6: $Acc \leftarrow$ validation accuracy
7: $NewDiff \leftarrow$ distance between $(1, Acc)$ and L
8: **while** $NewDiff > OldDiff$ **do**
      /* Determining the knee point */
9:     $K++$
10:    Obtain sub-array S_k of first k HwPCs from H
11:    Train and validate an Ensemble using S_k
12:    $Acc \leftarrow$ validation accuracy
13:    $OldDiff \leftarrow NewDiff$
14:    $NewDiff \leftarrow$ Distance between (k, Acc) and L
15: **end while**
16: $Result \leftarrow$ First $K-1$ HwPCs from H
---

accuracy (0 HwPCs yields 0 accuracy) to the point corresponding to the accuracy achieved in the validation of the model trained using all HwPCs. The latter is known as it was calculated in Step 1 of the methodology.

Subsequently, we iteratively proceed to use the ensemble to train models using an increasing number of HwPCs taken in order from the ranked list, as shown in Fig. 4a. We start by training a model with the highest-ranked HwPC, then a new model using the top two ranked HwPCs, and so on. In each case, we compute the distance between the reference line and the accuracy obtained by the model using a certain number of HwPCs, as shown in Fig. 4b. This iterative process concludes when this distance ceases to increase upon adding a new

HwPC, indicating that the knee point has been reached and that the increase in accuracy obtained becomes marginal from this point.

Finally, the minimum set of HwPCs capable of characterizing the dataset's regions consists of those for which the distance continued to increase.

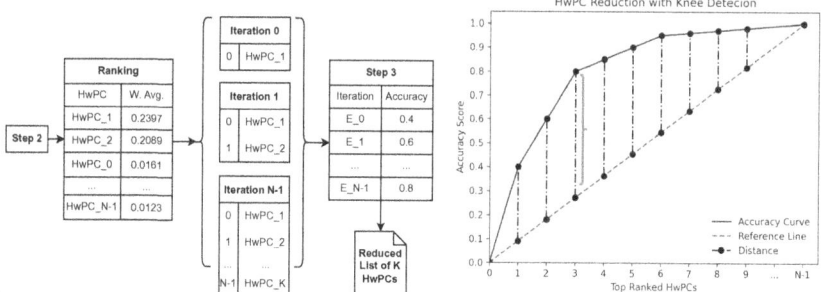

(a) Weight ranking and reduction process   (b) Knee detection of the accuracy curve

Fig. 4. Step 3: HwPC reduction considering the knee point.

It is worth noting that if the dataset used to apply the methodology includes representative regions of the space of possible parallel regions, the model generated for the reduced set of HwPCs would likely classify regions not included in the dataset with high accuracy.

5 Evaluation

In this section, we present the results obtained using the proposed ensemble methodology for different cases. First, we compare the results produced using our methodology with those reported in Alcaraz et al. [1]. Next, we assess the effectiveness of our methodology using a comprehensive dataset of OpenMP parallel regions on CPUs. Finally, we show that the methodology can also be applied to classify GPU kernels.

5.1 Comparison with PCA and Correlation-Based Methodology

We begin by comparing the results obtained using our methodology to those reported in [1]. Employing the same benchmark, STREAM [12], and the same hardware, a Xeon E5645 processor. STREAM comprises four patterns -Copy, Scale, Sum, and Triad- each exhibiting distinct memory access patterns and operation counts.

The HwPCs were collected using the preset events available in Performance Application Programming Interface (PAPI) [14]. In this architecture, the set of preset HwPCs included the following event types and the corresponding number of counters:

- **Branches**: 7
- **Cache L1**: 8
- **Cache L2**: 16
- **Cache L3**: 10
- **TLB**: 3
- **Cycles**: 3
- **Operations**: 3
- **Instructions**: 8

As a result of applying the PCA and correlation-based methodology, the number of HwPCs neccesary to classify these patterns was reduced from 58 to 20.

Using the proposed ensemble methodology, the number of HwPCs is reduced from 58 to 5, which includes a diverse set of event types:

- **Instructions**: PAPI_SR_INS
- **Operations**: PAPI_FP_OPS and PAPI_DP_OPS
- **Branches**: PAPI_BR_TKN
- **Cache L1**: PAPI_L1_ICH

Four of them (PAPI_DP_OPS, PAPI_FP_OPS, PAPI_BR_TKN, PAPI_SR_INS) are also present in the reduced set from [1], and the remaining one, PAPI_L1_ICH, is highly correlated with PAPI_BR_MSP (0.9781) from this set.

Table 2. Evaluation results for Xeon E5645.

Results/Methodology	PCA & Correlation	Ensemble 1	Ensemble 2
Reduced Set	20	5	5
Accuracy	99.98%	93.83%	99.20%
K Fold Accuracy	–	85.94%	96.10%

In [1], the reduced set was later used to train an Artificial Neural Network (ANN), which was utilized to predict the parallel code region based on the values of HwPCs. The training set consisted of 54 problem sizes (432000 entries), while the remaining 2 sizes were reserved for testing (16000 entries). Table 2 shows that the ANN accurately classified 99.98% of the test set in this case.

Using the proposed methodology with the same train/test split, the model (Ensemble 1 in the table) accurately classified 93.83% of the test set. Our stratified 5 fold cross validation, achieving an average cross validated score of 85.94%.

However, applying a random stratified train/validation/test split common in ML, 70% of data for training, 15% for validation, and 15% for testing, the model (Ensemble 2 in the table) was able to classify accurately 99.20% of the test set. We also performed a stratified 5 fold cross validation, achieving an average cross validated score of 96.10%.

Therefore, the proposed methodology achieves comparable results using only 5 automatically determined HwPCs, minimizing event multiplexing and thereby enhancing measurement precision.

5.2 Comprehensive Dataset of OpenMP Regions

Our methodology was further evaluated on a different architecture, a 32-core Xeon E5-4620, using a more comprehensive dataset consisting of 18 kernels. This dataset included 4 kernels from the STREAM benchmark [12], 12 benchmarks from the PolyBench suite [21,22], which comprises synthetic benchmarks representing common computational kernels in scientific and engineering applications. Finally, we included Collatz conjecture and a Friendly number calculator.

The HwPCs were collected using the preset events available in PAPI for this architecture. These events were separated into compatible groups, while taking into account the maximum number of events that can be read at the same time in one processor and if they can be accessed simultaneously [1]. We measured each group of HwPCs for multiple executions of the code regions, with different configuration combinations (number of threads, affinity policy, scheduling policy, and chunk size). The problem sizes were computed using the methodology presented in [2], which focuses on stressing the different memory levels available in the architecture. For each of the HwPC groups, problem sizes, and configurations, we conducted 100 executions for statistical significance. Table 3a shows the summary of the configurations for the executions of each region.

In this architecture, the set of preset HwPCs included the following event types and the corresponding number of counters:

- **Branches**: 6
- **Cache L1**: 5
- **Cache L2**: 14
- **Cache L3**: 9
- **TLB**: 2
- **Cycles**: 3
- **Operations**: 3
- **Instructions**: 8

Using the proposed ensemble methodology, the number of HwPCs is reduced from 50 to 6, which, again, include a diverse set of event types:

- **Instructions**: PAPI_SR_INS and PAPI_FDV_INS
- **Operations**: PAPI_FP_OPS and PAPI_DP_OPS
- **Branches**: PAPI_BR_NTK and PAPI_BR_MSP

As mentioned in Sect. 2, the number of kernels (18) and the large number of tested configurations (more than 12M) precludes us of using the PCA/Correlation based method of the previous subsection on the comprehensive dataset.

As in the previous case, we tested the results of the proposed ensemble methodology by training a model ensemble using a random stratified train/validation/test split (70% of the data for training, 15% for validation, and the remaining 15% for testing). The obtained accuracy on the test set was 96.95%, as shown in Table 3b. We also performed a stratified 5 fold cross validation, achieving an average cross validated score of 96.82%.

Once more, the proposed methodology achieves very good results using only 6 automatically determined HwPCs, minimizing event multiplexing and thereby

Table 3. Execution parameters and evaluation results for Xeon E5-4620.

(a) Execution parameters.

Execs./System	Xeon E5-4620
HwPC Sets	12
Threads	32
Problem Sizes	29
OpenMP Pars.	11
Reps.	100
Total	12,249,600

(b) Evaluation results.

Results/Method.	Ensembles
Reduced Set	6
Accuracy	96.95%
K Fold Accuracy	96.82%

enhancing measurement precision. Moreover, for a dataset including a significantly greater amount of regions and configurations, the methodology is still sharply reducing the number of HwPCs.

5.3 Applying the Methodology for Characterizing GPU Kernels

The last experiments have the objective of showing that the proposed methodology can be also applied for reducing the number of HwPCs necessary to characterize GPU kernels. HwPC data was collected on a set of benchmarks, either exhaustively or through random sampling, using the Kernel Tuning Toolkit (KTT) [15] on 2 different GPUs, the GeForce GTX 680 (Kepler) and the GeForce GTX 1070 (Pascal). For each configuration, data comprising tuning parameter values, execution time, and HwPC values was obtained on five kernels analyzed by Petrovič et al. in [16]: Convolution, Couloumb Sum, Nbody, Transposition, and GEMM, with the inclusion of the Reduction kernel for the Pascal GPU.

Using the ensemble methodology with the Kepler dataset (5 kernels), the number of HwPCs was reduced from 35 to 3, while for the Pascal dataset (6 kernels) it was reduced from 167 to 4. The resulting HwPCs are the following:

GTX 680 (Kepler):

- inst_fp_32
- l2_write_transactions
- inst_executed

GTX 1080 (Pascal):

- inst_per_warp
- gld_requested_throughput
- gst_requested_throughput
- dram_read_throughput

Given the smaller size of the datasets compared to the CPU ones, we opted for larger holdout datasets. Instead of the traditional 15/15 split for validation and testing, we implemented a random stratified train/validation/test split, allocating 70% of the data for training, 3% for validation, and 27% for testing. We believe that using 27% of the dataset for testing provides a more robust assessment of the effectiveness of our methodology in this context. Table 4 shows that the trained model achieves 99.94% accuracy on the Kepler dataset and 99.81%

accuracy on the Pascal dataset. We also performed a stratified 5 fold cross validation, achieving an average cross validated score of 99.99% on the Kepler dataset, and 99.43% on the Pascal dataset. It is highly probable that the cause of such sharp reduction in the number of HwPCs is the small number of kernels in the dataset. Nevertheless, the obtained results are also very promising for GPUs.

Table 4. Counters' reduction and evaluation results for GeForce GTX 680 (Kepler) and GeForce GTX 1080 (Pascal).

Results/System	GeForce GTX 680	GeForce GTX 1080
Full Set	35	167
Reduced Set	3	4
Accuracy	99.94%	99.81%
K Fold Accuracy	99.99%	99.43%

6 Related Work

The presented methodology involves the application of ML model ensembles to characterize a code region through a reduced set of HwPCs. There are several studies that make use of statistical techniques, and also pursue the objective of characterizing code regions.

On the one hand, there are approaches that involve the characterization of code regions via a representative dataset composed of multiple kernels and configurations. READEX [11] authors use Periscope Tuning Framework [13] and a representative dataset to record timing related data. This performance data is then used to discover relevant code regions in the application. Akash et al. [8] were able to determine parallel loop patterns using HwPCs and code graph representations of the code regions. On the other hand, other approaches focus on a specific application, exclusively collecting its data. In [18] the authors utilize CERE to characterize code regions, using clustering techniques to identify parallel regions with similar characteristics. The applications under consideration are decomposed into smaller code segments, *codelets*, which are then associated with corresponding OpenMP parallel regions. Artemis [20] uses collected execution data from instrumented parallel regions, and user provided features and execution policies for the code region. Extra-P [5] uses HwPCs and other metrics, such as the number of bytes an MPI function sends or receives, to generate a parallel profile of an application. In all the mentioned tools, there is a selection of which HwPCs should be used to characterize code regions. However, to the best of our knowledge, none of them uses a systematic methodology to determine the set of the most relevant HwPCs, as the one proposed in this work.

7 Conclusions and Future Work

In this paper, we introduced a novel method of reducing the HwPCs that characterize a parallel region. The proposed methodology, based on Machine Learning ensembles aimed to be automatic, and independent of hardware architecture. The ensemble methodology has been tested on CPUs and GPUs. The CPU tests were performed on 2 different sets corresponding to different architectures. During evaluation, we were able to significantly reduce the HwPCs required for characterization of a parallel code region. The reduced set only contained 5 and 6 HwPCs, and the ensemble methodology was able to correctly classify 99.20% and 96.95% of the parallel regions, respectively. To validate the architecture independence of the methodology, we evaluated it on 2 different GPU architectures with a small set of CUDA kernels. Although the collected databasets were not as large as in the CPU case, it is clearly demonstrated that the ensemble method drastically reduces the number of HwPCs necessary to characterize a CUDA kernel. The reduced set contains 3 and 4 HwPCs classifying kernels with 99.94 and 99.81% of accuracy, respectively. These results are significant, since the sheer amount of available HwPCs on GPUs yields impossible any manual effort. Currently, we are using ensembles of ML regression models to determine a reduced set of HwPCs for optimizing the values of tuning parameters.

References

1. Alcaraz, J., Sikora, A., César, E.: Hardware counters' space reduction for code region characterization. In: Yahyapour, R. (ed.) Euro-Par 2019. LNCS, vol. 11725, pp. 74–86. Springer, Cham (2019). https://doi.org/10.1007/978-3-030-29400-7_6
2. Alcaraz, J., et al.: Predicting number of threads using balanced datasets for openmp regions. PDP Spec. Issue 2021 Comput. **105**(5), 999–1017 (2023)
3. Arik, S.Ö., Pfister, T.: Tabnet: attentive interpretable tabular learning. arXiv preprint arXiv:1908.07442 (2019)
4. Breiman, L.: Random forests. Mach. Learn. **45**, 5–32 (2001)
5. Calotoiu, A., Hoefler, T., Poke, M., Wolf, F.: Using automated performance modeling to find scalability bugs in complex codes. In: Proceedings of the ACM/IEEE Conference on SC13, Denver, pp. 1–12. ACM (2013)
6. Chen, T., Guestrin, C.: XGBoost: a scalable tree boosting system. In: Proceedings of the 22nd ACM SIGKDD International Conference on Knowledge Discovery and Data Mining (KDD 16), pp. 785–794. ACM, New York (2016)
7. Cox, D.R.: The regression analysis of binary sequences. J. Roy. Stat. Soc.: Ser. B (Methodol.) **20**(2), 215–232 (1958)
8. Dutta, A., Alcaraz, J., TehraniJamsaz, A., Sikora, A., Cesar, E., Jannesari, A.: Pattern-based autotuning of openmp loops using graph neural networks. In: 2022 IEEE/ACM International Workshop on Artificial Intelligence and Machine Learning for Scientific Applications (AI4S), pp. 26–31 (2022)
9. Filipovič, J., Hozzová, J.A.N., Olha, J., Petrovič, F.: Using hardware performance counters to speed up autotuning convergence on gpus. J. Parall. Distrib. Comput. **160**, 16–35 (2022)
10. Hoerl, A.E., Kennard, R.W.: Ridge regression: biased estimation for nonorthogonal problems. Technometrics **12**(1), 55–67 (1970)

11. Kjeldsberg, P.G., Gocht, A., Gerndt, M., Riha, L., Schuchart, J., Mian, U.S.: Readex: linking two ends of the computing continuum to improve energy-efficiency in dynamic applications. In: Design, Automation Test in Europe Conference Exhibition, 2017, pp. 109–114 (2017)
12. McCalpin, J.: Memory bandwidth and machine balance in high performance computers. In: IEEE Technical Committee on Computer Architecture Newsletter, pp. 19–25 (1995)
13. Miceli, R., et al.: Autotune: a plugin-driven approach to the automatic tuning of parallel applications. In: Proceedings of the 11th International Workshop on the State-of-the-Art in Scientific and Parallel Computing (PARA 2012), vol. 7782, 328–342 (2013)
14. Mucci, P., Moore, S., Deane, C., Ho, G.: Papi: a portable interface to hardware performance counters (1999)
15. Petrovič, F., Filipovič, J.: Kernel tuning toolkit. SoftwareX **22**, 101385 (2023)
16. Petrovič, F., et al.: A benchmark set of highly-efficient CUDA and OpenCL kernels and its dynamic autotuning with kernel tuning toolkit. Futur. Gener. Comput. Syst. **108**, 161–177 (2020)
17. Polikar, R.: Ensemble based systems in decision making. IEEE Circuits Syst. Mag. **6**(3), 21–45 (2006)
18. Popov, M., Akel, C., Chatelain, Y., Jalby, W., de Oliveira Castro, P.: Piecewise holistic autotuning of parallel programs with CERE. Concurr. Comput. Pract. Exp. **29** (2017)
19. Tibshirani, R.: Regression shrinkage and selection via the lasso. J. Roy. Stat. Soc.: Ser. B (Methodol.) **58**(1), 267–288 (1996)
20. Wood, C., et al.: Artemis: automatic runtime tuning of parallel execution parameters using machine learning. In: Chamberlain, B.L., Varbanescu, A.-L., Ltaief, H., Luszczek, P. (eds.) ISC High Performance 2021. LNCS, vol. 12728, pp. 453–472. Springer, Cham (2021). https://doi.org/10.1007/978-3-030-78713-4_24
21. Yuki, T., Pouchet, L.N.: Polybench 4.0 (2015). https://web.cse.ohio-state.edu/~pouchet.2/software/polybench/
22. Yuki, T.: Understanding PolyBench/C 3.2 kernels. In: Rajopadhye, S., Verdoolaege, S. (eds.) Proceedings of the 4th International Workshop on Polyhedral Compilation Techniques, Vienna (2014)
23. Zou, H., Hastie, T.: Regularization and variable selection via the elastic net. J. Roy. Statist. Soc. Ser. B (Statist. Methodol.) **67**(2), 301–320 (2005)

Open Access This chapter is licensed under the terms of the Creative Commons Attribution 4.0 International License (http://creativecommons.org/licenses/by/4.0/), which permits use, sharing, adaptation, distribution and reproduction in any medium or format, as long as you give appropriate credit to the original author(s) and the source, provide a link to the Creative Commons license and indicate if changes were made.

The images or other third party material in this chapter are included in the chapter's Creative Commons license, unless indicated otherwise in a credit line to the material. If material is not included in the chapter's Creative Commons license and your intended use is not permitted by statutory regulation or exceeds the permitted use, you will need to obtain permission directly from the copyright holder.

ESIMD GPU Implementations of Deep Learning Sparse Matrix Kernels

Mohammad Zubair[1] and Christoph Bauinger[2]

[1] Old Dominion University, Norfolk, VA 23517, USA
zubair@cs.odu.edu
[2] Intel Corporation, Santa Clara, CA 95054, USA
christoph.bauinger@intel.com
http://www.cs.odu.edu/ mzubair

Abstract. We demonstrate that explicit SIMD programming on GPUs can outperform traditional programming environments such as CUDA and SYCL for three sparse matrix computations found in deep learning applications. Intel oneAPI's Explicit SIMD (ESIMD) SYCL extension API allows for simpler vectorization of arithmetic and memory operations which is critical in achieving good performance. We explore sparse matrix operations relevant to deep learning applications, namely the sparse-dense matrix multiplication (SPMM), the sampled dense-dense matrix multiplication (SDDMM), and the composition of the SDDMM with SPMM (FusedMM). Our ESIMD optimizations target the Intel Data Center GPU Max 1550. We evaluated performance on the test data set used by previous work, and our implementation outperforms state-of-the-art CUDA implementations on the latest NVIDIA hardware by up to a factor of 6.14. Additionally, our proposed implementation outperforms Intel's oneMKL implementation on Intel's GPU.

Keywords: Sparse Matrix Operations · Optimization · Machine Learning · Intel Data Center GPU

1 Introduction

The key to building and utilizing increasingly large machine learning (ML) models is efficient implementations of the training and inference. Graphics processing units (GPUs) have become relevant for ML applications [19,24], due to their high throughput in single precision (FP32) and reduced precision arithmetic (e.g., FP16, BF16), which is typically delivered by specialized hardware built into the devices [16,23]. Thus, in this contribution, we investigate three sparse matrix operations of particular interest for the training and inference of ML models on GPUs. Namely, the sparse-dense matrix multiplication (SPMM), the

---

This effort has been supported by the Intel oneAPI Center of Excellence at Old Dominion University. We want to thank Xiao Zhu of Intel, who provided support throughout this project, making resources available whenever we needed them.

© The Author(s), under exclusive license to Springer Nature Switzerland AG 2024
J. Carretero et al. (Eds.): Euro-Par 2024, LNCS 14801, pp. 33–46, 2024.
https://doi.org/10.1007/978-3-031-69577-3_3

sampled dense-dense matrix multiplication (SDDMM), and the composition of the SDDMM with SPMM, also termed as FusedMM operation [3–5,7,8,25]. The SPMM operation involves the multiplication of a sparse matrix with a dense matrix, resulting in a dense matrix. The SDDMM operation, in turn, multiplies two dense matrices followed by a sparse sampling. In other words, the output matrix of the SDDMM operation is sparse. The FusedMM operation merges the SDDMM and SPMM operations into a single operation, where the output of the SDDMM operation, which is a sparse matrix, is used as input to the following SPMM operation. Fusing the operations can increase the performance and thus benefit applications such as sparse transformer [7], where SPMM follows the SDDMM operation.

Sparse matrix operations have been studied extensively in the context of scientific computing [26] where the density of the matrices, which describes the fraction of non-zero entries in a matrix, is often less than 1%. The sparse matrices arising in ML, on the other hand, are relatively dense with densities up to 30% [4,7]. Nevertheless, these matrices are sufficiently sparse to warrant exploration of sparse matrix operations with compressed storage formats [7,8]. Several prior contributions have explored efficient implementations of sparse matrix operations, including SDDMM, SPMM, and FusedMM, on GPUs [5,7–9]. The major challenge in optimizing the performance of sparse matrix operations on GPUs is effectively utilizing the available memory bandwidth.

We found that SIMT programming models such as CUDA [21] or SYCL [20] introduce difficulties in achieving performance close to the theoretical peak hardware capabilities. Both programming models permit different threads in a warp/sub-group to take different paths. These different paths in the case of NVIDIA GPUs are mapped to a single path in real time using hardware (cf. [27], characteristics of the SIMT architecture). However, in the case of Intel's GPU architecture, different paths are mapped to SIMD hardware using appropriate assembly instructions. With the ESIMD API [13,14] Intel provides an extension to the SYCL standard which enables the explicit vectorization of GPU code by utilizing `simd` objects, thus addressing the underlying SIMD hardware directly. These `simd` objects enable the vectorization over SIMD-sizes different from the sub-group size (cf. [12] for details on sub-groups). Therefore, ESIMD offers finer control over the vectorization compared to standard SYCL. Since the `simd` objects are mapped to the registers, ESIMD also permits fine control over register usage. Additionally, ESIMD provides APIs for explicit memory load, store, and prefetch operations with parameters to control the caching behavior, and it simplifies the management of divergent branches in kernel code. The main disadvantage of ESIMD, in contrast to SYCL, is the lack of support for non-Intel GPUs.

The goals of the present contribution are to investigate i) how effective ESIMD is for the implementation of sparse matrix operations in deep learning applications, ii) the performance achievable on the Intel Data Center GPU Max 1550 [15], and iii) compare the results to other state-of the art implementations and hardware. In particular, in Sects. 2 and 3 we present our approaches and the conciseness of their ESIMD implementations. In Sect. 4 we compare the performance of our ESIMD implementations to the relevant functionalities provided by the Intel oneMKL on the same Intel GPU and to the performance of the best-known CUDA implementations [7,22] on Nvidia's H100 data center GPU. We demonstrate that our implementation outperforms the state-of-the-art oneMKL implementations for randomly generated sparse matrices by up to a factor of 3.4. We also outperform the CUDA implementations [7] on H100 by up to a factor 2.45 and the cuSPARSE implementations [22] by up to a factor 6.14 on the same randomly generated data set. For the sparse matrices from deep learning applications, we outperform the cuSPARSE library implementation by up to a factor 5.86 and by 1.6x on average in the SDDMM case and 1.21x on average in the SPMM case.

2 Overview of the Algorithms

In this section, we discuss our approach to parallelizing sparse matrix operations without giving details on how these algorithms are realized on a specific architecture. Table 1 gives an overview of all relevant quantities in the following descriptions. All dense matrices are stored in row-major order. The sparse matrices are stored in a compressed sparse row (CSR) format, which is described in detail in [26]. In the present context avalues $\in \mathbb{R}^{nnz}$, ia $\in \mathbb{N}^{M+1}$, and ja $\in \mathbb{N}^{nnz}$ denote the array of the matrix entries, the array of row offsets and the array of column indices in the CSR format, respectively.

Table 1. Overview of the relevant quantities and the notation used in the description of the algorithms.

$M \in \mathbb{N}$	Number of rows in a sparse matrix
$K \in \mathbb{N}$	Number of columns in a sparse matrix
$N \in \mathbb{N}$	Sometimes referred to as batch size
$\mathbf{A} \in \mathbb{R}^{M \times K}$	A sparse matrix of size $M \times K$
$\mathbf{B} \in \mathbb{R}^{K \times N}$	A dense matrix of size $K \times N$
$\mathbf{B}^T \in \mathbb{R}^{N \times K}$	The transpose of $\mathbf{B}$, with size $N \times K$
$\mathbf{D} \in \mathbb{R}^{K \times N}$	A dense matrix of size $K \times N$
$\mathbf{C} \in \mathbb{R}^{M \times N}$	A dense matrix of size $M \times N$
$\mathbf{E} \in \mathbb{R}^{M \times N}$	A dense matrix of size $M \times N$
$\mathbf{I}_A \in \{0,1\}^{M \times K}$	A sparse matrix of size $M \times K$
$\mathbf{O}_i \in \mathbb{R}^{1 \times \kappa}$	The row i, $1 \leq i \leq \mu$, of any matrix $\mathbf{O} \in \mathbb{R}^{\mu \times \kappa}$.
$\mathbf{O}_{i,j} \in \mathbb{R}$	jth element of $\mathbf{O}_i$, j, $1 \leq j \leq \kappa$.
$\alpha \in [0,1) \subset \mathbb{R}$	Sparsity. The fraction of matrix elements which are zero.
$nnz \in \mathbb{N}$	Non-zero elements in $\mathbf{A}$ computed as $nnz = MK(1-\alpha)$

2.1 Parallelizing SDDMM

The SDDMM operation is defined as follows.

$$\mathbf{A} = \mathbf{CB}^T \odot \mathbf{I}_A \qquad (1)$$

For this operation, a dense matrix $\mathbf{C}$ is multiplied with a dense matrix $\mathbf{B}^T$ followed by an element-wise product, which is indicated by the operation $\odot$, with a matrix $\mathbf{I}_A$. In a typical implementation, a dot product of a row of the matrix $\mathbf{C}$ with a column of $\mathbf{B}^T$ is computed only at a location of a non-zero entry in $\mathbf{I}_A$.

The parallelization is performed along the M rows of the resulting matrix $\mathbf{A}$ and the inner dimension N. For the sake of conciseness, we first describe the parallelization along the rows of the resulting matrix and ignore nested parallelism along the inner dimension N.

A total number of M work items are assigned to work concurrently, where a work item i, $1 \leq i \leq M$, computes all non-zeros of the row $\mathbf{A}_i$. Figure 1 illustrates this computation for a row $\mathbf{A}_i$ that has four non-zeros at column indices j_0, j_1, j_2, and j_3. The non-zero at j_0 is computed by multiplying the row $\mathbf{C}_i$ with a column j_0 of $\mathbf{B}^T$. The rest of the non-zeros are computed similarly. A high-level description of the algorithm for computing $\mathbf{A}_i$ is outlined in Alg. 1. Note that we use the CSR format for $\mathbf{A}$ in the high-level description in Alg. 1.

As indicated above, the parallelism in SDDMM operation can be increased by assigning more than one work item to each row of $\mathbf{A}_i$. This is important considering that otherwise, the occupancy of the Intel GPU would be sub-optimal when the number of rows M is not sufficiently large to fully occupy the device. In the case of the Intel GPU, M should be a multiple of 4096 per stack [16] for full occupancy. For example, we may assign two work items to compute the non-zeros of a row $\mathbf{A}_i$. In this case, a total of $2M$ work items are launched, where two consecutive work items, $2i$ and $2i+1$, collectively compute all non-zeros of $\mathbf{A}_i$, with each work item computing half of each of the inner products, updating the result atomically. Figure 1 illustrates this computation for $\mathbf{A}_i$ that has four non-zeros at column indices j_0, j_1, j_2, and j_3. The work item $2i$ computes non-zeros at column indices j_0 and j_1, and the work item $2i+1$ computes non-zeros at column indices j_2 and j_3. We typically partition the elements along the N dimension in chunks of a fixed size, which is denoted by NSZC and which is typically a multiple of 16 to ensure best memory bandwidth utilization by loading full cache lines (which are 64 bytes in size, i.e., 16 floats). A version of the algorithm, which increases the parallelism by splitting the rows of the resulting matrix $\mathbf{A}_i$ to the different work items instead of splitting the inner products, has shown better performance on small values of N and large values of K because of the higher level of parallelism that is achievable in those cases. It was discarded in favor of the version shown in Alg. 1 due to the otherwise lower performance.

2.2 Parallelizing SPMM

The SPMM operation multiplies a sparse matrix **A** with a dense matrix **B**, resulting in a dense matrix **C**, as shown below.

$$\mathbf{C} = \mathbf{AB} \tag{2}$$

Similar to the SDDMM implementation, our SPMM implementation parallelizes the computation over the M rows of the resulting matrix **C** first and increases the parallelism further by splitting the rows of the matrix **C** into multiple chunks assigned to different work items.

Without inner parallelism, a total of M work items are assigned to work concurrently, where a work item i, $1 \leq i \leq M$, computes a single row $\mathbf{C}_i$. This computation requires multiplying a sparse row $\mathbf{A}_i$ with selected elements of the **B** matrix to compute $\mathbf{C}_i$. This is again illustrated in Fig. 1.

A high-level description of the algorithm for computing a row $\mathbf{C}_i$ is outlined in Alg. 2. As before, we use the CSR format for **A** in Alg. 2. The main loop is over the non-zero elements in $\mathbf{A}_i$. In line 4, we obtain the j-th non-zero value in row i of **A**. The column index, k, associated with the j-th non-zero value is fetched in line 5. The for loop starting at line 6 performs a SAXPY computation [2], which is simply multiplying a scalar (s) with a vector ($\mathbf{B}_k$) and adding the result to another vector ($\mathbf{C}_i$).

As illustrated in Fig. 1, the parallelism can be increased further by partitioning each row into chunks of size NSZC (as before, NSZC is in general chosen as a multiple of 16 to ensure full usage of each loaded cache line) and assign these chunks to different work items. This is of particular interest when the size M is not a multiple of 4096 (on the Intel GPU), as indicated above.

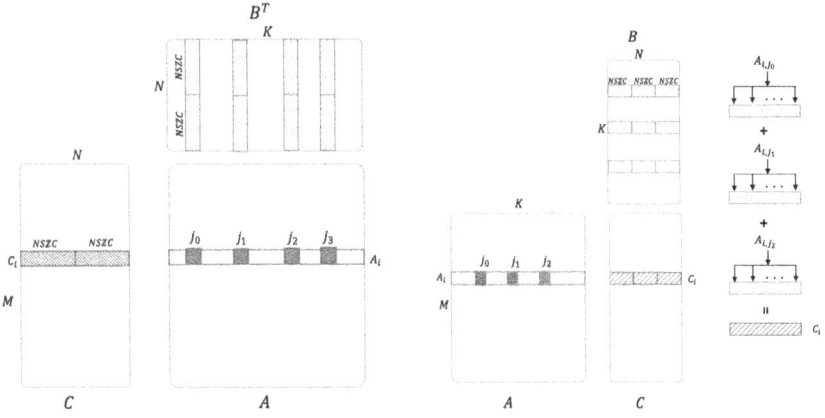

Fig. 1. Illustrations of the SDDMM (left) and SPMM (right) algorithms.

Algorithm 1 SDDMM-ROW	Algorithm 2 SPMM-ROW
1: Input: ia, ja, avalues, **B**, **C**, N, i	1: Input: ia, ja, avalues, **B**, **C**, N, i
2: Initialize: $\mathbf{C}[i,:] \leftarrow 0$	2: Initialize: $C[i,:] \leftarrow 0$
3: nnzr $\leftarrow$ ia$[i+1]$ − ia$[i]$	3: nnzr $\leftarrow$ ia$[i+1]$ − ia$[i]$
4: **for** $j \leftarrow 0$ **to** nnzr − 1 **do**	4: **for** $j \leftarrow 0$ **to** nnzr − 1 **do**
5: $\quad k \leftarrow$ ja[ia$[i]+j$]	5: $\quad s \leftarrow$ avalues[ia$[i]+j$]
6: $\quad dp \leftarrow 0$	6: $\quad k \leftarrow$ ja[ia$[i]+j$]
7: $\quad$ **for** $l \leftarrow 0$ **to** $N - 1$ **do**	7: $\quad$ **for** $l \leftarrow 0$ **to** $N - 1$ **do**
8: $\quad\quad dp \leftarrow dp + \mathbf{C}[i,l] * \mathbf{B}[k,l]$	8: $\quad\quad C[i,l] \leftarrow C[i,l] + s * B[k,l]$
9: $\quad$ **end for**	9: $\quad$ **end for**
10: $\quad$ avalues[ia$[i]+j$] $\leftarrow dp$	10: **end for**
11: **end for**	11: **return** C
12: **return** avalues	

Fig. 2. Pseudo-codes for the SDDMM (left) and SPMM (right) algorithms.

2.3 Parallelizing FusedMM

The FusedMM operation is a composition of SDDMM with SPMM. The composite operation avoids the explicit storage of the result of the SDDMM operation and can perform better than an implementation with the two operations applied one after another due to the reuse of registers and cached values.

$$\mathbf{E} = (\mathbf{CB}^T \odot \mathbf{I}_A)\mathbf{D} \qquad (3)$$

The parallel fused version of the SDDMM and SPMM operation is straightforward. We utilize one work item per row of the SPMM part of the algorithm. Thus, each work item first computes all non-zero values for a row of the sparse matrix **A** resulting from the SDDMM part. Once a work item has computed all the non-zero values of the relevant row in **A** (without storing them in global memory), we start the SPMM operation as outlined earlier.

3 ESIMD Implementation

In this section, we discuss ESIMD implementation details, where we account for the underlying vector architecture, number of registers, cache behavior, etc. To avoid redundancy, we focus on the SDDMM operation. The code for all the implementations can be found at [1].

Our SDDMM ESIMD kernel is launched with M work-groups, each consisting of NT items. A work-group i computes a row i of the sparse matrix of nnzr non-zeros in chunks of size MAXNNZ, to ensure efficient utilization of block-load instructions by maximizing the fraction of the loads which are actually utilized. The value MAXNNZ = 32 was chosen empirically. The associated SDDMM kernel code is shown in Fig. 3. In line 2, we assign the work-group id to the variable i, which denotes the row in the output matrix **A**, and j is assigned the local work item id that ranges from 0 to NT − 1. In lines 4- 6, a work-group i

loads the start and end indices of the row i in the CSR format, computes nnzr, the number of non-zero entries in row i, and returns in case there is nothing to do for that particular row. In line 8, we initialize the local `simd` object which holds the result. Line 9 loads a chunk of size NSZC of the row $\mathbf{C}_i$ into a `simd` object. Next, we set up a nested loop, where the outer loop is over the number of chunks nnzr/MAXNNZ of size MAXNNZ in the output matrix, and the inside loop is over the number of elements MAXNNZ in the output chunk a_row. In the outer loop, we load column indices for the current chunk into a `simd` object, col_idx, of size MAXNNZ. In the inside loop, we first load the column of $\mathbf{B}$ that is needed for the current iteration (line 16) into b_row. Next, in line 17, we multiply the two `simd` objects, c_row and b_row, reduce the result and store it in the correct position in a_row. After the inner loop, we atomically update the matrix $\mathbf{A}$ with the local values a_row. To keep our code segment simple, we avoid the details for handling the cases when nnzr is not a multiple of MAXNNZ, where N is not a multiple of NSZC, and where NT is not equal to N/NSZC.

We template the kernel on NT and NSZC and implemented a scheme that chooses the value of NT to be a positive integer less or equal to 32 and less or equal to $\lceil N/\text{NSZC} \rceil$ in dependence of the matrix size M such that the occupancy on the device is maximized. At the same time, we choose the chunk size NSZC as a power of two between 16 and 128. To achieve 100% occupancy on a single stack of the Intel GPU, one needs to launch 4096 ESIMD work items or a multiple thereof. In particular, we choose NT as the minimum positive integer, not larger than 32, to maximize the occupancy, which is given as follows

$$\text{Occupancy} = \frac{M \times \text{NT}}{4096} \bigg/ \left\lceil \frac{M \times \text{NT}}{4096} \right\rceil.$$

The rounded value in the denominator ensures that cases where $M \times \text{NT} > 4096$ are handled appropriately. For example, let $M = 1024$, then NT = 4 is chosen. For $M = 3072$ the choice of NT = 4 leads to 100% occupancy. We then choose NSZC as a power of two larger than 16 such that NT = $\lceil N/\text{NSZC} \rceil$. If that is not possible, we set NSZC = 16 and launch multiple work groups per row, each consisting of NT work items. For details on the shown ESIMD functions, we refer to [13].

Our SPMM operation is implemented with a concise and simple code similar to the SDDMM code shown in Fig. 3. It shows that the ESIMD API can be used to write vectorized code without sophisticated memory-access schemes (cf. Sect. V.B. in [7]), thus simplifying the algorithms significantly.

4 Experiments

In this section, we compare our implementations to the implementations available in oneMKL on the same Intel Data Center GPU Max 1550. Further, we compare our implementations to the *Sputnik* code presented in [7] and cuSPARSE [22] on a Nvidia H100 PCIe GPU. Our tests as well as the oneMKL tests were performed on a single stack of an Intel Data Center GPU Max 1550

```
1  #define MAXNNZ 32
2  int i = item.get_group(0);
3  int j = item.get_local_id(0);
4  simd<int,2> lrowptr2 = lsc_block_load(ia+i);
5  int nnzr = lrowptr2[1]-lrowptr2[0];
6  if (nnzr == 0) return;
7
8  simd<float,MAXNNZ> a_row;
9  simd<float,NSZC> c_row = lsc_block_load(C+i*N+j*NSZC);
10
11 for (int ii = 0; ii < nnzr/MAXNNZ; ii++) {
12   simd<int,MAXNNZ> col_idx = lsc_block_load(ja+lrowptr2[0]+ii*MAXNNZ)*N;
13
14   #pragma unroll
15   for (int l = 0; l < MAXNNZ; l++) {
16     simd<float,NSZC> b_row = lsc_block_load(B+col_idx[l]+j*NSZC);
17     a_row.select<1,1>(l) = reduce(c_row*b_row, std::plus<>());
18   }
19
20   lsc_atomic_update<atomic_op::fadd>(A+lrowptr2[0]+ii*MAXNNZ, a_row);
21 }
```

Fig. 3. ESIMD implementation of the SDDMM operation. NSZC and NT are template parameters which indicate the chunk size in the N dimension and the number of work items in N dimension, respectively. For simplicity, we skip details when N is not a multiple of NSZC, and $NT < N/NSZC$.

on an Intel-internal test system. The test system is a dual-socket system with two Intel Xeon Platinum 8480+ processors and 1 TB RAM. The code was compiled with Intel's icpx compiler (version 2024.0.0.20231017), which is included in Intel's oneAPI, version 2024.0. We used the compile options "-fsycl", "-O3" and, in the case of the oneMKL tests, "-qmkl". Further, we used an unreleased engineering GPU driver for the tests (agama-ci-devel/778). The theoretical peak global memory bandwidth of the device is approximately 1.6 TB/s. The theoretical peak FP32 multiply-add throughput is approximately 26 teraflops per second (Tflops/s).

The CUDA codes were tested on a dual-socket system with two Intel Xeon Platinum 8480+ processors, 512 GB RAM, and a Nvidia H100 GPU. For the cuSPARSE tests, we used NVHPC version 23.5 and compiled the code with nvcc and the "-arch=sm_90" flag. For the Sputnik code, we used NVHPC version 23.1 due to compilation issues with newer NVHPC versions. The g++ compiler was used as the host compiler for the Sputnik code. For both CUDA-based codes, the driver version was 535.129.03. The theoretical peak global memory bandwidth is 2 TB/s. The theoretical peak FP32 multiply-add throughput is approximately 51 Tflops/s.

4.1 Randomly Generated Sparse Matrices

The first set of experiments was performed on the randomly generated data set of given sizes which was introduced in [7] to model sparse matrices in Sparse Recurrent Neural Networks and which was used to show that the CUDA implementation in [7] outperforms various other implementations. Note that we utilize the same data set to enable a straightforward comparison. It consists of 24 different matrix sizes. Three different sparsities (0.7, 0.8, and 0.9) are tested for each matrix size. The non-zero values follow a uniform random distribution. Reference [7] is of particular interest considering that they outperform the approaches [8,28], and, at the time of their publication, cuSPARSE on a Nvidia V100 GPU. Under the assumption of an infinite cache model, the arithmetic intensities of these test cases range from approximately 9.85 to 60.1 flops per byte. Further, assuming that the theoretical peak bandwidth of the devices is achievable, this indicates that the larger problems are compute-bound while the smaller problems are memory-bound. Note that, in practice, the infinite cache assumption does not hold (reducing the arithmetic intensities) and the theoretical peak bandwidth is not achievable. Thus, even the larger problems may be memory bandwidth-bound.

Figure 4 shows the performance of our SDDMM implementation on the above-introduced randomly generated data set on a single stack of the Intel Data Center GPU Max 1550 compared to three other implementations for the matrices with size $N = 128$. The same set of benchmarks was performed for $N = 32$ and considered in the analysis below, although the results were not visualized. We compare against i) oneMKL's (included in oneAPI version 2024.0 [11]) dense blas::gemm implementation [17] on the same Intel GPU, ii) the SDDMM implementation introduced in [7] on a Nvidia H100 GPU, and iii) finally the cuSPARSE *cusparseSDDMM* function on a Nvidia H100 GPU. This comparison is highly disadvantageous for oneMKL since 70%–90% (depending on the sparsity of the workload) of the computed flops in a dense matrix-matrix multiplication are irrelevant for the output of SDDMM. Thus, although oneMKL blas::gemm achieves a peak performance of approximately 25 Tflops/s in the dense matrix multiplication, our specialized SDDMM implementation can outperform it for the sparse operation. The comparison to the dense matrix multiplication in oneMKL is due to the lack of a dedicated SDDMM functionality included in oneMKL. On average, our SDDMM implementation outperforms cuSPARSE, oneMKL, and Sputnik by factors 1.35, 1.82, and 1.84, respectively. Our implementation is at most 2.32, 3.35, and 4.13 times faster than cuSPARSE, oneMKL, and Sputnik, respectively and achieves a peak performance of 9.4 Tflops/s. Since the performance of our SDDMM implementation is bounded by the "SP Vector Add Peak" of 12.6 Tflops/s of the Intel GPU (as displayed by Intel's Advisor tool [10])—since we utilize a vectorized multiplication followed by a reduction—the peak performance of 9.4 Tflops/s of our code mark 75% of the theoretical peak of the device. The roofline analysis with Intel's Advisor tool shows efficient reuse of the cached data. In fact, for the particular 8k/8k/128/70% case, the data cached in L1 is utilized 50 times more often than data in the L3 cache, which is, in turn, reused approximately 180 times compared to the amount of data loaded from HBM.

We compare our results with the Sputnik code on a Nvidia V100 GPU [7]. We increase the peak performance from approximately 2.7 Tflops/s (achieved on the 4k/1k/128/70% case) to 9.4 Tflops/s (achieved on the 8k/8k/128/70% case). Further, the average performance gains achieved compared to [7] in the SDDMM case is a factor of approximately 4.3x with a maximum relative performance increase of approximately 10.4x (achieved on the 32k/8k/32/90% case).

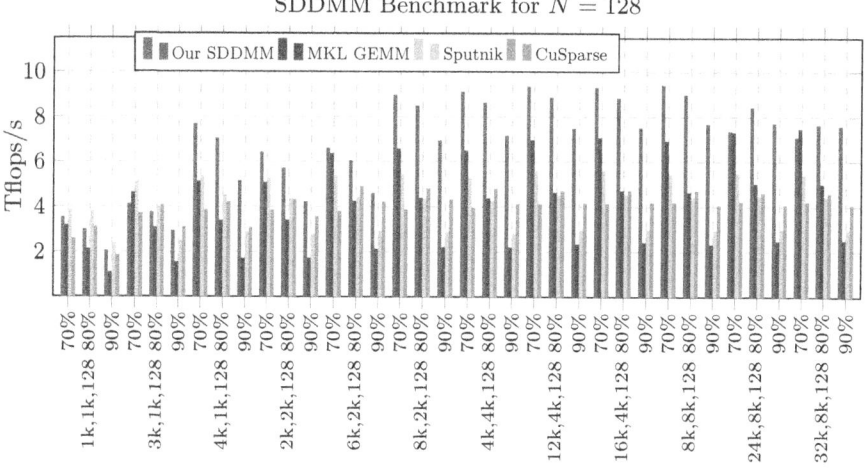

Fig. 4. Comparison of our SDDMM method with oneMKL blas::gemm on a single stack of the Intel Data Center GPU Max 1550 and the Sputnik [7] and cuSPARSE functions on a Nvidia H100. The x-axis indicates M/K/N/Sparsity, and the y-axis indicates the throughput in Tflops/s.

Figure 5, in turn, shows the performance of our SPMM implementation in comparison to oneMKL's sparse::gemm [18] implementation on Intel's Data Center GPU, which implements the SPMM operation, as well as the SPMM implementation from the Sputnik code [7], and the *cusparseSpMM* function from Nvidia's cuSPARSE on H100. Our implementation increases the performance on average by 1.34x, 1.46x, and 3.48x compared to oneMKL, Sputnik, and cuSPARSE, respectively. Compared to the three reference implementations, the maximum achieved speedups are 2.07x, 2.45x, and 6.14x, respectively. Our implementation achieves a peak throughput of 13.13 Tflops/s on the 8k/8k/128/70% case. These performance increases may be attributed to the high specialization of our SPMM implementation to the relevant matrix sizes and sparsities. In addition, tests showed that the matrix sizes of the random matrices are disadvantageous for cuSPARSE and that swapping the sizes of N and K results in a performance improvement of nearly 3x for the $N = 32$ ($K = 32$ after the swap), which indicates that cuSPARSE would perform significantly better on a more general set of matrices. This is tested and confirmed in Sect. 4.2, where the gap between the performance of our implementation and cuSPARSE is reduced. The memory access pattern and operation count for SPMM are similar to the SDDMM operation; however, we observed a better absolute peak performance for SPMM (13.13 Tflops/s) compared to SDDMM (9.4 Tflops/s). The main reason for the increased performance compared to SDDMM is that the main computation in the SPMM implementation is a multiply-add (MAD) operation. While the absolute performance of SPMM is better, it achieves a lower relative performance compared to the theoretical peak performance of the hardware. This is due to the performance of SPMM being bounded by the "SP Vector MAD Peak" of 25.2 Tflops/s. The SPMM performance is thus only up to 50% of the theoretical peak. Based on this data, there is still room for improvement of the performance of this operation. Compared to the SPMM results shown in [7], which were generated on a Nvidia V100 GPU, our code achieves a speedup of 2.63x on average and 4.34x at most.

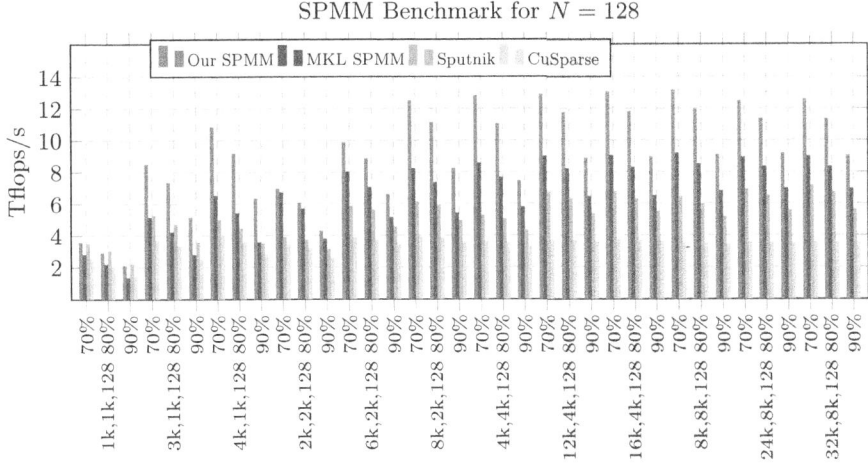

Fig. 5. Comparison of our SPMM method with oneMKL sparse::gemm on a single stack of the Intel Data Center GPU Max 1550 and the Sputnik [7] and cuSPARSE functions on a Nvidia H100. The x-axis indicates M/K/N/Sparsity, and the y-axis indicates the throughput in Tflops/s.

Finally, we compare the performance of our FusedMM operation to oneMKL's dense::gemm and sparse::gemm operation. For the oneMKL case, we are not including the time required for the sampling after the dense matrix multiplication for the SDDMM operation. Our FusedMM implementation increases the performance of oneMKL by approximately 2.02x on average and 3.30x at most. Our FusedMM implementation operation achieves on average 1.63x the throughput of our SDDMM implementation and 1.053x of our SPMM implementation.

The average performance is thus higher than in either of the cases before, underlining the importance of operator fusion for these kinds of operations. The peak performance of 12.46 Tflops/s for this operation represents 48% of the theoretical peak performance of the device.

4.2 ResNet-50 Data Set

The second data set we used to test the implementation is the ResNet-50 data set presented in [7], taken from [6]. In particular, we used the 1113 matrices of varying sizes and sparsities (excluding the so-called "initial_conv" matrices) representing ResNet-50 data. The batch sizes (the N value) of all matrices were padded to the next multiple of 16. The problems are significantly smaller than the random matrices in the previous section with arithmetic intensities (again under an infinite cache assumption) ranging from 0.2 to 61 flops per byte with a median arithmetic intensity of approximately 8.3 flops per byte. Most of these problems are thus memory bandwidth bound.

In the SDDMM case, our implementation achieves on average 1.6 times the performance of cuSPARSE. On 69% of the matrices, our implementation outperforms cuSPARSE. On 91% of the matrices, our implementation achieves at least half the performance of cuSPARSE. This is relevant considering that the H100 device has twice the theoretical peak single-precision throughput compared to a single stack of the Intel GPU. The minimum relative performance of our SDDMM is 0.28 times the performance of the cuSPARSE implementation. The maximum relative performance is 5.86 times the performance of cuSPARSE. We skip the comparison to oneMKL due to the missing SDDMM implementation in oneMKL.

In the SPMM case, our implementation outperforms cuSPARSE by a factor of 1.21 on average. In 71% of the cases, our implementation achieves a higher throughput than cuSPARSE. In 100% of the cases it achieves at least half the throughput of cuSPARSE. The minimum relative performance is 0.59 times the performance of cuSPARSE, and the maximum relative performance is 4.28 times that of cuSPARSE. Compared to the sparse::gemm function available in oneMKL, our implementation improves the performance by a factor of 1.72 on average and by a factor 3.52 at most.

Overall, these tests show that our implementation achieves competitive performance not just on the randomized data set but also on real-world data compared to state-of-the-art hardware and software.

5 Conclusion and Future Work

In this paper, we demonstrated that ESIMD APIs can effectively and concisely implement sparse matrix operations by enabling the writing of explicitly vectorized code. In particular, we showed that highly optimized ESIMD implementations of sparse matrix operations relevant to machine learning applications outperform the functionalities provided by the state-of-the-art oneMKL on the

Intel Data Center GPU Max 1550 and highly optimized CUDA implementations on a Nvidia H100 GPU. We plan to explore sparse matrix operations utilizing reduced precision data types and block sparse matrices for our future work.

Acknowledgements. This effort has been supported by the Intel oneAPI Center of Excellence at Old Dominion University. We want to thank Xiao Zhu and Ben Hörz of Intel, who provided support throughout this project, making resources available whenever we needed them. We also want to thank Peter Caday and Spencer Patty of Intel's oneMKL team for their support in optimizing our implementation.

Appendix: Disclaimers

Performance varies by use, configuration, and other factors. Learn more on the Performance Index site. Performance results are based on testing as of the dates shown and may not reflect all publicly available updates. No product or component can be absolutely secure. Your costs and results may vary. Intel technologies may require enabled hardware, software or service activation. ©Intel Corporation. Intel, the Intel logo, and other Intel marks are trademarks of Intel Corporation or its subsidiaries. Other names and brands may be claimed as the property of others.

References

1. ESIMD Implementation of Deep Learning Sparse Matrix Kernels. https://github.com/zubair23517/dlspm-esimd. Accessed 20 Mar 2024
2. Anderson, E., et al.: LAPACK Users' Guide. Society for Industrial and Applied Mathematics, Philadelphia, 3rd edn (1999)
3. Bharadwaj, V., Buluc, A., Demmel, J.: Distributed-memory sparse kernels for machine learning. In: 2022 IEEE IPDPS, pp. 47–58. IEEE Computer Society, Los Alamitos (2022). https://doi.org/10.1109/IPDPS53621.2022.00014
4. Gale, T., Elsen, E., Hooker, S.: The state of sparsity in deep neural networks. arXiv preprint arXiv:1902.09574 (2019)
5. Gale, T., Narayanan, D., Young, C., Zaharia, M.: Megablocks: efficient sparse training with mixture-of-experts (2022)
6. Gale, T., Zaharia, M., Young, C., Elsen, E.: RN50 Data Set (2020). https://storage.googleapis.com/sgk-sc2020/dlmc.tar.gz. Accessed 22 Nov 2023
7. Gale, T., Zaharia, M., Young, C., Elsen, E.: Sparse GPU Kernels for deep learning. In: Proceedings of the International Conference for High Performance Computing, Networking, Storage and Analysis (SC 2020). IEEE Press (2020)
8. Hong, C., Sukumaran-Rajam, A., Nisa, I., Singh, K., Sadayappan, P.: Adaptive sparse tiling for sparse matrix multiplication. In: Proceedings of the 24th Symposium on Principles and Practice of Parallel Programming (PPoPP 2019), pp. 300–314. Association for Computing Machinery, New York (2019). https://doi.org/10.1145/3293883.3295712
9. Hu, Y., et al.: Featgraph: a flexible and efficient backend for graph neural network systems. In: Proceedings of the International Conference for High Performance Computing, Networking, Storage and Analysis (SC 2020). IEEE Press (2020)

10. Intel Corporation: Intel Advisor GPU Roofline. https://www.intel.com/content/www/us/en/docs/advisor/user-guide/2023-2/analyze-gpu-roofline.html. Accessed 30 Oct 2023
11. Intel Corporation: Intel oneAPI. https://www.intel.com/content/www/us/en/developer/tools/oneapi/toolkits.html. Accessed 22 Nov 2023
12. Intel Corporation: Intel Thread Mapping. https://www.intel.com/content/www/us/en/docs/oneapi/optimization-guide-gpu/2023-2/thread-mapping-and-gpu-occupancy.html. Accessed 30 Oct 2023
13. Intel Corporation: DPC++ Explicit SIMD API (2023). https://intel.github.io/llvm-docs/doxygen/index.html. Accessed 25 May 2023
14. Intel Corporation: Explicit SIMD SYCL Extension (2023). https://www.intel.com/content/www/us/en/docs/dpcpp-cpp-compiler/developer-guide-reference/2023-1/explicit-simd-sycl-extension.html. Accessed 25 May 2023
15. Intel Corporation: Intel Data Center GPU Max 1550 (2023). https://www.intel.com/content/www/us/en/products/sku/232873/intel-data-center-gpu-max-1550/specifications.html. Accessed 14 July 2023
16. Intel Corporation: Intel Xe GPU Architecture (2023). https://www.intel.com/content/www/us/en/docs/oneapi/optimization-guide-gpu/2023-1/intel-xe-gpu-architecture.html. Accessed 17 July 2023
17. Intel Corporation: oneMKL blas::gemm (2023). https://www.intel.com/content/www/us/en/docs/onemkl/developer-reference-dpcpp/2024-0/gemm.html. Accessed 22 Nov 2023
18. Intel Corporation: oneMKL sparse::gemm (2023). https://www.intel.com/content/www/us/en/docs/onemkl/developer-reference-dpcpp/2024-0/oneapi-mkl-sparse-gemm.html. Accessed 22 Nov 2023
19. Intel Corporation: Tensorflow on GPUs (2023). https://github.com/intel/intel-extension-for-tensorflow. Accessed 27 Oct 2023
20. Khronos Group: SYCL (2020). https://www.khronos.org/sycl/. Accessed 24 Aug 2020
21. NVIDIA Corporation: CUDA C Programming Guide. http://docs.nvidia.com/cuda/cuda-c-programming-guide/#axzz4Hicq83a9. Accessed 14 July 2023
22. NVIDIA Corporation: cuSPARSE. https://developer.nvidia.com/cusparse. Accessed 24 Aug 2020
23. NVIDIA Corporation: Tensor Cores (2023). https://www.nvidia.com/en-us/data-center/tensor-cores/. Accessed 23 Nov 2023
24. PyTorch Project a Series of LF Projects, LLC: PyTorch on GPUs (2023). https://pytorch.org/docs/stable/notes/cuda.html. Accessed 27 Oct 2023
25. Rahman, M.K., Sujon, M.H., Azad, A.: Fusedmm: a unified sddmm-spmm kernel for graph embedding and graph neural networks. In: 2021 IEEE IPDPS, pp. 256–266 (2021). https://doi.org/10.1109/IPDPS49936.2021.00034
26. Saad, Y.: Iterative Methods for Sparse Linear Systems, 2nd edn. Society for Industrial and Applied Mathematics, Philadelphia (2003)
27. Volkov, V.: Understanding Latency Hiding on GPUs. Ph.D. thesis, EECS Department, University of California, Berkeley (2016). http://www2.eecs.berkeley.edu/Pubs/TechRpts/2016/EECS-2016-143.html
28. Yang, C., Buluç, A., Owens, J.D.: Design principles for sparse matrix multiplication on the GPU. In: Aldinucci, M., Padovani, L., Torquati, M. (eds.) Euro-Par 2018. LNCS, vol. 11014, pp. 672–687. Springer, Cham (2018). https://doi.org/10.1007/978-3-319-96983-1_48

Deconstructing HPL-MxP Benchmark: A Numerical Perspective

Greg Henry[✉], Eric Petit, Alexander Lyashevsky, and Peter Caday

Intel Corporation, Hillsboro, USA
{greg.henry,eric.petit,alexander.lyashevsky,peter.caday}@intel.com

Abstract. HPL-MxP has become a widely accepted benchmark for assessing high-performance computing (HPC) systems' capabilities for Artificial Intelligence (AI) workloads. However, the benchmark's representativeness of real-world HPC and AI workloads is unclear. In this paper, we discuss the HPL-MxP benchmark from a numerical perspective and propose new rules and data generation for numerically meaningful comparisons. We present experiments showing that the current HPL-MxP benchmark cannot be considered as a numerically relevant benchmark to prove superiority of a new format or algorithm. We propose to better specify these requirements for numerical formats to produce comparable performance numbers, and suggest new input data generation to make it numerically relevant. We validate our proposal on Int8, Int4, and BF16 implementations to demonstrate the numerical significance of the benchmark using our new generator.

1 Introduction

HPL-MxP, formerly HPL-AI [7], has emerged as a valuable metric for assessing high-performance computing (HPC) systems' capability for artificial intelligence (AI) workloads, and over the years, significant progress has been made in understanding its nuances [3]. Nevertheless, it is unclear if the benchmark is still representative of some real-world HPC and AI workloads. This paper analyzes the HPL-MxP benchmark from a numerical perspective and presents experiments to highlight the need for stronger specification of the benchmark's rules. This paper shows current HPL-MxP cannot be considered a numerically relevant benchmark for AI and HPC and cannot be used to demonstrate numerical superiority of a new low precision data format. Our proposed changes makes it more relevant to demonstrate usage of low-precision arithmetic in HPC workloads.

HPL-MxP has been extrapolated from HPL [16], a benchmark used for solving a system of equations $Ax = b$, where A is a double precision generated in a manner similar to the generators in the LAPACK linear algebra library. The system is solved using LU factorization with full row pivoting. Using only partial row pivoting or a different algorithm than LU is against the benchmark rules. The benchmark tests for theoretically double-precision error.

HPL-MxP also solves a FP64 system of equations $Ax = b$ like HPL, but with additional requirements. A lower-precision LU decomposition is used as a preconditioner in an iterative refinement scheme [8]. For instance, the reference code [11] carries out the LU decomposition in binary32 (single) precision and then iterates to refine the solution with double precision generalized minimal residual method solver, GMRES. The benchmark allows no more than 50 iterations of iterative refinement to reach the targeted residual error threshold corresponding to double-precision accuracy. However, a low precision variant of LU to estimate $x = A^{-1}b$ requires A to have a low condition number [7]. To match this requirement, the input matrix A is generated to exhibit diagonal row dominance, i.e. the sum of the element of its rows is lower that the diagonal element.

While the HPL-MxP benchmark has been a recent popular choice for evaluating high-performance computing (HPC) systems for low-precision performances, its relevance in the context of artificial intelligence (AI) workloads is also becoming less clear. Recent AI models, such as large language models, often involve a much larger number of smaller-sized parameters and matrices than usual dense algebra HPC applications, making it more important to focus on memory footprint and communication efficiency rather than peak floating-point performance. Furthermore they rely on various flavors of number encoding, not limited to fp16 or BF16. For example, recent research has shown that language models can be quantized to significantly reduce their memory footprint without sacrificing accuracy when trained with appropriate techniques, even using 8-bit BF8, int8, or 4-bit int4 formats for inference, fine-tuning and even most of the training operations. We must consider the specific requirements of targeted AI workloads when evaluating the performance of computing systems. In that regard, ML-PERF's recent introduction and extension to training and newer models appears more relevant [17]. Therefore we focus on improving HPL-MxP relevance for low precision arithmetic - inherited from AI - in HPC workloads.

In this paper, we develop arguments and experiments to support the following key messages:

- Because the input matrix is forced to be diagonally dominant, HPL-MxP's convergence criterion is not a reliable indicator of numerical superiority or even correctness. We suggest in this paper a new matrix generation process to have desired condition number without being diagonally dominant.
- Storage and compute numerical datatypes do not have to be the same in HPL-MxP. The reference code uses binary32 storage and binary32 compute for the low precision, and some kernels may also mix data and storage types, for instance, using lower-precision format such as Int4 storage and BF16 conversion to compute. The idea of compressing data for storage and communication is representative of the latest AI models (LLMs) where data is quantized in smaller formats to fit in memory (e.g., int4) and uncompressed for computation. A similar compression methodology could be applied to mixed precision HPC workloads.
- In solving the systems generated in HPL-MxP, diagonal and off-diagonal elements do not have to use the same format. Implementers could support this, but the reference code does not. Real workloads [1,4] could take advantage

of having spatial mixed precision decomposition, especially along the (block of) diagonal elements.
- We suggest that HPL-MxP or implementers should specify numerical datatypes for storage, compute, and both diagonal and off-diagonal element formats to facilitate comparisons between HPC systems and architectures. With new formats such as Int4 and BF8 emerging in the AI field, and the benchmark's current limitation of converging with almost any scheme, specifying these requirements ensures meaningful comparisons.

2 Related Works

Several works have focused on the HPL-MxP benchmark and related topics. The original HPL-MxP, formerly HPL-AI, by Haidar et al. [7] introduced the benchmark and discussed its performance on Nvidia tensor cores. This work has been followed by more in-depth analysis of similar LU+GMRES. Higham and Mary [8] propose the use of five lower-precision formats in GMRES. A broader survey opening to other aspects of mixed precision linear has been recently proposed by Anzt et al. [1].

In [3], Blanchard et al. reaches similar conclusions to ours on the numerical aspects of HPL-MxP's generated matrix. While they do not evaluate a fixed-point approach, they study the impact of other input matrices, like random orthogonal matrices. This is not particularly scalable since random $n \times n$ orthogonal matrices can be a harder problem than a double precision solve. To produce similar numerical challenges at scale, we improve their method by restricting the orthogonalization. Instead of generating a $n \times n$ orthogonal matrix from scratch, we focus on a Householder reflection matrix given by an orthogonal rank-k update $(I + VW^T$ where V, W are $n \times k$ with $k << n$.) This with rank-k update, the overhead of generating the data has no significant impact on the benchmark. Additionally, we evaluate fixed point approaches since they become prominent for large scale AI inference and fine tuning workloads [10].

Mixed precision in HPC does not only matter for benchmarks. There is a strong trend to take advantage of lower precision in real workloads [4,15]. For example Yong et al. [12] received the Gordon Bell prize in 2021 for Achieving Real-Time Simulation of Random Quantum Circuit. They used mixed precision simulation reaching 1.2 EFlops.

However, the main driver for the latest low-precision formats is AI applications, in particular deep neural networks. In 2015, Gupta et al. [6] propose the use of 16 bits and random rounding. Then floating point format proved to be more versatile with fp16 and BF16 to finally converge to a recent BF8 proposal [13]. However these approaches still use binary32, especially for accumulators, and qualifies as mixed precision. Inference uses much lower precision, such as int8 or int4. Recent work from Osorio et al. [14] also suggest that we can entirely suppress binary32 computation for training even on the latest transformers network.

Latest work has also focused on the use of low-precision formats for large language models (LLMs). For example LORA [10] is using low rank approximation and lower precision format to store weight updates, allowing fine-tuning of large model with lower memory footprint with minimum loss of accuracy. In Sect. 4.1 and algorithm 6 we show an example of using low rank approximation in HPL-MxP benchmark.

To evaluate random rounding, RR, impact on HPL-MxP we use emulation based on Verificarlo [5]. While RR has been shown to be efficient in AI workloads [6], proven to reduce error in many cases [2,4] and implemented in some dedicated architecture [4], our experiment in Sect. 4.1 shows it negatively impacts HPL-MxP, despite featuring a large dot-product [2], supporting our idea that HPL-MxP has significant blind-spots on the numerical behavior of AI and HPC workloads.

3 HPL-MxP Description and Implementation Notes

The HPL-MxP algorithm solves $Ax = b$ with double precision accuracy, while using low precision LU factorization for A and using the factorization result to accelerate the double precision solution in iterative refinement steps. However, some accuracy is required from the low precision LU, and if the linear systems condition number of A is too large, the algorithm will not converge.

Algorithm 1 describes the sequence of operations and expected precision level for each step. The LU part of line 1 represents more than 95% of the computation time at scale. Indeed, the benchmark rules do not enforce a given problem size and instead allow the best asymptotic performance, which is as big as memory allows.

Algorithm 1. HPL-MxP()
Compute x in Ax=b

Require: $A = Diag\_dominant\_random\_matrix(n, n)$
1: $\hat{L}\hat{U} \leftarrow compute\_LU(\hat{A})$ ▷ low prec
2: $x_0 \leftarrow solve(\hat{L}\hat{U}x_o = b)$ ▷ low prec
3: **while** $||r_i||_\infty \geq max\_res$ **do**
4:     $r_i \leftarrow b - Ax_i$ ▷ high prec, store low prec
5:     $x_i \leftarrow solve(\hat{L}\hat{U}u_i = r_i)$ ▷ low prec
6:     $x_{i+1} \leftarrow x_i + u_i$
7: **end while**

To resolve the limitations on the condition number, the HPL-MxP developers took the original HPL generator and added one new constraint: that the final matrix must be row diagonally dominant by algorithm 2.

While diagonal dominance keeps the overall condition number down, it has the unintended consequence of breaking the benchmark. Namely, now nearly any low precision LU will converge. If one looks at the generated matrix:

Algorithm 2. HPL_MxP_ref_gen(n,n)
Generate diagonally dominant n,n matrix

1: $A \leftarrow random(n,n,]\neg 0.5, 0.5[)$
2: **while** $i < n$ **do**
3: $\quad A_{i,i} \leftarrow \sum_j^n |A_{i,j}| - |A_{i,i}|$
4: $\quad i \leftarrow i + 1$
5: **end while**

- All diagonal elements have the same expected value (which is $n/4$) and it will converge to $n/4$ as n grows by the law of Large Numbers.
- From the previous property, the expected ratio between diagonal and off diagonal elements increases with problem size. Which means that at scale, especially with lower precision, only diagonal element matters.
- Since diagonal elements of the HPL-MxP matrix generator converge to the same (positive) value, they require a very narrow range of representation.
- The condition number converges to 1 when n increases.

From these observations, one can expect any low precision, quantized by the maximum diagonal element, to work fine, such as small integer fixed point. This will be verified in the following experiments.

4 Experiments

All our experiments derive from the reference CPU implementation [11]. Performance and validity at scale have been evaluated on Intel MAX GPU featuring BF16, int8 and int4. The RR (random rounding) has been emulated using Verificarlo on CPU. Additionally, we propose an optimized version to offload to accelerators using the following:

- Because of the diagonal dominant input, HPL-MxP does not require row pivoting for accuracy. But one can do column pivoting for performance. Instead of physically moving the columns, we track the new locations. This allows to reuse the column one processing unit happens to own. We enable implicit column pivoting and dynamic block size in the distributed memory case. This enables a distributed memory LU to use the block-size it needs.
- The ideal block-size to reach peak performance is a function of precision. Required block sizes may get huge with the lowest precision, pressuring storage of the fp64 version of the block. For instance, if FP32 starts to get close to its peak GEMM performance on outer products of size 256, BF16 might require a size closer to 1024, and BF8 or Int8 a size of 2048.
- Because of the random nature of the input matrix, it can be generated locally. There is no need to store the blocks of the FP64 input matrix at all times. Not storing all FP64 data allows handling even larger problems.
- Once the GEMM step is done in each LU blocked iteration, most of the data is not needed until the next GEMM step. Therefore, we propose a Streaming

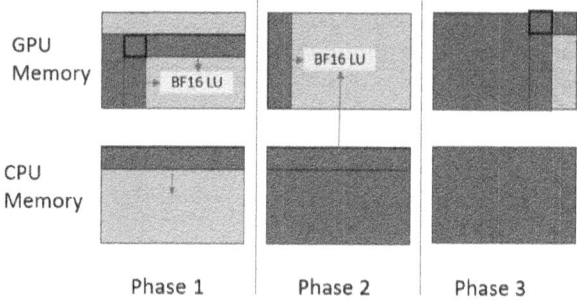

Fig. 1. SFG algoritm illustration of the three phases depicted in Algorithms 3, 4, 5.

Factorization Algorithm (SFG). This maximizes the size of the problem that can be handled within fixed GPU memory size. If both a CPU and GPU are used together, we use CPU memory as an external memory subsystems of the GPU with our 3 phases Algorithms 3, 4 and 5 depicted below.

Algorithm 3. LU_GPU_Kernel_Phase1_top

Require: $A^{gpu} = A(N, 0:N/2)$ ▷ is on GPU,
Require: $A^{cpu} = A(N, N/2:N)$ ▷ is on CPU
1: **while** $i < N/2$ **do**
2:     $H \leftarrow panel(A_{i,i}, k, N)$ ▷ factorize horizontal panel
3:     $L_H, U_H \leftarrow factorize(H^{gpu})$ ▷ factorize top half of vertical panel
4:     $L_V, U_V \leftarrow factorize(V^{gpu})$ ▷ Async copy overlapped with GEMM
5:     $Async\_Swap(H^{gpu}, H^{cpu})$ ▷ partial GEMM update
6:     $pannel(A^{gpu}_{i,i}, k, k) \leftarrow GEMM(U_H, L_V)$
7:     $i \leftarrow i + K$
8: **end while**

The phase 1 of the algorithm is given in Algorithm 3 and illustrated in Fig. 1. During this phase we do partial LU factorization using the upper part of each column of A, then swap factorized horizontal block from the GPU with the corresponding unfactorized block of the CPU in preparation of the next phase. At the end of phase 1, the CPU memory contains the upper part of A factorization, the GPU memory contains the unfactorized bottom part.

The phase 2 of the algorithm is given in Algorithm 4 and illustrated in Fig. 1. This phase computes the bottom left part by asynchronously loading only the required panel to compute the current block of GEMM update and factorize, until we reach the end of the bottom left panel. At the end of this step only the bottom right panel of A in unfactorized and stored on GPU.

The phase 3 of the algorithm illustrated in Fig. 1 is a straight forward factorization of the bottom right part of the matrix. The global algorithm given in Algorithm 5 consist in initializing the matrix, do the vertical split and load half

Algorithm 4. LU_GPU_Kernel_Phase2_bot

Require: $A^{gpu} = A(N, N/2 : N)$ ▷ bottom on GPU,
Require: $A^{cpu} = A(N, 0 : N/2)$ ▷ factorized top on CPU
1: **while** $i < N/2$ **do**
2:   ▷ U_H is asynchronously copied back from CPU overlapped with V^{gpu} factorization
3:   $Async\_load(U\_H)$
4:   $L_V, U_V \leftarrow factorize(V^{gpu})$ ▷ factorize the bottom part of vertical panel
5:   $pannel(A^{gpu}{}_{i,i}, k, k) \leftarrow GEMM(U_H, L_V)$ ▷ GEMM update
6:   $i \leftarrow i + k$
7: **end while**

Algorithm 5. LU_SFG()
LU Streaming Factorization Algorithm

Require: $A = HPL\_MxP\_ref\_gen(n, n)$
1: $(\hat{A}_{top}, \hat{A}_{bot}) \leftarrow vertical\_split(A)$
2: $Load\_GPU(\hat{A}_{top})$ ▷ Factorize the top half
3: $LU\_GPU\_Kernel\_Phase1\_top()$ ▷ Factorize the rest of the top half with GPU-side bottom half vertical panels and CPU-side factorized horizontal panels as inputs.
4: $LU\_GPU\_Kernel\_Phase2\_Bottom\_left()$ ▷ Factorize the bottom right half with standard LU
5: $LU\_GPU\_Phase3\_Bottom\_right()$

---

on the GPU, and then start the three phases in sequential order. At the end of Algorithm 5 the entire matrix is factorized.

While this SFG algorithm does not directly change the precision profile we used, it may impact the accuracy. Indeed, it allows much larger problem sizes and reorders the computation, which impacts accuracy and reproducibility. Furthermore, it relies on the fact that we do not need column pivoting. Finally, the FP64 input matrix does not need to be stored during LU and can be locally regenerated later. All of those are directly related to the nature of the input matrix generator from the benchmark. All in all, there are many ways to "game" the HPL-MxP benchmark rules. These optimizations might be partially irrelevant to iterative refinement algorithms on real data.

4.1 Exploring Low Precision

For the first experiment, we started GMRES without calling LU for a preconditioner. The HPL-MxP iterative refinement code still managed to converge due to the diagonal dominance. The number of extra GMRES iterations is very low (going from 5 to 8 iterations on average). The fact that the LU is no longer necessary, obsoletes any reason to guarantee accuracy. Furthermore, many bugs or illegal transformations can remain hidden.

Our next experiment is to approximate the matrix multiply in LU instead of using lower precision. That is, if we consider matrix-multiplication to be a rank-N update operation, then we can estimate matrix-multiplication with a rank-1 approximation as described in the following Algorithm 6. These types of low rank approximation techniques are also used in machine learning [10].

Algorithm 6. Low_rank_GEMM(A,B)
Compute approximate $AB \approx A*B$ with a rank 1 update

1: **while** $i < n$ **do**
2: $\quad row1\_A[i] \leftarrow average(A[i][:])$
3: $\quad col1\_B[i] \leftarrow average(B[:][i])$
4: $\quad Diag\_AB[i] = ddot(A[i][:], B[:][i])$
5: $\quad i \leftarrow i + 1$
6: **end while**
7: $AB \leftarrow dger(row1\_A, col1\_B)$
8: $\qquad\qquad\qquad\qquad\qquad\qquad$ ▷ Reset the diagonal to high acc diag elements
9: $Diag(AB) = Diag\_AB$

Algorithm 6 takes the mean value of the element of A rows, denoted a_i and the mean value of the element of B columns, denoted b_j, then instead of computing $A*B$ in $2n^3$ flops, this quantity is estimated by $a_i * b_j^T$, in FP64, and further refine the output by only computing more accurately the diagonal elements of $A*B$. The algorithm relies on two standard BLAS routines, DDOT and DGER. The first does a dot product in $O(n)$ flops, the second does a rank-1 vector outer product update in $O(n^2)$ flops. The overall algorithm yields an approximate matrix-multiplication, GEMM, algorithm doing an order of magnitude less flops, $O(kn^2)$ for rank k, instead of $O(n^3)$. Replacing the GEMM in LU with this experimental algorithm also converges 100% of the time with HPL-MxP without any significant change in GMRES behavior. It is hard to justify using lower precision in LU when one can remove the majority of the flops, which account for more than 95% of the execution time, and still get the right result.

However, we are not making the number of floating point operations required to strictly follow HPL-MxP guidance. In the next experiment, we compute full LU with different profiles of lower precision, strictly matching the HPL-MxP benchmark rules of required complexity of operations.

In all cases of Fig. 2, the same non-pivoted reference LU code is run with FP32 data. All the DTRSM double-precision-triangular-solves updates are using FP32 data. But the GEMM, $C = C - A*B$, inside LU uses different formats depending on the run. We remove FP16 from the plot as it completely overlaps with the BF16 results.

- BF16 input (RNE), FP32 output: A and B were first rounded down to BF16 (using RNE), but C is allowed to accumulate and be stored using FP32; $FP32 \leftarrow FP32 + BF16 * BF16$. The results are left in FP32 format, which is appropriate for all other steps in the algorithm. This format did the best with the smallest initial residual for all problem sizes.

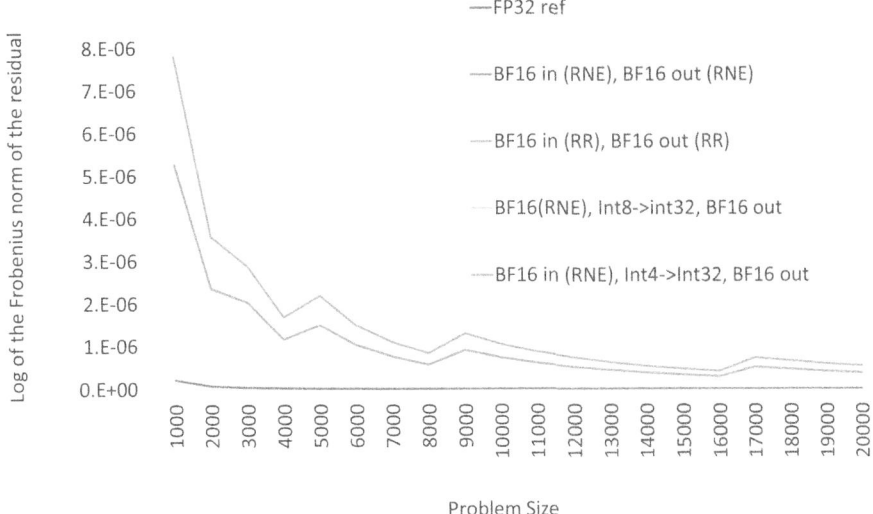

Fig. 2. Original HPL-MxP first residual accuracy with Different LU GEMMs precision. Lower is better

- BF16 input (RNE), BF16 output (RNE): Everything starts like the previous case, but after C is computed in FP32, it is rounded down before storing into BF16, saving half the memory space and bandwidth. In order to do the local LU, the BF16 data is temporarily up-converted to FP32 again, and those computations remain done in FP32 as before.
- BF16 input (RR), BF16 output (RR): Everything like the previous case, but using Random Rounding. The intuition being that RR can improve error bounds on dot product in some circumstance [2]. With the very particular data of HPL-MxP, it just made the problem worse instead of helping to reach the objective as in AI [6] or HPC workloads using low precision [15], but it is still converging. As mentioned earlier this is another indication of the need to make this benchmark more numerically relevant.
- BF16 input (RNE), Int8→Int32 computation, BF16 output: In this case, we still store the data as BF16 (using RNE), but we reduce the GEMM precision further using int8. HPL-MxP have a very small numeric range with its current generator, which is biased toward fixed-point calculations. Before the GEMM, the BF16 data is converted to Int8 via quantization focusing on the maximal elements. The GEMM computation assumes Int32 accumulation (and hence, error-free). Once the Int32 data is collected in blocks, it is converted back to BF16 and stored for the next iteration.
- BF16 input (RNE), Int4→Int32 computation, BF16 output: This experiment was identical to the previous one, but instead of converting the BF16 data into Int8, the quantization maps to Int4. It is interesting to note that Int4 does not have much precision at all, and yet experimentally, it does not behave substantially different than full BF16 or int8 at scale.

For all the versions in Fig. 2, we monitor the first residual after the LU computation as a function of the problem size. This first residual is decreasing with problem size for all versions, including small integers. The conclusion is that, as predicted, while the dimension of the problem n increases, the format precision matters less to the final result. Since the goal of the implementation is to reach the largest n possible to maximize FLOPS, it is easy to understand that it is not a desirable behavior. It suggests that if a computer does Int8 significantly faster than BF16 or FP16, it should always use Int8 for GEMM in HPL-MxP. This is particularly true with latest AI accelerator units such as tensor cores on Nvidia GPU, Intel Xeon with AMX, or latest Intel MAX GPU. Indeed, the addition of dedicated hardware can makes these units more than $30x$ faster than FP32 and $2x$ faster than BF16 counterpart. There may be a few more refinement iterations, but since that is a lower order cost and complexity, it does not offset the gain in LU. It will converge with high accuracy as long as the condition number of the original matrix is low enough.

4.2 Improving the Input Data

We still believe this benchmark could have value with improved input data: the condition number needs to be low, but not necessarily 1, and the way diagonal dominance is currently required prevents any relevant numerical measurement and validation at scale. In particular, the low precision LU can be completely wrong and bugged, the algorithm might still converge because of the diagonal dominance! In comparison, a broken LU for the FP64 HPL benchmark would not run properly and pass the residual check. In the original HPL, the errors will rapidly propagate and lead to horrific solutions.

The HPL-MxP generator must follow some constraints to be accepted. First it must be cost-effective and scalable and therefore be able to generate sub-blocks independently and in parallel. Second, it must return the same matrix for all users. Finally our goal is to have a behavior that is less sensitive to the problem scale, making larger runs as relevant as smaller ones.

To replace the naive matrix generation of HPL-MxP, we propose a new generator in Algorithm 7 matching these constraints, without diagonally dominant output, but still matching the constraint on the condition number.

The generator starts with a random B matrix of rank k and dimension (n, k). We assume k to be a small block-size, much lower than n. We then get the Q matrix from the QR decomposition of B. To control the condition number of the LU decomposition, we generate a diagonal matrix with random values in a range $[1.0, cond]$, and make sure 1.0 and $cond$ are used so that the min and max value on the diagonal are exactly 1 and $cond$ respectively with a ratio equal to $cond$. Finally, we multiply the $V_n * I_{n,n}$ diagonal matrix by Q to get our final random matrix of rank n with the target condition number.

Row pivoting has to be put back into HPL-MxP, and this makes it more realistic. The reason it was left out is the diagonal dominance. A positive aspect of having scaled random orthogonal matrix is that the true inverse is known,

Algorithm 7. QR_gen(n, k, cond)
Generate random matrix of dim n, with rank k update (where $k \ll n$) and condition number cond

1: $B_{n,k} \leftarrow HPL\_MxP\_ref\_gen(n,k)$
2: $Q_{n,n} \leftarrow QR(B_{n,k})$ ▷ $O(kn^2)$
3: **while** $i < n$ **do**
4: $\quad V_n[i] \leftarrow random([1.0, cond])$
5: $\quad i \leftarrow i+1$
6: **end while**
7: $V_n[0] \leftarrow 1.0; V_n[n-1] \leftarrow cond$
8: $A \leftarrow Q_{n,n} * (V_n * I_{n,n})$ ▷ matrix-scaling $O(n^2)$

allowing to easily compute the reference solution. Note that Algorithm 5 needs to be transposed and split horizontally to support the required row pivoting.

We reproduce our previous experiment with the new generator and a 1.1 condition number. The 1.1 is chosen to match the measured condition number of the nearly diagonal matrix generated by the old HPL-MxP generator for the same target matrix dimension. We also test with larger condition numbers, the large accumulator (FP32 output) allowing to safely use less precision while still converging. The results are shown in Fig. 3. The top figure is the first residual after LU. It shows that the new input data are less sensitive to problem size and we can now see a clear difference in the behavior of the various formats. Int4 will converge, however the number of GMRES iterations increases greatly. This is both an expected and desirable behavior for the benchmark and allows to measure trade-offs between numerical formats. The bottom plot shows the approximate residual on the tenth GMRES iteration for different problem sizes. The benchmark has become more challenging. All formats still converge, but now we see distinguishable behavior. For instances with the original generator there is no significant difference between BF16 with FP32 storage from BF16 with BF16 storage. However, we did not find logical explanation for the BF16 input (RNE), Int8→Int32 going upward with n while similar variant with int4 remains flat.

An interesting side conclusion of observing convergence with small integers, is that for 5-level GMRES [8] or similar works, it is numerically relevant to study the potentiality of using low integer fixed point format, as the newest architectures provide higher throughput and energy efficient hardware for it.

5 Discussion and Perspective

With the experiments done in this paper we reach the following conclusions:

1. The former name HPL-AI being replaced by HPL-MxP is a logical move. The current benchmark does indeed not represent AI/ML workloads. The community has proposed ML-Perf [17] for that purpose. In which case HPL-MxP should focus on low and mixed precision for HPC.

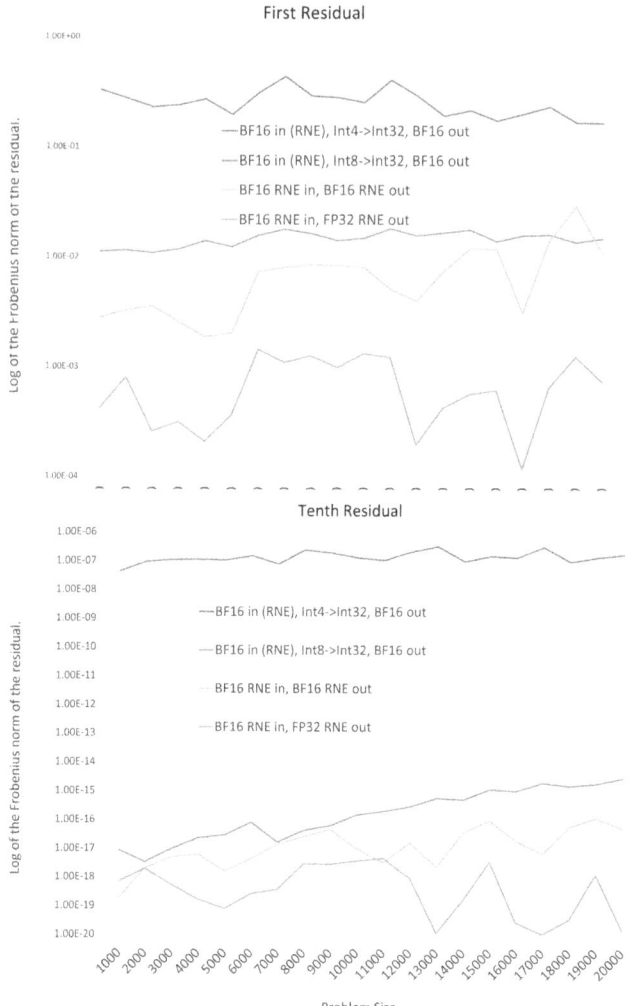

Fig. 3. HPL-MxP (New Generation with Condition Request of 1.1) first (and tenth) log of Frobenius residual accuracy with Different LU GEMMs. Lower is better.

2. With current inputs, the iterative refinement part is useless both for performance and accuracy validation. Most of the performance goes into LU, and the accuracy could be measured on LU only. With the new proposed input data we actually see a difference in GMRES behavior.
3. The rules ask for "$2/3n^3$ flops" complexity. It does not make sense with Integer or other formats that may arise. We suggest to call it "operations" and specifically call attention in the rules to allowing small precision fixed point alternatives.

4. We suggest to specify formats for the various parts of the algorithm with the benchmark submission.
5. An alternative is to generate data for which the vendors are challenged to propose the fastest solution to obtain a given residual for low precision LU. This is enabled by our QR based random matrix generator.

Contrary to algorithms that keep high precision for critical part of their problem [9], HPL-MxP and similar approaches are handling the entire problem in lower precision in some phase of the computation which results in a strong and unavoidable limitation on the maximum condition number. In that regard, HPL-MxP alone will always have blind-spots. While proposing stronger requirements on the numerical format to use, potentially limiting the study to the LU part, we claim that a new set of benchmarks based on true mixed precision should be developed in the future to support the development on hardware capable of handling mixed precision for HPC. The AI part having its own dedicated benchmark. However, with little improvements like the ones we propose, it could provide a useful metric performance-wise like HPL did for years in the top500.

6 Conclusion

In conclusion, while HPL-MxP has been a widely adopted benchmark for evaluating the performance of HPC systems on low precision workloads in the last few years, it has limitations that make it less relevant for incoming AI and HPC workloads. Additionally, the requirement for diagonal dominance in the input matrix and the use of BF16 for storage and computation restrict what the benchmark is representative of to a narrow range of use-cases. Furthermore, the latest AI models, such as LLMs, involve a much larger number of smaller-sized matrix of parameters than HPC applications, making it more important to focus on memory footprint and communication efficiency rather than peak floating-point performance. For instance we explain how using the CPU memory as an additional storage for the GPU algorithm drastically increases the addressable problem size. The use of quantization and compression techniques has also become more prevalent in the AI field to address the memory constraints of modern systems. Therefore, we suggest that HPL-MxP submissions should report specific datatypes for storage, compute, and both diagonal and off-diagonal element formats to facilitate fair comparisons between HPC systems. We proposed a new data generator matching all HPL-MxP design constraint while allowing significant evaluation of various numerical format encoding. Additionally, the benchmark should aim to be more agile to match the fast pace of arithmetic evolution coming from the AI field and support various fixed-point formats. While some latency is understandable for comparing the same generation of systems, the domain it represents - AI and HPC intersection - is still consolidating, and the benchmark needs to keep pace to remain relevant.

References

1. Anzt, H., et al.: Approximate computing for scientific applications. In: Bosio, A., Ménard, D., Sentieys, O. (eds.) Approximate Computing Techniques: From Component- to Application-Level, pp. 415–465. Springer, Cham (2022). https://doi.org/10.1007/978-3-030-94705-7_14
2. Arar, E.M.E., Sohier, D., de Oliveira Castro, P., Petit, E.: Stochastic rounding variance and probabilistic bounds: a new approach (2022)
3. Blanchard, P., Higham, N.J., Lopez, F., Mary, T., Pranesh, S.: Mixed precision block fused multiply-add: error analysis and application to GPU tensor cores. SIAM J. Sci. Comput. (2020)
4. Croci, M., Fasi, M., Higham, N.J., Mary, T., Mikaitis, M.: Stochastic rounding: implementation, error analysis and applications (2022)
5. Denis, C., de Oliveira Castro, P., Petit, E.: Verificarlo: checking floating point accuracy through Monte Carlo arithmetic. In: 23nd IEEE Symposium on Computer Arithmetic ARITH (2016)
6. Gupta, S., Agrawal, A., Gopalakrishnan, K., Narayanan, P.: Deep learning with limited numerical precision. In: Proceedings of the 32nd International Conference on International Conference on Machine Learning (ICML 2015), vol. 37. JMLR.org (2015)
7. Haidar, A., Tomov, S., Dongarra, J., Higham, N.J.: Harnessing GPU tensor cores for fast fp16 arithmetic to speed up mixed-precision iterative refinement solvers. In: Proceedings of the International Conference for High Performance Computing, Networking, Storage, and Analysis (SC 2018). IEEE Press (2018)
8. Higham, N.J., Mary, T.: Five level GMRES for mixed-precision preconditioning. SIAM J. Sci. Comput. (2018)
9. Higham, N.J., Mary, T.: Mixed precision algorithms in numerical linear algebra. Acta Numer. **31**, 347–414 (2022). https://doi.org/10.1017/S0962492922000022
10. Hu, E.J., et al.: Lora: low-rank adaptation of large language models (2021)
11. Laboratory, I.C.: Hpl-mxp reference implementation (2019). https://bitbucket.org/icl/hpl-ai/src/main/. Accessed Apr 2023
12. Liu, Y., et al.: Closing the "quantum supremacy" gap: achieving real-time simulation of a random quantum circuit using a new sunway supercomputer. In: Proceedings of the International Conference for High Performance Computing, Networking, Storage and Analysis (SC 2021). ACM (2021)
13. Micikevicius, P., et al.: Fp8 formats for deep learning. arXiv preprint arXiv:2209.05433 (2022)
14. Osorio, J., Armejach, A., Petit, E., Henry, G., Casas, M.: A bf16 FMS is all you need for DNN training. IEEE Trans. Emerg. Topics Comput. (2022)
15. Paxton, E.A., Chantry, M., Klöwer, M., Saffin, L., Palmer, T.: Climate modeling in low precision: effects of both deterministic and stochastic rounding. J. Climate (2022)
16. Petite, A., Whaley, C., Dongarra, J., Cleary, A.: (2004–2018). https://netlib.org/benchmark/hpl/
17. Reddi, V.J., Cheng, C., Kanter, D., Mattson, P., et al.: Mlperf inference benchmark. In: 2020 ACM/IEEE 47th Annual International Symposium on Computer Architecture (ISCA) (2020)

ImageMap: Enabling Efficient Mapping from Image Processing DSL to CGRA

Bizhao Shi[1,2], Tuo Dai[1,2], Sunan Zou[1,2], Xinming Wei[1,2], and Guojie Luo[1,2(✉)]

[1] School of Computer Science, Peking University, Beijing, China
{bshi,daitoto,zousunan,xinming.wei,gluo}@pku.edu.cn
[2] Center for Energy-Efficient Computing and Applications, Peking University, Beijing, China

Abstract. Image processing has broad application scenarios and fast-developing algorithms, requiring hardware platforms with both high energy efficiency and flexible programmability. Coarse-grained Reconfigurable Arrays (CGRAs) show great potential with their regular parallel architectures and word-level spatio-temporal reconfigurability. However, the mapping of image processing applications on CGRAs faces two main challenges: 1) low-level CGRA programming with multiple constraints brings difficulties for developers; 2) the gaps between coarse-grained image pipelines and the fine-grained pipelined loops executed on CGRA generate a huge program transformation space. In order to tackle these challenges, we propose ImageMap, an efficient mapping framework from Halide, an image processing DSL, to CGRAs. Firstly, we propose multi-level partitioning with the extended Halide scheduling primitives to decompose the complex applications systematically. Secondly, we propose a hierarchical program exploration algorithm specialized for CGRAs with the consideration of partitioning and CGRA performance modeling. Thirdly, we build an automatic compilation framework with several compilation optimization techniques to improve the mapping quality. In the experimental evaluations, ImageMap performs better than existing work across multiple CGRA architectures and common image processing applications.

Keywords: Image Processing · Coarse-grained Reconfigurable Array · CGRA Mapping

1 Introduction

Image processing has many applications, covering many scenarios from edge to the data center [5, 22], such as remote sensing [4], aerospace engineering [8], and medical diagnosis [19]. Continuously evolving algorithms with diverse constraints of application scenarios place high demands on the agility and portability of software programming as well as the high energy efficiency and reconfigurability of execution hardware platforms.

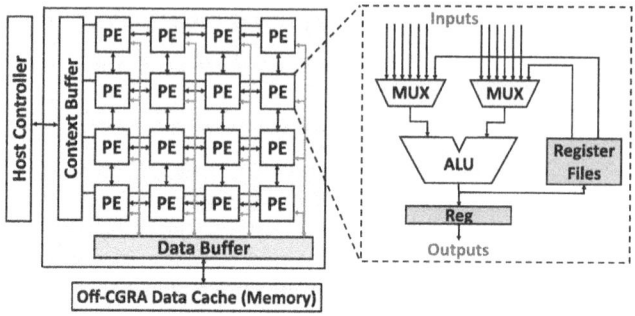

Fig. 1. A typical CGRA architecture with a 4 × 4 mesh-connected PE array.

To improve the efficiency of programming for image processing algorithms, recent software-related studies [11,16,20] extract the common computation and data access patterns and develop domain-specific languages (DSLs). Among these DSLs, Halide [20] becomes very popular because of its decoupled representations of the algorithmic functions and scheduling directives, enabling simplified high-level expressions and focused optimizations. Furthermore, Halide also provides good portability across different devices with its code generation mechanism.

As for the hardware implementations, there have been many specialized optimizations for the common platforms. Many studies focus on the auto-scheduling techniques to generate high-performance code for general purpose processors (GPPs) [1,3]. The other studies [13,18] optimize the accelerator architectures with agile design methodology on field programmable gate arrays (FPGAs). However, due to the instruction-driven execution of GPPs and the redundant bit-level reconfigurability of FPGAs, they both struggle to achieve the best trade-off between programmability and energy efficiency in the image processing domain.

Recently, coarse-grained reconfigurable arrays (CGRAs) have been an attractive acceleration platform because of the regular parallel architectures and the word-level spatiotemporal reconfigurability. The parallelism and pipelining of CGRA make it very advantageous in executing the nested loops in image processing. In particular, CGRAs provide temporal reconfigurability by periodically switching the configurations, enabling a more flexible mapping granularity and improving area efficiency. Figure 1 shows a typical 4 × 4 mesh-connected CGRA. Each PE has multiplexer and register files for data routing and an ALU for arithmetic operations. Besides, there are on-chip context buffer and data buffer for configuration switching and data caching.

However, the application mapping of image processing on CGRAs is still challenging for two reasons: 1) The CGRA programming is usually general but low-level. The classical method to program CGRAs is to construct general C/C++ programs or build data flow graphs (DFGs) for the fine-grained kernels [9]. The compilers perform operator scheduling, operator placement, and data routing through systematic or heuristic methods. The lack of domain-specific features in programming and the multiple constraints in CGRA mapping are burdensome for programmers. 2) A huge optimization space exists when mapping the high-level Halide programs to spatiotemporal reconfigurable CGRAs. Different scheduling and transformations will lead to different performance outcomes. Therefore, it is essential to effectively traverse the program transformation spaces and select the truly promising candidates.

There have been several studies that partially address the two challenges. At the CGRA programming level, AHA [12] provides an agile compilation flow from Halide to CGRAs. However, the specialized CGRA architectures are spatial-only without temporal reconfigurability tightly coupled with their optimization approaches and compilation flow. Therefore, migrating to existing multi-context CGRAs and their mapping flows takes much work. For the program transformation exploration, IP [24] and PBP [15] propose different schemes to obtain the optimized schedules. However, they are mainly based on the polyhedral model and enumerate the transformation candidates with limited scalability, which brings difficulties applied in image processing pipelines.

To tackle these challenges, we propose ImageMap, an end-to-end application mapping framework for compiling Halide programs to multi-context CGRAs. ImageMap first defines multi-level partitions from high-level Halide programs to fine-grained CGRA kernels. Then ImageMap extends the Halide framework for CGRA from three dimensions: 1) extended scheduling primitives for the multi-level partitioning, 2) an efficient auto-scheduling algorithm with a performance model, and 3) efficient CGRA loop scheduling support. More concretely, the main technical contributions of this paper are as follows:

- ImageMap proposes a multi-level partitioning method for CGRA to reduce the mapping complexity in the image processing domain, bridging the fine-grained loops on CGRA and the multi-stage image processing pipelines. The extended partition-related primitives also provide a clear interface for program transformation.
- ImageMap proposes an efficient auto-scheduling algorithm for CGRA with the consideration of partition-related primitives. With the effective performance model, ImageMap generates valuable schedules efficiently.
- The evaluations demonstrate that ImageMap achieves better performance compared to the other key prior works. Specifically, ImageMap achieves up to $5.08\times/1.26\times/1.29\times$ geomean speedups compared to Halide [20], Halide-Tuner [26], and PBP [15], respectively.

2 Background

2.1 Halide

Halide [20] is a popular image processing DSL, with the most prominent feature – decoupled computational and scheduling representation. In terms of computation, Halide supports efficient representation for the common computation patterns (e.g., *element-wise, convolution, reduction*) in the image processing domain.

In terms of scheduling, Halide provides a set of scheduling primitives for loop transformations and parallel optimizations (e.g., *reorder*, *fuse*, *tile*, *unroll*, and *vectorize*). The decoupled expression allows the SW and HW programmers to focus on the algorithmic and scheduling parts for functional development and performance optimization, respectively. The Halide programs will be lowered to Halide IR for further optimization and code generation for different backends.

2.2 CGRA Mapping

As CGRAs execute the computation-intensive innermost loops in a pipelined fashion, the studies on CGRA mapping can be divided into two main directions: a) loop scheduling and b) program transformation. Loop scheduling optimizes the pipelining performance of the computation-intensive innermost loops through modulo scheduling, while program transformation optimizes the program structures through loop transformations to minimize the overall latency.

- **Loop Scheduling.** Loop scheduling aims to find a feasible mapping between the loop representations, i.e., data flow graphs (DFGs), and the hardware representations, i.e., Modulo Routing Resource Graph (MRRG) and Time Extended CGRA (TEC). Loop scheduling usually contains three main constraint groups: operator scheduling, operator placement, and data routing. To optimize the throughput of the pipelined executed loops, the modulo scheduling techniques are widely applied to make the mapped initiation interval (II) as close as possible to the theoretical lower bound – minimum II (MII) [2]. Currently, there have been many loop scheduling methods with different formulations and optimization heuristics [6,7,10,25]. In order to get the minimum mapped II, the compilers usually work in a trial-and-error fashion and start mapping the DFG with MII until they find a successful mapping.
- **Program Transformation.** Program transformation focuses on the overall performance, i.e., latency of the applications [14,15,24]. Considering the huge gap between the overall program and the fine-grained loops executed on CGRA, there are many scheduling choices with different spatial-temporal behaviors (also with different performances). Previous studies have proposed some transformation spaces using loop transformation directives to explore the promising candidates. Different exploration strategies and candidate evaluation strategies are proposed. With the profiled candidates, they enable the multiple loop scheduling processes to get the best transformation with all feasible innermost loops.

3 Methods

3.1 Multi-level Partitioning and Halide Primitives Extensions

In order to decompose the complex image pipelines systematically, ImageMap introduces four partitioning levels: a) inter-stage partitioning, b) memory-aware partitioning, c) micro-stage partitioning, and d) spatiotemporal partitioning. Figure 2 demonstrates the examples and effects of each-level partitioning.

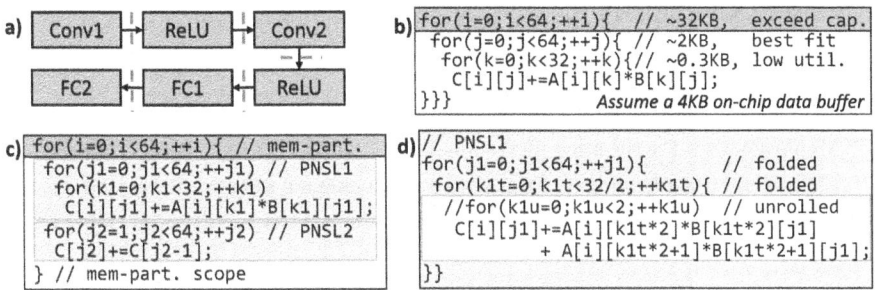

Fig. 2. Multi-level Partitioning in ImageMap: a) inter-stage partitioning, b) memory-aware partitioning, c) micro-stage partitioning, and d) spatiotemporal partitioning.

Besides, as the partitioning information will be inserted in the Halide program as a part of scheduling representation, the relationship between the conventional scheduling primitives and the partitioning-related primitives should be clarified. The following paragraphs will introduce the partitions and corresponding scheduling directives.

- **Inter-stage Partitioning:** In image processing applications, multiple algorithmic stages with various computation and memory access patterns are organized in a pipeline. The interaction between stages in the pipeline is primarily through producer-consumer data dependencies. Considering the fine-grained innermost loops executed on CGRA, partitioning the image processing pipelines into distinct stages will significantly reduce the mapping complexity. The compilation flow can optimize the schedule for each stage independently according to the corresponding patterns. Figure 2 part a) shows a simple convolutional neural network. The inter-stage partitioning will separate these operators and enable independent intra-stage explorations.
- **Memory-Aware Partitioning:** The image processing pipelines usually have large memory footprints with multiple intermediate buffers. Considering the limited on-chip data buffer on CGRAs, it is essential to indicate a proper data caching level for three reasons: 1) off-CGRA data access (loading in and writing back) during the pipelined execution harms the throughput significantly and should be eliminated; 2) if the on-chip data buffer is under-utilized, we also need to raise the caching level and the spatiotemporal granularity for the innermost loop; 3) a specific data caching level enables advanced compilation optimizations, such as addressing simplification. Figure 2 part b) shows a GEMM stage under a CGRA with a 4KB data buffer. At different levels, the sizes of the corresponding active set are various. The loop j is the best caching level with 50% utilization of the on-CGRA data buffer.
- **Micro-stage Partitioning:** Besides the two partitioning dimensions introduced above, we need to control the CGRA execution further with fine-grained partitioning. The proposed micro-stage partitioning is to extract the perfectly nested sub-loops (PNSLs) in the scope of one stage. With the different coarse-grained schedules (e.g., stage fusion and split), the fine-grained

Table 1. The extended primitives in ImageMap.

Partitioning Dimension	Primitive Definition		Factor
Inter-stage Partitioning	[Reused]	`func.compute_root()`	None
Memory-aware Partitioning	[Extended]	`func.buffer_at(t)`	Loop Index t
Micro-stage Partitioning	[Extended]	`func.nested_at(t)`	Loop Index t
Spatiotemporal Partitioning	[Extended]	`func.unrolled_at(t)`	Loop Index t

loop nesting relationships can be various. Besides, the CGRA behavior within one PNSL is regular and suitable for performance modeling. Therefore, we use the micro-stage partitioning as the interface. ImageMap utilizes the hierarchical feature to efficiently explore the transformation opportunities, where the stage and PNSL are considered units to explore the coarse-grained and fine-grained program transformation spaces. Figure 2 part c) shows a synthetic program with two PNSLs under the memory-aware partitioning scope.

- **Spatiotemporal Partitioning:** During the fine-grained exploration within each PNSL, the innermost loop may have different spatiotemporal granularity (e.g., loop tripcount and #DFG nodes), which leads to different on-chip buffer and PE array utilization as well as the performance and energy efficiency. Therefore, achieving a good trade-off between the temporally folded loops and the spatially unrolled operators is necessary. Besides, given the execution of CGRAs, the unrolled loop dimensions should be lowered to the innermost loop rather than simply generating duplicated loops. Therefore, ImageMap defines a specific partitioning to constrain the unrolling dimensions clearly. Figure 2 part d) shows an unrolled loop $k1u$ with a factor of 2.

Given the definitions of the multi-level partitioning, here we introduce the extended scheduling primitives in Halide for the explicit representations (listed in Table 1). For the inter-stage partitioning, ImageMap reuses the built-in primitive `compute_root()` and decouples the analysis and exploration automatically. The other three partitioning dimensions need a specific loop level with the index t to indicate their scopes. Combined with the other native Halide primitives, ImageMap provides a comprehensive scheduling space for CGRAs with sufficient compilation information. Next, we will introduce the proposed auto-scheduling method specialized for CGRA using these primitives.

3.2 Auto-scheduling Algorithm

A Halide program is usually represented as a directed acyclic graph (DAG). In order to effectively explore the schedule space with the consideration of CGRA executions, ImageMap proposes a hierarchical method by dividing the overall space into three coarse-to-fine sub-spaces: 1) inter-stage relationships, 2) inter-loop orders, 3) spatiotemporal granularity. Inter-stage relationships' space mainly explores the possible fusion choices between the adjacent stages at different loop levels. As the coarse-grained stage fusions may cause the different loop

Algorithm 1: Auto-scheduling Algorithm for CGRA

Input: Image Processing Pipeline P with N stages, Maximum Fusion Depth d, Top-K Schedule Candidate Capacity K
Output: Best Schedule with Mapping Configurations $Config$

1   $P_r \leftarrow$ getReverseTopologicalSort(P);
2   Initialize an $N \times N$ $costMatrix$ with the value $+\infty$;
3   Initialize an $N \times N \times K$ $topSchedule$ with the empty schedule;
4   Initialize an array f with the size of N.
5   **for** $i \leftarrow 0$ **to** N **do**
6 | $costMatrix[i][i], topSchedule[i][i] \leftarrow$ intraStageExploration($P_r[i]$);
7   **end**
8   **for** $i \leftarrow 0$ **to** N **do**
9 | **for** $j \leftarrow i+1$ **to** $\min(i+d, N)$ **do**
10 | $fusionCandidates \leftarrow$ stageFusionExploration($P_r[i:j]$);
11 | **forall** $cand$ **in** $fusionCandidates$ **do**
12 | $cost, sche \leftarrow$ intraStageExploration($cand$);
13 | **if** $cost < costMatrix[i][j]$ **then**
14 | $costMatrix[i][j] \leftarrow cost$;
15 | $topSchedule[i][j] \leftarrow (cand, sche)$;
16 | **end**
17 | **end**
18 | **end**
19   **end**
20   $f[0] \leftarrow cost[0][0]$;
21   **for** $i \leftarrow 1$ **to** N **do**
22 | **for** $j \leftarrow \max(1, i-d)$ **to** i **do**
23 | $f[i] \leftarrow \min(f[i], f[j-1] + cost[i][j])$;
24 | record the best j for i;
25 | **end**
26   **end**
27   enumerate all of the best inter-stage partitioning (j);
28   $config \leftarrow$ get the best mapping config from $topSchedule$ through loop scheduling;
29   **return** $config$
30   **Function** stageFusionExploration($stage\_list$):
31 | $fusionChoices \leftarrow$ Queue();
32 | $fusionChoices$.append(($stage\_list[0], 0$));
33 | **while** $fusionChoices$.top()[1] $<$ len($stage\_list$) **do**
34 | $top, level \leftarrow fusionChoices$.top(); $fusionChoices$.pop();
35 | $memParts \leftarrow$ generate the memory-aware partitioning for top;
36 | $nextFusions \leftarrow$ enumerate fusions with different $memParts$ for top and $stage\_list[level + 1]$;
37 | **forall** $\bar{f}$ **in** $nextFusions$ **do**
38 | $fusionChoices$.push(($f, level + 1$));
39 | **end**
40 | **end**
41 | $topK \leftarrow$ select top-K candidates in $fusionChoices$ with **evaluate()** function;
42 | **return** $topK$;
43   **Function** intraStageExploration($stage$):
44 | $tilingPool \leftarrow$ List();
45 | $memParts \leftarrow$ generate the default memory-aware partitioning for $stage$;
46 | $outTilings \leftarrow$ generate loop tiling-and-reorder with different $memParts$;
47 | $tilingPool$.append("compute_root()", evaluate($stage$.compute_root()));
48 | **forall** $tiling$ **in** $outTilings$ **do**
49 | $tilingPool$.append($tiling$, evaluate($stage.tiling$));
50 | **end**
51 | $tilingPool \leftarrow$ select top-K candidates in $tilingPool$;
52 | **forall** $tiling$ **in** $tilingPool$ **do**
53 | generate the micro-stage partitioning greedily for $tiling$;
54 | $PNSLs \leftarrow$ extract all of the PNSLs from $tiling$;
55 | **forall** $pnsl$ **in** $PNSLs$ **do**
56 | $fineSche \leftarrow$ generate reordering and tiling-for-unroll for $pnsl$;
57 | $topFineSche \leftarrow$ select top-K candidates in $fineSche$ with **evaluate()**.
58 | **end**
59 | select and store top-K schedules for the current $tiling$ with $topFineSche$.
60 | **end**
61 | $cost, sche \leftarrow$ select the overall $topK$ schedules in $tilingPool$ with **evaluate()**.
62 | **return** $cost, sche$

nesting hierarchies, the inter-stage relationships will be explored first. Within one (fused) stage, the inter-loop transformations (e.g., tiling and reordering) lead to different computation orders and memory access patterns for the image regions. Therefore, ImageMap will then explore the subspace of inter-loop orders and determine the memory-aware and micro-stage partitioning levels. Thirdly, within one PNSL, the fine-grained loops will directly impact the execution performance. ImageMap extracts each PNSL and explores the loop unrolling opportunities.

According to the guidance of hierarchical exploration, we design an efficient auto-scheduling algorithm in Algorithm 1. The algorithm inputs contain three parts: 1) the target image processing pipeline, 2) the maximum fusion depth constraint, and 3) the capacity of promising schedule candidates. At the top level, the algorithm searches for the optimal inter-stage partitioning in a dynamic programming-like style (Lines 5–18): it first explores the intra-stage exploration without any inter-stage fusion. Then, it explores the stage fusion opportunities with a limited depth. It is clear that the inter-stage data dependencies in the pipelines create an enormous fusion exploration space. Here, we add three constraints for stage fusion: 1) We only fuse up to d consecutive stages with linear dependencies, greatly reducing the searching complexity. In the context of CGRAs, too complex stage fusions lead to fragmented loop nesting and affect efficiency. 2) We only enumerate the fusions that can cause different memory-aware partitions. Memory-aware partitioning is performed greedily by maximizing data buffer utilization. It can be evaluated according to the static analysis for the active set within this loop level. If the stage fusion cannot cause different memory partitioning, we claim that this fusion is ineffective for CGRA execution. Besides, we will evaluate the computation and memory access through an analytical model (introduced in Sect. 3.3) and select K top fusion candidates for further fine-grained explorations (Lines 11–17).

Within each (fused) stage, the intra-stage exploration is performed in a beam search-like style (Line 43–62). To explore the various schedules comprehensively, the intra-stage exploration first enumerates the loop tilings. Here, we limit the tiled loop level to be higher than the corresponding memory-partitioning level. If the high-level loops are tiled, the newly generated loop should be lowered under the memory-partitioning level through loop reordering. With the combinations of (outer) loop tilings, we evaluate the tiling and select the top-K candidates for further fine-grained explorations. In order to maintain the schedules with diverse data buffering hierarchy, we additionally evaluate the similarity of two schedules through a tree edited distance [21]-like metric. It is worth to mention that although the memory-aware partitioning does not guide the exploration process explicitly, the marked data caching level is still important for performance modeling and addressing simplification in the compilation optimization.

In the fine-grained schedule explorations, the algorithms first generate the micro-stage partitioning under the corresponding memory partitioning level. If the sub-loops under memory partitioning are perfectly nested, the corresponding PNSL level is marked as the same level as memory-aware partitioning. If not, more than one PNSL partition will be inserted greedily under the memory partitioning level. Within each PNSL, the loop reordering and unrolling are explored to generate the kernels with different spatiotemporal granularities. The loop unrolling dimensions must be lowered to the innermost loops through tiling-reordering-unrolling. For each PNSL, we finally collect top-K schedules and return to the stage-level evaluation.

After all of the explorations, the algorithm traverses the pipelines and records the best inter-stage partitions as well as the top-K schedules within the corresponding (fused) stage. To get the final mapping configurations, parallel loop scheduling processes are enabled to find the first feasible schedule in *topSchedules*.

3.3 Performance Profiling

In the auto-scheduling algorithm, it is clear that the ranking and selections of promising schedules are determined by the `evaluate()` function. Therefore, effective performance profiling can improve the quality and efficiency of the overall compilation. Here, we introduce an analytical scheme for latency estimation.

Based on the micro-stage partitions, we first model the latency for each PNSL through the behavior analysis: the CGRA executes the innermost loops in pipeline, while the other loops within the PNSL are temporal-folded:

$$Cycles_{PNSL} = \prod_{out\ loops} TC_{loop} \times (MII \times (TC_{inner} - 1) + Latency_{inner}) \quad (1)$$

where TC, MII, and $Latency_{inner}$ denote the loop tripcount, MII, and iteration latency of the innermost loops. Based on the PNSL-level formulation, we further model the stage-level latency by adding the data access analysis:

$$Cycles_{stage} = Cycles_{compute} + Cycles_{memory} \quad (2)$$

$$Cycles_{compute} = \sum (\prod_{pnsl\ out\ loops} TC_{loop} \times Cycles_{pnsl}) \quad (3)$$

$$Cycles_{memory} = \sum (\prod_{mem\ out\ loops} TC_{loop} \times Vol_{mem}/BW) \quad (4)$$

where the overall computational latency is accumulated through repeated executions for multiple PNSLs. Memory-related latency is caused by data loading and writing back at the memory-partitioning level. Therefore, we count the latency according to the related data volume and streaming memory bandwidth. The latency for the entire image processing pipeline is modeled as follows:

$$Cycles_{pipeline} = \sum_{stage} Cycles_{stage} \quad (5)$$

With the analytical profiling method, we can easily evaluate the scheduling candidates and rank them based on the estimated latency. During the exploration of the program transformation space and the generation of the final mapping configurations, several compilation optimizations are used to further enhance performance. Therefore, we will introduce the overall compilation flow and the proposed optimization strategies for CGRA next.

3.4 ImageMap Framework and Compilation Optimizations

The extended scheduling primitives and the CGRA-specialized auto-scheduling algorithm are integrated into the Halide framework. With the Halide IR system and compilation infrastructure, we can easily lower the high-level algorithm and scheduling information to the code generation phase. Considering the low programming levels for CGRAs, we will introduce the compilation workflow of ImageMap and the optimization strategies during the code generation.

Figure 3 shows the overall workflow of ImageMap. With the input Halide program, the autoscheduler will be called to explore the program transformation space and insert the scheduling representations, where the abstract CGRA architecture information is considered as a set of input arguments. Then, the Halide compiler will lower the high-level programs to Halide IR and perform common optimizations (e.g., bound inference, sliding window optimization, and loop flattening). With the generated Halide IR graph, the code generator will perform two optimization passes to improve the quality of CGRA loop schedul-

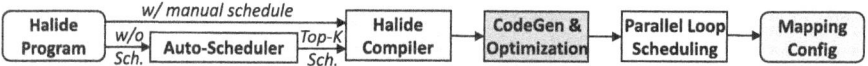

Fig. 3. ImageMap Compilation Workflow

ing and generate the backend representations (DFG or C code with pragmas) for CGRA mappers. Finally, the multiple scheduling processes are enabled in parallel to generate the feasible mapping configurations for all PNSLs efficiently.

Specifically, the optimization passes transform the program representations from two perspectives: a) data rearrangement with address simplification and b) high fan-out reduction through re-computation. The data rearrangement pass focuses on the complex address calculations due to loop tiling and unrolling. For CGRA, the required data needs to be placed tightly in the limited on-chip data buffer; for program execution, simplified address calculation will effectively improve the performance of resource-limited CGRA. Therefore, this pass uses the memory-aware partitioning level as a unit to arrange the required data closely, determine the access area of each array, and modify the starting offset of address calculation and the address interval of block access. As for the fan-out reduction pass, it considers that high fan-out brings challenges to data routing in loop scheduling, affecting the performance and even the success rate of mapping. Therefore, this pass will re-compute the high fan-out nodes without increasing the MII. It is worth noticing that the computation and constant nodes are easily replicated, while the data access usually involves critical load/store resources requiring more conservative balancing between re-computation and data routing.

As for the parallel loop schedulings, it is natural for the application to map from Halide to CGRAs. From the perspective of CGRA execution, there is no spatiotemporal overlap in the execution of different innermost loops. And different PNSLs within the same memory-aware partitioning share the same data placement scheme. From the perspective of Halide programs, the data interactions between stages or PNSLs usually depend on the global image arrays or temporary buffers. Therefore, DFGs of the different pipelined loops are independent of each other and without complex input/output nodes, which enables independent loop schedulings in parallel.

4 Evaluations

4.1 Experiment Setup

ImageMap is implemented on the top of Halide, and the back-end mapper for loop scheduling is developed based on SAT-MapIt [23]. Besides, there are three baselines for comparisons: 1) Halide: the original Halide programs with default schedules; 2) PBP [15], the state-of-the-art CGRA mapper focuses on the program transformation exploration under the guidance of polyhedral model; 3) HalideTuner [26], a tuning-based general auto-scheduler. We select four CGRA architectures for evaluations: 1) a 3×3 CGRA with a 6KB data buffer; 2) a 4×4 CGRA with an 8KB data buffer; 3) a 6×6 CGRA with a 12KB data buffer; and 4) an 8×8 CGRA with a 16 KB data buffer. For energy efficiency reasons, we limit the size of the context buffer to 8. The performance will be evaluated through an in-house cycle-accurate simulator. As for the benchmarks, we select eight typical Halide applications used in [1,13,17]: 1) Matmul: $1024 \times 1024 \times 1024$ general matrix multiplication; 2) Harris: Harris corner detection; 3) Dilation: maximum over 3×3 window; 4) Stencil Chain: 5×5 kernel chained 16 times; 5) IIR Blur: blur with four-pass IIR filters; 6) ConvReLU: 3×3 convolutional layer with 32 output channels and a ReLU activation; 7) Unsharp: unsharp masking filtering; 8) VGG16: VGG-16 network with 224×224 RGB images. The input images for cases 1)-7) are the size of 2160×3840. The batch size is set to 16.

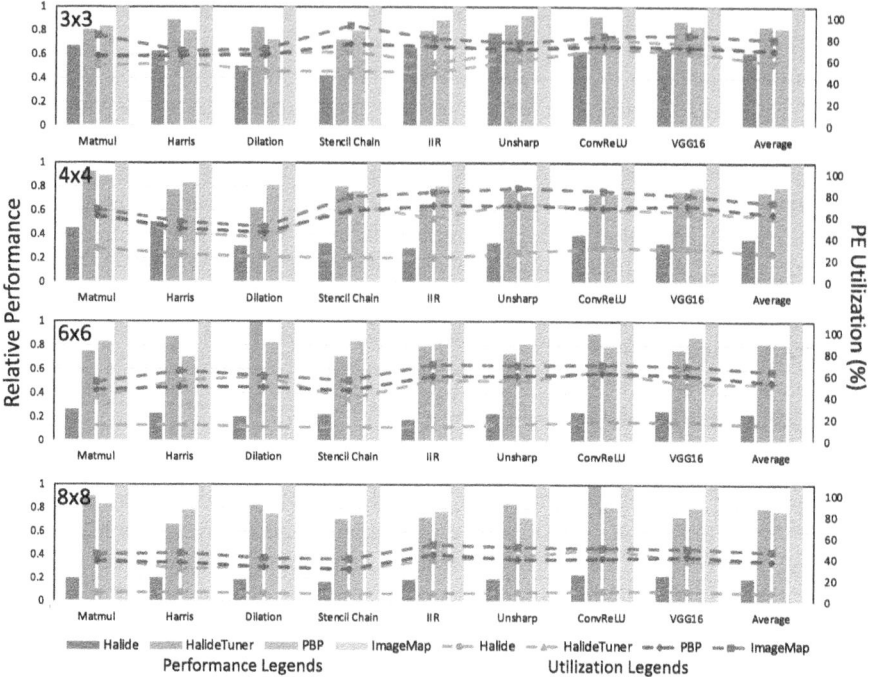

Fig. 4. Relative performance and PE array utilization evaluation.

4.2 Overall Performance Evaluation

Figure 4 shows the relative performance and PE array utilization of ImageMap and three baselines. Here, we set the maximum fusion depth d as three and the capacity of top schedule candidates K as 32. It is clear that ImageMap can perform better in all cases. The speedups achieved by ImageMap are $1.62\times/1.19\times/1.21\times$ on 3×3 CGRA, $2.76\times/1.32\times/1.26\times$ on 4×4 CGRA, $4.44\times/1.23\times/1.24\times$ on 6×6 CGRA, and $5.08\times/1.26\times/1.29\times$ on 8×8 CGRA compared to Halide, HalideTuner, and PBP, respectively. For the original Halide with default schedules, it only achieves high PE utilization on small PE arrays (57.6% on 3×3). With the increasing PE array size, the kernels with fine spatiotemporal granularity lead to low PE utilization and poor performance. HalideTuner and PBP both perform program transformation optimizations to improve performance and efficiency. HalideTuner is designed for CPUs and has some redundant (ineffective) design choices for CGRA. Besides, the implicit hierarchical searching strategies embedded in the Halide techniques of HalideTuner also cause limited compilation efficiency for CGRAs. For PBP, it enumerates the loop fusions and explores the inter-loop fine-grained transformations with depth-first-search. However, there is no consideration of data access in PBP, which makes it favor candidate schedules with too large active sets and causes low execution efficiency. In contrast, the success of ImageMap mainly depends on two parts: 1) The hierarchical exploration

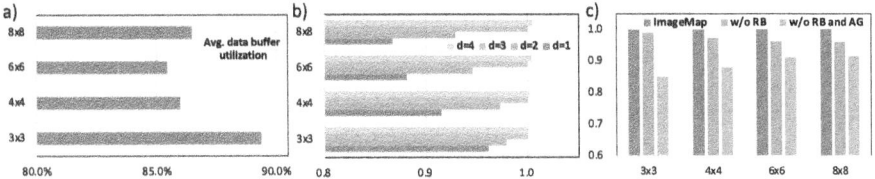

Fig. 5. Detailed evaluations: a) data buffer utilization; b) the impact of different fusion depths d on performance; c) ablation study for the proposed compilation optimizations.

with the two coarse-grained partitions (inter-stage and memory-aware) reduces the searching complexity, while also recording a set of loop nestings with various compute-memory behaviors for fine-grained search. Besides, the fine-grained search (with micro-stage and spatiotemporal partitioning) explores kernels with different spatiotemporal granularities and efficiently utilizes PE arrays. 2) The memory-aware partitioning and performance model effectively characterizes the utilization of data buffers and avoids the stalls caused by data access misses during the pipeline execution.

As for the PE array utilization, ImageMap has an obviously higher PE array utilization (79.8%, 72.8%, 64.0%, and 46.8% on 3×3, 4×4, 6×6, and 8×8 CGRAs, respectively) than the baselines. In Halide applications, the frequent access of data buffers make the PEs with load/store functions a critical resource. This limitation hinders the spatial expansion of the kernel, leading to a gradual decrease in PE utilization on larger CGRAs.

The above results demonstrate the superior performance and execution efficiency of ImageMap in mapping image processing applications to CGRA.

4.3 Detailed Evaluations

In order to demonstrate the effectiveness of the proposed optimization techniques, we conduct three detailed evaluations shown in Fig. 5. First, we show the average data buffer utilization among the four CGRA architectures in Fig. 5 part a). We find that for different buffer capacities, the promising schedules selected by ImageMap can utilize more than 80% of the data buffer and avoid off-CGRA data access during the pipeline execution. Thanks to the memory-aware partitioning, it explicitly indicates the data caching level and maximizes the utilization of the on-chip data buffer through the auto-scheduling process.

Secondly, we evaluate the impact of different fusion depths d on the overall performance shown in Fig. 5 part b). Considering the regular data dependencies between adjacent stages in the image processing pipeline, the stage fusions bring various memory access patterns, loop nesting relationships, and pipeline kernel expressions, but at the cost of higher exploration complexity. For small CGRAs, the pipelined loops can often achieve high PE utilization by unrolling, so the benefits of stage fusion mainly come from improving memory access efficiency. For larger CGRAs, stage fusion can not only optimize memory access but also improve array utilization in fine-grained kernel fusions. Therefore, with the increasing of d (from d=1 to d=3), the performance improves significantly on 6×6 and 8×8 CGRAs. However, when d continues to increase, the benefits tend to be saturated due to the limitations of the CGRA execution model, and the search overhead will increase significantly. Therefore, we choose d=3 for the end-to-end performance evaluations.

Thirdly, we conduct an ablation study for the proposed compilation optimizations in Fig. 5 part c), where RB denotes the re-balancing between recomputation and data routing, and AG denotes the on-chip data re-arrangement and address simplifications. We can see that both strategies can help improve performance. For small PE arrays, RB has a smaller trade-off space, while the simplification of the DFGs in AG shows greater benefits. For large arrays, the performance constraints are not only limited by the load/store units but also by data routing in the complex kernel, which will be improved through re-computation.

Through the above evaluations, we demonstrate the reasonableness and effectiveness of the proposed optimizations and parameter selections in ImageMap. Here we also have some discussions about the compilation time overhead. ImageMap takes seconds to minutes for the compilation. We think it is acceptable. The specific compilation time is closely related to the number of image processing pipeline stages, fusion depth, and the size of the CGRA array. To control the compilation overhead, we enhance the loop scheduling back-end and manually mine some common operators in the Halide programming to reduce the mapping overhead. In the future, automatically identifying common operators or repeated substructures will be very helpful in reducing the mapping overhead.

5 Conclusion

This paper proposes ImageMap, an efficient compilation framework for mapping image processing applications to multi-context CGRAs. ImageMap first defines four-level partitions and extends them as Halide scheduling primitives. Then, it designs an efficient auto-scheduling algorithm for CGRAs based on the partitions. Experimental results demonstrate the advanced performance of ImageMap compared to other key prior works.

Acknowledgments. We thank Sicheng Li and Yen-kuang Chen at Alibaba DAMO Academy for their valuable advice. This work was partly supported by the National Key R&D Program of China (Grant No. 2022YFB4500500) and the National Natural Science Foundation of China (Grant No. 62090021).

References

1. Adams, A., et al.: Learning to optimize Halide with tree search and random programs. ACM TOG **38**(4), 1–12 (2019)
2. Allan, V.H., et al.: Software pipelining. ACM CSUR **27**, 367–432 (1995)
3. Anderson, L., et al.: Learning to schedule Halide pipelines for the GPU. arXiv preprint arXiv:2012.07145 (2020)
4. Bagloee, S.A., et al.: Autonomous vehicles: challenges, opportunities, and future implications for transportation policies. J. Mod. Transport. **24**(4), 284–303 (2016)
5. Bhabatosh, C., et al.: Digital Image Processing and Analysis. PHI Learning Pvt, Ltd (2011)
6. Chin, S.A., et al.: An architecture-agnostic integer linear programming approach to CGRA mapping. In: Proceedings of the DAC, pp. 1–6 (2018)
7. Dave, S., et al.: RAMP: resource-aware mapping for CGRAs. In: Proceedings of the DAC (2018)
8. Dong, X., et al.: Automatic inspection of aerospace welds using x-ray images. In: Proceedings of the ICPR, pp. 2002–2007. IEEE (2018)
9. Guo, Y., et al.: Pillars: an integrated CGRA design framework. In: Third Workshop on Open-Source EDA Technology (WOSET) (2020)
10. Guo, Y., et al.: Formulating data-arrival synchronizers in integer linear programming for CGRA mapping. In: Proceedings of the DAC, pp. 943–948. IEEE (2021)
11. Hegarty, J., et al.: Darkroom: compiling high-level image processing code into hardware pipelines. ACM TOG **33**(4), 144–1 (2014)
12. Koul, K., et al.: AHA: an agile approach to the design of coarse-grained reconfigurable accelerators and compilers. ACM TECS **22**(2), 1–34 (2023)
13. Li, J., et al.: HeteroHalide: from image processing DSL to efficient FPGA acceleration. In: Proceedings of the FPGA, pp. 51–57 (2020)
14. Liu, D., et al.: Polyhedral model based mapping optimization of loop nests for CGRAs. In: Proceedings of the DAC, pp. 1–8 (2013)
15. Liu, D., et al.: Polyhedral-based pipelining of imperfectly-nested loop for CGRAs. In: Proceedings of the ICCAD, pp. 1–9 (2021)
16. Mullapudi, R.T., et al.: PolyMage: automatic optimization for image processing pipelines. In: Proceedings of the ASPLOS, pp. 429–443 (2015)
17. Mullapudi, R.T., et al.: Automatically scheduling Halide image processing pipelines. ACM TOG **35**(4), 1–11 (2016)
18. Pu, J., et al.: Programming heterogeneous systems from an image processing DSL. ACM TACO **14**(3), 1–25 (2017)
19. Qiao, L., et al.: FPGA-accelerated iterative reconstruction for transmission electron tomography. In: Proceedings of the FCCM, pp. 152–156. IEEE (2021)
20. Ragan-Kelley, J., et al.: Halide: a language and compiler for optimizing parallelism, locality, and recomputation in image processing pipelines. In: Proceedings of the PLDI, pp. 519–530 (2013)
21. Schwarz, S., Pawlik, M., Augsten, N.: A new perspective on the tree edit distance. In: Beecks, C., Borutta, F., Kröger, P., Seidl, T. (eds.) Similarity Search and Applications, pp. 156–170. Springer, Cham (2017). https://doi.org/10.1007/978-3-319-68474-1_11
22. Shi, B., et al.: Efficient super-resolution system with block-wise hybridization and quantized winograd on FPGA. IEEE TCAD **42**(11), 3910–3924 (2023)
23. Tirelli, C., et al.: SAT-MapIt: a SAT-based modulo scheduling mapper for coarse grain reconfigurable architectures. In: Proceedings of the DATE, pp. 1–6. IEEE (2023)

24. Yin, S., et al.: Joint affine transformation and loop pipelining for mapping nested loop on CGRAs. In: Proceedings of the DATE, pp. 115–120. IEEE (2015)
25. Zhao, Z., et al.: Towards higher performance and robust compilation for CGRA modulo scheduling. IEEE TPDS **31**(9), 2201–2219 (2020)
26. Zingales, G.P.E.T.: HalideTuner: generating and tuning Halide schedules with OpenTuner. Ph.D. thesis, Massachusetts Institute of Technology (2015)

Predicting GPU Kernel's Performance on Upcoming Architectures

Lucas Van Lanker[1,3]([✉]), Hugo Taboada[1,2], Elisabeth Brunet[3], and François Trahay[3]

[1] CEA, DAM, DIF, 91297 Arpajon, France
{lucas.vanlanker,hugo.taboada}@cea.fr
[2] CEA, Laboratoire en Informatique Haute Performance pour le Calcul et la simulation, Université Paris-Saclay, 91680 Bruyères-le-Châtel, France
[3] Télécom SudParis, Institut Polytechnique de Paris, Inria, 91000 Évry, France
{elisabeth.brunet,francois.trahay}@telecom-sudparis.eu

Abstract. With the advent of heterogeneous systems that combine CPUs and GPUs, designing a supercomputer becomes more and more complex. The hardware characteristics of GPUs significantly impact the performance. Choosing the GPU that will maximize performance for a limited budget is tedious because it requires predicting the performance on a non-existing hardware platform.

In this paper, we propose a new methodology for predicting the performance of kernels running on GPUs. This method analyzes the behavior of an application running on an existing platform, and projects its performance on another GPU based on the target hardware characteristics. The performance projection relies on a hierarchical roofline model as well as on a comparison of the kernel's assembly instructions of both GPUs to estimate the operational intensity of the target GPU.

We demonstrate the validity of our methodology on modern NVIDIA GPUs on several mini-applications. The experiments show that the performance is predicted with a mean absolute percentage error of 20.3 % for LULESH, 10.2 % for MiniMDock, and 5.9 % for Quicksilver.

Keywords: Performance projection · GPU architecture · Roofline model

1 Introduction

Designing a supercomputer is a complex task that requires balancing multiple properties including the price of components, and their performance. GPUs are a major part of the design space to explore, as new generations of GPUs deliver ever-better performance. Due to the high price of high-end GPUs, estimating the performance of an application on a target GPU architecture is crucial before committing to buy new hardware.

Predicting GPU applications' performance is quite challenging: GPUs rely on many cores and a complex memory hierarchy, vendors may use closed source documentation that hides artifacts such as memory bank conflict or code divergence, and applications require fine tunings to use the GPU to its full potential.

As we will see in the related work section, to project performance, several approaches exist, such as simulation, statistical model with machine learning, and analytical model. However, they are either too much time-consuming, or they cannot be applied to large applications. In this context, less accurate but faster methods such as performance projection models become interesting.

In this paper, we propose a methodology for predicting the performance of kernels running on a target GPU, as presented in Fig. 1. The proposed method runs a program on an existing GPU once, and it projects the application performance on a target GPU. With a single sample run, we characterize the application behavior according to different criteria such as its computational intensity, data placement, and other properties that can be measured, analyzed, and modeled. Our methodology compares the assembly code of the application on both the source GPU and the target GPU and uses the model in order to project the application performance on the target GPU.

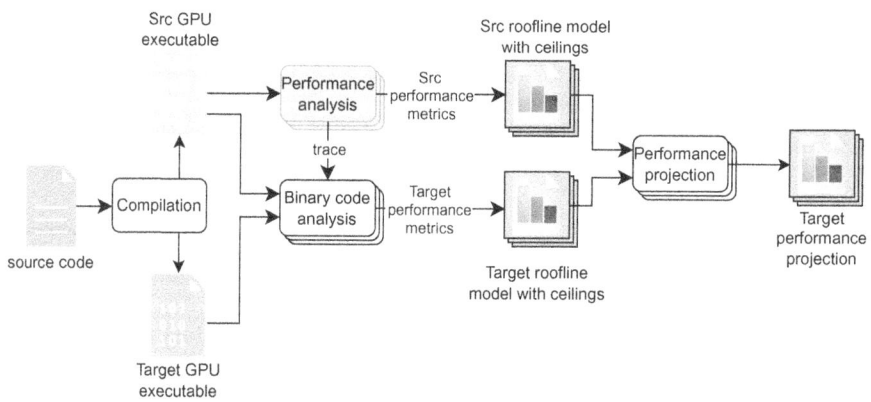

Fig. 1. Summary of the proposed projection workflow.

The contributions of this paper are the following:

- We propose a kernel performance projection methodology for GPUs from the run of a kernel on a given source GPU to a target one based on roofline models of GPUs with kernel-specific ceilings;
- We implement the methodology for NVIDIA GPUs. Our implementation combines a comparison of the assembly-code of both GPUs with a performance projection on both roofline models;
- We validate our methodology by projecting multiple mini-applications (Hydro1d, UVMBench, Quicksilver, LULESH, miniMDock) running on V100 GPUs to several modern NVIDIA GPUs like A100 and H100. In this evaluation, our methodology achieves a mean absolute percentage of error (MAPE) comprise between 10.3 % and 17.0 %.

The remainder of this paper is organized as follows. In Sect. 2, we describe how to modify a roofline model to take into account the characteristics of a kernel. In Sect. 3 we describe how we predict the performance of a kernel that would run on a target GPU. We present the implementation details of our methodology in Sect. 4. Section 5 presents the experimental evaluation of our implementation. We discuss related work in Sect. 6. Finally, we conclude the paper in Sect. 7.

2 Roofline Model of a GPU with Kernel-Specific Ceilings

As introduced in [21], the roofline model of a machine gives its upper bound in terms of performance and memory bandwidth. These bounds can be estimated based on the hardware characteristics($Perf^{Peak}$ and BW^{Peak}), or by measurement with benchmark applications such as HPL [17] and STREAM [14] ($Perf^{Max}$ and BW^{Max}). Depending on an application operational intensity (OI) and its performance, the roofline model indicates the optimization level of the application and its limiting hardware component. Several works have extended the roofline model for GPUs [6,12,22–24]. In particular, the NVIDIA Nsight Compute (ncu) profiler [16] defines a hierarchical roofline which relies on the OI of all GPU's cache levels (e.g. BW_{L1}^{Max}, BW_{L2}^{Max}, BW_{DRAM}^{Max}).

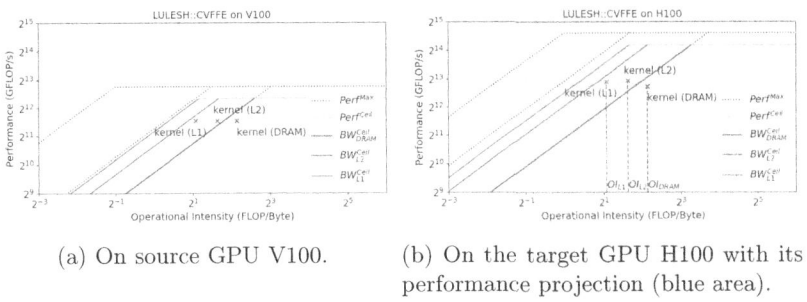

(a) On source GPU V100.　　(b) On the target GPU H100 with its performance projection (blue area).

Fig. 2. Roofline models with ceilings for the LULESH CVFFE kernel.

The roofline model describes the maximum attainable performance on a given machine for a given operational intensity, as depicted by Eq. 1.

$$roofline(OI) = min(BW^{max} \times OI, Perf^{max}) \quad (1)$$

However, this upper bound to performance could only be reached with a perfect compute efficiency and memory efficiency, which is unrealistic. To better understand how a given kernel performs, we refine the roofline model by adding ceilings of the compute and memory capacities. These ceilings are noted $Perf^{Ceil}$, BW_{L1}^{Ceil}, BW_{L2}^{Ceil}, and BW_{DRAM}^{Ceil} in Fig. 2.

Compute Efficiency. Roofline models usually model GPU maximum performance $Perf^{max}$ by relying only on Fused Multiply-Add (FMA) instructions performance. Nevertheless, the compute efficiency of a kernel is dependent on its floating-point operation mix [8,22]. Indeed, kernels use other floating-point instructions such as ADD, or MUL. In Eq. 2, we enhance the roofline $Perf^{max}$ term of Eq. 1 by averaging the maximum performance of both FMA and ADD+MUL operations as summed in Eq. 2:

$$Perf^{mix}(k) = Perf^{max}_{FMA} \times \frac{N_{FMA}}{N_{FMA} + N_{ADD} + N_{MUL}} \\ + Perf^{max}_{ADD\_MUL} \times \frac{N_{ADD} + N_{MUL}}{N_{FMA} + N_{ADD} + N_{MUL}} \qquad (2)$$

where N_{FMA} (respectively ADD, MUL) corresponds to the number of FMA instructions in the studied kernel k, and $Perf_{FMA}$ (resp. ADD_MUL) is the maximum performance of only FMA instructions.

To go further, we also take into account the GPU warp usage, which is the mean number of active threads per warp instruction divided by the size of a warp, which gives the performance ceiling of $Perf^{ceil}(k)$ the kernel k as described in Eq. 3, and represented with a yellow horizontal line in Fig. 2a.

$$Perf^{ceil}(k) = \frac{active\_thr\_per\_instr}{warp\_size} \times Perf^{mix}(k) \qquad (3)$$

Memory Performance. A kernel performance may also be limited by its memory performance. A kernel accesses data located in various place of the memory hierarchy, as illustrated in Fig. 3, where the DRAM is the main memory of the GPU, L2 a coherent cache level shared by all streaming multiprocessors (SM), L1 a cache private to each SM, and the shared memory (Sh.M), which is a fast memory shared by all the threads of a CUDA block.

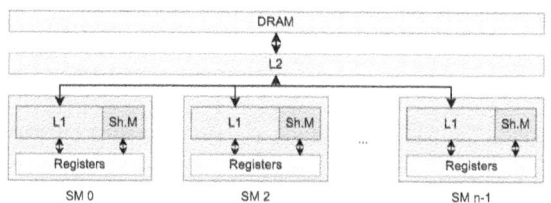

Fig. 3. Memory hierarchy of a GPU.

We assume that the time for getting data from a memory location depends on the memory location bandwidth, as described in Eq. 4.

$$t_{mem}(k) = \frac{N_{mem}(k)}{BW^{max}_{mem}} \qquad (4)$$

where N_{mem} is the number of bytes accessed by the kernel that hits the memory level mem, and BW^{max}_{mem} its maximum bandwidth as used in the roofline model.

Furthermore, we model the shared memory differently, as it is physically located in the L1 cache in our studied GPUs which is divided in memory banks.

The time for getting data from the shared memory (t_{ShM}) depends on the bank conflicts and the number of clock cycles needed to handle the memory requests. To be optimal, the number of accessed bytes per clock cycle (N_{ShM_pc}) should be 128 ($N_{ShM\_pc}^{max}$), due to the 32 banks, each with a bandwidth of 4 bytes per clock cycle [15], hence our definition of t_{ShM} in Eq. (5).

$$t_{ShM}(k) = \frac{N_{ShM}(k)}{N_{ShM\_pc}(k)} \times \frac{N_{ShM\_pc}^{max}}{BW_{ShM}^{max}} \qquad (5)$$

Then we update the roofline model with bandwidth ceilings for L1, L2, and DRAM (BW_{L1}^{ceil}, BW_{L2}^{ceil} and BW_{DRAM}^{ceil} in Fig. 2a). For each memory location, the bandwidth ceiling takes into account all the data access that traverse the memory location, e.g., L2 bandwidth ceiling is the bandwidth for the data coming from both the L2 cache, and the DRAM. Overall these bandwidth ceilings are computed as a weighted harmonic mean of bandwidths, as described by Eqs. 6, 7, and 8.

$$BW_{L1}^{Ceil}(k) = \frac{N_{L1}(k) + N_{ShM}(k) + N_{L2}(k) + N_{DRAM}(k)}{t_{L1}(k) + t_{ShM}(k) + t_{L2}(k) + t_{DRAM}(k)} \qquad (6)$$

$$BW_{L2}^{Ceil}(k) = \frac{N_{L2}(k) + N_{DRAM}(k)}{t_{L2}(k) + t_{DRAM}(k)} \qquad (7)$$

$$BW_{DRAM}^{Ceil}(k) = \frac{N_{DRAM}(k)}{t_{DRAM}(k)} \qquad (8)$$

where $N_{mem}(k)$ is the number of memory access to the memory location mem performed by kernel k.

3 Projecting the Roofline Model with Ceilings to a Target GPU

In order to predict the performance of a kernel on a target GPU, we first build its roofline model with ceilings on both source and target GPU following the method described in Sect. 4.2, as illustrated in Fig. 2.

Then, we measure the performance of the kernel itself $Perf_s^{Meas}(k)$ on the source GPU, as well as its three OIs ($OI_{L1}(k)$, $OI_{L2}(k)$, and $OI_{DRAM}(k)$), before projecting it on the target GPU using formula (9) which is presented by C. Gavoille et al. in [8] and Kwack et al. in [13].

The idea is to consider for each OI the ratio between the measured performance of the kernel $Perf_s^{Meas}(k)$ and the corresponding roofline $roofline_{s_{mem}}(OI_{s_{mem}}, k)$ on the source GPU, and to project this ratio by using the corresponding roofline and the OI of the target GPU $roofline_{t_{mem}}(OI_{t_{mem}}, k)$.

$$Perf_t(mem, k) = \frac{Perf_s(k)}{roofline_{s_{mem}}(OI_{s_{mem}}, k)} \times roofline_{t_{mem}}(OI_{t_{mem}}, k) \qquad (9)$$

Thus, we obtain three performance values $Perf_t(L1, k)$, $Perf_t(L2, k)$, and $Perf_t(DRAM, k)$ which give an interval of performance to expect, as illustrated by the blue area in Fig. 2b. Finally, we compute the kernel execution time by dividing $FLOP$ by the performance interval.

4 Implementation

We implemented our performance projection methodology for NVidia GPUs. This Section details the metrics that are collected when characterizing a kernel and a GPU. We also describe how we analyze the assembly instructions of a kernel in order to estimate its OIs.

4.1 Collecting Metrics

Our performance projection methodology requires to gather capabilities of both target and source GPUs. Reminding that the target GPU is unavailable, the theoretical peak $Perf_t^{Peak}$ and BW_t^{Peak} performance can be retrieved from the target GPU specification. The measured $Perf_t^{Max}$ and BW_t^{Max} performance are either obtained thanks to publicly available benchmarks results, or estimated if the $Peak/Max$ ratio is assumed to be similar for the source GPU and the target GPU. Source GPU capabilities are actually measured. We collect the maximum performance $Perf_s^{Max}$ using the High Performance Linpack (HPL) [17] benchmark, and the peak bandwidth BW_s^{Max} using the STREAM bandwidth [14] for each memory level. Application-specific performance data are also retrieved for each kernel during a profiling execution. We run the application with the ncu profiler and collect several metrics for each kernel, such as the execution time, the number of bytes accessed at each memory level, and the number of FLOPs.

4.2 Estimating the Target Operational Intensity

As depicted in Fig. 2a, we first characterize the actual kernel performance on the source GPU obtained by a profiling run. During this run, the amount of data accessed through the L1, L2, and DRAM are also gathered and we compute three operational intensities of the kernel on the source GPU. Following Eq. (10), the OI for a memory level is defined as the number of FLOPs per byte written or read at this cache level, with N_{mem}^+ the number of bytes traversing the memory level mem.

$$OI_{mem}(k) = \frac{FLOP(k)}{N_{mem}^+(k)} \qquad (10)$$

Now, in order to accurately project the kernel performance on a target GPU, it is necessary to estimate the kernel memory usage, and its OIs on the target GPU. While the memory usage is considered as roughly similar from one GPU to another in our current implementation, our model takes in consideration the fact that an OI may differ because both GPUs may provide different instruction sets. We estimate the target OI by analyzing the kernel assembly instructions (SASS) of the target machine binary, and comparing it with SASS instructions traces we profiled on the source GPU. In fact, since the intermediate PTX language of a kernel is the same for all GPUs, we only need to compare instructions that implement special functions, e.g. divisions or logarithms, which will be translated into multiples different floating operations depending on the GPU [1,24] and that the other instructions are executed the same way for both machines. Thus, we compare the basic blocks of the control-flow graph for both GPUs that contain such special functions: for these blocks, the SASS traces of the source GPU give the number of active threads, and we assume that the same number of threads are active in the equivalent blocks in the SASS instructions of the target GPU.

5 Experiments

In this Section, we evaluate our performance projection methodology. For this purpose, we run 5 mini-applications, i.e. Hydro1D, UVMBench, Quicksilver, LULESH, and MiniMDock on an NVidia V100 GPU, and we project their performance on the modern A100 and H100 NVidia GPUs. Effective runs of the latter allow us to compare and validate our projection with actual performance as depicted in Figs. 4, 5, 6, 7, 8 and 9. In these Figures, the leftmost blue bar is the average execution time per kernel when running on the V100, the black segment is the predicted performance interval on the target GPU, and the other colored bars are the actual performance measured on the target GPUs. Additionally, the small red line is the mean point of the projection interval. To assess the precision of the prediction, we compute the mean absolute percentage error (MAPE) between the mean prediction, and the actual performance measurement.

Table 1. Characteristics of used machines.

GPU	V100	A100-40	A100-80	H100
Compute Capability	7.0	8.0	8.0	9.0
$Perf^{Max}$ (GFLOP/s)	6890	9476	9476	24979
BW_{DRAM}^{Max} (GB/s)	846	1375	1678	1907
BW_{L2}^{Max} (GB/s)	2460	4710	4710	7758
BW_{L1}^{Max} (GB/s)	13963	19492	19492	25330
$nvcc$ version	V12.0.140	V11.6.55	V12.0.140	V12.0.140
CUDA driver version	530.30.02	510.85.02	530.30.02	530.30.02
OS	RHEL 8.8	RHEL 8.8	RHEL 8.8	RHEL 8.8
CPU	2 × 16c Xeon Gold 6226R @ 2.9 GHz	2×64c AMD Rome@2.6 GHz	2 × 16c Xeon Gold 6226R @ 2.9 GHz	2 × 64c Epyc Milan @ 2.8 GHz
CPU RAM	512 GiB	256 GiB	512 GiB	512 GiB

5.1 GPU Test-Bed Description

Table 1 summarizes up the characteristics of the different NVidia GPUs used for our experiments.

5.2 Hydro1D

Hydro1D is a mini-application that solves a hydrodynamic problem. It is mainly a loop composed of 9 consecutive kernels. Each kernel computes a single cell per thread, and there is no reuse of data, such as the DRAM bandwidth is the main limiting factor. We run this application with 50,000,000 cells on the V100 GPU. Figure 4 shows our projection results of the different inner kernels. For all kernels, the prediction intervals are narrow, and predictions are accurate: the percentage error ranges from −5.83% to 4.45%.

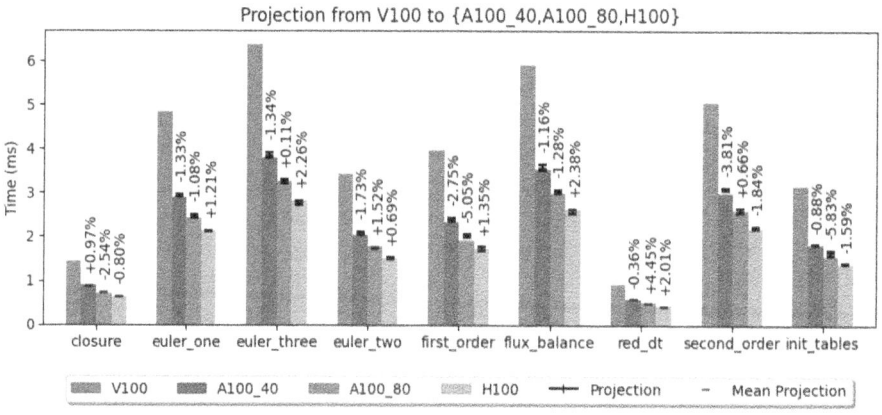

Fig. 4. Performance projection of Hydro1d kernels.

We may specify that we used the Stream Init bench, instead of the Stream Triad one, in order to measure the bandwidth to use for the *init_tables* kernel as it only writes data, which means a higher bandwidth on the GPU. However, this initialization kernel remains not really relevant in the whole projection performance of Hydro1D.

5.3 UVMBench

UVMBench [9] is a test suite composed of diverse mini-apps, which all have different memory patterns accesses, so that they challenge our memory bandwidth weightings. For this paper, we focus on the polybench 1.0 and KNN mini-apps with parameter configuration listed in Table 2.

Table 2. UVMBench Parameters.

Benchmark	Parameters	Benchmark	Parameters
KNN	$nb = 16384$	COVAR	$N = 8192; M = 2048$
2DConv	$N_{I,J} = 4096$	FDT2D	$N_{X,Y} = 2048$
2MM	$N_{I,J,K,L} = 2048$	GEMM	$N_{I,J,K} = 2048$
3DConv	$N_{I,J} = 1024; N_K = 256$	MVT	$N = 32768$
3MM	$N_{I,J,K,L,M} = 4096$	SYRK	$N = M = 1024$
ATAX	$N_{X,Y} = 32768$	SR2K	$N = M = 1024$
COOR	$N = 8192; M = 2048$	GRAMMSC	$N = 32768; M = 131072$

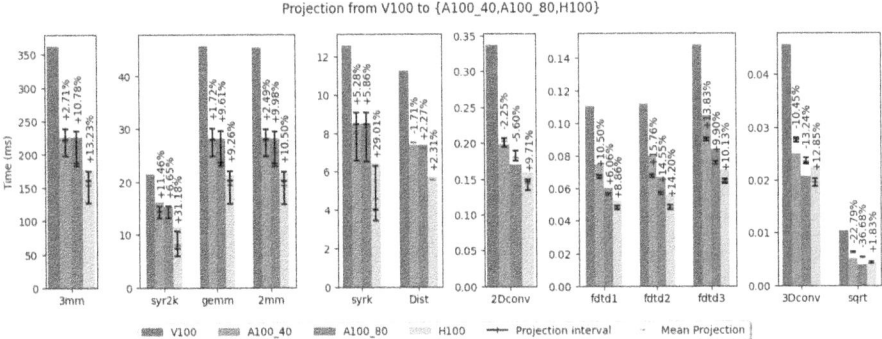

Fig. 5. Performance projection of UVMBench for intensive kernels.

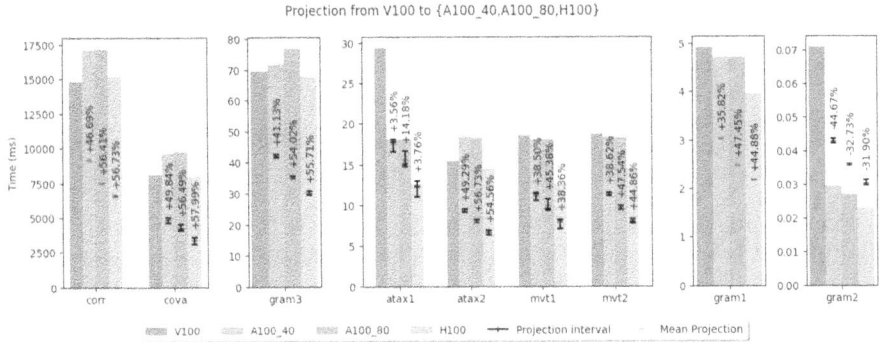

Fig. 6. Performance projection of UVMBench for kernels that under-use GPUs.

We separate the results in two parts: Fig. 5 reports the performance prediction results for standard kernels, and Fig. 6 reports the performance prediction for kernel that under-use GPUs.

The results for standard kernels show that the performance projection interval are mostly correctly predicted. Some projection intervals are wide (e.g.

SYRK, SYR2K, GEMM), which often means that the OI for the DRAM is high, so that the projection is made by taking the maximum performance in Eq. (9), which is quite different from one GPU generation to another, see Table 1.

Figure 6 shows that when under-using GPUs, several kernels (e.g. corr, or gram3) do not benefit from running on powerful GPUs due to their lack of parallelism. Since our performance projection does not take this into account, the prediction are inaccurate.

5.4 Quicksilver

Quicksilver [18] is a proxy application that solves a Monte-Carlo particle transport problem. The GPU version is made with a unique kernel and works with unified memory, which may imply memory latency. The application is composed of loops in which batches of particles are computed in the kernel one after the other, such that at the beginning of an iteration, a maximum amount of particles are computed during a single kernel, while at the end only the remaining particles are computed. Our testing case is the "Coral2_P1_1" problem with nParticles = 1000000.

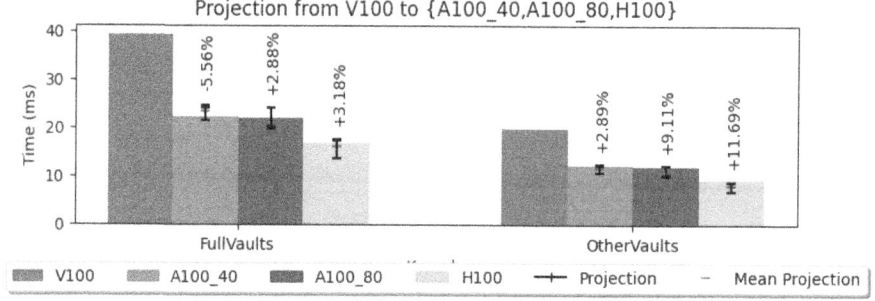

Fig. 7. Performance projection of Quicksilver.

Figure 7 presents our projection from the V100 GPU to the other GPUs on two different key moments of the kernel. The "FullVaults" case appears at the beginning of the time step when lots of particles are computed during the kernel, whereas "OtherVaults" is for the other cases. Cases with very few particles (using less than 30 blocks of threads) are excluded. It has to be noted that Quicksilver has a very low number of active threads per warp instructions: about 6 over 32, which makes it a very poor performing kernel. Despite not having taken into account this particular metric for weighting the bandwidths used for the projection, our prediction remains correct with a MAPE of 5.9 %.

5.5 LULESH

LULESH [10] is a mini-application that models 3D Lagrangian hydrodynamics. It is composed of a typical loop that iterates on a kernel that computes a time

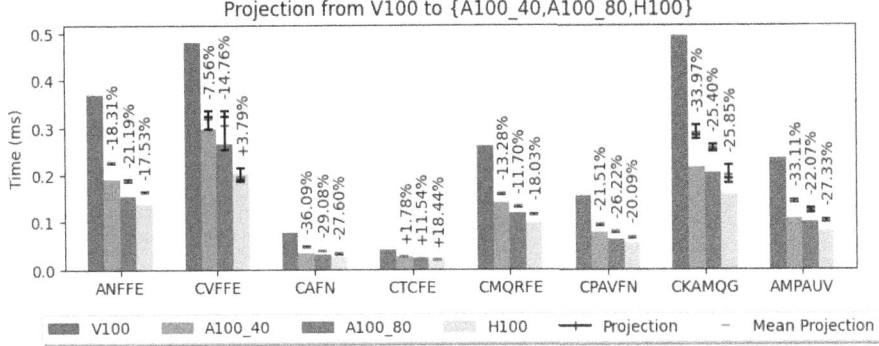

Fig. 8. Performance projection of LULESH.

step in which each thread computes a single mesh. The DRAM bandwidth is here the main restricting factor.

As depicted in Fig. 8, the projected execution time is often higher than the actual measured execution time on the target GPUs. The V100 seems to have a different behaviour than the other GPUs with these kernels, probably due to it smaller L2 cache size. Indeed, it implies a lower memory reuse for data that may be in L2 during runs on others GPU architecture. Even if we correctly calculated that the OI at level L1 is higher on V100, because of more local memory operations made in the other GPUs, the OI at DRAM level is far lower on V100 due to more memory transfers between the DRAM and the L2 cache according to the profiler. If we had taken in consideration the cache size, then the prediction would have been correct, since the DRAM bandwidth is the main restraining factor for these kernels. Overall, the MAPE is about 20.26 %.

5.6 MiniMDock

MiniMDock [19] is a molecular docking mini-application for which we use the default input 7cpa ligand and 100 LGA runs. This application makes use of the shared memory for its main kernel, but also not all threads of a warp are used during each instruction.

Figure 9 presents the projection of three kernels : two initialization kernels, CALC_INITPOP and GEN_AND_EVAL_NEWPOPS, and the computation kernel one PERFORM_LS. The measured performance on the target GPUs are in the predicted intervals, except when projecting performance to the H100 GPU.

While bandwidths are modeled assuming that all warp threads are active, the use of a performance analysis tool shows that, on average, only 26 threads over 32 per instruction are here active, which leads to inaccurate projections.

The projection error for both the A100s is virtually the same because the DRAM OI is high (above 1000 FLOP/Byte), which means that the DRAM bandwidth, which is the main difference between the two A100s, has virtually no influence in our performance model, hence the same performance projected.

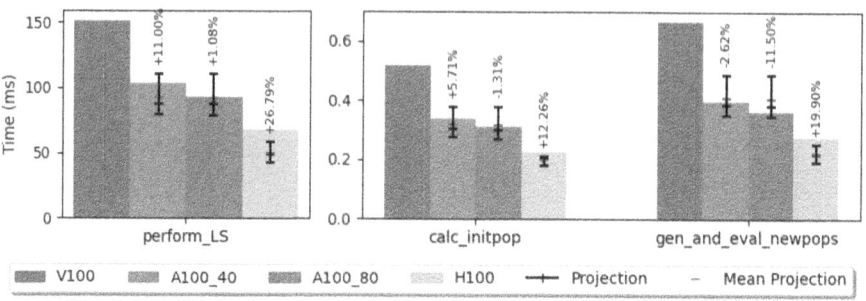

Fig. 9. Performance projection of MiniMDock.

6 Related Work

Several approaches have been used to project the performance from one architecture to another, including simulation, statistical model with machine learning and analytical model.

Simulators such as Gem5 [5] can accurately estimate the performance of an application on a target computer architecture. However, such simulation consume extensive resources and they are not viable for large applications. In this context, less accurate but faster methods such as performance projection models become interesting. For example, Domke et al. [7] propose a method to easily and quickly calculate the upper bound in performance improvements when changing cache components. As a result, modeling the behavior of a CPU only takes a few hours, instead of months with cycles-accurate simulators.

Simulators like GPGPU-SIM [3] and its extension Accel-Sim [11] reproduce the behaviour of a GPU by analyzing the instructions of a kernel obtained during a previous execution on a GPU, and on characteristics of the targeted GPU. Despite their precision, their large overhead and large size of traces needed to run such simulations make them impractical for real-life applications.

Instead of simulating the whole GPU and the kernel, which is resource consuming, one can reduce the cost of performance projection by using a performance model. Micro-benchmarks first characterize the GPU. Then, metrics are collected by analyzing the kernel, e.g. by executing it. Depending on the number of parameters to collect and to use, one can construct either machine learning (ML) models [4] to handle many parameters at a cost of a time-consuming data collection and a training for each studied GPU, or analytical models [20], which relies on simplified assumptions where kernels are classified depending on their main restraining factor. Moreover, CPU performance prediction are good work starting point. In [2], a machine learning model analyzes cross CPU-GPU applications first with only a CPU, before projecting their performance on a GPU. While in [8,13], the roofline model has been used for projecting an application performance on CPU architectures, based on its performance on a source CPU.

7 Conclusion

Throughout this paper, we present a methodology to get a performance interval of a given kernel for a target GPU by first analyzing the performance of the kernel on a source GPU. We base our performance prediction on a roofline model with multiple ceilings that are specific to the kernel. These ceilings characterize the behaviour of a kernel depending on its instruction mix, cache hits and warp efficiency. Moreover, we estimate the operational intensity of the kernel on the target GPU by comparing the assembly instructions of its executable with traces obtained on the source GPU. We then used a set of modern NVIDIA GPUs (V100, A100 40 & 80 GB, and H100) to evaluate our methodology on several mini-apps (Hydro1d, UVMBench, Quicksilver, LULESH and MiniMDock). This methodology is quite fast to run, since it only requires to profile the kernel of interest with a sample run on a source GPU to project its performance on other GPUs. The evaluation shows that we correctly project the performance from the V100 GPU to the other GPUs on our studied kernels.

In the future, we plan to extend this methodology to predict the performance of the whole application, and not only of its kernels. Moreover, modifications may be needed for predicting on AMD and Intel GPUs and also for exploring the impact of the unified memory.

Acknowledgments. We thank the University of Oregon and the OACISS team for the use of their machines.

Disclosure of Interests. The authors have no competing interests to declare that are relevant to the content of this article.

References

1. Abdelkhalik, H., Arafa, Y., Santhi, N., Badawy, A.H.: Demystifying the nvidia ampere architecture through microbenchmarking and instruction-level analysis. In: 2022 IEEE High Performance Extreme Computing Conference (HPEC), pp. 1–8 (2022)
2. Ardalani, N., Lestourgeon, C., Sankaralingam, K., Zhu, X.: Cross-architecture performance prediction (XAPP) using CPU code to predict GPU performance. In: Annual IEEE/ACM International Symposium on Microarchitecture (MICRO) (2015)
3. Bakhoda, A., Yuan, G.L., Fung, W.W.L., Wong, H., Aamodt, T.M.: Analyzing CUDA workloads using a detailed GPU simulator. In: IEEE International Symposium on Performance Analysis of Systems and Software (2009)
4. Benatia, A., Ji, W., Wang, Y., Shi, F.: Machine learning approach for the predicting performance of SpMV on GPU. In: IEEE 22nd International Conference on Parallel and Distributed Systems (ICPADS) (2016)
5. Binkert, N., et al.: The gem5 simulator. ACM SIGARCH Comput. Archit. News **39**, 1–7 (2011)
6. Ding, N., Awan, M., Williams, S.: Instruction roofline: an insightful visual performance model for GPUs. Concurrency Comput. Pract. Experience **34**, e6591 (2022)

7. Domke, J., et al.: At the locus of performance: quantifying the effects of copious 3D-stacked cache on HPC workloads. ACM Trans. Archit. Code Optim. **20**(4), 1–26 (2023)
8. Gavoille, C., Taboada, H., Carribault, P., Dupros, F., Goglin, B., Jeannot, E.: Relative Performance Projection on Arm Architectures. In: Cano, J., Trinder, P. (eds.) Euro-Par 2022: Parallel Processing. Lecture Notes in Computer Science, vol. 13440. Springer, Cham (2022). https://doi.org/10.1007/978-3-031-12597-3_6
9. Gu, Y., Wu, W., Li, Y., Chen, L.: UVMBench: a comprehensive benchmark suite for researching unified virtual memory in GPUs. arXiv:2007.09822 (2020) (2020)
10. Karlin, I., Keasler, J., Neely, R.: Lulesh 2.0 updates and changes. Tech. rep. (2013)
11. Khairy, M., Shen, Z., Aamodt, T.M., Rogers, T.G.: Accel-Sim: an extensible simulation framework for validated GPU modeling. In: ACM/IEEE 47th Annual International Symposium on Computer Architecture (ISCA) (2020)
12. Konstantinidis, E., Cotronis, Y.: A quantitative roofline model for GPU kernel performance estimation using micro-benchmarks and hardware metric profiling. J. Parallel Distrib. Comput. **107**, 37–56 (2017)
13. Kwack, J., Arnold, G., Mendes, C., Bauer, G.H.: Roofline analysis with cray performance analysis tools (CrayPat) and roofline-based performance projections for a future architecture. Concurrency Comput. Pract. Experience **31**, e4963 (2019)
14. McCalpin, J.D.: Memory bandwidth and machine balance in current high performance computers. IEEE Comput. Soc. Tech. Committee Comput. Archit. (TCCA) Newsl. **2**(19–25) (1995)
15. NVIDIA: CUDA C++ Programming Guide (2020). https://docs.nvidia.com/cuda/cuda-c-programming-guide/index.html
16. NVIDIA: Nvidia Nsight Compute. https://docs.nvidia.com/nsight-compute/NsightCompute/index.html
17. Petitet, A., et al.: HPL - a portable implementation of the high-performance linpack benchmark for distributed-memory computers (2008)
18. Richards, D., Brantley, P., Dawson, S., Mckenley, S., O'Brien, M.: Quicksilver, version 00 (2016). https://www.osti.gov/biblio/1313660
19. Thavappiragasam, M., Scheinberg, A., Elwasif, W., Hernandez, O., Sedova, A.: Performance portability of molecular docking miniapp on leadership computing platforms. In: IEEE/ACM International Workshop on Performance, Portability and Productivity in HPC (P3HPC) (2020)
20. Wang, Q., Chu, X.: GPGPU performance estimation with core and memory frequency scaling. IEEE Trans. Parallel Distrib. Syst. **31**(12), 2865–2881 (2020)
21. Williams, S., Waterman, A., Patterson, D.: Roofline: an insightful visual performance model for multicore architectures. Commun. ACM **52**(4), 65–76 (2009)
22. Yang, C., Kurth, T., Williams, S.: Hierarchical roofline analysis for GPUs: accelerating performance optimization for the NERSC-9 perlmutter system. Concurrency Comput. Pract. Experience **32**, e5547 (2020)
23. Yang, C., Wang, Y., Kurth, T., Farrell, S., Williams, S.: Hierarchical roofline performance analysis for deep learning applications. In: Intelligent Computing: Proceedings of the 2021 Computing Conference, vol. 2, pp. 473–491 (2021)
24. Yang, C., et al.: An empirical roofline methodology for quantitatively assessing performance portability. In: IEEE/ACM International Workshop on Performance, Portability and Productivity in HPC (P3HPC) (2018)

Bringing Auto-Tuning to HIP: Analysis of Tuning Impact and Difficulty on AMD and Nvidia GPUs

Milo Lurati[1,2], Stijn Heldens[2], Alessio Sclocco[2], and Ben van Werkhoven[2,3](✉)

[1] VU Amsterdam, Amsterdam, Netherlands
[2] Netherlands eScience Center, Amsterdam, Netherlands
[3] Leiden Institute of Advanced Computer Science, Leiden, Netherlands
b.van.werkhoven@liacs.leidenuniversity.nl

Abstract. Many studies have focused on developing and improving auto-tuning algorithms for Nvidia Graphics Processing Units (GPUs), but the effectiveness and efficiency of these approaches on AMD devices have hardly been studied. This paper aims to address this gap by introducing an auto-tuner for AMD's HIP. We do so by extending Kernel Tuner, an open-source Python library for auto-tuning GPU programs. We analyze the performance impact and tuning difficulty for four highly-tunable benchmark kernels on four different GPUs: two from Nvidia and two from AMD. Our results demonstrate that auto-tuning has a significantly higher impact on performance on AMD compared to Nvidia (10x vs 2x). Additionally, we show that applications tuned for Nvidia do not perform optimally on AMD, underscoring the importance of auto-tuning specifically for AMD to achieve high performance on these GPUs.

Keywords: Auto-tuning · GPU Programming · HIP · CUDA

1 Introduction

Graphics Processing Units (GPUs) are widely used in High-Performance Computing (HPC) and artificial intelligence because of their high parallel processing power and ability to accelerate complex workloads [10,14]. Eight out of nine supercomputers funded by EuroHPC JU use GPUs as the main source of compute power[1]. GPUs excel in terms of compute performance and energy efficiency for tasks that involve large data sets and dense computation, making them increasingly vital in various scientific domains [31].

GPU programming models – such as HIP, CUDA, and OpenCL – allow developers to create highly parallel functions, called *kernels*. However, GPU programmers are confronted with a myriad of implementation choices and optimization techniques related to thread organization, memory usage, and computation

---
[1] https://eurohpc-ju.europa.eu/supercomputers/our-supercomputers_en (Accessed March 2024).

strategies to achieve optimal compute performance [11]. The optimal kernel configuration depends on the specific GPU architecture and the task at hand, and finding this configuration is a process known as performance tuning; automating this process is called auto-tuning [4].

While auto-tuning techniques have been extensively studied for Nvidia GPUs [3,9,15,17,18,21,23,30], their effectiveness on AMD GPUs has received considerably less attention. The studies that do consider AMD GPUs predominantly use OpenCL [25,26,29]. In 2016, AMD introduced HIP: an open-source GPU programming model that enables applications to run on both AMD and Nvidia GPUs through a single source code. HIP creates new opportunities for auto-tuning. For example, OpenCL on AMD was restricted to at most 256 threads per block [6,13,24,33], whereas HIP increases this limit to 1024.

After a long period of market dominance by Nvidia, the HPC landscape is rapidly diversifying with the first generation of exascale supercomputers featuring for example Intel [2] and AMD GPUs [1]. Europe's #1 supercomputer LUMI, which uses AMD's MI250X GPUs, is part of this trend. It is urgent that we understand how the lessons learned from optimizing and tuning applications predominantly on Nvidia GPUs for over a decade, can be migrated to GPUs from different vendors.

To this end, this paper introduces the first auto-tuning tool for HIP kernels and studies the performance impact of tuning HIP kernels on AMD GPUs. Since HIP applications can run on both AMD and Nvidia GPUs, we subsequently compare the impact, tuning difficulty, and performance portability of tuned HIP applications on both AMD and Nvidia GPUs.

The contributions of this work are as follows:

- We extend Kernel Tuner [29], an open-source Python tool for auto-tuning GPU applications, with support for HIP by integrating PyHIP, an open-source Python library to access the HIP runtime library and compiler [32].
- We compare performance and portability of four highly-optimized auto-tuned HIP kernels on two AMD and two Nvidia GPUs.
- We show that GPUs by Nvidia are generally easier to tune than those from AMD, both manually and using optimization algorithms, while the performance impact of tuning the same code on AMD GPUs is much larger compared to Nvidia (10x vs 2x).
- We show that kernels tuned for AMD generally perform well on Nvidia GPUs, but not the other way around.

These findings demonstrate that it is even more important to use auto-tuning for HIP applications on AMD GPUs, compared to Nvidia, and thus emphasize the need for new tools that enable auto-tuning HIP code for AMD GPUs.

2 Related Work

Auto-tuning is widely used in various contexts such as optimizing numerical libraries, compilers, and application performance [4]. Examples of applications

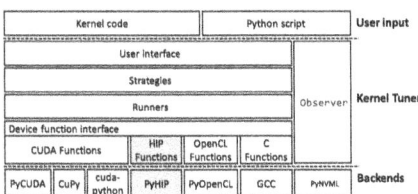
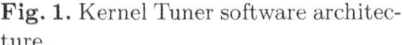
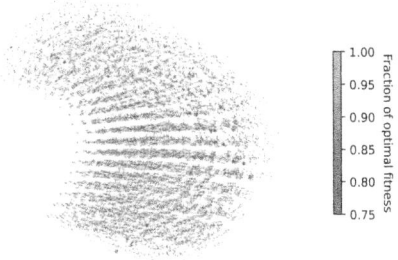

Fig. 1. Kernel Tuner software architecture.

Fig. 2. Fitness Flow Graph of 2D Convolution search space for A4000.

using auto-tuning include FFTW [8] for optimizing Fast Fourier Transforms on CPUs [28] and MAGMA for linear algebra [3]. In this paper, we focus on software-level auto-tuning, and in particular on the automatic tuning of code that targets GPUs.

There are several generic auto-tuners targeting GPU code. CLTune [20] is an auto-tuner for OpenCL. KTT [7] tunes parameters in OpenCL, CUDA, and GLSL applications focusing on pipelines of multiple kernels. ATF [23] focuses on OpenCL and CUDA kernels that have interdependent parameters.

HIP was released by AMD in March 2016 and is increasingly being adopted as a programming model for HPC applications, such as AMBER[2], NAMD[3], PeleC[4], and AMReX[5]. However, HIP is, to the best of our knowledge, not supported by any current auto-tuning framework.

In general, most auto-tuning studies have focused primarily on auto-tuning applications for Nvidia GPUs [7,9,15,17,18,21,23,27,30]. Many auto-tuning studies have included one or more AMD GPUs using OpenCL [12,13,20,24,29,33]. To the best of our knowledge, this paper is the first study to investigate and compare the impact, tuning difficulty, and performance portability on both AMD and Nvidia GPUs for auto-tuned HIP applications.

3 Design and Implementation

The layered software architecture of Kernel Tuner, extended to accommodate our contributions, is shown in Fig. 1. This revised architecture incorporates the HIP functions interface built on top of PyHIP[6].

Users of Kernel Tuner create a small Python script that describes how the GPU code can be tuned. The strategies layer implements a great variety of optimization algorithms, which in turn rely on a runner. The runners interact with

---

[2] https://ambermd.org/GPUSupport.php.
[3] http://www.ks.uiuc.edu/Research/namd/alpha/2.15_amdhip/.
[4] https://amrex-combustion.github.io/PeleC/.
[5] https://amrex-codes.github.io/amrex/docs_html/GPU.html.
[6] https://github.com/jatinx/PyHIP.

the diverse set of supported compilers and hardware through a unified device function interface, which abstracts the device-specific functionalities offered by various backends such as PyCUDA, CuPy, and PyHIP. This allows the higher-level layers (e.g. runners, optimization strategies) to operate independently of the underlying hardware and runtime.

The HIP backend in Kernel Tuner builds on PyHIP, a Python wrapper for HIP. We have made various contributions to PyHIP to increase its coverage of the HIP Runtime API and simplified the installation procedure. To integrate the new HIP backend with the rest of Kernel Tuner several changes were made. Due to the very high similarity between CUDA and HIP kernels, Kernel Tuner is not able to automatically detect the kernel language. To solve this problem, we require the user to manually specify when HIP is used.

Kernel Tuner performs empirical measurements of the execution time of each kernel configuration it compiles and benchmarks. As with CUDA, the execution time of HIP kernels is measured by recording events before and after the kernel and calling `hipEventElapsedTime` to retrieve the execution time.

Finally, to support loop-unrolling, a code optimization that aims to improve program performance by reducing loop overhead, while increasing instruction-level parallelism [11], we have extended support in Kernel Tuner to auto-tuning partial loop unrolling factors in CUDA kernels to also support HIP kernels.

4 Evaluation Metrics

We compare auto-tuning GPU codes for either vendor along three main axes: performance impact of auto-tuning, the tuning difficulty, and the performance portability of tuned kernels.

Tuning Impact. To quantify the performance impact of auto-tuning we analyze the statistical properties of the performance distribution of the full tuning search space of a kernel. More specifically, we define *tuning impact* as the factor between the performance of the *global optimum* and the *median* performance of configurations in the space. The rationale is that without auto-tuning one can expect to achieve performance that is the most common among configurations, and with auto-tuning the application can achieve optimal performance. In addition, violin plots are used to visualize the performance distributions relative to the optimum across devices, allowing for direct comparison and pattern identification.

Tuning Difficulty. For some tuning spaces, the global optimum may be a statistical outlier in terms of performance, but that does not necessarily mean that the global optimum is also difficult to find for an optimization algorithm. To assess the respective tuning difficulty on GPUs from the different vendors, we quantify how difficult it is for an optimization algorithm to arrive at a configuration of acceptable performance. For this, we use *the proportion of centrality* [24].

The proportion of centrality is computed on a fitness flow graph (FFG), which has directed edges between neighbouring points with better fitness values, as shown in Fig. 2. The idea is that a random walk on the FFG simulates the path taken by a local search algorithm. We use PageRank [5] centrality to quantify the likelihood of arriving at a local minimum. Given a proportion p, consider f_{opt} as the optimal fitness, $L(X)$ as the set of local minima of X, and $L_p(X)$ as the collection of local minima with fitness values less than $(1+p)f_{opt}$. P-proportion of centrality is defined, with c_G as the centrality function, as:

$$C_p(G, X) = \frac{\sum_{x \in L_p(X)} c_G(x)}{\sum_{x \in L(X)} c_G(x)} \quad (1)$$

Table 1. Tunable parameters for Convolution, Hotspot, and Dedispersion kernels.

Parameter	Convolution	Hotspot	Dedispersion
block_size_x	$16k$ for k in $1, 2, \ldots, 16$	$1, 2, 4, 8, 16, 32k$ for k in $1, 2, \ldots, 32$	$1, 2, 4, 8, 16, 32$
block_size_y	$1, 2, 4, 8, 16$	$1, 2, 4, 8, 16, 32$	$8k$ for k in $4, 5, \ldots, 32$
tile_size_x	$1, 2, 3, 4$	$1, 2, 3, 4, 5, 6, 7, 8, 9, 10$	$1, 2, 3, 4$
tile_size_y	$1, 2, 3, 4$	$1, 2, 3, 4, 5, 6, 7, 8, 9, 10$	$1, 2, 3, 4, 5, 6, 7, 8$
read_only	$0, 1$		
use_padding	$0, 1$		
use_shmem	$0, 1$		
temporal_tiling_factor		$1, 2, 3, 4, 5, 6, 7, 8, 9, 10$	
loop_unroll_factor_t		$1, 2, 3, 4, 5, 6, 7, 8, 9, 10$	
sh_power		$0, 1$	
tile_stride_x			$0, 1$
tile_stride_y			$0, 1$

Performance Portability. Performance portability examines how well a configuration that gives optimal performance on one device or set of devices, performs when moving to another device. We use the metric defined by Pennycook et al. [22], denoted as $\mathbf{\Psi}$, which measures the performance portability across a set of devices H for configuration x of kernel p as:

$$\mathbf{\Psi}(x, p, H) = \frac{|H|}{\sum_{i \in H} \frac{1}{e_i(x,p)}} \quad (2) \qquad e_i(x, p) = \frac{P_i(x, p)}{\max_{x \in X} P_i(x, p)} \quad (3)$$

Here, $e_i(x, p)$ represents the *performance efficiency* of configuration x for kernel p on device i as the ratio of the achieved performance $P_i(x, p)$ to the highest observed performance across all configurations called X.

5 Experimental Setup

In this section, we introduce the benchmark applications and the hardware and software used to compare auto-tuning HIP code on AMD and Nvidia GPUs.

Benchmark Kernels. For the evaluation, we use four benchmark kernels taken from the CLBlast library [19] (namely GEMM) and the BAT benchmark suite [27] (namely Convolution, Hotspot, and Dedispersion). The problems implemented by these kernels and an explanation of their tunable parameters can

Table 2. GPUs used in our experiments. *Only one out of two dies of MI250X is used.

GPU	Year	Architecture	Cores	Memory	Cache	Bandwidth (GB/s)	Peak SP (GFLOPS/s)
AMD W6600	2021	RDNA 2	1792	16 GB GDDR6	32 MB L3	224	10404
AMD MI250X*	2021	CDNA 2	7040	64 GB HMB2e	8 MB L2	1638	28160
Nvidia A4000	2021	Ampere	6144	8 GB GDDR6	4 MB L2	448	17800
Nvidia A100	2020	Ampere	6912	40 GB HMB2	40 MB L2	1555	19500

Table 3. GEMM tunable parameters, as explained in [19].

Parameter	Values
MWG	16, 32, 64, 128
NWG	16, 32, 64, 128
KWG	16, 32
MDIMC	8, 16, 32
NDIMC	8, 16, 32
MDIMA	8, 16, 32
NDIMB	8, 16, 32
VWM	1, 2, 4, 8
VWN	1, 2, 4, 8
STRM	0, 1
STRN	0, 1
SA	0, 1
SB	0, 1

Table 4. Statistical properties of the benchmarks. *Tuning impact* is the maximum over the median.

		W6600	MI250X	A4000	A100
Convolution (GFLOP/s)	median	137	380	2284	4117
4,362 configurations	maximum	4370	11460	7393	13637
	impact	31.9x	30.1x	3.2x	3.3x
Hotspot (GFLOP/s)	median	94	334	92	632
10,5412 configurations	maximum	229	1781	177	1776
	impact	2.5x	5.3x	1.9x	2.8x
Dedispersion (GB/s)	median	427	667	470	1085
11,130 configurations	maximum	582	1586	532	1154
	impact	1.4x	2.4x	1.1x	1.1x
GEMM (GFLOPS/s)	median	1154	7799	4802	10748
116,928 configurations	maximum	6010	19807	10502	17145
	impact	5.2x	2.5x	2.2x	1.6x

be found in [19,27]. The tunable parameter values are listed in Table 1 and 3. For GEMM, the input matrices are 4096 × 4096. The full source code of the kernels, input problem dimensions, and analysis tools are provided in the accompanying GitHub repository[7].

Hardware and Software Description. For the evaluation, we focus on four different GPU models available in the DAS-6 cluster and the LUMI supercomputer. The GPU specifications are listed in Table 2. On DAS-6 we use Rocky-8 Linux 4.18.0, ROCM 6.0.2 with AMD clang 17.0.0, and CUDA 12.2 with GCC 9.4.0. For the MI250X, LUMI is running SUSE Linux 5.14.21, ROCM 5.2.3 with AMD clang 14.0.0. Note that the MI250X is a multi-chip module with two individually operating GPU dies and we use only a single die. All measurements have been performed with Kernel Tuner 1.0.0b6, into which our modifications have been merged. For proportion of centrality calculation and visualization, we adapted the code from Schoonhoven et al. [24].

6 Evaluation

In this section, we first present the results on the four benchmark applications by analyzing the tuning impact, tuning difficulty, and performance portability.

---
[7] https://github.com/MiloLurati/AutoTuning_AMD_vs_Nvidia_GPUs.

We also present the top five best performing configurations in each auto-tuning search space to discuss how the results obtained by the tuner can be explained by properties of the hardware.

6.1 Convolution

Figure 3 presents the performance distributions of the convolution kernel tuning space on all four GPUs showing rather bottom-heavy distributions, meaning that the optimal configurations are extreme outliers in terms of performance. This is, however, even more pronounced for the two AMD devices. It is quite clear from these results that manual performance optimization of the convolution kernel is, if not impossible, at least very unlikely to result in optimal performance.

The median and maximum of each kernel on each device are shown in Table 4, showing how important tuning is for this kernel, in absolute performance: tuning provides a ∼30x performance improvement for the AMD GPUs, and a ∼3x improvement for the Nvidia ones. A whole order of magnitude difference between the two vendors, meaning the impact of auto-tuning is high for our AMD devices.

Figure 4 shows the proportion of centrality of the convolution, for all platforms, at different levels of acceptable optima p, ranging from 0% (the global optimum) to 15%. Here we see that, while manual tuning was more difficult for the AMD GPUs, the results for this experiment are different. Instead of a vendor split, we see that finding the global optimum of the A100 is more difficult than finding the optimum of the other devices, and that by relaxing the constraints on the optimum the A4000 becomes easier to tune than the rest.

Table 5 shows the top 5 configurations for each device. A first observation is that these configurations are different for each device. However, we can observe certain patterns. All GPUs prefer small thread blocks, with at most 256 threads, but while the two AMD devices, and the A4000, prefer one-dimensional block configurations, the A100 prefers two-dimensional ones. So, even if the total number of threads is similar, the distribution of threads in the two-dimensional block is not. Another similarity between the GPUs is that all configurations use some form of tiling in the y dimension, to compensate for the lack of thread-level parallelism within thread blocks. In contrast, tiling in the x dimension is mainly used by the MI250X and the A4000, and not by the other two devices. Two more

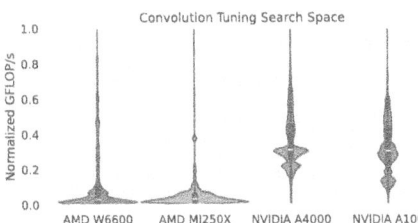

Fig. 3. 2D Convolution tuning search space.

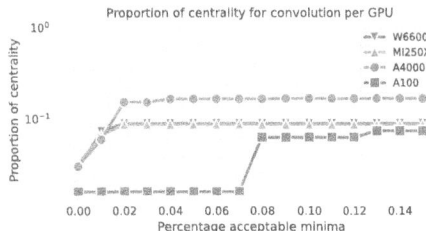

Fig. 4. 2D Convolution proportion of centrality.

Table 5. Top configurations for convolution. Parameters match Table 1. Performance in TFLOP/s.

W6600		MI250X		A4000		A100	
Parameters	Perf.	Parameters	Perf.	Parameters	Perf.	Parameters	Perf.
128 1 1 4 1 0 0	4.37	64 1 2 4 1 0 0	11.46	256 1 2 4 0 0 0	7.39	32 4 1 3 1 0 1	13.64
32 1 1 4 1 0 0	4.35	128 1 2 4 1 0 0	11.46	32 1 2 4 0 0 0	7.36	128 2 1 3 1 0 1	12.69
64 1 1 4 1 0 0	4.33	256 1 2 4 1 0 0	11.29	128 1 2 4 0 0 0	7.31	128 1 1 3 1 0 1	12.27
256 1 1 4 1 0 0	4.32	128 1 1 4 1 0 0	11.28	256 1 1 4 0 0 0	7.30	48 2 1 4 1 0 1	12.09
16 16 4 2 1 1 1	3.65	64 1 1 4 1 0 0	11.23	32 1 4 4 0 0 0	7.30	48 2 1 3 1 0 1	12.08

facts to highlight are that the A100 is the only GPU to consistently prefer using shared memory, but without padding to avoid bank conflicts, which is only used by one configuration in the top 5 on the W6600 with a 16 × 16 thread block size.

6.2 Hotspot

Next, we study the Hotspot kernel. Figure 5 shows a clear separation between consumer and server grade GPUs, with the consumer GPUs having more configurations that lead to reasonably good performance, and the server grade GPUs showing that only a few configurations achieve high performance. As shown in Table 4, the impact of auto-tuning the hotspot kernel varies from 1.9x on the A4000 to 5.3x on the MI250X.

The consumer grade GPUs are also easier to tune for optimization algorithms, as shown in Fig. 6, although in this case the tuning difficulty of the two AMD devices is not that different from each other once we relax the amount of acceptable configurations.

Table 6 shows the top 5 configurations on all four devices. Again, we see that no configuration appears twice, underlining the need to tune for each device individually. The A4000 stands out, it is has the worst performance of all four GPUs and is the only GPU that does not store the power input data in shared memory. Also, the A4000 does not use temporal tiling, and instead uses relatively

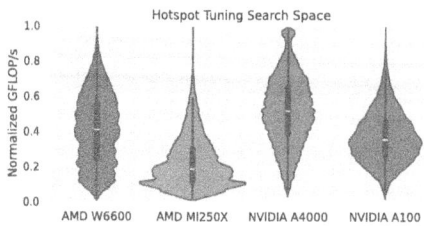

Fig. 5. Hotspot tuning search space.

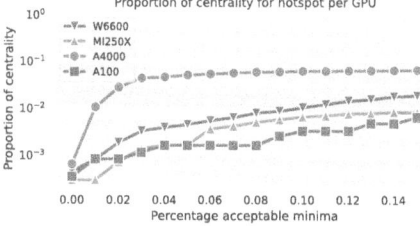

Fig. 6. Hotspot proportion of centrality.

Table 6. Top configurations for Hotspot. Parameters match Table 1. Performance in GFLOP/s.

W6600		MI250X		A4000		A100	
Parameters	Perf.	Parameters	Perf.	Parameters	Perf.	Parameters	Perf.
8 32 4 2 3 3 1	229.31	16 32 2 1 5 5 1	1781.16	64 1 8 2 1 1 0	177.93	8 32 4 1 4 4 1	1776.14
16 16 4 2 3 3 1	227.13	16 32 2 1 4 4 1	1738.68	64 2 8 2 1 1 0	177.59	4 32 4 1 9 1 1	1770.40
8 32 8 1 3 3 1	226.72	32 32 4 1 4 4 1	1723.78	32 2 8 3 1 1 0	177.40	4 32 5 2 7 1 1	1763.47
8 32 7 1 4 4 1	226.70	32 16 2 1 4 4 1	1690.77	64 2 8 3 1 1 0	177.31	8 32 4 1 4 2 1	1747.24
16 32 4 1 3 3 1	226.49	16 32 6 1 8 8 1	1685.52	32 2 4 8 1 1 0	177.29	8 32 6 1 4 4 1	1741.92

small block sizes combined with spatial tiling. All to reduce register usage and improve thread-level parallelism at the cost of data reuse in shared memory.

The other GPUs all use some degree of temporal tiling, which computes multiple calls of the kernel in a single kernel call, trading increased SM-level resource usage and even redundant work for reduced DRAM traffic. The AMD GPUs prefer to fully unroll the temporal tiling loop, where this preference is less pronounced on the A100. The MI250X uses large thread blocks, up to 1024 threads, much larger than the A100, showing that while the distributions, and even performance, of the two devices are similar, the optimal configurations are not.

6.3 Dedispersion

Now we shall look at the Dedispersion kernel. In Fig. 7, we can see a clear distinction in the distribution of the MI250X compared with the other GPUs, where the optimum is clearly an outlier in terms of performance. In particular, looking at the median values, the A100 and A4000 achieve respectively the 94% and 88% of the optimum, making these devices not difficult to tune manually.

In terms of absolute performance, shown in Table 4, we can see that the MI250X achieves the highest overall performance, and over 96% of its peak bandwidth, and while it is more difficult to tune than the others, the impact is also higher. The proportion of centrality (Fig. 8) shows that the MI250X remains difficult even if we include more configurations in the acceptable range. In contrast, the A100 achieves only 74% of its peak, but the majority of configurations come close to the optimal performance on A100.

Table 7 shows the top configurations on each device for the Dedispersion kernel. One thing that stands out is that all GPUs have a strong preference for large thread blocks, something that we could not have found using OpenCL instead of HIP for the AMD GPUs. More importantly, all GPUs prefer to do more work in the y-dimension, either per block or per thread, which is the one dimension where data reuse can be exploited. In particular, the W6600 benefits from its large L3 cache (32MB), achieving up to 582 GB/s, which is more than double of its theoretical peak memory bandwidth.

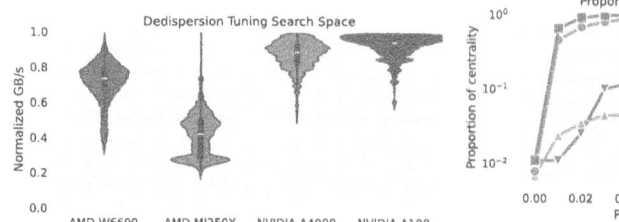
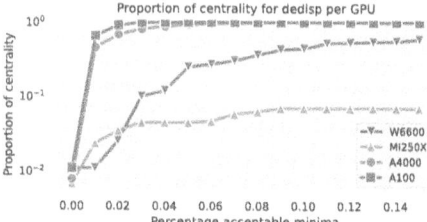

Fig. 7. Dedispersion tuning search space.

Fig. 8. Dedispersion proportion of centrality.

Table 7. Top configurations for Dedispersion. Parameters match Table 1. Performance in GB/s.

W6600		MI250X		A4000		A100	
Parameters	Perf.	Parameters	Perf.	Parameters	Perf.	Parameters	Perf.
32 32 1 1 0 0	582.19	8 32 1 1 0 0	1586.43	8 96 1 6 0 1	532.46	4 64 1 3 0 1	1154.54
2 96 1 1 0 0	575.18	8 64 1 1 0 0	1584.01	8 96 1 4 0 1	532.32	8 96 1 7 0 1	1153.83
16 64 1 1 0 0	573.26	4 64 1 1 0 0	1579.71	16 48 1 5 0 1	532.25	8 96 3 7 1 1	1153.06
2 128 1 8 0 1	568.87	16 32 1 1 0 0	1576.24	8 64 1 5 0 1	532.00	16 48 1 7 0 1	1151.78
4 112 1 1 0 0	568.40	4 32 1 1 0 0	1576.03	8 64 1 7 0 1	531.99	4 64 1 4 0 1	1151.38

6.4 GEMM (General Matrix Multiplication)

Finally, we study the GEMM kernel. In Fig. 9 we notice that the shape of the violin plots for the W6600 and the MI250X are quite similar, although the median performance of the W6600 is barely 20% of the optimum. The outlier for GEMM is the A100, for which the distribution is more top heavy with half of the configurations within 60% of the optimum. However, Table 4 shows that the speedup over the median is still 1.6x even for the A100. The GEMM kernel on the A100 achieves 88% of the theoretical peak performance of the GPU.

Looking at the proportion of centrality in Fig. 10 we see that, while the optimal configurations are outliers on all GPUs, including more configurations in the acceptable range makes tuning easier for all devices. The Nvidia GPUs do become easier to tune, compared to AMD, even after a modest increase of the optimality criterion.

Table 8 shows again that no single configuration appears in the top 5 for more than one GPU. At the same time, there is a lot of similarity between the top configurations on all four GPUs. For example, all GPUs prefer to store both matrix A and B in shared memory and use a 16 as the loop blocking value for the K loop (KWG, 3rd column in Table 8). The thread block dimensions (MDIMC & NDIMC, 4th and 5th columns) shows that AMD GPUs overall prefer larger thread blocks than the A4000 and the A100. The two server grade GPUs strongly prefer to assign 8 by 8 blocks of work to each thread ($\frac{MWG}{MDIMC}$ in x and $\frac{NWG}{NDIMC}$ in y dimension), while the top configurations for the A4000 uses 16 in either x

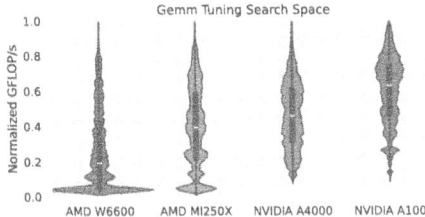
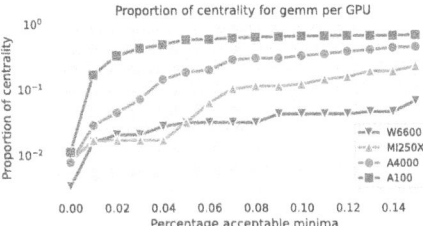

Fig. 9. GEMM tuning search space.

Fig. 10. GEMM proportion of centrality.

or y, and the W6600 uses 4 in the x or y dimension. We see here the effects of the small cache size of A4000, that prefers to rely on data reuse in registers, compared with the large L3 cache of the W6600, that instead prefers relying more heavily on the hardware managed cache.

Table 8. Top configurations for GEMM. Parameters match Table 3. Performance in GFLOPS/s.

W6600	
Parameters	Perf.
128 128 32 32 16 32 16 1 2 1 1 1 1	6010.47
128 128 32 32 16 16 16 2 2 1 1 1 1	6010.17
128 128 32 32 16 32 32 2 2 1 1 1 1	5992.99
128 128 32 32 16 16 32 2 2 1 1 1 1	5985.31
128 128 32 16 32 32 16 2 2 1 1 1 1	5982.45

MI250X	
Parameters	Perf.
128 128 16 16 16 32 32 4 2 1 1 1 1	19806.86
128 128 16 16 16 32 32 4 4 1 1 1 1	19718.46
128 128 16 16 16 32 32 4 4 1 0 1 1	19686.09
128 128 16 16 16 16 16 2 2 1 1 1 1	19651.96
128 128 16 16 16 16 16 4 2 1 1 1 1	19569.83

A4000	
Parameters	Perf.
128 128 16 16 8 8 8 4 4 1 1 1 1	10502.17
128 128 16 8 16 16 16 4 4 1 1 1 1	10489.60
128 128 16 16 8 16 16 4 4 1 1 1 1	10479.14
128 128 16 16 8 16 8 4 4 1 1 1 1	10469.28
128 128 16 8 16 16 8 4 4 1 1 1 1	10418.63

A100	
Parameters	Perf.
128 64 16 16 8 32 8 2 4 1 1 1 1	17145.04
64 128 16 8 16 16 16 4 4 1 1 1 1	17138.06
128 64 16 16 8 8 8 4 4 1 1 1 1	17135.74
128 64 16 16 8 16 8 4 4 1 1 1 1	17123.11
64 128 16 8 16 16 8 4 4 1 1 1 1	17116.28

6.5 Performance Portability

Next, we consider the performance portability of our benchmarks. Given that the performance portability score Ψ is computed over a specific set of devices H, we can consider different aspects of performance portability by using different subsets of devices for H. For instance, by identifying the configuration with the optimal Ψ score for $H = \{\text{W6600}, \text{MI250X}\}$ we can determine the most portable configuration across the two AMD devices. In this work, we consider the following seven options for H:

- Each of the four GPUs individually.
- The two AMD devices together: W6600 and MI250X.
- The two Nvidia devices together: A4000 and A100.
- All four devices together.

For each combination of subset H and kernel, we calculated the performance portability $\mathbf{P}$ across all configurations and selected the one with the highest score. Figure 11 shows the results for each of the three kernels. From these results, we can make the following observations.

For the dedispersion and GEMM kernels, we observe that a highly portable configuration exists that achieves an application efficiency of at least 85% across all devices (bottom row). However, for the convolution and the hotspot kernel, we do not find a configuration that qualifies as performance-portable, as each configuration results in a performance loss of at least 15% on one or more devices.

Another observation is that, in general, configurations performing well on Nvidia tend to not translate to good performance on AMD. This is especially evident when looking at GEMM and convolution, where configurations exists that obtain more than 80% of the performance on both Nvidia devices (sixth row), but achieve abysmal performance of less than 10% on AMD. Similar patterns can be observed for the other two kernels, albeit with less pronounced differences. Figure 13 shows the average results, revealing that the configuration most portable across Nvidia gives 93% of the performance on Nvidia and only 41% on AMD. These findings underscore the necessity of re-tuning applications previously optimized for Nvidia GPUs when porting to AMD.

However, the converse is not true, and configurations that perform well on AMD typically also perform well on Nvidia. For example, for GEMM, the configuration that exhibits the highest portability across AMD (fifth row) also delivers 97% of the performance on the A4000 and 96% on the A100. On average, when considering the most portable configurations for AMD across the four kernels, we find AMD gives 97% of the optimal performance and Nvidia achieves 81%.

Another observation is that the convolution kernel presents an especially difficult target to tune for, since configurations that perform well on each GPU individually (top four rows), perform poorly on the other devices. Especially the optimal configurations for the A100, delivers poor performance on AMD.

7 Discussion

In this section, we look at the results of all experiments presented in Sect. 6 and provide some highlights on tuning impact, difficulty, and performance portability for all applications and GPUs.

We defined the tuning impact as the performance improvement of the optimum over the median of the tuning space. There are clear differences between the impact on performance of auto-tuning on AMD and Nvidia GPUs: the average performance improvement, over all applications, for AMD is 10 times, while

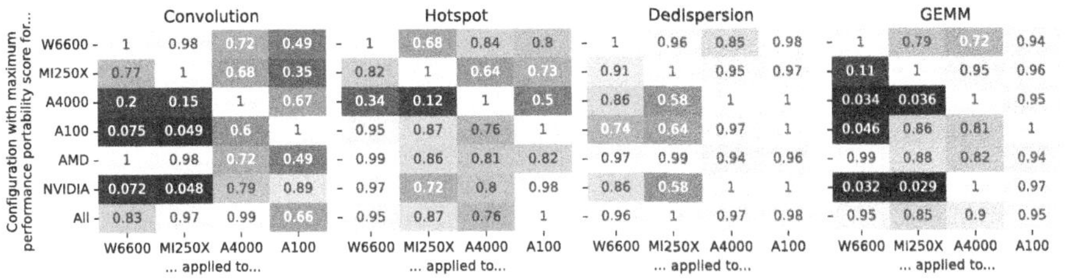

Configuration with maximum performance portability score for...
Convolution
W6600 - 1 0.98 0.72 0.49
MI250X - 0.77 1 0.68 0.35
A4000 - 0.2 0.15 1 0.67
A100 - 0.075 0.049 0.6 1
AMD - 1 0.98 0.72 0.49
NVIDIA - 0.072 0.048 0.79 0.89
All - 0.83 0.97 0.99 0.66
W6600 MI250X A4000 A100
... applied to...
Hotspot
1 0.68 0.84 0.8
0.82 1 0.64 0.73
0.34 0.12 1 0.5
0.95 0.87 0.76 1
0.99 0.86 0.81 0.82
0.97 0.72 0.8 0.98
0.95 0.87 0.76 1
W6600 MI250X A4000 A100
... applied to...
Dedispersion
1 0.96 0.85 0.98
0.91 1 0.95 0.97
0.86 0.58 1 1
0.74 0.64 0.97 1
0.97 0.99 0.94 0.96
0.86 0.58 1 1
0.96 1 0.97 0.98
W6600 MI250X A4000 A100
... applied to...
GEMM
1 0.79 0.72 0.94
0.11 1 0.95 0.96
0.034 0.036 1 0.95
0.046 0.86 0.81 1
0.99 0.88 0.82 0.94
0.032 0.029 1 0.97
0.95 0.85 0.9 0.95
W6600 MI250X A4000 A100
... applied to...

Fig. 11. Performance portability results. Each row considers a different subset H and shows the results for the configuration x with a maximum $\Phi(x, p, H)$ score as defined by Eq. 2. Values shown are the application efficiencies $e_i(x, p)$ of x as defined in Eq. 3 for the different devices.

for Nvidia it is only 2x. Our results show that auto-tuning is crucial to achieving high performance for all applications and GPUs in our experiments, but the performance impact is much larger for AMD GPUs than for Nvidia GPUs.

Auto-tuning is not only more important in terms of achieved performance on AMD compared to Nvidia, it is also more difficult. We observe that for all applications the optimum is more of an outlier for AMD than it is for Nvidia. This does not mean that tuning these applications on the A4000 or A100 is particularly easy, but rather that tuning for the W6600 or the MI250X is, on average, more difficult.

In Fig. 12, we see the averaged proportion of centrality for all the applications, showing that while the global optimum is difficult to find for both vendors, if we relax the constraint on optimality the Nvidia GPUs become easier to tune than the AMD GPUs. We can conclude that, for our benchmarks, tuning HIP kernels is overall more difficult for AMD than for Nvidia.

By using the performance portability metric, we assessed how well a kernel tuned for one specific GPU performs on the other devices. A final observation from Fig. 13 is that configurations that perform well on the A4000 often fall short on AMD devices. On average, the configuration that achieves optimal performance on the A4000, only attains an average performance of ~22% on the MI250X and ~36% on the W6600.

Average Proportion of Centrality over all Kernels
AMD
Nvidia
Proportion of centrality
10^0
10^{-1}
10^{-2}
0.00 0.02 0.04 0.06 0.08 0.10 0.12 0.14
Percentage acceptable minima

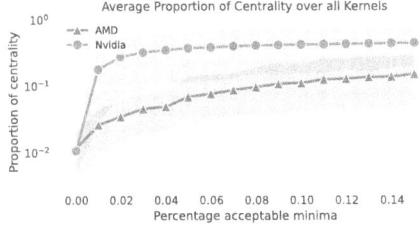

Fig. 12. Average proportion of centrality.

Average
Configuration with maximum performance portability score for...
W6600 - 1 0.85 0.78 0.8
MI250X - 0.65 1 0.8 0.75
A4000 - 0.36 0.22 1 0.78
A100 - 0.45 0.61 0.79 1
AMD - 0.99 0.93 0.82 0.8
NVIDIA - 0.48 0.34 0.9 0.96
All - 0.92 0.92 0.9 0.9
W6600 MI250X A4000 A100
... applied to...
1.0
0.8
0.6
0.4
0.2
0.0

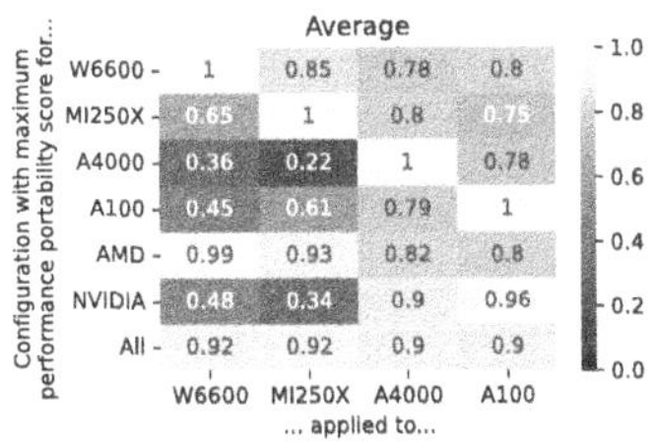

Fig. 13. Data from Fig. 11 averaged over kernels.

8 Conclusions

In this paper, we compared the auto-tuning effectiveness between AMD and Nvidia GPUs. We integrated support for HIP into Kernel Tuner, now available in the production-ready version 1.0 of the tool, enabling us to auto-tune GPU kernels on both AMD and Nvidia devices. We have compared the impact, tuning difficulty, and performance portability on AMD and Nvidia using four different kernels: 2D convolution, hotspot, dedispersion, and GEMM.

For all four kernels, we see larger differences between the global optimum and the average performance within the search spaces on AMD, compared to Nvidia. This shows that auto-tuning is crucial for achieving high performance on AMD, while manual or no optimization may still yield relatively good performance on Nvidia hardware. Overall, the impact on performance of tuning the same HIP code on AMD GPUs is much larger (10x vs 2x) compared to Nvidia GPUs.

Our evaluation also shows that it is easier for an optimization algorithm to find near-optimal implementations on Nvidia, compared to AMD. Generally, AMD-tuned kernels perform well on Nvidia, but the reverse is not consistently true. Thus, while HIP enables *code* portability, it does not guarantee *performance* portability. Given that many current GPU applications are written in CUDA and optimized for Nvidia, re-tuning is crucial when migrating to HIP for AMD execution. Fortunately, the extensions to Kernel Tuner presented in this paper make it possible to tune GPU kernels using HIP on AMD.

This study opens up several avenues for future research. Future work could include a broader array of computational kernels and a broader range of devices from both vendors to fully assess the generalizability of the findings. Also, the disparity in performance portability between Nvidia and AMD GPUs when using HIP suggests a need for deeper investigation into the underlying reasons for these differences. This could involve analyzing the architectural differences between the GPUs of both vendors and how they interact with the HIP programming language. Finally, our extensions to Kernel Tuner bring us one step closer to investigating the effectiveness of auto-tuning for optimizing the energy efficiency of applications on AMD GPUs.

Acknowledgment and Artifact Availability. The CORTEX project has received funding from the Dutch Research Council (NWO) in the framework of the NWA-ORC Call (file number NWA.1160.18.316). Funded by the European Union. The ESiWACE3 project has received funding from the European High Performance Computing Joint Undertaking (JU) under grant agreement No 101093054. The code is available in the repository [16].

References

1. Frontier: OLCF's Exascale Future (2018). https://www.olcf.ornl.gov/2018/02/13/frontier-olcfs-exascale-future/
2. U.S. Department of Energy and Intel to deliver first exascale supercomputer, Argonne National Laboratory (2019). https://www.anl.gov/article/us-department-of-energy-and-intel-to-deliver-first-exascale-supercomputer
3. Agullo, E., Demmel, J., et al.: Numerical linear algebra on emerging architectures: the PLASMA and MAGMA projects. In: Journal of Physics: Conference Series. IOP Publishing (2009)
4. Balaprakash, P., Dongarra, J., et al.: Autotuning in high-performance computing applications. In: IEEE, Proceedings (2018)
5. Brin, S., Page, L.: The anatomy of a large-scale hypertextual web search engine. Comput. Netw. ISDN Syst. **30**(1–7), 107–117 (1998)
6. Dolbeau, R., Bodin, F., et al.: One OpenCL to rule them all? In: 6th International Workshop on Multi-/Many-core Computing Systems (MuCoCoS). IEEE (2013)
7. Filipovič, J., Petrovič, F., et al.: Autotuning of OpenCL kernels with global optimizations. In: Autotuning and Adaptivity Approaches for Energy Efficient HPC Systems (2017)
8. Frigo, M., Johnson, S.G.: FFTW: an adaptive software architecture for the FFT. In: International Conference on Acoustics, Speech and Signal Processing (1998)
9. Grauer-Gray, S., Xu, L., et al.: Auto-tuning a high-level language targeted to GPU codes. In: Innovative Parallel Computing. IEEE (2012)
10. Heldens, S., Hijma, P., et al.: The landscape of exascale research: a data-driven literature analysis. ACM Comput. Surv. **53**(2), 1–43 (2020)
11. Hijma, P., Heldens, S., et al.: Optimization techniques for GPU programming. ACM Comput. Surv. **55**(11), 1–81 (2023)
12. Hou, K., Feng, W., et al.: Auto-tuning strategies for parallelizing sparse matrix-vector (SPMV) multiplication on multi-and many-core processors. In: International Parallel and Distributed Processing Symposium Workshops. IEEE (2017)
13. Komatsu, K., Sato, K., et al.: Evaluating performance and portability of OpenCL programs. In: 5th International Workshop on Automatic Performance Tuning (2010)
14. LeCun, Y., et al.: Deep learning. Nature **521**, 436–444 (2015)
15. Li, Y., Dongarra, J., Tomov, S.: A note on auto-tuning GEMM for GPUs. In: Allen, G., Nabrzyski, J., Seidel, E., van Albada, G.D., Dongarra, J., Sloot, P.M.A. (eds.) ICCS 2009. LNCS, vol. 5544, pp. 884–892. Springer, Heidelberg (2009). https://doi.org/10.1007/978-3-642-01970-8_89
16. Lurati, M., Heldens, S., Sclocco, A., van Werkhoven, B.: Artifact of the paper: Bringing auto-tuning to HIP: analysis of tuning impact and difficulty on AMD and Nvidia GPUs (2024). https://doi.org/10.5281/zenodo.11617999
17. Magni, A., Grewe, D., et al.: Input-aware auto-tuning for directive-based GPU programming. In: Proceedings of the 6th Workshop on General Purpose Processor Using Graphics Processing Units (2013)
18. Nath, R., Tomov, S., et al.: An improved magma GEMM for fermi graphics processing units. Int. J. High Perform. Comput. Appl. **24**(4), 511–515 (2010)
19. Nugteren, C.: CLBlast: A tuned OpenCL BLAS library. In: International Workshop on OpenCL (2018)
20. Nugteren, C., Codreanu, V.: CLTune: a generic auto-tuner for OpenCL kernels. In: 9th International Symposium on Embedded Multicore/Many-core Systems-on-Chip (2015)

21. Nukada, A., Matsuoka, S.: Auto-tuning 3-D FFT library for CUDA GPUs. In: Conference on High Performance Computing Networking, Storage and Analysis (2009)
22. Pennycook, S.J., Sewall, J.D., et al.: A metric for performance portability (2016)
23. Rasch, A., Schulze, R., et al.: Efficient auto-tuning of parallel programs with interdependent tuning parameters via auto-tuning framework (ATF). ACM Trans. Archit. Code. Optim. (TACO) **18**(1), 1–26 (2021)
24. Schoonhoven, R., van Werkhoven, B., et al.: Benchmarking optimization algorithms for auto-tuning GPU kernels. IEEE Trans. Evol. Comput. **27**(3), 550–564 (2022)
25. Sclocco, A., Bal, H.E., et al.: Auto-tuning dedispersion for many-core accelerators. In: IEEE 28th International Parallel and Distributed Processing Symposium (2014)
26. Sclocco, A., Heldens, S., et al.: AMBER: a real-time pipeline for the detection of single pulse astronomical transients. SoftwareX (2020)
27. Tørring, J.O., van Werkhoven, B., et al.: Towards a benchmarking suite for kernel tuners. In: International Parallel and Distributed Processing Symposium Workshops (IPDPSW). IEEE (2023)
28. Vuduc, R., Demmel, J.W.: Code generators for automatic tuning of numerical kernels: experiences with FFTW position paper. In: Taha, W. (ed.) SAIG 2000. LNCS, vol. 1924, pp. 190–211. Springer, Heidelberg (2000). https://doi.org/10.1007/3-540-45350-4_14
29. van Werkhoven, B.: Kernel Tuner: a search-optimizing GPU code auto-tuner. Future Gener. Comput. Syst. **90**, 347–358 (2019)
30. van Werkhoven, B., Maassen, J., et al.: Optimizing convolution operations on GPUs using adaptive tiling. Future Gener. Comput. Syst. **30**, 14–26 (2014)
31. van Werkhoven, B., Palenstijn, W.J., Sclocco, A.: Lessons learned in a decade of research software engineering GPU applications. In: ICCS (2020)
32. Xavier, J.: Python interface to HIP and hiprtc library (2022)
33. Yu, C.L., Tsao, S.L.: Efficient and portable workgroup size tuning. Trans. Parallel Distrib. Syst. **31**, 455–469 (2019)

A Mechanism to Generate Interception Based Tools for HPC Libraries

Bengisu Elis[1](✉)[iD], David Boehme[2][iD], Olga Pearce[2][iD], and Martin Schulz[1][iD]

[1] Technical University of Munich, Boltzmannstr. 3, Garching 85748, Germany
{bengisu.elis,martin.w.j.schulz}@tum.de
[2] Lawrence Livermore National Laboratory, 7000 East Ave, Livermore, CA 94550-9234, USA
{boehme3,pearce8}@llnl.gov

Abstract. Software tools are integral components of the HPC software stack and provide invaluable measurements and insights into application run time and system behaviour to end users, code developers and system administrators. However, most tools currently do not support performance analysis at the granularity of libraries, which are the most important level of abstraction for code when developing modern applications. To overcome this limitation, we present a novel infrastructure that can auto-generate tool interfaces that enable interception at library-level. This opens the door to deploying tools at the right level of abstraction and with that to many use cases previous impossible or infeasible. We demonstrate an implementation of our approach alongside several use cases that show how such library-level tooling can support application and system optimization.

Keywords: Performance tools · Tools interface · Interception tools · Automated tool generation

1 Introduction

Software tools are integral components of the HPC software stack and provide invaluable measurements and insights about application run time and system behaviour to end users, code developers and system administrators. Most tools, however, provide either full application data or can focus on individual procedures or statements; modern HPC applications, on the other hand, greatly depend on software libraries for many functionalities, such as numerical solvers and communication. Thus, adding support to gain performance and debugging insight at a library call granularity is critical to gain an understanding of the performance of modern applications.

For this purpose, library call interception is a common technique and can provide specific tuning abilities, especially for libraries that do not have built-in profiling interfaces or information access. However, interception based tools come with inherent limitations, such as hard maintenance to endure compatibility with changing library APIs, not allowing more than one user to perform simultaneous interception of library calls and prevention of building collaborative tools targeting different libraries. As a consequence, an automatic generation of tools and tool interfaces is needed to provide the ability to efficiently and quickly target a range of application libraries.

In this paper we, therefore, propose a mechanism to auto-generate both an interception infrastructure to be added to libraries as well as interception based tools. The auto-generation enables us to target arbitrary libraries only based on their interfaces as well as to follow interface changes and to apply tools to a large number of libraries within an application. Further, our approach can support multiple tools intercepting the same library calls simultaneously by providing a complimentary, library-specific interception infrastructure.

We achieve this with a software tool that is capable of parsing library header files provided by the application/library developers and then uses the information to generate a specific interception layer containing a tool interface that can support chains of interception tools and that can then be used inject the needed tool functionality(ies). We verify our design by implementing a prototype and applying it to use cases previously not (easily) feasible with state of the art tools. Moreover, we analyze the performance impact of our generated tools and tools' interface and show that our tools have low overhead.

The specific contributions of this paper are:

1. A prototype implementation of a tool generator that enables:
   - Automatic generation of API wrappers based on header files (e.g., parsing mpi.h and generating function wrappers, as shown in Sect. 2.1)
   - Specific analysis of arbitrary libraries (e.g., parameter tracking in the Hypre library demonstrated in Sect. 2.2)
   - Collaborative tools (e.g., distinguishing memory consumption of two libraries, demonstrated in Sect. 2.4).
   - Tool chaining (e.g., multiple tools intercepting calls simultaneously, shown in Sect. 2.3)
2. Overhead analysis of auto generated tools and the tools interface.

2 Gaps in Current Library Introspection Methods

State of the art library introspection methods use either a built-in information access provided by the library developers or implement interception based tools to intercept library calls from the application. These approaches have certain limitations. In this section we cover four different limitations of the state of the art and how generation of tools and tool's interface with a toolchain support, as shown in Figure 1, can help overcome these limitations.

2.1 Automatic Generation of Library Function Wrappers

Interception based tools require wrapper implementations of the target library functions, which will be linked with the library calls in the application. However, library APIs change over time with changes in function signatures, new functions, or deprecated functions. After such changes the set of tool wrappers must be updated to maintain compatibility with and full coverage of the library.

A concrete example is the Message Passing Interface (MPI), the de-facto inter-process communication standard for HPC applications. Optimization and performance analysis of communication is one of the core themes of HPC, making MPI performance tools a core component of the application development process. Moreover, the MPI standard and its implementations have been around for 30 years by now with 4 major version updates. Although MPI aims to provide backward compatibility, naturally there are some additions to the MPI API with which the tools are required to keep up. There exist several tool interfaces for MPI (PMPI, PnMPI [10], QMPI) that provide support for interception based tools. However any tool implemented for these interfaces depend on wrapper functions, which must be implemented and maintained by tool developers with each change in MPI standard API. Hence, MPI is a great example to demonstrate why auto-generation of tool wrappers is necessary. Indeed, there are several simple tools like `wrap.py` [4] that automate the generation of basic MPI function wrappers. Although these tools work well, they are MPI specific and similar wrappers can be generated by our general tool generator concept and used as MPI performance tools. With our automatic tool and interface generator structure we remove these limitations and enable automated tool extension and updates for any library.

2.2 Parameter Tracking

Currently, if a library doesn't have a tools interface that exposes metrics and runtime values of some variables used by the library functions, then it is hard to perform specific analysis for that particular library. This issue can be mitigated by using interception based tools and performing the specific analysis via the information obtained at runtime via function wrappers. An example is Hypre, a library for the solution of large, sparse linear systems of equations on parallel computers [7]. Hypre does not have a tool interface that exposes runtime data about the state of the variables, data structures or function calls in the library.

With solver libraries, data compression can help improve resource consumption and optimize performance. When making decisions about data compression for large scientific applications, it is useful to obtain information about the values used in the data domain such as the range of magnitude of values, patterns (sparsity, density etc.), common exponents, etc. To obtain information about the data domain, application developers can track input parameters passed to solver library functions to identify certain patterns or magnitude ranges and decide on eligible data compression methods. Our tool generation mechanism enables generating a tool that can track function parameters. This tool can then be used to track, record and plot a histogram of the input vectors for each call of certain library functions and identify patterns in the data domain to make decisions on how to compress data.

2.3 Tool Chaining

On modern HPC systems, different stakeholders often need to collect data simultaneously at run time. For example, system administrators may want to monitor application resource utilization, while regular users may want to collect performance data for application tuning, and library developers may want to test new implementation optimizations without changing actual library code and while collecting performance data simultaneously.

As an example, consider the various use cases for tracking `malloc` calls in the C standard library. Malloc calls have a significant impact on application performance when used in bad patterns, such as over-allocation, lots of small allocations, short-lived allocations or similar. Therefore, application developers might want to record time stamps for malloc calls. Meanwhile, system monitoring tools used by system administrators may want to be able to track memory consumption of running applications. Such simultaneous data collection from multiple users is difficult with existing library call interception methods. Our tool chaining feature helps overcome this limitation and enables multiple tools to intercept library calls at run time independent of each other.

2.4 Analysis of Different Library Calls by Collaborative Tools

Although some tools can chain interception tools, e.g., QMPI or PnMPI, these interfaces do not support collaborative operation of MPI tools with tools for other libraries, a generic approach does not exist so far. Our generated interface enables collaborative operation of any library, which allows relational performance analysis between different libraries. Users can perform such analysis by generating tools that intercept multiple libraries independently, which then can communicate with each other via shared variables. Communication can be used either to compute relational metrics at runtime or to change program logic.

For example, the users may gather information about calls to a certain library from other libraries, e.g., which libraries have the highest number of calls to certain functions in another library. A concrete example would be tracking memory allocations of libraries: to optimize memory allocation and provide portable interfaces for different processor and accelerator architectures, there are different memory management library implementations, e.g., the Umpire library at LLNL [2]. By enabling collaborations between the tools in the tool chain, we can now identify which calls to the Umpire library come from which other libraries and with that enable new optimizations.

3 Tool and Interface Architecture Design

In this section we describe the design, the requirements and the concepts of our tool interface generator and its accompanying tools.

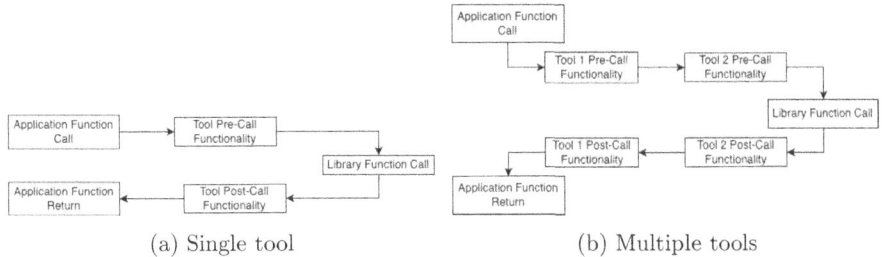

Fig. 1. Function interceptions of library call in toolchain

3.1 Generated Tools

The generated tools are a collection of function wrappers that can be applied around library calls. They are hooked into the application at run time via the toolchain also generated by our approach (see below). Additional auxiliary functions and variables help tools to communicate and register themselves with the interface. In the registration phase tools provide the interface with the information regarding which functions among the tuned library they are intercepting. Further, the tool generation mechanism generates minimal wrapper function templates to enable tool-chaining.

The actual logic of the tool itself, which can then be included into the generated code infrastructure, must be provided by the tool developer in two parts, in the form of pre-call and post-call functionality, to be executed around the call to the routine for the original functionality, i.e., the wrapped code. The execution order of the pre- and post-call functionalities of a tool are shown in Fig. 1a. The interception of a library function by multiple tools in the tool-chain with pre- and post-call logic is depicted in Fig. 1b. With the pre-call logic a developer can manipulate the function call parameters, algorithm optimizations and implementation or obtain "before call" timestamps. The post-call logic can obtain information such as return values of the library call or obtain "after call" timestamp. In addition, through changing function call parameters or return types tools can manipulate the execution of other tools in the toolchain.

3.2 Generated Tools Interface

The generated interface enables hooking and chaining of generated tools and must be compiled with or linked into the application before execution. If re-linking the application is not possible, the interface allows the use of dynamic runtime pre-loading methods, such as LDPRELOAD. The interface is designed to cause negligible overhead and linking it to application by default should not hurt the performance when there are no tools in the toolchain.

The interface receives registrations from tools and initializes necessary data and structures the tools need to ensure functionalities, such as interception, tool chaining and collaboration of the tools. The coverage of the intercepted library functions are provided by the tool developer when generating the interface. Although full coverage of all functions in a library is not required, the set of the functions intercepted by the generated interface should be a superset of the functions intercepted by any of the tools in the toolchain.

3.3 Generation Infrastructure

The core of our approach is the generator that can produce both the interface and the matching tools. It takes as input the library header to describe the calls to be intercepted, as well as the description of the tool functionality, and then automatically combines them. It works in two stages:

Stage 1: Tools Interface Generation. This stage is triggered by a single command and the resulting output is the source code of a matching interface library, which satisfies the properties in Sect. 3.2. For the interface generation, the generator expects a complete list of functions to be intercepted by the generated interface, which can be extracted from library header files.

Stage 2: Tool Generation. In the second stage the tools that can be plugged into the tool-chain are generated, in the form of individual C source code files that then can be compiled as shared libraries. For the tool generation, the generator expects the same list of library functions to be intercepted as the interface generation stage. By configuring the generated tool code, the tool developer can opt-out of the interception of certain functions. During tool registration phase the interface can discover which functions the tool intercepts.

4 Implementation

In this section we discuss our generator implementation together with the tool and tool's interface codes produced by it.

4.1 Generated Tools Interface

The generated tools interface is compiled as a shared library. Normally it is statically linked into the application. The interface uses an initialization phase to register tools added by the user and to set up necessary data structures to ensure its functionalities. The initialization phase takes place before the `main` function of the application. During the initialization phase the interface checks if the `TOOLS` environment variable is set, which contains a colon separated list of paths to the tool libraries requested by the application user. The order of the paths in the `TOOLS` variable determines order of the tools in the toolchain. By simply setting and unsetting the `TOOLS` variable, the toolchain can be plugged in and out of the execution flow without recompilation or relinking of the application. When the `TOOLS` variable is not set, the thin interface layer intercepts the function calls only with a single additional function call.

To ensure the toolchain execution, it is the interface's responsibility to provide the tools with the correct function pointers to be called in the tool's wrappers. To meet this requirement one of the data structures initialized during initialization phase are function look-up tables. Function look-up tables establish the correct order of function executions by storing function pointers to the tool wrappers in correct order. The tools call the next wrapper in line in the toolchain by requesting pointers from the function look up tables.

The interface has two sets of wrappers one is to intercept the function call from the application and to trigger the toolchain. The second set of wrappers is called at the bottom layer by the last tool in the chain, which calls the actual library function. Moreover the interface provides a function that returns the function pointer to be executed next in the toolchain.

4.2 Generated Tools Implementation

The generated tools are compiled as dynamic libraries. Each tool contains an enum array whose elements correspond to the intercepted library functions. If the tool is to intercept calls of a certain library function, the corresponding enum array element is set to the name of the wrapper function that is to intercept the library call. If the tool developer doesn't wish a certain tool to intercept a certain function then she can replace the function name in the corresponding element of the array with the string NULL. Doing so makes the tools' interface skip this particular wrapper. Apart from the interception array, tools implement a function with a declaration that is known to the interface. This function returns the information regarding library functions to be intercepted by the tool when the tool registers with the interface.

The tools must perform some basic tasks, such as requesting next function pointers to be called, declaring function pointer type, and calling the next function. A code snippet to perform these steps is shown in Listing 1.1. Any tool logic that is performed before and after these tasks are called pre- and post-call functionalities, respectively. The tool generator adds the user provided pre- and post-call functions in their respective places in the code.

```
int Tool_library_function_name (input parameters ) {

    pre_call_logic();

    // request funciton pointer
    void* f_dl=NULL;
    TABLE_QUERY(_library_function_name,&f_dl,\
        (*VECTOR_GET(v, i)).table );
    // request funciton level in the chain
    int new_level=QMPI_GET_LEVEL (i,\
        _library_function_name, v);
    //declaring function pointer type
    typedef int (*_library_function_name_func) ( input parameters );
    //call fucnitop pointer
    int ret = ((_library_function_name_func) f_dl) (input parameters );

    post_call_logic();

    return ret;
}
```

Listing 1.1. Sample tool wrapper function specification

4.3 Generator Implementation

The tool and interface generator is implemented in Python and relies on the *pyclibrary* python module to parse function prototypes. Both for tool and interface generation it requests header file paths in which the list of functions to be intercepted are declared. The interface generation should precede the tool generation as the tools are linked with the interface as well when compiling tools.

The interface generation is triggered by a cmake command and the header path can be passed by the INCLUDE_PATH variable. The user may provide multiple header paths to generate an interface supporting multiple libraries simultaneously. The tool generation is triggered by running a Python script with the same header paths as the interface generation. In order to have the generator add the pre- and post-call functionalities requested by the tool developer, the pre and post-call function calls are passed to the tool generator as parameter. The tool generator places the provided calls into all wrapper functions in their respective positions. In addition, the tool generator produces prepost.c and prepost.h files. In these files, the tool developer can declare and define the pre- and post-call functions passed to the tool generator. For all tools there is only one prepost.c and one prepost.h file. The pre- and post-call functions can be declared as inline in order to avoid additional context switch overheads due to function calls in the wrapper routines.

5 Use Case Analysis

In this section we verify that our tool and interface generation infrastructure can fill the gaps mentioned in Sect. 2. As a sample code, we use the AMG benchmark and three of its dependencies, namely Umpire, Hypre and MPI. AMG is a parallel algebraic multigrid solver benchmark for linear systems arising from problems on unstructured grids [13]. We generate the interface and tools by using the prototype implementation explained in Sect. 4 for AMG's libraries. To better illustrate how the tools in the toolchain are placed and used, Figs. 2a and 2b show the toolchain for each use case setup.

5.1 Automatic Generation of Library Function Wrappers

In this section we show how our general generator structure can produce interception based tools for MPI that are compatible with the version of the API used by the tool users. Our generation software prototype enables generation of a tools interface and matching tools that enable the interception of all MPI functions in the mpi.h header file.

For verification purposes we generated a tool that measures the total time spent for MPI operations throughout the application runtime. We verify our results by comparing them with results obtained from the existing mpiP MPI tool. MpiP is a profiling tool for MPI which collects and statistically analyzes MPI calls in the application. It relies on the PMPI interface and uses function wrappers to intercept MPI function calls. These wrappers are generated by

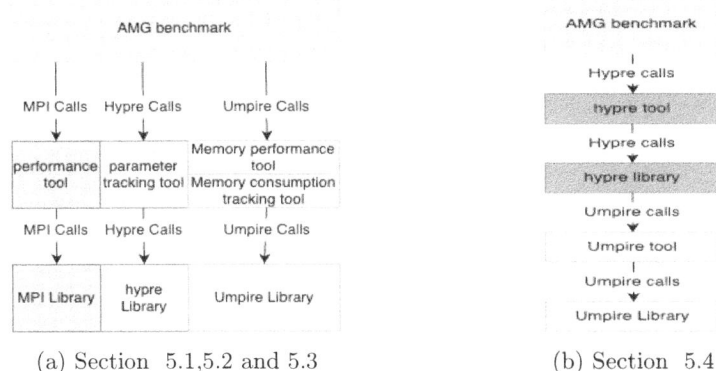

(a) Section 5.1,5.2 and 5.3 (b) Section 5.4

Fig. 2. Toolchain Representation

parsing a hard coded file which needs to be updated with every API change. [12].

Our example tool and the interface are generated by passing the mpi.h file to both the interface and tool generators. Time measurement code is added at generation and time stamps are recorded in pre- and post-call stages. Some additional minor manual modifications to the code, such as memory allocation for a variable to accumulate individual time measurements and a one line code for reporting the result, take up three lines of code in total.

We execute the AMG benchmark 20 times to measure total MPI time with the mpiP tool and with our auto generated tool. We calculate the average of each set of 20 measurements obtained from mpiP and auto-generated tools. mpiP measures average total MPI time of 1,242 sec whereas our tool measures an average of 1,157 sec. The Figure 3 shows the box plots for the set of measurements taken by the mpiP and auto generated tool.

This difference is due to mpiP having additional functionalities, such as extra statistics and file output compared to just measuring MPI time, even when the mpiP file output and call-site printing functions are disabled. It does show that our generated tools are streamlined and only expose necessary overhead.

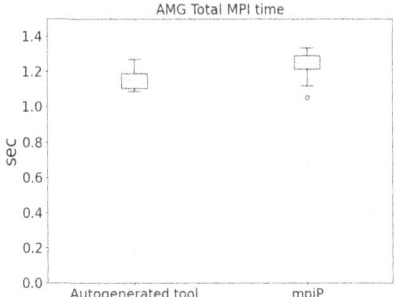

5.2 Parameter Tracking

In this section we verify how our general generator structure can produce interception based tools for the Hypre library. Our generated tool tracks the runtime values of the input parameters passed to the library functions. This information is useful when deciding which data compression methods are useful for the data

Fig. 3. MPI time measurements by mpiP and the auto-generated tool.

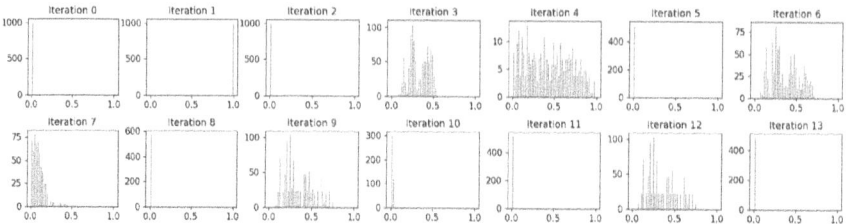

Fig. 4. Values of vector y for calculation $y = y + \alpha * p$ over AMG iterations

used by the application, e.g., by identifying data ranges, data patterns, common exponents or matrix sparsity information over iterations.

The demonstrate our functionality, we look into the example of parameters passed to the AxpY function. We record the values in the y vector at every iteration of the application and record these values in a file. We generate all wrappers in the tool without any pre- and post-call functionality and add the necessary implementation in Axpy wrappers to record input vector y in a file for each call of Axpy manually. Later, the recorded values are plotted in histograms for each iteration to see magnitude of each value in the y vector. These histograms are shown in Fig. 4. For simplicity, only the first 14 iterations shown. The histograms show that the y vector values change between 0 and 1.

5.3 Tool Chaining

Our interface enables multiple tools intercepting calls to a single library during the execution of an application. These tools may be added to the tool-chain by different users (e.g., end users vs. administrators) with interests in different aspects of runtime behavior of an application.

To demonstrate this, we add a performance tool in the tool chain and a high watermark tracker tool for tracking memory consumption of the application. Performance tools are frequently used by the regular users, whereas memory consumption tracker tools might be used by system administrators. The prototype implementation allows adding tools to the tool-chain by appending paths to the corresponding tools to the TOOLS environment variable. When executed by `mpirun -n 1 ./amg` command our memory utilization tool reports 8GB memory high watermark and the performance tools reports 0.9 sec spent in total for memory allocations in Umpire.

5.4 Collaborative Tool Functionality

This use case looks into the functionality of the generated interface to enable collaborative tools, using Hypre and Umpire. For both, hypre and Umpire, no native interfaces exist that enable tools working together to produce comparative information about performance metrics, resource utilization and function calls.

To show this functionality, we extract information regarding which Umpire calls originated in the application code itself or in the Hypre library. We keep track of the high watermark of calls for each source of calls. Similar to the previous use case, we generate the interface both for Umpire and hypre as well as a tools that intercept each library. The hypre library updates a variable that is also accessible by the Umpire tool via a function provided by the generated interface. Hence by checking the state of this variable, the Umpire tool can execute a different code path depending on whether the call comes from hypre or the application. The execution flow is illustrated in Fig. 2b.

In original AMG benchmark all Umpire function calls come from hypre. To demonstrate our structure better we added a memory allocation of 8 KB directly into AMG. When executed with the `mpirun -n 1 ./amg` command, our tool reports 8 GB for hypre and 8 KB for the application as high watermark of Umpire memory allocations by `umpire_allocator_allocate` function.

6 Overhead Analysis

For the experiments in this section we use a single Intel Icelake-based node, which has two Xeon Platinum 8360Y CPUs sockets, each with 36 cores and 2 way hyper threading. The memory attached consists of 512GB DDR4 RAM and 24 modules of 128GB NVDIMM Optane 200 series. The compiler used is gcc v11.2.0 and the MPI installation is Open MPI v4.1.2.

6.1 Generated Interface Overhead

In order to measure the overhead introduced by the interface we compile the application with and without linking the generated tools interface. As the application we use the AMG benchmark of LLNL The interface is generated for MPI and tools intercept all MPI calls. We execute each version of the benchmark 50 times and report the average of 50 executions. For the interface linked compilation of the AMG the toolchain is set to be empty and the time difference between two averages only comes from the linked in generated interface. Both compilations are executed by the following command.

```
time mpirun -np 144 --hostfile hostfile \
                --oversubscribe amg -laplace -n 100 100 100
```

The oversubscribe flag is used to be able to utilize all available cores on the system. Additionally, for this configuration of the AMG benchmark, the mpiP tool reports that MPI takes on average 3.23% of total runtime of each process. We choose AMG to represent a scenario close to real life application characteristic and we use the widely used MPI to show the interface overhead. The average number of MPI calls per rank in the AMG execution is 16364 with maximum number of 33695 calls.

Figure 5a shows the comparisons of the two executions and highlights that the interface introduces negligible overhead. This is further illustrated in Fig. 5b with

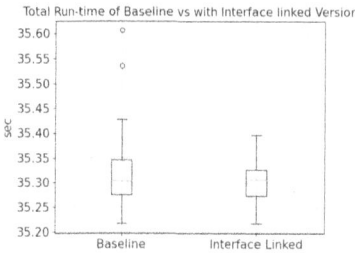
(a) Runtime comparison

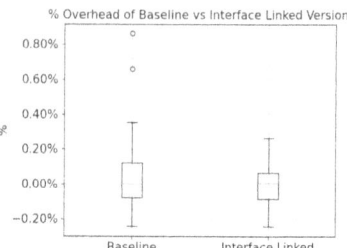
(b) Percentage overhead compared to baseline.

Fig. 5. AMG application runtime comparisons with and without generated MPI interface linking

the percentage runtime distribution of baseline and interface linked benchmark executions in comparison to baseline median. It shows that only linking the interface without any tools attached introduces at most 0.25% overhead.

6.2 Toolchain Scaling

To measure the overhead introduced by the toolchain, we generate an empty MPI interception tool with only the essential functionalities added by the tool generator in the wrappers. These functionalities are required at minimum to establish and execute the toolchain structure and tools don't include any other functionality. To demonstrate the overhead of each additional empty tool, we linearly increase the number of empty tools in the toolchain and measure the overall run time of the application for each toolchain size.

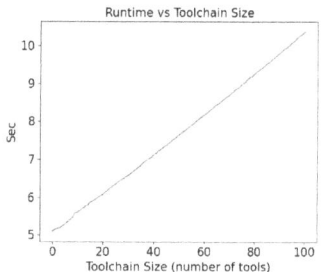

Fig. 6. Runtime overhead of scaling toolchain size

We used a point to point blocking communication ping-pong benchmark from the OSU micro benchmarks suite to showcase the scaling behavior. For each execution of the ping pong benchmark, ping pong communication is repeated for all message sizes from 1 byte to 4MB with increments of square of the previous message size and executed with 2 MPI ranks on a single node to introduce the worst case scenario with on-node contention. The toolchain size changes from 0 tools to 100 tools in the chain and for each different toolchain size the execution is repeated 20 times and their averages are plotted in Fig. 6. It shows linear scaling of the toolchain leads to linear increase in runtime and each additional tool presents 1% overhead of the total runtime which is 51 msec. The average number of MPI calls per rank in ping pong benchmark is 602006. Our results have shown that each additional tool layer presents 84nsec average overhead per

MPI function call. However, it is important to note that a ping pong benchmark is almost only made up of MPI operations. Hence, results of this experiment represent the overhead of a worst case scenario with majority of the function calls in the application being intercepted by the toolchain.

7 Related Work

There is plethora of HPC performance tools for tuning and profiling, as well as many built-in interfaces for HPC programming models and libraries, e.g., CUPTI for CUDA [1] and OMPT for OpenMP [5]. However, most HPC libraries do not have such built-in interfaces, e.g., almost all numerical libraries. Our mechanism is useful when such interfaces are not provided and function interception is used for tooling purposes.

Runtime symbol linking is a well established method to dynamically link wrappers to application at runtime. For example users can set LD_PRELOAD to a dynamic library path with wrappers to a certain library functions. However runtime linking doesn't enable toolchaining and users can intercept application calls only by a single tool. To address this issue, Gotcha can enable intercepting application function calls and tool chaining similar to our generated tools interface [9]. However, unlike our mechanism, Gotcha is platform dependent and currently only supports x86_64 and PPC64 binaries. Also, it doesn't provide an auto generation mechanism for interception tools. Tool developers have to learn and use Gotcha's provided API to produce compatible tools.

PnMPI and QMPI tool's interfaces of MPI offer toolchaining and interception based tool support for MPI applications similar to our generated interface [6]. However, these interfaces and libraries only intercept MPI calls and do not provide a mechanism to produce interception tools for MPI. The wrap library of LLNL generates such PMPI wrappers but it is MPI specific and doesn't work for other libraries [8].

TAU [11] and Score-P [3] have their own automated wrapper generators which enable intercepting arbitrary library calls. However these generators do not enable toolchainig for their generated tools.

8 Conclusion

The function call interception is a powerful method for HPC tools to gain deep insight into application runtime. State of the art methods to support these tools have limitations. In this paper we investigated a tools generation and an interface generation mechanism that enables chaining of automatically generated interception based tools for user provided set of library functions. We showed the specific limitations this mechanism addresses together with overhead analysis of our prototype implementation. Also we elaborated the design and implementation of the prototype to clarify how such a mechanism can be realized. As future work we plan to update the C header parsing mechanism to use dwarf data to support compiled languages, e.g. C++, Fortran.

Acknowledgements. Funded by the European Union. This work has received funding from the European High Performance Computing Joint Undertaking (JU) and Sweden, Finland, Germany, Greece, France, Slovenia, Spain, and Czech Republic under grant agreement No 101093261. This work was performed under the auspices of the U.S. Department of Energy by Lawrence Livermore National Laboratory under Contract DE-AC52-07NA27344 (LLNL-CONF-864058).

References

1. Overview - cupti 12.4 documentation 2024 (2024). https://docs.nvidia.com/cupti/overview/overview.html
2. Beckingsale, D., McFadden, M., Dahm, J., Pankajakshan, R., Hornung, R.: Umpire: application-focused management and coordination of complex hierarchical memory (2020). https://doi.org/10.1147/JRD.2019.2954403
3. Brendel, R., Wesarg, B., Tschüter, R., Weber, M., Ilsche, T., Oeste, S.: Generic library interception for improved performance measurement and insight. Programming and Performance Visualization Tools, pp. 21–37 (2019). https://doi.org/10.1007/978-3-030-17872-7_2
4. Chan, A., Gropp, W., Lusk, E.: User's guide for MPE extensions for MPI programs. Tech. rep., Technical Report ANL-98/xx, Argonne National Laboratory, 1998. The updated ... (1998)
5. Eichenberger, A.E., et al.: OMPT: an OpenMP tools application programming interface for performance analysis. In: Rendell, A.P., Chapman, B.M., Müller, M.S. (eds.) IWOMP 2013. LNCS, vol. 8122, pp. 171–185. Springer, Heidelberg (2013). https://doi.org/10.1007/978-3-642-40698-0_13
6. Elis, B., Yang, D., Pearce, O., Mohror, K., Schulz, M.: QMPI: a next generation MPI profiling interface for modern HPC platforms. Parallel Comput. **96**, 102635 (2020). https://doi.org/10.1016/j.parco.2020.102635
7. Falgout, R.D., Jones, J.E., Yang, U.M.: The design and implementation of hypre, a library of parallel high performance preconditioners. In: Lecture Notes in Computational Science and Engineering, pp. 267–294 (2004). https://doi.org/10.1007/3-540-31619-1_8
8. Gamblin, T.: LLNL/wrap: MPI wrapper generator, for writing PMPI tool libraries. https://github.com/LLNL/wrap
9. Poliakoff, D., LeGendre, M.: Gotcha: an function-wrapping interface for HPC tools. Program. Perform. Vis. Tools, 185–197 (2019). https://doi.org/10.1007/978-3-030-17872-7_11
10. Schulz, M., De Supinski, B.R.: PnMPI tools: a whole lot greater than the sum of their parts. In: Proceedings of the 2007 ACM/IEEE Conference on Supercomputing, pp. 1–10 (2007)
11. Shende, S., Malony, A.D., Spear, W., Schuchardt, K.: Characterizing i/o performance using the tau performance system. In: Applications, Tools and Techniques on the Road to Exascale Computing, pp. 647–655. IOS Press (2012)
12. Vetter, J., Chambreau, C.: MPIP: lightweight, scalable MPI profiling (2005)
13. Yang, U.M., et al.: BoomerAMG: a parallel algebraic multigrid solver and preconditioner. Appl. Numer. Math. **41**(1), 155–177 (2002)

OMPGPT: A Generative Pre-trained Transformer Model for OpenMP

Le Chen[1]([✉]), Arijit Bhattacharjee[1], Nesreen Ahmed[2], Niranjan Hasabnis[2], Gal Oren[3], Vy Vo[2], and Ali Jannesari[1]

[1] Iowa State University, Ames, IA, USA
lechen@iastate.edu
[2] Intel Labs, Hillsboro, USA
[3] Technion – Israel Institute of Technology, NRCN, Hiafa, Israel

Abstract. Large language models (LLMs)such as ChatGPT have significantly advanced the field of Natural Language Processing (NLP). This trend led to the development of code-based large language models such as StarCoder, WizardCoder, and CodeLlama, which are trained extensively on vast repositories of code and programming languages. While the generic abilities of these code LLMs are helpful for many programmers in tasks like code generation, the area of high-performance computing (HPC) has a narrower set of requirements that make a smaller and more domain-specific model a smarter choice. This paper presents OMPGPT, a novel domain-specific model meticulously designed to harness the inherent strengths of language models for OpenMP pragma generation. Furthermore, we leverage prompt engineering techniques from the NLP domain to create Chain-of-OMP, an innovative strategy designed to enhance OMPGPT's effectiveness. Our extensive evaluations demonstrate that OMPGPT outperforms existing large language models specialized in OpenMP tasks and maintains a notably smaller size, aligning it more closely with the typical hardware constraints of HPC environments. We consider our contribution as a pivotal bridge, connecting the advantage of language models with the specific demands of HPC tasks.

Keywords: Large Language model · OpenMP · HPC

1 Introduction

Recent advancements in transformer-based [24] large language models (LLMs) have revolutionized artificial intelligence and machine learning. These models have shown remarkable performance in natural language processing (NLP) tasks, leading to the development of code-based LLMs such as StarCoder [15], WizardCoder [18], and CodeLlama [20], which are specifically designed for programming language tasks. However, applying these models to High-Performance Computing (HPC) tasks presents unique challenges.

L. Chen, A. Bhattacharjee and A. Jannesari—Equal contribution.

- Training data diversity: Advanced LLMs like GPT3 and CodeLlama are trained on both natural language (NL) and programming languages (PL), enabling them to interpret NL prompts and generate appropriate PL code. In contrast, models like Starcoder, trained solely on code, struggle with NL prompts and are limited to code generation tasks.
- Performance consistency. Using NL as input can lead to variability in LLM outputs due to different phrasing of the same question by users, posing challenges for consistent performance and post-processing.
- Output processing. LLMs typically return answers in NL, necessitating additional effort to extract relevant information for practical use.

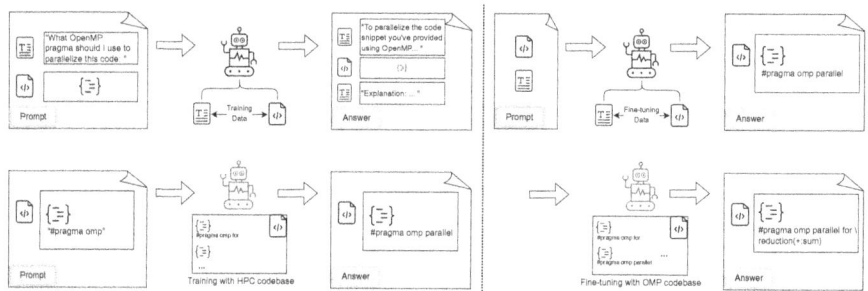

Fig. 1. 🯅 (black): Traditional LLMs require extensive NL and PL training data for generating OpenMP pragmas, leading to an increased complexity and larger model size. Users usually carefully craft prompts and interpret outputs to obtain accurate OpenMP pragmas. 🯅 (blue): **OMPGPT** is tailored for HPC code, with nearly half of its training data being OpenMP code. It aligns OpenMP pragmas with their scope during training to match GPT model instincts. OMPGPT not only addresses the limitations of current LLMs but also benefits from the **Chain-of-OMP** prompt engineering technique. (Color figure online)

To address these challenges, we propose the OMPGPT model and the chain-of-OMP prompt engineering method for automatic parallelization via OpenMP pragma generation. As illustrated in Fig. 1, OMPGPT is a domain-specific model trained on an extensive HPC dataset of C and C++ code, converting OpenMP pragma generation into a code generation problem. This approach follows the instinct of LLMs and eliminates the need for training NL data to understand the task objective. The Chain-of-OMP method enhances OMPGPT's performance by incrementally refining prompts with preconditions for OpenMP pragma generation, aligning with the structure of OpenMP pragmas. The contributions of this work are as follows:

- We introduce OMPGPT, a compact 0.76B domain-specific language model (smallest among our baseline models) tailored for OpenMP pragma generation with competitive performance to larger LLMs.

- We propose a novel OpenMP clause-based prompting technique, Chain-of-OMP, which enhances OMPGPT by providing targeted hints.
- Our comprehensive evaluation demonstrates OMPGPT's superior performance in OpenMP pragma generation compared to the state-of-the-art models MonoCoder [11] and GPT-3.5 and highlights the effectiveness of the Chain-of-OMP method in boosting OMPGPT's capabilities.

2 Background

2.1 Generative Pre-trained Transformers and Code LLMs

The emergence of Generative Pre-trained Transformers (GPT) has revolutionized Natural Language Processing (NLP) and extended its influence to programming languages, with models like GPT-3.5 capable of generating source code. GPT models are autoregressive, generating text sequentially from left to right, which enables them to produce contextually appropriate responses in natural language tasks. This led to the development of Large Language Models (LLMs) for code (Code LLMs), which are able to understand and generate programming code. Code LLMs are trained on extensive datasets containing code snippets and are designed to assist in code completion, quality improvement, and streamlining the software development process. However, challenges remain in ensuring the models can generate contextually and functionally meaningful code.

StarCoder [15] is a 15B parameter model trained for code generation or completion. The training dataset, the Stack [13], has 1 trillion tokens sourced from a large collection of permissively licensed GitHub repositories. CodeLlama [20] is a code-generating LLM based on Llama2 [22] by Meta, specialized for code by training with code-specific datasets. It has parameter sizes of 7B, 13B, and 34B, trained with 500B tokens of code data. Most code LLMs (e.g., StarCoder) have been trained on raw code data without instruction fine-tuning. However, the recent WizardCoder [18], enables Code LLMs with instruction fine-tuning by adapting the Evol-Instruct methods for coding tasks, and it was shown to improve the performance of code generation.

2.2 LLMs on Code-Related Tasks for HPC

LLM models show potential in HPC tasks by leveraging their ability to capture complex code patterns and boost efficiency. Although not specifically designed for HPC, their adaptability makes them valuable for code-related HPC challenges [23]. HPC predominantly uses C, C++, and Fortran for low-level control and parallelism optimization capabilities. Focusing on these primary languages allows smaller, more efficient models tailored to specific HPC tasks with direct inputs. Recently, research in applying LLMs to HPC has been emerging. For example, LM4HPC [4] stands as the first attempt to adapt LLMs to the HPC domain. Building upon this, a subsequent study by Ding et al. [8] introduced a Llama-based Question and Answer model specifically tailored for HPC tasks.

Despite these advancements, these early efforts predominantly rely on existing LLMs, indicating a nascent stage in developing HPC-focused language models.

One important HPC task is sequential code parallelization. OpenMP (Open Multi-Processing) [7] is the mainstream API that supports multi-platform shared-memory multiprocessing programming in C, C++, and Fortran. It enables developers to write parallel code using multiple cores on a single machine. Various works [5,6] have applied machine learning techniques to predict OpenMP pragmas for sequential code parallelization.

2.3 Prompt Engineering

Prompt engineering is a key technique in LLMs for crafting input prompts that elicit specific outputs. Chain-of-thought (CoT) [25] is a prominent method where a series of intermediate reasoning steps enhances an LLM's complex reasoning ability. Instead of a single prompt, CoT guides the model through phases of small hints, helping it grasp the deeper meaning of the query. This approach has significantly improved LLM performance in areas like arithmetic and common sense reasoning.

3 Approach

3.1 OMPGPT Design

As highlighted in Sect. 1, existing Large Language Models (LLMs) encounter significant limitations when applied to HPC tasks, particularly in the realm of OpenMP pragma generation. In designing OMPGPT, we consider several criteria to ensure its suitability and efficacy for OpenMP code generation:

1. **Training Data Relevance**: The quality of the training dataset is essential to any language model. OMPGPT is trained on HPC code in the most common programming languages in the HPC field.
2. **Model Compatibility**: The OMPGPT model size is aligned with the hardware configurations prevalent in most HPC clusters.
3. **Flexibility and Adaptability**: OMPGPT is designed to be flexible and adaptable, capable of handling a variety of OpenMP pragma generation tasks without the need to craft prompts
4. **Performance Efficiency**: OMPGPT is expected to outperform previous small language models and be competitive compared to advanced LLMs.
5. **User Accessibility**: Recognizing the varied nature of HPC ecosystems, OMPGPT is designed for a diverse array of users, regardless of their OpenMP knowledge background.

3.2 OMPGPT Training & Inference

Dataset. HPCorpus, introduced by Kadosh et al. [10], is an extensive HPC database derived from GitHub repositories containing C, C++, and Fortran code. Notably, approximately 45% of the repositories use some form of parallel programming. The primary parallel programming mode is OpenMP, making HPCorpus suitable for training models for OpenMP tasks. We use C and C++ code from HPCorpus for our model's training and fine-tuning, with 144,522 C code repositories and 150,481 C++ code repositories, totaling 8,781,759 C code functions and 68,233,984 C++ code functions (a total of 72.39 GB). Figure 2 shows the distribution of OpenMP pragmas in the HPCorpus OpenMP subset used for OMPGPT fine-tuning. We allocate 10% of the data as a test set for both training and fine-tuning to maintain evaluation integrity.

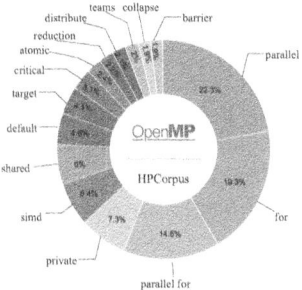
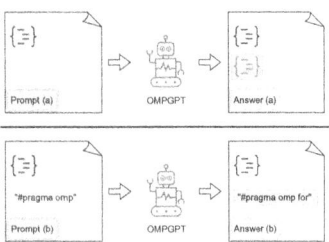

Fig. 2. Distribution of OpenMP Pragmas in the HPCorpus OpenMP subset with the top 15 most frequently occurring pragmas.

Fig. 3. Basic prompt for OMPGPT. (a): prompt for code generation. (b): prompt for OpenMP pragma generation.

Data Processing. Our data pre-processing for OMPGPT includes the following:

1. **Trimming natural language**: OMPGPT is trained solely on code. Therefore natural language text such as comments are removed.
2. **OpenMP Pragma Positioning**: Our approach, unlike previous studies, places OpenMP pragmas after their scopes, leveraging GPT models' instinct to overcome the constraints of current LLMs. This strategy aligns with the findings of the previous work in [19] but diverges by training OMPGPT from scratch to generate OpenMP pragmas, a capability not present in conventional pre-trained models. This unique training methodology tailors OMPGPT to the demands of OpenMP pragma generation and enhances its ability to understand and process the HPC-specific code structures.
3. **Filtering code by size**: Following practices used in previous research, such as PolyCoder [26], we filter out large code segments (more than 100 tokens or greater than 1 MB) from HPCorpus.

Hardware. In all experiments, we utilized a single node on an HPC cluster equipped with a dual-socket AMD EPYC Rome 7402 (24 cores/socket) and 512 GB DDR4-3200 RAM, along with 4 x NVIDIA A100 40GB HBM2e Tensor Core GPUs connected via NVLink3 to each other.

OMPGPT Training: We leveraged the GPT-Neo 2.7B [2] model architecture as a foundation. However, we have tailored the model to better suit our needs by downsizing the number of layers to 8 while maintaining 32 attention heads per layer. The model features a hidden dimension of 2560. We employ the Star-Coder tokenizer for tokenization, which utilizes a vocabulary comprising 49,152 tokens. This configuration results in a total parameter count of 0.76 billion for OMPGPT, making it more compact than our baseline models.

OMPGPT Inference. We convert the OpenMP pragma generation problem into a code generation task by replacing the OpenMP pragmas in training. Figure 3 (a) illustrates inference with OMPGPT for code generation. Originating from a GPT-based model, OMPGPT inherits the capability for generation tasks given input code. OMPGPT is trained on pre-processed OpenMP code where pragmas are moved to the end of loops. When prompted with a prefix like `#pragma omp`, as shown in Fig. 3 (b), OMPGPT demonstrates its specialized ability to generate relevant OpenMP pragmas. This highlights OMPGPT's aptitude for intuitively continuing code sequences tailored to the syntax and structure of OpenMP directives, showcasing practical utility for real-world programming scenarios.

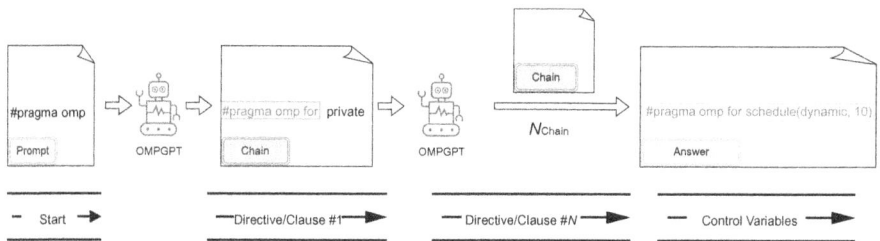

Fig. 4. Chain-of-OMP. Start phase: using the standard OpenMP pragma generation prompts for OMPGPT. Directive/clause generation phase: the first generated Directive/clause is augmented to the previous input as the input for the next chain. This phase is updated till it number of chains reaches parameter N_{chain}. The final Control variable generation phase generates the last component to complete the chain-of-OMP and generate the OpenMP pragma.

3.3 Chain-of-OMP

Chain-of-thought (CoT) [25] facilitates complex reasoning in NLP tasks by guiding LLMs through intermediate steps. Inspired by the "think step by step" methodology, we developed Chain-of-OMP, a novel prompt engineering technique to enhance OMPGPT in generating OpenMP pragmas.

We consider an OpenMP pragma as comprising three major components:

- Directive Prefix (#pragma omp): This universal prefix signals the presence of an OpenMP directive to the compiler. Within our model, this prefix is used in prompts to orient OMPGPT towards generating OpenMP pragmas, steering it away from generic code generation. We represent it as <prefix>.
- Directives and Clauses. This segment outlines the type of parallel or work-sharing construct being utilized and details its specific behavior. We represent them as <dc>.
- Control Structure. A control structure typically immediately follows the directives. It is essential for the behavior of directives like #omp parallel reduction. We represent it as <cs>.

In OpenMP syntax, these three components are listed sequentially (i.e., <prefix><dc><cs>), perfectly fitting the instinct of LLMs. Leveraging this, Chain-of-OMP operates as an automated sequence of prompts, as depicted in Fig. 4. The process begins with standard OpenMP pragma generation prompts (i.e., <prefix>). The output from the first stage is then refined, retaining only the generated directive/clause, which is subsequently passed to the next OMPGPT client to generate the following component. In other words, we only retain <prefix><dc> part of the generated output and ignore the rest. This retained part is then fed as the prompt for the next stage. In general, the components of an OpenMP pragma expand incrementally, with one element added at each inference stage, until it reaches a user-defined limit, N_{chain}. The input I_n for a chain component chain_n is defined by Eq. 1.

$$I_n = concat(I_{n-1}, \text{first generated directive/clause in } O_{n-1}) \qquad (1)$$

where I_n, O_n stands for the input and output of chain_n. concat stands for the concatenate operation. OpenMP pragmas have a different number of components. Consequently, we need a different number of chains to generate the complete OpenMP pragma. We let the user set the maximum number of chains limit by setting N_{chain}. The default value of N_{chain} is 256 to avoid an infinity loop. The value aligns with the commonly used maximum output length of LLMs. The design of Chain-of-OMP has the following advantages:

- Mimicking Expert User Inquiry: This approach closely replicates the querying process employed by experienced OpenMP users. Instead of requesting a complete pragma with a basic prompt (using just #pragma omp), skilled users often provide more specific information, such as directives (e.g., #pragma omp for), to refine their inquiry about the remaining parts of the pragma. Chain-of-OMP embodies this nuanced approach, leading to more targeted and accurate pragma generation.
- Enhancing Performance Across Various LLMs: By selectively retaining the initial directive/clauses and discarding the rest, Chain-of-OMP effectively narrows the search space for subsequent chains. This approach is akin to the strategy in the classic Monty Hall problem, where a "pick again" method

theoretically increases the chances of accuracy. Such a strategy is anticipated to improve OpenMP pragma generation accuracy not just for OMPGPT but for other LLMs as well.
- Automation of the Process: A key strength of Chain-of-OMP is its fully automated chain generation capability. This contrasts traditional chain-of-thought techniques, where users typically need to craft prompts for each step manually. Users usually do not need to specify the value of N_{chain}, as the model will stop when it predicts there is an end of a pragma. Explicitly defining N_{chain} is also an option for expert users who want the model to run n chain stages. The automation in Chain-of-OMP streamlines the process, making it more efficient and user-friendly.

3.4 Fine-Tuning

Due to the complexity of OpenMP pragmas, previous works either train an ML model or fine-tune a language model for specific tasks covering a limited selection of pragmas. In our work, we have employed a strategic fine-tuning approach to demonstrate the enhanced performance of OMPGPT after fine-tuning and to facilitate a comprehensive comparison with baseline models.

We fine-tune the pre-trained OMPGPT model using the AdamW optimizer [17], a variant of the Adam optimizer known for its effectiveness in large models and datasets. This process incorporates a linear warm-up phase over the initial 100 steps. The warm-up phase gradually increases the learning rate from zero to the initial learning rate set for training, helping to stabilize the model's learning process in its early stages. Following the warm-up, we implement a linear decay in the learning rate for the remaining steps. This decay approach gradually reduces the learning rate, allowing for finer adjustments to the model's weights as it converges toward optimal performance.

4 Evaluation

4.1 Model Perplexity

Task Definition. This subsection evaluates the general knowledge of OpenMP code possessed by the base model. We assess its ability to generate code using perplexity score, a common metric in language processing. Perplexity essentially measures how surprised a model is by the next word in a sequence. Lower perplexity indicates the model can better predict upcoming elements and thus has a better understanding of the language. In this context, we use perplexity to gauge the model's grasp of OpenMP code structure.

Evaluation Setup. As described in Sect. 3.2, we use 10% of the HPCorpus dataset as a test set unknown to OMPGPT. We calculate OMPGPT's perplexity (PP) using the following Eq. 2.

$$PP = \exp\left(-\frac{1}{N}\sum_{i=1}^{N}\log P(w_i|w_1, w_2, \ldots, w_{i-1})\right) \quad (2)$$

where $P(w_i, w_1, w_2, \ldots, w_{i-1})$ is the probability of the first word w_i occurring, given the sequence of the subsequent words $w_1, w_2, \ldots, w_{i-1}$. We use prompt (a) in Fig. 3 for general code generation and calculate the perplexity. We compare the perplexity result of OMPGPT with MonoCoder and other open-source language models.

Baselines. Table 1 compares perplexity scores on OpenMP code for various open-source code LLMs. These models have different parameter sizes and were all trained with extensive parallel learning (PL) data, enabling their code generation capabilities. However, most of them are generic models and are included here for perplexity evaluation only. MonoCoder stands out as the only model specifically focused on OpenMP. Additionally, it was trained and tested with the HPCorpus dataset, making it a well-suited baseline for our later investigation of OpenMP pragma generation.

Table 1. Perplexity Comparison across Open-source Language Models.

Model	Size (B)	C	C++
OMPGPT	**0.76**	3.54	3.66
MonoCoder	0.89	3.51	3.69
PolyCoder	2.7	2.33	2.99
GPT-Neo	2.7	3.69	2.87
GPT-J	6	2.82	2.47
CodeX	12	2.55	1.95
StarCoder	15.5	1.71	2.01
GPT-NeoX	20	2.37	2.32

Results. As shown in Table 1, OMPGPT achieves competitive scores (3.54 for C and 3.66 for C++) despite its smaller size (0.76B) compared to models like PolyCoder (2.7B) or GPT-J (6B). While larger models like StarCoder (15.5B) generally achieve lower perplexity, OMPGPT demonstrates efficiency by competently bridging this gap with larger models. This trend suggests a correlation between model size and perplexity, but the efficiency of OMPGPT is notable, given its significantly smaller size. It competently bridges the gap with larger models, indicating a promising direction for efficient model design in the code generation tasks.

4.2 OpenMP Pragma Generation with OMPGPT Base Model

Task Definition. OMPGPT is trained with the preprocessed OpenMP code in HPCorpus. The capability of generating any OpenMP pragma distinguishes OMPGPT from most existing code-oriented Large Language Models (LLMs). This task evaluates OMPGPT's performance on the 15 most prevalent OpenMP pragmas found in the HPCorpus test set to assess this capability.

Evaluation Setup. We followed the Prompt (b) in Fig. 3, where the input code is followed by the hint `#pragma omp` to signal to OMPGPT that we are performing the pragma prediction instead of generic code generation. Evaluation metrics focus on accuracy, specifically gauging the congruence between OMPGPT's outputs and the original OpenMP pragmas.

We employed a strict matching criterion, wherein a generated pragma is considered correct only if it precisely matches the corresponding pragma in the test dataset. For instance, although the following two OpenMP pragmas are functionally equivalent, they are not deemed correct under this strict criterion:

```
#pragma omp parallel for reduction(+:sum) private(var)
```

```
#pragma omp parallel for private(var) reduction(+:sum)
```
Results. Figure 5 compares OMPGPT with its base model GPT-Neo. Notably, OMPGPT outperforms GPT-Neo, indicating the performance gain is achieved as OMPGPT successfully learned the task of OpenMP pragma generation. However, as shown in the figure, the strict matching criterion results in lower scores, highlighting the challenge of achieving perfect accuracy in this task.

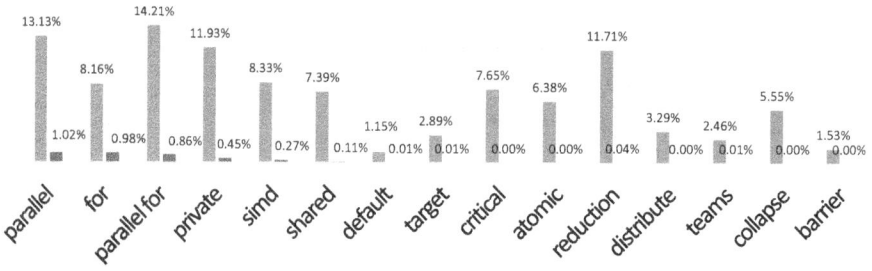

Fig. 5. Pragma Generation Accuracy. Blue: OMPGPT. Red: GPT-Neo. (Color figure online)

4.3 OpenMP Pragma Generation Using Chain-of-OMP

Task Definition. As shown in Sect. 4.2, OMPGPT's base model can generate OpenMP pragmas, but accuracy is limited due to the complexities of OpenMP syntax. This section evaluates our proposed Chain-of-OMP method, assessing its effectiveness in improving pragma generation compared to basic prompts. This comparison will highlight Chain-of-OMP's ability to address these syntactic challenges.

Evaluation Setup. We evaluate chain-of-OMP for four specific OpenMP clauses: `for schedule`, `collapse`, `teams`, and `target`. These pragmas are well-aligned with the three-component structure outlined earlier. We compare Chain-of-OMP's accuracy with the base prompt to quantify its performance improvement.

Results. Table 2 showcases the accuracy gains achieved by Chain-of-OMP. For `for schedule`, Chain-of-OMP significantly improves accuracy from 1.3% to 7.8%, representing a substantial 600% increase. Similar improvements are observed for `collapse` (0.1% to 2.4%, a 2300% increase) and `target` (2.9%

Table 2. Chain-of-OMP effectiveness evaluation with OMPGPT.

	Basic Prompt	Chain-of-OMP
for schedule	1.3%	7.8%
collapse	0.1%	2.4%
teams	0.1%	0.3%
target	2.9%	16.9%

to 16.9%, a 580% increase). The smaller improvement for teams (0.1% to 0.3%) is due to limited training data for this specific pragma.

4.4 Fine-Tuning OMPGPT for Specific Pragma Generation

Task Definition. As discussed in Sect. 3.4, fine-tuning is necessary due to the complexity of OpenMP pragmas. We fine-tuned OMPGPT for three sub-tasks: private, reduction, and SIMD. We evaluate its performance against two baselines: MonoCoder (fine-tuned for pragma generation) and GPT-3.5 (not fine-tuned due to time/cost constraints). We also applied Chain-of-OMP with the fine-tuned OMPGPT for each sub-task, setting the number of chains N_{chain} to 2 based on the evaluation clauses' structure.

Evaluation Setup. We used the test set from our fine-tuning dataset for each sub-task. We employed precision, recall, F1-score, and accuracy metrics. The evaluation consisted of two subtests:

1. Subtest 1 (Clause Matching): This subtest checks if the predicted clause matches the expected clause.
2. Subtest 2 (Stricter Matching): This stricter subtest requires both the predicted clause and its control structure to match the expected ones.

For both GPT-3.5 and Monocoder, we used the same test set employed for OMPGPT to ensure a fair comparison. Results for MonoCoder are reported from its original paper since it uses the same dataset splits as OMPGPT. We note that some entries in Tables 3 and 4 were unavailable for MonoCoder since they were not reported in their paper.

Table 3. Fine-tuning results for private, reduction, and SIMD on the first test (Subset 1). P = Precision, R = Recall, F1 = F1 Score, Acc = Accuracy. Note Monocoder does not support SIMD.

Model	private				reduction				SIMD			
	P	R	F1	Acc	P	R	F1	Acc	P	R	F1	Acc
OMPGPT	0.94	0.91	0.92	0.96	0.92	0.91	0.915	0.98	0.88	0.82	0.85	0.93
MonoCoder	0.89	0.83	0.86	0.94	0.99	0.81	0.891	0.98	-	-	-	-
GPT-3.5	0.4	0.16	0.23	0.77	0.53	0.57	0.549	0.92	0.51	0.55	0.53	0.84

Results. Tables 3 and 4 show the performance on the two subtests for private, reduction, and SIMD clauses (MonoCoder doesn't support SIMD). Overall, OMPGPT consistently outperforms both MonoCoder and GPT-3.5 models in the two subtests. As expected, the performance drops for all models in the second subtest (clause and control structure). However, notably, the Chain-of-OMP prompt improves the accuracy of OMPGPT in predicting both the clause and control structure correctly in the second subtest.

Table 4. Fine-tuning results for `private`, `reduction`, and `SIMD` on the second test (Susbet 2). Note Monocoder does not support SIMD.

Model	private				reduction				SIMD			
	P	R	F1	Acc	P	R	F1	Acc	P	R	F1	Acc
OMPGPT	0.74	0.61	0.67	0.51	0.78	0.71	0.74	0.57	0.64	0.69	0.66	0.42
Chain-of-OMP	0.76	0.77	0.76	0.64	0.77	0.78	0.77	0.60	0.66	0.73	0.69	0.58
MonoCoder	-	-	-	0.48	-	-	-	0.52	-	-	-	-
GPT-3.5	0.23	0.34	0.27	0.14	0.71	0.55	0.62	0.51	0.61	0.55	0.58	0.40

The effectiveness of Chain-of-OMP is showcased by analyzing two selected OpenMP pragmas, as detailed in Sect. 4.3. Furthermore, we extended our evaluation to include a smaller set comprising ten samples of the top 15 most common pragmas in this test. This testing led to two significant observations:

- Consistent Performance Enhancement: Chain-of-OMP consistently maintained or improved performance across all test sets. In no instance did its application lead to a performance decline.
- Notable Improvement in Majority of Tasks: Impressively, Chain-of-OMP improved performance in 11 out of the 15 pragma generation tasks, demonstrating its substantial efficacy in enhancing OpenMP pragma generation across various tasks.

5 Related Work

Recent works have explored language models (LMs) for HPC tasks as described in [11]. Studies have fine-tuned existing code LLMs for tasks such as race detection [8] and generating parallel code like MPI routines [19]. The latter work also explored the task of generating accurate OpenMP pragmas. In contrast, [12] formulated predicting OpenMP pragmas as a multi-label classification task.

One of the most recent studies utilizing LLMs for OpenMP pragma generation is MonoCoder [11]. This work fine-tunes a domain-specific language model on the HPCorpus dataset specifically for OpenMP pragma generation. OMPGPT stands out from MonoCoder due to its novel training approach. By strategically repositioning OpenMP pragmas during training, OMPGPT aligns with the left-to-right processing inherent to GPT models. This approach, along with the proposed Chain-of-OMP prompting technique, leads to consistent performance improvements over MonoCoder.

Chain-of-thought prompting improves LM reasoning ability, showing promise on math word problems, commonsense reasoning [25], and summarizing software components [21]. This prompting strategy has also enhanced code generation from models like ChatGPT [14,16] and bug reproduction from reports [9]. Most relevantly, it has been applied to correcting compilable code [3].

6 Conclusion and Future Work

While large language models have transformed natural language processing they struggle with domain-specific problems like HPC tasks. This work presents OMPGPT, a 0.76B domain-specific model trained for OpenMP pragma generation on HPC data. Our evaluation shows that OMPGPT outperforms larger LLMs like GPT-3.5. Moreover, our novel chain-of-OMP prompting technique assists OMPGPT in improving accuracy through step-by-step prompts. Our findings suggest that smaller LLMs can achieve excellent performance on specific tasks with proper domain training and prompting techniques. This paves the way for more accessible and efficient LLMs.

Future work includes evaluating Chain-of-OMP on other OpenMP clauses, extending context windows beyond loop snippets, training LLMs from scratch on our data with Chain-of-OMP prompting, and exploring this approach for other HPC tasks [1].

Acknowledgement. This project was funded by NSF (#2211982) and Intel Labs. We would like to thank them for their generous support. Additionally, we extend our gratitude to the Research IT team (https://researchit.las.iastate.edu/) of Iowa State University for their continuous support in providing access to HPC clusters for conducting the experiments of this project.

References

1. Bhattacharjee, A., Daley, C.S., Jannesari, A.: OpenMP offload features and strategies for high performance across architectures and compilers. In: 2023 IEEE International Parallel and Distributed Processing Symposium Workshops (IPDPSW), pp. 564–573 (2023)
2. Black, S., Gao, L., Wang, P., Leahy, C., Biderman, S.: GPT-Neo: large scale autoregressive language modeling with Mesh-Tensorflow. If you use this software, please cite it using these metadata **58**, 2 (2021)
3. Chen, L., et al.: CompCodeVet: a compiler-guided validation and enhancement approach for code dataset. arXiv preprint arXiv:2311.06505 (2023)
4. Chen, L., Lin, P.-H., Vanderbruggen, T., Liao, C., Emani, M., de Supinski, B.: LM4HPC: towards effective language model application in high-performance computing. In: McIntosh-Smith, S., Klemm, M., de Supinski, B.R., Deakin, T., Klinkenberg, J. (eds.) OpenMP: Advanced Task-Based, Device and Compiler Programming: 19th International Workshop on OpenMP, IWOMP 2023, Bristol, UK, September 13–15, 2023, Proceedings, pp. 18–33. Springer Nature Switzerland, Cham (2023). https://doi.org/10.1007/978-3-031-40744-4_2
5. Chen, L., Mahmud, Q.I., Jannesari, A.: Multi-view learning for parallelism discovery of sequential programs. In: 2022 IEEE International Parallel and Distributed Processing Symposium Workshops (IPDPSW), pp. 295–303. IEEE (2022)
6. Chen, L., Mahmud, Q.I., Phan, H., Ahmed, N., Jannesari, A.: Learning to parallelize with OpenMP by augmented heterogeneous AST representation. In: Proceedings of Machine Learning and Systems **5** (2023)
7. Dagum, L., Menon, R.: OpenMP: an industry standard API for shared-memory programming. IEEE Comput. Sci. Eng. **5**(1), 46–55 (1998)

8. Ding, X., et al.: HPC-GPT: integrating large language model for high-performance computing. In: Proceedings of the SC'23 Workshops of The International Conference on High Performance Computing, Network, Storage, and Analysis, pp. 951–960 (2023)
9. Feng, S., Chen, C.: Prompting is all you need: automated android bug replay with large language models. In: Proceedings of the 46th IEEE/ACM International Conference on Software Engineering, pp. 1–13 (2024)
10. Kadosh, T., Hasabnis, N., Mattson, T., Pinter, Y., Oren, G.: Quantifying OpenMP: statistical insights into usage and adoption. In: 2023 IEEE High Performance Extreme Computing Conference (HPEC), pp. 1–7. IEEE (2023)
11. Kadosh, T., et al.: Domain-specific code language models: unraveling the potential for HPC codes and tasks. arXiv preprint arXiv:2312.13322 (2023)
12. Kadosh, T., Schneider, N., Hasabnis, N., Mattson, T., Pinter, Y., Oren, G.: Advising OpenMP parallelization via a graph-based approach with transformers. In: McIntosh-Smith, S., Klemm, M., de Supinski, B.R., Deakin, T., Klinkenberg, J. (eds.) OpenMP: Advanced Task-Based, Device and Compiler Programming: 19th International Workshop on OpenMP, IWOMP 2023, Bristol, UK, September 13–15, 2023, Proceedings, pp. 3–17. Springer Nature Switzerland, Cham (2023). https://doi.org/10.1007/978-3-031-40744-4_1
13. Kocetkov, D., et al.: The stack: 3 TB of permissively licensed source code. Preprint (2022)
14. Li, J., Li, G., Li, Y., Jin, Z.: Structured chain-of-thought prompting for code generation. arXiv preprint arXiv:2305.06599 (2023)
15. Li, R., et al.: StarCoder: may the source be with you! arXiv preprint arXiv:2305.06161 (2023)
16. Liu, C., et al.: Improving ChatGPT prompt for code generation. arXiv preprint arXiv:2305.08360 (2023)
17. Loshchilov, I., Hutter, F.: Decoupled weight decay regularization. arXiv preprint arXiv:1711.05101 (2017)
18. Luo, Z., et al.: WizardCoder: empowering code large language models with Evol-instruct. arXiv preprint arXiv:2306.08568 (2023)
19. Nichols, D., Marathe, A., Menon, H., Gamblin, T., Bhatele, A.: Modeling parallel programs using large language models. arXiv preprint arXiv:2306.17281 (2023)
20. Roziere, B., et al.: Code Llama: open foundation models for code. arXiv preprint arXiv:2308.12950 (2023)
21. Rukmono, S.A., Ochoa, L., Chaudron, M.R.: Achieving high-level software component summarization via hierarchical chain-of-thought prompting and static code analysis. In: 2023 IEEE International Conference on Data and Software Engineering (ICoDSE), pp. 7–12. IEEE (2023)
22. Touvron, H., et al.: Llama 2: open foundation and fine-tuned chat models. arXiv preprint arXiv:2307.09288 (2023)
23. Valero-Lara, P., et al.: Comparing Llama-2 and GPT-3 LLMs for HPC kernels generation. arXiv preprint arXiv:2309.07103 (2023)
24. Vaswani, A., et al.: Attention is all you need. In: Advances in Neural Information Processing Systems, vol. 30 (2017)
25. Wei, J., et al.: Chain-of-thought prompting elicits reasoning in large language models. Adv. Neural. Inf. Process. Syst. **35**, 24824–24837 (2022)
26. Xu, F.F., Alon, U., Neubig, G., Hellendoorn, V.J.: A systematic evaluation of large language models of code. In: Proceedings of the 6th ACM SIGPLAN International Symposium on Machine Programming, pp. 1–10 (2022)

Scheduling, Resource Management, Cloud, Edge Computing, and Workflows

Scheduling Distributed I/O Resources in HPC Systems

Alexis Bandet[1]([✉])[iD], Francieli Boito[1][iD], and Guillaume Pallez[2][iD]

[1] Univ. Bordeaux, CNRS, Bordeaux INP, Inria, LaBRI, UMR 5800,
33400 Talence, France
{alexis.bandet,francieli.zanon-boito}@inria.fr
[2] Inria, Rennes, France
guillaume.pallez@inria.fr

Abstract. This paper presents a comprehensive investigation on optimizing I/O performance in the access to distributed I/O resources in high-performance computing (HPC) environments. I/O resources, such as the I/O forwarding nodes and object storage targets (OST), are shared by applications. Each application has access to a subset of them, and multiple applications can access the same resources. We propose heuristics to schedule these distributed I/O resources in two steps: for each application, determining *how many* (allocation) and *which* (placement) resources to use. We discuss a wide range of information about applications' characteristics that can be used by the scheduling algorithms. Despite the fact that a higher level of application knowledge is associated with better performance, we demonstrate the robustness of our solutions in scenarios where information is limited or inaccurate. This research provides insights into the trade-offs between the depth of application characterization and the practicality of scheduling I/O resources.

Keywords: HPC · parallel I/O · parallel file system · object storage targets · I/O forwarding · scheduling · resource allocation

1 Introduction and Related Work

In large high-performance computing (HPC) platforms, applications access persistent data by performing I/O operations to a remote shared parallel file system (PFS), such as Lustre or BeeGFS. Because of the gap between processing and I/O speeds, and with processing power ever increasing, many HPC applications spend a large portion of their time on I/O. This access is often synchronous—meaning the application occupies the compute resources while waiting to complete I/O transfer. Therefore, improving I/O performance promotes a more efficient usage of the expensive and power-hungry HPC compute resources.

Parallel file systems cut files into fixed-size stripes and distribute them across a number of storage targets (OSTs) for parallel access. Depending on the files that they access, all compute nodes may require access to the same OSTs at the same time. Thus, to mitigate contention, a layer of I/O forwarding nodes (or simply "I/O nodes") is sometimes placed between compute nodes and the PFS [1]. Both OSTs and I/O nodes are I/O resources, and it is important to notice both are potentially shared by running applications. Other shared resources include burst-buffer nodes, present in some systems [5,20]. When applications access the same I/O resources concurrently, their I/O performance can be slowed down [24], and hence they occupy compute resources for longer. In addition to wasting resources, the fact that I/O performance depends on what others are doing in the system leads to higher performance variability [13], which makes execution time less predictable and, consequently, complicates resource management [9].

Shared I/O Access Scheduling. Many techniques have been proposed to mitigate contention, mainly PFS access scheduling [9,15,17], burst-buffers [2] and I/O-aware batch scheduling [6,19]. However, these efforts usually see the shared I/O infrastructure as a single resource of a certain bandwidth, whereas in practice it is a distributed set of resources from which each application can use a subset. In addition, using X% of the OSTs, for example, does not grant a job X% of the PFS' peak performance [8,12]. Indeed, depending on their characteristics, each application is impacted differently by the number of used I/O resources [14,26].

Forwarding Node Scheduling. Xu et al. [23] present an I/O infrastructure where I/O resources can be dynamically selected for each file the applications access. That selection is done based on real-time monitoring data to avoid congestion. Some machines, such as Sunway TaihuLight [18] allow for real-time reconfiguration. From a scheduling perspective, the historical approach to deal with distributed I/O resources was to use a fixed forwarding-node mapping (FFM) [21], where even though the compute nodes are connected to all forwarding nodes, the system uses an exclusive, static mapping between the forwarding and the compute nodes. This led many forwarding nodes to stay idle, while some may be saturated [18]. Recent approaches have provided a mix of exclusive access, and opportunistic use of other forwarding nodes [4,26]. In the algorithm by Bez et al. [4], the allocation and placement are obtained by optimizing the sum of applications' bandwidths and favoring exclusive access as much as possible. We use this algorithm as a comparison to our solutions. Another approach is that proposed by Ji et al. [18]. They assign statically less than half of the I/O nodes to applications. The rest of the I/O nodes are allocated based on historical data (mostly the number of compute nodes performing I/O and I/O volume).

OST Scheduling. Yang et al. [25] reduce the problem of placing applications on I/O nodes *and* OSTs to the maximum flow problem, using their I/O load and the current monitored load of the resources. We evaluate a non-exclusive allocation version of this approach. The strategy by Wang et al. [22] also considers all layers at once. The OST with the lowest-cost path is selected for each of the application's compute nodes. The cost of a path depends on manually-set weights given to layers according to their importance for performance.

In this paper, we present a comprehensive study of the problem of scheduling shared I/O resources—I/O nodes, OSTs, etc.—to HPC applications with the goal of mitigating contention and improving I/O and system performance. We tackle this problem by proposing heuristics to answer two questions: 1) *how many* resources should we give each application (allocation heuristics), and 2) *which* resources should be given to each application (placement heuristics). These questions are not independent, as using more resources often means sharing them. Nonetheless, our two-step approach allows for simpler heuristics that would be usable in practice. Our main contributions are:

- We accurately model the problem of scheduling distributed I/O resources, and propose allocation and placement algorithms.
- An important aspect, which impacts how "implementable" algorithms are, is their requirements input-wise. Indeed this information is often not available or at least imprecise. We discuss the quality of various input parameters and study their impact with the goal of answering questions about the importance of accurate application description, and how robust the heuristics are to inaccurate information.

The rest of this paper is organized as follows: Sect. 2 formally states the studied problem, and then Sect. 3 discusses the proposed heuristics. We then evaluate these results in Sect. 4. We provide concluding remarks in Sect. 5.

2 Model

This section describes our platform (shown in Fig. 1) and application models.

2.1 Platform Model

We assume that we have a parallel platform composed of compute nodes and remote shared storage. To access this storage, each application must communicate first through distributed I/O resources, which can be I/O nodes, OSTs, burst buffer nodes, etc. There are N I/O resources. We consider that access to compute nodes are exclusive (congestion-free), hence in this work we focus on a performance model for I/O.

Capacity Sharing. When multiple applications access concurrently an I/O resource, they share equally its capacity. In other words, the bandwidth of each I/O resource is divided by the number of applications using it at this time.

2.2 Application Model and I/O Behavior

K applications run concurrently on the platform. Each application is a series of phases that alternate between computation and I/O subphases [11,16,17]. We study the synchronous I/O case where compute and I/O subphases cannot overlap. The key parameters describing an application and used in the rest of this paper are summarized in Table 1.

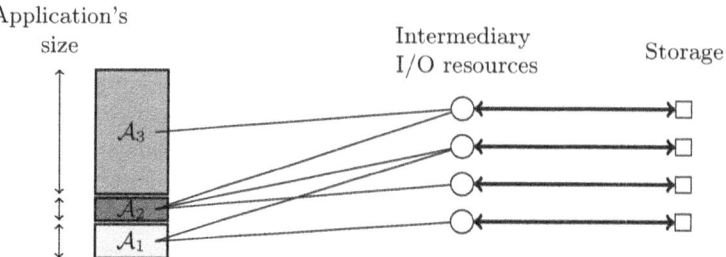

Fig. 1. Representation of the architecture: three applications $\mathcal{A}_1$ (resp. $\mathcal{A}_2$, $\mathcal{A}_3$) use two (resp. three, one) I/O resources. The number of I/O resources is not necessarily correlated to the size (number of compute nodes) of the application.

Table 1. Key parameters for application $\mathcal{A}_j$.

Q_j	Number of compute resources
p_j	Number of phases (compute then I/O)
$t_{\text{cpu}}^{(i)}$	Length of the compute subphase of phase $i \leq p_j$
$v_{\text{io}}^{(i)}$	Volume of I/O transferred in phase $i \leq p_j$
T_{cpu}^j	Accumulated compute time over all compute (sub)phases
V_{io}^j	Accumulated volume of I/O over all I/O (sub)phases
b_j	I/O bandwidth as a function of the number of I/O resources

The length of each I/O subphase depends on the number of I/O resources allocated to application $\mathcal{A}_j$. The bandwidth of $\mathcal{A}_j$ as a function of I/O resources is given by: $n \mapsto b_j(n)$. If $\mathcal{A}_j$ uses n_j I/O resources, when there is no congestion, its aggregated I/O time (for amount of data V_{io}) is: $\text{T\_cf}_{\text{io}}^j(n) = \frac{V_{\text{io}}}{b_j(n)}$.

When there is no congestion, during a total time $T_{\text{cpu}}^j + \text{T\_cf}_{\text{io}}^j(n)$, $\mathcal{A}_j$ occupies n I/O resources during a time $\text{T\_cf}_{\text{io}}^j(n)$, and we have:

$$\text{I/O-Stress}(j, n) = \frac{n \cdot \text{T\_cf}_{\text{io}}^j(n)}{T_{\text{cpu}}^j + \text{T\_cf}_{\text{io}}^j(n)}$$

In the rest of this paper, for clarity and when there is no ambiguity, we remove the index j when talking about an application variable.

Characteristic Values. For application $\mathcal{A}_j$, we define two characteristic values:

$$n_{\text{perf}}^j = \text{argmin}_n \text{T\_cf}_{\text{io}}^j(n) = \text{argmax}_n b_j(n) \quad (1)$$

$$n_{\text{sys}}^j = \text{argmin}_n \text{I/O-Stress}(j, n) \quad (2)$$

n_{perf}^j corresponds to the number of I/O resources that minimizes the I/O transfer time of $\mathcal{A}_j$; n_{sys}^j corresponds to the number of I/O resources that minimizes the stress (I/O-Stress) on the system due to $\mathcal{A}_j$.

Independence of I/O Transfers. An I/O subphase over n I/O resources can be seen as n independent I/O transfers. This means that if an application is using multiple I/O resources, and its performance is slowed-down on one of those, then the other transfers are *not* slowed down. However, an I/O subphase only ends when all its I/O transfers are over (See Fig. 2).

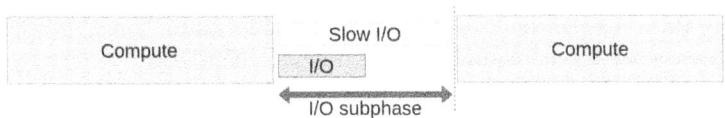

Fig. 2. Independence of I/O transfers with $n = 2$

2.3 Measuring Performance

More details on the evaluation objectives are given in the companion report [3].
A solution is described by two elements:

- the number of I/O resources each application uses ($\pi = (n_1, \ldots, n_K)$);
- a mapping of the applications over the I/O resources.

At a given time t, and given a schedule π, we define its I/O load as:

$$\text{I/O-load}(\pi) = \frac{1}{N} \sum_{i=1}^{K} \text{I/O-Stress}(i, \pi(i)) \qquad (3)$$

Intuitively, this is a lower bound on the expectation of I/O time occupied by π per unit of time. By definition, I/O-load is minimized for the schedule $\pi_{\text{sys}} = (n^1_{\text{sys}}, \ldots, n^K_{\text{sys}})$. If I/O-load > 1, then the system is *saturated*. In such a scenario, typical I/O time needed by applications exceeds system capabilities.
We define the following optimization criteria to evaluate a schedule π:

I/O Performance. The first objective, Mean-I/O-SlowDown, measures the I/O performance of the system from an application perspective: it aims at answering the question (*on average, how reduced was my I/O bandwidth?*). To have a better qualitative understanding of the Mean-I/O-SlowDown, we measure separately the speed reduction (slowdown) caused by not using the number of I/O resources that minimizes I/O time (ρ_j^{io}), and due to congestion (ρ_j^{con}).

Machine Utilization. The second objective, Machine-Idletime, measures the proportion of time when the compute nodes are *not* being used for computing. Intuitively, it focuses from a system administrator perspective, where a fair treatment of applications (from an I/O perspective) may forget the fact that not all applications use the machine similarly.

3 Algorithms for Scheduling I/O resources

As mentioned in Sect. 2.3, a solution is defined by two questions: the number of I/O resources each application will use and the mapping of applications over the multiple I/O resources. In this section we present heuristics to provide the answers - respectively allocation (Sect. 3.1) and placement (Sect. 3.2) algorithms. While an application is accurately described by the elements described in Sect. 2, in practice this data can be hard to collect and inaccurate. Thus, in Sect. 3.3 we further discuss the input required by the different heuristics.

3.1 Allocation Algorithms

We propose five allocation policies:

- **Random**: each application receives a randomly picked number of I/O resources. This serves as a baseline.
- **Static**: application $\mathcal{A}_j$, running on Q_j compute nodes (out of Q^{cpu} in the system) receives $\frac{Q_j \cdot N}{Q^{cpu}}$ I/O resources, rounded to the closest positive integer. For the case of I/O nodes, this policy represents what happens in HPC systems where the mapping from compute nodes to them is static.
- **BestBdw (BBA)** allocates n_{perf}^j to each $\mathcal{A}_j$, i.e., the number of I/O resources that minimizes its I/O time. While this policy minimizes ρ^{io}, in some cases it may increase I/O-load and make applications share more I/O resources, which leads to more congestion and hence to an increased ρ^{con}.
- **Nsys-Allocator (NSYSA)** gives π_{sys}, i.e., it allocates n_{sys}^j to each $\mathcal{A}_j$ to minimize the I/O-load.
- **TCPU-Allocator (TA)**, detailed in Algorithm 1, starts at π_{sys} and then repeatedly increases the number of I/O resources of the application that maximizes the utilization of compute resources (the sum of CPULoad) while respecting the constraint that I/O-load must be smaller or equal to 1 (so the I/O system is not saturated).

$$\text{CPULoad}(i, n) = Q_i \cdot \frac{T_{\text{cpu}}^i}{T_{\text{cpu}}^i + \text{T\_cf}_{\text{io}}^i(n)}$$

TA aims at being a compromise between BBA and NSYSA. Note than when the I/O-load of π_{perf} is below 1, then it behaves as BBA.

3.2 Placement Algorithms

Three placement algorithms are considered.

- **Random-Placement (RandP)** randomly assigns I/O resources to applications. This policy reflects what happens in practice in many HPC systems, where I/O behavior is not taken into consideration for placement.

```
Data: K applications
Result: An allocation π
1  π ← initialized as π_sys;
2  done ← False;
3  while not done do
4  |  π̃ ← π;
5  |  loadDiff ← an array of size K, filled with -1;
6  |  initIOLoad ← I/O-load(π);
7  |  for i from 1 to K do
8  |  |  n ← π(i);
9  |  |  while n ≠ n^i_{perf} & loadDiff(i) < 0 do
10 |  |  |  n ← n + 1;
11 |  |  |  if initIOLoad + (I/O-Stress(i,n)/N - I/O-Stress(i,π(i))/N) ≤ 1
   |  |  |  then
12 |  |  |  |  loadDiff(i) ← CPULoad(i,n) - CPULoad(i, π̃(i));
13 |  |  |  |  π̃(i) ← n;
14 |  idx ← argmax(loadDiff);
15 |  if loadDiff(idx) < 0 then
16 |  |  done ← True;
17 |  else
18 |  |  π(idx) ← π̃(idx);
19 return π;
```

Algorithm 1: TCPU-Allocator (TA)

- **Greedy-Non-Clairvoyant (GNC)** aims at providing a balanced number of applications per I/O resource. It sorts applications by decreasing number of I/O resources (computed by the allocation algorithm), then it places each of them going over the I/O resources in a round-robin fashion.
- **Greedy-Clairvoyant (GC)** strives for a balanced load across the I/O resources. It sorts applications by decreasing congestion-free I/O ratio $T\_cf_{io}/(T_{cpu} + T\_cf_{io})$, then it greedily places them on the I/O resources the least stressed.

3.3 On the Difficulty of Instantiating an Algorithm

The eight described algorithms use different information about applications, as summarized in Table 2. The colors represent how easy to obtain we consider these values to be:

- Easy ( ): the number of compute resources used by each application can be obtained from the resource manager. Similarly to the total number of available compute and I/O resources, it is easily obtained and reliable.
- Medium (orange): aggregated information such as the total amount of transferred data and compute time of an application can be obtained from previous

Table 2. Heuristics and their input

		Allocation					Placement		
		Random	Static	BBA	NSYSA	TA	Random	GNC	GC
Easy	Q_j		x			x			
Medium	V_{io}^j				x	x			x
	T_{cpu}^j				x	x			x
	n_{perf}			x					
Hard	b_j				x	x			x

runs, for example with profiling tools such as Darshan [10], or provided by the user. In both cases, the actual observed values could vary and this data is only semi-reliable. n_{perf}, is considered in this category because it does not require the whole evaluation and bandwidth values.

- Hard (red): for an application $\mathcal{A}_j$, obtaining the bandwidth as a function of the number of I/O resources (b_j) requires multiple previous runs and is naturally sensitive to variability. The system could accumulate this information over time (so it would only be available to *some* of the running applications), or the user could provide it (less reliable).

4 Evaluation

4.1 Evaluation Methodology

The evaluation in this paper relies on data from real executions. The evaluation is done on a time-based simulator, available at https://gitlab.inria.fr/hpc_io/ionode_simulator along with instructions to reproduce our results.

Datasets. We use two sets of data with several applications $\mathcal{A}_j$ and b_j, i.e., bandwidth measurements for different numbers of I/O resources.

1. Data on 189 applications on the MareNostrum supercomputer was made publicly available by Bez et al. [4]. We use it for the use case of scheduling I/O nodes.
2. The second dataset (use case of OST scheduling) [7] is generated by running the IOR benchmark with different configurations in the PlaFRIM experimental platform, using numbers of OSTs for BeeGFS varying from 1 to 8. The I/O infrastructure of this platform has been detailed in [8]. The 301 configurations all write to a shared file, while covering various values for numbers of nodes, processes per node, request size, contiguous vs. 1D-strided file layout, and total amount of data.

Workload Generation Protocol. We make the hypothesis that the algorithms' behavior depends on the I/O stress on the system. Hence in our generation of the application sets, we cover various I/O-load values.

In all the experiments we consider that we have $N = 20$ I/O resources, and $Q^{cpu} = 480$ compute resources. The number of applications K depends on the experiment, so does the target I/O-load: Θ. Given K and Θ, to generate $\mathcal{A}_j$:

- we pick an I/O bandwidth profile uniformly at random in the dataset;
- the number of phases p_j is picked uniformly at random in $\{2, 3, 4, \cdots, 20\}$;
- Q_j is computed so that 10% (resp. 30%, 60%) of applications use 75% (resp. 20%, 5%) of the compute resources (large, medium, and small applications);
- for all applications, we set $T_{\text{cpu}}^j + \text{T\_cf}_{\text{io}}^j(1) = 5000\text{s}$ (common horizon). Then, we set $T_{\text{cpu}}^j / \text{T\_cf}_{\text{io}}^j(1) = X$, where X is picked uniformly at random in $[0, b]$. The bound b is computed so that $\mathbb{E}(\text{I/O-Stress}(j,1)) = \frac{\Theta N}{K}$: b is the solution to $\log(1+b) = b\frac{\Theta N}{K}$ (computed analytically). Consequently:

$$V_{\text{io}}[j] = 5000 \cdot b_j(1)/(1+X); \quad T_{\text{cpu}}^j = 5000\left(1 - 1/(1+X)\right)$$

By construction, this generation has the property I/O-load$(\pi_1) = \Theta$.

In a second step and for the evaluation, we categorize the sets of applications that we have generated by their minimum I/O-load, i.e., I/O-load$(\pi_{\text{sys}}) \leq \Theta$.

Evaluation Protocol. Each studied scenario is evaluated with over 100 different application sets, randomly generated as described above. The metrics are measured on an interval where the state of the system is constant (i.e. no application finishes), but of a sufficient length (i.e. each application should have performed at least a complete phase compute+I/O). In addition to our solutions, we compare to the MCKP algorithm [4].

4.2 Results

In this section we provide various elements to compare the different heuristics. We first compare the algorithms in a setup where their inputs are reliable, then we loosen the quality of the input information to study the robustness of our algorithms; finally, we discuss the fact that the results hold with another bandwidth model.

To compare the algorithms, we study the optimization criteria presented in Sect. 2.3. The comparison between the algorithms is performed when I/O-load(π_{sys}) varies. This value corresponds to the level of stress on the I/O system: we hypothesize that this is what impacts the most the performance of the algorithms in relation to each other.

Evaluation with Accurate Input Data. In this first set of experiments, we consider that the algorithms have access to precise application profiles. This gives us ideal performance behavior.

As a first step, we study the placement heuristics. In Fig. 3, we present the performance ratio in terms of Mean-I/O-SlowDown when using GNC (Fig. 3a) or RandP (Fig. 3b) instead of the more informed heuristic GC for all allocation algorithms. To read Fig. 3a (resp. Figure 3b), when the TA line is at 2%, that

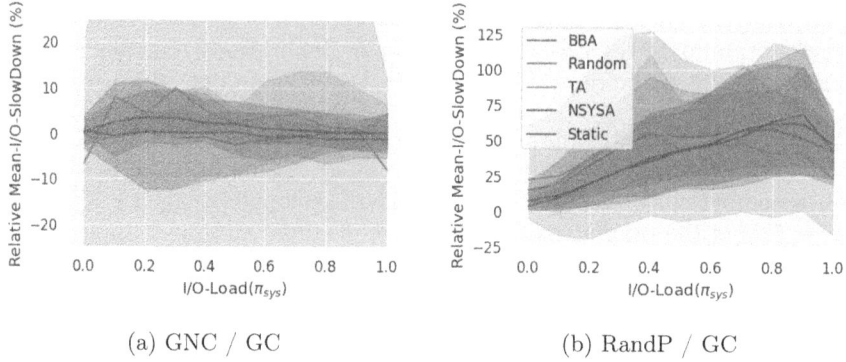

Fig. 3. Relative Mean-I/O-SlowDown for different algorithm combinations when I/O-load(π_{sys}) increases. Placement are compared with GC. Lines show the mean value, and the area around them is the percentile interval (10th–90th).

means that on average, TA-GNC (resp. TA-RandP) has a Mean-I/O-SlowDown 2% worse than that of TA-GC.

The first key observation that we can make is that choosing either GC or GNC for placement has very little impact on performance (except for Random allocation). Nonetheless, this is not true for RandP, which confirms that placement plays a part in the performance.

By studying the load imbalance between I/O resources (i.e. the difference between the most loaded I/O resources and the least loaded I/O resources), we can show that there is a real difference in behavior between GC and GNC. This difference is even more notable with Random allocation. The fact that the I/O performance is not impacted hints that while we manage to stay below a certain level of I/O stress per I/O resource, improving this equilibrium does not matter. These results are available in the companion report [3]. Hence, we conclude that placement can be done greedily with limited information. *Based on this observation, in the rest of this section, we only use GNC as the placement algorithm.*

User-Observed Performance. To compare the allocation heuristics, we decompose the I/O-SlowDown into their I/O and congestion components in Fig. 4, where we show their behavior when I/O-load(π_{sys}) varies. By design, BBA decreases the portion of I/O time due to I/O resources allocation (ρ^{io}) to its bare minimum, at the cost of a much higher congestion overhead (ρ^{con}) than that of NSYSA or Static. As I/O-load(π_{sys}) increases, this cost increases linearly and may become a problem at very high I/O-load values. On the contrary, the congestion overhead with allocation algorithms that take into account the system I/O-load (NSYSA and TA) do not vary as much when I/O-load(π_{sys}) increases. Nonetheless, that comes at the cost of increased I/O time due to I/O resources allocation. Finally, MCKP [4] performs worse than all the other studied policies for these objectives. Indeed, it seeks to optimize the sum of applications' band-

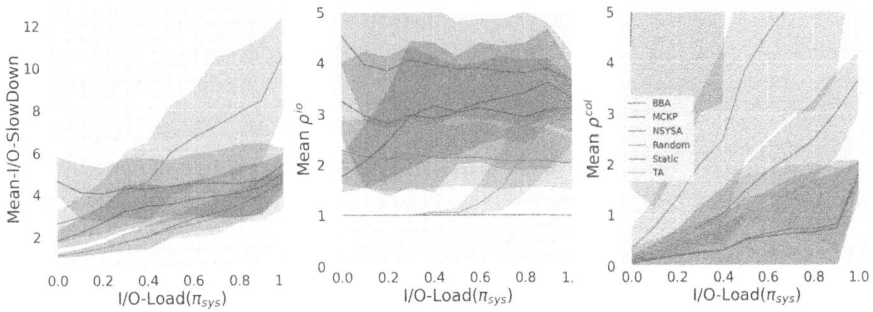

Fig. 4. Mean-I/O-SlowDown (left) separated into its two main components: I/O resources allocation ρ^{io} and congestion ρ^{con}. The lines show the mean value, and the area around them is the percentile interval (10th-90th). To improve visibility, MCKP results were omitted from the first plot: they range from 1.30 to 158.97.

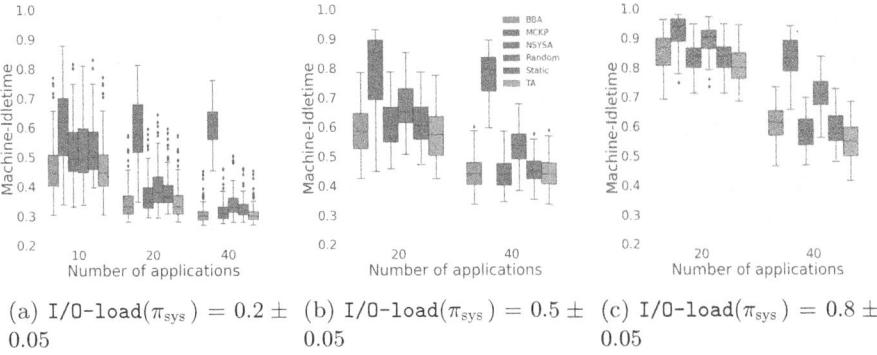

(a) I/O-load(π_{sys}) = 0.2 ± 0.05 (b) I/O-load(π_{sys}) = 0.5 ± 0.05 (c) I/O-load(π_{sys}) = 0.8 ± 0.05

Fig. 5. Machine-Idletime for allocation algorithms at increasing I/O-load(π_{sys}). The y axes do *not* start at 0. The lower the better.

widths due to I/O resources allocation, and has hence a tendency of favoring a few applications (the highest bandwidth ones) in detriment of others.

Machine Utilization. Solely looking at Mean-I/O-SlowDown tends to encourage equal treatment between all applications (big or small). From a system administrator perspective, it may be more interesting to have an application that occupies a large part of the machine to perform its I/O fast, even if it at the cost of worse performance for smaller applications.

To evaluate this, we study the Machine-Idletime in Fig. 5. We can make two observations:

- At low values of I/O-load(π_{sys}), the relative allocation algorithm performance in terms of Machine-Idletime are the same as those for Mean-I/O-SlowDown (BBA and TA perform the best). This is not surprising: I/O has less impact.

– However, at larger I/O-load(π_{sys}), we start to see a real difference of performance between TA and BBA, even though their respective I/O performance were similar, giving an advantage to the heuristic that considers more information (TA).

Static is an interesting heuristic: it uses little information about the applications and still can get good machine utilization results when the I/O-load is high.

Robustness to the Quality of the Input. In Sect. 4.2, we were able to demonstrate the fact that under low I/O-load, BBA was the most efficient allocation algorithm, whereas under a heavier I/O-load, one should rather use TA which provides the same I/O performance from an application perspective but improves on system utilization.

As shown in Sect. 3.3, there is however an important difference between these two algorithms: their input. In particular, TA requires a full I/O profile of the applications whereas BBA only requires the number of I/O nodes that provides the maximum bandwidth.

In this section, we run the same simulations as before, but giving algorithms partial (and potentially wrong) information to study how robust they are. Essentially all applications are classified into four profiles (Ascent, Descent, Peak, Neutral). Then the bandwidth function within a profile is identical for all applications within said profile. Details are provided in the companion report [3].

In Fig. 6, we study the performance of three combinations of algorithms (TA+GNC; BBA+GNC; BBA+GC) with poor input accuracy. To do so, we use all generated scenarios, and plot them as a function of I/O-load(π_{sys}). Note that GNC is not impacted by the lack of accuracy: its behavior does not change. Similarly, BBA is impacted by the lack of accuracy only for some of the applications with a bandwidth profile Peak and Neutral.

Specifically, in Fig. 6a, we compare their performance to what was observed with accurate information: if the value is 2%, for example, it means that the

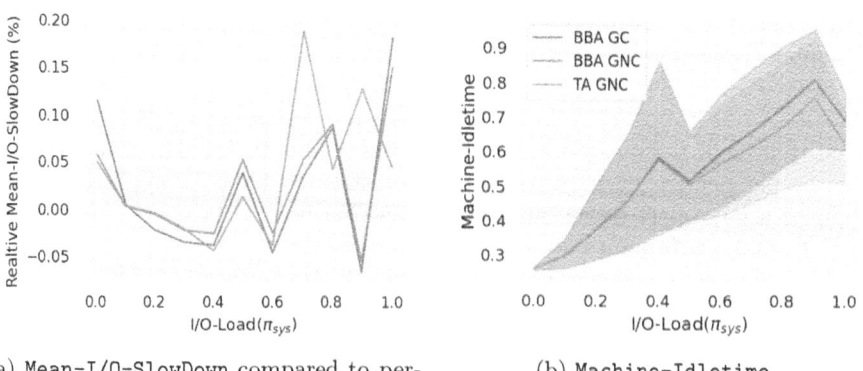

(a) Mean-I/O-SlowDown compared to performance with exact information (%)

(b) Machine-Idletime

Fig. 6. Performance of three scheduling solutions with partial input information

algorithm with inaccurate information performed 2% worse than with accurate information.

We can observe that they have very similar performance. As expected, the allocation algorithm where the behavior differs the most is TA, which is the one that requires the most information. Yet this difference is still negligible (less than 1%). With respect to the mapping algorithm, GC performs almost identically to GNC except in cases with extremely low I/O-load, i.e. when the Mean-I/O-SlowDown is close to 1, the error in prediction is most impactful.

We confirm their absolute impact by plotting their Machine-Idletime (Fig. 6b) which confirms that even with inaccurate information TA is the best solution. More generally, we observe that the various algorithms are quite robust to some inaccuracy in I/O behavior, and that the main claims of our work with respect to choosing allocation and placement algorithms hold.

Scheduling of OSTs. In this final set of experiments, we evaluate our algorithms on a different context: OST scheduling. The main difference with I/O nodes lies on the performance obtained depending on the number of resources allocated to the application.

Overall the main observation [3] is the same as previously: when there is little I/O stress on the system, then BBA performs better than I/O stress-aware algorithms such as NSYSA. Then as the stress increases, its performance quickly degrades. The main difference here is that the cut-off point is much earlier. These results confirm that TA is an excellent alternative that is able to match the performance of BBA when needed, while being I/O stress aware.

Static's performance are excellent for this use case. This is interesting because i) for OSTs, Static is not what is typically used in practice; and ii) it is quite natural and easy to implement. Unfortunately, the fact that this behavior is highly dependent on application profile (i.e. we did not see the same behavior with the I/O nodes dataset) makes the Static allocation algorithm unreliable.

5 Conclusion

In this work we have investigated the problem of allocating subsets of distributed I/O resources to applications in order to optimize their I/O performance and the platform utilization.

Our contributions include both allocation and placement algorithms. In their design, we have taken into account a trade-off between simplicity and efficiency. To this regard we have shown that the placement algorithm can be quite naive: balancing the absolute number of applications per I/O resource, without considering their I/O load, leads to results as good as I/O-aware placement. This naive algorithm gives more leeway to optimize placement based on other reasons (such as proximity to the applications).

In contrast, we have shown that the allocation algorithm is more important for I/O performance, and one should use a more fine-tuned algorithm rather than a naive approach such as peak bandwidth or a static approach that allocates a number of I/O resources proportional to the number of compute resources.

An important contribution of our work is the robustness study: indeed, I/O behavior has been shown to be quite volatile and hard to predict. Hence a very efficient heuristic that is not robust to volatility in its input can become quite useless. In this work we have studied different types of input that algorithms could use, and the limits of each algorithm based on these inputs. In addition, we have shown that our presented heuristics are robust to inaccuracy in input information. We believe that this opens avenues in terms of I/O behavior prediction, which is a hard problem: indeed exact information may not be needed for some of the I/O scheduling algorithms. This should considerably simplify the design of I/O analysis tools.

Acknowledgments. As part of the "France 2030" initiative, this work has benefited from a State grant managed by the French national research agency (*Agence Nationale de la Recherche*) attributed to the Exa-DoST project, and bearing the reference ANR-22-EXNU-0004. It was also supported by the "Adaptive multitier intelligent data manager for Exascale (ADMIRE)" project, funded by the European Union's Horizon 2020 JTI-EuroHPC Research and Innovation Programme (grant 956748). Experiments were carried out using the PlaFRIM experimental testbed, supported by Inria, CNRS (LABRI and IMB), Université de Bordeaux, Bordeaux INP and *Conseil Régional d'Aquitaine* (see https://www.plafrim.fr).

References

1. Almási, G., et al.: An overview of the blue gene/L system software organization. In: Kosch, H., Böszörményi, L., Hellwagner, H. (eds.) Euro-Par 2003. LNCS, vol. 2790, pp. 543–555. Springer, Heidelberg (2003). https://doi.org/10.1007/978-3-540-45209-6_79
2. Aupy, G., Beaumont, O., Eyraud-Dubois, L.: Sizing and partitioning strategies for burst-buffers to reduce to contention. In: IEEE IPDPS, pp. 631–640. IEEE (2019)
3. Bandet, A., Boito, F., Pallez, G.: Allocation and placement algorithms for scheduling distributed I/O resources in HPC systems. Technical report hal-04593977, Inria (2024). https://inria.hal.science/hal-04593977
4. Bez, J.L., Boito, F.Z., Miranda, A., Nou, R., Cortes, T., Navaux, P.O.A.: Towards on-demand I/O forwarding in HPC platforms. In: PDSW, pp. 7–14 (2020)
5. Bez, J.L., et al.: Access patterns and performance behaviors of multi-layer supercomputer I/O subsystems under production load. In: HPDC 2022, New York, NY, USA, pp. 43–55 (2022)
6. Bleuse, R., Dogeas, K., Lucarelli, G., Mounié, G., Trystram, D.: Interference-aware scheduling using geometric constraints. In: Aldinucci, M., Padovani, L., Torquati, M. (eds.) Euro-Par 2018. LNCS, vol. 11014, pp. 205–217. Springer, Cham (2018). https://doi.org/10.1007/978-3-319-96983-1_15
7. Boito, F.: Write performance with different numbers of OSTs for BeeGFS in PlaFRIM (2024). https://doi.org/10.5281/zenodo.10518127
8. Boito, F., Pallez, G., Teylo, L.: The role of storage target allocation in applications' I/O performance with BeeGFS. In: CLUSTER, Heidelberg, Germany (2022)
9. Boito, F., Pallez, G., Teylo, L., Vidal, N.: IO-SETS: simple and efficient approaches for I/O bandwidth management. TPDS **34**(10), 2783–2796 (2023)

10. Carns, P., Harms, K., Allcock, W., Bacon, C., Lang, S., et al.: Understanding and improving computational science storage access through continuous characterization. ACM Trans. Storage **7**(3), 8:1–8:26 (2011)
11. Carns, P., Latham, R., Ross, R., Iskra, K., Lang, S., Riley, K.: 24/7 Characterization of petascale I/O workloads. In: Cluster, pp. 1–10. IEEE (2009)
12. Chowdhury, F., Zhu, Y., Heer, T., Paredes, S., Moody, A., et al.: I/o characterization and performance evaluation of beeGFS for deep learning. In: ICPP (2019)
13. Costa, E., Patel, T., Schwaller, B., Brandt, J.M., Tiwari, D.: Systematically inferring I/O performance variability by examining repetitive job behavior. In: SC 2021. ACM (2021)
14. Devarajan, H., Mohror, K.: Extracting and characterizing I/O behavior of HPC workloads. In: CLUSTER, pp. 243–255 (2022)
15. Dorier, M., Antoniu, G., Ross, R., Kimpe, D., Ibrahim, S.: CALCioM: mitigating I/O interference in HPC systems through cross-application coordination. In: IEEE IPDPS, pp. 155–164 (2014)
16. Dorier, M., Ibrahim, S., Antoniu, G., Ross, R.: Using formal grammars to predict I/O behaviors in HPC: the Omnisc'IO approach. IEEE TPDS **27**(8), 2435–2449 (2016)
17. Gainaru, A., Aupy, G., Benoit, A., Cappello, F., Robert, Y., Snir, M.: Scheduling the I/O of HPC applications under congestion. In: IEEE IPDPS (2015)
18. Ji, X., et al.: Automatic, application-aware I/O forwarding resource allocation. In: USENIX CFST, FAST 2019, pp. 265–279. USENIX Association (2019)
19. Liu, Y., Gunasekaran, R., Ma, X., Vazhkudai, S.S.: Server-side log data analytics for I/O workload characterization and coordination on large shared storage systems. In: SC 2016, pp. 819–829 (2016)
20. Lopez, A., Valat, S., Narasimhamurthy, S., Golasowski, M.: Ephemeral data access environment: Concept and architecture. Technical report, IO-SEA project (2022)
21. Vishwanath, V., et al.: Accelerating I/O forwarding in IBM blue gene/P systems. In: SC 2010, pp. 1–10. IEEE (2010)
22. Wang, F., Oral, S., Gupta, S., Tiwari, D., Vazhkudai, S.S.: Improving large-scale storage system performance via topology-aware and balanced data placement. In: ICPADS 2014, pp. 656–663 (2014)
23. Xu, W., et al.: Hybrid hierarchy storage system in MilkyWay-2 supercomputer. Front. Comp. Sci. **8**(3), 367–377 (2014)
24. Yang, B., Ji, X., Ma, X., Wang, X., Zhang, T., et al.: End-to-end I/O monitoring on a leading supercomputer. In: NSDI. USENIX Association (2019)
25. Yang, B., Zou, Y., Liu, W., Xue, W.: An end-to-end and adaptive I/O optimization tool for modern HPC storage systems. In: IPDPS 2022, pp. 1294–1304 (2022)
26. Yu, J., Liu, G., Dong, W., Li, X., Zhang, J., Sun, F.: On the load imbalance problem of I/O forwarding layer in HPC systems. In: ICCC (2017)

Light-Weight Prediction for Improving Energy Consumption in HPC Platforms

Danilo Carastan-Santos[1], Georges Da Costa[2]([✉]), Millian Poquet[2], Patricia Stolf[2], and Denis Trystram[1]

[1] Univ. Grenoble Alpes, CNRS, INRIA, Grenoble INP, LIG, Grenoble, France
{danilo.carastan-dos-santos, denis.trystram}@univ-grenoble-alpes.fr
[2] Université de Toulouse, IRIT, CNRS, Toulouse, France
{georges.da-costa,millian.poquet,patricia.stolf}@irit.fr

Abstract. With the increase of demand for computing resources and the struggle to provide the necessary energy, power-aware resource management is becoming a major issue for the High-performance computing (HPC) community. Including reliable energy management to a supercomputer's resource and job management system (RJMS) is not an easy task. The energy consumption of jobs is rarely known in advance and the workload of every machine is unique and different from the others.

We argue that the first step toward properly managing energy is to deeply understand the energy consumption of the workload, which involves predicting the workload's power consumption and exploiting it by using smart power-aware scheduling algorithms. Crucial questions are (i) how sophisticated a prediction method needs to be to provide accurate workload power predictions, and (ii) to what point an accurate workload's power prediction translates into efficient energy management.

In this work, we propose a method to predict and exploit HPC workloads' power consumption, with the objective of reducing the supercomputer's power consumption while maintaining the management (scheduling) performance of the RJMS. Our method exploits workload submission logs with power monitoring data, and relies on a mix of light-weight power prediction methods and a classical EASY Backfillling inspired heuristic.

We base this study on logs of Marconi 100, a 980 servers supercomputer. We show using simulation that a light-weight history-based prediction method can provide accurate enough power prediction to improve the energy management of a large scale supercomputer compared to energy-unaware scheduling algorithms. These improvements have no significant negative impact on performance.

Keywords: Machine learning · HPC · Resource management · Power capping · Simulation

---

INP—Institute of engineering Univ. Grenoble Alpes.

© The Author(s), under exclusive license to Springer Nature Switzerland AG 2024
J. Carretero et al. (Eds.): Euro-Par 2024, LNCS 14801, pp. 152–165, 2024.
https://doi.org/10.1007/978-3-031-69577-3_11

1 Introduction

High-Performance Computing (HPC) technology is becoming more accessible and less expensive to build, which opens the door to new fields to capitalize on the large computational capabilities afforded only by such large systems. However, as opposed to the production cost, the power consumption of HPC platforms only increases, reaching levels [16] in the order of the power consumption of a small city. Besides the carbon footprint issue [2] raised by this increase in the power consumption, current climate events may heavily strain the electricity grids [22] that power HPC platforms. To avoid outages, it has become crucial for HPC platform maintainers to deploy measures to ease the strain in the electricity grid, which is typically achieved by enforcing a power capping over time in the platform. The platform's resource manager must therefore adapt to the available power during this power constrained period.

Most existing works propose methods to predict the power consumption of the workload, coupled with a speed scaling (DVFS) method, to adapt to the available power. The drawback is the risk of unforeseeable effects on Quality of Service (QoS). Only few works in the literature propose a full framework, including a workload power prediction method feeding energy data at the submission time to a resource manager. These few works often result in complex and/or heavyweight optimization schemes that are perceived to be either too risky that might disrupt regular functioning, or too expensive in terms of computational resources, thus reducing the (constrained) power available for the applications.

In contrast with related works, this work aims to adapt to the available power and deal with the power constraints *as lightweight and simple as possible*. We exploit power consumption data to develop models to predict the power consumption of an HPC application in advance. These models feed power consumption predictions of arriving applications to a scheduler, and the scheduler uses these predictions to comply with the power constraints while keeping the supercomputer operational. Our experimental results highlight that a lightweight, history-based predictor of the mean power consumption – which is arguably one of the simplest descriptors of an applications' power consumption – coupled with an EASY Backfilling [12] inspired scheduler can make a close to optimal use of the available power in constrained periods.

We organize the rest of this paper as follows: Sect. 2 presents related works in the literature, Sect. 3 presents preliminary concepts needed to understand our work's context, and Sects. 4 and 5 present our methods to predict HPC applications power consumption and to schedule them in an HPC platform, respectively. We present and discuss our experimental results in Sect. 6, and we present our concluding remarks and future perspectives in Sect. 7.

2 Related Work

This section provides an overview of the related works regarding supercomputer's power monitoring/predictions and prediction-aided HPC resource management.

The reader can consult Kocot *et al.* [15] work for a more comprehensive survey on energy-aware resource management in HPC platforms.

Many works propose to exploit predictions to improve the performance of HPC resource management. For instance, Zrigui *et al.* [23] used a coarse grain prediction of jobs into long and short to design a scheduling algorithm taking this information into account for the minimization of the maximum completion time of a set of jobs. In [13], the authors propose a new scheduling algorithm that outperforms the popular EASY backfilling algorithm by 28% considering the average bounded slowdown objective taking into account predictions on the job running times. In the context of predicting the power consumption, Storlie *et al.* [21] developed a framework that predicts energy consumption of arriving jobs. They build a statistical model to approximate the power used by HPC jobs using hierarchical Bayesian modeling with hidden Markov and Dirichlet process models. The goal of their model is to enable the use of an individual node-capping power strategy shown to be more effective for limiting energy consumption than a uniform one. It is the most wholesome model in comparison to the others, though it comes with a high level of complexity. Bugbee *et al.* [5] proposed another model by combining *a priori* (resource manager's meta-data) and *in situ* data (collected during jobs execution). They focus on the specific applications that exhibit a periodic behavior, which accounts for only 45% of the total workload. Another limitation is that developing fine-tuned models for each possible application may be impractical and too resource demanding. Borghesi *et al.* [3] and more recently Saillant *et al.* [19] and Antici *et al.* [1] proposed Machine Learning (ML) and Rote-Learning approaches that rely on resource manager meta-data in order to predict the power consumption of a HPC workload. They combine this information measurements using the RAPL [14] interface. Borghesi *et al.* [3] introduced the idea that the mean value is a good descriptor of the HPC applications' power consumption. We distinguish from these works in two aspects: (i) we explore and compare a prediction method that do not rely on ML to predict the power consumption, and (ii) we further investigate on how the predicted mean power value can be useful to a resource manager to adapt to the constrained power. In [20], the authors focused on large-scale parallel jobs for predicting the energy of a parallel application just by observing a few of its active nodes (as opposed to monitor all the deployed nodes). Chapsis *et al.* [7] propose a power prediction and a resource management framework that includes the power variability due to hardware manufacturing. Their work involves a fine-grained monitoring of the applications and using hardware specific features (hardware counters) to predict the power consumption. Such an approach can be computationally expensive, especially due to the overhead introduced in the computing nodes by the fine-grained monitoring of numerous counters. The approach we propose in this paper intents to reach a balance in the granularity of the used information: providing coarse grained information on the power profile while using only resource manager related information and past, coarse-grained, monitored executions on the platform.

3 Preliminary Concepts

Modern HPC platforms contain large number of nodes. They usually are homogeneous[1]. Many users submit parallel applications (hereafter referred to as jobs) to be executed in the HPC platform, and these jobs can arrive at any point in time (i.e., online job submission). The jobs' submissions are managed by the Resources and Jobs Management System (RJMS). It decides when and where to process each job. Typical meta-data available to the RJMS for a given job j is its arrival time (r_j), requested number of processors (q_j) and an estimation of its processing time $(\tilde{p}_j)$ which is provided by the user who submitted j. Resources allocation and execution is usually represented in a Gantt chart (Fig. 1).

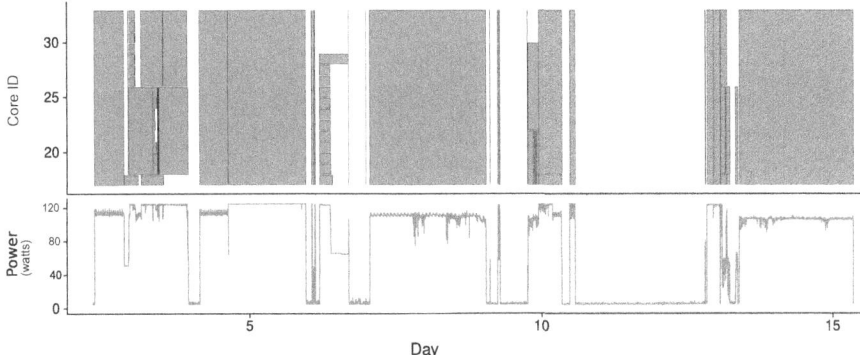

Fig. 1. The two sources of data used in a single, 32-core processor example: (top) data coming from the RJMS regarding the jobs' execution and allocation (processing time *versus* cores allocated), and (bottom) data coming from a power monitoring tool of the computing node (power *versus* time).

RJMS needs even more information when scheduling jobs under power capping. It needs at least a power profile which will serve as a power constraint over a certain time window. Recent HPC platforms are deployed with energy consumption monitoring tools such as IPMI [8], wattmeters, or software modules (often using RAPL [14]). Such an energy monitoring tool can provide power consumption data at the computing node level, as a time series of the power consumption of the computing node in function of time (bottom graph in Fig. 1).

We can cross the RJMS's jobs data with the computing nodes' power monitoring data to get an idea about the power consumption of the jobs. In the case of jobs that share a same computing node (stacked rectangles in Fig. 1), the resulting power consumption is in function of each of the jobs' energy consumption plus potential interference between the jobs, which makes it hard to distinguish each of the jobs' contribution to the power consumption of the node.

---

[1] The term homogeneous in this paper means that all computing nodes have the same CPU/accelerators configuration.

When taking into account jobs that had exclusive access to computing nodes, however, we can identify a power consumption profile of the jobs. The exact jobs' power profile can only be known after the jobs' execution.

In this work we focus on exploiting the jobs' power consumption profiles to perform better scheduling under power constraints *in the simplest way possible*. We choose simplicity because (i) sophisticated methods often leads to heavy-weight computations whose power consumption can reduce or at some point nullify the power savings from better scheduling, and (ii) sophisticated methods are often hard to explain/justify which hinders their deployment in practice [11].

More specifically, we focus on the following research questions:

1. Which **simple piece of information** regarding the jobs' power profile contribute to better scheduling under power constraints?
2. How to predict this simple piece of information **before the jobs' execution**? How much prediction accuracy can we achieve?

We consider as simple piece of information (hereafter referred to as jobs' power consumption for simplicity) the **mean** and **maximum** metrics of the jobs' power consumption profile. We decide to study the mean and the maximum because these two metrics can have different impacts in the scheduling with power constraints. We uncover these impacts in Sect. 6.5.

4 Predicting the Power Consumption of HPC Jobs

For each job, the RJMS follows the same algorithm before the job's execution: (i) read all the meta-data of the job (including the user's id); (ii) predict the mean and max power consumption of the job; (iii) provide the job to the scheduler along with power information. The RJMS also has access to past measures, including meta-data and power consumption of past jobs.

We propose two job power prediction methods with an increasing level of complexity to predict the jobs power consumption: the first method uses the power consumption of previous users' jobs (users' job history). The second method uses previous jobs' power consumption data and jobs metadata (Table 1) with Machine Learning (ML) regression methods.

4.1 The First Method: Predicting Power Consumption with Users' Jobs History.

For a job j of a given user and a sliding window size s in seconds, we predict the power consumption of the job $\hat{P}_j$ as follows,

$$\hat{P}_j = \frac{\sum_{j' \in W} \theta_{j'} P_{j'}}{\sum_{j' \in W} \theta_{j'}} \qquad (1)$$

$$W = \{j' \mid r_j \geq C_{j'} \geq (r_j - s)\} \qquad (2)$$

$$\theta_{j'} = \left(1 - \left(\frac{r_j - C_{j'}}{s}\right)\right)^{\alpha} \tag{3}$$

where $C_{j'}$ is the completion time of a previously executed job j' of same user who submitted j, and $P_{j'}$ is the measured mean power of j'. The power consumption of a previous job $P_{j'}$ can be known at the time we predict $\hat{P}_j$ since $C_{j'} \leq r_j$.

Equation 1 is a weighted average of previous jobs j' of the user that finished within a sliding time window with size s (Eq. 2). We assign the weight $\theta_{j'}$ (Eq. 3) in function of how long in the past j' finished compared to the arrival time of j. A value of $\theta_{j'} = 0$ means that j' finished at the oldest allowed date, and $\theta_{j'} = 1$ means that the j' finished exactly at the arrival time of j. The parameter α changes the way we penalize older jobs by changing the $\theta_{j'}$ behavior between 0 and 1, from a linear $\alpha = 1$, to a super-linear $\alpha = 2$ or sub-linear $\alpha = 0.5$ fashion.

In this paper, we considered the *max* and the *mean* power consumption as we assume that both metrics have different effects when used for performing scheduling decisions. These effects are explored in more detail in Sect. 6.5.

4.2 The Second Method: Predicting Using Supervised Regression

The former prediction method can not harness the jobs' metadata (e.g., requested resources, submission time, expected processing time, etc.) to potentially provide better predictions. We can circumvent this problem by using supervised regression with the hypothesis of increasing the prediction accuracy, using the jobs' metadata and the power consumption history as input features.

We propose an online learning method to predict the jobs' power consumption. The method retrains the prediction models at periodic time intervals (e.g., at the end of each week) in order to adapt, as the jobs' history increases and changes. In this context, online still refers to the behavior of the RJMS using all past data, and only meta-data of the arriving jobs. For an *already passed* week with index w (i.e., week 0, 1, 2, ...), let $t(w)$ be the timestamp of when the models will be retrained at the end of week w. Then, we define our job dataset $\mathbf{J}_{train}$ as follows.

$$\mathbf{J}_{train} = \{j \mid C_j < t(w)\} \tag{4}$$

In other words, $\mathbf{J}_{train}$ contains the jobs' history. Then, we train a predictor $\hat{f}(j)$ of the jobs' power consumption that minimizes the Mean Squared Error (MSE, Eq. 5).

$$MSE = \frac{1}{|\mathbf{J}_{train}|} \sum_{j \in \mathbf{J}_{train}} \left(P_j - \hat{f}(j)\right)^2 \tag{5}$$

After training a predictor $\hat{f}(j)$ we use it to predict the power consumption $\hat{P}_{j'}$ for all jobs $j' \in \mathbf{J}_{inference}$, where $\mathbf{J}_{inference}$ is defined as follows.

$$\mathbf{J}_{inference} = \{j' \mid t(w) \leq r_{j'} \leq t(w+1)\} \tag{6}$$

In other words, we use the jobs history to train a model at week w that already passed, and use this model to perform predictions of the power consumption of the jobs that will arrive online at week $w + 1$. At the end of week $w + 1$ (i.e., at timestamp $t(w + 1)$) the training procedure repeats, generating a new predictor $\hat{f}(j)$, which will be used for week $w+2$. A particular situation is for week $w = 0$, where there is no such dataset to train a regression model. In this case we can use $\hat{f}(j) = \hat{P}_j$ (Eq. 1). We present the choice of regression methods to train $\hat{f}(j)$, and how we exploit the jobs' data (i.e., the features of j) in Sect. 6.2.

5 Scheduling with Jobs' Power Profile Prediction

As the focus of this article is on the impact of power prediction, we will use a simple and classical EASY backfilling algorithm [12]. This algorithm is used in production in a large number of HPC centers. We assume that the platform is static: no failure of nodes nor new nodes during the experiment. We also assume that the servers will always be switched on. We finally assume there is no constraints on the applications related to the host they can run on. All these assumptions enable us to focus on the impact of the prediction framework, further studies on these hypotheses are kept as perspectives.

The implemented EASY uses a first-come first serve (FCFS) policy and works as follows. EASY is executed when these events occur: a new task arrives, a task finishes. Tasks are stored in a queue in their order of arrival—the order of this queue will never be changed. EASY starts the oldest jobs in the queue until either finishing the queue or arriving on a job (called high-priority job) that cannot start due to lack of resources. In the later case, EASY will try to *backfill* jobs, that is to say start remaining task right now if they do not impact the high-priority job estimated starting time.

The only modification we have made to the classical EASY is how to check whether resources are available. Classical EASY only checks whether there are enough available nodes/cores. Here, our implementation named EASY+PC also checks whether there is enough power w.r.t. a given power cap. We assume that an estimator (such as the ones we propose) can estimate the power needed for a job. Based on this estimator, EASY+PC estimates the currently used power and the requested power for each job in the queue. All of EASY+PC decisions are based solely on these estimations.

6 Results

6.1 Jobs' Power Prediction: Dataset Description

This work uses the trace collected from the Marconi100 supercomputer [4]. Marconi100 consisted of 980 computing nodes, each of which consisted of a two-socket IBM POWER9 AC922 (32 cores in total), and four NVIDIA Volta V100 GPUs. The trace contains jobs' meta-data such as jobs submission times, processing times, anonymized user ids, and node ids allocated to the jobs. It also contains data about the nodes' total power consumption, measured at each 20-second periods, using an IPMI module installed in the nodes.

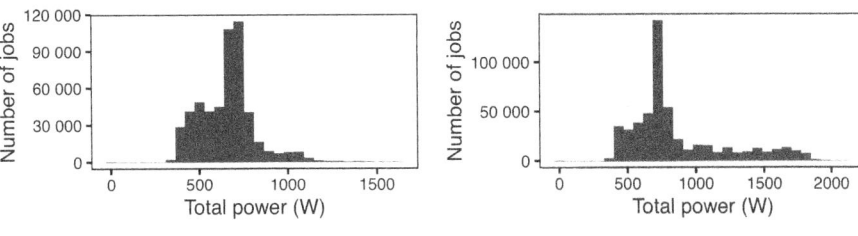

(a) Mean total power consumption (b) Max total power consumption

Fig. 2. Distributions of the actual mean and maximum power consumption of the filtered jobs in the Marconi100 trace.

From this trace we used the data regarding the operation of the Marconi100 from January 2022 to September 2022. To circumvent the limitation mentioned in Sect. 3, we filtered out the jobs that shared a node from the original trace. We also filtered out jobs that run in less than a minute because they have a too small number of power measurements. After this filtering we end up having a job dataset submissions from 576 users, accounting for 523,204 jobs.

Figure 2 shows the mean and max power consumption of the computing nodes for each of the jobs in the dataset. We can observe a peak density of jobs with mean and max consumption of around 700 W. This insight in itself could serve as a prediction if the whole distribution was clear and concentrated at around 700 W. However, the jobs distribution is not so clear for other power values, which justifies the need of more sophisticated prediction methods.

6.2 Jobs' Power Prediction: Experimental Setting

For the history based power prediction method (Sect. 4), we set the parameter α (Eq. 3) with a value of 2. This choice is based on the hypothesis that recent jobs have more importance than older jobs when predicting the power consumption. An $\alpha = 2$ puts more weight into recent jobs, and the weight decreases fast for older jobs. We set the sliding window size s to account for the whole user's job history, which translates to s being completion time of the first finished job of a user. We decided on this design to avoid eventual empty sliding windows during the prediction process. For the regression based power prediction method, we use the features presented in Table 1. Features 1 to 4 are standard job data that can be obtained at job submission, and features 5 to 7 are lagged features (i.e., a standard feature engineering technique), which can be obtained by using the user's job submission history.

We trained predictors $\hat{f}(j)$ using a selection of regression methods in the `scikit-learn` [17] library: (i) Linear Regression (`LinearRegression`), (ii) Random Forest (`RandomForestRegressor`), (iii) Support Vector Regression with Linear Kernel (`LinearSVR`), and (iv) Stochastic Gradient Descent Regression (`SGDRegressor`). For each training week and method, we applied

Table 1. Features used in the mean power consumption regression methods

Feature	Description
1	Submission time (hour of the day)
2	Number of processors (q_j)
3	Number of nodes
4	Requested processing time $\tilde{p}_j$
5	The sliding window history prediction $\hat{P}_j$ (Eq. 1)
6	Standard deviation $\sigma(\{P_{j'} \mid j' \in W\})$
7	The power consumption P_{j^*} where j^* is the last finished user job

scikit-learn's recursive feature elimination technique to choose the appropriate subset of features from Table 1 to use according to the training data. We perform this feature elimination and we set each of the regression methods hyper-parameters with a 5-fold cross validation scheme.

6.3 How to Predict Jobs' Power Information before the Jobs' Execution? How much prediction accuracy can we achieve?

Figure 3 shows the mean absolute percentage error (MAPE) of the methods used to predict the mean and the max jobs' power consumption. The boxplots represent the distribution of the prediction performance for each of the 576 users present in our job dataset. For the mean power consumption, we achieve a prediction MAPE from 0.115 (using jobs' history method, Sect. 4) to 0.128 (using linear regression, Sect. 4). This translates into a prediction accuracy of 88.5% and 87.2%, respectively. For predicting the maximum power consumption, we achieve a prediction MAPE from 0.195 (jobs' history method) to 0.215 (linear regression), which translates to a prediction accuracy of 80.5% and 78.5%, respectively. For both predicting the mean and the maximum power consumption, we can not clearly distinguish which prediction method is better. We can observe, however, that our jobs' history prediction method achieves equivalent prediction performance than the more sophisticated ML methods.

This is an important finding. Because we develop these prediction methods to reduce the energy consumption of operating supercomputers, we must reduce the energy consumption overhead induced by introducing these methods as much as possible. Achieving a high level of power prediction performance with the lowest level of energy consumption is therefore a priority. Although all of the regression methods used can be seen as lightweight when compared to neural network methods, a simple jobs' history based method is clearly much less energy demanding than a Machine Learning regression method, which requires much more processing steps (i.e., normalizing data, selecting the best features and finding the best hyper-parameters with cross-validation, etc.).

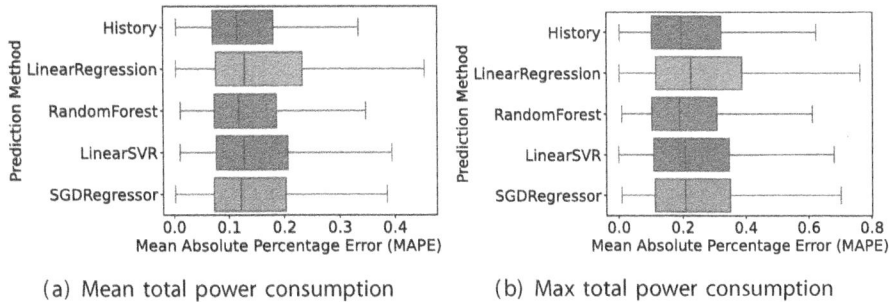

(a) Mean total power consumption   (b) Max total power consumption

Fig. 3. Mean Absolute Percentage Error of the mean and maximum power consumption prediction methods for the jobs in the Marconi100 trace.

6.4 Jobs Scheduling with Power Prediction: Experimental Setup

We simulate 30 different workloads using EASY+PC (Sect. 5) with various powercap values and with various job power predictors. Each workload consists of jobs taken from the filtered Marconi100 supercomputer dataset (Sect. 6.1). Jobs are selected following workload trace replay guidelines [10].

EASY+PC applies a power constraint solely during the first 3 h of each simulation. The powercap values we use range from 10% to 70% of the highest dynamic power consumption of the Marconi100 dataset in 2022 (955080 W).

We study EASY+PC's behavior depending on the information it uses to determine the power consumption of a job: (i) predicted mean and (ii) predicted max use the users' job history prediction method (Sect. 4.1), (iii) real mean and (iv) real max are the mean and max power consumption obtained from the workload dataset, and (v) naive uses the maximum reachable power consumption of a job (i.e., 2100 W * q_j, where 2100 W is the maximum single-node power value present in the Marconi100 dataset in 2022). naive is used as a baseline predictor to evaluate the accuracy of the other predictors proposed.

We use Batsim [9] and SimGrid [6] to perform the scheduling simulations, using a SimGrid representation of the whole 980-node of Marconi100. We use the schedule produced by the simulators plus the time-series data about the jobs' power consumption from the Marconi100 dataset to calculate the total power consumption. Taking into account the 30 workloads and the job power predictors, our experimental campaign consists of 1950 simulation instances. Additionally, each workload is executed on EASY (without powercap) to serve as baseline and evaluate both impacts on total power consumption and QoS.

6.5 Which Jobs' Power Information Contribute to Better Scheduling Under Power Constraints?

Figures 4 and 5 summarizes results of our simulation campaign (Sect. 6.4) by aggregating data from all workloads together. 1 workload has been excluded from Fig. 5 as powercapping greatly increases scheduling performance on it. Values

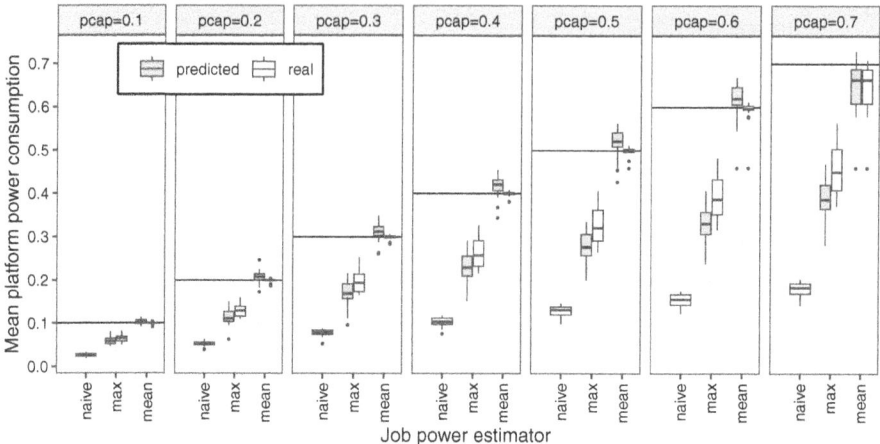

Fig. 4. Distribution of the platform power consumption during the powercap-constrained 3-hour time window. Powercap is the horizontal black line. All power values (y axis, facet powercap `pcap`) are expressed as a proportion of the maximum dynamic power range. Standard boxplots (Q_{1-3}, 1.5 IQR).

given in the remaining of this section are computed by (workload, powercap) group, and then averaged on all groups. They analyze (I) the extent to which each predictor is able to use the power at its disposal while powercap is active, and (II) how they degrade QoS performance (through turnaround time) compared to baseline EASY's.

Since `naive` considers the maximum achievable node power for the whole jobs' duration, EASY+PC is incapable of harnessing the power consumption fluctuations that occur during job execution to better use the available power. This incapability leads to a severe power under-utilization (74%), and a significant increase in the turnaround time (15%).

`max` provides better information about the maximum power consumption than `naive`, thus better harnessing the fluctuations. `max` still remains, however, as a "conservative" method which hypothesizes that the maximum value occurs all the time during the jobs' execution. Such hypothesis helps assuring that EASY+PC does not trespass the power cap (it never did, even when using our `max` prediction method), though this results in power under-utilization and increase in the turnaround time (respectively around 44% and 11%).

More "aggressive", `mean` hypothesizes that the mean power is the value that occurs most of the time during the jobs' execution. This hypothesis gives more flexibility to EASY+PC to harness the jobs' power fluctuations. The drawback is the increased risk of trespassing the powercap. In our experiments, the `mean` method is the one that makes the best use of the available power (3% power over-utilization) and the one that increases the turnaround time the least (6%). Using `mean` trespasses the powercap in most instances (95%) but the trespassing

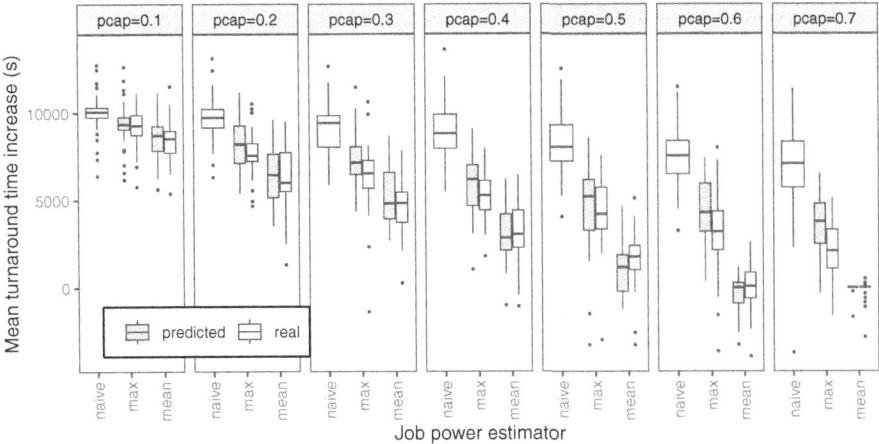

Fig. 5. Distribution of the performance degradation (compared to EASY) for 29/30 workloads. The turnaround time of a job is the amount of time the job spends in the system (from submission to finish). The workload mean turnaround time is the arithmetic mean all the jobs' turnaround time. Standard boxplots.

is small: the maximum instantaneous powercap break observed is in average and median 14% above the powercap.

Lastly, the prediction accuracy of the mean method (Sect. 6.3) results in satisfactory performances when compared to using real mean values. Please note that real values are baselines and cannot be obtained before the jobs' execution.

7 Conclusion

We presented in this paper two main contributions: a complete integrated environment from monitored data to the jobs execution and an evaluation of several jobs' power consumption prediction methods. In particular, we showed that "lightweight" (frugal) predictions used in the scheduling module lead to similar performance improvements, when compared to more costly and sophisticated predictions or compared to the optimal value. Simple history prediction method (such as mean) is sufficiently good to express the jobs' power profiles during scheduling, which fosters "lower-tech" scheduling algorithms.

The proposed approach focused on the capability to take into account these lightweight predictors for a classical and widely used EASY scheduling policy. From this positive experience on EASY, the next step is to investigate new scheduling policies harnessing the new information from the predictors, but also adding actual monitoring values to improve the quality of its decision. It would also be interesting to refine the jobs' model, to take into account phases of long duration applications. Using such information would help to improve the management of short duration jobs.

Acknowledgements and Artifact Availability. Experiments presented in this paper were carried out using the Grid'5000 testbed. This work was supported by the research program on Edge Intelligence of the Multi-disciplinary Institute on Artificial Intelligence MIAI at Grenoble Alpes (ANR-19-P3IA-0003), ENERGUMEN (ANR-18-CE25-0008), the France 2030 NumPEx Exa-SofT (ANR-22-EXNU-0003) and Cloud CareCloud (ANR-23-PECL-0003) projects managed by the French National Research Agency (ANR), REGALE (H2020-JTI-EuroHPC-2019-1 agreement n. 956560), and LIGHTAIDGE (HORIZON-MSCA-2022-PF-01 agreement n. 101107953). A CC-BY public copyright licence has been applied by the authors to the present document and will be applied to all subsequent versions up to the Author Accepted Manuscript arising from this submission, in accordance with the grants' open access conditions. We thank Salah Zrigui for starting the study on the job energy profiles. We also thank Francesco Antici for curating and sharing the Marconi100 dataset. The experiments described in this article have been made with open science and reproducibility concerns in mind. Code, data and documentation to reproduce our work is available on Zenodo [18].

References

1. Antici, F., Yamamoto, K., Domke, J., Kiziltan, Z.: Augmenting ml-based predictive modelling with NLP to forecast a job's power consumption. In: Proceedings of the SC'23 Workshops of The International Conference on High Performance Computing, Network, Storage, and Analysis, pp. 1820–1830 (2023)
2. Bates, N., et al.: Electrical grid and supercomputing centers: an investigative analysis of emerging opportunities and challenges. Informatik-Spektrum **38**(2), 111–127 (2015)
3. Borghesi, A., Bartolini, A., Lombardi, M., Milano, M., Benini, L.: Predictive modeling for job power consumption in HPC systems. In: Kunkel, J.M., Balaji, P., Dongarra, J. (eds.) ISC High Performance 2016. LNCS, vol. 9697, pp. 181–199. Springer, Cham (2016). https://doi.org/10.1007/978-3-319-41321-1_10
4. Borghesi, A., et al.: M100 ExaData: a data collection campaign on the CINECA's marconi100 tier-0 supercomputer. Sci. Data **10**(1), 288 (2023)
5. Bugbee, B., Phillips, C., Egan, H., Elmore, R., Gruchalla, K., Purkayastha, A.: Prediction and characterization of application power use in a high-performance computing environment. Stat. Anal. Data Mining ASA Data Sci. J. **10**(3), 155–165 (2017)
6. Casanova, H., Giersch, A., Legrand, A., Quinson, M., Suter, F.: Versatile, scalable, and accurate simulation of distributed applications and platforms. J. Parallel Distrib. Comput. **74**(10), 2899–2917 (2014)
7. Chasapis, D., Moretó, M., Schulz, M., Rountree, B., Valero, M., Casas, M.: Power efficient job scheduling by predicting the impact of processor manufacturing variability. In: Proceedings of the ACM International Conference on Supercomputing, pp. 296–307 (2019)
8. Da Costa, G., Pierson, J.M., Fontoura-Cupertino, L.: Mastering system and power measures for servers in datacenter. Sustain. Comput. Inform. Syst. **15**, 28–38 (2017). https://doi.org/10.1016/j.suscom.2017.05.003
9. Dutot, P.F., Mercier, M., Poquet, M., Richard, O.: Batsim: a realistic language-independent resources and jobs management systems simulator. In: 20th Workshop on Job Scheduling Strategies for Parallel Processing, Chicago, United States (2016). https://hal.science/hal-01333471

10. Emeras, J.: Workload Traces Analysis and Replay in Large Scale Distributed Systems. Theses, Université de Grenoble (2013)
11. Feitelson, D.G., Rudolph, L., Schwiegelshohn, U., Sevcik, K.C., Wong, P.: Theory and practice in parallel job scheduling. In: Feitelson, D.G., Rudolph, L. (eds.) JSSPP 1997. LNCS, vol. 1291, pp. 1–34. Springer, Heidelberg (1997). https://doi.org/10.1007/3-540-63574-2_14
12. Feitelson, D.G., Weil, A.M.: Utilization and predictability in scheduling the IBM SP2 with backfilling. In: Proceedings of the First Merged International Parallel Processing Symposium and Symposium on Parallel and Distributed Processing, pp. 542–546. IEEE (1998)
13. Gaussier, E., Glesser, D., Reis, V., Trystram, D.: Improving backfilling by using machine learning to predict running times. In: Proceedings of the International Conference for High Performance Computing, Networking, Storage and Analysis. SC 2015. Association for Computing Machinery, New York (2015)
14. Khan, K.N., Hirki, M., Niemi, T., Nurminen, J.K., Ou, Z.: RAPL in action: experiences in using RAPL for power measurements. ACM Trans. Model. Perform. Eval. Comput. Syst. **3**(2) (2018). https://doi.org/10.1145/3177754
15. Kocot, B., Czarnul, P., Proficz, J.: Energy-aware scheduling for high-performance computing systems: a survey. Energies **16**(2), 890 (2023)
16. Oak Ridge National Laboratory: Frontier's architecture (2023). https://olcf.ornl.gov/wp-content/uploads/Frontiers-Architecture-Frontier-Training-Series-final.pdf. Accessed 29 Nov 2023
17. Pedregosa, F., et al.: Scikit-learn: machine learning in Python. J. Mach. Learn. Res. **12**, 2825–2830 (2011)
18. Poquet, M., Carastan-Santos, D., Da Costa, G., Stolf, P., Trystram, D.: Artifact data of article "light-weight prediction for improving energy consumption in HPC platforms. Euro-Par 2024 (2024). https://doi.org/10.5281/zenodo.11173631
19. Saillant, T., Weill, J.-C., Mougeot, M.: Predicting job power consumption based on RJMS submission data in HPC systems. In: Sadayappan, P., Chamberlain, B.L., Juckeland, G., Ltaief, H. (eds.) ISC High Performance 2020. LNCS, vol. 12151, pp. 63–82. Springer, Cham (2020). https://doi.org/10.1007/978-3-030-50743-5_4
20. Shoukourian, H., Wilde, T., Auweter, A., Bode, A.: Predicting the energy and power consumption of strong and weak scaling HPC applications. Supercomput. Front. Innovations **1**(2), 20–41 (2014)
21. Storlie, C., Sexton, J., Pakin, S., Lang, M., Reich, B., Rust, W.: Modeling and predicting power consumption of high performance computing jobs (2015)
22. Wikipedia: 2021 Texas power crisis (2023). https://en.wikipedia.org/wiki/2021_Texas_power_crisis. Accessed 29 Nov 2023
23. Zrigui, S., de Camargo, R.Y., Legrand, A., Trystram, D.: Improving the performance of batch schedulers using online job runtime classification. J. Parallel Distrib. Comput. **164**, 83–95 (2022)

EKRM: Efficient Key-Value Retrieval Method to Reduce Data Lookup Overhead for Redis

Yiming Yao[1]($\boxtimes$), Xiaolin Wang[1], Diyu Zhou[1,2], Liujia Li[1], Jianyu Wu[1], Liren Zhu[1], Zhenlin Wang[3], and Yingwei Luo[1]

[1] National Key Laboratory for Multimedia Information Processing, School of Computer Science, Peking University, Beijing 100871, China
{yim,liujia_li}@stu.pku.edu.cn, {wxl,jywu2017,zhuliren,lyw}@pku.edu.cn, diyu.zhou@epfl.ch
[2] The Swiss Federal Institute of Technology in Lausanne, Lausanne, Switzerland
[3] Michigan Technological University, Houghton, USA
zlwang@mtu.edu

Abstract. As an open-source key-value system, Redis has been widely used in internet service stations. A key-value lookup in Redis usually involves several chained memory accesses, and the address translation overhead can significantly increase the lookup latency. This paper introduces a new software-based approach that can reduce chained memory accesses and total address translation overhead of lookup requests by placing key-value entries in a specially managed memory space organized as huge pages with a fast hash table and enabling a fast lookup approach with simple hash functions, while keeping the integrity of Redis data structure. The new approach brings up to 1.38× average speedup for the key-value retrieval process, and significantly reduces misses in TLB and last-level cache. It outperforms SLB, an address caching software approach and has match the performance to STLT, a software-hardware co-designed address-centric design.

Keywords: Key-Value store · Redis · Hash function · Translation lookaside buffer · Address translation · Chained memory access · Huge page

1 Introduction

The volume of data has experienced explosive growth in the past decade, and various applications have increasing demand for accessing large amounts of data with low latency. To address this challenge, in-memory key-value systems such as Redis [28], Memcached [29] have become an important layer in the client/server architecture.

Cloud services often rely on key-value store as a key infrastructure, because it enables a simple and flexible data model with high performance and scalability

[12–15]. Cloud service providers use Redis [30], Memcached [29], and their variants for various purposes in the production environments. For key-value store systems, the data are not only diverse in types and characteristics but also mainly stored in memory, which allows for faster access and lower latency than disk-based storage structures. These features, combined with high access volume, pose many different challenges for the design of key-value systems. As the most critical performance factor for key-value storage, maximizing the data retrieval speed is still the most important goal. The hash table is a critical part of typical key-value systems. To ensure the security and integrity of the data, the hash function must have a certain complexity to resist malicious attacks. Hash tables often use linked lists to solve collisions and have the problem of poor locality. Under a large number of key-value accesses, the hash table accesses can become an important performance bottleneck.

In typical key-value store applications, accessing a record in memory involves certain kinds of index and data structure traversal, which is a process composed of multiple address translations. Before actually accessing the record associated with a key, the hash function needs to convert the key to an integer, then the index data structure needs to convert the integer to the virtual address of the target record, and then *Memory Management Unit*(MMU) tries to convert the virtual address to the physical address of the record through *Translation Lookaside Buffer* (TLB). A TLB miss will lead to expensive *Page Table Walk* (PTW). This process is shown in Fig. 1.

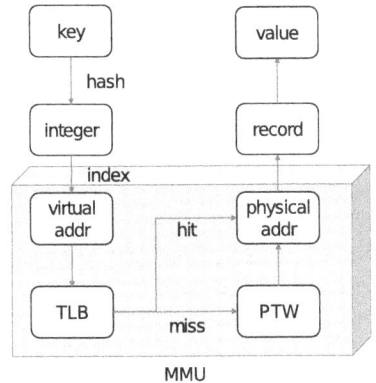

Fig. 1. The process of data retrieval of a key-value system

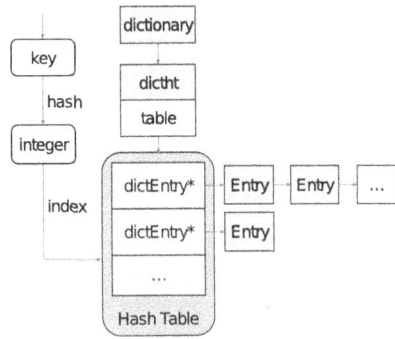

Fig. 2. The process of data retrieval in Redis dictionary

Redis uses ziplist or dictionary for key-value store. Ziplist is for small amounts of data storage. In the Redis dictionary, the value is retrieved from the key by the following steps shown in Fig. 2. First, the key is mapped to the hash table of the dictionary by a hash function, and the hash table stores pointers to key-value entries that are the virtual addresses. The virtual address is converted to the physical address by the TLB, and then the value entry is obtained from memory by the physical address. These steps are repeated for each memory access, causing large address translastion overhead. Due to the high data volume demand for key-value stores, a key-value system actually requires a TLB that is much larger than the hardware can offer to reach a sufficient TLB hit ratio, and if a TLB miss occurs in address translation, the system needs to perform PTW to obtain the page table entry, which means additional overhead. Research work [2] has shown that the overhead from address translation and key finding could account for more than 50% in data retrieval.

Our optimization focuses on the process of key-value retrieval. This paper develops a software solution, EKRM that can reduce chained memory accesses and TLB misses, while being simple to be implemented in Redis and also compatible with many other methods. The main contribution of the paper is that, EKRM significantly accelerate data retrieval in Redis by reducing total addressing translation and memory access overhead. It surpasses the address caching method SLB [4] and achieves performance comparable to the software-hardware co-designed address-centric approach STLT [2].

2 Related Work

Key-value store efficiency has been studied in depth in the past decades. It is widely used to accelerate lookup in hash table by software and hardware in previous work. The idea of hardware-based caching addresses has been widely used in key-value stores to get the physical address of the data in a more efficient way. SDC [8] is a high-performance software-defined cache which uses a part of the space in last level cache to assist the lookup, enabling programs to use cache as a look-aside key-value buffer. HTA [10] is a software-hardware co-designed method that creates a cache for hash table, which is cache-friendly and can serve most of the hash lookup work by hardware. The limitations of these methods are that the record size are limited and the main reliance on hardware cache creates the tension between the capacity and cost.

SLB [4] uses a software cache that stores the addresses of recently accessed records. It has demonstrated promising performance but requires much more storage and needs a trade-off between the capacity and cost. STLT [2] was proposed based on the concept of address-centric approach. It reduces address translation overhead and enhances TLB's performance as address translation accounts for a large part of the total time spent on a key-value lookup. STLT is a kind of look-aside buffer that bypasses the index, while it places the index, virtual address, and page table entries in the cache instead of the value. It can bring up to 1.4 times acceleration on Redis in a simulation experiment, but needs hardware support to be fully implemented in a real environment. This paper also proposes a scheme that can reduce total address translation overhead, but uses a relatively low-cost approach by software.

Besides, there are some typical relevant solutions that accelerate data retrieval in key-value store. pRedis [6] is an improved scheme for cache replacement algorithm in key-value store, which mainly solves the problem that traditional cache replacement algorithm cannot balance locality and miss penalty by a new approach to evaluate the miss penalty of each access. Cavast [7] uses the characteristic of pages in modern operating systems to place data in appropriate positions of cache, thereby reducing the eviction of frequently accessed keys. WIDX [9] is a unit specially designed for hash tables, consisting of a hash calculation unit and a walker, which can reduce the overhead from the main hash table.

3 Motivation

In Sect. 1, we introduced the main optimization difficulties and bottlenecks of the current key-value system and some existing optimization schemes. We summarize the most important issues as follows. First, hash tables with linked lists have the characteristics of poor locality. Under a large number of key-value accesses, hash table access has become an important performance bottleneck. Second, the virtual address to physical address conversion overhead resulting from Redis multiple chained memory accesses accounts for a large part of the data retrieval process. We use the following experiment to illustrates this issue. We divided the cost of data retrieval into the three following parts: the cost of address translation and memory access related to hash tables and entries, the cost of key hash and compare to find the corresponding entry, and other cost like data maintenance to finish a single command. We record the ratio of the cumulative total time from key to value to the total execution time of these commands. The results are collected using 0.1 to 1000 million of distinct keys and $10\times$ GET operations generated by YCSB. The overhead of the previous two parts increases from 49.6% to 63.1% and among which the overhead of address translation and memory access related to hash tables and entries increases from 34.5% to 52.3% as shown in Fig. 3. As the number of stored keys grows, address translation and memory access overhead related to the hash table and entries can become the bottleneck. This cost is impacted by the design of Redis as we mentioned above.

In Sect. 2, we introduced some typical methods to accelerate data retrieval in a key-value store. Based on the experiment above, we focus on optimizing the hash table and related parts in Redis dictionary to reduce the overhead of address translation and memory access, as optimizing this part is of great significance to the acceleration of the data retrieval in Redis. Our idea is to better organize the hash table entries indexed by hash functions, so that Redis can find the corresponding entry of a key faster. The general idea is to create a specially managed memory space to hold key-value entries. This space is divided into two parts and the first part is used as a hash table which can be directly indexed by some simple hash functions. The second part is for handling hash collisions. If we can find the entry corresponding to the key indexed by a hash function, there will be no need for executing the original lookup method. The original data structure of Redis is still unchanged, therefore the lookup methods in Redis dictionary still works, keeping the integrity of the Redis data structure. The advantage of this design is that, first, it can reduce the access frequency of the original hash table because a large part of the entries can be directly found

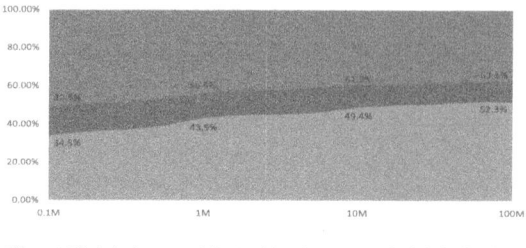

Fig. 3. Breakdown of the execution time of Redis. The results were collected using different numbers from 0.1 million to 100 million of distinct keys and 10× GET operations generated by YCSB. We use Unix domain socket to transmit data and do not count network transmission overhead.

in the first part of the space, second, these new hash functions map the keys to a continuous address space for holding entries, and third, our design can be regard as a bypass approach for a regular value request, retaining the ability to resist potential hash attacks.

When Redis manages a huge number of key-value pairs, finding entries within regular-page memory could result in large address translation overhead. To further reduce TLB misses and total translation overhead, we consider using huge pages specially for the memory space mentioned above.

4 EKRM Design

This section presents the detail design of EKRM to accelerate key-value lookup operations.

4.1 Design Overview

To reduce the occurrences of hash function collisions and resist hash attacks, Redis usually uses relatively complex functions like *SipHash* or *MurmurHash*, and uses a chaining method to solve hash collisions. Therefore, it often takes multiple address accesses to find the required entry from the key, resulting in a large latency.

To be compatible with the original design of Redis, EKRM's scheme is as follows. EKRM stores the entries of the dictionary within a continuous address space of huge pages, and these entries are indexed by fast hash functions with lower computational complexity, which mainly perform simple bitwise operations on the key. When inserting key-value pairs, EKRM prefers to allocate the entry in the position indexed by the fast hash functions. If a hash collision happens and can not be resolved, the entry will be placed in the second part of the huge page space. The second part is managed by a free list in which one available position is linked to the next, and EKRM can allocate an available position dynamically. It is feasible to allocate memory for the second part when the space is not enough to hold entries. When the hash collision ratio is not high, most of the entries can be quickly indexed by a fast function in the first part, which reduces the number of memory accesses in the key-value query process. To increase the hit ratio of the fast lookup approach, EKRM uses two fast hash functions $H1$ and $H2$ that work like Cuckoo hashing [11]. Besides, there is extra space to store metadata in the design of the Redis entry data structure, so several databases in Redis can share the fast hash table by marking their serial numbers in entries.

4.2 EKRM Operations

EKRM supports INSERT, GET, and DELETE operations.

INSERT. The operation attempts to insert a new key-value pair into Redis and the *key* should not be in any existing entries. If the position in fast hash table indexed by any fast hash function $H1$ or $H2$ is available, a new entry of the key-value pair will be placed into the corresponding position, otherwise EKRM will work like Cuckoo hashing and attempts to move the entry of *key2* that occupies index $H1(key)$ to position $H2(key2)$ or $H1(key2)$. In order to control the overhead, at most one entry in fast hash table is allowed to migrate in an INSERT operation. When all the above attempts fail, the entry will be placed into the second part of the space. After the position of the entry is determined, EKRM still needs to execute the original insertion process to maintain the original hash table and linked lists in Redis. If an entry in the fast hash table is moved, its relevant information in Redis dictionary should be updated.

GET. The operation attempts to look up the corresponding value to the given key. If any of the two hash functions in the fast hash table indexes the corresponding entry to the key, the operation is successful, otherwise, the original lookup approach of Redis will be used. In this operation, the fast lookup method does not conflict with the original one and can be regarded as a bypass approach.

This process is illustrated in Fig. 4 and an example is shown. The entries in the fast hash table in Fig. 4 can be directly indexed by the fast hash functions $H1$ and $H2$, and the entries in the second part can only be accessed by the linked lists from the original Redis hash table. In the hash table directed by fast hash functions, a hash line contains one 32-byte entry. For example, if the key-value pair is *Bob:002*, there will be two lookup approaches. By fast hash function $H2$ in Fig. 4, we get index 1 and find the corresponding entry in the table line, or by calculating Redis hash function, we get index 1 and find the entry through a linked list from *Alice* to *Bob*. The fast lookup approach is prioritized.

DELETE. The operation attempts to delete a key-value pair in Redis. EKRM finds the entry and marks its position as available, and updates the free list if necessary. The Redis structure will also be updated according to the original method.

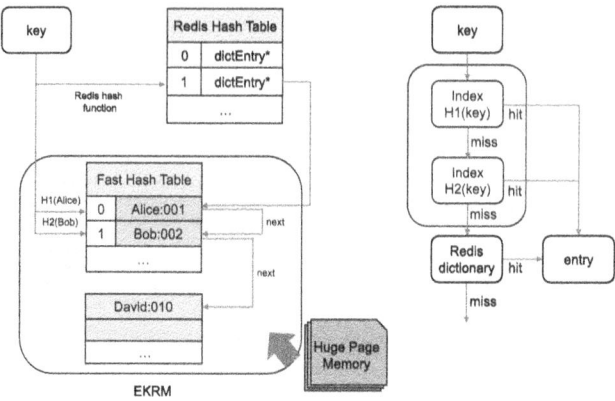

Fig. 4. The process of data retrieval in EKRM

4.3 Other Supports

Linux operating system supports allocating 2MB and 1GB huge pages, and we set */proc/sys/vm/nr_hugepages* to control the usage of huge pages. Note that we do not use transparent huge pages. In the code implementation, we use the *mmap()* function to map a memory space to the allocated huge pages. Before starting Redis, we need to estimate the working set size, and allocate suitable memory of huge pages and divide it into two reasonably sized regions. The probability of success lookup by fast hash functions can be increased at the cost of additional memory overhead.

Redis generally does not recommend using huge pages to take advantage of the Copy-on-Write (CoW) mechanism of forked processes to achieve persistent storage and data security in the *Redis Database* (RDB) and *Append Only File* (AOF) functions [28]. In addition to the time-consuming page table copying, some study shows that there will also be additional delays caused by the usage of huge pages [16,17]. Note that we only allocate huge page memory specifically for storing key-value entries. To address these problems, we set the address space that organizes as huge pages to be Copy-on-Write free, to avoid the extra overhead caused by a large number of huge pages after Redis forks a sub-process. We record a backup of the huge page space, and start recording the latest updates that occur in the memory space after the RDB sub-process is created, and delete the records after the sub-process finishes. Generally, these changes do not have much impact on performance in our tests.

5 Evaluation

In this section, we evaluate the performance of the proposed EKRM on different workload distributions of Redis and provide speedup analysis, sensitivity studies on the design, and discuss some special cases.

5.1 System Configurations

We perform our experiment in a 64-bit X86-64 system shown in Table 1. The L1d TLB for general 2M pages is 4-way, 32 entries and for 4K pages is 4-way, 64 entries. The L2 shared TLB for 4K and 2M pages is 6-way, 1536 entries.

Table 1. System Configurations

Component	Parameter
ISA	64-bit X86-64
CPU	16 core, Intel Xeon Silver 4216 CPU @ 2.10GHz
L1d TLB	2M/4M pages: 4-way, 32 entries 1G pages: 4-way, 4 entries 4K pages: 4-way, 64 entries
L2 TLB	4K/2M pages: 6-way, 1536 entries
L1d Cache	512KB
L2 Cache	16MB
L3 Cache	22MB

5.2 Benchmarks and Datasets

Zipfian distribution was observed in most database workloads by Cooper et al. [3], who proposed the *Yahoo! Cloud Serving Benchmark* (YCSB) based on it. The same distribution was confirmed for key-value stores in production environments by other studies [18–20]. Spatial locality in key-value store was reported by recent studies [21,22].

Considering that the keys to be looked up in the real world often have a certain distribution pattern, we set the search or update frequency of different keys to have a Zipfian, Uniform, or Latest distribution, among which Zipfian distribution has an alpha value of 0.99, and Latest distribution data satisfies that the data inserted recently is more likely to be accessed. We use YCSB for generating data and set 5% of requests as UPDATE operations and the others as GET operations. ETC is the closest workload to a general-purpose one, with the highest miss ratio of more than 19% in all Facebook's Memcached pools [25]. We export the data stream generated by mutilate [31] and run it on our Redis testing program. These workloads have 10 million keys and 100 million key accesses. The size of the keys is set to 24 bytes.

Data retrieval efficiency is an essential part that influences performance of Redis. As we have discussed in Sect. 3, our optimization work accounts for a large portion of the total execution time excluding network overhead, we exclude other components of Redis in our measurement, including data fetching, data validation, conversions between input/output commands, and their internal representations and other possible overhead. Those components are not the target of EKRM, but the focus of other complementary techniques. We intend not to consider the overhead of network communication and other data maintenance work within Redis, in order to focus on the overhead of data retrieval in Redis. In our testing program, we repeatedly execute the functions of data retrieval or modification for each requested key in the Redis program in a loop and record the total time usage.

We use *Siphash* as the default hash function for Redis. In three YCSB workloads, the tests are divided into two phases. The first phase contains *SET* operations that insert data into Redis, and the second phase performs search or update operations including *GET* and *SET*. We first run YCSB on the general redis-server, and then export the testing traces from the database.

5.3 Speedup on Redis

In the following experiment, we set the memory usage of 2 MB huge pages as 1 to 8 times of the total size of the entries and set the size of the second part of as 1/4 of the first part. A comparative method to EKRM is SLB, the software-implemented address caching method introduced in Sect. 2. We use the original Redis program as the baseline and measure the speedup effect of both methods.

The speedups are shown in Fig. 5. The memory usage of SLB refers to the extra memory for address caching besides the origin memory to store entries, while EKRM places these entries in a special memory space. On average, EKRM brings up to 1.38× average speedups while SLB only brings 1.16× average speedups with 8× memory usage of the total size of the entries on these workloads. EKRM also shows a significant advantage against SLB with different sizes of memory usage. Choosing the memory usage as about 2× of all entries' size is a relatively suitable option for EKRM, as the speedup has obvious improvement compared to the size of 1×, while further increasing it will reduce the sensitivity. The results show that EKRM consistently outperforms SLB in our workloads substantially and can run without extra memory demands.

We also compare the performance of EKRM with STLT using SniperSim [26] simulating the 64-bit X86, Gainestown architecture. The datasets and testing program are the same as above. As is shown in Fig. 6, STLT can brings 1.38× speedups on average to Redis and EKRM brings 1.31× speedups on average when using 2× memory of the total entries size. Our software-implemented method can match the performance of hardware-supported STLT.

Speedup Analysis. We record a hit when the entry is successfully indexed by either of the fast hash functions and record a miss when both of them fail. We measure dTLB and last-level cache (LLC) misses by Linux perf [27], which is a useful tool for performance analysis. The results are compared to the original Redis version.

The speedup of EKRM for address translation and memory access is the result of the combination of dTLB miss reduction and cache miss reduction.

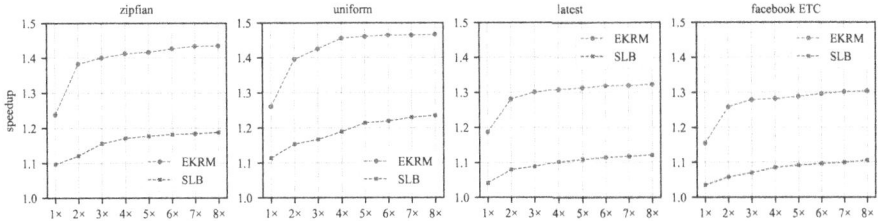

Fig. 5. The speedup of EKRM and SLB in workloads of different memory usage from 1× to 8× of the total entries size

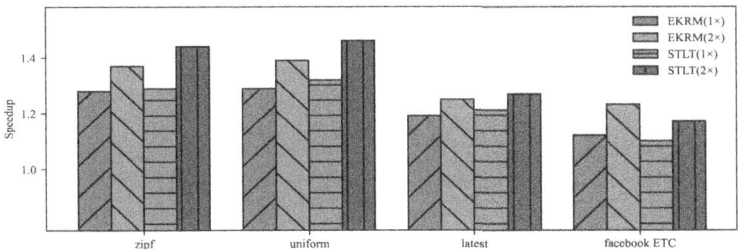

Fig. 6. The speedup of EKRM and STLT of 1× and 2× memory usage in workloads

Figure 7 shows the average hit ratio by fast hash functions and the average dTLB miss reduction on workload in Sect. 5.2. EKRM has a significant effect on reducing dTLB misses in the four workloads. The average number of dTLB misses declines by 52%. For data randomly generated in the key space of three YCSB distributions, the average hit ratio of the fast hash functions can reach about 90% with huge page memory usage of 2× size of the total inserted entries. EKRM has a relatively lower hit ratio on ETC workload due to compulsory misses.

EKRM has the highest speedup on the workload of Uniform distribution, while has the lowest speedup on the workload of Latest distribution in 3 YCSB workloads. Among the three distributions, Latest has the best data locality, Zipf modest, and Uniform the worst, so the original Redis program performs the best on the workload of Latest distribution and performs the worst on the workload of Uniform distribution. The dTLB reduction by EKRM also shows that the original Redis program suffers from the most severe dTLB misses on the workload of Uniform distribution and the least in Latest distribution. Additionally, the query requests under the Latest distribution are more often related to the data that have been inserted recently, and these data have a lower probability of being hit by the fast hash functions compared to the earlier data due to possible hash collision, while retrieving these data by the original Redis approach is less likely to suffer from dTLB miss and cache miss. The decline of the hit ratio by the fast hash functions on the workload of Latest distribution in Fig. 7 shows this problem. The worse the locality of the workload in these distributions, the

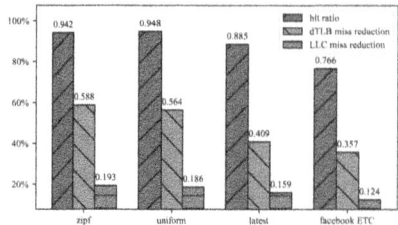 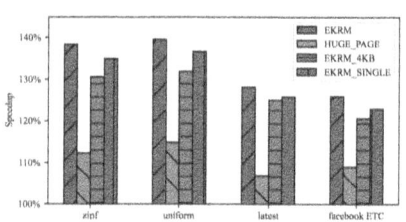

Fig. 7. The hit ratio, dTLB miss reduction and LLC miss reduction of EKRM with huge page memory usage of 2× size of the total inserted entries

Fig. 8. Speedup for different EKRM configurations

more advantage EKRM has over the original Redis. Speedup on facebook ETC workload is the worst, as it has the lowest hit ratio caused by compulsory misses [25], and this means EKRM has to perform more original lookups, leading to more dTLB misses and LLC misses.

Breakdown of Speedup. We conduct an ablation study for EKRM by configuring it in different ways. Figure 8 shows their speedups over original Redis.

HUGE_PAGE is the configuration that only uses huge page memory to store entries and does not enable fast lookup approach. EKRM_4KB allocates 4KB size pages for the fast hash table and otherwise works the same as EKRM. EKRM_SINGLE uses only a single fast hash function. The main contribution of speedup comes from the fast lookup. EKRM_4KB without usage of huge pages still shows obvious speedup over original Redis.

5.4 Case Studies

Parallel Optimization in Situation of High Miss Ratio. In Sect. 5.3, our experiment shows that although our fast lookup method can speed up key-value lookup in most cases, it may increase the overhead in the situation of a high miss ratio. One solution is that when EKRM detects that the miss ratio of keys is significantly high, it prioritizes the original lookup method of Redis to some extent. The effectiveness of this feature depends on how frequently we monitor and how aggressively we adjust.

Since our fast lookup approach and the original approach are independent and our design can be regarded as a bypass solution, using parallel optimization can be an effective way. Two threads are dispatched to execute the fast lookup and Redis hash, respectively, and once one thread successfully finds the entry, the other task is terminated. If the overhead by synchronization is low enough, parallel optimization will work effectively in situations of high miss ratio. To reduce the overhead of synchronization between threads, establishing a low-cost communication mechanism based on hardware is a possible solution.

We use instruction-level synchronization based on register renaming dependency to implement the optimization in the Gem5 simulator [32], and our parallel version shows 10% performance improvement compared to the sequential version when the miss ratio is higher than 30%. Therefore, EKRM can be potentially accelerated by parallel lookups.

Numbers of Entries of an Index. We study the speedup of using different numbers of entries of an index in EKRM. The speedup is almost the same when using 1 or 2 entries by an index, and decreases when using more. Using 2 entries can increase the hit ratio in the fast hash table while increasing dTLB misses and LLC misses, which is mainly caused by extra key comparison.

Memory Usage. EKRM requires additional memory for a larger index table to increase the hit ratio of fast hash functions. In our implementation, it is required to allocate the huge page memory space in advance with an estimate of the size of the working set. By adding a rehash method which has been implemented in Redis, the size of our index table can be also adjustable but it brings up more overhead.

In our design, EKRM is suitable for accelerating data retrieval when memory is relatively abundant and the size of the working set is relatively stable. When allocated with an appropriate size of memory and with a relatively stable size of the working set, EKRM has little chance of suffering from fragmentation. When the memory is insufficient, Redis will start the elimination strategy and EKRM can consider replacing entries in the fast hash table that are seldom accessed.

6 Conclusion and Future Work

This paper presents a new method to accelerate key-value lookup in Redis. It specially focuses on reducing chained memory access and data addressing overhead, utilizing an efficient lookup method using fast hash functions. The new solution places the entries of key-value records into a continuous address space organized as huge pages and enables most of them to be quickly indexed. The new method reduces TLB miss in the lookup process and preserves the integrity of Redis, and addresses the CoW and fragmentation problems caused by the usage of huge pages in some ways. Experiments on various request distributions show that it brings up to $1.38\times$ speedups on the key-value retrieval process for a set of Redis workloads.

For future work, EKRM can be explored to work in parallel by a mechanism with less synchronization overhead. Accelerating EKRM with a mechanism like direct segment [5] instead of huge page is possible to further lower the address translation overhead. Additionally, bypassing infrequently accessed entries in last-level-cache [23,24] is a possible approach.

Acknowledgments. The research is supported in part by the National Key R&D Program of China under Grant No. 2022YFB4500701, and by the National Science Foundation of China (Nos. 62032001, 62032008, 62372011).

References

1. Kwon, M., Lee, S., Choi, H., Hwang, J., Jung, M.: Realizing strong determinism contract on log-structured merge key-value stores. ACM Trans. Storage **19**, 1–29 (2023). https://doi.org/10.1145/3582695
2. Ye, C., Xu, Y., Shen, X., Liao, X., Jin, H., Solihin, Y.: Hardware-based address-centric acceleration of key-value store. In: 2021 IEEE International Symposium On High-Performance Computer Architecture (HPCA), pp. 736–748 (2021)
3. Cooper, B., Silberstein, A., Tam, E., Ramakrishnan, R., Sears, R.: Benchmarking Cloud Serving Systems with YCSB. Association for Computing Machinery (2010). https://doi.org/10.1145/1807128.1807152
4. Wu, X., Ni, F., Jiang, S.: Search lookaside buffer: efficient caching for index data structures. In: Proceedings of the 2017 Symposium on Cloud Computing, pp. 27–39 (2017). https://doi.org/10.1145/3127479.3127483
5. Basu, A., Gandhi, J., Chang, J., Hill, M., Swift, M.: Efficient virtual memory for big memory servers. In: Proceedings of the 40th Annual International Symposium on Computer Architecture, pp. 237–248 (2013). https://doi.org/10.1145/2485922.2485943
6. Pan, C., Luo, Y., Wang, X., Wang, Z.: PRedis: penalty and locality aware memory allocation in redis. In: Proceedings of the ACM Symposium on Cloud Computing, pp. 193–205 (2019). https://doi.org/10.1145/3357223.3362729
7. Wang, K., Liu, J., Chen, F.: Put an elephant into a fridge: optimizing cache efficiency for in-memory key-value stores. Proc. VLDB Endow. **13**, 1540–1554 (2020). https://doi.org/10.14778/3397230.3397247
8. Ni, F., Jiang, S., Jiang, H., Huang, J., Wu, X.: SDC: a software defined cache for efficient data indexing. In: Proceedings of the ACM International Conference on Supercomputing, pp. 82–93 (2019). https://doi.org/10.1145/3330345.3330353
9. Kocberber, O., Grot, B., Picorel, J., Falsafi, B., Lim, K., Ranganathan, P.: Meet the Walkers: Accelerating Index Traversals for in-Memory Databases. Association for Computing Machinery (2013). https://doi.org/10.1145/2540708.2540748
10. Zhang, G., Sanchez, D.: Leveraging caches to accelerate hash tables and memoization. In: Proceedings of the 52nd Annual IEEE/ACM International Symposium on Microarchitecture, pp. 440–452 (2019). https://doi.org/10.1145/3352460.3358272
11. Pagh, R., Rodler, F.: Cuckoo hashing. J. Algorithms **51**, 122–144 (2004). https://www.sciencedirect.com/science/article/pii/S0196677403001925
12. Lepers, B., Balmau, O., Gupta, K., Zwaenepoel, W.: KVell: the design and implementation of a fast persistent key-value store. In: Proceedings of the 27th ACM Symposium on Operating Systems Principles, pp. 447–461 (2019). https://doi.org/10.1145/3341301.3359628
13. Zhang, K., Hu, J., He, B., Hua, B.: DIDO: dynamic pipelines for in-memory key-value stores on coupled CPU-GPU architectures. In: 2017 IEEE 33rd International Conference on Data Engineering (ICDE), pp. 671–682 (2017)
14. Kaiyrakhmet, O., Lee, S., Nam, B., Noh, S., Choi, Y.: {SLM-DB}: {Single-Level} {Key-Value} store with persistent memory. In: 17th USENIX Conference on File and Storage Technologies (FAST 2019), pp. 191–205 (2019)
15. Zhang, T., et al.: FPGA-accelerated compactions for {LSM-based}{Key-Value} store. In: 18th USENIX Conference on File and Storage Technologies (FAST 2020), pp. 225–237 (2020)
16. Liu, H., Liu, R., Liao, X., Jin, H., He, B., Zhang, Y.: Object-level memory allocation and migration in hybrid memory systems. IEEE Trans. Comput. **69**, 1401–1413 (2020)

17. Heo, T., Wang, Y., Cui, W., Huh, J., Zhang, L.: Adaptive page migration policy with huge pages in tiered memory systems. IEEE Trans. Comput. **71**, 53–68 (2020)
18. Chen, J., et al.: {HotRing}: a {Hotspot-Aware}{In-Memory}{Key-Value} store. In: 18th USENIX Conference on File and Storage Technologies (FAST 2020), pp. 239–252 (2020)
19. Atikoglu, B., Xu, Y., Frachtenberg, E., Jiang, S., Paleczny, M.: Workload analysis of a large-scale key-value store. In: Proceedings of the 12th ACM SIGMETRICS/PERFORMANCE Joint International Conference on Measurement and Modeling of Computer Systems, pp. 53–64 (2012)
20. Wu, X., Zhang, L., Wang, Y., Ren, Y., Hack, M., Jiang, S.: Zexpander: a key-value cache with both high performance and fewer misses. In: Proceedings of the Eleventh European Conference on Computer Systems, pp. 1–15 (2016)
21. Cao, Z., Dong, S., Vemuri, S., Du, D.: Characterizing, modeling, and benchmarking {RocksDB}{Key-Value} workloads at Facebook. In: 18th USENIX Conference on File and Storage Technologies (FAST 2020), pp. 209–223 (2020)
22. Gilad, E., et al.: EvenDB: optimizing key-value storage for spatial locality. In: Proceedings of the Fifteenth European Conference on Computer Systems, pp. 1–16 (2020)
23. Gaur, J., Chaudhuri, M., Subramoney, S.: Bypass and insertion algorithms for exclusive last-level caches. In: Proceedings of the 38th Annual International Symposium on Computer Architecture, pp. 81–92 (2011)
24. Park, J., Park, Y., Mahlke, S.: A bypass first policy for energy-efficient last level caches. In: 2016 International Conference on Embedded Computer Systems: Architectures, Modeling and Simulation (SAMOS), pp. 63–70 (2016)
25. Atikoglu, B., Xu, Y., Frachtenberg, E., Jiang, S., Paleczny, M.: Workload analysis of a large-scale key-value store. SIGMETRICS Perform. Eval. Rev. **40**, 53–64 (2012). https://doi.org/10.1145/2318857.2254766
26. Carlson, T., Heirman, W., Eyerman, S., Hur, I., Eeckhout, L.: An evaluation of high-level mechanistic core models. ACM Trans. Archit. Code Optim. **11** (2014). https://doi.org/10.1145/2629677
27. Linux kernel. https://git.kernel.org/pub/scm/linux/kernel/git/torvalds/linux.git. Accessed 15 Mar 2024
28. Redis. https://redis.io/. Accessed 15 Mar 2024
29. Memcached. https://memcached.org/. Accessed 15 Mar 2024
30. Redis documentation. https://redis.io/docs/management/optimization/latency/. Accessed 15 Mar 2024
31. Mutilate. https://github.com/leverich/mutilate. Accessed 15 Mar 2024
32. Gem5. https://github.com/gem5/gem5. Accessed 15 Mar 2024

Automated Data Management and Learning-Based Scheduling for Ray-Based Hybrid HPC-Cloud Systems

Tingkai Liu[1], Huili Tao[1], Yicheng Lu[1], Zhongbo Zhu[1], Marquita Ellis[2], Sara Kokkila-Schumacher[2], and Volodymyr Kindratenko[1](✉)

[1] University of Illinois at Urbana-Champaign, 1205 W. Clark Street, Urbana, IL 61801, USA
{tingkai2,huilit2,yl53,zhongbo2,kindrtnk}@illinois.edu
[2] IBM Thomas J. Watson Research Center, 1101 Kitchawan Road, Yorktown Heights, NY 10598, USA
{m.ellis,saraks}@ibm.com

Abstract. HPC-Cloud hybrid systems are gaining popularity among scientists for their ability to manage sudden demand spikes, resulting in faster turnaround times for HPC workloads. However, deploying workloads on such systems currently requires complicated configurations, particularly for data migration across HPC clusters and Cloud. Additionally, existing schedulers lack support for workload scheduling on such hybrid systems. To address these issues, we have designed and implemented an HPC-Cloud bursting system based on Ray, an open-source distributed framework. Our system integrates automated data management with learning-based scheduling at the function level, using a dynamic label-based design. It automatically prefetches data files based on demand and detects data movement and execution patterns for future scheduling decisions. The developed framework is evaluated with two workloads: machine learning model training and image processing. We compare its performance against naive data fetching under various network speeds and storage locations. Results indicate the effectiveness of our system across all scenarios. The system is open-sourced and the source code and replication packages for reproducing experimental results are provided.

Keywords: Cloud bursting · HPC · Data movement · Scheduling

Replication package: github.com/HPC-cloud-burst-with-ray/paper-reproduce

1 Introduction

The integration of High-performance computing (HPC) clusters with Cloud resources has been attracting interest within the scientific community [12]. Traditional HPC infrastructure encounters inherent constraints due to its rigidity

---
H. Tao, Y. Lu and Z. Zhu—Equal Contribution.

and limited scalability. In response to these limitations, Cloud resources could facilitate the handling of smaller tasks that do not require the full power of an HPC system, while providing flexibility in managing spikes in computational demands and acting as an extension of HPC clusters to augment the requirements of high-throughput jobs.

The attractiveness of HPC-Cloud frameworks is amplified with the recent demand to train and run large-scale machine learning models such as large language models [4]. Recent research has demonstrated the feasibility of training models across multiple Cloud providers or hybrid HPC-Cloud environments even in the presence of limited network connectivity [5], further showing the potential of HPC-Cloud frameworks.

Besides developing new tools or extending existing ones within the HPC community, such as Slurm© [20] or Torque [18], recent efforts have been directed towards adapting tools from the Cloud community, such as Kubernetes®[1] [8]. Among these adaptations, Ray™ [13], an open-source distributed framework, has increasingly attracted attention in the Cloud community due to its high efficiency and native support for machine learning tasks. Previous research has demonstrated the utility of leveraging Ray to bridge the gap between HPC clusters and Cloud environments [11]. Such design automates deployment of jobs across the two distinct infrastructures, and prioritizes ease-of-use via unified Python interface. However, its initial design requires manual data management and does not consider data movement overheads when making scheduling decisions. Given Ray's increasing popularity, we chose to develop our system on top of this framework. Nonetheless, the underlying concept could also be applied in other settings.

Our system aims to improve the user experience and performance of HPC-Cloud bursting on top of the Ray-based HPC-Cloud bursting framework [11]. It introduces automated data management capability and integrates data movement with learning-based scheduling. Specifically, our system detects the required data of remote functions, pre-assigns execution nodes for pending tasks, prefetches data to these execution nodes, and employs dynamic label-based scheduling for job dispatching. Meanwhile, our scheduler dynamically collects task execution profiles to improve scheduling decisions for subsequent tasks. With these enhancements, users are relieved from manually managing data movement, prefetching data reduces waiting times for data transmission, and the scheduler is equipped to differentiate between HPC resources and Cloud environments, leading to more informed scheduling decisions.

The remainder of the paper is organized as follows: Sect. 2 discusses the related work and necessary background. In Sect. 3, we detail the design and implementation of our system. Section 4 includes functionality and performance evaluation. Brief discussion and conclusions are presented in Sect. 5.

---

[1] The Linux Foundation® has registered trademarks and uses trademarks. For a list of trademarks of The Linux Foundation, please see their Trademark Usage page.

2 Related Work

Researchers have explored different approaches to integrate Cloud resources into HPC environments for running high throughput jobs while minimizing network demands. For instance, for users familiar with HPC tools, efforts have been made to incorporate Cloud resources as schedulable partitions within Slurm clusters [14]. Similarly, for users accustomed to the Cloud ecosystem, attempts have been made to integrate HPC resources as virtual nodes under Kubernetes [21]. More recently, with the increasing interest in distributed machine learning, the Ray distributed framework has also been utilized to facilitate the connection between HPC and Cloud environments [11].

While Slurm or Kubernetes operate as cluster-level schedulers, Ray operates at a more granular level, handling jobs at the level of individual Python functions. Unlike cluster schedulers that treat workloads as black boxes with limited information about resource requirements, Ray provides more detailed information about each submitted task. For example, it can retrieve each function's arguments, start time, end time, and other customizable scheduling constraints. This wealth of information provides the potential for the scheduler to make better decisions based on the specific characteristics of each task.

Various scheduling methods have been explored for HPC-Cloud hybrid systems and heterogeneous environments in general. Flux [2], for instance, represents a hierarchical scheduler designed for the next generation of data centers, aiming to seamlessly connect Cloud resources. Another approach involves a scheduling algorithm that requires users to estimate start and end times, catering to different types of workloads (rigid, on-demand, and malleable jobs) in HPC environments [6]. The Heterogeneous Earliest-Finish-Time (HEFT) algorithm [19], a classical approach for heterogeneous systems, has demonstrated its effectiveness in scheduling complex workloads across disparate computational resources with varying performance levels. An extension of HEFT, E-HEFT [16], was also proposed, specifically tailored for load balancing in Cloud environments.

These advanced schedulers are believed to be more effective in managing complex tasks with intricate internal dependencies. However, our focus is on the integration of data movement and scheduling. We design our scheduler to be customizable for exploring the potential of integrating with more advanced scheduling algorithms, which is shown in later sections.

The management of data movement and placement has also been investigated in various contexts. One prevalent solution involves the implementation of shared file systems, such as GPFS^{TM} [17] at the system level. Additionally, studies have explored strategies for data pre-placement across different data centers to enhance computational efficiency [10]. Both approaches have been employed to address data availability requirements in multi-cluster environments.

However, our focus on HPC-Cloud bursting considers a different scenario. Unlike long-running and relatively stable data centers, which are conducive for shared file systems or data pre-placement, HPC-Cloud bursting involves creation of Cloud resources only in response to burst demand. Upon completion of computations, these Cloud resources are promptly dismantled, along with the associated system setup. Consequently, there is a preference for lightweight and automatic setup mechanisms. As a result, this paper does not delve into discussions regarding full data synchronization or data pre-placement.

3 Design and Implementation

In this section, we outline the design and implementation of our system. We start with a high-level overview of our design, followed by a detailed explanation of the two key components: 1) data movement and dynamic labeling, and 2) scheduling with dynamic profiling. Finally, we present the complete workflow of our system.

3.1 Ray Cluster Background

A standard Ray cluster has a head node and one or more worker nodes. [15] The worker nodes consist of worker process(es), which are responsible for Ray task submission and execution, and Raylets. A Raylet is shared across a single worker node and consists of a scheduler, which we refer to as the original Ray scheduler, and a shared-memory object store. The Ray cluster head node, in addition to the components described for the Ray worker nodes, also hosts the Ray Global Control Service, driver process(es), and other Ray cluster-level services.

3.2 Overall System Design

Maintaining the original design choice of utilizing Ray to establish the connection between the HPC cluster and Cloud [11], we configure a Ray cluster to span both infrastructures. More precisely, the Ray head is placed on the login node of the HPC cluster, and Ray workers are distributed across the compute nodes of the HPC cluster and the Cloud nodes.

At a high level, the main performance benefits offered by our system come from data prefetching that hides the transmission wait times. For prefetching to be possible, rather than adopting the original Ray scheduler, which assigns pending tasks to specific nodes only when resources are available for execution, pre-assigning tasks to nodes is required. Task pre-assignment also needs to have reasonable load balancing across nodes. As a result, a learning-based scheduler that is able to predict task finish time is preferred. The high-level concept behind scheduling decisions is relatively straightforward: collecting task execution profiles and calculating speeds for each node, then making decisions based on predicted finish times with these speeds. However, integrating this scheduler with the Ray core to capture submitted jobs is a more complex design endeavor.

While modifying the original Ray scheduler may initially seem like the most straightforward solution, it's essential to consider the broader implications. Ray has a large user community, employing it for diverse purposes. Altering the Ray scheduler would be a disruptive change to Ray's functionality, potentially introducing compatibility issues with other components and workflows. Additionally, incorporating these changes directly into Ray itself could impose unnecessary overhead on users who do not need or benefit from them. Moreover, embedding such modifications into the core of Ray would limit users' ability to customize the framework to suit their specific needs, as extensive understanding of Ray core would be necessary to implement changes.

With these considerations in mind, we decided on the following design principles: first, our changes to Ray core should only add functionality without breaking existing ones. Second, the customizable component of our system should exist as a standalone component with compact interfaces into Ray core, so that users with limited knowledge of Ray core can easily use and customize it.

Building upon these considerations, we devised a dynamic label-based scheduling approach, where a label on a node indicates the presence of specific data. Rather than halting task submission or task execution until data is ready, we incorporate data as a label requirement for task execution. Tasks are scheduled exclusively to nodes with corresponding labels, effectively preventing job execution if the required data is absent. Meanwhile, upon completion of data movement to a specific node, we add a corresponding label to it, allowing the original Ray scheduler to place the task on the specific node that has the data, with its original behavior. Our scheduler, designed to function as a standalone process, is tasked with assigning label requirements to tasks, orchestrating data movement to nodes, and dynamically adding labels to nodes upon completion of data movement. Such dynamic label-based design achieves both node selection and data-availability-indication functionalities without altering the original behavior of the Ray scheduler.

Hence, our implementation can be divided into two parts: (1) incorporating the dynamic labeling feature into the Ray core and utilizing it to signify completion of data movement; (2) developing the scheduler as a standalone daemon to leverage the new feature, learn from runtime profiles, and make the actual scheduling decisions. These two parts are elaborated in the following sections.

3.3 Data Movement and Dynamic Labeling

In this section, we describe how we introduced dynamic labeling into Ray core as a non-destructive add-on, according to our design principles. While Ray initially supports node labeling during node startup, it lacks the capability to modify labels dynamically during runtime. Enabling dynamic labeling-based scheduling requires implementing this new feature for Ray core.

Our implementation involves introducing new user APIs and gRPC® channels to facilitate the entire workflow of dynamically adding labels. Ray adopts a centralized architecture with a two-level scheduler for scheduling tasks. Beside each worker node storing its own state, cluster-wide information is stored both at the head node and the worker nodes, with the head node maintaining an additional Global Control Store (GCS) serving as the "ground truth" global state. As a result, updating all instances that utilize label information in the correct order is essential for maintaining consistency.

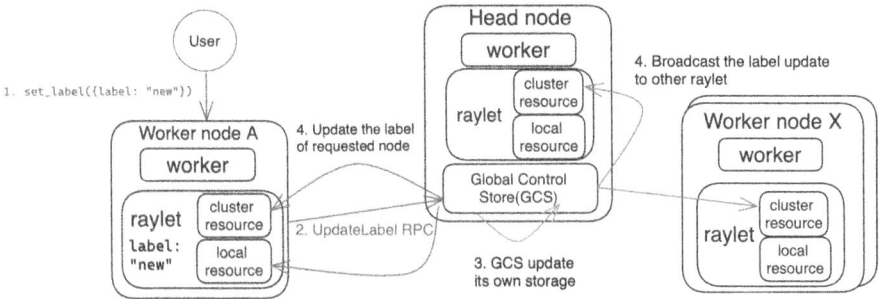

Fig. 1. The process of dynamic node labeling

Figure 1 presents the complete process of updating a node's label within the Ray cluster, with all arrows representing the newly implemented interfaces. For instance, if a user wishes to add a label called "new" to worker node A (located in the left part of Fig. 1), the following steps occur: first, the user invokes the `set_label` method on worker node A. This action triggers a gRPC request from the worker to the GCS, indicating the update of node A's label for centralized management. Upon receiving the request, the GCS updates its own table of node label information. Subsequently, the head node establishes connections with all active nodes' Raylets, broadcasting the label update details. On the worker side, upon receiving the label update, each Raylet updates their respective cluster resource managers. Additionally, the Raylet of node A, which is the node with the new label, updates its own local resources to reflect the updated label.

The newly added dynamic labeling is used to indicate the completion of data transmission. Once the scheduler pre-selects a node for a specific task to execute, it triggers a remote function at the designated worker node. In this remote function, the target worker node initiates data fetching from the data source (configured as environment variables). The data fetching method is dependent on the data source and could be configured accordingly. For example, if the data is located on a Network File System (NFS), a `rsync` command is used, and if the data is located on Amazon® Simple Storage Service® (S3) Cloud storage, Amazon Web Services (AWS®) Python APIs are used. Upon completion of data transmission, the scheduler initiates the previously described workflow to set a new label as the indication of data availability on the specific compute node. The specific label value used in our implementation is the absolute path of the data file. Consequently, tasks requiring this particular piece of data for execution are effectively scheduled to this node using the original Ray scheduler.

3.4 Scheduling System and Dynamic Profiling

In this section, we describe the scheduling system as a standalone component, which again follows our design principles. The scheduling system comprises two primary components: the storage server and the stateless controller daemon.

The storage server serves as a pivotal repository, housing essential information for task scheduling operations. It stores task specifications for each user task, such as task's unique ID and its resource requirements, and status information, such as the task state (running or pending), start and end times, and the status of its associated data transfer and label-binding task. With that information, a profiling API is also provided to plot out the entire execution timeline, which is utilized later for understanding our experimental results.

Among stored task specifications, task complexity score is an important property that is worth further explanation. Assuming that each worker executes a similar computational task, the complexity score of a task is assigned as its required data workset size. In the job submission process, the data workset of each task is provided as a function argument by the user. Its size is then obtained with a quick API query by our scheduling system, without doing the expensive file transmission. For example, if the data is located at AWS S3 Cloud storage, our system utilizes the AWS Python API to query the data size, without actually downloading the file. This complexity score is the key for later scheduling decisions.

Besides task information, the storage server also maintains node information, by aggregating runtime profiles of tasks executed on each worker node. Each node's processing speed is dynamically calculated based on task complexity scores and actual execution time, which is used for subsequent scheduling decisions. As an initial implementation, we assume a linear relationship between the task complexity score and its execution time, as a naive learning algorithm for node speed calculation. This could be replaced by more advanced algorithms, including machine learning based ones.

The stateless controller daemon contains the main logic of our scheduling loop, orchestrating scheduling operations in response to any changes in the status of Ray tasks. Upon the submission of a new task, the controller employs our scheduling algorithm to identify the most suitable node for task execution, leveraging profiling data for informed decision-making. Subsequently, it triggers the data transmission and label-binding task on the selected node, which executes as a non-blocking remote function. The controller retains only the binding task's ID and updates relevant information to the storage server. Once the binding task completes, the controller detects this change and recognizes that the user task has been scheduled and is now running. The actual dispatching of jobs after label assignment is handled by the original Ray scheduler.

Algorithm 1 describes how the controller selects the best node for a submitted user task, utilizing the task complexity score and node speed explained in the previous sections. The available resources of the worker node and the resource requirements of pending tasks are used to estimate the start time, which is when sufficient resources are available for the current task to be executed. Since it is possible that execution on an idle node may be slower than waiting to execute on the currently busy node, we use estimated start times and estimated execution times in order to estimate finish times, and choose the node with the earliest estimated finish time as the best node.

Algorithm 1. Algorithm for Choosing the Best Node

1: **Input:** task, nodeList
2: earliestFinishTime ← ∞
3: bestNode ← None
4: **for** node in nodeList **do**
5:     freeResources ← node[freeResources]
6:     estimatedTaskDuration ← $\frac{task[complexityScore]}{node[speed]}$
7:     **if** freeResources ≥ task[requiredResources] **then**
8:         estimatedStartTime ← currentTime
9:     **else**
10:        **for** submittedTask in node[orderedRunningAndPendingTask] **do**
11:            freeResources ← freeResources + submittedTask[requiredResources]
12:            **if** freeResources ≥ task[requiredResources] **then**
13:                estimatedStartTime ← submittedTask[estimatedFinishTime]
14:                break
15:    estimatedFinishTime ← estimatedStartTime + estimatedTaskDuration
16:    **if** estimatedFinishTime < earliestFinishTime **then**
17:        earliestFinishTime ← estimatedFinishTime
18:        bestNode ← node
19: **Output:** bestNode

3.5 The Overall Workflow

Bringing all of the components together, the complete system overview is shown in Fig. 2 with numbers indicating the control flow order. When a user submits a task, it is done via the original Ray remote function interface, with an argument indicating the required data. From this point onward, the entire scheduling process is transparent to the user. Within the Python runtime responsible for remote function submission, tasks requiring our system's involvement are detected, and a hard-requirement label is added to the task to indicate its data requirement. The task is then submitted to the unmodified original Ray scheduler as usual (step 1). As the required label is not present, the task is kept in the pending state. Simultaneously, our controller daemon is notified of this submission (step 1). Upon notification, the controller daemon employs the scheduling algorithm (Algorithm 1) to select the most suitable node. It then proceeds to launch the remote function on the chosen worker node (step 2), which is responsible for fetching data from the data source and dynamically setting the label (step 3). The label-setting instruction is then synchronized across the entire cluster using the mechanism described in Sect. 3.3 (step 4). Once the label-setting operation completes, the original Ray scheduler becomes aware of this and deploys the task to the selected worker node that has the required label, per its original behavior (step 5). Upon task completion, runtime profile information is updated to inform future scheduling decisions (step 6). This iterative process continues until all user tasks have been executed.

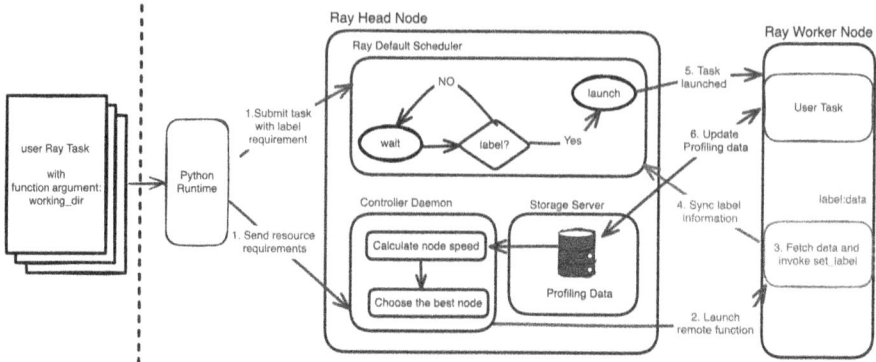

Fig. 2. The overall view of the scheduling workflow.

4 Use Cases and Evaluation

We evaluate our system using two workloads: machine learning model training and image processing. To understand the impact of data storage location, we conducted analyses of overall performance by deploying data on either the HPC cluster storage or AWS S3.

Given the variability in setups among different HPC clusters and the Cloud resources employed, we recognized the necessity to account for differing network speeds. While the network connection between Cloud resources and HPC clusters can vary, internal networks within the same Cloud provider often utilize stable private networks. Similarly, internal networks within HPC clusters, are also considered stable and high-performance. As a result, our experiment only varies the network speeds between the HPC cluster and Cloud, while maintaining their internal network speeds. To achieve this, and to avoid disruptions to the normal operations of public HPC clusters, we decided to simulate our HPC cluster on the Cloud resource in separate Virtual Private Cloud (VPC) on AWS. The communication between HPC compute node and the Cloud node requires the proxy of the HPC login node, mirroring the common HPC-Cloud connection.

For detailed analysis including fine-grained execution timelines, we configured our HPC-Cloud experimental system with the minimal resources necessary. Figure 3 illustrates the experimental setup. While the Cloud nodes utilize their own local SSD storage, all HPC nodes share a common NFS, mirroring the typical setup of HPC clusters. We will refer to this as the HPC NFS in our experiments. Furthermore, data may also reside in Amazon S3 storage, accessible by both Cloud nodes and HPC nodes via the network. We use uniform compute instances for all nodes, AWS r5.4xlarge [1], in order to minimize the impact of computation speed variability on measurements of our system's data prefetching enhancement.

The network speed restrictions required by our experiment are done with two methods. For limiting the network speed between the HPC nodes and the

Cloud nodes, the traffic control command, tc, available in the Linux® kernel is used. For the network between HPC nodes and Cloud S3 storage, AWS configuration APIs are used to restrict the download speed. In Fig. 3, only the network connections highlighted in yellow dashed lines are speed-restricted.

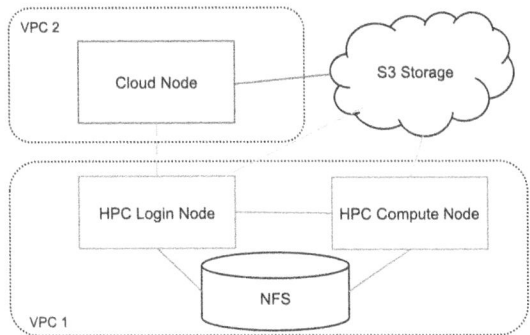

Fig. 3. The experiment cluster setup

The following subsections present the results of our experiments with different workloads. For each experiment, we stored data in two locations: HPC NFS storage and S3 Cloud Storage. We examine the total runtime of identical workloads under various network speeds between HPC and Cloud resources. The overall runtime with our system for data prefetching and scheduling is compared to a baseline implementation's runtime. The baseline uses Ray's original scheduler, and fetches necessary data when its absence is detected at execution time.

4.1 Machine Learning Model Training

The machine learning model training workload in our experiments involves training with an asynchronous parameter server [9]. In this setup, the processing of each distinct batch is executed in a remote function, by a Ray worker. Each worker fetches the latest gradients from the parameter server, then computes the forward propagation with its distinct batch of data, and finally transmits the updated gradients back to the parameter server. The parameter server aggregates the gradients and updates the model parameters accordingly. The training data is stored in either HPC NFS or S3 for each set of experiments. Consequently, workers lacking access to the data source must fetch the required data; this is where our system can help in data management and making scheduling decisions. In the baseline implementation, each worker function initiates an rsync command to fetch the data from the HPC NFS, or initiate downloads from Cloud S3 storage, if it detects the data required for training is not available after training process starts. For demonstration purposes, we utilized a subset of the PASS dataset [3] to train the MobileNetV3 [7] model. The training comprised 50

Table 1. Total execution time for parameter server training

Network Speed (Mbps)	Data at HPC NFS			Data at Cloud S3		
	Our System (s)	Baseline (s)	Improv. %	Our System (s)	Baseline (s)	Improv. %
30	475.49 ± 11.61	567.64 ± 15.83	16.23	553.82 ± 5.36	701.19 ± 29.76	21.02
50	443.62 ± 11.64	544.88 ± 20.93	18.58	490.08 ± 8.68	634.66 ± 3.56	22.78
80	431.80 ± 6.46	537.71 ± 9.18	19.70	463.82 ± 8.85	624.74 ± 0.28	25.76
100	420.11 ± 8.82	535.42 ± 9.20	21.54	455.14 ± 7.17	621.71 ± 12.80	26.79
150	415.43 ± 2.01	530.26 ± 12.66	21.66	445.45 ± 15.23	613.19 ± 1.92	27.36

batches, with each batch consisting of 100 images. We evaluate the total running time for completing all 50 batches of training under different setups.

Experimental results are shown in Table 1. Our system successfully reduces runtime when compared to the baseline method by saving data transmission time, as shown by the absolute improvement in overall execution time. However, the percentage of improvement decreases as network speed decreases. As mentioned earlier, each batch of training takes 100 small images. This makes the transmission time mostly influenced by the transmission setup time and the overhead of processing small files, rather than network speed. On the other hand, in-memory parameter exchange over the network occurs for each batch of training data, which causes longer overall execution time with slower network speeds. Under lower network speeds, while the transmission time – where our system excels – remains relatively stable, the total execution time increases. This results in a decrease in percentage improvement with slower network speeds.

4.2 Image Processing

Image processing workloads typically involve operations on a large number of images, including operations such as resizing, transpose, or applying a Gaussian Blur. For benchmarking purposes, in our experiment, each worker process takes a single large image of about 100MB, loads it into a tensor, and performs a transpose operation on it, representing a typical workload pattern. Further, we identified that at most two worker processes can run on each worker node concurrently due to memory constraints and for clear analysis and demonstration. Similar to the machine learning workload, with the baseline method, each worker process tries to fetch the data if it detects that the data is not available at execution time.

Table 2 shows the total runtime of processing all 30 images under different network setups, which again shows the effectiveness of our system. Different from the parameter server training workload, the image processing workload illustrates that our system can yield greater percentage improvements with slower network speeds. In this experiment, each task takes 100MB of data, making its transmission time notably impacted by the network speed. Moreover, since

Table 2. Total execution time for image processing

Network Speed (Mbps)	Data at HPC NFS			Data at Cloud S3		
	Our System (s)	Baseline (s)	Improv. %	Our System (s)	Baseline (s)	Improv. %
30	404.34 ± 1.04	470.74 ± 25.52	14.11	384.18 ± 12.02	408.31 ± 2.99	5.91
50	335.03 ± 14.49	396.89 ± 4.67	15.58	332.01 ± 13.93	363.46 ± 4.77	8.65
80	330.13 ± 6.20	373.19 ± 3.86	11.54	329.89 ± 6.09	358.53 ± 2.05	7.99
100	328.30 ± 2.97	368.29 ± 4.99	10.86	324.76 ± 3.12	342.42 ± 2.34	5.16
150	323.83 ± 2.98	360.28 ± 6.89	10.12	317.57 ± 6.15	327.97 ± 4.43	3.17

this workload is embarrassingly parallel, the actual execution time of each task remains unaffected by the network. With the execution time remaining stable while the transmission time increases, our system demonstrates better improvements on slower networks.

There is a noticeable decline in the improvement percentage at a network speed of 30 Mbps regardless of the initial data location. Further analysis of this phenomenon was conducted by plotting the execution timeline graph to gain insights into the entire execution process, by utilizing our system's profiling tool (the same profiling used for dynamic scheduling). The profiling tool is capable of plotting the entire execution timeline in HTML files that allows user interaction. For the purpose of analysis, Fig. 4 shows the relevant segment of this timeline.

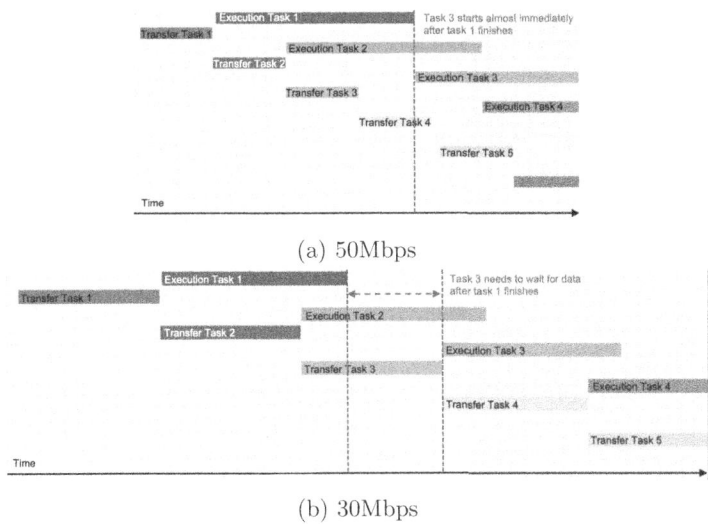

(a) 50Mbps

(b) 30Mbps

Fig. 4. Segment of execution timelines of image processing benchmark. Image data is originally located on HPC NFS and the execution timeline is shown for tasks running on the Cloud.

As shown in the figure, at the network speed of 50 Mbps, the data transmission finishes before the previous worker process finishes, allowing the next worker process to start execution as soon as the previous worker process completes. However, at a network speed of 30 Mbps, although transmission still occurs concurrently with execution, the network is so slow that ththe transmission does not complete by the time the previous worker process finishes. As a result, the subsequent worker process must still wait for the completion of data transmission, albeit for a shorter duration than if waiting for the entire file to transmit. This discrepancy causes a drop in improvement. This analysis also provides insights into how the percentage improvement can be maximized. Theoretically, the percentage improvement is maximized when the execution time is n times longer than the transmission time, where n is the maximum number of parallel worker process on each worker node.

4.3 Further Performance Analysis

Quantifying the absolute improvement in time is not as straightforward as measuring the total file transmission time. This complexity arises from dynamic scheduling, varying the number of tasks executed on HPC versus Cloud. Consider an example of 30 tasks: when the data transmission time is hidden by our scheduler, both HPC workers and Cloud nodes execute 15 tasks each. However, in the absence of our scheduler, while the HPC worker nodes may complete 15 tasks, the Cloud nodes might only finish 10, for example. Consequently, the original Ray scheduler (baseline), assigns more tasks to the HPC worker nodes, reducing the number of files transmitted to the Cloud (and also reducing the number of transmissions to hide). This results in the time improvement being less than the transmission time that was hidden by our scheduler.

The large standard deviation observed in some data points is mainly due to the way tasks are executed, where a small network disturbance can cause a big change in execution time. The completion time of the entire run is determined by the final task. For instance, a very small network disturbance may only slightly affect the total execution time. However, if the network disturbance goes beyond a certain threshold, the final task originally designated for the Cloud may instead be scheduled on an HPC node. In this case, the execution time change could be close to the execution time of a whole task. Averaging across multiple experiments can reveal underlying trends, but the large standard deviation remains due to the discrete factor.

It is also notable that the performance of the same workload when putting data at different locations varies. The machine learning model has better performance when data is stored on HPC NFS. This could be due to the larger overhead when accessing multiple small files from Cloud S3 storage. Conversely, the image processing workload performs better when data is stored at Cloud S3. This might be due to how we simulate different network speeds in our experiment. The restricted link for transmitting data from HPC to Cloud is also utilized by the Ray nodes' communication, resulting in lower bandwidth availability for data transmission. On the other hand, the bandwidth restriction to

Cloud S3 storage is made by AWS S3 configurations, which is unaffected by other communications.

In summary, our system improves performance in all scenarios, with the main benefits coming from reduction in transmission overhead. Perfect alignment of execution and transmission can yield the most significant performance benefits.

5 Conclusions

In this paper, we present our design and implementation of a novel HPC-Cloud bursting system that leverages the Ray distributed framework. Our system combines automated data management with learning-based scheduling, using the dynamic label-based design. With our system, data required by user-submitted tasks is automatically fetched to the respective worker node before computation can be scheduled on that node. Correspondingly, a learning-based scheduler that collects dynamic profiles is implemented for making pre-assignment decisions. We evaluated our system using two workloads. As evidenced by the data, our system consistently delivers benefits across various data locations and network speeds for the two workloads we tested, compared to the baseline data fetching method. This shows that our system not only improves the user experience but can also improve runtime performance. Our system allows for customization, including the utilization of advanced scheduling algorithms for more complex workloads. The system is open-sourced, and we provide packages for both general use and for reproducing the experimental results presented.

Acknowledgements. We would like to thank Carlos Costa and Claudia Misale for their technical support and discussion. This work is funded by the IBM-Illinois Discovery Accelerator Institute. We are grateful to Amazon for providing Cloud resources on AWS.

References

1. Amazon EC2 R5 instances. https://aws.amazon.com/ec2/instance-types/r5/
2. Ahn, D.H., Garlick, J., Grondona, M., Lipari, D., Springmeyer, B., Schulz, M.: Flux: a next-generation resource management framework for large HPC centers. In: 2014 43rd International Conference on Parallel Processing Workshops, pp. 9–17 (2014). https://doi.org/10.1109/ICPPW.2014.15
3. Asano, Y.M., Rupprecht, C., Zisserman, A., Vedaldi, A.: PASS: An ImageNet replacement for self-supervised pretraining without humans. NeurIPS Track on Datasets and Benchmarks (2021). https://thor.robots.ox.ac.uk/datasets/pass//license_pass.txt
4. Bommasani, R., et al.: On the opportunities and risks of foundation models. arXiv preprint arXiv:2108.07258 (2021)
5. Erben, A., Mayer, R., Jacobsen, H.A.: How can we train deep learning models across clouds and continents? An experimental study (2024)
6. Fan, Y., Lan, Z., Rich, P., Allcock, W., Papka, M.E.: Hybrid workload scheduling on HPC systems. In: 2022 IEEE International Parallel and Distributed Processing Symposium (IPDPS), pp. 470–480 (2022). https://doi.org/10.1109/IPDPS53621.2022.00052

7. Howard, A., et al.: Searching for MobileNetV3. In: 2019 IEEE/CVF International Conference on Computer Vision (ICCV), pp. 1314–1324 (2019). https://doi.org/10.1109/ICCV.2019.00140
8. Kubernetes: Production-grade container orchestration. https://kubernetes.io
9. Li, M., et al.: Scaling distributed machine learning with the parameter server. In: Proceedings of the 11th USENIX Conference on Operating Systems Design and Implementation, OSDI 2014, pp. 583–598. USENIX Association, USA (2014)
10. Lin, B., et al.: A time-driven data placement strategy for a scientific workflow combining edge computing and cloud computing. IEEE Trans. Industr. Inf. **15**(7), 4254–4265 (2019). https://doi.org/10.1109/TII.2019.2905659
11. Liu, T., et al.: Cloud-bursting and autoscaling for Python-native scientific workflows using Ray. In: Bienz, A., Weiland, M., Baboulin, M., Kruse, C. (eds.) High Performance Computing. LNCS, vol. 13999, pp. 207–220. Springer, Cham (2023). https://doi.org/10.1007/978-3-031-40843-4_16
12. Lofstead, G.F., Duplyakin, D.: Take me to the clouds above: bridging on site HPC with clouds for capacity workloads (2021). https://www.osti.gov/biblio/1856762
13. Moritz, P., et al.: Ray: a distributed framework for emerging AI applications. In: 13th USENIX Symposium on Operating Systems Design and Implementation (OSDI 2018), pp. 561–577 (2018)
14. Peng, Y., Skone, J., Christ, C., Runesha, H.: Skyway: a seamless solution for bursting workloads from on-premises HPC clusters to commercial clouds. In: Paris, J., Milhans, J., Hillery, B., Geva, S.B., Schmitz, P., Sinkovits, R.S. (eds.) PEARC 2021: Practice and Experience in Advanced Research Computing, Boston, MA, USA, 18–22 July 2021. ACM (2021). https://doi.org/10.1145/3437359.3465607
15. Ray v2 architecture (2022). https://docs.ray.io/en/latest/ray-contribute/whitepaper.html
16. Samadi, Y., Zbakh, M., Tadonki, C.: E-HEFT: enhancement heterogeneous earliest finish time algorithm for task scheduling based on load balancing in cloud computing. In: 2018 International Conference on High Performance Computing & Simulation (HPCS), pp. 601–609 (2018). https://doi.org/10.1109/HPCS.2018.00100
17. Schmuck, F., Haskin, R.: GPFS: a shared-disk file system for large computing clusters. In: Proceedings of the 1st USENIX Conference on File and Storage Technologies, FAST 2002, pp. 19-es. USENIX Association, USA (2002)
18. Staples, G.: TORQUE resource manager. In: Proceedings of the 2006 ACM/IEEE Conference on Supercomputing, SC 2006, p. 8-es. Association for Computing Machinery, New York (2006)
19. Topcuoglu, H., Hariri, S., Wu, M.Y.: Performance-effective and low-complexity task scheduling for heterogeneous computing. IEEE Trans. Parallel Distrib. Syst. **13**(3), 260–274 (2002). https://doi.org/10.1109/71.993206
20. Yoo, A.B., Jette, M.A., Grondona, M.: SLURM: simple Linux utility for resource management. In: Feitelson, D., Rudolph, L., Schwiegelshohn, U. (eds.) JSSPP 2003. LNCS, vol. 2862, pp. 44–60. Springer, Heidelberg (2003). https://doi.org/10.1007/10968987_3
21. Zhou, N., Georgiou, Y., Zhong, L., Zhou, H., Pospieszny, M.: Container orchestration on HPC systems. In: 2020 IEEE 13th International Conference on Cloud Computing (CLOUD), pp. 34–36 (2020)

Solving the Restricted Assignment Problem to Schedule Multi-get Requests in Key-Value Stores

Louis-Claude Canon[1], Anthony Dugois[1(✉)], and Loris Marchal[2]

[1] FEMTO-ST Institute, Univ. Bourgogne Franche-Comté, CNRS, Besançon, France
{louis-claude.canon, anthony.dugois}@femto-st.fr
[2] LIP, ENS Lyon, CNRS, Lyon, France
loris.marchal@ens-lyon.fr

Abstract. Modern distributed key-value stores, such as Apache Cassandra, enhance performance through *multi-get requests*, minimizing network round-trips between the client and the database. However, partitioning these requests for appropriate storage server distribution is non-trivial and may result in imbalances. This study addresses this optimization challenge as the Restricted Assignment problem on Intervals (RAI). We propose an efficient $(2-1/m)$-approximation algorithm, where m is the number of machines. Then, we generalize the problem to the Restricted Assignment problem on Circular Intervals (RACI), matching key-value store implementations, and we present an optimal $O(n \log n)$ algorithm for RACI with fixed machines and unitary jobs. Additionally, we obtain a $(4 - 2/m)$-approximation for arbitrary jobs and introduce new heuristics, whose solutions are very close to the optimal in practice. Finally, we show that optimizing multi-get requests individually also leads to global improvements, increasing achieved throughput by 27%–34% in realistic cases compared to state-of-the-art strategy.

Keywords: Key-Value Stores · Multi-Get · Scheduling · Restricted Assignment · Intervals · Approximation

1 Introduction

Many theoretical scheduling problems capture the essence of practical challenges in modern distributed systems. Among those, NoSQL databases such as distributed key-value stores (e.g., Dynamo [6] and Apache Cassandra [10]), which spread data over several servers and map items to unique keys, became central components in the architecture of online cloud applications, thanks to their excellent performance and capability to scale linearly with the dataset. They are often subject to high throughput, and must therefore be able to serve requests with low latency to meet user expectations. Hence, the proper scheduling of these requests is of paramount importance, and has a direct effect on the overall observed performance of the system [14]. Their wide adoption in the industry has led to the development of numerous optimization techniques, in particular to mitigate the well-known tail latency problem [5].

The API of modern distributed key-value stores offer various operations to interact with the dataset, among which single reads and writes are the most common. As the dataset is usually replicated on several servers (in order to ensure accessibility of data in case of node failure), each key is accessible at different *replica* servers, which unlocks the possibility to execute the corresponding read operation on any of these replicas. Most web-services often need to retrieve several data items to perform their own calculations. Thus, some APIs, such as Rein [13], provide a special type of operations called *multi-get* requests, which permit to retrieve several items from a given key set in a single round-trip. When executing such a multi-get request, the key-value store needs to partition the requested key set into several sub-operations at the destination of storage servers, and it should carefully balance the keys between these sub-operations in order to respond as quickly as possible. For example, TailX achieves better performance on heterogeneous workloads than a basic priority-based mechanism by taking into account an estimation of the actual service time of read operations [9].

In this paper, we show how the partitioning and scheduling of a multi-get request may be seen as the so-called Restricted Assignment problem, whose objective is to schedule jobs to machines in such a way that the makespan (i.e., maximum completion time) is minimized, with the additional constraint that a given job can be processed only by a particular subset of machines. Unfortunately, this problem is strongly **NP**-hard. Even though there is no polynomial algorithm with an approximation ratio better than $3/2$ unless $\mathbf{P} = \mathbf{NP}$ [11], algorithms with an approximation ratio of 2 or better have been proposed [7,8,11]. Moreover, the actual variant of the Restricted Assignment problem that applies to multi-get request partitioning is easier than the general problem. This enables us to develop low-cost, guaranteed algorithms, giving good results in practice.

Contributions. We express in Sect. 2 the partitioning of multi-get requests as the Restricted Assignment problem on Intervals (RAI) and extend in Sect. 3 an efficient algorithm proposed by Lin et al. [12] to the case with arbitrary jobs. We show that it is a $(2-1/m)$-approximation, running in time $O(m^2 + n \log n + mn)$, where m is the number of machines and n is the number of jobs (Theorem 1). Then, in Sect. 4, we further generalize the RAI problem to the Restricted Assignment problem on Circular Intervals (RACI) by allowing intervals that may begin at the end of the list of machines and go back to the start, which match the usual replication strategy of distributed key-value stores [6,10]. We iterate over ELFJ to develop a new $(4-2/m)$-approximation algorithm called DOUBLE ELFJ (DELFJ) with the same time complexity (Theorem 4) in Sect. 5. Finally, we derive two heuristics from DELFJ and evaluate their performance in simulations in Sect. 6. We find that, for individual multi-get requests, the solutions given by our heuristics largely improve from simple system-like greedy solutions and remain very close to the optimal (with a median ratio to the optimal of 1.031), and that the throughput of a series of multi-get requests is also increased by our heuristics.

2 Applicative Context and Formal Model

In this section, we introduce the partitioning of multi-get requests and give the formal definition of the corresponding scheduling problem.

Partitioning Multi-get Requests in Key-Value Stores. Key-value stores are low-latency databases where each data item is associated with a unique key [6,10]. In these systems, a *get* (or *read*) operation consists in retrieving the value that corresponds to a given key, whereas a *put* (or *write*) operation consists in adding a new association between a value and a key. As it is too large to fit on a single server, the overall dataset is split into several data partitions, and each partition is stored on a different server. Moreover, in order to guarantee accessibility of data in case of node failure, each partition is replicated on different physical servers. Although the replication strategy differs from one system to another, a common and practical way consists in arranging the servers on a virtual ring, and replicating the partition of each server i on its $k-1$ successors $i+1, i+2, \cdots, i+k-1$ (modulo the number of servers m), where k is a small integer ($k=3$ is a common value). In other words, servers are virtually ordered, and each key/value couple is stored on an interval of k different consecutive servers. The duration of a *get* operation depends on the size of the value being retrieved: even if most values are small, few values with a large size represent a substantial share of the total service time [5]. To some extent, value sizes can be estimated and used for scheduling optimization [9].

In contrast with *single* get operations, *multi-get* requests involve several keys. Such aggregated operations are useful, for instance, to reduce the number of network round-trips between a web-service and the database, as a single end-to-end request often requires to retrieve several data items before responding to the client [9,13]. In a multi-get request, the requested keys (which constitute the *key set* of the request) may be located in different data partitions, which are physically stored on different servers. Thus, the contacted server must split the multi-get request into several sub-requests: each sub-request contains a subset of the initial keys and is redirected towards a storage server holding these keys.

Partitioning a request into sub-requests can be seen as a scheduling problem, where servers correspond to machines, and each single get operation corresponds to a job, whose processing time is the time required to retrieve the data item from the store. Each job may be processed only by a subset of machines, which corresponds to the physical servers on which the requested key is located. The objective is to minimize the response time, that is, the largest completion time of all sub-requests, which corresponds to the maximum completion time of jobs, as illustrated in Fig. 1.

In key-values stores, any node may be used to query the database, hence many node may independently send jobs on worker node in a distributed work. However, tools have been proposed to ensure that all nodes have an up-to-date view of the system to make informed scheduling decisions [3].

The Restricted Assignment Problem. In the problem of scheduling jobs on unrelated machines (also known as the $R\,||\,C_{\max}$ problem in Graham's

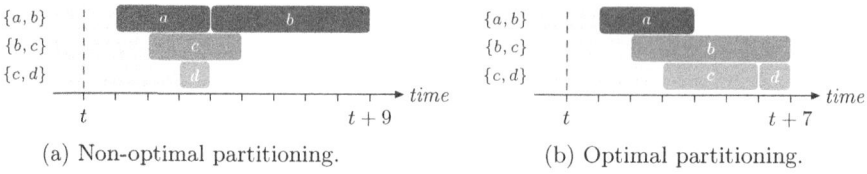

Fig. 1. Two possible partitions of the same multi-get request released at time t containing keys $\{a, b, c, d\}$. Gray areas represent earlier work on each server. Subset of values stored on each server are written on the left.

classification), we are given a set of n jobs $J = \{1, \cdots, n\}$ and a set of m machines $M = \{1, \cdots, m\}$, where each job $j \in J$ has a processing time $p_{ij} > 0$ on machine $i \in M$. The objective is to schedule (non-preemptively) the jobs on machines so as to minimize the makespan, that is to say, the maximum completion time of the jobs. We focus on a special case of this problem, called the Restricted Assignment (RA) problem and noted $P \mid \mathcal{M}_j \mid C_{\max}$, where each job $j \in J$ can be processed only on a subset of machines $\mathcal{M}_j \subseteq M$, which we call the *processing set* of j.

As the RA problem is known to be **NP**-hard in the strong sense, variants have been studied where some structure is brought in the processing sets of jobs. In this paper, we focus on *interval* processing sets. Let us note $\langle a, b \rangle$ the interval[1] ranging from machine a (inclusive) to machine b (inclusive, $a \leq b$). The Restricted Assignment problem on Intervals (RAI) defines for each job $j \in J$ its processing set as $\mathcal{M}_j = \langle a_j, b_j \rangle$. As a generalization of the classical makespan problem $P \mid\mid C_{\max}$, the RAI problem, noted $P \mid \mathcal{M}_j(interval) \mid C_{\max}$ in Graham's classification, remains **NP**-hard in the strong sense.

3 An Algorithm for the Restricted Assignment Problem on Regular Intervals

We focus here on the standard RAI problem $P \mid \mathcal{M}_j(interval) \mid C_{\max}$, for which Lin et al. [12] have proposed a polynomial algorithm when jobs are unitary. In this section, we generalize their approach to derive a tight $(2 - 1/m)$-approximation algorithm for the RAI problem with arbitrary jobs, running in time $O(m^2 + n \log n + mn)$ (Theorem 1).

We introduce Algorithm 1, called ESTIMATED LEAST FLEXIBLE JOB (ELFJ), which generalizes Lin et al.'s algorithm. ELFJ takes a time λ as parameter and builds a schedule that is guaranteed to finish before this time. In other words, λ denotes an upper bound on the optimal makespan, i.e., the better the quality of the bound, the closer ELFJ gets to an optimal schedule. The algorithm performs two steps. First, it sorts the jobs in non-decreasing order of interval upper bound b_j (in time $O(n \log n)$). Second, it greedily assigns jobs

---

[1] We will extend the interval definition later, thus we do not use the common notations of integer intervals.

Solving the Restricted Assignment Problem to Schedule Multi-get Requests   199

Algorithm 1. ESTIMATED LEAST FLEXIBLE JOB (ELFJ)
Input: jobs J, machines M and makespan λ
Output: an assignment μ
1: sort jobs in non-decreasing order of b_j
2: **for** all machines $i \in M$ **do**
3:     $\delta_i \leftarrow 0$
4:     **for** all unassigned jobs $j \in J$ such that $i \in \langle a_j, b_j \rangle$ **do**
5:        **if** $\delta_i + p_j \leq \lambda$ **then**
6:           $\mu_j \leftarrow i$
7:           $\delta_i \leftarrow \delta_i + p_j$
8: **return** μ

on machines (in time $O(mn)$), and returns an assignment vector μ, where μ_j denotes the machine on which job j is assigned. In the following, we explain how to choose λ to get various guarantees on the quality of the schedule.

Let us start with some notations and definitions. For any interval of machines $\langle \alpha, \beta \rangle$, where $1 \leq \alpha \leq \beta \leq m$, we define $K_{\langle \alpha, \beta \rangle}$ as the set of jobs whose processing set is included in $\langle \alpha, \beta \rangle$, i.e., $K_{\langle \alpha, \beta \rangle} = \{j \in J \text{ s.t. } \mathcal{M}_j \subseteq \langle \alpha, \beta \rangle\}$. We denote the total processing time of jobs in $K_{\langle \alpha, \beta \rangle}$ by $w_{\langle \alpha, \beta \rangle}$, i.e., $w_{\langle \alpha, \beta \rangle} = \sum_{j \in K_{\langle \alpha, \beta \rangle}} p_j$. Let $\tilde{w}_{\langle \alpha, \beta \rangle}$ represent the minimum average work that *any* schedule must perform on machines $\alpha, \cdots, \beta$, i.e.,

$$\tilde{w}_{\langle \alpha, \beta \rangle} = \frac{w_{\langle \alpha, \beta \rangle}}{\beta - \alpha + 1},$$

and let $\tilde{w}_{\max}$ be the maximum value of $\tilde{w}_{\langle \alpha, \beta \rangle}$ over all intervals (that is, $\tilde{w}_{\max} = \max_{1 \leq \alpha \leq \beta \leq m} \{\tilde{w}_{\langle \alpha, \beta \rangle}\}$). From these definitions, one may easily see that $\tilde{w}_{\max}$ is a lower bound on the optimal makespan $C_{\max}^{\text{OPT}}$ for a given instance $\mathcal{I}$ of the RAI problem. Let $\langle a, b \rangle$ be an interval of machines such that $\tilde{w}_{\max} = \tilde{w}_{\langle a, b \rangle}$. Then, in the best case, all jobs $K_{\langle a, b \rangle}$ are perfectly balanced on the interval $\langle a, b \rangle$ and finish no earlier than time $\tilde{w}_{\langle a, b \rangle}$. Note that if jobs are unitary, the lower bound can be refined to $\lceil \tilde{w}_{\max} \rceil$.

In the original paper, Lin et al. show that setting λ to $\lceil \tilde{w}_{\max} \rceil$ in ELFJ produces an optimal schedule when jobs are unitary. They also provide a procedure to compute $\tilde{w}_{\max}$ in this specific case. With a similar approach, we show in this section how to choose λ to get a guaranteed approximation ratio when processing times are arbitrary, and we develop a new procedure to find $\tilde{w}_{\max}$ efficiently in the general case.

Computing $\tilde{w}_{\max}$ for Arbitrary Jobs. We provide a new procedure to compute $\tilde{w}_{\max}$ in time $O(m^2 + n)$ for any instance of the RAI problem with arbitrary processing times. We notice that the set of intervals in a list of m machines can be represented by a graph, where nodes correspond to intervals. For all intervals $\langle \alpha, \beta \rangle$ such that $\alpha < \beta$, the node $\langle \alpha, \beta \rangle$ is the parent of two children nodes $\langle \alpha, \beta - 1 \rangle$ and $\langle \alpha + 1, \beta \rangle$. Let $J_{\langle \alpha, \beta \rangle}$ be the set of jobs whose processing set is exactly $\langle \alpha, \beta \rangle$, i.e., $J_{\langle \alpha, \beta \rangle} = \{j \in J \text{ s.t. } \mathcal{M}_j = \langle \alpha, \beta \rangle\}$, and let $v_{\langle \alpha, \beta \rangle}$ be their total processing time. We have a recursive relation between the values $w_{\langle \alpha, \beta \rangle}$: for a given interval $\langle\alpha,\beta\rangle$ that has two children intervals, the work $K_{\langle\alpha,\beta\rangle}$ includes the work $J_{\langle\alpha,\beta\rangle}$, the work $K_{\langle\alpha,\beta-1\rangle}$, and the work $K_{\langle\alpha+1,\beta\rangle}$, minus the work $K_{\langle\alpha+1,\beta-1\rangle}$, as it is included both in $K_{\langle\alpha,\beta-1\rangle}$ and $K_{\langle\alpha+1,\beta\rangle}$. Then, for any α,β, we have

$$w_{\langle\alpha,\beta\rangle} = v_{\langle\alpha,\beta\rangle} + w_{\langle\alpha,\beta-1\rangle} + w_{\langle\alpha+1,\beta\rangle} - w_{\langle\alpha+1,\beta-1\rangle},$$

with the convention $w_{\langle\alpha,\beta\rangle} = 0$ if $\alpha > \beta$. Values $v_{\langle\alpha,\beta\rangle}$ can be pre-computed in time $O(n)$ by scanning jobs, and the computation of values $w_{\langle\alpha,\beta\rangle}$ is done in time $O(m^2)$. Thus, $\tilde{w}_{\max}$ can be found in time $O(m^2 + n)$ and space $O(m^2)$, as shown in Algorithm 2.

An Approximation for Arbitrary Jobs. When jobs have arbitrary processing times, ELFJ does not produce an optimal schedule anymore. However, we show here that, subject to a small adaptation on the value of λ, it still gives a guaranteed solution in this more general case. In the following, $p_{\max}$ denotes the maximum processing time among all jobs of the instance.

Theorem 1. *Let* $\lambda = \tilde{w}_{\max} + \left(1 - \frac{1}{m}\right) p_{\max}$. *Then, ELFJ (Algorithm 1) is a tight $(2 - 1/m)$-approximation algorithm for RAI, and the full procedure runs in time $O(m^2 + n\log n + mn)$.*

We give here a sketch of the proof, and refer the reader to the linked research report for a detailed version [2]. Suppose that ELFJ does not produce a feasible schedule in time λ, i.e., there exists at least one job that is unassigned at the end of execution. Let j_0 be the first one. As a consequence, all machines $a_{j_0}, \cdots, b_{j_0}$ must finish after time $\lambda - p_{j_0}$, and we know that $b_j \leq b_{j_0}$ for all jobs j assigned on these machines (otherwise, j_0 would have been assigned by ELFJ). Let $\gamma \leq a_{j_0}$ be the first machine such that all machines $\gamma, \cdots, b_{j_0}$ finish after time $\lambda - p_{\max}$. As a consequence, we know that $a_j \geq \gamma$ for all jobs j assigned on these machines (otherwise, they would have been assigned before γ). The critical step of the proof is now to show that there exists a machine α between γ and a_{j_0} such that all jobs assigned on machines $\alpha, \cdots, b_{j_0}$ by ELFJ come from the set $K_{\langle\alpha,b_{j_0}\rangle}$. If

---

Algorithm 2. Computing $\tilde{w}_{\max}$

1: $v_{\langle\alpha,\beta\rangle} \leftarrow 0$ for all $0 \leq \alpha \leq \beta \leq m$
2: **for** all jobs $j \in J$ **do**
3: $\quad v_{\langle a_j,b_j\rangle} \leftarrow v_{\langle a_j,b_j\rangle} + p_j$
4: $\tilde{w}_{\max} \leftarrow 0$
5: **for** all l from 0 to $m - 1$ **do**
6: $\quad$ **for** all a from 1 to $m - l$ **do**
7: $\quad\quad b \leftarrow a + l$
8: $\quad\quad w_{\langle a,b\rangle} \leftarrow v_{\langle a,b\rangle} + w_{\langle a,b-1\rangle} + w_{\langle a+1,b\rangle} - w_{\langle a+1,b-1\rangle}$
9: $\quad\quad \tilde{w}_{\langle a,b\rangle} \leftarrow w_{\langle a,b\rangle}/(b - a + 1)$
10: $\quad\quad$ **if** $\tilde{w}_{\langle a,b\rangle} > \tilde{w}_{\max}$ **then**
11: $\quad\quad\quad \tilde{w}_{\max} \leftarrow \tilde{w}_{\langle a,b\rangle}$

this is the case, then we necessarily have $w_{\langle \alpha, b_{j_0}\rangle} > (b_{j_0} - \alpha + 1)(\lambda - p_{\max}) + (b_{j_0} - a_{j_0} + 1)(p_{\max} - p_{j_0}) + p_{j_0}$, which leads to the contradiction $\tilde{w}_{\max} < \tilde{w}_{\langle \alpha, b_{j_0}\rangle}$. To find such a machine α, we begin with the interval $\langle a_{j_0}, b_{j_0}\rangle$: if $a_j \geq a_{j_0}$ for all jobs j assigned on these machines, then $\alpha = a_{j_0}$ and we stop here; otherwise, we consider next the interval $\langle a_{j_1}, b_{j_0}\rangle$, where j_1 is a job assigned on $\langle a_{j_0}, b_{j_0}\rangle$ such that a_{j_1} is minimal. We repeat the process until we find α.

4 A General Framework for Circular Intervals

In this section, we present a generalization of the RAI problem to so-called *circular intervals*, which match the usual replication strategy of key-value stores.

Introducing Circular Intervals. Machines are linearly arranged in the standard RAI problem. In contrast, distributed key-value stores organize machines in a virtual *ring*, where the machines able to answer a query for a particular key are consecutively arranged in this ring. Thus, in addition to *regular* intervals $\langle a, b\rangle$ (with $a \leq b$), we introduce here *circular* intervals such that $a > b$. In this case, the corresponding set $\langle a, b\rangle$ includes machines $a, a+1, \cdots, m$ and machines $1, 2, \cdots, b$, i.e., $\langle a, b\rangle = \{a, a+1, \cdots, b\}$ if $a \leq b$, and $\langle a, b\rangle = \{1, 2, \cdots, b\} \cup \{a, a+1, \cdots, m\}$ otherwise. By extension, we call this generalized problem the Restricted Assignment problem on Circular Intervals (RACI).

For two given intervals $\langle a_g, b_g\rangle$ and $\langle a_h, b_h\rangle$, we say that $\langle a_g, b_g\rangle$ *precedes* $\langle a_h, b_h\rangle$ if and only if $a_g \leq a_h$ and $b_g \leq b_h$, and we note $\langle a_g, b_g\rangle \preceq \langle a_h, b_h\rangle$. For a given instance, let Z^* be the set of circular intervals that are associated to at least one job ($Z^* = \{\langle a_j, b_j\rangle$ s.t. $j \in J$ and $a_j > b_j\}$). We restrict ourselves to instances where the relation $\preceq$ is a total order on Z^*. In other words, for any $\langle a_g, b_g\rangle, \langle a_h, b_h\rangle \in Z^*$, we cannot have $\langle a_g, b_g\rangle \subset \langle a_h, b_h\rangle$. Although it is a particular case of RACI, it remains more general than RAI. Moreover, we assume that there are K types of jobs, and each job of type k has processing time $p(k)$.

An Optimal Procedure for K Job Types. We now introduce a general procedure that solves the RACI problem for the described restricted instances, assuming that one already knows an optimal algorithm $\mathcal{A}$ for the standard RAI problem with K job types.

Theorem 2. *Let $\mathcal{A}$ be an optimal algorithm for the RAI problem with K job types running in time $O(f(n))$. Then there exists a procedure solving the corresponding RACI problem on totally ordered circular intervals in time $O(n^K f(n))$.*

We begin with a few definitions, before giving the procedure and a quick sketch of the proof. Let J^* be the subset of jobs whose processing set is a circular interval ($J^* = \{j \in J$ s.t. $a_j > b_j\}$). We call J^* the *circular* jobs, and by extension, the jobs $J \setminus J^*$ are called *regular* jobs. We also partition J^* into K subsets $J_1^*, \cdots, J_K^*$, such that all jobs in J_k^* are of type k, and we note $n_k^* = |J_k^*|$. Moreover, in a given schedule, we say that a circular job j assigned between a_j (inclusive) and the last machine m (inclusive) is a *left* job. Equivalently, a circular job j assigned between the first machine 1 (inclusive) and b_j (inclusive) is a *right* job. Thus, a schedule π implicitly defines a partition of each set J_k^* into two subsets G_k and D_k, where G_k (resp. D_k) contains only left (resp. right) jobs. Figure 2 shows an example of such schedule.

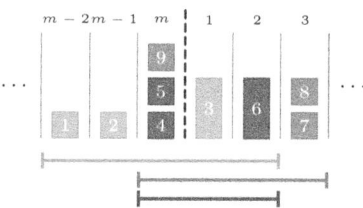

Fig. 2. Example of circular jobs in a schedule. Colors denote common processing intervals. Jobs 1, 2, 4, 5, 9 are left jobs. Jobs 3, 6, 7, 8 are right jobs. Jobs 1, 2, 4, 5, 7, 8, 9 are of type 1 (with $p(1) = 1$). Jobs 3 and 6 are of type 2 (with $p(2) = 2$). We have $G_1 = \{1, 2, 4, 5, 9\}$, $D_1 = \{7, 8\}$, $G_2 = \emptyset$, and $D_2 = \{3, 6\}$.

For now, consider only one type of jobs ($K = 1$). The intuition to compute an optimal schedule is to find which jobs in J^* should be assigned to the left or to the right. Assume that we know that r jobs of J^* must be assigned to the right in an optimal schedule. Intuitively, the r circular jobs with rightmost intervals should be put on the right, while the others should be put on the left. For example, consider only the small jobs in Fig. 2. If we suppose that $r = 5$ (arbitrarily), then we guess that the 2 red jobs and the 3 green jobs should be put between machines 1 and 3, and the 2 blue jobs should be put between machines $m - 2$ and m, as the red and green intervals are "more on the right" than the blue interval. To capture this intuition, we say that a schedule is *right-sorted* if and only if for all types k, the property $\langle a_j, b_j \rangle \preceq \langle a_{j'}, b_{j'} \rangle$ holds for any jobs $j \in G_k$ and $j' \in D_k$. In the linked report [2], we prove that, by successively swapping jobs of the same type, a non-right-sorted optimal schedule can always be transformed into another optimal solution that is right-sorted, i.e., there always exists at least one optimal right-sorted schedule.

For any vector $\mathbf{r} = (r_1, \cdots, r_K)$ such that $0 \leq r_k \leq n_k^*$ for all k, we introduce the polynomial function $\phi_\mathbf{r}$ that transforms any instance $\mathcal{I}$ of the (totally ordered) RACI problem into another instance $\mathcal{I}' = \phi_\mathbf{r}(\mathcal{I})$ that does not include any circular interval:

1. Sort jobs J^* by non-increasing order of b_j, and sort jobs with identical b_j by non-increasing order of a_j. Note that this corresponds to sorting jobs by non-increasing order of $\preceq$. As $\preceq$ is a total order on Z^*, all jobs are comparable.
2. For each type k, set $a_j = 1$ for the r_k first jobs of J_k^*, and $b_j = m$ for the $n_k^* - r_k$ other jobs, effectively removing circular intervals.

For a given instance $\mathcal{I}$ of RACI, let $\Pi(\mathcal{I})$ denote the set of all possible schedules, and for a given $\mathbf{r}$, let $\Pi_\mathbf{r}(\mathcal{I})$ be the subset that put exactly r_k jobs of type

k on the right, and $n_k^* - r_k$ jobs of type k on the left. Recall that $C_{\max}^{\text{OPT}}$ denotes the optimal makespan among all schedules $\Pi(\mathcal{I})$. We define analogously $C_{\mathbf{r}}^{\text{BEST}}$ as the *best possible makespan* among schedules $\Pi_{\mathbf{r}}(\mathcal{I})$. As the subsets $\Pi_{\mathbf{r}}(\mathcal{I})$ define a partition of $\Pi(\mathcal{I})$, we have $C_{\max}^{\text{OPT}} = \min_{\mathbf{r}} \{C_{\mathbf{r}}^{\text{BEST}}\}$. In the report [2], we prove the following two statements: applying an optimal algorithm to $\phi_{\mathbf{r}}(\mathcal{I})$ produces a valid solution for $\mathcal{I}$, and the makespan of this solution is at most $C_{\mathbf{r}}^{\text{BEST}}$. This implies that we can find an optimal solution for $\mathcal{I}$ by performing an exhaustive search of the best vector $\mathbf{r}$, proving Theorem 2. The first statement comes from the fact that any schedule for $\phi_{\mathbf{r}}(\mathcal{I})$ is right-sorted with r_k circular jobs on the right for all k, which means that it necessarily belongs to $\Pi_{\mathbf{r}}(\mathcal{I})$. The second statement comes from the fact that there always exists at least one optimal right-sorted schedule, thus, applying an optimal algorithm on $\phi_{\mathbf{r}}(\mathcal{I})$ will necessarily produce a schedule having the best possible makespan among $\Pi_{\mathbf{r}}(\mathcal{I})$.

Revisiting the Unitary Job Case. We study the application of this procedure on the ELFJ algorithm presented in Sect. 3. We show how to largely reduce the complexity compared to Theorem 2. ELFJ is an optimal algorithm for the standard RAI problem on unitary jobs, which consists in 3 distinct steps: computing the optimal makespan, in time $O(m^2 + n)$; sorting the jobs, in time $O(n \log n)$; performing the actual job assignment, in time $O(mn)$. By applying our framework around ELFJ, and because we have only one type of jobs in this specific case, we know from Theorem 2 that we can solve the generalized problem on totally ordered circular intervals in time $O(m^2 n + n^2 \log n + mn^2)$. The following theorem states that we can improve this solution even further by reducing its worst-case time complexity.

Theorem 3. *The totally ordered RACI problem with unitary jobs can be solved in time $O(m^2 + n \log n + mn)$.*

The proof of Theorem 3 explains how to eliminate any redundant work when applying the procedure from Sect. 4. In particular, finding the correct number of circular jobs that should be put on the right is needed only for the computation of the optimal makespan. The rest of the algorithm can then be processed only once. Furthermore, we can reduce the complexity when computing $\tilde{w}_{\max}$ by relying on a memoization matrix. The interested reader can find the complete proof in the linked research report [2].

5 An Approximation for the Restricted Assignment Problem on Circular Intervals

In this section, we introduce an approximation algorithm to assign jobs on circular intervals, based on the following intuition: under certain conditions, it is possible to split the problem into two sub-problems, such that each of them consider only regular intervals. On each of these sub-problems, we can use the $(2-1/m)$-approximation algorithm presented in Sect. 3 to get a guaranteed solution.

We consider jobs whose processing set is a circular interval, that is, $J^* = \{j \in J \text{ s.t. } a_j > b_j\}$, and we define the smallest "left" index of these intervals, namely $z_{left} = \min_{j \in J^*} \{a_j\}$, as well as their largest "right" index $z_{right} = \max_{j \in J^*} \{b_j\}$. We assume in this section that the "leftmost" circular interval does not intersect the "rightmost" circular interval, that is, $z_{left} > z_{right}$. This assumption holds in particular for intervals of size k if and only if $m \geq 2(k-1)$, as $z_{left} \geq m - (k-1) + 1$ and $z_{right} \leq k - 1$, i.e., $z_{left} - z_{right} \geq m - 2k + 3$.

Algorithm 3. DOUBLE ELFJ (DELFJ)

Input: jobs J and machines M
Output: an assignment μ
1: $J^* \leftarrow \{j \in J \text{ s.t. } a_j > b_j\}$
2: $\mu \leftarrow$ apply ELFJ on jobs $J \setminus J^*$
3: $z_{left} \leftarrow \min_{j \in J^*} \{a_j\}$
4: **for all** jobs $j \in J^*$ **do**
5: $\quad a_j \leftarrow a_j - z_{left} + 1$ ▷ shift left
6: $\quad b_j \leftarrow b_j + m - z_{left} + 1$ ▷ shift left
7: $\mu^* \leftarrow$ apply ELFJ on jobs J^*
8: **for all** jobs $j \in J^*$ **do**
9: $\quad \mu_j \leftarrow ((\mu_j^* + z_{left} - 2) \bmod m) + 1$ ▷ shift right
10: **return** μ

The proposed algorithm, named DOUBLE ELFJ (DELFJ) and presented in Algorithm 3, works as follows: regular jobs are first allocated on machines using the $(2 - 1/m)$-approximation algorithm ELFJ presented in Sect. 3. To allocate the remaining jobs (from J^*), we use the same algorithm. However, ELFJ only handles regular intervals. Hence, we first shift all intervals so that the leftmost circular intervals start on machine 1 before applying ELFJ (see Fig. 3), and we shift back the allocation in the end. Thanks to our assumption on z_{left} and z_{right}, we know that shifting the initially circular intervals will

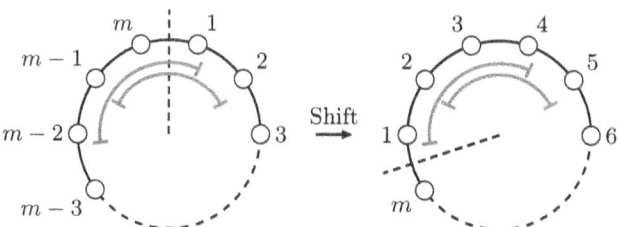

Fig. 3. Shifting the circular intervals "to the left" to transform them into regular intervals. In this example, there are two circular intervals (red and blue). Moreover, $z_{left} = m - 2$ and $z_{right} = 2$. The shifted machine corresponding to the machine with index i has index $i - z_{left} + 1$ if $i \geq z_{left}$, $i - z_{left} + 1 + m$ otherwise. (Color figure online)

result in all these intervals becoming regular. As the two categories of jobs are allocated separately using a $(2-1/m)$-approximation, we obtain a $(4-2/m)$-approximation algorithm, as stated in the following theorem (see full proof in the research report [2]).

Theorem 4. DOUBLE ELFJ *(Algorithm 3) is a tight* $(4-2/m)$-*approximation algorithm provided that* $z_{left} > z_{right}$.

6 Experimental Evaluation

We now derive a new heuristic from our guaranteed algorithm DELFJ to partition multi-get requests, and we perform a series of experiments to evaluate its practical performance.

Introducing the DSLFJ Heuristic. The drawback of DELFJ is that it uses ELFJ as a sub-algorithm: in each round, it keeps putting jobs on the same machine until it reaches λ, which differs from the optimal by a factor $2-1/m$. Our heuristic, called DOUBLE SEARCHED LFJ (DSLFJ), also assigns regular jobs in the first round and circular jobs in the second, but uses a different sub-algorithm to do so. This variant no longer computes an approximated objective value, but instead progressively searches for a feasible makespan by successively applying ELFJ, starting from $\lceil \tilde{w}_{\max} \rceil$. The searching procedure directly depends on how the makespan λ grows through iterations: a slow progression will yield a better final objective, but the worst-case time complexity will necessarily be higher. In the following, we consider two variants of DSLFJ, according to the growing function of λ: ARITHMETICALLY-SEARCHED LFJ (ASLFJ), which increments λ by 1 in each iteration, and GEOMETRICALLY-SEARCHED LFJ (GSLFJ), which doubles λ in each iteration. Their time complexities are respectively $O(m^2 + n \log n + mn \cdot p_{\max})$ and $O(m^2 + n \log n + mn \cdot \log p_{\max})$.

Experimental Settings. We test the quality of ASLFJ and GSLFJ in simulations. The key-value store is characterized by a number of machines m and a replication factor k, which defines the size of each interval of machines. We generate a dataset of 100 000 keys, and we uniformly assign each key to a random machine. Each key κ is associated a corresponding service time t_κ, which is drawn from an exponential distribution with mean 12. The processing time of each job is set to the service time of the corresponding requested key. Each multi-get request is parameterized by the number of keys n that are requested, and the chosen keys that are drawn according to a given popularity distribution. In the following, we consider the uniform distribution (each key has the same probability of being chosen) and the Zipf distribution (with bias 1.0), which is the default in most benchmarks [4]. We compare our heuristics with the following algorithms: RANDOM, which randomly assigns each job to a compatible machine; EFT-MIN, which assigns each job to the first compatible machine that completes the job the earliest; EFT-RAND, which is EFT-MIN with a randomized tie-breaking rule. EFT-MIN is a strategy that actual key-value stores tend

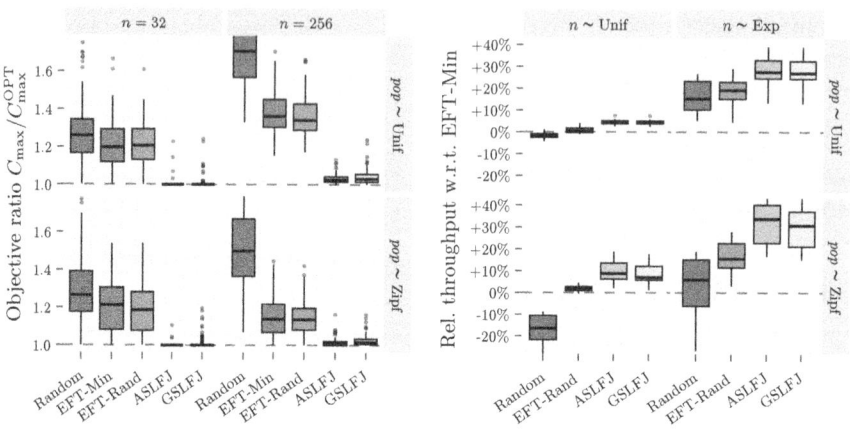

(a) Ratio between C_{max} and C_{max}^{OPT}. (b) Relative throughput w.r.t. EFT-Min.

Fig. 4. On the left, we plot the ratio between the makespan C_{max} given by each heuristic and the optimal makespan C_{max}^{OPT} in different settings (the lower the better). On the right, we plot the ratio between the saturating throughput given by each heuristic on 1000 multi-get requests and the saturating throughput given by EFT-MIN in different settings (the higher the better).

to use, even if it is never perfectly implemented in practice due to the usual constraints of distributed systems [14]. When the instance size is not prohibitive, we also compare our heuristics with the optimal solution of a Mixed Integer Linear Program (MILP) solver.

Results. We evaluate the response time of individual requests, and the maximum attainable throughput of the system on a saturating stream of requests. In both experiments, we set the number of machines to $m = 48$ and the replication factor to $k = 3$ (common value in practical systems [10]). The popularity distributions of keys are uniform ($pop \sim$ Unif, top row) and Zipf's law with bias 1.0 ($pop \sim$ Zipf, bottom row).

Response Time of Individual Requests. In Fig. 4a, we schedule one multi-get request made of several jobs, and we measure the ratio between the makespan C_{max} computed by each heuristic and the optimal makespan C_{max}^{OPT} computed by the MILP solver. We consider multi-get requests of size $n = 32$ (medium size, left column) and $n = 256$ (large size, right column). Each setting is simulated 100 times. We observe that ASLFJ and GSLFJ give close-to-optimal solutions in the considered settings: the median ratio of ASLFJ (resp. GSLFJ) is at most 1.025 (resp. 1.031), whereas EFT-MIN systematically has a median ratio between 1.139 and 1.362. Moreover, by counting the number of times each heuristic gives the best solution for each instance, we find that ASLFJ gives the best solution in 99% of the 400 tested cases. Comparatively, without taking ASLFJ into account, GSLFJ gives the best solution in 94% of the cases, whereas EFT-MIN is the best only in 5.25% of the cases, and even gives the worst solution in 16.25% of the cases.

This confirms that GSLFJ provides a good trade-off between quality and time complexity. Overall, the proposed heuristics give close-to-optimal response time, where EFT-MIN is between 15% and 35% slower on average.

Saturating Throughput of a Stream of Requests. In Fig. 4b, we test whether optimizing each individual request has an impact on the throughput. We schedule a workload of 1000 multi-get requests and measure the finishing time of the last request to complete. The saturating throughput is defined as the number of requests in the workload divided by this last finish time. In this figure, we plot the ratio between the saturating throughput of each heuristic and the one of the baseline EFT-MIN. We make the size of multi-get requests vary according to a uniform distribution between 1 and 256 ($n \sim$ Unif, left column) and an exponential distribution with mean 32 ($n \sim$ Exp, right column). We use this last setting as a realistic workload where small multi-get requests are a lot more probable than large ones. Each experiment is repeated 20 times. We observe that ASLFJ and GSLFJ improve the maximum attainable throughput in all tested settings. However, the improvement is more significant when the size of multi-get requests follows an exponential distribution. When keys have the same probability of being requested (top row), the median saturating throughput of ASLFJ (resp. GSLFJ) is greater than the one of EFT-MIN by 4.3% (resp. 4.3%) if $n \sim$ Unif, whereas it is greater by 27.5% (resp. 27%) if $n \sim$ Exp. For a Zipf popularity distribution (bottom row), the median saturating throughput of ASLFJ (resp. GSLFJ) is greater than the one of EFT-MIN by 8.8% (resp. 7%) if $n \sim$ Unif, whereas it is greater by 33.9% (resp. 30.8%) if $n \sim$ Exp. We noticed that ASLFJ and GSLFJ were particularly efficient for small multi-get requests (i.e., they find an optimal solution quasi-systematically when $n \leq 10^2$), which are in majority if $n \sim$ Exp. Over the 80 tested workloads, ASLFJ gives the best results in 86.25% of the cases. When ASLFJ is not taken into account, GSLFJ gives the best results in 97.5% of the cases.

Overall, we notice that our heuristics not only improve the response time of individual requests, but also improve the maximum load that the system is able to cope with. This is a non-trivial and interesting conclusion since throughput optimization is similar to load-balancing, which is usually an orthogonal objective to optimizing the individual performance of requests. Depending on the distribution of request sizes and key popularities, the improvement in throughput goes from 27% to 34% in realistic cases.

7 Conclusion

In this paper, we tackle the multi-get request partitioning problem that arises is modern key-value stores by modeling this as a scheduling problem, namely the Restricted Assignment problem on Intervals (RAI), and proposing approximation algorithms and heuristics to solve it. We first exhibit a $(2 - 1/m)$-approximation algorithm, and we further extend the RAI problem to *circular* intervals, which fit the configuration of actual replicated key-value stores. In this setting, we propose a general framework that, given an optimal algorithm for the RAI problem with at most K job types and running in time $O(f(n))$, computes an optimal solution for the RACI problem in time $O(n^K f(n))$. This enables us to revisit an optimal algorithm for the RAI problem when jobs are unitary to solve the corresponding RACI problem in time $O(m^2 + n \log n + mn)$. Moreover, we derive a new $(4 - 2/m)$-approximation algorithm in the general case, which we use as a basis to design new practical heuristics to partition multi-get requests. We evaluate these heuristics through extensive simulations, and we show that they not only improve the response time of individual multi-get requests compared to simple greedy strategies, leading to close-to-optimal allocations, but are also able to increase the maximum attainable throughput of the system by 27%–34% in realistic cases.

As a future work, the next step would be to implement and evaluate our heuristics in a real key-value store, e.g., Apache Cassandra. On the theoretical side, it remains unknown if there exists an efficient approximation algorithm for the particular instances of RACI where circulars intervals are not necessarily totally ordered, i.e., a given circular interval may be strictly included into another. Moreover, we conjecture that there exists an efficient approximation algorithm for RACI that improves on the $4 - 2/m$ guaranteed factor.

Acknowledgements and Artifact Availability. The Code is available in the Zenodo repository [1].

References

1. Canon, L.C., Dugois, A., Marchal, L.: Artifact of the paper: Solving the Restricted Assignment Problem to Schedule Multi-Get Requests in Key-Value Stores (2024). https://doi.org/10.5281/zenodo.11636529
2. Canon, L.C., Dugois, A., Marchal, L.: Solving the restricted assignment problem to schedule multi-get requests in key-value stores (extended version). Research report (2024). https://hal.science/hal-04516752
3. Canon, L.C., Dugois, A., Marchal, L., Rivière, E.: Hector: a framework to design and evaluate scheduling strategies in persistent key-value stores. In: Proceedings of the 52nd International Conference on Parallel Processing, pp. 535–545 (2023)
4. Cooper, B.F., Silberstein, A., Tam, E., Ramakrishnan, R., Sears, R.: Benchmarking cloud serving systems with YCSB. In: ACM Symposium on Cloud Computing, pp. 143–154 (2010)
5. Dean, J., Barroso, L.A.: The tail at scale. Commun. ACM **56**(2), 74–80 (2013)
6. DeCandia, G., et al.: Dynamo: amazon's highly available key-value store. In: SOSP 2007, pp. 205–220 (2007)
7. Ebenlendr, T., Krcál, M., Sgall, J.: Graph balancing: a special case of scheduling unrelated parallel machines. In: SODA, vol. 8, pp. 483–490 (2008)
8. Glass, C.A., Kellerer, H.: Parallel machine scheduling with job assignment restrictions. Nav. Res. Logist. **54**(3), 250–257 (2007)
9. Jaiman, V., Mokhtar, S.B., Rivière, E.: Tailx: scheduling heterogeneous multiget queries to improve tail latencies in key-value stores. In: IFIP DAIS, pp. 73–92 (2020)
10. Lakshman, A., Malik, P.: Cassandra: a decentralized structured storage system. ACM SIGOPS Oper. Syst. Rev. **44**(2), 35–40 (2010)

11. Lenstra, J.K., Shmoys, D.B., Tardos, É.: Approximation algorithms for scheduling unrelated parallel machines. Math. Program. **46**(1), 259–271 (1990)
12. Lin, Y., Li, W.: Parallel machine scheduling of machine-dependent jobs with unit-length. Eur. J. Oper. Res. **156**(1), 261–266 (2004)
13. Reda, W., Canini, M., Suresh, L., Kostić, D., Braithwaite, S.: Rein: taming tail latency in key-value stores via multiget scheduling. In: EuroSys, pp. 95–110 (2017)
14. Suresh, L., Canini, M., Schmid, S., Feldmann, A.: C3: cutting tail latency in cloud data stores via adaptive replica selection. In: USENIX NSDI, pp. 513–527 (2015)

PriCE: Privacy-Preserving and Cost-Effective Scheduling for Parallelizing the Large Medical Image Processing Workflow over Hybrid Clouds

Yuandou Wang[1](✉)[iD], Neel Kanwal[2][iD], Kjersti Engan[2][iD], Chunming Rong[2][iD], Paola Grosso[1][iD], and Zhiming Zhao[1](✉)[iD]

[1] Multiscale Networked Systems, University of Amsterdam, Amsterdam, The Netherlands
{y.wang,p.grosso,z.zhao}@uva.nl
[2] Department of Electrical Engineering and Computer Science, University of Stavanger, Stavanger, Norway
{neel.kanwal,kjersti.engan,chunming.rong}@uis.no

Abstract. Running deep neural networks for large medical images is a resource-hungry and time-consuming task with centralized computing. Outsourcing such medical image processing tasks to hybrid clouds has benefits, such as a significant reduction of execution time and monetary cost. However, due to privacy concerns, it is still challenging to process sensitive medical images over clouds, which would hinder their deployment in many real-world applications. To overcome this, we first formulate the overall optimization objectives of the privacy-preserving distributed system model, i.e., minimizing the amount of information about the private data learned by the adversaries throughout the process, reducing the maximum execution time and cost under the user budget constraint. We propose a novel privacy-preserving and cost-effective method called PriCE to solve this multi-objective optimization problem. We performed extensive simulation experiments for artifact detection tasks on medical images using an ensemble of five deep convolutional neural network inferences as the workflow task. Experimental results show that PriCE successfully splits a wide range of input gigapixel medical images with graph-coloring-based strategies, yielding desired output utility and lowering the privacy risk, makespan, and monetary cost under user's budget.

Keywords: Privacy · Cost-effectiveness · Hybrid Clouds · Medical Image splitting · Multi-Objective Optimization · Scheduling

1 Introduction

Modern medical image processing techniques utilize deep neural networks to extract hidden patterns and make predictions; however, running such machine learning-based inferences for large medical images is resource-hungry and time-consuming when computing resources are limited. Cloud computing can provide ample and highly scalable storage, computational resources, and ubiquitous access for distributed processing tasks. Hybrid Clouds (HCs) combine the economies and efficiencies of public cloud with the security and control of private cloud [1]. However, privacy concerns significantly complicate the development of an optimal cloud resource allocation plan for outsourcing computations on sensitive data processing tasks: (1) medical images often contain privacy-sensitive information in their metadata, which cannot be directly outsourced to the public cloud due to the risk of data leakage, (2) assigning distributed processing workloads to available cloud resources to meet multiple user requirements such as the reduction of time and monetary cost, known as Multi-Objective Optimal (MOO) workflow scheduling, is a typical NP-hard problem [2].

The problem of privacy-preserving and cost-effective scheduling in large (e.g., gigapixel) medical image processing over HCs has not yet been studied in detail, and we observed that this problem exhibits unique characteristics. For instance, although patching the original large image in a grid and dividing the patch-level dataset into multiple sub-datasets are common practices, the strategy employed for these practices is critical for both privacy preservation and resource provisioning for deployment in the cloud. Furthermore, although several studies have addressed workflow privacy in the context of cloud technology [2,3], there is a need for precise measurements of privacy metrics that align with the specific privacy-preserving approaches used for workflow scheduling.

This work aims to overcome those limits and solve the problem of privacy-preserving and cost-effective distributed inference tasks over clouds. To address this, we first formulate the research problem that minimizes the vulnerability, reduces the monetary cost, and minimizes the maximum execution time of the privacy-preserving distributed system under constraints. We propose a novel privacy-preserving and cost-effective algorithm called PriCE. Our experimental evaluation reveals the benefits of PriCE in privacy-preserving and cost-effective workflow scheduling when answering the following three sub-research questions: (I) "What are the trade-offs among privacy, cost, and execution time as split strategies related to the distributed processing of large images?" (II) "Can privacy-preserving split strategies improve resource planning and lead to Pareto optimality?" and (III) "How different are the Pareto optimal solutions from different split strategies?"

Our main contributions can be summarized as follows:

- We design and implement PriCE, which consists of multiple image-splitting strategies, image label perturbation, and multi-objective optimization procedures that can seek the Pareto front of resource provisioning for the privacy-preserving and cost-effective system model.
- We demonstrate how to analyze, quantify, compare, and understand different split strategies within PriCE and obtain the final assignment, estimated objective values of the cloud instances, by conducting experiments based on a use case for artifact detection tasks on gigapixel medical images.

The remainder of this paper is structured as follows. Section 2 presents related work to privacy-aware workflow scheduling in HCs. In Sect. 3, we propose our system model, provide critical metrics used for the methodology and evaluation, and formulate the research problem. Section 4 illustrates our proposed approach for problem-solving and Sect. 5 details the experimentation and evaluation. Finally, we conclude our work in Sect. 6.

2 Related Work

The scheduling of privacy-aware workflows has garnered increased attention in recent years, especially aiming to minimize costs and processing time while ensuring compliance with privacy requirements. Sharif *et al.* [2] target a resource allocation map based on privacy privileges over HCs that combine private, community, and public clouds, while using a healthcare workflow that consists of private, semi-private, and public tasks as a case for problem modeling. Their objective is to minimize the overall execution cost of workflows while satisfying concerns about their privacy and deadline. Zhou *et al.* [4] study the European (EU) data protection regulation—GDPR[1] in the geo-distributed cloud and formulate the geo-distributed process mapping problem that minimizes the cost of workflow applications while meeting data privacy constraints regarding the restrictions of the data movement between different cloud data centers. Lei *et al.*. [3] define a deadline-constrained cost optimization problem in a HC under the deadline and privacy constraints. Similarly, Wen *et al.* [5] propose a multi-objective privacy-aware scheduling algorithm to obtain a set of Pareto trade-off solutions between execution makespan and cost reductions while meeting the set of privacy protection constraints. As presented in Table 1, these works are close to our research problem in terms of data and task privacy constraints, time performance improvement, and cost reduction for resources planning over HCs; nonetheless, our work significantly differs from their works.

Table 1. Comparisons of the problem formulation.

Problem Model	Optimization Objective			Constraint(s)
	Time	Cost	Privacy	
Sharif *et al.* [2]	✗	✓	✗	task/data privacy, deadline
Lei *et al.* [3]	✗	✓	✗	deadline, privacy
Zhou *et al.* [4]	✗	✓	✗	data privacy, GDPR, deadline
Wen *et al.* [5]	✓	✓	✗	privacy protection
Ours	✓	✓	✓	user's budget

---

[1] General Data Protection Regulation (GDPR). https://gdpr.eu/.

We study the scheduling problem that minimizes the quantified amount of information about private data learned by the adversaries, lowers financial cost, and reduces the maximum execution time with different data-split strategies. To the best of our knowledge, this is a unique problem statement since the majority of the related works leave privacy as a constraint, instead of a quantified optimization objective.

3 Problem Formulation

3.1 System Model

We consider a system as depicted in Fig. 1. We remove the privacy-sensitive metadata from the original image $\mathcal{D}$ before splitting the large image into many image tiles to introduce data parallelism. We apply a privacy-preserving data splitting procedure in step ❶, in conjunction with image label encryption and image object serializing to preserve the data privacy. Data splitting aims to protect data privacy by fragmenting sensitive data and storing the fragments in different locations so that individual parts do not disclose identities or confidential information [6]. In step ❷, we transform the Convolutional Neural Network (CNN) inference model into several reusable fine-grained computational tasks; configuring the available resources such as private and public cloud resources in step ❸ can facilitate making plans for resource provision.

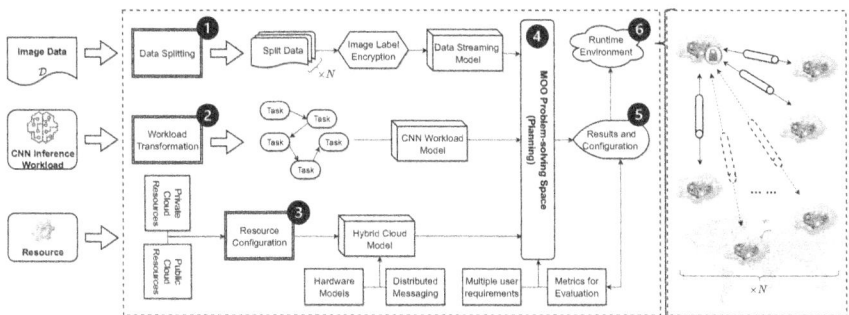

Fig. 1. Workflow of the system model and its related application scenario.

Based on the prepared data, workload, and HC model, step ❹ maps available resources to various workloads in a manner that optimizes their utilization and satisfies user requirements. The privacy-preserving and cost-effective problem is a classic MOO scheduling problem, where N workloads and split privacy-preserved datasets have to be scheduled on M identical cloud instances over HCs, with the multi-objective functions that minimize the information about sensitive data learned by adversaries, the financial expense of the total instances consumed, and the maximum execution time of the instance that completes the last workload, i.e., makespan. After obtaining the estimated results and configuration in step ❺, the application will be deployed and executed onto the runtime environment. The system should ensure that data storage and workload execution remain in place and continue to be effective even among changes, such as downtime, errors, or attackers, to the system or emerging threats, according to step ❻ [7]. Note that when constructing this model, we refer to the prior research experience and user requirements from several EU projects such as CLARIFY[2], BlueCloud2026[3], ENVRI-Hub NEXT[4], and LifeWatch ERIC[5].

3.2 Privacy-Preserving and Cost-Effective Metrics

To satisfy user demands, privacy-preserving and cost-effective data processing should consider goals such as privacy preservation, makespan, and monetary cost. Additionally, we use the semi-honest threat model to evaluate the robustness of the system [6]. HC service providers honestly fulfill their role in the storage and processing tasks, but may inspect the information that users store or process. The attacker typically tries to collude with a number of processing nodes storing the datasets to infer and reason sensitive information of the other nodes to gain insights without directly altering the data or system. We assume that once the attacker obtains the image datasets stored on the nodes, he will try to reconstruct the original image data by using sensitive information from image labels, e.g., the coordinates $(x, y)_{\text{coord}}$. The system should evaluate the results and configuration of the MOO problem-solving before the sub-datasets and CNN inference models are assigned to planned infrastructures.

To quantify the privacy-preserving goals, we introduce information-theoretic metrics since they assume a stronger adversary and are more efficient concerning both communication and computational demands [8,9]. Let $\mathcal{N}$ be the number of datasets $\{d_{p,1}, d_{p,2}, ..., d_{p,N}\}$ split from the entire image $\mathcal{D}$; the set $\{d_{e,1}, d_{e,2}, ..., d_{e,N}\}$ denotes the encrypted datasets. Let Z_i and S_i be the encrypted and private information of $d_{e,i}$ and $d_{p,i}$ ($i \in \mathcal{N}$), respectively. We denote the entropy that measures the randomness of S_i as $H(S_i) = -\sum_{j=1}^{n} p_j log_2 p_j$, where p_j denotes the probability of the unique coordinate information in S_i. The mutual information $I(S; Z) = H(S) - H(S|Z)$ between two random variables S and Z measures the dependence between S and Z, quantifying the average reduction in uncertainty about S that results from learning the value of Z.

Output Utility. The output utility is to measure how close the estimated value $\hat{Y}_i$ of a privacy-preserving distributed processing algorithm is to its desired output Y_i, for each node $i \in \mathcal{N} \subset M$,

$$u_i = I(Y_i; \hat{Y}_i), \quad \forall i \in \mathcal{N} \tag{1}$$

where $0 \leq u_i \leq I(Y_i; Y_i)$ and $u_i = I(Y_i, Y_i)$ indicates perfect output utility [9].

---

[2] CLARIFY project. http://www.clarify-project.eu/.
[3] Blue-Cloud2026 project. https://blue-cloud.org/about-blue-cloud-2026.
[4] ENVRI-Hub NEXT. https://envri-hub.envri.eu/.
[5] LifeWatch ERIC. https://www.lifewatch.eu/.

Privacy Risk. Let $\mathcal{V}$ denote the set of random variables containing all information collected by the adversaries throughout the whole process. The individual privacy of honest node $i \in \mathcal{N}_h$ quantifies the amount of information about the private data S_i learned by the adversaries, which is given by,

$$\rho_i = I(S_i; \mathcal{V}), \quad \forall i \in \mathcal{N}_h \subset \mathcal{N} \tag{2}$$

The smaller ρ_i, the more private the data is, hence, the lower the privacy risk the data is. Based on the definitions of the adversary model, the lower bound on individual privacy risk is formally stated by,

$$\rho_{i,min} = I(S_i; \{S_j, \hat{Y}_j\}_{j \in \mathcal{N}_c}), \quad \mathcal{N}_c = \mathcal{N} - 1 \tag{3}$$

where adversaries always have knowledge of the private data $\{s_j\}_j = S_j$ and estimated outputs over corrupted nodes $\{\hat{y}_j\}_j = \hat{Y}_j$, in which the maximum number of corrupted nodes $\mathcal{N}_c$ denotes $\mathcal{N} - 1$ out of $\mathcal{N}$ [9].

Total Cost and Makespan. To measure the total cost and makespan of employing cloud instances $\mathcal{N}$ over the HC model, we consider the pay-as-you-go pricing model. Let p_k be the unit price of the kth cloud instance over the HC that consists of commercial and private cloud resources M. The total monetary cost is given by,

$$\text{Cost} = \sum_{k=1}^{\mathcal{N}} (T_k^{(\text{compt.})} + T_k^{(\text{comm.})}) \times p_k \times x_k, \quad k \in M \tag{4}$$

where $x_k \in \boldsymbol{x}$ is a boolean value that if sub-dataset d_k from $\mathcal{D}$ and the inference model are mapping to the cloud instance k, then x_k equals 1; otherwise, 0. If k belongs to commercial cloud instances, then $p_k \in R^+$; otherwise, $p_k = 0$. $T_k^{(\text{comm.})}$ is the communication time when transferring the inference model and encrypted sub-dataset $d_{e,k}$ to the cloud instance k and $T_k^{(\text{compt.})}$ is the computation time when running the workload on k, respectively. Similarly, the makespan over distributed processing nodes is given by,

$$\text{Makespan} = \max((T_k^{(\text{compt.})} + T_k^{(\text{comm.})}) \times x_k), \quad k \in M \tag{5}$$

where the compute capacity, geographical location, and network bandwidth of the instance k impact the time of executing the privacy-preserving distributed application that typically consists of the time cost of on-site computation and communication overhead.

3.3 Multi-objective Optimization

The overall optimization objective of the system model intends to minimize the average lower bound on privacy risk f_1, the total monetary cost f_2, and the maximum completion time f_3 over a HC:

$$\min f_1 = \text{Average minimal privacy risk} = \bar{\rho}_{min}(s), \quad \forall s \in \mathcal{S} \tag{6}$$

$$\min f_2 = \text{Cost} = \sum_{k=1}^{\mathcal{N}} (T_k^{(\text{compt.})} + T_k^{(\text{comm.})}) \times p_k \times x_k, \quad \forall k \in M \tag{7}$$

$$\min f_3 = \text{Makespan} = \max((T_k^{(\text{compt.})} + T_k^{(\text{comm.})}) \times x_k), \quad \forall k \in M \tag{8}$$

with regards to the following constraints:

- The average privacy risk $\bar{\rho}_{min}$ is sensitive to privacy-preserving data-splitting strategy s in the set $\mathcal{S}$, since each strategy s generates unique sub-datasets of different sizes and image labels.
- The total number of split datasets $\mathcal{N}$ is expected to be the minimal number of the employed distributed processing nodes, which is limited to the maximum available resources of the HC model M.
- Each split dataset and its corresponding inferences should be mapped to only one instance at a time. Meanwhile, one instance only runs one processing task per time. The total monetary cost f_2 is limited by the user's *budget*.

4 PriCE: Privacy-Preserving and Cost-Effective Solution

This section presents the proposed PriCE solution and its algorithm pseudocode, as detailed in Algorithm 1. The solution primarily involves two key components: (1) privacy-preserving image splitting using graph-coloring, and (2) 3D Pareto trade-off solutions for resource planning.

4.1 Privacy-Preserving Image Splitting with Graph-Coloring

To cope with the diverse image samples of the privacy-preserving data-splitting procedure, we abstract the entire image as a grid graph where different patches with pixel size $p \times p$ are cropped from the original image $\mathcal{D}$, containing sensitive image labels and objects. The image label contains sensitive coordinate information to reconstruct the image and guide the outcome. One essential hypothesis is that the more adjacent image patches an attacker obtains, the higher the probability he could succeed in restoring the entire original image.

Let $G = (V, E)$ be a graph extracted from the entire patch dataset D cropped from the original image $\mathcal{D}$. Each patch is represented as a vertex $v \in V$. Two vertices v and μ of V such that $(v, \mu) \in E$ are called to be adjacent. Let $v = (x_i, y_i)$ and $\mu = (x_{i+1}, y_{i+1})$, we denote all possible adjacent relationships between v and μ as: (1) horizontal: $|x_{i+1} - x_i| = p$; (2) vertical: $|y_{i+1} - y_i| = p$; and (3) diagonal: $\sqrt{(x_{i+1} - x_i)^2 + (y_{i+1} - y_i)^2} = \sqrt{2} \times p$. With these characteristics, the positions of the patches can be identified in the original image. The graph-coloring-based splitting procedure is written in pseudo-code from step 1 to step 4.

Based on the assumption, we study different split strategies to scramble these identifications and reduce the risk of restoring the original dataset from the image fragments by the adversary. On the one hand, we adopt the graph-coloring-based

Algorithm 1: PriCE Method

Input: The original image $\mathcal{D}$, patch size p, split strategies $\mathcal{S}$, inference workloads Θ, and cloud instances M, budget B
Output: A new label system A_e, Pareto optimal solutions $\boldsymbol{x}^*$, and encrypted split datasets $d_{e,1}, d_{e,2}, ..., d_{e,N}$.

1 Patch set $D \leftarrow$ create_patches($\mathcal{D}, p$)
2 $G \leftarrow$ abstract_a_graph(D)
3 $\mathcal{N}, C \leftarrow$ **graph_coloring**$(G, s)_{s \in \mathcal{S}}$
4 $d_{p,1}, ..., d_{p,N} \leftarrow$ divide D_p into $\mathcal{N}$ sub data sets
5 **for** $d_{p,k} \in d_{p,1}, ..., d_{p,N}$ **do**
6 $\quad$ Data matrix A_p of size $(a \times b) \leftarrow S_k \leftarrow d_{p,k}$
7 $\quad$ $\bar{x} \leftarrow$ mean(A_p)
8 $\quad$ $\sigma \leftarrow$ std(A_p)
9 $\quad$ $A_{p,c} \leftarrow (A_p - \bar{x})/\sigma$ // Normalize the data
10 $\quad$ **Cov**$(A_{p,c}) \leftarrow \frac{1}{a-1} A_{p,c}^T A_{p,c}$ // Compute the covariance matrix of $A_{p,c}$
11 $\quad$ $\lambda, \boldsymbol{V} \leftarrow$ **eig**(**Cov**($A_{p,c}$)) // Compute eigenvalues and eigenvectors
12 $\quad$ $\lambda_{sort}, \boldsymbol{V}_{sort} \leftarrow$ **sort_eig**($\lambda, \boldsymbol{V}$)
13 $\quad$ $\boldsymbol{V}_k \leftarrow$ first k columns of $\boldsymbol{V}_{sort}$
14 $\quad$ $A_e \leftarrow A_{p,c} \boldsymbol{V}_k$ // Transform the original coordinate data
15 $\quad$ $d_{e,k} \leftarrow$ rename($d_{p,k}, A_e, r$) // Transform labels with random values r and perturbed coordinates A_e
16 $\bar{\rho}_{min}(s)_{s \in \mathcal{S}} \leftarrow \rho_{i,min}(s)_{s \in \mathcal{S}}, i \in \mathcal{N} \leftarrow$ **Eq. 3**
17 $totalC, maxTime, \boldsymbol{x} \leftarrow$ **prob.solve**($\mathcal{N}, \Theta, M, B$), derived from **Eqs. 6, 7, and 8**
18 $\boldsymbol{x}^* \leftarrow$ plot_Pareto_3D($\boldsymbol{x}$) // plot the 3D Pareto trade-off solutions
19 **return** $\boldsymbol{x}^*, A_e, \{d_{e,1}, d_{e,2}, ..., d_{e,N}\}$

split strategies [10–12], including 'largest_first', 'random_sequential', 'smallest_last', 'independent_set', 'connected_sequential', 'saturation_largest_first', to split the entire dataset D into different sub-datasets $d_{p,1}, ..., d_{p,N}$, such that no two adjacent vertices share the same color or dataset. On the other hand, we introduce a random data perturbation to preserve the sensitive coordinates on split datasets' labels by inserting random noise.

We extract $(x, y)_{\text{coord}}$ as a data matrix A_p of size $(a \times b)$, $a < b$, from $d_{p,k} \subset D$. After normalization, we compute the covariance matrix of the normalized matrix $A_{p,c}$, and then computed the eigenvalues λ and eigenvectors $\boldsymbol{V}$ so that we can get the top-k eigenvectors $\boldsymbol{V}_k$ to calculate A_e. Moreover, we transform the data into a new coordinate system and encrypt it into datasets $\{d_{e,1}, d_{e,2}, ..., d_{e,N}\}$. The pseudo-code is illustrated in step 5 to step 15. From the perturbed data, since we know the noise variance, we obtain the estimate coordinates $\hat{Y}$ from decryption by inversely transforming the eigenvector matrix $\boldsymbol{V}_k$ and A_e, i.e., $\hat{Y} = A_e \cdot \boldsymbol{V}_k^T$. Note that the size of the transformed data matrix A_e might differ from that of the original data matrix A_p. To address this discrepancy, we introduce random values r to compensate for the size difference. Consequently, we can obtain a set of split image datasets with encrypted labels $\{d_{e,1}, ..., d_{e,k}, ..., d_{e,N}\}$. Besides, since we know the mappings of original labels and their corresponding encrypted labels, it is easy to measure the output utility shown in Eq. 1. Furthermore, we calculate the average minimal privacy risk over the distributed datasets by Eq. 3. Empirical evidence indicates that the computation of eigenvalues and eigenvectors remains lightweight, even with up to 10,000 patches.

4.2 Pareto Trade-Off Solution Among Privacy, Cost, and Time

The number of split datasets $\mathcal{N}$ is directly related to the number of cloud instances that need to be rented. Given split data $\{d_{e,1}, d_{e,2}, d_{e,N}\}$, CNN inference workload Θ, hybrid cloud instances M, and user's budget B, our PriCE establishes a decision-making process based on MOO for resource planning.

The MOO problem is a classical integer programming problem since the variables x are restricted to be integers. We first find available optimal solutions of the bi-objective optimization problem that minimizes f_2 (Eq. 7) and f_3 (Eq. 8) under the *budget*, and together with all available split strategies that generate f_1 (Eq. 6), obtaining all feasible solutions as X. Due to the trade-offs among minimizing lower bound on privacy risk f_1, monetary cost reduction f_2, and makespan minimization f_3, we then seek Pareto trade-off solutions $x^* \in X$, where no solution is superior to another in all objectives (See Sect. 3.3). Pareto front is the set of all such non-dominated Pareto optimal solutions. From the mathematical point of view, the definition of the dominance between two candidate solutions can be expressed as x_1 dominates x_2 if $f_i(x_1) \leq f_i(x_2)$, $\forall i = 1, 2, ..., n$. Therefore, a solution $x^* \in X$ is called to be nondominated or Pareto optimal if and only if there does not exist any other point $x \in X$, such that $F(x) \leq F(x^*)$ and $f_i(x) < f_i(x^*)$ for at least one function [13], in which $F(x) = [f_1(x), f_2(x), f_3(x)]$. The MOO problem-solving procedure is written in the steps 16 to 18, as shown in Algorithm 1.

5 Experiments and Evaluation

This section details the experimental setup, demonstrates the visualized results, and evaluates the outcomes for validation. We implemented our algorithm PriCE in Python and evaluated the capability and quality of response of our algorithm via simulation when used to answer the questions in Sect. 1. It is important to note that the results presented here are, in whole or in part, based on data generated by the TCGA Research Network: https://www.cancer.gov/tcga. The original data and experimental results are available online[6].

5.1 Experimental Setup

We conducted extensive experiments on a dedicated remote server equipped with 6 cores/12 threads@3.6GHz, 64GB DDR4 RAM, and 2×512 GB NVMe SSD and a private GPU server equipped with a Tesla T4 16 GB device. To collect

---

[6] The source code is available online. https://github.com/yuandou168/PriCE.

benchmark data, we used a real-world CNN ensemble application for artifact detection developed by Kanwal *et al.* [14] as our CNN workloads. Specifically, it is the ensemble of five CNNs. The complexity of the inference workloads has been measured by the total parameters, FLOPs, batch size, and memory usage.

For the evaluation of solutions, we have investigated 25 commercial GPU servers offered by Fluidstack[7] and 2 private GPU servers offered by universities, located in different cities across the Netherlands, Norway, USA, Iceland, and India. Since these cloud instances have different configurations, we investigated their relative performance based on TPU review data about GPUs[8] and collected the workload performance over the private T4 GPU server offered by the university of Amsterdam. Besides, since the bandwidths are various with different geo-locations, we refer to fixed upload Internet speeds provided by SpeedTest[9] to simplify the network environments. More technical details have been presented in the source code.

5.2 Visualization

In this study, we utilized a WSI named 'TCGA-E9-A1N3-01Z-00-DX1' for demonstration, which is available on the TCGA repository[10]. In Fig. 2, we demonstrate that PriCE can effectively split a large medical image into different sub-datasets using a graph-coloring-based strategy, ensuring that no two adjacent patches are placed in the same sub-dataset.

Figure 2a represents the thumbnail picture of the original WSI and Fig. 2b is the binary mask pictures after removing the background of the large image. The patch nodes from the original image represent a set of colored images with the size of 224×224 pixels; each of them has a unique label that contains the coordinate information of the image to identify its position in the original image. First, we can see that PriCE can perform graph-coloring-based splitting with the coloring assignment to distribute image samples for the WSI. For example, we obtain eight sub-datasets with the 'random sequential' graph-coloring strategy. Then, we adopt the data perturbation method to the split patch labels to hide the sensitive coordinate information; meanwhile, we examine the output utility that measures how close the estimated label of the privacy-preserving algorithm is to its desired output. In Fig. 2c, we plot the reconstructed graph with identified coordinates after the decryption procedure.

For more complex and diverse WSIs, we can apply our method to extract various graphs by adding patch nodes and edges, choose, and run different strategies to generate different split datasets. Practically, we tested our PriCE for a number of TCGA WSIs. The outcomes always match the original coordinates, achieving the perfect output utility.

---

[7] Cloud GPU servers. https://console2.fluidstack.io/virtual-machines.
[8] GPU Database–TechPowerUp. https://www.techpowerup.com/gpu-specs/.
[9] Network Speed Test.https://www.speedtest.net/performance.
[10] https://portal.gdc.cancer.gov/image-viewer/MultipleImageViewerPage?caseId=03c143e0-d8a1-4d60-a4a3-df0501fc6b6e.

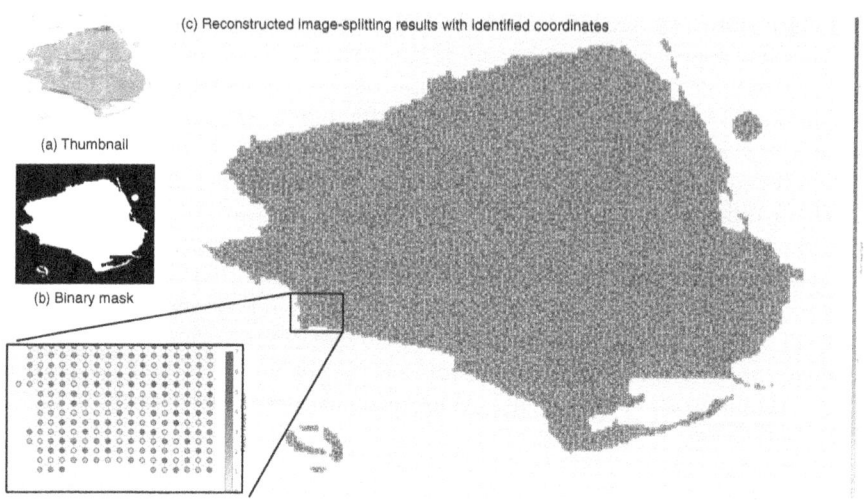

Fig. 2. Visualization of the image-splitting: (a) the thumbnail picture of the original medical image, (b) the binary mask picture, and (c) the reconstructed graph from estimated coordinates after decryption.

5.3 Reduction of the Average Lower Bound on Privacy Risk

We bring a unique perspective by introducing our novel PriCE algorithm with 'graph-coloring-based split' strategies (i.e., $\mathcal{S}_{graph}$), which we compare with the commonly used 'average split with shuffle or without shuffle' ones (i.e., $\mathcal{S}_{avg}$). Table 2 presents the overall comparisons of the number of split dataset and the average minimal privacy risk scores of the image-splitting strategies. Using graph-based split strategies, we achieved the minimum number $\mathcal{N}$ of split datasets of varying sizes. However, the average split strategy is not able to obtain that number except for customizing it by users. To make the comparisons fair, we custom the same $\mathcal{N}$ when splitting the datasets in the average cases.

The results show that (1) in the average split cases for the same number $\mathcal{N}$, the minimal privacy risk scores with shuffle ('is_shuffled_True') and without shuffle ('is_shuffle_False') are very close to each other; (2) when the number of split datasets is four, the privacy risk scores of all cases are almost the same, though the one with 'saturation_largest_first' is higher than the others; (3) as the number of datasets increases, the corresponding average minimal privacy risk score decreases; and (4) for the same number of split datasets, the average minimal privacy risk obtained by most graph-coloring-based split methods are generally lower but accompanied by a larger standard deviation. When $\mathcal{N} = 7$, the difference between graph and average-based strategies is over 0.04, which is higher than when $\mathcal{N} = 5$, 6, or 8, where the differences are below 0.02, 0.04, and 0.03, respectively. As a result, the number of datasets $\mathcal{N}$ and corresponding split strategies significantly affect the privacy risk.

Table 2. Comparisons of split strategies, the number of split datasets, and the average minimal privacy risk scores.

	Strategy	$\mathcal{N}$	$\bar{\rho}_{min}$		
			x_{coord}	y_{coord}	$\sum(x,y)$
Graph-based Split	saturation_largest_first	4	0.1835±0.001	0.1389±0.0007	0.3224
	smallest_last	5	0.1523±0.0564	0.1169±0.0409	0.2692
	connected_sequential	6	0.1281±0.0738	0.0987±0.055	0.2268
	independent_set	7	0.1108±0.0798	0.0859±0.0597	0.1967
	largest_first	8	0.1101±0.058	0.0879±0.0445	0.198
	random_sequential	8	0.1106±0.0571	0.0881±0.0437	0.1987
Average Split w/wo Shuffle	is_shuffled_True	4	0.1832±0.0004	0.1386±0.0005	0.3218
	is_shuffled_True	5	0.1613±0.0003	0.1255±0.0002	0.2868
	is_shuffled_True	6	0.1448±0.0005	0.1145±0.0005	0.2593
	is_shuffled_True	7	0.132±0.0003	0.1061±0.0005	0.2381
	is_shuffled_True	8	0.1213±0.0007	0.0989±0.0007	0.2202
	is_shuffled_False	4	0.1831±0.0009	0.1386±0.0002	0.3217
	is_shuffled_False	5	0.1615±0.0011	0.1251±0.0008	0.2866
	is_shuffled_False	6	0.1448±0.001	0.1147±0.0006	0.2595
	is_shuffled_False	7	0.1318±0.0007	0.106±0.0006	0.2378
	is_shuffled_False	8	0.1213±0.0005	0.0985±0.0007	0.2198

5.4 Evaluation by Simulations

For Pareto optimal resource planning, we successfully obtained the Pareto trade-off solutions out of all feasible solutions from various split strategies under budget constraints through simulation experiments. Figures 3 and 4 depict the Pareto trade-off solutions selected using the 3D Pareto front, comparing them across graph-based and average-based split strategies and two budget constraints.

When the budget is limited to 120, we have identified four Pareto optimal solutions out of ten feasible solutions (4/10) in Fig. 3a, within the scenario using only average split strategies ($s \in \mathcal{S}_{avg}$). In contrast, we have found four out of six Pareto trade-off solutions (4/6) within the scenarios using only graph-based split strategies ($s \in \mathcal{S}_{graph}$), as shown in Fig. 3b. When decreasing the budget to 100, there are eight feasible solutions in the only average split case ($s \in \mathcal{S}_{avg}$), compared to ten solutions under the budget=120, as seen in Fig. 3c. This reduction is attributed to the absence of bi-objective optimal solutions for f_2 and f_3 identified by the problem solver when the number of average split datasets is eight. Remarkably, for the graph-coloring-based split, our PriCE method could still identify all Pareto trade-off resource planning solutions under the budget=100, as depicted in Fig. 3d.

When combining both average and graph-based strategies ($s \in \mathcal{S}_{all}$), there are four Pareto trade-off solutions out of sixteen (4/16) when the budget is constrained by 120, as illustrated in Fig. 4a. Notably, when compared to the separate

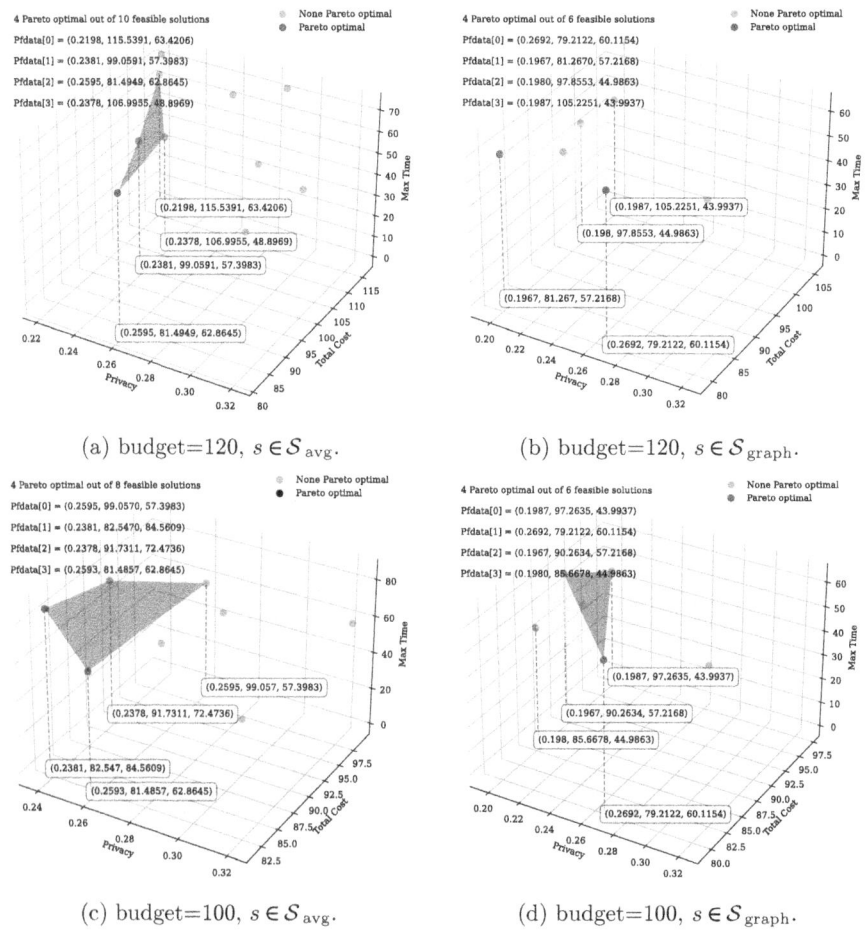

(a) budget=120, $s \in \mathcal{S}_{\text{avg}}$.

(b) budget=120, $s \in \mathcal{S}_{\text{graph}}$.

(c) budget=100, $s \in \mathcal{S}_{\text{avg}}$.

(d) budget=100, $s \in \mathcal{S}_{\text{graph}}$.

Fig. 3. The 3D Pareto trade-off solutions are compared as follows: (a) and (c) solutions fall within the only average split strategies $\mathcal{S}_{\text{avg}}$, while (b) and (d) solutions are derived from the only graph-coloring-based split strategies $\mathcal{S}_{\text{graph}}$.

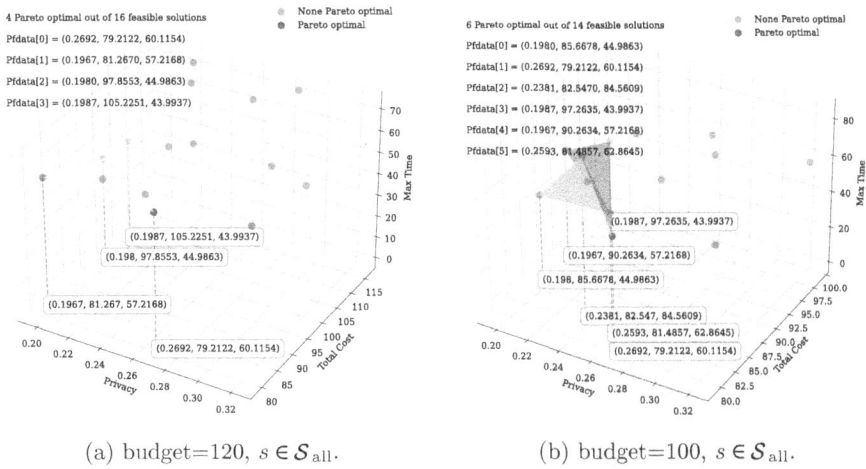

Fig. 4. Comparisons of the 3D Pareto trade-off solutions with all combined strategies $\mathcal{S}_{\text{all}}$ under two budget constraints: (a) budget = 120, and (b) budget = 100.

cases, all four Pareto trade-off solutions (4/4) originate from the graph-coloring-based split strategies. Furthermore, when combining all feasible solutions from all split strategies and budget = 100, as depicted in Fig. 4b, the majority of Pareto trade-off solutions (4/6) for the privacy-preserving and cost-effective problem are derived from the graph-coloring-based split strategies, with the remaining 2/6 solutions originating from the average split strategies. It can be inferred that when the budget becomes more constrained, privacy will be sacrificed. We have observed when the split datasets are unbalanced, the resource allocation plan exhibits greater resilience in matching with heterogeneous cloud instances. This increased resilience arises from the enhanced diversity in execution times and costs, which maximizes the opportunities for efficient task assignments.

6 Conclusion and Future Work

This paper investigates the workflow scheduling problem of privacy-preserving and cost-effective distributed inference using multiple GPU servers over hybrid clouds. We propose a novel solution, PriCE, which employs various image splitting strategies to enhance privacy and cost-efficiency. To the best of our knowledge, this is the first approach to address a privacy-aware scheduling problem that minimizes privacy risk while reducing makespan and cost within a budget in a privacy-preserving distributed system. We conducted a comprehensive experimental evaluation using a real-world application for medical image artifact detection. The results demonstrate that PriCE successfully takes the large number of patches from a gigapixel image and splits them using multiple graph-coloring-based strategies, yielding the desired output utility while lowering privacy risk, makespan, and monetary cost under the user's budget. Further improvements in implementation might include making better use of secure distributed messaging or secrets handling across multiple clouds with high-level automated operations. Additionally, exploring the trade-offs between privacy overhead versus time and monetary cost in more complex scenarios could provide valuable insights.

Acknowledgment. We thank Mr. Zongxiong Chen for discussing the methodology and Mr. Aditya Shankar for reviewing the manuscript. This work has been partially funded by the European Union's Horizon research and innovation program by CLARIFY (860627), BlueCloud-2026 (101094227), ENVRI-Hub Next (101131141), OSCARS (101129751), EVERSE (101129744), BioDT (101057437, via LifeWatch ERIC), by the LifeWatch ERIC and by the Dutch NWO LTER-LIFE project.

References

1. Mazhelis, O., Tyrväinen, P.: Economic aspects of hybrid cloud infrastructure: User organization perspective. Inf. Syst. Front. **14**, 845–869 (2012)
2. Sharif, S., et al.: Privacy-aware scheduling SaaS in high performance computing environments. IEEE Trans. Parallel Distrib. Syst. **28**(4), 1176–1188 (2016)
3. Lei, J., Wu, Q., Xu, J.: Privacy and security-aware workflow scheduling in a hybrid cloud. Future Gener. Comput. Syst. **131**, 269–278 (2022)
4. Zhou, A.C., et al.: Privacy regulation aware process mapping in geo-distributed cloud data centers. IEEE Trans. Parallel Distrib. Syst. **30**(8), 1872–1888 (2019)
5. Wen, Y., et al.: Scheduling workflows with privacy protection constraints for big data applications on cloud. Future Gener. Comput. Syst. **108**, 1084–1091 (2020)
6. Domingo-Ferrer, J., et al.: Privacy-preserving cloud computing on sensitive data: a survey of methods, products and challenges. Comput. Commun. **140**, 38–60 (2019)
7. Wang, Y., et al.: Towards a privacy-preserving distributed cloud service for preprocessing very large medical images. In: 2023 IEEE International Conference on Digital Health (ICDH), pp. 325–327. IEEE (2023)
8. Kraskov, A., Stögbauer, H., Grassberger, P.: Estimating mutual information. Phys. Rev. E **69**(6), 066138 (2004)
9. Li, Q., et al.: Privacy-preserving distributed processing: metrics, bounds and algorithms. IEEE Trans. Inf. Forensics Secur. **16**, 2090–2103 (2021)
10. Matula, D.W., Beck, L.L.: Smallest-last ordering and clustering and graph coloring algorithms. J. ACM (JACM) **30**(3), 417–427 (1983)
11. Kubale, M.: Graph Colorings, vol. 352. American Mathematical Society (2004)
12. Deo, N., Kowalik, J.S., et al.: Discrete optimization algorithms: with Pascal programs. Courier Corporation (2006)
13. Marler, R.T., Arora, J.S.: Survey of multi-objective optimization methods for engineering. Struct. Multidiscip. Optim. **26**, 369–395 (2004)
14. Kanwal, N., et al.: Equipping computational pathology systems with artifact processing pipelines: a showcase for computation and performance trade-offs. arXiv preprint arXiv:2403.07743 (2024)

A $1.25(1+\epsilon)$-Approximation Algorithm for Scheduling with Rejection Costs Proportional to Processing Times

Olivier Beaumont[1,2], Rémi Bouzel[3], Lionel Eyraud-Dubois[1,2], Esragul Korkmaz[1,2(✉)], Laercio Pilla[1,2], and Alexandre Van Kempen[3]

[1] Inria Center of the University of Bordeaux, Talence, France
{olivier.beaumont,lionel.eyraud-dubois,
esragul.korkmaz,laercio.pilla}@inria.fr
[2] LaBRI, UMR 5800, Talence, France
[3] Qarnot Computing, Montrouge, France
{remi.bouzel,alexandre.vankempen}@qarnot-computing.com

Abstract. We address an offline job scheduling problem where jobs can either be processed on a limited supply of energy-efficient machines, or offloaded to energy-inefficient machines (with an unlimited supply), and the goal is to minimize the total energy consumed in processing all tasks. This scheduling problem can be formulated as a problem of scheduling with rejection, where rejecting a job corresponds to process it on an energy-inefficient machine and has a cost directly proportional to the processing time of the job. To solve this scheduling problem, we introduce a novel $\frac{5}{4}(1+\epsilon)$ approximation algorithm $\mathcal{BEKP}$ by associating it to a Multiple Subset Sum problem. Our algorithm is an improvement over the existing literature, which provides a $(\frac{3}{2} - \frac{1}{2m})$ approximation for scheduling with arbitrary rejection costs. We evaluate and discuss the effectiveness of our approach through a series of experiments, comparing it to existing algorithms.

Keywords: Scheduling with rejection · Approximation algorithm · Energy minimization

1 Introduction

In this paper, we consider a scheduling problem with the possibility of job rejection, where the cost of rejecting a job is proportional to its processing time. The inspiration for this problem comes from the recent existence of cloud providers that recycle the heat produced by computation to heat buildings or other facilities. For example, Qarnot Computing[1] [3] installs its computing units in water boilers that are used in swimming pools or large apartment buildings to provide

---
[1] https://qarnot.com/.

hot water. As computing jobs run on these boilers, the energy used for computing is reused to heat the water, eliminating the need for costly air conditioning to cool the machine and reducing the overall carbon footprint.

However, there may not be enough of these energy-efficient machines available to run all of the required jobs in a reasonable amount of time. In this case, it may be necessary to offload some of this workload to other less efficient compute units, either within the cloud provider or to another conventional public provider. From the point of view of scheduling jobs on the boiler, this corresponds to *rejecting* some jobs, and the goal is to minimize the additional energy required to process these jobs on the less efficient machines. As a first approximation, it is reasonable to assume that the energy required to run a job is proportional to its processing time.

Scheduling with rejection is a valuable concept applicable in various real-life scenarios [12]. For instance, it has been used to model the context of make-to-order production with a limited amount of resources [5], where the cost of rejection corresponds to a lack of income from not producing the item. When modeling our problem, we introduce several additional assumptions to formalize the job scheduling problem in a more interesting and simple way. These assumptions, while extending beyond the initial scope, result in a potentially practical model in other contexts. For example, as minimizing the makespan of the accepted jobs plus the total penalty for rejected jobs is a common objective function in the works for scheduling with rejection, we consider the same objective function. This assumption corresponds for example to the case where a customer rents a boiler to process their jobs and wants to minimize the total energy (or financial cost), which is equal to the total usage of the boiler plus the additional cost of outsourcing some of the jobs to other less efficient machines. Another example is the case where a maintenance operation needs to be scheduled on a boiler. Similarly, to simplify our problem, as a first step, we assume an offline setting and no deadline constraints on the jobs.

The best-known approximation algorithm for scheduling with rejection is reported in a paper by Liu and Lu [8], with an approximation factor of $\frac{3}{2}$. The main contribution of our paper is to exploit the assumption that the rejection cost is proportional to the processing time to obtain a polynomial-time practical approximation algorithm with an improved approximation factor of $\frac{5}{4}(1+\epsilon)$ for any positive ϵ. Our algorithm is based on techniques adapted from an algorithm for the Multiple Subset Sum problem [4], together with ad hoc bounds on the makespan of an optimal solution.

The rest of the paper is organized as follows. We discuss related work and our problem formulation in Sects. 2 and 3, respectively. In Sect. 4, we present a scheduling algorithm for the case where we are given a target makespan T. This algorithm provides a solution with a makespan of at most $\frac{5}{4}T$ with a guarantee on the cost of rejected jobs. In Sect. 5, we use bounds on the makespan of an optimal solution to approximate it within a factor of $1+\epsilon$ in reasonable time. In Sect. 6, we perform an experimental study to assess the practical behavior of our algorithm compared to prior solutions. Finally, we present conclusions and perspectives in Sect. 7.

2 Related Works

For a comprehensive overview of scheduling with rejection, we refer the reader to the surveys by Slotnick [13] and Shabtay et al. [12].

Bartal et al. [1] introduced the problem of scheduling with job rejection. Their objective is to minimize the makespan of accepted jobs plus the sum of penalties associated with rejected jobs. For the online setting, they present a $(1 + \phi)$-competitive algorithm, where ϕ represents the golden ratio. For the offline setting, they introduce a fully polynomial approximation algorithm for fixed m and a polynomial approximation algorithm for arbitrary m. In addition, they propose a $(2 - \frac{1}{m})$ approximation algorithm for the offline problem with $\mathcal{O}(n \log n)$ complexity.

Ou et al. [11] improve the approximation of Bartal et al. with a heuristic that achieves a worst-case bound of $\frac{3}{2} + \epsilon$ and $\mathcal{O}(n \log n + \frac{n}{\epsilon})$ complexity. Liu and Lu [8] provide a $(\frac{3}{2} - \frac{1}{2m})$ approximation algorithm with $\mathcal{O}(n^3 log n)$ complexity, improving on the work of Ou et al. [11]. In addition to this solution for the identical release date problem, Liu and Lu also present solutions for both the single machine and the parallel machine problems in presence of release dates.

The problem of scheduling with rejection has also been investigated, with the goal of optimizing the sum of weighted completion times of scheduled jobs plus the sum of penalties for rejected jobs. Engels et al. [6] propose general techniques to address offline scheduling with rejection problems with this objective. Epstein et al. [7] focus on the single-machine online problem, where jobs have unit processing times and the weight of each job's completion time is equal to 1. Liu [9] considers the single-machine problem with partial rejection and devises both polynomial-time optimal and pseudopolynomial-time optimal algorithms.

In their work, Mor and Shabtay [10] explore two objectives in scheduling with rejection for single-machine problems. One approach aims to minimize the sum of total late work and rejection cost, while another focuses solely on minimizing total rejection cost, providing an upper bound on total late work.

In our paper, we present a new heuristic to improve on the $(\frac{3}{2} - \frac{1}{2m})$ approximation provided by Liu and Lu [8]. In our setting, the rejection costs are proportional to the processing times of the jobs. We then relate the problem to a Multiple Subset Sum Problem (MSSP).

MSSP consists in allocating a set of n items into m identical bins, each with a positive capacity c. Each item i has a positive weight w_i. The goal is to distribute the items among the bins so as to maximize the total sum of weights of the items in the bins. This problem is known to be strongly NP-hard, and finding an optimal solution is challenging. However, solving MSSP is of practical importance in various domains such as logistics, cutting and packing, where efficient resource allocation is essential to optimize operations.

Caprara et al. [4] propose an algorithm for MSSP that guarantees to obtain at least a fraction $\frac{3}{4}$ of the maximum possible weight sum. The complexity of this approximation algorithm is $\mathcal{O}(m^2 + n)$. In their work, they introduce two basic ideas that are relevant in our context. These ideas are explained below.

First, they divide the set of items into five subsets based on their weights relative to the capacity of the bin. In the first step, the subset containing the smallest items is excluded (all other items are considered large). The bounds on the weights of all subsets are used to identify all possible valid *combinations* of large item subsets that can be simultaneously allocated to any bin. This limited set of combinations is then explicitly used to build the approximation algorithm. In the second step, they greedily allocate small items, once other large items have been allocated. They prove that any polynomial-time algorithm that achieves a ratio $\frac{3}{4}$ of the maximum weight sum for MSSP without considering small items can be transformed into one that achieves $\frac{3}{4}$ for the general MSSP (with small items) with the same time complexity. In our work, we adapt these ideas to build the approximation algorithm.

3 Problem Formulation

We consider a scheduling problem where a set of non-preemptive jobs J are to be scheduled on m identical machines. Each job i is characterized by its processing time p_i and can either be processed on one of the energy-efficient machines (corresponding to boilers in the context of Qarnot) or rejected at a cost $\rho \cdot p_i$. This rejection cost represents the cost of offloading the job to other machines (e.g., a public cloud), which are assumed to be in unlimited supply.

A solution $\mathcal{S}$ specifies (i) whether each job is accepted or rejected and (ii) assigns each accepted job i to a machine $j \leq m$. The makespan $C^{\mathcal{S}}$ of a solution is the maximum load on any energy-efficient machine, $C^{\mathcal{S}} = \max_{j \leq m} \sum_{i \text{ assigned to } j} p_i$. We denote as $R^{\mathcal{S}}$ the total processing time (or *area*) of the rejected jobs in $\mathcal{S}$: $R^{\mathcal{S}} = \sum_{i \text{ rejected}} p_i$. The objective of our problem is to minimize the cost $Z^{\mathcal{S}}$, defined as the sum of the occupation of all the machines plus the rejection cost:

$$Z^{\mathcal{S}} = m \cdot C^{\mathcal{S}} + \rho \cdot R^{\mathcal{S}}. \tag{1}$$

Given a target makespan T, we denote with $R^*(T)$ the smallest possible area of rejected jobs among the solutions of makespan at most T. More formally, $R^*(T) = \min_{\mathcal{S}, C^{\mathcal{S}} \leq T} R^{\mathcal{S}}$. This definition leads to the following result:

Lemma 1. *For two values T_1 and T_2 such that $T_1 \leq T_2$, then $R^*(T_2) \leq R^*(T_1)$.*

Table 1 provides a summary of the main notations used in this paper. In the following sections, we present an approximation algorithm for this scheduling problem. We start in Sect. 4 with finding a good solution when a bound on the makespan is given, and then use this bound in Sect. 5 to build the overall approximation algorithm.

4 Scheduling with a Bound on Makespan

In this section, we assume that we are given a bound T on the makespan. We present an algorithm called *FillMaxArea* which, given a set of jobs J, a number of machines m and the bound T, outputs a solution $\mathcal{S}$ with $C^{\mathcal{S}} \leq \frac{5}{4}T$ and $R^{\mathcal{S}} \leq R^*(T)$.

Table 1. Notation employed throughout this paper

m	Number of machines
n	Number of jobs
J	Set of jobs
p_i	Processing time of job i for $i \in \{1, 2, ..., n\}$
W	Area of all jobs in J ($W = \sum_{i \in \{1,2,...,n\}} p_i$)
ρ	Rejection cost coefficient
C^S	Makespan of the accepted jobs in schedule S
A^S	Area of the accepted jobs in schedule S
R^S	Area of the rejected jobs in schedule S
Z^S	Cost of the schedule S: $Z^S = mC^S + \rho R^S$
OPT	An optimal schedule which minimizes the cost
$R^*(T)$	Minimum possible area of rejected jobs within makespan T ($min_{S, C^S \leq T} R^S$)

4.1 Job Types

From a given makespan bound T, we can group jobs from J according to their processing time. This idea is similar to Caprara et al. [4], using different cutoff values adapted to the context of scheduling with rejection costs.

$$G = \{i \mid \frac{3}{4}T < p_i \leq T\} \quad N_1 = \{i \mid \frac{1}{2}T < p_i \leq \frac{3}{4}T\}$$
$$N_2 = \{i \mid \frac{3}{8}T < p_i \leq \frac{1}{2}T\} \quad N_3 = \{i \mid \frac{1}{4}T < p_i \leq \frac{3}{8}T\} \quad P = \{i \mid p_i \leq \frac{1}{4}T\}$$

where jobs in G, N_1, N_2, and N_3 are called *long* jobs, while jobs in P are called *short* jobs. We define a *combination* $(Set_1, Set_2, ...)$ as a mapping of jobs to a machine, where exactly one job from each set (a set can occur multiple times) is scheduled on the same machine. For example, (N_3, N_3, N_2) represents two jobs from N_3 and one job from N_2 assigned to a machine in any order.

Lemma 2. *In a schedule with maximum makespan of T, only the following combinations of long jobs are valid:*

$$(G), (N_1), (N_2), (N_3)$$
$$(N_2, N_1), (N_3, N_1), (N_2, N_2), (N_3, N_2), (N_3, N_3)$$
$$(N_3, N_3, N_2), (N_3, N_3, N_3)$$

Proof. Consider one machine in a schedule, with makespan at most T. We split the proof depending on the number l of long jobs this machine processes.

For $l = 1$, any long job guarantees that the makespan bound T is respected. Thus, singleton possibilities are (G), (N_1), (N_2) and (N_3).

For $l = 2$, the combination (N_1, N_1) can not be assigned to that machine: indeed, jobs in N_1 are such that $p_i > \frac{1}{2}T$, so that processing any two of them is not feasible within makespan T. All other combinations of length 2 are valid. Thus, the possible pairs are (N_2, N_1), (N_3, N_1), (N_2, N_2), (N_3, N_2), (N_3, N_3).

For $l = 3$, if two jobs from N_2 are assigned to a machine, even assigning one extra N_3 job is not feasible since the total processing time exceeds $(\frac{3}{8} + \frac{3}{8} + \frac{1}{4})T = T$. Thus, set combinations with longer jobs are not valid either. Therefore, the only possible triplets are (N_3, N_3, N_2) and (N_3, N_3, N_3).

Finally, $l \geq 4$ is not feasible, since any long job has $p_i > \frac{1}{4}T$. □

In addition, it is possible to bound the maximum total processing time of any of these combinations.

Lemma 3. *For any of the combinations provided in Lemma 2, the overall processing time of any valid combination is at most $\frac{5}{4}T$.*

Proof. The proof is trivial, by enumerating all valid combinations and summing the upper bounds of its subset for each element.

4.2 Algorithm

FillMaxArea algorithm is based on these two lemmas. By guaranteeing that the long jobs assigned to each machine obey one of the combinations in Lemma 2, we can guarantee that the resulting solution $\mathcal{S}$ satisfies $C^{\mathcal{S}} \leq \frac{5}{4}T$.

Our long job assignment algorithm is based on the *AssignFrom* routine, whose pseudocode is given in Algorithm 1. Given the list of combinations and the number l of machines, *AssignFrom* creates l machine assignments by successively picking the jobs with the largest processing times from the first combination of available jobs. For example, $AssignFrom(\{(N_2, N_1), (N_3, N_1), (N_2, N_2)\}, l)$ selects the largest job from N_2 and the largest job from N_1 until one of them is empty, and then proceeds with the combination (N_3, N_1), and so on.

Algorithm 1. $AssignFrom(combs, l)$

1: $Result \leftarrow \emptyset$
2: Remove all combinations from *combs* where at least one set within the combination is empty
3: **while** $|Result| \leq l$ and *combs* is not empty **do**
4: Denote by $(K_1, K_2, ..., K_k)$ the first combination in *combs*
5: $j_1 \leftarrow$ the largest job from K_1
6: $j_2 \leftarrow$ the largest remaining job from K_2
7: Continue until $j_k \leftarrow$ the largest remaining job from K_k
8: $Result = Result \cup (j_1, j_2, ..., j_k)$
9: Remove all combinations from *combs* where at least one set within the combination is empty
10: **return** $Result$

The *FillMaxArea* algorithm, whose pseudocode is given in Algorithm 2, starts by scheduling the long jobs first, and completes the schedule with a greedy assignment of the short jobs without exceeding the makespan bound $\frac{5}{4}T$. To decide which long jobs to accept, we set values for $l_0, l_1, l_2,$ and l_3 that represent the number of machines running no long job, one long job, two long jobs, and three long jobs, respectively. For each of these cases, we use the *AssignFrom* routine with a careful ordering of the combinations identified in Lemma 2. If we run out of jobs in this process, we discard the current solution with quadruplet $j = (l_0, l_1, l_2, l_3)$ and move on to the next possible quadruplet solution. Once an assignment has been computed for all possible quadruplets, the result of $FillMaxArea$ is the one that maximizes the total processing time of all assigned jobs.

Algorithm 2. $FillMaxArea(J, m, T)$

1: Generate G, N_1, N_2, N_3 and P subsets of J
2: **for** each $j = (l_0, l_1, l_2, l_3)$ such that $l_0 + l_1 + l_2 + l_3 = m$ and $l_1 + 2l_2 + 3l_3 \le n$ **do**
3:     $X_j \leftarrow \emptyset$
4:     $X_j \leftarrow X_j \cup AssignFrom(\{(G), (N_1), (N_2), (N_3)\}, l_1)$
5:     $X_j \leftarrow X_j \cup AssignFrom(\{(N_2, N_1), (N_3, N_1), (N_2, N_2), (N_3, N_2), (N_3, N_3)\}, l_2)$
6:     $X_j \leftarrow X_j \cup AssignFrom(\{(N_3, N_3, N_2), (N_3, N_3, N_3)\}, l_3)$
7:     **if** $l_0 + |X_j| < m$ **then**
8:        Discard X_j and continue
9:     Add jobs from P greedily (in any order) to X_j, keeping makespan $\le \frac{5}{4}T$
10: $X^* = \{X_j | \max_j A^{X_j}\}$
11: **return** X^*

4.3 Proof

We now prove a guarantee on the solution produced by $FillMaxArea$: its makespan is at most $\frac{5}{4}T$, and it rejects not more work (in terms of total processing time) than any solution with makespan at most T.

Lemma 4. *For any T, let $\mathcal{S}$ be the solution obtained by $FillMaxArea(J, m, T)$. Then, $C^{\mathcal{S}} \le \frac{5}{4}T$ and $R^{\mathcal{S}} \le R^*(T)$.*

Proof. $C^{\mathcal{S}} \le \frac{5}{4}T$ is a direct consequence of Lemma 3. We focus on proving $R^{\mathcal{S}} \le R^*(T)$. Let us denote by $\mathcal{S}_0$ any solution with makespan at most T: we aim to prove that $R^{\mathcal{S}} \le R^{\mathcal{S}_0}$, or equivalently $A^{\mathcal{S}} \ge A^{\mathcal{S}_0}$.

Lemma 2 defines the list of valid combinations for long jobs in $\mathcal{S}_0$. Let $j = (l_0, l_1, l_2, l_3)$ denote the number of machines with zero, one, two, and three long jobs in $\mathcal{S}_0$, respectively, and consider the solution X_j constructed by $FillMaxArea$ for this particular quadruplet. By construction, $A^{\mathcal{S}} \ge A^{X_j}$. Let us now prove that $A^{X_j} \ge A^{\mathcal{S}_0}$.

Let us consider the small jobs first, and distinguish between two possibilities:

Case 1: At least one small job in P is rejected in X_j. Since a small job is only rejected if it cannot be scheduled to finish before $\frac{5}{4}T$, and since the processing time of any short job is at most $\frac{1}{4}T$, this ensures that all machines have a workload of at least T. Thus, the total number of accepted jobs satisfies $A^{X_j} \ge m \cdot T \ge A^{\mathcal{S}_0}$, since $\mathcal{S}_0$ has a makespan of at most T.

Case 2: All small jobs are accepted in X_j. In this case we can ignore the small jobs and we will prove that $A^{X_j} \geq A^{S_0}$ when restricted to long jobs. Indeed, since S_0 cannot accept more small jobs than X_j, this will imply $A^{X_j} \geq A^{S_0}$ for all jobs.

In the following, we will denote *singleton* a machine that processes a single long job, *pair* a machine that processes two long jobs, and *triplet* a machine that processes three long jobs. Both X_j and S_0 have l_1 singletons, l_2 pairs, and l_3 triplets. In the rest of the proof, we show that S_0 can be transformed into a solution that uses the same number of each *type* of jobs as X_j, without decreasing the total accepted area, where the type of a job refers to the specific long job subset to which it belongs. We will use two possible transformations: *replace*, where an accepted job is exchanged for a rejected job with a longer processing time, and *swap*, where two accepted jobs assigned to different machines are swapped. The first operation increases the total accepted area, while the second does not modify it. Along with the transformations, we will make sure to use only *valid* combinations from the list of Lemma 2.

We start the transformation by considering the l_1 singletons. In X_j, the jobs assigned to these machines are the l_1 longest jobs from J. We build S_1 from S_0 by applying a transformation for each of these longest jobs:

1. If it is rejected in S_0, we *replace* it with the smallest job in a singleton of S_0. This increases the total accepted area of S_0.
2. If it is scheduled either in a pair or triplet in S_0, we *swap* this large job with the smallest job in a singleton of S_0.

The resulting schedule is denoted S_1, and satisfies ($\mathcal{P}_1$): its singletons process the same set of jobs as the singletons of X_j. In particular, the number of each type of job processed by the singletons is the same.

Based on ($\mathcal{P}_1$), and given that $FillMaxArea$ schedules as many N_1 jobs as possible in the pairs, the number of N_1 jobs present in a pair is not greater in S_1 than in X_j. If the number of N_1 jobs processed on a pair is greater in X_j, then S_1 must contain more (N_2, N_2), (N_3, N_2), or (N_3, N_3) combinations than C_j, and therefore rejects more N_1 jobs (since N_1 jobs cannot be processed on a triplet). We can *replace* any job in such a combination with a rejected N_1 job until the number of N_1 jobs in pairs is the same as in X_j. This results in either (N_2, N_1) or (N_3, N_1) combinations, both of which are valid. The resulting solution is denoted S_2 and satisfies ($\mathcal{P}_1$) and ($\mathcal{P}_2$): it processes the same number of N_1 jobs on pairs as X_j.

X_j cannot use less N_2 jobs than S_2 for the pairs, because $FillMaxArea$ prioritizes N_2 jobs over N_3 jobs. Let us assume that the number of N_2 jobs processed on a pair is greater in X_j than in S_2. Then the missing N_2 jobs in S_2 can either be rejected or scheduled in a (N_3, N_3, N_2) triplet. We can *swap* all N_2 jobs in a (N_3, N_3, N_2) combination with N_3 jobs from (N_3, N_2) or (N_3, N_3). Here, the possible set combinations we get are either (N_2, N_2) or (N_3, N_2) and (N_3, N_3, N_3), which are all valid. If X_j still uses more N_2 jobs in pairs, then there are rejected N_2 jobs in S_2. We can *replace* one N_3 job from a (N_3, N_2)

or (N_3, N_3) combination with each of these rejected N_2 jobs. This results in (N_2, N_2) or (N_3, N_2) valid combinations. The resulting solution is denoted S_3 and satisfies $(\mathcal{P}_1)$, $(\mathcal{P}_2)$ and $(\mathcal{P}_3)$: it processes the same number of N_2 and N_3 jobs on pairs as X_j.

Finally, if X_j schedules more N_2 jobs on triplets than S_3, this implies that there are rejected N_2 jobs in S_3. We can *replace* one N_3 job from a (N_3, N_3, N_3) combination of S_3 with each of these rejected N_2 jobs. This results in a valid (N_3, N_3, N_2) combination. This solution is denoted S_4, and since it satisfies $(\mathcal{P}_1)$, $(\mathcal{P}_2)$, $(\mathcal{P}_3)$ in addition to having the same number of N_2 jobs in triplets, we have shown that S_4 uses the same number of G, N_1, N_2, and N_3 jobs as X_j.

Finally, we use the fact that when choosing a job from a long job set, $FillMaxArea$ always chooses the largest available job. This implies that $A^{X_j} \geq A^{S_4}$. Since all transformations either increase or do not change the accepted area, we know that $A^{S_4} \geq A^{S_0}$, which concludes the proof. □

From this lemma, we can deduce the following bound on the cost of S:

Lemma 5. *For any T, let S be the solution obtained by $FillMaxArea(J, m, T)$. We can bound its cost by: $Z^S \leq \frac{5}{4}Tm + \rho R^*(T)$.*

Proof. This follows directly from $Z^S = mC^S + \rho R^S$ and Lemma 4. □

5 $\mathcal{BEKP}$ Approximation Algorithm

If we have an optimal solution OPT with respect to the objective function Z, we can compute the solution $FillMaxArea(J, m, C^{OPT})$. From Lemma 5 we get a $\frac{5}{4}$-approximation. In this section, we show how to obtain an approximation of C^{OPT} (with ϵ as the precision coefficient) with controlled complexity. In the end, we obtain the $\mathcal{BEKP}$ algorithm, which is a $\frac{5}{4}(1+\epsilon)$ approximation for any positive number ϵ.

The idea behind $\mathcal{BEKP}$ is to first compute an upper bound U and a lower bound L on the optimal makespan T^{OPT}, and then build different schedules with the $FillMaxArea$ algorithm for each makespan value C_i such that

$$C_i \in \{L, (1+\epsilon)L, ..., (1+\epsilon)^k L\}. \quad (2)$$

The number of iterations k is the smallest value that satisfies $(1+\epsilon)^k L \geq U$, and can be computed as $k = \lceil \log_{1+\epsilon}(\frac{U}{L}) \rceil$. We will now show how to compute U and L so that $\frac{U}{L}$ is bounded, which provides a bound for k.

5.1 Computing Bounds on the Optimal Makespan

Let us define the following function:

$$f(C) = Cm + \rho R^*(C), \quad (3)$$

which represents the minimum possible cost for a schedule with a makespan of C, since $R^*(C)$ is the minimum possible area of rejected jobs for any schedule with that makespan.

We start by providing two lower bounds on $f(C)$. The first one is:

$$f(C) \geq Cm. \tag{4}$$

For the second one, given the total workload $W = \sum_i p_i$, we know that $Cm + R^*(C) \geq W$, which implies that $R^*(C) \geq W - Cm$. Together with (3), this yields the second lower bound:

$$f(C) \geq \rho W - (\rho - 1)Cm. \tag{5}$$

Let us also define a target value H as $H = \dfrac{4\rho W}{5}$.

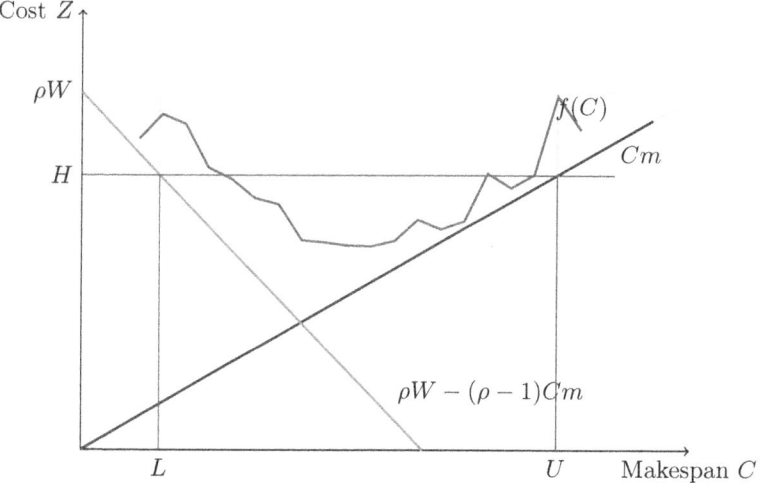

Fig. 1. Sketch of the graph of $f(C)$ (in red), highlighting how the bounds U and L are computed (Color figure online)

Let us sketch the possible graph of the cost function $f(C)$ and the two bounds in Fig. 1. The function $f(C)$ is shown in red, the first bound (4) is shown with a blue line, and the second bound (5) is shown in brown. Finally, the target value H is displayed as a green horizontal line.

We define U and L as the values of C such that the first and second bounds are equal to H. This is shown in Fig. 1, and we get $U = \dfrac{4\rho W}{5m}$. Similarly, given the second bound (5) and the target, we can compute their intersection: $L = \dfrac{\rho W}{5m(\rho-1)}$.

These values for U and L yield a ratio $\dfrac{U}{L} = 4(\rho - 1)$, which gives a bound on the number of iterations k. For example, if we assume a rejection cost coefficient of $\rho \leq 10$, then $4(\rho - 1) \leq 36$. If the precision is set to $1 + \epsilon = 1.05$, Equation (2) specifies at most 74 different makespan values, which leads to a practical number of iterations. With these values, $\mathcal{BEKP}$ is a $\frac{5}{4} * 1.05 = 1.3125$ approximation algorithm. The tradeoff between number of iterations and performance guarantee can be adjusted when considering different values for ϵ.

5.2 $\mathcal{BEKP}$ Algorithm

Algorithm 3. $\mathcal{BEKP}(J, m)$

1: X_0 = the solution where all jobs are rejected
2: $U = \frac{4\rho W}{5m}$ and $L = \frac{\rho W}{5m(\rho - 1)}$ and $k = \lceil \log_{1+\epsilon} \frac{U}{L} \rceil$
3: **for** each $C_i \in \{L, (1+\epsilon)L, (1+\epsilon)^2 L, ..., (1+\epsilon)^k L\}$ **do**
4:   $X_i = FillMaxArea(J, m, C_i)$
5: **return** schedule with the lowest cost among X_0 and all X_i

---

$\mathcal{BEKP}$ is specified in Algorithm 3, where ϵ is a fixed parameter. The algorithm considers several possible schedules: the solution where all jobs are rejected, denoted by X_0, whose cost is $Z^{X_0} = \rho W$, and the result of $FillMaxArea(J, m, C_i)$ for each value C_i between L and U as in Equation (2). The result of $\mathcal{BEKP}$ is the lowest cost schedule among all these candidates.

Theorem 1. *For any positive ϵ, BEKP is a $\frac{5}{4}(1+\epsilon)$ approximation algorithm.*

Proof. Consider an arbitrary set of jobs J to be scheduled on m machines. Let OPT be a schedule for this instance with optimal cost: we will compare Z^{OPT} with the cost of one of the X_i schedules considered in $\mathcal{BEKP}$. We consider two cases, depending on the value of C^{OPT} relative to L and U:

If $C^{OPT} < L$ or $C^{OPT} > U$, we know from $Z^{OPT} \geq f(C^{OPT})$ and our lower bounds (4) and (5) that $Z^{OPT} \geq H = \frac{4\rho W}{5}$. On Fig. 1 this can be interpreted as $f(C^{OPT})$ being located in one of the red triangle areas. Since $Z^{X_0} = \rho W$, we get $Z^{X_0} \leq \frac{5}{4} Z^{OPT}$.

If $L \leq C^{OPT} \leq U$, then there exists an index i such that $C^{OPT} \leq C_i \leq (1+\epsilon)C^{OPT}$. Let us denote this solution as X_i. By Lemma 5 we know that $Z^{X_i} \leq \frac{5}{4}mC_i + \rho R^*(C_i)$. Since $C^{OPT} \leq C_i$, we obtain by Lemma 1 that $R^*(C_i) \leq R^*(C^{OPT})$. Finally, since $C_i \leq (1+\epsilon)C^{OPT}$, we can derive:

$$Z^{X_i} \leq \frac{5}{4}(1+\epsilon)mC^{OPT} + \rho R^*(C^{OPT}) \leq \frac{5}{4}(1+\epsilon)Z^{OPT}$$

In both cases, we identify a schedule X considered by $\mathcal{BEKP}$ that satisfies $Z^X \leq \frac{5}{4}(1+\epsilon)Z^{OPT}$. Since the result of $\mathcal{BEKP}$ has a cost not greater than X, this concludes the proof. □

5.3 Complexity

As discussed in Sect. 5.1 and the ratio $\frac{U}{L} = 4(\rho - 1)$, the number of calls to $FillMaxArea$ in Algorithm 3 is $\mathcal{O}(\log_{1+\epsilon} \rho)$. In $FillMaxArea$ (Algorithm 2), the number of quadruplets to test is $\mathcal{O}(m^3)$, and for each of them we call $AssignFrom$ and greedily schedule the jobs in P. For a quadruplet, the complexity of all $AssignFrom$ calls is $\mathcal{O}(m)$ in total. We can assume that the jobs are sorted by increasing processing time at the beginning of $\mathcal{BEKP}$, incurring a one-time $\mathcal{O}(n \log n)$ complexity. Scheduling the jobs greedily can be done in $\mathcal{O}(n)$.

In total, the complexity of $\mathcal{BEKP}$ is $\mathcal{O}(m^3(m+n) \log_{1+\epsilon} \rho)$. This can be compared to the algorithm proposed by Liu and Lu [8], whose complexity is $\mathcal{O}(n^3 \log n)$: we expect our approach to be significantly faster in scenarios with fewer machines and a larger number of jobs.

6 Experiments

In this section, we evaluate $\mathcal{BEKP}$ in terms of total solution cost (computed as in Eq. 1). To provide reference points, we compare our approach to two existing solutions: a naive solution $\mathcal{LPT}$ that accepts all jobs and schedules them using the Longest Processing Time-first method, and the algorithm proposed by Liu et al. [8], denoted $\mathcal{LIULU}$. Each method has been implemented in a straightforward manner without deep emphasis on performance optimization. In addition, we also compute a lower bound on the solution cost, with an Integer Linear Programming formulation that estimates the makespan of a set of jobs with the standard lower bounds $\max_i p_i$ and $\frac{\sum_i p_i}{m}$, and optimally decides which jobs to accept. This can be formulated as minimizing $Cm + \sum_{i \in J} \rho(1 - x_i) p_i$, subject to the constraints $\forall i \in J, C \geq x_i p_i$ and $C \geq \sum_{i \in J}(x_i p_i)/m$, where x_i is a boolean decision variable equal to 1 if the job is accepted and 0 otherwise. All experiments were performed sequentially on the Miriel nodes (each consisting of two INTEL Xeon E5-2680v3 12-core 2.50 GHz processors with 128 GB of memory) of the Plafrim supercomputer[2].

We generated random instances in which job processing times follow a lognormal distribution with a mean of 3. We use three different values for the standard deviation σ: 0.5, 0.7, and 1.0. As σ increases from smaller to larger values, the variance in processing times between jobs also increases. We set the number of machines m to 20. We present results for two values of ρ: 1.5 and 4. For each case, we generate 30 different random sets of jobs.

In Fig. 2, each grid column corresponds to a different rejection coefficient, while each row corresponds to a different number of jobs. The x axis represents the different standard deviations used to generate the processing times, and the y axis represents the relative cost of each method compared to the lower bound (where a limit is set for better visualization). The results for each method over the 30 random instances are shown with a boxplot showing the median, first and

---
[2] https://www.plafrim.fr.

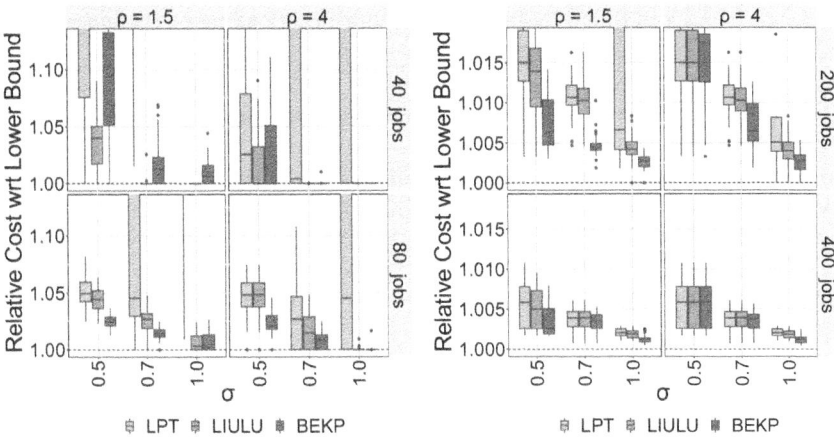

Fig. 2. Comparison of $\mathcal{LIULU}$, $\mathcal{LPT}$ and $\mathcal{BEKP}$ using $m = 20$ for different number of jobs, different values for ρ and σ

third quartiles, with whiskers extending to the lowest and highest values. Small black dots represent outliers.

In Fig. 2, we observe that $\mathcal{LPT}$ can yield significantly higher cost solutions compared to the other two methods, especially when there is a small number of jobs and a large variance in the processing times of the jobs. In our experiments, this high cost reached up to 4 times the value of the lower bound. On the other hand, both $\mathcal{BEKP}$ and $\mathcal{LIULU}$ provide low-cost solutions thanks to their rejection capabilities, with neither exceeding the lower bound by more than a factor of 1.2. $\mathcal{BEKP}$ consistently achieves results close to $\mathcal{LIULU}$, and in most cases provides improved solutions at reasonable cost.

7 Conclusion and Perspectives

We address an offline job scheduling problem where jobs are assigned to a limited set of energy-efficient machines, with the option of offloading them to less energy-efficient machines when necessary. This problem can be viewed as a scheduling problem with rejection, where rejection means using less energy-efficient machines, with an energy overhead proportional to the job processing time. We introduce $\mathcal{BEKP}$, a novel $\frac{5}{4}(1+\epsilon)$ approximation algorithm with a time complexity of $\mathcal{O}(m^3(m + n \log n))$. In comparison, the state-of-the-art algorithm of Liu and Lu [8] provides a $(\frac{3}{2} - \frac{1}{2m})$-approximation ratio with a time complexity of $\mathcal{O}(n^3 \log n)$ for scheduling tasks with arbitrary rejection costs. Therefore, our proposed algorithm improves both the approximation ratio and the algorithmic complexity with respect to the total number of jobs. Our experimental evaluation shows that our algorithm also produces good quality solutions in practice, in most cases with similar or better cost compared to Liu and Lu's approach. This work opens up interesting perspectives. Improving the algorithmic complexity of the algorithm could help open it up to more practical cases. The assumption that the rejection cost is proportional to the processing time can be extended to other contexts, such as jobs with quality of service requirements, where this realistic assumption could also lead to improved performance guarantees.

Acknowledgments and Artifact Availability. Our work is done in the context of the Inria – Qarnot Pulse project: https://www.inria.fr/en/pulse. The code is available in the Zenodo repository [2] with all explanations to reproduce the results.

Disclosure of Interests. The authors have no competing interests to declare that are relevant to the content of this article.

References

1. Bartal, Y., Leonardi, S., Marchetti-Spaccamela, A., Sgall, J., Stougie, L.: Multiprocessor scheduling with rejection. SIAM J. Discret. Math. **13**(1), 64–78 (2000)
2. Beaumont, O., Bouzel, R., Eyraud-Dubois, L., Korkmaz, E., Pilla, L., Van Kempen, A.: Artifact of the paper: A $1.25(1+\epsilon)$-Approximation Algorithm for Scheduling with Rejection Costs Proportional to Processing Times (2024). https://doi.org/10.5281/zenodo.11580038
3. Bouzel, R., Ngoko, Y., Benoit, P., Saintherant, N.: Distributed grid computing manager covering waste heat reuse constraints. In: 2021 Design, Automation & Test in Europe Conference & Exhibition (DATE), pp. 294–299. IEEE (2021)
4. Caprara, A., Kellerer, H., Pferschy, U.: A 3/4-approximation algorithm for multiple subset sum. J. Heuristics **9**(2), 99–111 (2003)
5. Cesaret, B., Oğuz, C., Sibel Salman, F.: A tabu search algorithm for order acceptance and scheduling. Comput. Oper. Res. **39**(6), 1197–1205 (2012). Special Issue on Scheduling in Manufacturing Systems
6. Engels, D.W., Karger, D.R., Kolliopoulos, S.G., Sengupta, S., Uma, R.N., Wein, J.: Techniques for scheduling with rejection. In: Bilardi, G., Italiano, G.F., Pietracaprina, A., Pucci, G. (eds.) ESA 1998. LNCS, vol. 1461, pp. 490–501. Springer, Heidelberg (1998). https://doi.org/10.1007/3-540-68530-8_41
7. Epstein, L., Noga, J., Woeginger, G.J.: On-line scheduling of unit time jobs with rejection: minimizing the total completion time. Oper. Res. Lett. **30**(6), 415–420 (2002)
8. Liu, P., Lu, X.: New approximation algorithms for machine scheduling with rejection on single and parallel machine. J. Comb. Optim. **40**(4), 929–952 (2020)
9. Liu, Z.: Scheduling with partial rejection. Oper. Res. Lett. **48**(4), 524–529 (2020)
10. Mor, B., Shabtay, D.: Single-machine scheduling with total late work and job rejection. Comput. Ind. Eng. **169**, 108168 (2022)
11. Ou, J., Zhong, X., Wang, G.: An improved heuristic for parallel machine scheduling with rejection. Eur. J. Oper. Res. **241**(3), 653–661 (2015)
12. Shabtay, D., Gaspar, N., Kaspi, M.: A survey on offline scheduling with rejection. J. Sched. **16**, 3–28 (2013)
13. Slotnick, S.A.: Order acceptance and scheduling: a taxonomy and review. Eur. J. Oper. Res. **212**(1), 1–11 (2011)

DProbe: Profiling and Predicting Multi-tenant Deep Learning Workloads for GPU Resource Scaling

Zechun Zhou[ID], Jingwei Sun[✉][ID], Hengquan Mei, Peng Sun, and Guangzhong Sun[ID]

University of Science and Technology of China, Hefei, China
{zhouzechun,hengquanmei}@mail.ustc.edu.cn, {sunjw,gzsun}@ustc.edu.cn,
peng.sunshine@gmail.com

Abstract. The surge in deep learning services has precipitated the development of modern large-scale GPU datacenters, which cater to the computational demands of multi-tenant deep learning workloads. These facilities implement virtual cluster partitioning to maintain isolation across product groups. Dynamically adjusting resource allocation across virtual clusters can effectively enhance resource utilization. However, efficient GPU resource scaling hinges on accurately forecasting resource demand trends, which is a task complicated by significant variations in GPU utilization among diverse deep learning instances. For this issue, we propose DProbe, a system designed to predict resource demand trends within virtual clusters, employing fine-grained profiling of multi-tenant deep learning workloads. Initially, DProbe employs a job profiler that integrates model-specific attributes with runtime hardware metrics to perform performance modeling for deep learning instances. Resource demands are then estimated through a multi-level approach, considering the distribution of instances across varying levels of GPU utilization. Additionally, DProbe incorporates a multi-task trend predictor to anticipate future resource demand trends, based on historical traces. DProbe's predictions enable efficient resource scaling across virtual clusters. We evaluate DProbe using production traces across five scheduling policies and effectively reduce the average job queuing delay by 22.4% to 50.7%.

Keywords: Workload Characterization · Workload Prediction · Cloud Computing · Resource Management

1 Introduction

Over the past years, Deep Learning (DL) technologies have been widely adopted in various production domains. To address the escalating computational demands of DL tasks, enterprises and research institutes often build large-scale multi-tenant GPU datacenters [9,12,27]. These facilities offer comprehensive services spanning the entire DL pipeline, from feature engineering and model training to evaluation and inference, accommodating DL tasks from multiple product groups across various frameworks. Analogous to conventional cloud infrastructures, multi-tenant DL datacenters often partition virtual clusters to maintain isolation across product groups [9]. Dynamically adjusting resource allocation across virtual clusters to achieve load balancing is an effective means of enhancing resource utilization.

For CPU workloads in conventional cloud services, Auto-scaling mechanisms that dynamically adjust both Pod-level (Kubernetes' minimal deployment units) and node-level resources to optimize resource utilization have emerged as prominent solutions [23]. Considering the cyclically fluctuating business demands of cloud applications, Pod-level Auto-scaling allocates the requisite number of Pods in response. Given the substantial homogeneity of Pods servicing the same cloud application, node-level Auto-scaling adjusts the number of CPU nodes for corresponding virtual clusters based on the number of Pods. The high isolation and homogeneity among CPU instances facilitate the assessment of overall workload resource demands. Researchers have explored proactive Auto-scaling implementation in multiple cloud service scenarios based on demand prediction for cloud workloads, such as web services [11] and public cloud services [32].

However, the resource scaling approaches for CPU workloads fall short when applied to DL workloads in GPU-sharing-enabled datacenters. Due to differences in model architecture, there is strong heterogeneity in resource utilization among DL instances. The resource contention between DL instances sharing a single GPU is also more pronounced [10]. In this scenario, assessing the resource demands of DL workloads proves to be challenging [28], as it cannot solely rely on the overall workload volume or the total number of Pods. For DL workloads, designing GPU-sharing policies to minimize co-location slowdowns is a hot topic. To facilitate the evaluation of GPU-sharing policies, existing works [10,27,31] typically maintain fixed scales for virtual clusters. Some of these works [9,10] have explored GPU resource scaling based on coarse-grained demand forecasts following the determination of specific policies, effectively improving resource utilization. Motivated by these studies, our research aims to refine demand predictions for GPU resource scaling to optimize DL workload scheduling further.

In this paper, we present DProbe, a system designed to predict resource demand trends within virtual clusters, employing fine-grained profiling of multi-tenant GPU-sharing DL workloads. Initially, DProbe employs a job profiler that integrates model-specific attributes with runtime hardware metrics to perform performance modeling for DL instances. Specifically, it profiles the runtime metrics of representative models as targets, and extracts their computational graphs as features to build a performance prediction model based on Graph Attention Network (GAT) [26], enabling accurate identification of resource utilization levels for all submitted jobs. Resource demands are then estimated through a heuristic multi-level approach, considering the distribution of instances across varying levels of GPU utilization. Additionally, DProbe incorporates a multi-task trend predictor to anticipate future resource demand trends, based on historical traces. DProbe's predictions enable efficient resource scaling across virtual clusters. The main contribution of our work lies in designing accurate resource demand predictions for GPU-sharing DL workloads, thereby facilitating load balancing across clusters through scaling.

To evaluate the prediction accuracy of DProbe, we compare its performance against state-of-the-art baselines using production traces from SenseTime [9], Microsoft [12] and Alibaba [27]. DProbe demonstrates the best prediction performance, with Mean Absolute Percentage Errors (MAPEs) of only 14.2%, 11.7%, and 18.9% across the three traces. Moreover, we evaluate the impact of DProbe-based resource scaling on scheduling efficiency across five policies [9,10,31] via trace-driven simulation experiments. The results demonstrate that DProbe-based scaling can reduce the average job queuing delay by 22.4% to 50.7%, validating its effectiveness as a framework for optimizing DL workload scheduling.

2 System Design

In this section, we offer a detailed introduction to the system design of DProbe. Figure 1 illustrates the overview of DProbe's architecture. It consists of two main modules: the job profiler (Sect. 2.1) and the demand predictor (Sect. 2.2).

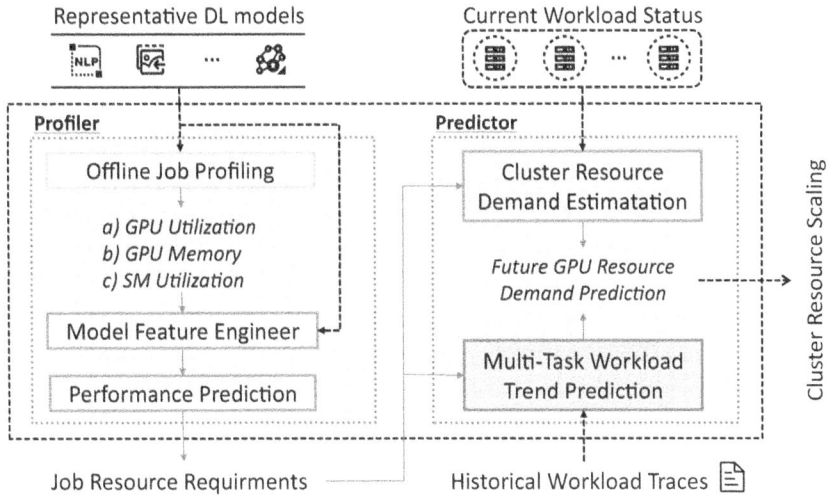

Fig. 1. Overview of DProbe's architecture.

2.1 Job Profiler of DProbe

DProbe focuses on the resource demand prediction of DL workloads in GPU-sharing-enabled datacenters. In these datacenters, DL jobs can share GPUs through NVIDIA MPS or vGPU technologies. Apart from workloads requiring exclusive access due to latency sensitivities, such as inference and cross-node jobs, GPU-sharing can effectively increase throughput for other workloads, primarily training workloads [10]. Assessing the resource demands for GPU-sharing workloads is challenging. DProbe's job profiler performs performance modeling for these DL workloads to accurately assess their resource utilization levels.

Online Job Profiling. To understand different resource utilization levels among DL workloads, DProbe performs online profiling on representative DL models, collecting their runtime hardware metrics before setting up other modules. Our analysis involves various DL workloads with different configurations, spanning multiple domains such as computer vision, natural language processing, reinforcement learning, and recommendation, summarized in Table 1. They can be distinguished based on their backbone network architectures, including Convolutional Neural Network (CNN), Recurrent Neural Network (RNN), Transformer, and Actor-Critic (for reinforcement learning). We utilize NVIDIA-SMI and DCGM[1] to collect runtime metrics for these DL models on three different hardware platforms, including GPU utilization (%), GPU memory occupancy (MB), and SM utilization (%), with results averaged from profiling data. All experiments are conducted in our implementation environment (Sect. 3.1).

Table 1. Summary of representative models in DL workloads.

Arch	Model	Dataset	Batch size
CNN	AlexNet [14]	ImageNet	$\{4n \mid 2 \leq n \leq 32\}$
CNN	ResNet-18, 34 [7]	ImageNet	$\{4n \mid 2 \leq n \leq 32\}$
CNN	MobileNetV2 [21]	ImageNet	$\{4n \mid 2 \leq n \leq 32\}$
CNN	VGG-11, 13 [24]	ImageNet	$\{4n \mid 2 \leq n \leq 32\}$
RNN	LSTM [2]	WikiText2	$\{4n \mid 16 \leq n \leq 32\}$
RNN	GRU [3]	WikiText2	$\{4n \mid 16 \leq n \leq 32\}$
Transformer	Swin Transformer [15]	ImageNet	$\{2n \mid 2 \leq n \leq 8\}$
Transformer	ViT-S [4]	ImageNet	$\{2n \mid 2 \leq n \leq 8\}$
Transformer	Transformer [25]	WikiText2	$\{2n \mid 2 \leq n \leq 8\}$
Transformer	BERT [13]	WikiText2	$\{2n \mid 2 \leq n \leq 8\}$
Transformer	GPT-1 [19]	WikiText2	$\{2n \mid 2 \leq n \leq 8\}$
Actor-Critic	PPO [22]	LunarLander	$\{4n \mid 2 \leq n \leq 32\}$
Actor-Critic	TD3 [5]	BipedalWalker	$\{4n \mid 2 \leq n \leq 32\}$

Performance Prediction Model. Given the diverse and quickly updating nature of DL models, relying solely on online profiling for representative workloads is insufficient. For new model architectures not encountered during online

---
[1] https://developer.nvidia.com/dcgm/.

Table 2. Operator feature representation.

Node Features	Description
Operator Type	Type of the operator (e.g., Conv2d, MaxPool2d).
Hyperparameter	Operator Hyperparameters (e.g., kernel size, channel size).
Operator FLOPs	Number of floating-point operations of the operator.
Operator Tensor Size	The size of the operator input and output tensor shape.
GPU FLOPS	GPU peak floating-point operations per second.
Temporary Tensor Size	The size of temporary variables used by the operator.

analysis, re-profiling them is inconvenient and wastes cluster computational resources. Therefore, DProbe further extracts the computational graph and hyperparameters of each model in Table 1 as features and utilizes the GPU runtime metrics as the targets, constructing a performance prediction model based on GAT [26]. We use ONNX[2] to obtain the computational graphs for DL models. ONNX defines a common set of operators, enabling AI developers to represent DL models with common computational graphs.

Given a computational graph $G = (V, E)$, where V represents operators as nodes, and E represents forward/backward propagation as asymmetric edges, the number of nodes is $|V| = N$. The input of the performance prediction model of DProbe is the adjacency matrix A of this graph and the feature vectors of all nodes $\boldsymbol{h} = \{\boldsymbol{h}_1, \boldsymbol{h}_2, \cdots, \boldsymbol{h}_N\}, \boldsymbol{h}_i \in \mathbb{R}^F$. All the adopted features are summarized in Table 2, where the upper part can be automatically extracted from the model architecture, while the lower part, serving as an optional supplement, needs to be manually inputted. Denoting the neighbor set of node i as $\mathcal{N}_i$, the GAT module aggregates information by computing self-attention coefficients for the concatenation of its feature vector h_i with each neighbor's feature vector:

$$e_{ij} = a([W\boldsymbol{h}_i || W\boldsymbol{h}_j]), \quad \alpha_{ij} = softmax_j(e_{ij}), \quad j \in \mathcal{N}_i, \tag{1}$$

where $a(\cdot)$ represents a feedforward layer and $W \in \mathbb{R}^{\tilde{F} \times F}$ is the weight matrix for the feature transformation. Then, a linear combination is performed to obtain the intermediate representation $\tilde{\boldsymbol{h}} = \{\tilde{\boldsymbol{h}}_1, \tilde{\boldsymbol{h}}_2, \cdots, \tilde{\boldsymbol{h}}_N\}, \tilde{\boldsymbol{h}}_i \in \mathbb{R}^{\tilde{F}}$ for all nodes:

$$\tilde{\boldsymbol{h}}_i = \sigma(\sum_{j \in \mathcal{N}_i} \alpha_{ij} W \tilde{\boldsymbol{h}}_j), \quad i = 1, 2, \cdots, N. \tag{2}$$

The intermediate representation is finally mapped to three GPU runtime metrics (GPU utilization, GPU memory occupancy, and SM utilization) via fully connected layers. When encountering a new model, DProbe predicts its resource utilization offline based on its model-specific attributes using the performance prediction model. Thus far, DProbe's job profiler can characterize all submitted jobs in production environments, allowing us to estimate cluster resource demands.

---
[2] https://onnx.ai/.

2.2 Demand Predictor of DProbe

Resource Demand Estimation. We employ a heuristic approach to estimate the resource demands of currently running and pending workloads, tailored to GPU-sharing policies designed for DL workload scheduling. Efficient GPU-sharing requires minimizing co-location slowdown. It is evident that in time-sharing GPU scenarios implemented using technologies such as vGPU, noticeable slowdowns primarily manifest when the cumulative utilization of co-located DL tasks surpasses 100%. This finding is also applicable to the MPS sharing mode [10,31]. For example, the average GPU utilization for the BERT model across all configurations in our online profiling exceeds 95%, indicating that it is susceptible to co-location slowdowns. Conversely, all configurations of the PPO model have an average GPU utilization below 15%. GPU-sharing scheduling policies tend to allocate resources exclusively to BERT to ensure its performance, while favoring letting PPO share its idle computational resources to improve resource utilization [10]. Thus, GPU-sharing scheduling can be modeled as a bin packing problem with job priorities, where resource demand estimation corresponds to determining the number of bins.

However, as the scale of scheduling increases, directly solving the bin packing problem incurs significant costs. To simplify this problem and benchmark diverse GPU-sharing scheduling policies [10,27,31], we quantify the resource utilization levels of jobs based on their runtime metrics described in Sect. 2.1, thereby categorizing jobs into four types: $Level = 1$, $Level = 2$, $Level = 3$, and $Exclusive$. $Exclusive$ jobs demand exclusive access to GPUs to meet quality-of-service requirements. Jobs are designated as $Level = 1$ if they exhibit an average GPU utilization below 25% and GPU memory occupancy under 3 GB, resulting in minimal interference with co-located tasks. Conversely, jobs with average GPU utilization and SM utilization exceeding 70% are classified as $Level = 3$, susceptible to co-located slowdowns, thus requiring exclusive GPU access or pairing with tiny jobs to maintain training speed. SM utilization serves as a supplementary metric to reflect the spatial computational resource occupancy in MPS sharing mode. Jobs with moderate resource utilization fall into $Level = 2$.

In this simplified proxy problem, jobs labeled as $Level = 1$, $Level = 2$, $Level = 3$, and $Exclusive$ are considered to require 30%, 50%, 70%, and 100% fractional GPUs, respectively. Given the current quantities of GPUs requested from four types of jobs: ω_1, ω_2, ω_3, and ω_E, we can simulate a bin packing process benchmarking a specific sharing policy to estimate resource demand. For example, under a strictly exclusive scheduling policy, the GPU resource demand estimation of current workloads is $\omega_1 + \omega_2 + \omega_3 + \omega_E$. Under a local optimal sharing scheduling policy aimed at maximizing resource utilization, the GPU resource demand estimation of current workloads is the number of bins obtained by finding the optimal solution to the proxy bin packing problem. With estimates of resource demand for each virtual cluster, efficient scaling to ensure load balance and enhance resource utilization becomes feasible. To achieve efficient scaling of GPU resources, it is essential not only to be aware of the GPU demands of current workloads but also to understand their future fluctuation trends. DProbe extends this analysis by forecasting future workload trends based on historical trace data, offering insights into potential demand shifts.

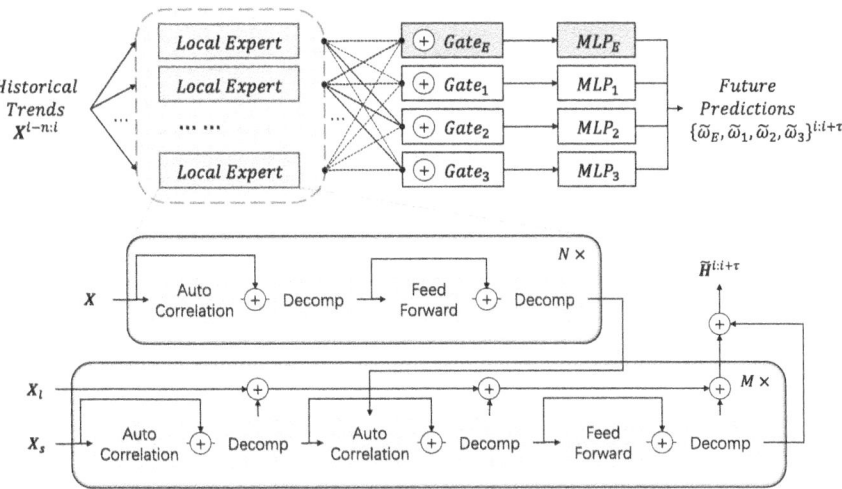

Fig. 2. Overview of the multi-task trend predictor.

Workload Trend Prediction. The multi-task trend predictor in DProbe is responsible for providing multi-objective joint predictions for four workload type quantity trends. Our design is inspired by the multi-gate mixture-of-experts structure [16]. Figure 2 illustrates the architecture of the trend predictor. In DProbe's trend predictor, we adopt Autoformer [29] as the backbone network, i.e., each local expert. The workflow of the local expert is illustrated in the lower part of Fig. 2. Given the workload trend series X up to time i, Autoformer utilizes the query Q, key K, and value V of X to calculate autocorrelation coefficients instead of self-attention coefficients to uncover sequential trend information:

$$\alpha(Q, K, V) = \sum_{i=1}^{k} Roll(V, \tau_i) \times softmax_i(\lim_{L\to\infty} \frac{1}{L} \sum_{t=1}^{L} Q_t K_{t-\tau_i}), \qquad (3)$$

where τ_i is one of multiple selected time delays, and $Roll(X, \tau)$ represents a shift operation on X with time delay τ. Autoformer decomposes seasonal trends and long-term trends based on embedded decomposition layers:

$$X_l = AvgPool(Padding(X)), \quad X_s = X - X_l, \qquad (4)$$

where the long-term trend X_l is obtained through the moving average on the sequence along with padding operations. The encoder exclusively extracts seasonal trend patterns, while the decoder aggregates both seasonal and long-term trend patterns to obtain an intermediate representation of future trend $\tilde{H}_{i:i+\tau}$.

As depicted in the upper part of Fig. 2, local experts are employed to extract specific patterns of seasonal and long-term trends from the historical traces. Subsequently, there is a type-specific gating network layer that aggregates pattern information from all experts. The final forward prediction for future workloads is rendered by four distinct multi-layer perceptrons, utilizing aggregated trend patterns as their input. Combining workload trend predictions $\{\tilde{\omega}_1, \tilde{\omega}_2, \tilde{\omega}_3, \tilde{\omega}_E\}^{i:i+\tau}$ with the current workload $\{\omega_1, \omega_2, \omega_3, \omega_E\}$, enables more precise resource demand estimation and more efficient scaling.

3 Evaluation

In this section, we evaluate DProbe from three perspectives: performance metric prediction, resource demand prediction, and resource scaling optimization.

3.1 Experimental Setup

Our experiments utilize a physical cluster to obtain profiling data, comprising three distinct systems, each characterized by GPUs from different generations that exhibit notable performance disparities. The configurations of these systems are itemized in Table 3. DProbe conducts runtime metric collection independently across these systems to bolster its generalizability. For the experiment workloads listed in Table 1, DProbe employs NVIDIA-SMI and DCGM to gather data on GPU utilization, memory occupancy, and SM utilization metrics. The ONNX framework is used for extracting computational graph representations and hyperparameters of DL models. We develop DProbe's DL-based modules using Python 3.9, PyTorch 1.13.1, and CUDA 11.7. To assess the effectiveness of DProbe in optimizing resource scaling, we also implement a scheduling event simulator that utilizes real-world production traces.

Table 3. The machine configurations for implementation.

Specification	System-1	System-2	System-3
GPU Model	A100 (80 GB)	RTX 3090 (24 GB)	RTX 2080Ti (12 GB)
GPU Number	2	8	8
GPU Arch	Ampere	Ampere	Turing
CPU Model	Intel Xeon w5-2455X	Intel XeonGold 6326	Intel XeonE5-2680 v4
CPU Core	12	32	28
Memory	256 GB	256 GB	128 GB
System	Ubuntu 20.04	Ubuntu 20.04	CentOS 7
CUDA	11.7	11.3	10.2

3.2 Evaluation of Performance Metric Prediction

To construct a test set for evaluating DProbe's performance prediction, we enhance the set of known workloads listed in Table 1 by introducing new hyperparameter configurations. Specifically, this test set includes known Transformer workloads with batch sizes ranging from $\{2n \mid 8 < n \leq 12\}$, as well as other known workloads with batch sizes ranging from $\{4n \mid 32 < n \leq 40\}$. Moreover, the test set is augmented with additional DL models, including ResNet-50 [7], VGG-16 [24], MobileNetV3 [8], ViT-T [4], and GPT-2 [20], with batch sizes spanning $\{2n \mid 2 \leq n \leq 8\}$. DProbe's performance prediction model extracts the computational graphs of workloads from this test set and predicts three GPU runtime metrics: GPU utilization, GPU memory occupancy, and SM utilization. We evaluate the performance prediction by calculating the MAPE between its predictions and the actual profiled values. For known workloads with new configurations, the MAPEs for the three metrics are 4.2%, 2.1%, and 5.7%, respectively. For new workloads, the MAPEs for the three metrics are 9.5%, 2.7%, and 11.2%, respectively. The performance prediction model can effectively discern the resource utilization levels of each submitted job.

3.3 Evaluation of Resource Demand Prediction

We use three large-scale production traces to evaluate the accuracy of resource demand prediction, as summarized in Table 4. We maintain the original job submission traces without any rescaling or modification. The records from the last two weeks of each trace are used as the testbed, while the remaining workload records are utilized as the training and validation sets. The prediction of future resource demand trends is conducted at an hourly granularity. For one-step prediction, the demand trend of the recent day's historical trace is used as input to predict the resource demands for the next three hours. In the testbed, the impact of GPU-sharing policy on resource demand is implemented benchmarking to the scheduler Lucid [10]. We manually implement the most efficient resource scaling for virtual clusters based on perfectly accurate future traces, which serves as the ground truth for our evaluation.

Table 4. The trace configurations for evaluation.

Trace	Source	#GPUs	#Jobs	Duration
Venus [9]	SenseTime (2020)	1,080	247k	6 months
Philly [12]	Microsoft (2017)	864	103k	3 months
PAI [27]	Alibaba (2020)	6,742	1.26M	2 months

The following models serve as baselines in our evaluation, including general time series forecast models and state-of-the-art models specifically designed for workload prediction:

1. Auto-Regressive-Integrated-Moving-Average (ARIMA): is a classical statistical model widely applied for time series forecasting.
2. Long-Short-Term-Memory (LSTM): is a type of deep neural network widely used in sequential tasks, also suitable for time series forecasting.
3. LoadDynamics [11]: is a self-optimized, generic workload prediction framework based on LSTM, designed for web service scenarios.
4. Wasserstein-Adversarial-Transformer (WAT) [1]: is a prediction framework based on an adversarial training Transformer, designed for cloud clusters.
5. Cluster-Energy-Saving (CES) [9]: adopts GBDT to predict future GPU demand in clusters based on the trends of active GPU numbers.
6. GA^2M [10]: presents an interpretable algorithm to predict the workload throughput of GPU clusters, indirectly guiding resource scaling.

Except for CES and GA^2M, other predictors primarily focus on forecasting the total number of Pods. Consequently, we fine-tune them to predict the resource demands of GPU clusters. The performance of all models in predicting future resource demand trends is assessed using the MAPE. Table 5 presents the evaluation results of resource demand predictions. While predictors not tailored for GPU workloads perform poorly, CES and GA^2M achieve partial success in extracting specific trend patterns, showing notable results on the Philly and Venus traces, respectively. DProbe demonstrates the best prediction performance, with MAPEs of only 14.2%, 11.7%, and 18.9% across the three traces, owing to its refined trend decomposition and joint forecasting.

Table 5. Evaluation of resource demand predictions with MAPE (%).

	ARIMA	LSTM	LoadDynamics	WAT	CES	GA^2M	DProbe
Venus	37.1	28.3	29.0	23.1	19.4	17.0	**14.2**
Philly	32.9	24.1	22.7	21.4	15.9	25.8	**11.7**
PAI	49.5	43.2	40.5	34.8	24.7	36.1	**18.9**

3.4 Evaluation of Resource Scaling Optimization

Referencing the SenseTime Group's production trace simulator[3], we perform trace-driven simulation on the Venus trace testbed to evaluate resource scaling optimization. The simulated environment is a homogeneous cluster equipped with NVIDIA RTX3090 GPUs. The simulation is at the event level, reflecting job execution rates and co-location slowdowns as recorded in the original trace [9,10]. Our primary objective in these simulation experiments is to achieve a balanced workload distribution across virtual clusters within Venus. In the vanilla scheduling policies designed for Venus, the scale of each virtual cluster remains fixed. However, the dynamic nature of heterogeneous workloads often leads to

---
[3] https://github.com/S-Lab-System-Group/Lucid/.

load imbalances among virtual clusters. DProbe's predictions enable effective resource scaling to enhance scheduling efficiency.

We evaluate the enhancement effects of DProbe on the following five scheduling policies: (1) First-Come-First-Served (FCFS), (2) Shortest-Job-First (SJF), (3) Quasi-Shortest-Service-First (QSSF) [9], (4) Horus [31], and (5) Lucid [10]. Specifically, QSSF heuristically assigns priority based on job resource demands and estimated completion times. Horus prioritizes jobs by assessing the co-located training interference each job might cause to others within the queue. Lucid employs pre-scheduling profiling to facilitate efficient GPU-sharing and minimize queuing delays, especially for shorter jobs. Horus and Lucid represent state-of-the-art scheduling policies designed for GPU-sharing DL workloads. The resource saving efficiency via GPU-sharing varies among policies.

We measure the job completion time (JCT) and queuing delay for all jobs in five vanilla scheduling policies, comparing the results with those enhanced by DProbe-based scaling. Figure 3 illustrates the evaluation results, where Subfigs. 3(a) and 3(b) depict the average queuing delay and the 95% percentile (P95) tail queuing delay, respectively. Compared to the vanilla scheduling policies, the DProbe-enhanced scaling successfully reduces the average queuing delay by 22.4% to 50.7%, and the P95 queuing delay by 13.3% to 35.1%. Subfigure 3(c) illustrates the Cumulative Distribution Function (CDF) of JCT measured under FCFS scheduling, where Optimal represents the resource scaling that is manually implemented based on perfectly accurate future traces. DProbe-enhanced scaling significantly reduces the JCT for all jobs, averaging 41.8%, and is approaching the level of Optimal scaling.

4 Related Work

DL Model Characterization. As DL models become more complex, concerns regarding the performance modeling and optimization of DL models have arisen in both the industrial and research communities. Lots of existing works designed graph-based algorithms to predict the performance of DL models based on their computational graphs, encompassing aspects such as inference latency [6], training interference [31], GPU occupancy [17], etc. Regarding GPU utilization optimization, Lucid [10] conducted online profiling to optimize co-location efficiency for DL jobs. Antman [30] analyzed the SM utilization of each job to enhance GPU-sharing efficiency. In DProbe's job profiler, we integrated model-specific attributes and runtime hardware metrics to perform performance modeling for resource scaling.

Cluster Characterization. Extensive prior works have conducted comprehensive trace analysis for conventional CPU workloads in HPC [18] and cloud systems [32]. However, the existing methods for characterizing DL workloads within large-scale GPU datacenters are not as comprehensive. The rise of large-scale DL datacenters in recent years has been notable, but the availability of publicly accessible production traces for research purposes is limited. Jeon et al. [12] analyzed DL job traces from Microsoft datacenter to explore the impact of training

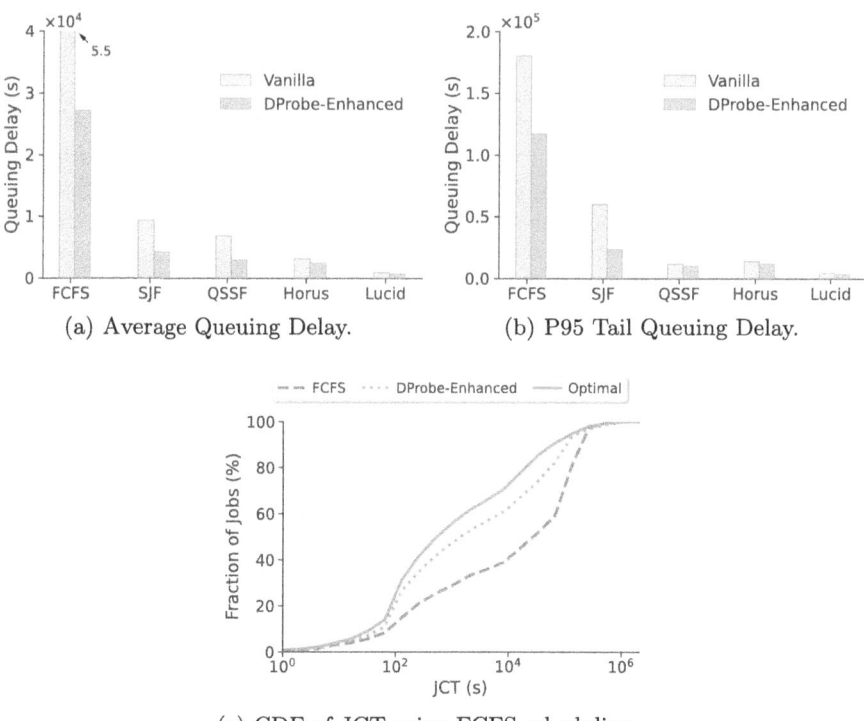

Fig. 3. Evaluation results of resource scaling optimization.

job locality on GPU utilization. Hu et al. [9] presented workload characterization and prediction-based resource management for the SenseTime datacenter. Alibaba Group[4] publicly shared a portion of their production traces in PAI. Lots of prior works by Alibaba Group conducted characterization for PAI traces [27,28]. Our work was inspired by the characterization of these production traces and involved evaluation experiments with them.

Prediction-Based Resource Management. Comprehensive workload characterization and prediction can enhance the resource management of large-scale clusters. For conventional cloud workloads, lots of prior work has focused on leveraging accurate predictions to enhance the efficiency of Auto-scaling [23] in multiple cloud service scenarios, such as web services [1,11] and public cloud services [32]. For DL datacenters, Hu et al. [9] designed a resource demand prediction model to dynamically activate GPU resources. Lucid [10] predicted the throughput of DL workloads to dynamically adjust its GPU-sharing policy. Our work leveraged the accurate predictions of DProbe to achieve more efficient GPU resource scaling.

---

[4] https://github.com/alibaba/clusterdata/.

5 Conclusion

In this paper, we propose DProbe, a system designed to predict resource demand trends for GPU resource scaling in DL datacenters. Specifically, we design a two-dimensional job profiler to comprehensively recognize the resource utilization levels of various DL workloads. On this basis, DProbe predicts future GPU demand trends for cluster resource scaling based on a demand predictor. We evaluate DProbe using production traces across five scheduling policies and successfully reduce the average job queuing delay by 22.4% to 50.7%, validating its effectiveness as a framework for optimizing DL workload scheduling. In the future, we plan to further design an end-to-end scheduling policy for GPU-sharing DL workloads based on DProbe's characterization. Besides, we plan to extend its ability for more scheduling objectives.

References

1. Arbat, S., Jayakumar, V.K., Lee, J., Wang, W., Kim, I.K.: Wasserstein adversarial Transformer for cloud workload prediction. In: Proceedings of the AAAI Conference on Artificial Intelligence (AAAI), pp. 12433–12439 (2022)
2. Bahdanau, D., Cho, K., Bengio, Y.: Neural machine translation by jointly learning to align and translate. In: International Conference on Learning Representations (ICLR) (2015)
3. Cho, K., van Merrienboer, B., Gulcehre, C., Bougares, F., Schwenk, H., Bengio, Y.: Learning phrase representations using RNN encoder-decoder for statistical machine translation. In: Proceedings of the Conference on Empirical Methods in Natural Language Processing (EMNLP) (2014)
4. Dosovitskiy, A., et al.: An image is worth 16x16 words: transformers for image recognition at scale. In: International Conference on Learning Representations (ICLR) (2021)
5. Fujimoto, S., Hoof, H., Meger, D.: Addressing function approximation error in actor-critic methods. In: International Conference on Machine Learning (ICML), pp. 1587–1596 (2018)
6. Gao, Y., Gu, X., Zhang, H., Lin, H., Yang, M.: Runtime performance prediction for deep learning models with graph neural network. In: IEEE/ACM 45th International Conference on Software Engineering: Software Engineering in Practice (ICSE-SEIP), pp. 368–380 (2023)
7. He, K., Zhang, X., Ren, S., Sun, J.: Deep residual learning for image recognition. In: Proceedings of the IEEE Conference on Computer Vision and Pattern Recognition (CVPR), pp. 770–778 (2016)
8. Howard, A., et al.: Searching for MobileNetV3. In: Proceedings of the IEEE/CVF International Conference on Computer Vision (ICCV), pp. 1314–1324 (2019)
9. Hu, Q., Sun, P., Yan, S., Wen, Y., Zhang, T.: Characterization and prediction of deep learning workloads in large-scale GPU datacenters. In: Proceedings of the International Conference for High Performance Computing, Networking, Storage and Analysis (SC), pp. 1–15 (2021)
10. Hu, Q., Zhang, M., Sun, P., Wen, Y., Zhang, T.: Lucid: a non-intrusive, scalable and interpretable scheduler for deep learning training jobs. In: Proceedings of the 28th ACM International Conference on Architectural Support for Programming Languages and Operating Systems (ASPLOS), pp. 457–472 (2023)

11. Jayakumar, V.K., Lee, J., Kim, I.K., Wang, W.: A self-optimized generic workload prediction framework for cloud computing. In: IEEE International Parallel and Distributed Processing Symposium (IPDPS), pp. 779–788 (2020)
12. Jeon, M., Venkataraman, S., Phanishayee, A., Qian, J., Xiao, W., Yang, F.: Analysis of large-scale multi-tenant GPU clusters for DNN training workloads. In: USENIX Annual Technical Conference (ATC), pp. 947–960 (2019)
13. Kenton, J.D.M.W.C., Toutanova, L.K.: BERT: pre-training of deep bidirectional Transformers for language understanding. In: Proceedings of the Conference of the North American Chapter of the Association for Computational Linguistics (NAACL), pp. 4171–4186 (2019)
14. Krizhevsky, A., Sutskever, I., Hinton, G.E.: ImageNet classification with deep convolutional neural networks. In: Advances in Neural Information Processing Systems (NeurIPS) (2012)
15. Liu, Z., et al.: Swin Transformer: hierarchical vision transformer using shifted windows. In: Proceedings of the IEEE/CVF International Conference on Computer Vision (ICCV), pp. 10012–10022 (2021)
16. Ma, J., Zhao, Z., Yi, X., Chen, J., Hong, L., Chi, E.H.: Modeling task relationships in multi-task learning with multi-gate mixture-of-experts. In: Proceedings of the 24th ACM SIGKDD International Conference on Knowledge Discovery & Data Mining (KDD), pp. 1930–1939 (2018)
17. Mei, H., Qu, H., Sun, J., Gao, Y., Lin, H., Sun, G.: GPU occupancy prediction of deep learning models using graph neural network. In: IEEE International Conference on Cluster Computing (CLUSTER), pp. 318–329 (2023)
18. Patel, T., Liu, Z., Kettimuthu, R., Rich, P., Allcock, W., Tiwari, D.: Job characteristics on large-scale systems: long-term analysis, quantification, and implications. In: Proceedings of the International Conference for High Performance Computing, Networking, Storage and Analysis (SC), pp. 1–17 (2020)
19. Radford, A., Narasimhan, K., Salimans, T., Sutskever, I.: Improving language understanding by generative pre-training (2018). https://openai.com/research/language-unsupervised
20. Radford, A., et al.: Language models are unsupervised multitask learners (2019). https://openai.com/research/better-language-models
21. Sandler, M., Howard, A., Zhu, M., Zhmoginov, A., Chen, L.C.: MobileNetV2: inverted residuals and linear bottlenecks. In: Proceedings of the IEEE Conference on Computer Vision and Pattern Recognition (CVPR), pp. 4510–4520 (2018)
22. Schulman, J., Wolski, F., Dhariwal, P., Radford, A., Klimov, O.: Proximal policy optimization algorithms (2017). https://openai.com/research/openai-baselines-ppo
23. Shen, Z., Subbiah, S., Gu, X., Wilkes, J.: CloudScale: elastic resource scaling for multi-tenant cloud systems. In: Proceedings of the 2nd ACM Symposium on Cloud Computing (SoCC), pp. 1–14 (2011)
24. Simonyan, K., Zisserman, A.: Very deep convolutional networks for large-scale image recognition. In: International Conference on Learning Representations (ICLR) (2015)
25. Vaswani, A., et al.: Attention is all you need. In: Advances in Neural Information Processing Systems (NeurIPS) (2017)
26. Veličković, P., Cucurull, G., Casanova, A., Romero, A., Liò, P., Bengio, Y.: Graph attention networks. In: International Conference on Learning Representations (ICLR) (2018)

27. Weng, Q., et al.: MLaaS in the wild: workload analysis and scheduling in large-scale heterogeneous GPU clusters. In: 19th USENIX Symposium on Networked Systems Design and Implementation (NSDI), pp. 945–960 (2022)
28. Weng, Q., et al.: Beware of fragmentation: scheduling GPU-Sharing workloads with fragmentation gradient descent. In: USENIX Annual Technical Conference (ATC), pp. 995–1008 (2023)
29. Wu, H., Xu, J., Wang, J., Long, M.: Autoformer: Decomposition Transformers with auto-correlation for long-term series forecasting. In: Advances in Neural Information Processing Systems (NeurIPS), pp. 22419–22430 (2021)
30. Xiao, W., et al.: AntMan: dynamic scaling on GPU clusters for deep learning. In: 14th USENIX Symposium on Operating Systems Design and Implementation (OSDI), pp. 533–548 (2020)
31. Yeung, G., Borowiec, D., Yang, R., Friday, A., Harper, R., Garraghan, P.: Horus: interference-aware and prediction-based scheduling in deep learning systems. IEEE Trans. Parallel Distrib. Syst. **33**(1), 88–100 (2021)
32. Zhou, Z., et al.: AHPA: Adaptive horizontal pod autoscaling systems on Alibaba cloud container service for Kubernetes. In: Proceedings of the AAAI Conference on Artificial Intelligence (AAAI), pp. 15621–15629 (2023)

sAirflow: Adopting Serverless in a Legacy Workflow Scheduler

Filip Mikina[1], Pawel Zuk[2], and Krzysztof Rzadca[1]

[1] Institute of Informatics, University of Warsaw, Warsaw, Poland
krzadca@mimuw.edu.pl
[2] University of Southern California, Los Angeles, USA
pawelzuk@isi.edu

Abstract. Serverless clouds promise efficient scaling, reduced toil and monetary costs. Yet, serverless-ing a complex, legacy application might require major refactoring and thus is risky. As a case study, we use Airflow, an industry-standard workflow system. To reduce migration risk, we propose to limit code modifications by relying on change data capture (CDC) and message queues for internal communication. To achieve serverless efficiency, we rely on Function-as-a-Service (FaaS). Our system, sAirflow, is the first adaptation of the control plane and workers to the serverless cloud—and it maintains the same interface and most of the code. Experimentally, we show that sAirflow delivers the key serverless benefits: scaling and cost reduction. We compare sAirflow to MWAA, a managed (SaaS) Airflow. On Alibaba benchmarks on warm systems, sAirflow performs similarly while halving the monetary cost. On highly parallel workflows on cold systems, sAirflow scales out in seconds to 125 workers, reducing makespan by 2x–7x.

Keywords: Function-as-a-Service · FaaS · cloud applications · software migration

1 Introduction

Serverless cloud [8] products (AWS Lambda, GCP Cloud Run, Azure Functions, OpenWhisk) propose a new kind of contract between the provider and the customer. The customer supplies just the code of the function to execute, while the provider manages resources at the granularity of individual invocations. For customers, this reduces the toil of maintaining infrastructure, and often reduces monetary costs, as typically, the customer pays only for the consumed resources. The providers can optimize hardware while providing highly dynamic horizontal scaling: from zero when a function is not invoked to hundreds of concurrent invocations. This invocation-by-invocation management of resources *by providers* has received considerable attention [8]: e.g., avoiding cold-starts by optimizing the environment pre-warming and evictions [20]; reducing response latency in a warm system by changing how invocations are allocated to workers [5], or by more efficient scheduling at a worker node [35]. Comparatively, *applications* received less attention; and most of the serverless applications described in the literature [24] seem to be built from scratch. Yet, research and industry alike operate on proven, tested and well-understood legacy systems. Throwing away old code and starting from scratch is risky [10]. Yet, there are few blueprints for refactoring towards serverless [36].

The research question we address in this paper is: How can we effectively refactor a complex, legacy application to reap the benefits of serverless computing, including seamless scalability and cost-effectiveness, without introducing significant disruptions to its existing code structure?

As an example of a legacy application we take Airflow, an industry standard for authoring, scheduling, running and monitoring workflows, in particular, data processing pipelines [26]. Airflow is widely used in the industry, both on-premises and as a SaaS offering (AWS' MWAA, Google's Cloud Composer, and Azure's Data Factory Managed Airflow).

The primary challenge in refactoring Airflow lies in its reliance on a metadata database updated with SQL queries from many code locations. To overcome this obstacle, we utilize database-level change data capture (CDC) to transform metadata updates into events then transmitted to the control plane. This pattern allows us to transform Airflow's architecture into event-drive one. Functions from the original Airflow control plane execute as serverless functions (lambdas) that are triggered by events delivered through message queues. For example, when a user submits a new DAG, a CDC-triggered event invokes the scheduler. Similarly, we launch user-defined work on serverless offerings: a FaaS executor for shorter tasks (up to 15 min.); and a universal Container-as-a-Service (CaaS) executor. When a task ends, an event triggers a metadata update, that, in turn, triggers the scheduler. No sAirflow code continuously pulls or runs in the background.

The Contribution of this Paper is as Follows: (1) We propose a new software design pattern for adapting to serverless legacy, database-driven applications: to minimize changes in the code, keep the database interactions; and rely on change data capture (CDC) to produce events driving the control plane. (2) sAirflow is the first serverless adaptation of Airflow's control plane and executors. This enables sAirflow to scale horizontally in seconds to 125 executors and to halve monetary costs. sAirflow thus efficiently surfaces through a legacy system the key advantages of FaaS: elasticity and usage-based pricing.

This paper is organized as follows. We start by reviewing related work in Sect. 2. We then describe Function as a Service (FaaS) and Airflow in Sect. 3. Section 4 describes the design and the key implementation details of sAirflow. Section 5 describes how sAirflow is deployed to the cloud; it also describes the evaluation method. Section 6 describes results of experiments comparing sAirflow with MWAA.

The source code is available at https://github.com/fiffeek/beeflow.

2 Related Work

Workflow Management Systems (WMSs): [13] is a recent survey. Popular WMS include Airflow, Pegasus [9], FuncX [15,32] (both mostly used in scientific computing), Pachyderm [14] (bioinformatics), Argo Workflows (big data) and Kubeflow (ML). We evaluate sAirflow on workflows derived from Alibaba Cloud [38], following [21], advocating real-world-based traces.

Running Workflows in the Cloud: A survey [22] classifies the available approaches, challenges, and evaluation techniques for scientific workflows in the cloud. In particular, [7,18,28] focus on systems approaches to achieve a reliable and scalable scientific WMS. Improvements often concentrate on the scheduling algorithm [3,31] with, e.g., reinforcement learning [17], or prediction of task execution times [19]. sAirflow uses a complementary approach: by switching to a different execution model (serverless), we reduce the platform and worker costs.

Serverless Computing: In contrast to many papers optimizing serverless backends [5,20,35], we take the perspective of a developer of serverless applications. Our contribution is analogous to adaptations of existing systems to FaaS: Unix shell [27], MapReduce [11], or parallelizing Python [2]. A survey [24] of 89 serverless applications does not analyze whether an application was migrated to serverless. A serverless blueprint [30] does not address the challenges of starting from a legacy system. CDC was proposed as one of possible methods to *interoperate* with legacy systems in the software architecture context [25], but they do not specifically target *migrating* large, legacy code, nor they quantify performance.

Serverless Workflow Management Frameworks (WMF): Some serverless WMFs are built from scratch [1,16], thus introducing migration risks and incompatibilities. [16] introduces a container-based WMF; similarly to sAirflow, they rely on messages for internal communication. analyzes serverless-based WMF. [29] extends FaaS with stateful, addressable instances to run workflows (compatible with Durable Functions, not Airflow). [23] uses serverless containers in HyperFlow by extending the executors to run on AWS Lambda and AWS Fargate; HyperFlow orchestrates a one-off workflow, in contrast to Airflow's continously-running control plane coordinating recurring runs of multiple workflows. [6] states that FaaS-based workflow orchestrators (AWS Step Functions or Apache OpenWhisk Composer) are more cost-efficient and easier to scale than Airflow. Our sAirflow addresses this exact shortcoming.

Apache Airflow Extensions and Serverless: Airflow scheduler improvements include [12,33]; they propose adding components to predict resource requirements. [39] provides an Airflow executor (a plugin) allowing job scheduling on AWS Batch and managed Kubernetes. While this plug-in partly addresses the scaling of executors, the control plane is always running—in contrast to sAirflow that additionally uses serverless architecture for the control plane.

3 System Context: FaaS and Airflow

FaaS and Related Serverless Offerings: A *function* is the core building block in a FaaS platform. A programmer defines a function by writing code, packaging it, specifying its memory limits, and defining the invoking triggers. As serverless applications are event-driven, the programmer must bind the invocation of a function to an event: e.g., a direct HTTP call; or a periodic, cron-like schedule. For resiliency, event producers should be decoupled from consumers. A queuing broker (e.g. Kafka) temporary queues events, thus allowing multiple producers and consumers, or consumers to go briefly offline.

FaaS has, however, certain limitations. First, the maximum time of a single function run is limited (e.g., 15 min in AWS). Second, a *cold start* occurs when new resources are assigned for an invocation; a cold start increases the response time by between 300 ms and 24 s [4]—a significant delay for short functions. Third, the functions are expected to be stateless, as the environment is ephemeral. Therefore, state must be stored externally (e.g., in blob storage) which may significantly slow down some applications.

Apache Airflow: a Workflow Scheduler: Airflow processes *DAGs* (workflows) of *tasks*. Tasks are the smallest units of work, with user-defined processing, e.g., copying files or creating a database table from a query. Dependencies between tasks are defined through an API or special operators in the task code. A workflow can be launched manually or scheduled to run, e.g., every day at 4 am. A single execution of a workflow is internally represented by a *DAG run*. Similarly, a single execution of a task is a *task instance*.

The scheduler monitors and orchestrates all tasks and DAGs. By default, once per minute, the scheduler collects DAGs, parses tasks' statuses, and adjusts the metadata on the DAGs and the tasks.

Tasks are launched through local or remote *executors*. A *local executor* launches a task in a child OS process. A *remote executor* sends a task to an external service responsible for queueing and launching. For example, the Kubernetes executor contacts a pre-configured Kubernetes cluster and uses this cluster's API to request a pod that will execute the task.

4 sAirflow: Design and Implementation

We had the following design requirements for sAirflow. (1) *Compatibility* with all Airflow interfaces. (2) *Scalability, Performance and Availability* at least on par with the managed Airflow. (3) *Reproducibility* by persisting infrastructure in code. (4) *Precise intervention* by limiting the modifications of the Airflow source code. (5) *Pay-as-you-use:* Minimize fixed costs. sAirflow achieves all but the last goal, as the database (with the accompanying CDC mechanism), an external dependency, are not pay-as-you-use. Currently, even the AWS serverless database, Aurora, does not scale down to 0; and additionally, it does not support CDC, thus requiring extensive changes in Airflow code (Sect. 4.2), contradicting our penultimate goal. However, we emphasize these are just external

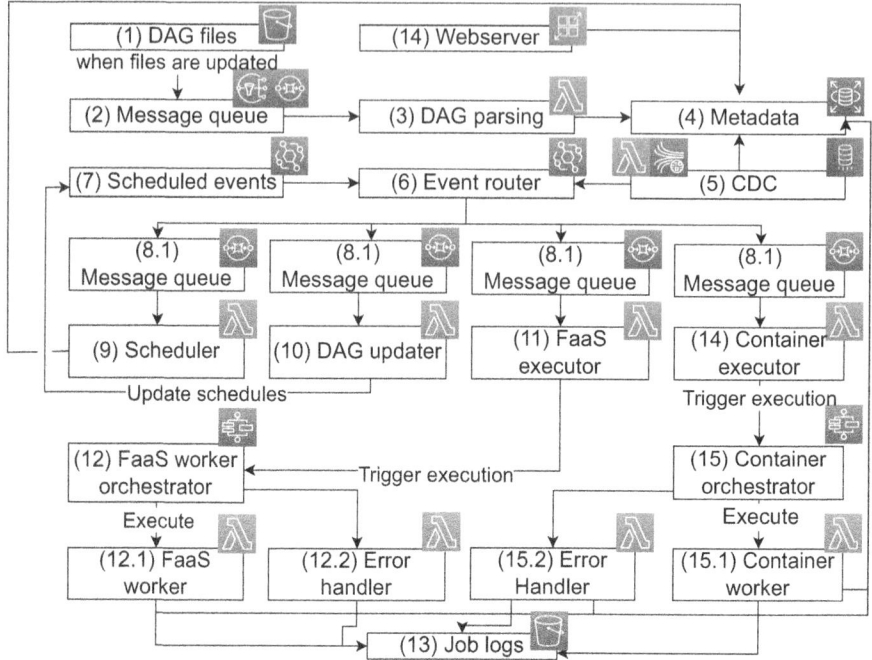

Fig. 1. sAirflow on AWS (icons' source: AWS)

dependencies that, in the future, could be replaced with pay-as-you-use products, if the cloud provider introduces them (as, e.g., Google's recent Datastream for CDC).

Figure 1 presents the high-level design of sAirflow. The figure maps sAirflow architecture to the standard serverless idioms (e.g., a message queue); and then to concrete AWS products (e.g., SQS). As other providers are comparable, porting sAirflow to, e.g., GCP, would require minor code changes.

4.1 Control Flow

We introduce the event-based architecture of sAirflow by describing the flow of control in the system, with component numbers referring to Fig. 1. An Airflow user submits a new (or updated) workflow which is persisted as a DAG file in the blob storage (1). The storage sends notifications via a message queue (2). The notification triggers a function (3) that parses the DAG files and updates the Metadata DB (4). To reduce the load when multiple DAGs are uploaded, we batch these invocations. A similar flow is triggered from the web UI (14).

Changes in the metadata DB are captured by the Change Data Capture (CDC) (5) that produces an event routed to the Event Router (6). Applying CDC to Airflow was the key architectural difficulty we had to solve (Sect. 4.2)

The Event Router (6) routes the following events:

A *change of a parsed DAG* is routed to a function (10) that parses the schedule and updates the scheduled events in EventBridge, a cron-like module (7).

A *periodic event* represents a single launch of a workflow that, e.g., is scheduled daily at 4am. This event is routed to the Airflow scheduler (9). The scheduler creates a new *DAG run* in the metadata DB (4).

A *DAG run* event is routed to the scheduler (9), Sect. 4.3. The scheduler determines if new tasks should be created and which tasks should be executed. Upon deciding to run a task, the scheduler changes the task's status in the metadata DB (4) to queued, triggering a *task queued* event.

A *task queued* event is routed to one of two executors (workers): the Function Executor (11) for invocations of up to 15 min.; or the Container Executor (14). Executors start the user-defined task (12.1) and handle failures (12.2), Sect. 4.4. We stress that executors do not actively wait for the completion of the user work. Once the task is completed (or fails), the executor saves logs (13) and updates the metadata DB (4), triggering a *task finished/failed* event.

A *task finished/failed* event is routed to the scheduler (9), that reruns a task, queues its successors, or marks the DAG run as complete.

4.2 Change Data Capture (CDC)

In serverless architecture, propagating database changes in an event-driven manner requires additional effort. A Change Data Capture (CDC) pattern allows us to reuse most Airflow code (rather than reimplement all database interactions). In AWS cloud, CDC is provided through Database Migration Service (DMS), an external dependency. DMS creates an event on a change in the SQL database and forwards it to a pre-configured destination. We use Amazon Kinesis Data Streams, coupled with a short function (executed as AWS Lambda) to pre-parse the event (e.g., remove redundancies).

DMS introduces a significant delay to the control loop. Typically, it takes 1–1.5 s between the change in the database and the event being delivered to the event router. Our experiments will later show this delay considerably affects sAirflow performance.

The alternative to CDC is to manually inject code that generates events near each DB modification. Apart from the volume of the code modifications needed, the problem with that approach is the joint, transactional nature of the event and the database change. A naive implementation has a *dual write problem*: if the process fails after the database change but before the event is sent, the event might be lost; and if we reverse the order, the event might be consumed by a reader before the change in the database is committed (and visible to the reader).

4.3 Scheduler

Airflow scheduler determines which tasks to launch. Airflow runs the scheduler as a separate, always-running thread, even if workflows are executed only sporadically. Moreover, all previous attempts to serverless Airflow kept this always-on scheduler (Sect. 2). The change of the Airflow scheduler's architecture to event-based—without major refactoring, and retaining Airflow scheduling semantics—was one of the key difficulties while working on sAirflow.

In sAirflow, an event triggers the execution of a scheduling algorithm—for example, an event produced when a task has just been completed. A single pass of the scheduler is executed in a single FaaS invocation. To increase reliability, Airflow can be configured to run multiple, redundant schedulers. In contrast, sAirflow's reliability directly relies on the guarantees provided by FaaS (e.g., multiple availability zones for AWS Lambda). In Airflow, most of the scheduler code executes in a critical section. For consistency, sAirflow feeds the scheduler from a single-shard message queue. The algorithm, however, is largely not modified:

1. For each DAG ready to execute: create a DAG run.
2. For each task in each DAG run with all predecessors completed: create a scheduled task instance.
3. For each scheduled task instance, label it queued.

In contrast to Airflow which might launch some (short) tasks and then actively poll their state running the scheduling loop, sAirflow consistently relies on changes in the metadata database, delivered to external executors.

4.4 Executors and Workers

An executor starts a task instance and then monitors its execution. sAirflow moves the task handling logic to AWS Step Functions; this enables sAirflow to avoid always-on workers polling the state of the user task. AWS Step Functions executes the user code (as a lambda or in a container, details follow). If the user code fails, AWS Step Functions calls a short sAirflow lambda that handles this failure.

sAirflow provides two executors (Function and Container), but the framework algorithm is common:

1. **Invoke execution**: AWS services invoke sAirflow code in an isolated environment. The environment contains a handler that intakes the metadata about the task to execute. The metadata is then passed to the worker.
2. **Pull configuration**: The worker downloads the deployment configuration from the blob storage.
3. **Pull DAG files**: The worker downloads the DAG files defining the workload.
4. **Start task**: The worker starts the task using LocalTaskJob, a standard Airflow component that executes the task in the process of the worker. When a task completes (or fails), this component modifies the metadata DB.
5. **Push logs**: When a task completes, logs are collected throughout the runtime and sent to the blob storage. sAirflow needs minor modifications to push the logs and not close the logging sinks (thus, a single Lambda instance can serve for multiple invocations).

The function executor and the container executor differ by what service they use to run the worker. The *Function Executor* uses FaaS, AWS Lambda. While FaaS scales extremely well, the execution duration is limited (in AWS, to 15 min). This executor forwards task instances from an AWS SQS to a serverless orchestrator, AWS Step Functions.

In the *Container Executor*, the worker launches code in a container through an external service, AWS Batch with AWS Fargate. Containers typically have unbounded execution duration. As in a standard managed container service, a container must specify the limits on the memory, CPU and number of copies. AWS Batch on AWS Fargate supports horizontal scaling (including to 0), thus is consistent with our pay-per-use requirement. AWS Fargate does not limit the duration of execution but typically scales out slower than AWS Lambda [23] and with a significant start-up overhead. On each invocation, the start-up might involve downloading an image and initializing a container, which results in a minutes-long delay. While [23] reports a 1-min start time, in our experiments, we additionally observed significant variance.

5 Deployment and Evaluation Method

To benchmark the performance, we deploy sAirflow in the cloud and compare it to a SaaS solution, Amazon Managed Workflows for Apache Airflow (MWAA). Cloud has myriad configuration and deployment options; our goal is to create environments that are as similar to each other as possible to achieve fair comparison at a reasonable cost. In this section, we describe how we deploy and configure both systems and then how we generate the workflows.

Managed Workflows for Apache Airflow: We run MWAA with a *small* environment (as the large environment is four times more expensive). By default, MWAA uses the Celery executor, with 5 tasks on each worker node. Unless explicitly specified, this parameter was not changed. The environment starts with one worker and might be scaled to 25 workers. Thus, MWAA can run up to 125 tasks concurrently (a *large* environment might support more tasks, but the scalability issues would simply be deferred). Each worker has 1vCPU and 2 GB of RAM, so each task gets roughly 0.2vCPU and 400 MB of RAM. MWAA runs two schedulers in parallel (high availability setting), which might be an advantage compared with sAirflow's single scheduler: both schedulers run the scheduling loop processing the workload, which could improve the task throughput.

sAirflow: For a fair comparison, we match sAirflow's configuration to MWAA. Both systems use Airflow 2.4.3. The resources used by sAirflow's services are scaled to ones used by MWAA. The worker functions have a memory limit of 340 MB (which corresponds to vCPU of around 0.2 as AWS allocates 1vCPU per 1769 MB of memory. The scheduler uses 512 MB of RAM (around 0.35vCPU). We use *db.t3.small* (2vCPU, 2 GB memory) instance with PostgreSQL (without high availability and *SQL proxy*).

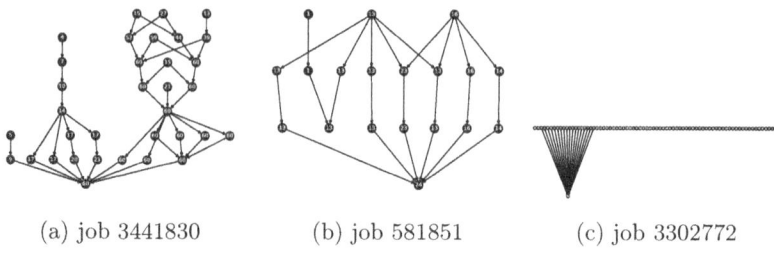

(a) job 3441830 (b) job 581851 (c) job 3302772

Fig. 2. Sample DAGs obtained from jobs in the Alibaba trace. Note that the last DAG is highly parallel (77 tasks in total, 76 of which run in parallel on start-up). Some of the tasks do not have a downstream dependency.

Workloads: We experiment both on synthetic and on realistic workflows, characterized by: n, the number of tasks in the DAG; p_i, the duration of execution of a task in seconds; and T, the period: the DAG executes every T minutes. When measuring *warm* starts, we use $T = 5$ which allows AWS Lambda to reuse previously allocated resources. In contrast, when measuring *cold* starts, we use $T = 30$: AWS Lambda should always spawn new resources for each invocation. When $T = 5$, we run the given DAG for an hour (12 invocations); when $T = 10$, we also run the DAG for an hour (but with 6 invocations); finally, when $T = 30$, we run the DAG for 1.5 h (and get 3 invocations). We do not increase the runtime of experiments (to get more invocations), as MWAA would get too expensive.

As common in evaluating schedulers [34], tasks in both realistic and synthetic DAGs `sleep()` for time p: this does not influence the results, as both MWAA and sAirflow execute tasks in isolated environments with static CPU and memory limits. Additionally, workload traces do not contain all information needed to run the tasks (e.g., binaries, environments or parameters).

We use synthetic *chain* and *parallel* DAGs; and realistic DAGs generated from Alibaba cloud traces [38]. A *chain DAG* has tasks sequentially executing one after another (no parallelism). The optimal execution time of a chain DAG is $n * p$. A *parallel DAG* models highly-parallelizable workloads: after a short startup task, n tasks can be executed in parallel. The optimal execution time is p. Finally, for *Alibaba* DAGs, we extract the DAG shapes and task durations from the batch jobs of Alibaba cloud traces [38]. After filtering out chain and parallel DAGs, we select 30 different DAGs at random. To reduce the costs of experiments, we limit the runtime of any task to at most 60 s.

Figure 2 shows three examples of derived DAGs. For example, the DAG in (Fig. 2a) has $n = 34$ tasks: 13 tasks were shortened to 60 s. The *critical path*, i.e., the path with the longest duration, is 439 s, while the *longest path*, i.e., the path with the maximum number of nodes, is 8 nodes.

Metrics: The key metric, measuring the overall efficiency of the system, is the *DAG makespan*, the difference between DAG's start and end times reported by Airflow. More formally, denoting by v_i the task's ready time, s_i the start time, and by c_i the completion time, the makespan is $C_{\max}(D) = \max_{i \in D} c_i - \min_{i \in D} v_i$. Additionally, to better understand performance, we also report the *task duration*, $(c_i - s_i)$: the difference between the duration and the workload p_i shows the per-task overhead of the system; and the *task wait time*, $(s_i - v_i)$, showing the start-up overhead.

6 Experimental Evaluation Results

For a comprehensive performance comparison, we consider three setups. We start with the *function (FaaS) executor* in two variants, cold (Sect. 6.1) and warm (Sect. 6.2). Then, Sect. 6.3, we run sAirflow with the *container executor*: as it cannot reuse environments, all the executions are cold. We conclude with cost estimation (Sect. 6.4). Due to limited space, we show only the key trends and results; for transparency, all metrics and all results are in the Appendix [37].

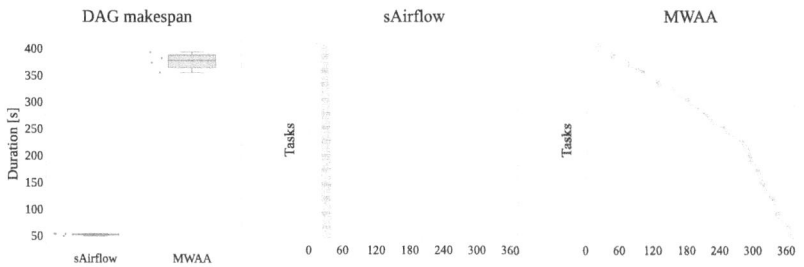

Fig. 3. Parallel DAGs, $p = 10$, $T = 30$, $n = 125$ (cold starts). sAirflow shortens the makespan by 7.2x (left). Gantt charts (middle, right) show a single run.

6.1 Function Executor and Cold Starts

To measure how the systems handle sporadic load, we run Parallel DAGs with $p = 10$ and $n \in \{16, 32, 64, 125\}$. Due to space constraints, Fig. 3 shows the largest $n = 125$ (full results in the Appendix [37]). We run parallel DAGs to focus on workload with enough work. Thus, any inefficiencies will be directly caused by scaling problems. MWAA is configured to start with one worker and horizontally scale out to up to 25 (supporting 125 concurrent invocations). sAirflow is similarly limited to 125 concurrent FaaS invocations. The 30 min interval between runs ($T = 30$) ensures that both systems de-provision resources between consecutive runs.

sAirflow is much faster in scaling out to match the demand, exposing Lambda's horizontal scaling with minimal overheads. The managed version of Airflow needs up to $5\,min$ to add a new worker node (Fig. 3, right), whereas sAirflow starts all workers almost immediately, thus completing the whole workload in less than a minute (Fig. 3, first column). Due to MWAA's long horizontal scaling time, sAirflow reduces the makespan by, on average: 1.9 times ($n = 16$), 3.7 times ($n = 32$), 6.13 times ($n = 64$) and 7.2 times ($n = 125$).

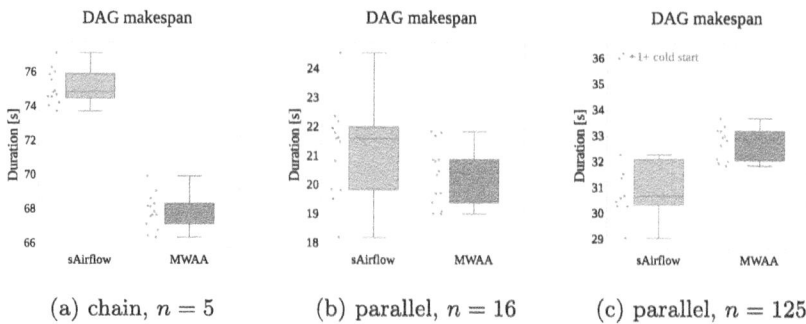

(a) chain, $n = 5$ (b) parallel, $n = 16$ (c) parallel, $n = 125$

Fig. 4. Warm system, $p = 10$, $T = 5$. The first DAG run is not reported.

In sAirflow, the recorded task durations ($c_i - s_i$) increase when more tasks try to start at the same time: a 10-second-long task takes 12 s to complete when $n = 64$ and 17 s when $n = 128$. In these settings, the transactional nature of the internal Airflow's code becomes a bottleneck.

6.2 Function Executor and Warm Starts

To measure the performance under constant load, we now focus on warm invocations. To ensure MWAA is run warm, we disable horizontal scaling by equating the minimum and the maximum number of workers (equal to 25, thus 125 parallel tasks). In sAirflow, we pre-warm the system with a single invocation of the DAG: this invocation warms the lambdas executing the control plane code, as well as the workers. To isolate this effect, we used a one-task DAG and we measured the cold start increasing the waiting time to almost 12 s (vs a median of 2.5 s on a warm system). To focus on warm performance, we now exclude the first DAG invocation from the results unless explicitly stated. However, there is no guarantee that the remaining invocations are all warm—occasional cold starts do happen, and we will take them into account when describing results.

Chain. DAGs emphasize the per-task overheads (Fig. 4a): sAirflow is on the average 0.8 s slower than MWAA when launching a task, a consequence of the lack of real-time CDC data streaming on AWS. As multiple events have to be sent in sequence to execute the next task: the previous task's completion triggers the scheduler, which marks the next task as queued, which in turn triggers the push of another event. This sequence results in a higher latency due AWS DMS overheads: it might take up to 1 s to push the event out of the database through Kinesis to EventBridge.

Parallel. DAGs: When fewer tasks run in parallel ($n = 16$, Fig. 4b, and $n = 32$), MWAA's and sAirflow's DAG execution times are comparable. MWAA is marginally faster for $n = 16$ (by 1.2 s); and similar to sAirflow for $n = 32$. The task wait time for sAirflow is shorter and less variable due to sAirflow's event-driven architecture, in contrast with MWAA's polling executor. sAirflow is faster

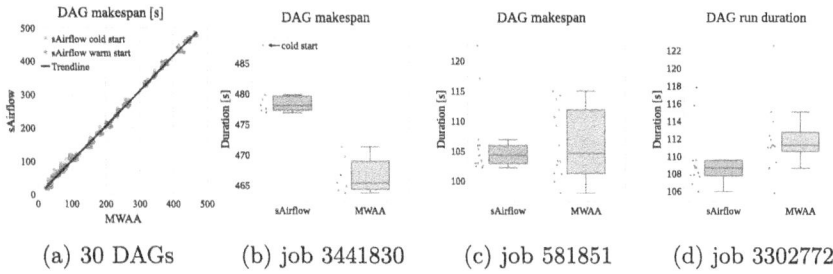

Fig. 5. Alibaba DAGs: makespans on all DAGs (left) and a detailed analysis on the three DAGs from Fig. 2.

than MWAA on larger DAGs with more parallelism, $n = 64$ and $n = 125$, Fig. 4c. Each of the two outliers in Fig. 4c can be traced to a cold start of a FaaS worker.

Alibaba Traces: Comparable Performance: DAGs derived from the Alibaba traces show that performance on realistic, industrial workloads confirms the observed trends, with sAirflow outperforming MWAA when parallelism is sufficient. In this analysis, we include the first cold-start execution for sAirflow. Overall, makespans are similar (as emphasized by the trend line in the scatterplot, Fig. 5a). A detailed analysis of three example DAGs confirms the earlier trends. On chain-like DAGs, such as the one in Fig. 2a, sAirflow's makespan is minimally worse than MWAA (Fig. 5b): 478 s for sAirflow vs. 465 s for MWAA. The task wait time is the same in both systems, while the per-task overheads are higher in sAirflow; thus, the overall makespan is longer (478 s for sAirflow vs. 465 s for MWAA). There are 8 nodes on the critical path for the DAG; thus, the 13 s increase can be attributed to the per-task overheads. The DAG from Fig. 2b shows a workload where both systems perform similarly (Fig. 5c). Where sAirflow loses in terms of the task duration overhead, it gains on better performance concerning the task wait time. Finally, the DAG in Fig. 2c is similar to our parallel DAG, with over 70 tasks that can be executed in parallel; as expected, sAirflow completes the DAG slightly faster than MWAA.

6.3 Container Executor

We measure sAirflow using container workers (AWS Batch with AWS Fargate). Due to space constraints, we only report the key metrics; full results are available in the Appendix [37]. Launching even a single task DAG on a container worker increases the waiting time to 100.5 s (from 2.5 s with FaaS worker). Yet, beyond that delay, sAirflow with container workers still efficiently scales horizontally: a parallel DAG with $n = 32$ tasks of $p = 10$ s completes in approx. 140 s (compared with approx. 160 s needed by cold-starting MWAA).

6.4 Monetary Cost Estimates

While the cloud pricing changes, we believe that the qualitative price difference between on-demand VMs and transient serverless should remain relatively stable, rendering the cost comparison based on current prices at least qualitatively correct in the longer term. We assume systems run continuously over 24 h; we analyze costs with four types of workload (heavy, sporadic parallelizable, sporadic light, and constant light, see Appendix [37] for the exact definitions and results). We lower-bound MWAA costs by assuming that MWAA'a autoscaling bugs are resolved. We upper-bound sAirflow costs by excluding the free tier, and assuming the database and the CDC are always available (while with a sporadic load, CDC might be switched off).

Overall, sAirflow halves the fixed cost. The total cost of sAirflow is lower by 17–48%. As serverless products eliminate paying for idle resources, sAirflow is cheaper on sporadic and unpredictable workloads. sAirflow, due to the platform's elasticity, also eliminates the need to account for the worst-case load when deploying the service (in contrast to MWAA, that cannot reliably downscale). In both systems, the costs are driven principally by the size of the database.

7 Conclusions

We show how to adapt an existing, complex application, Apache Airflow, to the serverless cloud. Our prototype uses FaaS for Airflow's control plane, message queues populated by change data capture (CDC) for internal messaging, and FaaS and CaaS for workers. Through micro-benchmarks and 30 real-world DAGs derived from the Alibaba Cloud traces, we compare the performance of our system with a commercially-maintained version on AWS (MWAA). Our results show that sAirflow with FaaS workers scales notably better than MWAA. When a workflow has enough parallelism, a cold system scales in seconds to 125 workers, reducing completion times by 2x–7x. Conversely, sequential workflows, particularly with long tasks requiring containers, highlight increased latencies stemming from propagating CDC events (approx. 2 s); and launching containers through a queuing system (approx. 90 s).

Adopting a comprehensive, legacy system like Apache Airflow to serverless illustrates the difficulties and effort involved. Our extensive experiments show the performance penalty directly resulting from gaps in the current serverless offerings: the SQL database and the CDC process. Ideally, these two capabilities should be integrated into a single cloud-native serverless service.

Acknowledgements. This research was supported by Polish National Science Center grant Opus (UMO-2017/25/B/ST6/00116), and by the Department of Energy under grant DE-SC0024387.

References

1. Jiang, Q., Lee, Y.C., Zomaya, A.Y.: Serverless execution of scientific workflows. In: International Conference on Service-Oriented Computing, pp. 706–721 (2017)
2. Jonas, E., Pu, Q., Venkataraman, S., Stoica, I., Recht, B.: Occupy the cloud: distributed computing for the 99%. In: Proceedings of SoCC, pp. 445–451 (2017)
3. Kijak, J., Martyna, P., Pawlik, M., Balis, B., Malawski, M.: Challenges for scheduling scientific workflows on cloud functions. In: CLOUD, pp. 460–467 (2018)
4. Manner, J., Endress, M., Heckel, T., Wirtz, G.: Cold start influencing factors in function as a service. In: UCC Proceedings, pp. 181–188. IEEE (2018)
5. Aumala, G., Boza, E., Ortiz-Aviles, L., Totoy, G., Abad, C.: Beyond load balancing: package-aware scheduling for serverless platforms. In: Proceedings of CCGRID. IEEE (2019)
6. Barcelona-Pons, D., Garcia-Lopez, P., Alvaro, R., Gomez-Gomez, A., Paris, G., Sanchez-Artigas, M.: FaaS orchestration of parallel workloads. In: WOSC (2019)
7. Cai, Z., Li, X., Ruiz, R.: Resource provisioning for task-batch based workflows with deadlines in public clouds. IEEE TCC **7**(3), 814–826 (2019)
8. Castro, P., Ishakian, V., Muthusamy, V., Slominski, A.: The rise of serverless computing. Commun. ACM **62**(12), 44–54 (2019)
9. Deelman, E., et al.: The evolution of the pegasus workflow management software. Comput. Sci. Eng. **21**(4), 22–36 (2019)
10. Fairbanks, G.: Ignore, refactor, or rewrite. IEEE Softw. **36**(2), 133–136 (2019)
11. Giménez-Alventosa, V., Moltó, G., Caballer, M.: A framework and a performance assessment for serverless MapReduce on AWS Lambda. FGCS **97**, 259–274 (2019)
12. Ilyushkin, A., Bauer, A., Papadopoulos, A.V., Deelman, E., Iosup, A.: Performance-Feedback Autoscaling with Budget Constraints for Cloud-based Workloads of Workflows (2019). arXiv: 1905.10270
13. Mitchell, R., et al.: Exploration of workflow management systems emerging features from users perspectives. In: Big Data, pp. 4537–4544 (2019)
14. Novella, J.A., et al.: Container-based bioinformatics with Pachyderm. Bioinformatics **35**(5), 839–846 (2019)
15. Chard, R., et al.: Funcx: a federated function serving fabric for science. In: Proceedings of the 29th International Symposium on High-Performance Parallel and Distributed Computing, pp. 65–76 (2020)
16. Dessalk, Y.D., Nikolov, N., Matskin, M., Soylu, A., Roman, D.: Scalable execution of big data workflows using software containers. In: MEDES. ACM (2020)
17. Farid, M., Latip, R., Hussin, M., Abdul Hamid, N.A.W.: Scheduling scientific workflow using multi-objective algorithm with fuzzy resource utilization in multi-cloud environment. IEEE Access **8**, 24309–24322 (2020). https://doi.org/10.1109/ACCESS.2020.2970475
18. Lopez, P.G., Arjona, A., Sampe, J., Slominski, A., Villard, L.: Triggerflow: trigger-based orchestration of serverless workflows. In: DEBS. ACM (2020)
19. Pham, T.-P., Durillo, J.J., Fahringer, T.: Predicting workflow task execution time in the cloud using a two-stage machine learning approach. IEEE Trans. Cloud Comput. **8**(1), 256–268 (2020). https://doi.org/10.1109/TCC.2017.2732344
20. Shahrad, M., Fonseca, R., Goiri, I., Chaudhry, G., Bianchini, R.: Characterization and Optimization of the Serverless Workload at a Large Cloud Provider. USENIX (2020)
21. Versluis, L., et al.: The workflow trace archive: open-access data from public and private computing infrastructures. TPDS **31**(9) (2020)

22. Ahmad, Z., et al.: Scientific workflows management and scheduling in cloud computing: taxonomy, prospects, and challenges. IEEE Access **9**, 53491–53508 (2021)
23. Burkat, K., et al.: Serverless containers - rising viable approach to scientific workflows. In: eScience (2021)
24. Eismann, S., et al.: The state of serverless applications: collection, characterization, and community consensus. IEEE TSE **48**(10), 4152–4166 (2021)
25. Gilbert, J., Price, E.: Software Architecture Patterns for Serverless Systems: Architecting for Innovation with Events, Autonomous Services, and Micro Frontends. Packt Publishing, Birmingham (2021)
26. Harenslak, B.P., de Ruiter, J.: Data Pipelines with Apache Airflow. Simon and Schuster, New York (2021)
27. Mahéo, A., Sutra, P., Tarrant, T.: The serverless shell. In: Middleware: Industrial Track, pp. 9–15 (2021)
28. Ahmad, Z., Jehangiri, A.I., Mohamed, N., Othman, M., Umar, A.I.: Fault tolerant and data oriented scientific workflows management and scheduling system in cloud computing. IEEE Access **10**, 77614–77632 (2022)
29. Burckhardt, S., et al.: Netherite: efficient execution of serverless workflows. VLDB **15**(8), 1591–1604 (2022)
30. Copik, M., Calotoiu, A., Taranov, K., Hoefler, T.: FaasKeeper: a Blueprint for Serverless Services (2022). arXiv: 2202.05711
31. Kamran, A., et al.: A unified mechanism for cloud scheduling of scientific workflows. IEEE Access **10**, 71233–71246 (2022)
32. Li, Z., et al.: FuncX: federated function as a service for science. IEEE Trans. Parallel Distrib. Syst. **33**(12), 4948–4963 (2022)
33. Lin, E., et al.: Global Optimization of Data Pipelines in Heterogeneous Cloud Environments (2022). arXiv: 2202.05711
34. Przybylski, B., Pawlik, M., Zuk, P., Lagosz, B., Malawski, M., Rzadca, K.: Using unused: non-invasive dynamic FaaS infrastructure with HPC-whisk. In: Supercomputing. IEEE (2022)
35. Zuk, P., Przybylski, B., Rzadca, K.: Call scheduling to reduce response time of a FaaS system. In: CLUSTER, pp. 172–182. IEEE (2022)
36. Hamza, M., Akbar, M.A., Smolander, K.: The journey to serverless migration: an empirical analysis of intentions, strategies, and challenges. In: Kadgien, R., Jedlitschka, A., Janes, A., Lenarduzzi, V., Li, X. (eds.) PROFES 2023. LNCS, vol. 14483. Springer, Cham (2024). https://doi.org/10.1007/978-3-031-49266-2_7
37. Mikina, F., Zuk, P., Rzadca, K.: sAirflow: Adopting Serverless in a Legacy Workflow Scheduler (2024). arXiv: 2406.01374
38. Alibaba, Clusterdata: Public trace data sets of production clusters. https://github.com/alibaba/clusterdata/tree/master/cluster-trace-v2018
39. Elzeiny, A.: Apache Airflow: Native AWS Executors. https://github.com/aelzeiny/airflow-aws-executors

Hurry: Dynamic Collaborative Framework For Low-Orbit Mega-Constellation Data Downloading

Handong Luo, Wenhao Liu, Qi Zhang, Ziheng Yang, Quanwei Lin,
Wenjun Zhu, Kun Qiu(✉), Zhe Chen(✉), and Yue Gao(✉)

Fudan University, Shanghai, China
{hdluo23,liuwh23,qizhang23,zhyang22,qwlin22}@m.fudan.edu.cn,
{wenjun,qkun,zhechen,gao.yue}@fudan.edu.cn

Abstract. Low-orbit mega-constellation network, which utilize thousands of satellites to provide a variety of network services and collect a wide range of space information, is a rapidly growing field. Each satellite collects TB-level data daily, including delay-sensitive data used for crucial tasks, such as military surveillance, natural disaster monitoring, and weather forecasting. According to NASA's statement, these data need to be downloaded to the ground for processing within 3–5 h. To reduce the time required for satellite data downloads, the state-of-the-art solution known as CoDld, which is only available for small constellations, uses an iterative method for cooperative downloads via inter-satellite links. However, in LMCN, the time required to download the same amount of data using CoDld will exponentially increase compared to downloading the same amount of data in a small constellation. We have identified and analyzed the reasons for this degradation phenomenon and propose a new satellite data download framework, named Hurry. By modeling and mapping satellite topology changes and data transmission to Time-Expanded Graphs, we implement our algorithm within the Hurry framework to avoid degradation effects. In the fixed data volume download evaluation, Hurry achieves 100% completion of the download task while the CoDld only reached 44% of download progress. In continuous data generation evaluation, the Hurry flow algorithm improves throughput from 11% to 66% compared to the CoDld in different scenarios.

Keywords: Satellite Network · Satellite Downloading · LEO Satellite

1 Introduction

Low-orbit Mega-Constellation Network (LMCN) is an emerging and rapidly developing field. In recent years, constellation projects like Starlink [3], OneWeb [1], and Starshield [2] have been proposed and are gradually being deployed. These large low-Earth-orbit (LEO) constellations utilize tens of thousands of satellites orbiting the Earth to provide services such as Internet communication, Earth observation, and space data collection.

Each LEO satellite generates approximately 1TB of data daily [22,24], containing information for services like military surveillance [19], natural disaster monitoring [26], and weather forecasting [14]. Due to the limited processing capabilities of satellites [25], this data needs to be downloaded to the ground for processing within 3–5 h [11] according to NASA's statement. How to rapidly download data from high-speed moving satellites to the ground through fixed ground stations is a challenging problem.

Current research largely focuses on using ground-satellite links (GSL) [15] for data transmission [7,8,23,24]. However, communication between satellites and ground stations only lasts for 5–15 min at a time, occurring 6–8 times daily [6]. Utilizing inter-satellite links (ISL) [4] enables satellites to transfer data among themselves, accelerating data downloading. Research utilizing ISL has shown that the CoDld algorithm, which employs iterative methods and bipartite graph matching, can fully utilize GSL bandwidth in small constellations (typically ranging from 10 to 66 satellites) like Iridium [12] and Globalstar [10]. However, in LMCN where the number of satellites ranges from 500 to 12,000 [9], the CoDld algorithm suffers from severe degradation, with download speeds decreasing as the download progresses. The time require to download the last 25% of the data is 326 times longer than that for the first 25%.

In this paper, we analyze the cause of this degradation, terming it the Proximal Station Bias Degradation (PSBD), an algorithmic degradation phenomenon where data on satellites requires more hops to reach the ground station as the downloading progresses. This is mainly due to the fact that data closer to ground stations is prioritized for downloading, while data farther away from the ground stations is suspended during its download process. To address this degradation and accelerate satellite data downloading, we propose a flow planning algorithm. This algorithm models and maps the predicted satellite dynamic topology and data generation into Time-Expanded Graphs [18] to calculate transmission schemes. We also establish the *Hurry* framework to dynamically adjust the transmission scheme based on its actual execution.

We integrate the Hurry framework as a plugin into the Plotinus [13], a satellite digital twin system, to validate our algorithm's performance. Our algorithm can achieve 100% completion of a single download task while the CoDld algorithm can only reach 44% download progress. In experiments with continuous data generation, our algorithm can improve throughput by 11%–66% compared to the CoDld in different scenarios.

This paper contributes by:

1. Identifying and thoroughly analyzing the PSBD phenomenon in existing satellite data downloading algorithms like CoDld, especially when applied to LMCN.
2. Introducing *Hurry*, a dynamic satellite downloading framework designed to optimize satellite data download time, implementing a transmission scheme generation algorithm based on Time-Expanded Graphs [18] within this framework.

3. Validating the performance of the Hurry framework and the flow planning algorithm using the Plotinus, a satellite digital twin system.

The paper is organized as follows: Sect. 2 describes the background and the PSBD phenomenon. Section 3 provides an overview of the Hurry framework. Section 4 gives the problem formulation, details, and the specific algorithm design. Section 5 describes the evaluation, and we conclude in Sect. 6.

2 Background

2.1 Constellation, Links, and Download

In this paper, we focus on the Walker Delta satellite constellation. In this satellite constellation, inter-satellite links (ISL) and ground-satellite links (GSL) form the foundation of the satellite network. ISL enables direct communication between satellites, while GSL is the direct communication link between satellites and ground stations. Under the +Grid ISL structure [5], each satellite can establish connections with four adjacent satellites: two for connecting with adjacent satellites in the same orbital plane, and another two for connecting with satellites that have the same numerical designation in neighboring orbits.

Currently, in satellite download algorithms that only utilize GSL, the state-of-the-art method is Umbra [24], which employs network flow-based graph: Time-Expanded Graphs to manage the data volume transmitted to ground stations. The algorithm proposed in this paper is innovated by this study. The exploration of using ISL to accelerate satellite data downloading is initially put forward by the CoDld algorithm. Zhang [28] subsequently introduce an energy-efficient variant of CoDld [17], and Wu [27] extend the model to encompass multiple ground stations. To the best of our knowledge, all existing researches on satellite downloading are based on small constellations comprising merely a few dozen satellites (typically ranging from 10 to 200 satellites).

2.2 CoDld Algorithm

The CoDld algorithm employs an iterative method to construct a download schedule for the satellite network. For i-th satellite S_i in the network, the algorithm maintains two key variables: remaining download time and remaining contact time with the ground station. The remaining download time indicates how long the time required by S_i to fully download its data, while the remaining contact time signifies how much ground station contact time S_i can still be allocated for communication with the ground station. During each iteration, satellites waiting to download data and satellites with spare contact time are paired by a maximum bipartite graph matching algorithm. Upon successful matching, data will be transmitted to the satellite that has available contact time through inter-satellite links, thereby being relayed to the ground. This iterative process continues until all satellites have completed their data downloads or the contact time with the ground station is fully utilized. A notable characteristic of this algorithm is that if a satellite has data yet to be downloaded, it will not accept any data from other satellites until its data download is completed (Fig. 1).

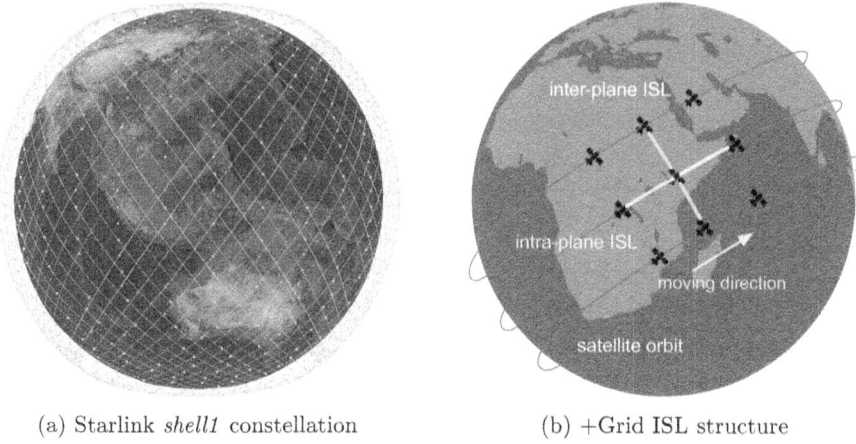

(a) Starlink *shell1* constellation (b) +Grid ISL structure

Fig. 1. Walker Delta satellite constellation and +Grid ISL structure

2.3 Proximal Station Bias Degradation

PSBD is an algorithmic degradation phenomenon in which data from satellites requires an increasing number of hops to reach the ground station during the download process. This phenomenon is caused by the imbalanced distribution of data across the satellite network during download, where data closer to ground stations is given priority for downlink, while data farther from the ground stations remains suspended during its download process.

Figure 2a shows the distribution of data download progress in the satellite network when the PSBD phenomenon occurs. Satellites closer to the ground station in Manhattan were given priority to download all satellite data, while those farther away did not begin downloading, creating an area where no data exists on the satellites. All data needed for download were located on satellites far from the ground station. Figure 2b shows the process of satellites distant from the ground station transmitting data to the ground station via inter-satellite links. Since data offloading only takes place on satellites one hop away, the data must survive multiple time-consuming inter-satellite offloading before it can be transmitted to the ground. The number of hops for data offloading will continue to increase as the area where no data exists on the satellites expands, further slowing down the download speed.

As we have mentioned before, existing solutions such as CoDld cannot prevent the degradation effect, which may cause a download suspension. Thus, a new algorithm that can solve PSBD needs to be proposed to increase the downloading speed in LMCN.

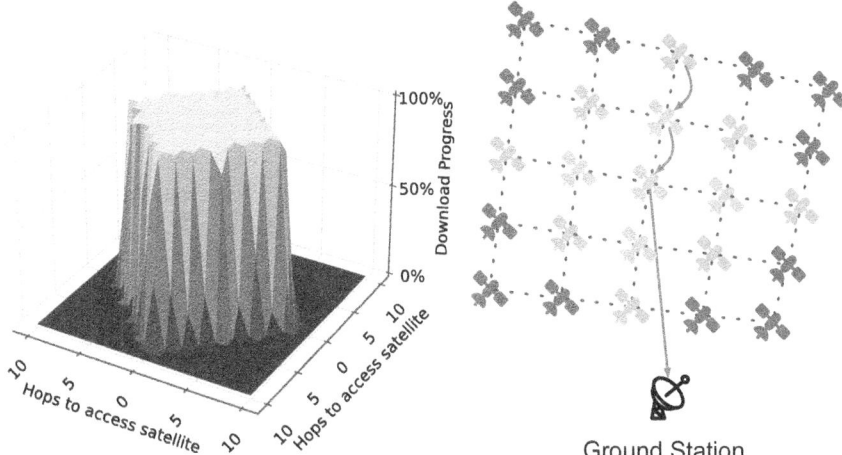

(a) **Uneven distribution of data download progress across satellite constellation during PSBD events.** The x-axis and y-axis coordinates represent the number of hops needed for the satellite to reach the access satellite within the current orbital plane and between orbital planes, respectively. The z-axis coordinate represents the current satellite's data download progress.

(b) **Transmission process of satellite data download via inter-satellite Links.** Green satellites represent those that have completed data downloads, orange satellites represent those currently downloading data, and blue satellites represent those that have not yet started downloading data.

Fig. 2. The PSBD phenomenon and its consequences

3 Overview of Hurry

In this section, we will provide an overview of the Hurry framework. The overall design of Hurry, as shown in Fig. 3, is composed of four submodules: data capture, satellite selection, flow planning, and satellite monitoring.

Data Capture module captures data from the satellite constellation as the initial state of our system. It collects three key pieces of data: location of the ground station, the Two Line Element (TLE) orbit descriptors of the satellite, and download plan of each satellite. The first two types of data can be easily obtained from ITU software or public websites like Space-Track or CelesTrak. TLE descriptors should be updated periodically to ensure accurate satellite orbit positioning.

Satellite Selection module uses its emulator to emulate the satellite position in each time slot. It calculates the distance between the satellite and ground station to determine the visible satellites for each ground station at a given time. The ground station then selects satellites in its visible satellite list to establish a data connection. After the connection is established, the satellite sends the data generated by itself or from other satellites to the ground station.

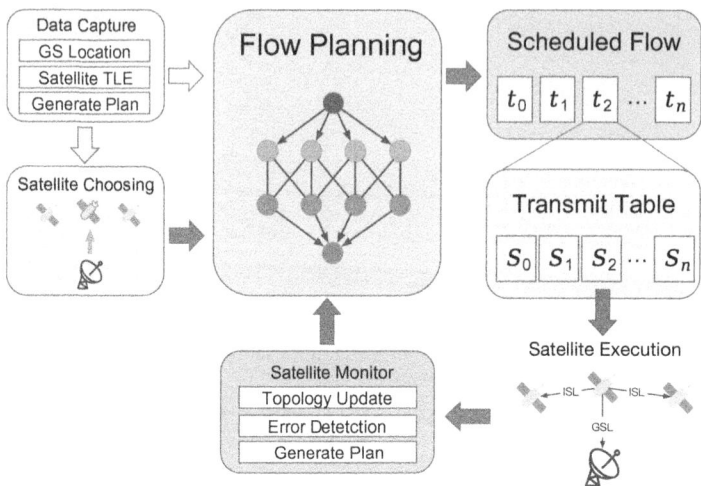

Fig. 3. Overall architecture design for Hurry framework

Flow Planning module takes the data from the Data Capture model and the Satellite Selection model as input and generates a transmission plan. It determines the direction and volume of data transmission from satellites to ground stations or between satellites.

Satellite Monitoring module monitors the satellite's queuing status and the unpredictable topology change of the satellite constellation. If the queue state of a satellite does not meet the predefined threshold, the monitor module sends a signal to the flow planning module to adjust the plan. This module also tracks the topology change of the satellite constellation owing to the high mobility of LEO satellite constellations.

4 Flow Planning

4.1 Problem Formulation

First, we provide the problem formulation and optimization objective of the flow planning module. Formally, denote the set of satellites as

$$\mathcal{S} = \{S_1, S_2, \ldots, S_n\}$$

In this paper, we adopt a discrete-time framework, where the interval from time point t to $t+1$ is considered as time unit. Within this time unit, each satellite S_i captures and generates new data $P_{S_i}^t$. Satellites can transmit data to other satellites through inter-satellite links (ISL) over a interval from time t to time $t+1$. Let (B_{S_i,S_j}^t) denote the bandwidth available between satellites S_i and S_j during this interval (Table 1).

Table 1. Terms of Definition

Notation	Definition
t	The t-th timeslot
n	The total number of satellite
m	The total number of ground station
S_i	Satellite i
S_i^t	Node for Satellite i at time slot t
G_i	Ground station i
G_i^t	Node for Ground station i at time slot t
D	Transmit plan matrix
D_{S_i,G_j}^t	Data amount transferred from S_i to G_j at time t
D_{S_i,S_j}^t	Data amount transferred from S_i to S_j at time t
B_{S_i,S_j}^t	The bandwidth between S_i and S_j at time t
B_{S_i,G_j}^t	The bandwidth between S_i and G_j at time t
$B_{G_j}^t$	The bandwidth from G_j to Data Center at time t
$Q_{S_i}^t$	The data stored at satellite at time t
$Q_{S_i}'^t$	The actual observed queue length for S_i at time t
$P_{S_i}^t$	S_i generated data between time $t-1$ and time t
P_{total}	S_i total data volume generated by all satellites
T	The total number of time slots satellite generated data

Next, the set of ground stations is

$$\mathcal{G} = \{G_1, G_2, \ldots, G_m\}$$

If the satellite is connected to the ground station within the time interval from t to $t+1$, it can transfer a data amount of B_{S_i,G_j}^t; if not connected, $B_{S_i,G_j}^t = 0$. The satellite is capable of storing data generated by itself and received from other satellites. $Q_{S_i}^t$ represents the amount of data stored on satellite S_i at time t. Since typical satellites have storage of multiple TBs [24], we consider the storage capacity of satellites to be sufficient for data storage.

Our goal is to compute a **data transmission plan**, which can be formulated as two matrices D_{S_i,S_j}^t and D_{S_i,G_k}^t, representing the amount of data satellite S_i transferred to its neighboring satellite S_j or to the ground station G_k within the time interval from t to $t+1$. D is subject to the following constraints:

– A satellite communicates with at most one ground station at a time:
 $\forall t, S_i, G_j \neq G_k, D_{S_i,G_j}^t = 0 \vee D_{S_i,G_k}^t = 0$.
– A ground station communicates with at most one satellite at a time:
 $\forall t, G_k, S_i \neq S_j, D_{S_i,G_k}^t = 0 \vee D_{S_j,G_k}^t = 0$
– A satellite's transfer speed to the ground station cannot exceed GSL bandwidth:
 $\forall t, S_i, G_j, D_{S_i,G_j}^t \leq B_{S_i,G_j}^t$.

- A satellite's transfer speed to another satellite cannot exceed ISL bandwidth: $\forall t, S_i, S_j, D^t_{S_i,S_j} \leq B^t_{S_i,S_j}$ where $i \neq j$.
- A satellite cannot transmit more data than it store:
$\forall t, i, (\sum_{j=0}^{n} D^t_{S_i,S_j} + \sum_{k=0}^{m} D^t_{S_i,G_k}) \leq Q^t_{S_i}$.

The data stored on the satellite can be calculated based on the previously generated and transmitted data as follows:

$$Q^t_{S_i} = \sum_{j=0}^{t-1} P^j_{S_i} + \sum_{k=0}^{t-1}\sum_{j=0}^{n} D^k_{S_i,S_j} - \sum_{k=0}^{t-1}(\sum_{j=0}^{n} D^k_{S_i,S_j} + \sum_{j=0}^{m} D^k_{S_i,G_j}) \tag{1}$$

Optimization Objective: Our optimization goal is to minimize the time taken to download all the data from the satellites after the last data generation time slot T. Mathematically, we define the download completion time T_Download as the shortest time such that the total stored data on all satellites at time T_Download is 0. Thus, we can express our optimization problem as:

$$T_\text{Download} = \min\{t \in \mathbb{N} \mid t \geq T \text{ and } \sum_{i=1}^{n} Q^t_{S_i} = 0\} \tag{2}$$

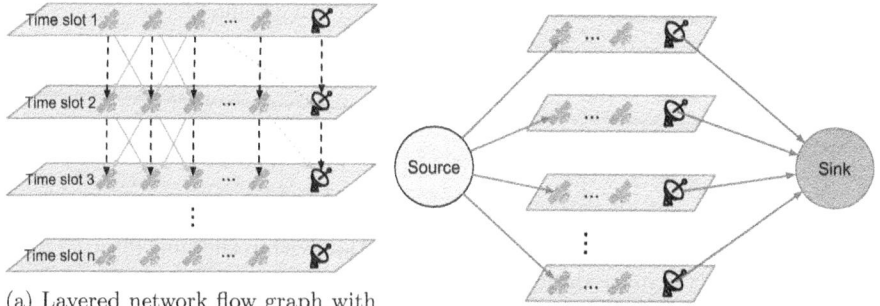

(a) Layered network flow graph with edges between satellite node and ground station node

(b) Layered network flow graph with source and sink node

Fig. 4. Layered network flow graph

4.2 Transmission Plan Generating

Generating the transmission plan requires solving the layered network flow graph using the Min-Cost Max-Flow algorithm. First, as illustrated in Fig. 4a, we treat each time slot required for the transmission plan as a layer of network flow graph. For each satellite S_i and ground station G_j, we create corresponding nodes S^t_i and G^t_j in each graph layer.

Firstly, for data generation, if satellite S_i produces data between T_{j-1} and T_j, an edge from the source node to S_i^t is established with a flow capacity of $P_{S_i}^t$, representing the generated data. Simultaneously, for each ground station G_i at every time slot, an edge is drawn from G_i^t to the sink node with a capacity of $B_{G_i}^t$, depicting the bandwidth available for uploading data to the cloud for processing.

Algorithm 1. Adaptive Doubling Strategy for Transmission Plan
---
1: $T_{gen} \leftarrow 0, M \leftarrow 1, G \leftarrow \emptyset$
2: **while** True **do**
3:     $G \leftarrow$ Generate layered flow graph (length=$T_{gen} + M$)
4:     $P_{\text{transmit}} \leftarrow$ Maxflow$(G, \text{source}, \text{sink})$
5:     **if** $P_{\text{transmit}} == P_{\text{total}}$ **then**
6:        $T_{gen} \leftarrow T_{gen} + \lfloor M/2 \rfloor$
7:        break
8:     **else**
9:        $M \leftarrow M * 2$
10:    **end if**
11: **end while**
12: **return** $T_{gen} + 1$

We use the following step to create the edge between the satellite nodes and the ground station node:

1. Edges between satellite S_j^t and ground station G_i^{t+1} nodes are drawn with a flow capacity B_{S_j,G_i}^t if they are scheduled to communicate within the time slot t to $t+1$.
2. If satellite S_i can transmit data to S_j within the time slot t to $t+1$, an edge from S_i^t to S_j^{t+1} is created with a capacity B_{S_i,S_j}^t.
3. Edges of infinite capacity link the same satellite and ground station nodes across consecutive time slots S_i^t to S_i^{t+1} and G_i^t to G_i^{t+1}, symbolizing the data store capability.

For each edge in the network flow graph, we assign a cost of 1 to encourage rapid data transfer to the ground.

4.3 Adaptive Transmission Plan Update

For packet loss and link failures, we use the Satellite Queue Deviation Index (SQDI) to assess the need to update the transmission plan. The SQDI is calculated as

$$\text{SQDI} = \frac{1}{n}\sum_{i=1}^{n}\left|Q'^t_i - Q^t_i\right| + \max_{i=1}^{n}\left|Q'^t_i - Q^t_i\right| \qquad (3)$$

which triggers a plan update when it exceeds the threshold θ. To update the transmission plan, we need to reconstruct the network flow graph from the current time slot, adding edges from the source to each satellite node S_i^t at the beginning of the graph. These edges have a capacity of Q'^t_i, representing the current data status of each satellite.

4.4 Generation Acceleration

To address the challenge of increased latency from extended computation times, we have developed an adaptive doubling strategy in Algorithm 1. This strategy efficiently identifies the optimal length T_{gen} for transmission plan generation, where T_{gen} is the minimum time necessary for completing data downloading.

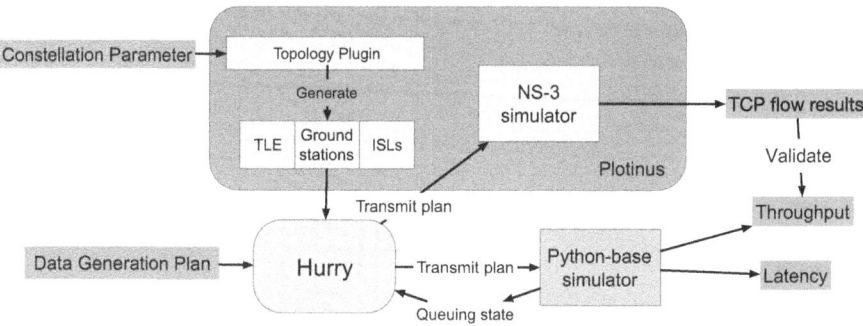

Fig. 5. The evaluation process of Hurry

5 Experimental Evaluation

5.1 Evaluation Environment

We implement the Hurry framework as a plugin into the Plotinus [13] to validate the performance of our algorithm. The specific validation process is illustrated in Fig. 5, where we use Constellation Parameters as input to the Topology Plugin in Plotinus, which generates the satellite TLE, ground station locations, and inter-satellite link topology information required by Hurry. We use starlink *shell1* as our experimental satellite constellation. We set the bandwidth for inter-satellite and satellite-to-ground links for light load scenarios at 10 Gbps. In moderate load scenarios, the bandwidth is set to 5 Gbps for both types of links, and for heavy load scenarios, it is reduced to 1 Gbps.

5.2 Baseline Algorithms

We use the following algorithms as baselines to compare the performance of our algorithm under different scenarios: 1) **CoDld**: The original CoDld algorithm; 2) **CoDld Modify**: An adjustment to the original CoDld algorithm that incorporates iterative logic to enable data offloading and downloading cycles as soon as satellites generate data; 3) **Greedy with ISL**: Satellites use Floyd algorithm to find the shortest path (in terms of hops) to the ground station; 4) **Greedy without ISL**: This algorithm only initiates data transmission when a satellite has a direct connection to the ground station.

Table 2. Algorithm performance for satellite data downloads. Each entry in the table represents the time it takes for the corresponding algorithm to download 99% of 0.25 GB of data generated by each satellite over a 10-s period.

	Downloading time (s)								
GSL bandwidth	1 Gbps			5 Gbps			10 Gbps		
ISL bandwidth	1 Gbps	5 Gbps	10 Gbps	1 Gbps	5 Gbps	10 Gbps	1 Gbps	5 Gbps	10 Gbps
Greedy (no ISL)	30008	30008	30008	29735	29735	29735	29735	29735	29735
Greedy with ISL	18029	15854	15853	18029	15618	15423	18029	15618	15369
CoDld	6594	6021	6021	7037	6660	6660	7184	6850	6850
CoDld Modify	6456	5727	5727	7043	6594	6594	6989	5943	5943
Hurry	65	65	65	52	26	26	52	25	25

5.3 Overall Performance

To verify the performance of the proposed algorithm, we test the time required to download satellite data under different link bandwidth combination scenarios. The experimental results are shown in Table 2. Our algorithm consistently outperforms the baseline algorithm in various scenarios, reducing the download time by more than 99%. Our algorithm's download time under heavy load exceeds twice that of medium and light loads. However, in the CoDld algorithm and its modified version, the download times across different bandwidths essentially remain consistent. For the Greedy with ISL algorithm, its download time is approximately three times that of the CoDld algorithm. When the ISL bandwidth is 5 Gbps or higher, its download time can be reduced by 17% compared to when the bandwidth is 1 Gbps.

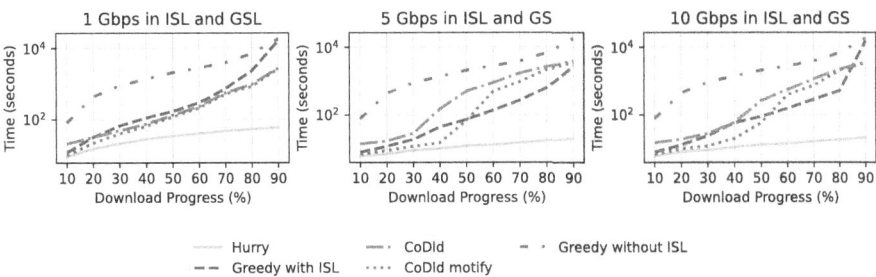

Fig. 6. Time to reach download progress for different inter-satellite link and ground station-satellite link bandwidths.

In Fig. 6, we present the time required by the Hurry and baseline algorithms to reach corresponding progress milestones in the download process under various combinations of ISL and GSL bandwidths. Hurry maintains an almost constant rate from the beginning to the end of the downloading, whereas the time

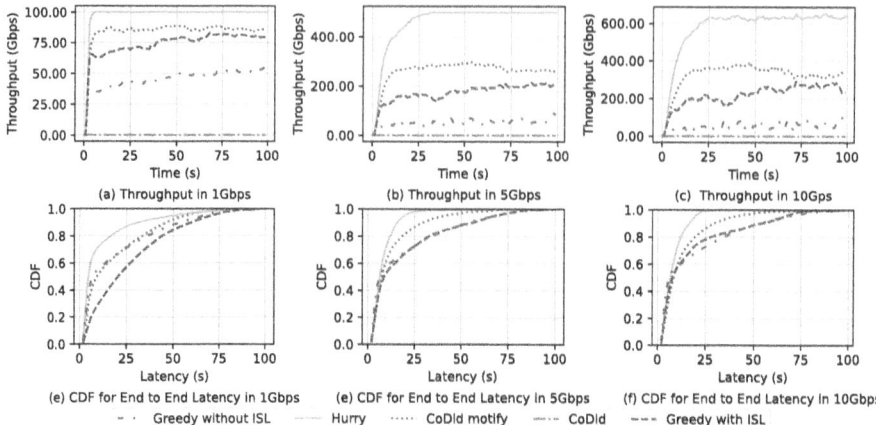

Fig. 7. Throughput over time in different ISL and GSL bandwidths, and latency CDF in different scenarios.

taken by other algorithms to complete corresponding progress milestones sharply increases as the download proceeds. At 10% transmission progress, the Hurry, CoDld Modify, and Greedy with ISL algorithms require roughly the same amount of time. As the transmission continues, the gap between the CoDld Modify and the original CoDld algorithms gradually narrows in the graph, with the time taken for corresponding progress levels showing exponential growth. On the other hand, the time for corresponding progress in the Greedy with ISL algorithm initially grows exponentially but then completes the transmission rapidly towards the end. The Greedy without ISL algorithm takes significantly longer for data transmission than all other algorithms. For the flow planning algorithm, the primary bottleneck under heavy load is the bandwidth of the GSL, while under light and moderate loads, most of the time is consumed by the delay caused by data transmission between satellites.

5.4 Performance of Long-Time Generation

We test the performance of our algorithm and the baseline algorithms in a scenario where each satellite continuously generates data at a rate of 400 Mbps. As shown in Fig. 7(a)(b)(c), the throughput indicates that our algorithm, under a combination of 1 Gbps ISL and GSL bandwidths, improved the overall throughput by approximately 11% compared to the CoDld Modify algorithm, which has the highest throughput among the baselines. At bandwidths of 5 Gbps and 10 Gbps, the throughput increased by 66% and 50%, respectively.

During transmission, our algorithm and CoDld Modify maintain consistent throughput after reaching their maximum values. The throughput of the Greedy with ISL algorithm gradually increases over time. The throughput of the Greedy without ISL algorithm slowly increases at low GSL bandwidths and remains unchanged at medium and high GSL bandwidths. The throughput of the original

CoDld algorithm is consistently zero due to its lack of support for dynamic data generation. The CoDld Modify algorithm, affected by the Proximal Station Bias Degradation (PSBD) phenomenon, can only effectively transmit data within a few hops of the ground station.

Figure 7(d)(e)(f) illustrates the CDF graph of the packets transmitted by the flow planning algorithm and the baseline in the continuous data generation experiment. Our algorithm exhibits lower latency than the baseline in every bandwidth experiment, with the delay further decreasing as the bandwidth of ISL and GSL increases. The latency of the CoDld modify algorithm is superior to that of Greedy with ISL across all three bandwidths due to the fact that Greedy with ISL encounters more congestion phenomena during data transmission.

6 Conclusion

In this paper, we introduce the Hurry framework and the flow planning algorithm, which significantly reduce the satellite data downloading time in Low-orbit Mega-Constellation Networks (LMCN), identifying and thoroughly analyzing the Proximal Station Bias Degradation (PSBD) phenomenon present in the existing CoDld algorithm within LMCN. By modeling and mapping the changes in satellite topology and data transmission onto Time-Expanded Graphs, the flow planning algorithm is able to generate an efficient transmission plan. In our experiments conducted using the Plotinus satellite digital twin system, in the fixed data volume download evaluation, Hurry achieves 100% completion of the download task while the CoDld has reached only 44% download progress. Furthermore, in scenarios of continuous data generation, Hurry increases throughput by 11% to 66%, highlighting its capability to adjust transmission plan for optimal efficiency dynamically. As a potential future direction, we are looking forward to extending our Hurry to improve the performance of various applications such as distributed learning systems [20,21], ISAC [16], etc. in LEO satellite networks.

References

1. Eutelsat OneWeb. https://oneweb.net/
2. SpaceX - starshield. https://www.spacex.com/starshield/
3. Starlink. https://www.starlink.com/
4. Arora, H., Goyal, R.: A review on inter-satellite link in inter-satellite optical wireless communication. J. Opt. Commun. **38**(1), 63–67 (2017)
5. Bhattacherjee, D., Singla, A.: Network topology design at 27,000 km/hour. In: Proceedings of the 15th International Conference on Emerging Networking Experiments and Technologies, pp. 341–354 (2019)
6. Cakaj, S., Fischer, M., Scholtz, A.: Practical horizon plane for low earth orbiting (LEO) satellite ground stations, pp. 62–67
7. Castaing, J.: Scheduling downloads for multi-satellite, multi-ground station missions (2014)
8. Chen, H., Zhai, B., Wu, J., Du, C., Li, J.: A satellite observation data transmission scheduling algorithm oriented to data topics. Int. J. Aerosp. Eng. **2020**, 1–16 (2020)

9. Curzi, G., Modenini, D., Tortora, P.: Large constellations of small satellites: a survey of near future challenges and missions. Aerospace **7**(9), 133 (2020)
10. Dietrich, F.J., Metzen, P., Monte, P.: The globalstar cellular satellite system. IEEE Trans. Antennas Propag. **46**(6), 935–942 (1998)
11. NASA Earth Science Data Systems: LANCE: NASA Near Real-time Data and Imagery — Earthdata. Earth Science Data Systems NASA
12. Fossa, C.E., Raines, R.A., Gunsch, G.H., Temple, M.A.: An overview of the IRIDIUM (R) low earth orbit (LEO) satellite system. In: Proceedings of the IEEE 1998 National Aerospace and Electronics Conference. NAECON 1998. Celebrating 50 Years (Cat. No. 98CH36185), pp. 152–159. IEEE (1998)
13. Gao, Y., et al.: Plotinus: a satellite internet digital twin system. PTP J. Commun. Inf. Netw. **9**(1), 23–32 (2024)
14. Geer, A.J., et al.: All-sky satellite data assimilation at operational weather forecasting centres. Q. J. R. Meteorol. Soc. **144**(713), 1191–1217 (2018)
15. Hou, Z., Yi, X., Zhang, Y., Kuang, Y., Zhao, Y.: Satellite-ground link planning for LEO satellite navigation augmentation networks. IEEE Access **7**, 98715–98724 (2019)
16. Hu, J., Chen, Z., Zheng, T., Schober, R., Luo, J.: HoloFed: environment-adaptive positioning via multi-band reconfigurable holographic surfaces and federated learning. IEEE J. Sel. Areas Commun. **41**, 3736–3751 (2023)
17. Jia, X., Lv, T., He, F., Huang, H.: Collaborative data downloading by using intersatellite links in LEO satellite networks. IEEE Trans. Wireless Commun. **16**(3), 1523–1532 (2017)
18. Köhler, E., Langkau, K., Skutella, M.: Time-expanded graphs for flow-dependent transit times. In: Möhring, R., Raman, R. (eds.) ESA 2002. LNCS, vol. 2461, pp. 599–611. Springer, Heidelberg (2002). https://doi.org/10.1007/3-540-45749-6_53
19. Korody, P.: Satellite surveillance within US borders. Ohio St. LJ **65**, 1627 (2004)
20. Lin, Z., Chen, Z., Fang, Z., Chen, X., Wang, X., Gao, Y.: FedSN: a general federated learning framework over LEO satellite networks. arXiv preprint arXiv:2311.01483 (2023)
21. Lin, Z., et al.: Efficient parallel split learning over resource-constrained wireless edge networks. IEEE Trans. Mobile Comput., 1–16 (2024)
22. Ma, Y., et al.: Remote sensing big data computing: challenges and opportunities **51**, 47–60. https://doi.org/10.1016/j.future.2014.10.029
23. Maillard, A., et al.: Adaptable data download schedules for agile earth-observing satellites. J. Aerosp. Inf. Syst. **13**(3), 280–300 (2016)
24. Tao, B., Masood, M., Gupta, I., Vasisht, D.: Transmitting, fast and slow: scheduling satellite traffic through space and time. In: Proceedings of the 29th Annual International Conference on Mobile Computing and Networking, pp. 1–15 (2023)
25. Theis: Spacecraft computers: state-of-the-art survey **16**(4), 85–97. https://doi.org/10.1109/MC.1983.1654358. Conference Name: Computer
26. Visser, S.J., Dawood, A.S.: Real-time natural disasters detection and monitoring from smart earth observation satellite. J. Aerosp. Eng. **17**(1), 10–19 (2004)
27. Wu, L., Yang, L., Huang, H., Jia, X.: Optimal satellite data downloading to multiple ESs by ISL offloading in LEO satellite networks. In: 2019 15th International Conference on Mobile Ad-Hoc and Sensor Networks (MSN), pp. 188–193. IEEE. https://doi.org/10.1109/MSN48538.2019.00045
28. Zhang, M., Zhou, W.: Energy-efficient collaborative data downloading by using inter-satellite offloading. In: 2019 IEEE Global Communications Conference (GLOBECOM), pp. 1–6. IEEE (2019)

Optimizing Service Replication and Placement for IoT Applications in Fog Computing Systems

Farah Ait-Salaht[✉], Maher Rebai, and Nora Izri

Léonard de Vinci Pôle Universitaire, Research Center,
92 916 Paris La Défense, Courbevoie, France
{farah.ait_salaht,maher.rebai,nora.izri}@devinci.fr

Abstract. Fog Computing extends Cloud Computing to the network edge, enhancing distributed computing to meet the growing needs of Internet of Things (IoT) applications requiring real-time or near-real-time analysis. This research focuses on efficiently managing the vast amounts of data generated by IoT devices and the continuous data streams they produce, employing an advanced replication and placement strategy for application components across distributed Fog Computing nodes. This approach enables scalable and parallel data processing to adapt to demand fluctuations, prevent over-provisioning, and maintain low response times, making it particularly effective for the dynamic nature of data stream processing in IoT applications. In this paper, we propose an Optimal IoT Service Replication and Placement (SRP) model, formulated as a constraint satisfaction problem, that considers the diverse requirements of IoT applications and the available infrastructure resources. Our model is designed to be adaptive and extensible, addressing the challenge of workload variability through real-time optimization. Numerical evaluations confirm the superior performance and scalability of our model over existing methods, while maintaining quality of service constraints. This highlights the potential of our approach to improve efficiency and resource management in Fog Computing environments.

Keywords: Fog Computing · Service replication · Service placement · IoT applications · Constraint Programming

1 Introduction

In the rapidly evolving landscape of the Internet of Things (IoT) and the Fog Computing [5], the seamless and efficient handling of data flow has emerged as a critical challenge. The proliferation of IoT devices has led to an unprecedented increase in data generation, necessitating robust systems capable of processing and analyzing data close to the source. This paradigm shift towards decentralization aims to reduce latency, enhance bandwidth utilization, and improve overall system responsiveness. However, the dynamic and distributed nature of IoT applications, coupled with the fluctuating demands of data flow, presents significant challenges in service replication and placement within Fog Computing environments.

IoT applications are commonly designed within a service-oriented architecture, which breaks down complex systems into logically distinct and complementary microservices. This architecture is represented as a directed acyclic graph (DAG), where each service acts as a modular component dedicated to executing specific facets of the application's logic [21]. To accommodate fluctuating data rates and varying workload demands, these components require the capability to dynamically scale, employing sophisticated replication and parallelization techniques [19]. These techniques ensure that each service component can process part of the incoming data flow in parallel, leveraging the distributed computing resources of the Fog network to maintain and enhance system performance and responsiveness.

Therefore, a paramount challenge in Fog environments is the optimization of service replication and placement, an essential mechanism for ensuring high availability, fault tolerance, and effective load balancing. Replication involves deploying multiple instances of services across distributed nodes to meet the varied demands of users and applications. However, the distributed and heterogeneous nature of Fog networks adds complexity to the replication process, necessitating careful consideration of several factors, including network topology, resource availability, workload characteristics, and Quality of Service (QoS) requirements. In this context, we propose an innovative approach to tackle service replication by formulating the problem as a constraint satisfaction problem, aimed at optimizing service replication in Fog networks. Building on the Service Placement model by Aït-Salaht et al. [1], which offers a general formulation for optimal IoT service placement, we aim to expand this model to develop an optimal Service Replication and Placement model (SRP) for efficiently managing workload demands. A key innovation of our approach is its focus on scalability and adaptability, addressing the complexities of deploying interconnected service sets across geographically distributed and heterogeneous environments.

The remainder of this paper is organized as follows: Sect. 2 explores related literature, emphasizing key insights. Section 3 introduces the problem definition and system model. Section 4 elaborates on our proposed methodology. Section 5 presents and discusses the numerical evaluation of our model. Finally, Sect. 6 concludes the paper and outlines future research directions.

2 Related Work

The literature extensively investigates the deployment and replication challenges of IoT applications within Fog Computing networks, Edge, and distributed environments, categorizing the research into two distinct areas. The first examines data replication and placement issues [3, 29–31], while the second focuses on IoT applications modeled as a DAG, emphasizing the determination of replication degrees and the strategic placement of application components across the computing network. Our research aligns with the latter, revealing that most studies address these challenges in isolation, with few pieces of literature exploring their joint optimization. Typically, research initially focuses on component placement, neglecting the replication factor, which is only adjusted in response to declining performance. This often necessitates frequent application rescheduling, incurring considerable overhead.

The placement problem has been thoroughly investigated in the literature, taking into account various modeling assumptions and optimization goals, for example, [1,6,7,13]. Conversely, numerous studies on the replication issue concentrate on adjusting the number of application component replicas in response to observed changes in monitored performance metrics. Some research utilizes threshold-based policies [11,14] predicated on the utilization rates of either system nodes or service instances, while others employ more sophisticated strategies for making scaling decisions, including queuing theory [18], game-theory [20], reinforcement learning [26], etc. to efficiently manage workload variability.

A distinctive single-stage approach for determining both the placement and parallelism degree of application services is presented by Cardellini et al. [8,9], that delve into the joint optimization of component replication and placement for Distributed Streaming Processing (DSP) applications. The authors introduced an Integer Linear Programming (ILP) formulation integrated into a Storm-based prototype for evaluating real data stream applications. Madsen et al. [19] propose an ILP model that calculates the replication of co-location groups, alongside load balancing among them, based on a heuristic aimed at minimizing inter-node traffic.

Furthermore, De Souza et al. [12] unveiled a mixed-integer linear programming model to optimize task placement and parallelism degree of DSP tasks across Cloud and Edge computing environments. This model aims to strike a balance between minimizing end-to-end latency and reducing the monetary costs of resource utilization. In [4], the authors established an operator performance model to predict data processing delays under various operator parallelism levels in stream processing jobs running across heterogeneous networks. Utilizing this model, they systematically explored how different topological changes impact the performance of data stream applications in a geo-distributed environment. Peng et al. [22] tackled the challenges of joint operator scaling and placement for Distributed Stream Processing applications within Edge Computing environments, highlighting the importance of time-critical and latency-sensitive tasks. They developed a queuing-network-based model for QoS estimation, modeled the problem within an integer-programming framework, and proposed a two-stage solution approach. Finally, Shi et al. [28] addressed the challenge of replicating and deploying applications in a Multi-Cloud environment, taking into account location awareness and budget constraints. They proposed a genetic algorithm-based method that optimizes the average application response time, including execution time and network latency, while conforming to budgetary limitations.

In this paper, we propose a model that seeks to offer improvements in efficiency, flexibility, and scalability compared to existing solutions. Indeed, our goal is to provide a model that is both understandable and easy to grasp, and also proficient in effectively tackling the challenges of one-stage optimization of replication and placement of IoT applications within Fog computing environments.

Table 1. Main notation adopted for the problem description.

Symbol	Description
G^I	Fog infrastructure network graph
$\mathcal{H}$	Computing host nodes in G^I
$\mathcal{E}$	Logical links in G^I
$U(g)$	Available resources (CPU, RAM, ...) at host $g \in \mathcal{H}$
$LAT(e)$	Latency on Fog link $e \in \mathcal{E}$
$BW(e)$	Bandwidth on Fog link $e \in \mathcal{E}$
$G^a = \langle \mathcal{V}^a, \mathcal{L}^a \rangle$	Graph of application $a \in \mathcal{A}$, comprising its components and links
$u(i)$	Resources required (REQCPU, REQRAM, etc.) for service $i \in \mathcal{V}^a$
$\Phi^a, \phi^a(i)$	Set of fixed components and their designated network node
C_i	Cost of deploying service i on computing node
$Reqlat(k)$	Maximum acceptable latency for link $k \in \mathcal{L}^a$
$Reqbw(k)$	Required bandwidth for link $k \in \mathcal{L}^a$
λ_i	Incoming data rate for component $i \in \mathcal{V}^a$
λ_{i,m_i}	Data rate entering the m_i-th replica of component i
$\mu_{i,g}$	Processing rate of component i at node g
K_i	Maximum replication degree for service i
$\mathcal{A}, \mathcal{C}, \mathcal{L}$	Set of applications, components and links to deploy on Fog network
r_i	Number of replicas for service i
$P_{i,m}$	Instantiation indicator for replica m of service i
$h_{i,m}$	Host node for replica m of service i
s_{k,m_u}	Host for source component u's replica m_u of link $k = (u,v) \in \mathscr{L}$
t_{k,m_v}	Host for sink component v's replica m_v of link k
$n_{k,m_u,m_v,j}$	Node at position j on path for link $k = (u,v)$, connecting m_u-th instance of component u to m_v-th instance of component v
p_{k,m_u,m_v}	Position of t_{k,m_v} in path n
$a_{k,m_u,m_v,j}$	Arc between nodes in path of link k
$l_{k,m_u,m_v,j}, b_e$	Latency on arc $a_{k,m_u,m_v,j}$ and bandwidth on Fog link $e \in \mathcal{E}$

3 System Model and Problem Definition

In this section, we introduce the system model that describes the Fog infrastructure and IoT applications, addressing the complex issue of service replication and placement. Extending our prior work on service placement challenges within Fog Computing frameworks [1], this section depicts the extensions made and outlines critical attributes essential for the effective management of the Service Replication and Placement (SRP) problem in Fog contexts. For clarity and ease of reference, Table 1 summarizes the symbols and notations used in the paper.

3.1 Computing Infrastructure Model

The Fog Computing infrastructure can be modeled as a fully connected directed graph $G^I = \langle \mathcal{H}, \mathcal{E} \rangle$, where $\mathcal{H}$ represents the set of host nodes, and $\mathcal{E}$ encompasses the links and logical network connections between these nodes. The infrastructure's nodes may include Cloud nodes (data centers), Edge servers, Fog nodes (resources offering computational power and/or storage, such as base stations, access points, and computers), and IoT devices (sensors and actuators), each positioned at potentially different hierarchical layers. Every network node $g \in \mathcal{H}$ is characterized by its resource capacities $U(g) = \langle \text{CPU}(g), \text{RAM}(g), \ldots \rangle$, including processing speed $\text{CPU}(g)$, memory $\text{RAM}(g)$, disk space, energy, etc. Network nodes are interconnected through a set of links $\mathcal{E}$, with $\mathcal{E} = \mathcal{H} \times \mathcal{H}$. Each link $e = (u, v) \in \mathcal{E}$, is defined by the network latency $LAT(e)$ between the source node u and the sink node v, as well as the bandwidth of the link $BW(e_{i,j})$.

3.2 IoT Application Model

An IoT application can be envisioned at various levels of abstraction: as a monolithic component, a collection of interdependent components, or a Directed Acyclic Graph (DAG), as discussed in [2]. In this paper, we consider a service-oriented architecture, defining an application as a DAG, $G^a = \langle \mathcal{V}^a, \mathcal{L}^a \rangle$, where $\mathcal{V}^a$ denotes the set of all components (also referred to as services) of application a, and $\mathcal{L}^a \subseteq \mathcal{V}^a \times \mathcal{V}^a$ represents the inter-dependencies, data flow, and communication requirements among these components (see Fig. 1.a). Each application component is a self-contained processing element designed to perform a specific function (e.g., filtering, mapping, aggregation, join, etc.). The application graph includes at least one data source and one data sink. We denote by $\mathcal{A}$ as the set of applications intended for deployment within the Fog network.

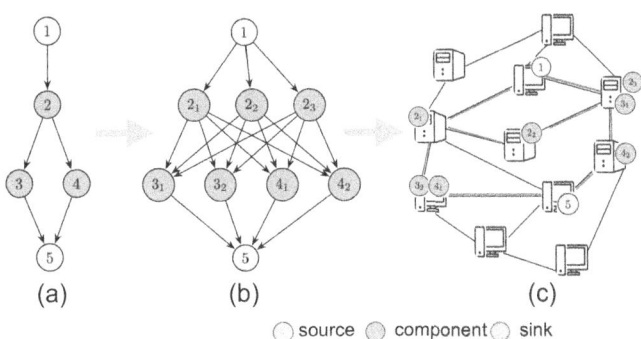

Fig. 1. Example of: (a) a DAG application, (b) replication of the application components, and (c) application placement on computing resources [9].

Each application component i, within $\mathcal{V}^a$, has requirements for CPU and memory to process incoming events, denoted by $\text{REQCPU}(i)$ and $\text{REQRAM}(i)$, respectively. Additional requirements may be specified. A component has an input data flow rate, λ_i, and can output to one or more streams, with the assumption that the output flow is evenly distributed across all outputs. The processing rate of component i at resource node g in $\mathcal{H}$ is given by $\mu_{i,g}$, calculated as $\mu_{i,g}$, where $\lambda_i < \mu_{i,g}$. Some application components are considered fixed, necessitating deployment on specific infrastructure nodes. These fixed components are represented by $\Phi^a \subseteq \mathcal{V}^a$, with $\phi^a(i) \in \mathcal{H}$ indicating the deployment node for component i. Each component i in $\mathcal{V}^a$ is associated with a deployment cost, C_i.

A link $k \in \mathcal{L}^a$ is defined by the ordered pair $k = (u, v)$, with both u and v belonging to the set $\mathcal{V}^a$, serving to identify the source and sink components of link k, respectively. For each link k, the maximum allowable latency is denoted by ReqLat(k), establishing the latency constraints between connected components. Additionally, the bandwidth requirements for each link are specified by ReqBW(k), highlighting the data transmission capacity needed to support the inter-component communication effectively.

3.3 Problem Definition: Service Replication and Placement

In Fog Computing systems, the strategic deployment of a set of applications $\mathcal{A}$ within the computing infrastructure G^I involves assigning application components $\mathscr{C} = \bigcup_{a \in \mathcal{A}} \mathcal{V}^a$ and their interconnecting links $\mathscr{L} = \bigcup_{a \in \mathcal{A}} \mathcal{L}^a$ to the infrastructure's nodes $\mathcal{H}$ and links $\mathcal{E}$, respectively. The goal is to allocate resources for all components $\mathscr{C}$ without exceeding the capacity limits of network nodes and to secure network paths for each link $k \in \mathscr{L}$ ensuring adherence to specific bandwidth and latency requirements. This placement guarantees compliance with the infrastructure's networking and resource constraints, thereby enabling efficient and responsive application performance.

Service Replication and Placement: To manage fluctuating workload conditions and maintain acceptable performance levels, a data parallelism technique [15] is employed. This approach involves replicating each application component into multiple parallel instances, with each instance processing a portion of the incoming data flow concurrently. Implementing this strategy significantly improves the system's scalability and responsiveness by evenly distributing the workload across several instances. The core challenge in joint service replication and placement lies in determining the optimal number of replicas for each application component $i \in \mathscr{C}$ and their strategic deployment across the computing nodes within $\mathcal{H}$. Accommodating the dynamic demands of service replication and placement requires ensuring that all application links, including those from replication instances, are supported on the physical network in a way that satisfies the application's communication needs, This is an NP-hard problem [8]. Figure 1 illustrates a schematic of this replication and placement strategy, leveraging data parallelism to adaptively manage workloads, and provides a clear illustration of the methodology.

4 A Constraint-Based SRP Model

Expanding on our foundational model [1] concerning service placement within Fog Computing systems, this paper delves into the complex issue of joint service replication and placement over Fog networks. We introduce the CP-SRP model (for Constraint Programming Service Replication and Placement) that uses the formalism of a constraint satisfaction problem to establish a comprehensive framework for the elastic and optimal management of service replication and placement. The CP-SRP model employs an enriched set of decision variables and constraints, tailored to optimize the replication and strategic deployment of services across the Fog infrastructure. This section outlines the set of decision variables, their domains and the set of the considered constraints.

4.1 CP-SRP Decision Variables

We identify, respectively, a set of decision variables related to replication, nodes, and links, as follows: The model introduces new decision variables for explicitly managing service replication, determining the optimal replication count for each application component, and their distribution within the infrastructure. The decision variable r_i represents the number of instances for each service $i \in \mathscr{C}$. For simplification, it is assumed that each component i can be instantiated up to K_i times, where K_i denotes the maximum allowed number of replicas for service i. Additionally, a binary variable $P_{i,m}$ indicates whether the m-th replica of service i is instantiated, for all $i \in \mathscr{C}$ and $1 \leq m \leq K_i$.

Updates to node-associated variables, we extend the model CP-SPP [1] to accommodate the SRP problem with multiple instances of each service component. We update the decision variable $h_{i,m}$ to specify the host node of each instance m of service i. For each link $k = (u,v)$ within the set $\mathscr{L}$, where u represents the source component and v the sink component of this link, we have the variables s_{k,m_u} and t_{k,m_v} that represent the nodes hosting the m_u-th and m_v-th instances of the source and sink components of k, respectively. The variable $n_{k,m_u,m_v,j}$ denotes the host node at position j in the path from the source to sink instance, enhancing the model's precision in depicting component flows. Additionally, the variable p_{k,m_u,m_v} defines the position of t_{k,m_v} in n_{k,m_u,m_v}, considering the position of $s_{k,m_u} = 0$.

Regarding the arcs-related variables, we identify for each link $k = (u,v) \in \mathscr{L}$, the variable $a_{k,m_u,m_v,j}$ that denotes the arc between node positions in the path from the m_u-th instance of the source component u to the m_v-th instance of the sink component v. Variables $l_{k,m_u,m_v,j}$ and $b_{a_{k,m_u,m_v,j}}$ represent the latency and bandwidth on these arcs, respectively.

4.2 CP-SRP Constraints

The CP-SRP model categorizes its constraints into three primary categories: node-related, replication-related, and arc-related constraints. We use several well-known predicates in our constraints, such as ALLDIFFERENT for ensuring unique host assignments [25], REGULAR for maintaining path continuity [23], and BINPACKING to enforce resource constraints [27].

Node-Related Constraints. These constraints are integral for maintaining the integrity and functionality of the Fog infrastructure, focusing on resource capacity, node positioning, path integrity, data flow, and locality.

To prevent the aggregate demand from application components and their replicas from exceeding the nodes' available capacities for critical resources like CPU and RAM, Binpacking constraints are applied.

$$\text{BINPACKING}(\langle h, \text{REQCPU}\rangle, \text{CPU}), \text{ AND BINPACKING}(\langle h, \text{REQRAM}\rangle, \text{RAM}). \quad (1)$$

Node positioning and path integrity ensure precise deployment for source and sink components (Eq. 2, and 3), eliminate cycles (Eq. 4), enforce specific endpoint terminations (Eq. 5), preserve path continuity for application link sharing a component (Eq. 6), and align node-related variables (Eq. 7). The formalization of these constraints is expressed through the following equations:
$\forall k = (u,v) \in \mathscr{L}, \forall m_u \in [1, K_u], \forall m_v \in [1, K_v],$

$$P_{u,m_u} \land P_{v,m_v} \Rightarrow n_{k,m_u,m_v,0} = s_{k,m_u} \; \& \; n_{k,m_u,p_{k,m_u,m_v}} = t_{k,m_v} \quad (2)$$

$$s_{k,m_u} = t_{k,m_v} \iff p_{k,m_u,m_v} = 1 \quad (3)$$

$$\text{ALLDIFFERENT}(n_{k,m_u,m_v,j}, \; \forall j \in [1, |\mathcal{H}|]) \quad (4)$$

$$P_{u,m_u} \land P_{v,m_v} \Rightarrow n_{k,m_u,p_{k,m_u,m_v}+1} = \alpha \; \& \; \text{REGULAR}(n_{k,m_u,m_v}, \text{``}[\hat{\;}\alpha]+[\alpha]+\text{''}) \quad (5)$$

$$t_{k,m_v} = s_{k',m_{u'}}, \; \forall k' = (u',v') \in \mathscr{L}, \forall m_{u'} \in [1, K_{u'}], \text{ where } v = u' \quad (6)$$

$$s_{k,m_u} = h_{u,m_u} \text{ and } t_{k,m_v} = h_{v,q_v} \quad (7)$$

The locality constraint dictates that specific components must reside on designated nodes: $h_{i,m} = \phi^a(i), \; \forall m \in [1, K_i], \forall i \in \Phi^a, \forall a \in \mathcal{A}$.

Data flow conservation ensures an equilibrium between the sum of incoming and outgoing data flow rates for each application component and its replicas. This balance, denoted by $\lambda_{i,m_i} = \Lambda^{out}_{i,m_i}$ for the m_i-th instance of component i where $\lambda_{i,m_i} = \lambda_i/r_i$, and Λ^{out}_{i,m_i} represents the total outgoing data rate, maintains data integrity and continuity across the application's architecture.

$$\sum_{m_i=1}^{K_i} \lambda_{i,m_i} = \sum_{m_i=1}^{K_i} \Lambda^{out}_{i,m_i}, \text{ and thus, } \lambda_i = \sum_{m_i=1}^{K_i} \Lambda^{out}_{i,m_i}. \quad (8)$$

Replication-Related Constraints. These constraints focus on ensuring unique hosting (Eq. 9) for each component instance (this constraint can be removed if such a requirement is not mandatory), adherence to the specified replication counts (Eq. 10), and systematic index-based instantiation of deployed services' replications (Eq. 11).

$$\text{ALLDIFFERENT}(h_{i,m}, \forall m \in [1, K_i]), \; \forall i \in \mathscr{C}. \quad (9)$$

$$\sum_{m=0}^{K_i} P_{i,m} = r_i, \; \forall i \in \mathscr{C}. \quad (10)$$

$$r_i < j \Rightarrow P_{i,m} = 0, \text{ and } r_i \geq j \Rightarrow P_{i,m} = 1, \; \forall m \in [1, K_i], \forall i \in \mathscr{C}. \quad (11)$$

Arc-Related Constraints. To maintain service quality, the CP-SRP model enforces two critical constraints on network arcs: bandwidth and latency management. For bandwidth management, the model employs a BinPacking constraint to prevent the total bandwidth demands of primary services and their replicas from exceeding the capacities of any physical link $e \in \mathcal{E}$. This constraint is articulated as:

$$\text{BinPacking}(\langle b, Reqbw \rangle, BW). \tag{12}$$

Regarding latency optimization, the model ensures that end-to-end latency across all links remains within acceptable thresholds, which is vital for the responsiveness of services. This is specified by the following conditions for all $k = (u,v) \in \mathcal{L}$, $m_u \in [1, K_u]$, and $m_v \in [1, K_v]$:

$$l_{k,m_u,m_v,j} = LAT(a_{k,m_u,m_v,j}), \quad \forall j = 0, \ldots, |\mathcal{H}|, \tag{13}$$

$$\sum_{j=0}^{|\mathcal{H}|} l_{k,m_u,m_v,j} \leq Reqlat(k). \tag{14}$$

4.3 Multi-objective Function

The CP-SRP allows for the flexible definition of the objective function, enabling the customization to meet specific optimization goals (e.g., energy consumption, latency, availability, etc.). In this paper, we propose to enhance QoS by minimizing joint response time and deployment cost in the Fog network. The essential components are summarized as follows:

Response time (Rt): combines computation delay (D_{comp}) and communication delay (D_{comm}), defined as: $Rt = D_{\text{comp}} + D_{\text{comm}}$.

Applying the M/M/1 queuing theory model for both application components and processing services, we estimate the computation delay for the m-th instance of service i on host $h_{i,m}$ as follows: $D_{\text{comp},i,m} = \frac{1}{\mu_{i,h_{i,m}} - \lambda_{i,m}}$, and the total computation delay across all services and replicas as: $D_{\text{comp}} = \sum_{i \in \mathcal{C}} \max_{m \in [1, r_i]} D_{\text{comp},i,m}$.

The communication delay is given by:

$$D_{\text{comm}} = \max_{\pi \in \Pi^a} \sum_{k=(u,v) \in \pi} \max_{m_u, m_v} \sum_{j=0\ldots|\mathcal{H}|-1} l_{k,m_u,m_v,j}. \tag{15}$$

It considers the worst end-to-end delay from sources to sinks, capturing the delay along a path π for all source-sink paths Π^a in G^a.

Deployment Cost (TC): accounts for the financial expense of hosting IoT application components and their replicas: $TC = \sum_{i \in \mathcal{C}} C_i \cdot r_i$, where C_i and r_i represent the cost and number of replicas for the i-th component, respectively.

For the **objective function** (F) description, we chose a simple additive weighting technique [32] to facilitate comparison with the approach in [10].

$$F = w_r \frac{Rt}{Rt_{\max}} + w_c \frac{TC}{TC_{\max}}, \tag{16}$$

where weights w_r, $w_c \geq 0$ and $w_r + w_c = 1$ correspond to the different QoS attributes. $Rt_{\max}$ and $TC_{\max}$ are the worst-case bounds for response time, and total cost respectively. Each metric is normalized to range between $[0, 1]$, with 1 indicating the best case and 0 the worst.

4.4 Optimization of the CP-SRP Problem

The goal of the Service Replication and Placement optimization is to ideally determine both the number of replicas and their placement for application components within a Fog network, aiming to minimize the objective function F. Constraint Programming [17] is used for its effective problem modeling and solution identification capabilities, making it a pivotal tool in achieving optimal or near-optimal solutions through domain reduction and constraint propagation. The efficacy of CP in addressing the SRP optimization relies on search strategies that streamline complex decision variables and highlight critical factors for constraint satisfaction. For the resolution of our model, we propose the integration of depth-first search with strategies such as weighted degree and smallest values first, facilitating a detailed exploration of the search space.

5 Numerical Experiments

In this section, we evaluate the CP-SRP model through a series of numerical experiments aimed at showcasing the model's performance.

5.1 Implementation of CP-SRP Model

We implement and solve the elaborated Constraint Programming-based Service Replication and Placement model using the Choco constraint programming solver [24]. Choco is chosen for its frequent recognition at international solver competitions MiniZinc[1]. It is a free, open-source Java library focused on Constraint Programming, designed to articulate real-world combinatorial challenges as constraint satisfaction problems and resolve them through constraint programming techniques. The CP-SRP algorithm inputs the infrastructure network and the set of application graphs to be deployed, producing either all feasible solutions or the optimal solution if an objective function is specified.

5.2 Experiment Setup

In order to compare our model with the model provided in the literature and more precisely to the work presented in [7,10], we propose to consider the following experimental setup. We select a segment of the ANSNET computing network as our experimental environment, which is a geographically distributed network comprising 15 interconnected computing nodes. The benchmark application employed is that which addresses a query from the DEBS 2015 Grand

---

[1] https://www.minizinc.org/challenge.html.

Challenge [16], where data streams from New York City taxis are analyzed to identify the top-10 most frequent routes over the last 30 min, as depicted in Fig. 2. The application's Directed Acyclic Graph (DAG) operates as follows: The *data source* component retrieves datasets from Redis; the *parser* component excludes irrelevant and invalid data. Subsequently, the *filterByCoordinates* component forwards only those events pertinent to a designated area to the *computeRouteID* component, which identifies the routes taken by taxis. The *countByWindow* component then calculates the frequency of these routes within the last 30 min, supported by the *metronome* component that tracks the passage of time. Lastly, the *partialRank* and *globalRank* components determine the top-10 most frequent routes.

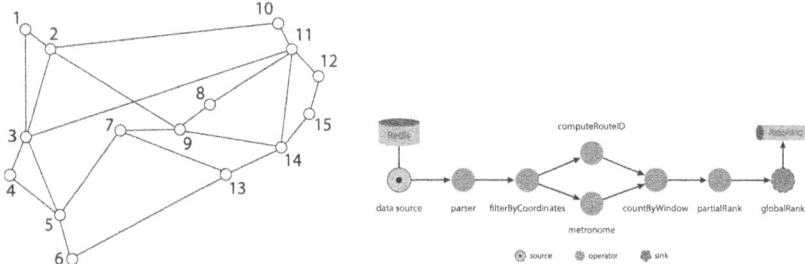

Fig. 2. Subset of ANSNET network (left). Reference IoT application (right).

Within the computing network, we designate each computing node with a memory capacity of 5 GB and a processing speed of 10 GHz. The infrastructure network's edges are defined by edge latencies of 20 ms and bandwidths of 100 Mbps. For the application requirements, it is considered that each application component necessitates a memory and CPU requirement of 1 GB and 2 GHz, respectively, with a bandwidth of 10 Mbps and a latency of 200 ms per application link. It's assumed that each application component can be replicated up to $K_i = 3$ times, with the exception of the source and sink services (*data source* and *globalRank*), as well as the *metronome* component, due to it complexity in parallelization. For simplification purposes, the response time of an application component $i \in \mathscr{C}$, under the incoming load λ_{i,r_i}, is modeled using an M/M/1 queue, where $\mu = 200$ tuples/s represents the service rate for each application service regardless of the network host node of the components. Additionally, a deployment cost of 1 unit is attributed to each service.

5.3 Impact of Replication

These initial experiments are designed to demonstrate the effectiveness of the CP-SRP model for handling the workflow variations and the benefits of replication when the application is subjected to an increasing traffic load. The model is evaluated using three configurations of weights: ($w_r = 0.8$, $w_c = 0.2$), ($w_r = 0.5$,

$w_c = 0.5$), and ($w_r = 0.2$, $w_c = 0.8$). The incoming traffic load is progressively increased from 20 tuples/s to 180 tuples/s, causing the bottleneck component to impose a load on the underlying computing node that ranges from 10% to 90% of its capacity. Figure 3 illustrates the results in terms of response time (in seconds) and the total number of instantiated services within the deployed application.

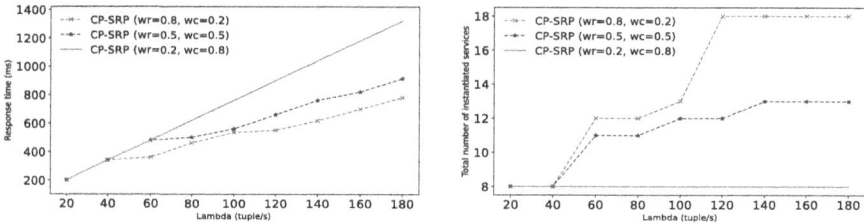

Fig. 3. Impact of replication on the application performance. Response time (left), Total number of components instances (right).

From Fig. 3.a, we observe that when the system becomes overloaded beyond 100 tuples/s, at which point the response time significantly increases, becoming up to 3 times higher than under medium load conditions. A similar outcome is noted when CP-SRP is set with ($w_r = 0.2$, $w_c = 0.8$), where application cost is prioritized over response time, leading CP-SRP to minimize the replication of application components. Conversely, when CP-SRP is configured with ($w_r = 0.8$, $w_c = 0.2$), replication is leveraged to decrease the application response time. Figure 3.b displays the number of instantiated components. It reveals that, as the incoming load surpasses 100 tuples/s, CP-SRP with ($w_r = 0.8$, $w_c = 0.2$) begins to replicate the bottleneck components incrementally up to 18 instances i.e., when every service has been replicated. As indicated in Fig. 3.a, this strategy is advantageous for the response time.

5.4 Scalability of CP-SRP Model

In these second experiments, we aim to benchmark our model against existing Service Replication and Placement resolution approaches, particularly focusing on its scalability and performance characteristics. We compare our approach, the CP-SRP model, with the one developed by Cardellini et al. [9], denoted as ODRP, which addresses the combined challenge of data stream processing replication and placement. Additionally, we compare our model with an ILP model we devised based on Flow formalization. Table 2 summarizes the numbers of variables and resolution times for each model given varying numbers of computing nodes and maximum numbers of replications K_i for application components. In this scenario, we consider a fully connected Ansnet network with different infrastructure sizes, from $|\mathcal{H}| = 8$ to $|\mathcal{H}| = 32$, and the application outlined in the first numerical evaluations.

Table 2. Number of variables and execution time under CP-SRP, ILP and ODRP [8] approaches.

|H|	Metrics	$K_i = 2$			$K_i = 3$			$K_i = 4$		
		ILP	CP-SRP	ODRP	ILP	CP-SRP	ODRP	ILP	CP-SRP	ODRP
8	Variables	5776	7194	15912	12108	13576	216552	20756	21956	1956312
	Res. time (s)	23.4	5.1	1.1	109.3	21.1	34.4	4154.1	92,7	-
15	Variables	19594	13136	147120	41508	24672	5320560	71534	39827	-
	Res. time (s)	357.6	18.8	8.8	-	23.2	-	-	217,8	-
24	Variables	49456	21066	843000	105228	39225	-	181748	63092	-
	Res. time (s)	-	43.9	55.8	-	309.08	-	-	613.7	-
32	Variables	87424	28418	2514336	186348	52465	-	322148	84076	-
	Res. time (s)	-	134.7	170.2	-	455.8	-	-	966.4	-

From this table, it is evident that the number of variables and resolution time rapidly grow even for $K_i = 2$ and a small number of nodes. Indeed, the complexity of the different formulations is influenced by the maximum degree of component replication K_i, which affects the number of service and links, and the cardinality of the sets of decision variables. We observe that the ODRP model provided by Cardellini et al. encounters scalability issue when the computing network exceeds 15 nodes, and the maximum number of replicas is greater than or equal to 3, a limitation similarly observed in the ILP model.

However, our CP-SRP model distinctly demonstrates its capability to solve various problem instances effectively within reasonable time frames. Moreover, unlike other models, the number of variables in CP-SRP remains relatively low, offering a significant advantage for addressing larger problem instances. Additionally, the CP-SRP model provides intermediate feasible results, and the timings specified herein correspond to the best solution achieved.

6 Conclusion

In this paper, we presented and assessed a constraint programming-based technique tailored for optimizing service replication and placement within IoT applications. Our model aims for comprehensiveness, flexibility, and easy upgradability, accommodating the diverse computing and networking resources prevalent in Fog environments. It offers customization for various Quality of Service (QoS) metrics, whose relevance may vary based on the application's specific context. Through extensive experimental analysis, we demonstrated our approach's scalability compared to existing models and highlighted the advantages of jointly optimizing service replication and placement in enhancing IoT application performance. For future work, we plan to evaluate larger problem instances, delineate our model's scope by varying data flow proportions, consider complex compositional application patterns, and incorporate a dynamic mechanism for real-time service deployment adjustments, including service migrations.

References

1. Aït Salaht, F., et al.: Service placement in fog computing using constraint programming. In: IEEE SCC, pp. 19–27 (2019)
2. Aït Salaht, F., Desprez, F., Lebre, A.: An overview of service placement problem in fog and edge computing. ACM Comput. Surv. **53**(3), June 2020
3. Aral, A., et al.: A decentralized replica placement algorithm for edge computing. IEEE TNSM **15**(2), 516–529 (2018)
4. Arkian, H., Pierre, G., Tordsson, J., Elmroth, E.: Model-based stream processing auto-scaling in geo-distributed environments. In: ICCCN, pp. 1–10. IEEE (2021)
5. Bonomi, F., Milito, R., Zhu, J., Addepalli, S.: Fog computing and its role in the internet of things. In: MCC, pp. 13–16. ACM (2012)
6. Brogi, A., Forti, S.: QoS-aware deployment of IoT applications through the fog. IEEE Internet Things J. **4**(5), 1185–1192 (2017)
7. Cardellini, V., et al.: Optimal operator placement for distributed stream processing applications. In: ACM DEBS, pp. 69–80. ACM, New York (2016)
8. Cardellini, V., et al.: Joint operator replication and placement optimization for distributed streaming applications. In: EAI VALUETOOLS, pp. 263–270 (2017)
9. Cardellini, V., et al.: Optimal operator replication and placement for distributed stream processing systems. ACM SIGMETRICS **44**(4), 11–22 (2017)
10. Cardellini, V., et al.: Optimal operator deployment and replication for elastic distributed data stream processing. CCPE **30**(9), e4334 (2018)
11. Cardellini, V., Nardelli, M., Luzi, D.: Elastic stateful stream processing in storm. In: HPCS, pp. 583–590. IEEE (2016)
12. De Souza, F.R., et al.: An optimal model for optimizing the placement and parallelism of data stream processing applications on cloud-edge computing. In: SBAC-PAD, pp. 59–66. IEEE (2020)
13. Donassolo, B., Fajjari, I., Legrand, A., Mertikopoulos, P.: Fog based framework for IoT service provisioning. In: IEEE CCNC, January 2019
14. Heinze, T., Pappalardo, V., Jerzak, Z., Fetzer, C.: Auto-scaling techniques for elastic data stream processing. In: ACM DEBS, pp. 318–321 (2014)
15. Hirzel, M., Soulé, R., Schneider, S., Gedik, B., Grimm, R.: A catalog of stream processing optimizations. ACM Comput. Surv. **46**(4), 1–34 (2014)
16. Jerzak, Z., Ziekow, H.: The debs 2015 grand challenge. In: ACM DEBS, pp. 266–268. Association for Computing Machinery, New York (2015)
17. Kotecha, P.R., Bhushan, M., Gudi, R.D.: Efficient optimization strategies with constraint programming. AIChE J. **56**(2), 387–404 (2010)
18. Lohrmann, B., Janacik, P., Kao, O.: Elastic stream processing with latency guarantees. In: IEEE ICDCS, pp. 399–410. IEEE (2015)
19. Madsen, K.G.S., Zhou, Y., Cao, J.: Integrative dynamic reconfiguration in a parallel stream processing engine. In: ICDE, pp. 227–230. IEEE (2017)
20. Mencagli, G.: A game-theoretic approach for elastic distributed data stream processing. ACM TAAS **11**(2), 1–34 (2016)
21. Pahl, C., Jamshidi, P.: Microservices: a systematic mapping study. CLOSER **1**, 137–146 (2016)
22. Peng, Q., Xia, Y., Wang, Y., Wu, C., Luo, X., Lee, J.: Joint operator scaling and placement for distributed stream processing applications in edge computing. In: Yangui, S., Bouassida Rodriguez, I., Drira, K., Tari, Z. (eds.) ICSOC 2019. LNCS, vol. 11895, pp. 461–476. Springer, Cham (2019). https://doi.org/10.1007/978-3-030-33702-5_36

23. Pesant, G.: A regular language membership constraint for finite sequences of variables. In: Wallace, M. (ed.) Principles and Practice of Constraint Programming, pp. 482–495 (2004)
24. Prud'homme, C., Fages, J.G., Lorca, X.: Choco Documentation. TASC - LS2N CNRS UMR 6241, COSLING S.A.S. (2017). http://www.choco-solver.org
25. Régin, J.: A Filtering Algorithm for Constraints of Difference in CSPs. In: Proceedings of the 12th National Conference on Artificial Intelligence, Seattle, WA, USA, July 31 - August 4, 1994, vol. 1, pp. 362–367 (1994)
26. Russo, G.R., et al.: Reinforcement learning based policies for elastic stream processing on heterogeneous resources. In: ACM DEBS, pp. 31–42 (2019)
27. Shaw, P.: A Constraint for Bin Packing. In: Wallace, M. (ed.) Principles and Practice of Constraint Programming - CP 2004. Springer, Heidelberg (2004)
28. Shi, T., et al.: Location-aware and budget-constrained application replication and deployment in multi-cloud environment. In: ICWS, pp. 110–117. IEEE (2020)
29. Taghizadeh, J., et al.: An efficient data replica placement mechanism using biogeography-based optimization technique in the fog computing environment. J. Ambient. Intell. Humaniz. Comput. **14**(4), 3691–3711 (2023)
30. Taghizadeh, J., Ghobaei-Arani, M., Shahidinejad, A.: A metaheuristic-based data replica placement approach for data-intensive IoT applications in the fog computing environment. Softw. Practice Exp. **52**(2), 482–505 (2022)
31. Torabi, E., Ghobaei-Arani, M., Shahidinejad, A.: Data replica placement approaches in fog computing: a review. Clust. Comput. **25**(5), 3561–3589 (2022)
32. Yoon, K.P., Hwang, C.L.: Multiple Attribute Decision Making: An Introduction. Sage Publications (1995)

Deadline-Driven Enhancements and Response Time Analysis of ROS2 Multi-threaded Executors

Zhengda Wu, Yixiao Feng, Mingtai Lv, Sining Yang(✉), and Bo Zhang

Academy of Military Science, Beijing 100091, China
{wuzhengda22,lvmingtai22}@alumni.nudt.edu.cn,
{fengyixiao15,yangsining16,zhangbo10}@nudt.edu.cn

Abstract. The second-generation Robot Operating System, ROS2, has gained significant interest due to its enhanced real-time capabilities. Although some studies are conducted on ROS2 multi-threaded executors to improve real-time capabilities, the existing scheduling schemes of multi-threaded executors may incur high latency for low-priority chains and priority inversion. Therefore, it remains a challenging problem to meet the real-time constraints of chain instances for multi-threaded executors. In this paper, we design a Chain-Instance-Level Earliest Deadline First (CIL-EDF) scheduling scheme for multi-threaded executors and present a comprehensive response time analytical model (RTAM) for the proposed scheduler; In this scheduler, callback instances are prioritized based on the corresponding chain instances of deadline to meet the real-time constraints for chain instances. Besides, the proposed RTAM is capable of analyzing chains with both arbitrary and constrained deadlines, as well as accounting for the impact of mutually-exclusive callback groups. To validate the scheduler and analytical model, we conduct a series of case studies. The results demonstrate the CIL-EDF outperforms the default and Chain-Level scheduling schemes of multi-threaded executors in terms of worst-case response time and schedulability, and the RTAM can safely upper-bound response times under all chain instances that are schedulable in the system.

Keywords: ROS2 Multi-threaded Executor · Earliest Deadline First scheduling scheme · response time analysis

1 Introduction

Robot Operating System [2] (ROS) is an open-source middleware framework widely used in robotics application development. Due to its software modularity and composability, ROS improves the efficiency of robotics application development. However, over the decades, ROS has revealed a major shortcoming in its lack of real-time capability, which limits its use in safety-critical domains with high real-time requirements. In this background, the ROS community released the second generation of the robot operating system in 2017, ROS2 [9], which was redesigned based on the ROS framework. The primary objective of ROS2 is to improve the real-time capability of the framework ROS2 integrates the Data Distribution Service (DDS) for robust end-to-end data communication and is compatible with real-time operating systems. Although ROS2 can provide better real-time support for robot applications compared to ROS, it has still does not guarantee the stringent timing constrains for hard real-time or safety-critical applications.

The executor [5] is the core component in ROS2 for real-time capability, with two types provided: single-threaded executors and multi-threaded executors. Single-threaded executors sequentially executes the ready callbacks in the single thread; Multi-threaded executors distributes the ready callbacks to multiple threads execute them in a parallel mode.

In the research work of single-threaded executors, Choi et al. [6] proposed PiCAS, a scheduling scheme based on prioritization at the Chain-Level, enhance real-time performance for higher-priority chains. But this potentially increased latency for lower-priority chains due to frequent preemptions. To overcome this problem, Arafat et al. [3] proposed an Earliest Deadline First (EDF) scheduling scheme for single-threaded executors, which can maintain lower levels of average response time and worst-case response time (WCRT) of chains.

As robotic applications become increasingly complex, it is becoming essential to leverage the parallel processing capabilities of multi-core platforms through multi-threaded executors. Sobhani et al. [13] implemented the PiCAS scheduling scheme proposed in [6] on multi-threaded executors, which can well guarantee that high-priority chains meet real-time constraints. However, the execution of low-priority chains is likely to be disproportionately preempted by high-priority chains resulting in large latency.

The existing scheduling schemes for ROS2 multi-threaded executors encounter the following issues:

- The default scheduling scheme for ROS2 multi-threaded executors is based on the round-robin approach, which periodically updating a common set, *ReadySet*, at polling points [8,13]. The fair scheduling scheme may lead to priority inversion issues and is inadequate for applications with strict real-time requirements.
- Sobhani et al. [13] extends PiCAS [6] from single-threaded executors to multi-threaded executors. However, in the PiCAS scheduling scheme, low-priority chains are at risk of frequent preemption by higher-priority chains, particularly in overload scenarios, this can lead to further degradation, rendering low-priority chains unable to execute.

The existing scheduling schemes of multi-threaded executors may incur high latency for low-priority chains and priority inversion. In this paper, to address this issue, we design a Chain-Instance-Level Earliest Deadline First (CIL-EDF) scheduling scheme for ROS2 multi-threaded executors.[1] Our proposed scheduling

---

[1] Source code available here: https://github.com/Wuzhengda55/CIL-EDF-for-ROS2-multi-threaded-Executors.

scheme addresses the limitations of the default scheduling scheme and the existing Chain-Level scheduling scheme of multi-threaded executors. The contributions of our work are as follows:

- To the best of our knowledge, we propose the first CIL-EDF scheduling scheme for ROS2 multi-threaded executors. To implement this scheme, we redesign the scheduling unit and the architecture of multi-threaded executors, and introduce a fault correction mechanism. This scheme enables finer granularity in priority assignment at the Chain-Instance-Level compared to the Chain-Level scheduling scheme.
- We propose a comprehensive response time analytical model (RTAM) for chains running on ROS2 multi-threaded executors for the proposed scheduler; this model can analyze chains with both arbitrary and constrained deadlines and also take the effect of mutually exclusive callback groups into account.
- For evaluation, we conducted case studies derived from tasks executed by autonomous robots. The results demonstrate the superior performance of the CIL-EDF scheduling scheme in terms of WCRT and schedulability, compared with the existing scheduling schemes of ROS2 multi-threaded executors. And show that our model can safely upper-bound the response time of chains under all chain instances that are schedulable in the system.

2 Related Work

Many studies have been conducted on improving the real-time capability of ROS. Satio et al. [11] introduced a real-time scheduling framework for ROS applications, enhancing ROS with a real-time library that contained heterogeneous laxity-based scheduling techniques. Wei et al. [18] designed a platform that integrates real-time and non-real-time task execution environments, running real-time ROS nodes on RTOS and non-real-time ROS nodes on the Linux system. Satio et al. [10] proposed a priority-based information transmission algorithm within the ROS framework, enabling publishers to send data to subscribers in predefined priority. Suzuki et al. [14] presented a coordination mechanism for ROS nodes executing on both CPUs and GPUs, along with an offline scheduling algorithm that assigns priorities to nodes using slackness as a determinant. However, these studies have been only focused on for ROS and have not encompassed formal modeling and analysis to guarantee strict real-time constraints.

To guarantee that ROS2 applications meet the strict real-time constraints, it is imperative for designers to designers must formally model and analyze their timing behaviors. Casini et al. [5] provided the first formal modeling and analysis of the timing behavior of ROS2 single-threaded executors, providing a foundation for subsequent analyses. Tang et al. [15] improved enhanced the RTAM of presented in [5] and proposed a priority allocation method to optimize the response time of task chains. Blaß et al. [4] improved the RTAM of in [5] by considering variations in the actual execution time of chains and further exploring scheduling properties in single-threaded executors. Yi Wang et al. [16] proposed an RTAM that focusesd on the case scenarios when where chains are modeled as a DAGs and generate more precise results and complete in less time than compared to [4]. Harun Teper et al. [17] focused on cause-effect chains and proposed a RTAM of cause-effect chains in ROS2. PiCAS [6] is the first work to address the lack of real-time capability in single-threaded executors, by introducing a new scheduling scheme based on prioritization at the Chain-Level. Arafat et al. [3] proposed an EDF scheduling scheme for single-threaded executors. This scheme addresses the potential issue of significantly high latency for low-priority chains, as identified in the scheduling scheme proposed in [6].

In the realm of formal modeling and analysis of response times for chains in ROS2 multi-threaded executors, Jiang et al. [8] were the first to provide a formal description of multi-threaded executors, and also to proposed introduce a RTAM for chains with constrained deadlines on multi-threaded executors. Additionally, they discovered the risk of increased response time when merging the workloads of multiple single-threaded executors into one multi-threaded executor. Sobhani et al. [13] proposed a RTAM for chains with constrained and arbitrary deadlines on multi-threaded executors. The model incorporated the impact also considers the effects of mutually-exclusive callback groups. Additionally in addition, they implemented the PiCAS [6] scheduling scheme on multi-threaded executors and proposed a complementary corresponding RTAM for this context.

3 System Model

In this section, We model the workload of ROS2 systems running on multi-core platforms, structuring the system to comprise n chains $\Gamma = \{\Gamma_0, \Gamma_1, \Gamma_2, ..., \Gamma_{n-1}\}$. Concerning temporal aspects, our model adopts a discrete time framework, wherein all timing parameters are expressed as integer multiples of processor clock cycles. Subsequently, we detail the modeling for callbacks, chains, and executors[2].

Callbacks. The callback $C_{<i,j>}$ represents the j-th callback of the Γ_i, where $0 \leq j \leq ||\Gamma_i|| - 1$. We can model each callback as:

$$C_{<i,j>} := \{E_{<i,j>}, \chi_{<i,j>}\} \tag{1}$$

- $E_{<i,j>}$: The worst-case execution time (WCET) of $C_{<i,j>}$.
- $\chi_{<i,j>}$: $\chi_{<i,j>} \in \{\chi_T, \chi_R\}$, $\chi_{<i,j>}$ represents the type of $C_{<i,j>}$, χ_T represents the callback type as a timer callback, and the first callback $C_{<i,0>}$ in the Γ_i is usually of type χ_T. χ_R represents the callback type as a regular callback. A regular callback $C_{<i,j>}$ is triggered by the message from the previous callback $C_{<i,j-1>}$ in the Γ_i.

Chains. The chain $\Gamma_i = \{C_{<i,0>}, C_{<i,1>}, \cdots, C_{<i,||\Gamma_i||-1>}\}$ consists of $||\Gamma_i||$ callbacks, where the callbacks are characterized by sequential execution; that is, the $C_{<i,j>}$ can only begin execution after the $C_{<i,j-1>}$ has finished execution. We can model the Γ_i as:

$$\Gamma_i := \{E_i, T_i, D_i\} \tag{2}$$

---

[2] The background of ROS2 system is in appendix [1].

- E_i: The WCET of the Γ_i. $E_i = \sum_{j=0}^{\|\Gamma_i\|-1} E_{<i,j>}$.
- T_i: The release period of instances of the Γ_i. From the perspective of callbacks, T_i also serves as the release period of instances of the $C_{<i,0>}$.
- D_i: The relative deadline of the Γ_i. The deadline of chain instances is determined by summing the release time of chain instances with their relative deadline.

We define the response time of released instances of the Γ_i as the interval between the release time of the $C_{<i,0>}$ and the completion time of execution for $C_{<i,\|\Gamma_i\|-1>}$, denoted as R_i. If $R_i \leq D_i$, the instances released by the Γ_i are considered schedulable.

For ROS2 multi-threaded executors, chains can be categorized into two types: constrained deadline chains, characterized by relative deadline that do not exceed the release period ($\forall D_i \leq T_i$), and arbitrary deadline chains, in which the relative deadlines can extend beyond the release period ($\exists D_i > T_i$).

Lemma 1. *In ROS2 multi-threaded executors, for any chain Γ_i, there can be a maximum of $\lceil \frac{D_i}{T_i} \rceil$ schedulable instances simultaneously in the system.*[3]

Executors. The multi-threaded executor $\omega = \{t_0, t_1, \ldots, t_{m-1}\}$ has m built-in threads, each running on a different CPU core. The supply-bound function [12] $sbf_i(\Delta)$ for the thread t_i denotes the minimum guaranteed execution time that thread offers over an interval of length Δ. This leads to the subsequent definition:

Definition 1. *The supply-bound function $sbf_\omega(\Delta)$ of a ω is the aggregate of supply-bound functions of its m threads:*

$$sbf_\omega(\Delta) = \sum_{i=0}^{m-1} sbf_i(\Delta) \qquad (3)$$

Definition 2. *To determine the minimum interval Δ for thread t_i needs to allocate an execution time of x, the inverse function of $sbf_i(\Delta)$ [7] is formulated:*

$$\overline{sbf_i}(x) = \min\{\Delta | sbf_i(\Delta) = x\} \qquad (4)$$

Lemma 2. *In ROS2 multi-threaded executors, for any given chain Γ_i, the execution progress varies among instances coexisting simultaneously.see footnote 3*

4 Proposed Scheduler

In this section, we first explain the operation rules of our proposed scheduler, and then introduce the design of the proposed scheduler from scheduling unit, executor architecture and fault correction mechanism.

---

[3] The proof of Lemma 1 and Lemma 2 are in appendix [1] .

4.1 Operation Rules of Proposed Scheduler

The operation rules of the CIL-EDF scheduling scheme for ROS2 multi-threaded executor are as follows:

1) Chain instances are prioritized in ascending order based on their deadlines.
2) The priority of callback instances matches that of their corresponding chain instances.
3) Threads access [13] the ready set in a mutually-exclusive manner, scheduling the callback instance with the highest priority.

4.2 Design of the Scheduling Unit

In the default scheduling scheme of ROS2 multi-threaded executors, executors utilize the callback handles as scheduling units. Handles can only provide information regarding the callback type to executors and cannot convey attributes pertinent to chains (such as release period, relative deadlines, etc.). Therefore, to equip executors with the capability to consider chain attributes in the scheduling of callback instances, we have done the following work:

1) We introduce the *CallbackExecutable* structure [3] to multi-threaded executors. The structure associates **callback-related** and **chain-related** attribute parameters. Transitioning the scheduling unit for the multi-threaded executor from callback handles to the *CallbackExecutable* structure. From the perspective of chains, as shown in Fig. 1. The execution is based on the callback pointed to by the handle when executors schedule a *CallbackExecutable*.

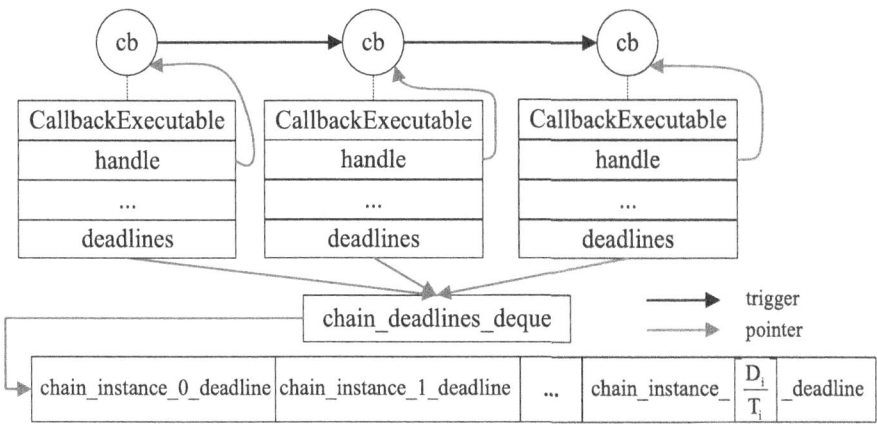

Fig. 1. Chains perspective of *CallbackExecutable* structure.

2) In the CIL-EDF scheduling scheme, executors schedule callback instances based on the deadline of corresponding chain instances, which means all

callback instances from the same chain instances are based on the same deadline. Therefore, the **deadlines** field of all *CallbackExecutable* structures corresponding to callbacks of a chain point to the same vector, **chain_deadlines_deque**, which is designed to store the deadline of chain instances. By Lemma 1, the Γ_i can have at most $\lceil \frac{D_i}{T_i} \rceil$ simultaneously schedulable instances. Hence, we set the size of the *chain_deadlines_deque* to store the deadlines of different instances of chains. For the deadline of chain instances, once its final callback instance is scheduled, it does no effect on subsequent executions. Additionally, timer instances can determine the time interval from the current moment to the next release instance by the *time_until_trigger* field. Thus, we use the queue structure to manage the deadline of chain instances, where the head element represents the deadline of instances. When callback instances are scheduled by executors, its queue updating rule is shown in Fig. 2.

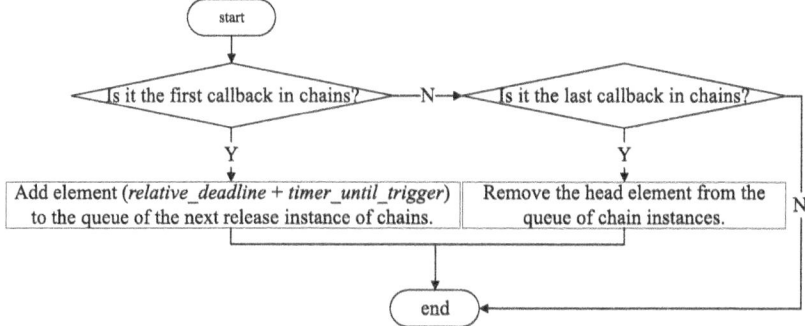

Fig. 2. Updating rule of the queue of chain instances.

3) For determining which chain instance the corresponding callback instance of *CallbackExecutable* belongs to when executors schedule it. By Lemma 2, executors do not schedule instances released by the same callback of different instances of the same chain at any given time. Therefore, we included an indicator variable, **cur_index**, in the *CallbackExecutable* structure to indicate which chain instance the current callback instance belongs to. Our rule for updating *cur_index* is as follows: For Γ_i, after any callback instance is scheduled by executors, setting *cur_index* to $(cur\_index + 1)\% \lceil \frac{D_i}{T_i} \rceil$, indicating that the next time this callback instance is scheduled, it belongs to the next chain instance. Figure 3 shows an example of it illustrates the updating process of *cur_index* for the first callback of the chain.

4.3 Design of the Executor Architecture

As shown in Fig. 4 of the scope of this work, the architecture of single-threaded executors was redesigned in [6], and we extended this design to multi-threaded

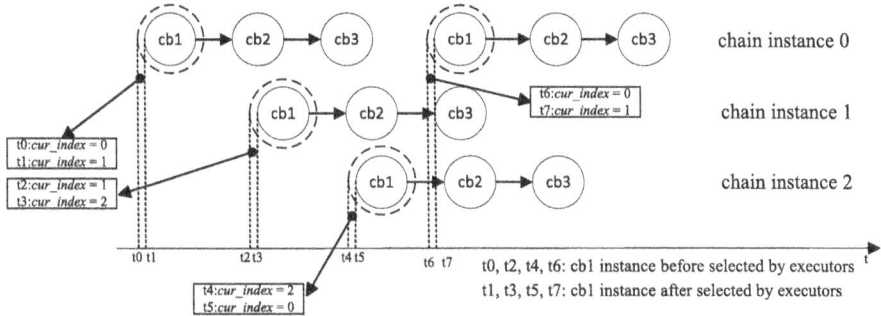

Fig. 3. The process of updating the *cur_index*. The chain comprising three callbacks, and it can be a maximum of three schedulable instances simultaneously running.

executors. The *ReadySet* is replaced with a priority queue, **ReadyQueue**, as it couldn't prioritize callback instances based on the deadline of chain instances. Additionally, to reduce runtime overhead, executors include a hash table called **CallbackMap**. The *CallbackMap* maps callback handles to *CallbackExecutable* structures, storing the structures of all callbacks in the system. This enables the *ReadyQueue* to add new callback instances by simply adding pointers to the *CallbackExecutable* structures; eliminating the need to include the structures directly. To prevent priority inversion [3,6], *ReadyQueue* is updated after each non-preemptive execution of callback instances, In contrast, *ReadySet* is updated only when the set is empty.

4.4 Fault Correction Mechanism

The fault correction mechanism of multi-threaded executors handles the following issues: when instances released by the Γ_i encounter unschedulable situations, indicating that the number of simultaneous instances may exceed $\lceil \frac{D_i}{T_i} \rceil$. From updating the rule of the queue of chain instances, it can be inferred that when the number of simultaneous instances of Γ_i exceed $\lceil \frac{D_i}{T_i} \rceil$ for chain instances with the same *cur_index*, the later released chain instances will inherit the deadline of the earlier released chain instances before the last callback instance of the earlier released chain instances scheduled by executors, thus causing priority inversion.

To minimize the impact of priority inversion, we have introduced the fault correction mechanism [3] for multi-threaded executors: In *CallbackExecutable* structures, we include a **counter** field to record the release times of callback instances. When prioritizing callback instances in executors' *ReadyQueue*, instances with equal deadline are prioritized in ascending order based on the *counter* field. With this mechanism, for any chains, their instances with the same *cur_index*, the priority of later-released chain instances is lower than that of earlier-released chain instances, ensuring that the earlier released chain instances are not preempted by later ones. Once the last callback instance of the earlier released chain instances is scheduled by executors, the later released chain

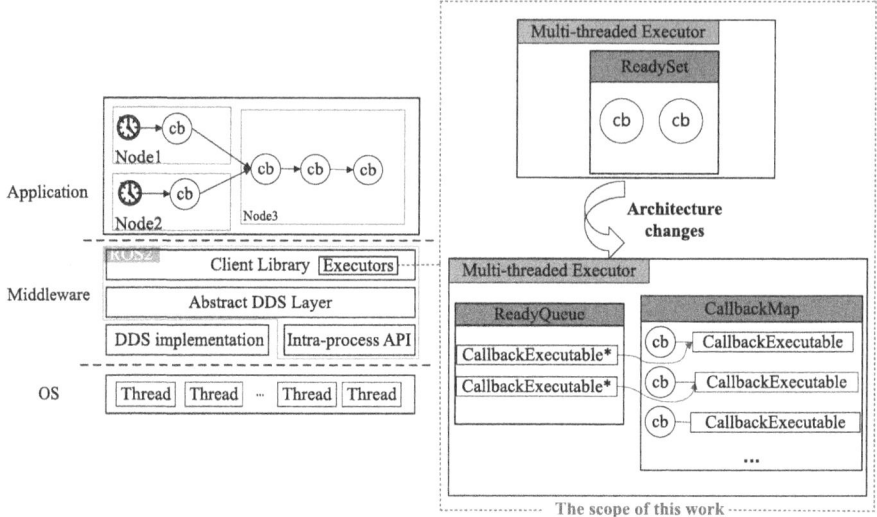

Fig. 4. Executor architecture changes.

instances no longer inherit the deadline of the earlier released chain instances, and priority inversion is automatically eliminated.

5 Response Time Analytical Model

This section introduces our proposed RTAM. We first review previous work. Then, focusing on our proposed scheduler, we develop a RTAM can analyze chains with both arbitrary and constrained deadlines and can take into account the effect of mutually-exclusive callback groups.

Based on the theoretical foundations of works in [13], For ROS2 multi-threaded executors, to calculate the WCRT of a given chain Γ_i, it is required to determine the maximum time interval from the release time of the first callback instance to the completion of the first execution unit for the last callback instance in the chain. Then, the response time R_i of the chain can be upper-bounded by $\Delta + \overline{sbf}(E_{<i,||\Gamma_i||-1>} - 1)$. The following constraint is satisfied:

$$\begin{cases} dbf(\Delta) < sbf_\omega(\Delta), \\ sbf_\omega(\Delta) \leq m \cdot \Delta. \end{cases} \quad (5)$$

where $dbf(\Delta)$ represents the demand-bound function of Γ_i.

We derive the following theorem to calculate the upper-bound of response time for chains under the CIL-EDF scheduling scheme on a ROS2 multi-threaded executors.[4]

---
[4] all proofs are in the appendix [1].

Theorem 1. On a ROS2 multi-threaded executor with m threads, based on the CIL-EDF scheduling scheme, if $dbf(\Delta) < sbf_\omega(\Delta)$, the response time of chain $\Gamma_i = \{C_{<i,0>}, C_{<i,1>}, \ldots, C_{<i,\|\Gamma_i\|-1>}\}$ with a constrained deadline can be upper-bounded by $R_i = \Delta + \overline{sbf_c}(E_{<i,\|\Gamma_i\|-1>} - 1)$, holds for the following $dbf(\Delta)$:

$$dbf(\Delta) = m \cdot (E_i - E_{\langle i, \|\Gamma_i\|-1\rangle}) \\ + \sum_{\forall \Gamma_j \in \Gamma \wedge D_j < D_i} \left\lfloor \frac{\Delta}{T_j} \right\rfloor \cdot E_j + \min(E_j, \Delta - \left\lfloor \frac{\Delta}{T_j} \right\rfloor \cdot T_j) \\ + \sum_{\forall \Gamma_k \in \Gamma - \{\Gamma_i\}} \min(E_k, \Delta) \quad (6)$$

$dbf(\Delta)$ can be solved through fixed-point iteration with an initial condition of $\Delta = E_i - E_{\langle i, \|\Gamma_i\|-1\rangle}$.

Theorem 2. On a ROS2 multi-threaded executor with m threads, based on the CIL-EDF scheduling scheme, if $dbf(\Delta) < sbf_\omega(\Delta)$, the response time of chain $\Gamma_i = \{C_{<i,0>}, C_{<i,1>}, \ldots, C_{<i,\|\Gamma_i\|-1>}\}$ with an arbitrary deadline can be upper-bounded by $R_i = \Delta + \overline{sbf_c}(E_{<i,\|\Gamma_i\|-1>} - 1)$, holds for the following $dbf(\Delta)$:

$$dbf(\Delta) = m \cdot (E_i - E_{\langle i, \|\Gamma_i\|-1\rangle}) \\ + \sum_{\forall \Gamma_j \in \Gamma \wedge D_j < D_i} \left\lceil \frac{\Delta}{T_j} \right\rceil \cdot E_j \\ + (\sum_{\forall \Gamma_k \in \Gamma} \left\lceil \frac{D_k}{T_k} \right\rceil \cdot \min(E_k, \Delta) - \min(E_i, \Delta)) \quad (7)$$

$dbf(\Delta)$ can be solved through fixed-point iteration with an initial condition of $\Delta = E_i - E_{\langle i, \|\Gamma_i\|-1\rangle}$.

Theorem 3. With mutually-exclusive callback groups, On a ROS2 multi-threaded executor with m threads, based on the CIL-EDF scheduling scheme, if $dbf(\Delta) < sbf_\omega(\Delta)$, the response time of the chain $\Gamma_i = \{C_{<i,0>}, C_{<i,1>}, \ldots, C_{<i,\|\Gamma_i\|-1>}\}$ can be upper-bounded by $R_i = \Delta + \overline{sbf_c}(E_{<i,\|\Gamma_i\|-1>} - 1)$, holds for the following $dbf(\Delta)$:

$$dbf(\Delta) = RHS \text{ of } Eq.(6) \text{ or } Eq.(7) \\ + \sum_{j=0}^{\|\Gamma_i\|-1} m \cdot mutually\_execlusive\_blocking\_time(C_{<i,j>}, \Delta) \quad (8)$$

Algorithm 1. $mutually\_exclusive\_blocking\_time(C_{<i,j>}, \Delta)$

1: $blocking\_time = 0$
2: $group = callback\_group(C_{<i,j>}) - \{C_{<i,j>}\}$
3: **for all** $C_{<k,y>} \in group$ **do**
4:     **if** $k \neq i$ **then**
5:         $blocking\_time += \left\lceil \frac{D_k}{T_k} \right\rceil \cdot E_{<k,y>}$
6:         **if** $D_k < D_i$ **then**

7: $\qquad blocking\_time+ = \left\lceil \frac{\Delta}{T_k} \right\rceil \cdot E_{<k,y>}$
8: $\qquad$ **end if**
9: $\quad$ **end if**
10: **end for**
11: **return** $blocking\_time$

6 Evaluation

This section evaluates our proposed CIL-EDF scheduling scheme for ROS2 multi-threaded executors by comparing it with the default scheduling scheme and PiCAS scheduling scheme. We conduct case studies to compare the performance of the CIL-EDF scheduling scheme in terms of WCRT and schedulability with the existing scheduling schemes of multi-threaded executors, and present the results of the RTAM.[5] The title of each subplot represents: "CD" represent chains with constrained deadline. "AD" represent chains with arbitrary deadlines. "R" and "M" represent the settings of reentrant groups and mutually exclusive callback groups. The numbers represent the number of threads in multi-threaded executors.

Figure 5 illustrates the distribution of observed response times for each chain under different configurations. Evaluations see footnote 5 for chains with arbitrary deadlines have twice the workload than chains with constrained deadlines. In the evaluation of chains with constrained deadlines, in most cases, the CIL-EDF scheduling scheme shows a slight advantage over the other two in WCRT. in the evaluation of chains with arbitrary deadlines, the difference between the WCRT of chains under different scheduling schemes is very large. We observed that when the number of threads is 2, Γ_4 and Γ_5 experienced "starvation" under the PiCAS scheduling scheme. This occurred due to their low priority in the PiCAS scheduling scheme and the system overloaded, executors keep prioritizing instances of higher priority chains. Except for Γ_0 and Γ_1 in some cases, where the PiCAS scheduling scheme yields better WCRT than the CIL-EDF scheduling scheme. In most cases, the WCRT of chains under CIL-EDF scheduling scheme is significantly superior to the other two.

Table 3 and Table 4[6] presents the schedulability of each chain under different configurations. Overall, the CIL-EDF scheduling scheme demonstrates significant advantages over the other two in WCRT and schedulability, especially if the system is heavily loaded.

From Fig. 6, for chains with constrained deadlines, the results of the RTAM could safely upper-bound the WCRT. But for chains with arbitrary deadlines, we observe that except when the number of threads is set to 4, the results of the RTAM can safely upper-bound the WCRT of chains. In other cases, the results of the RTAM are smaller than the actual WCRT. The reason is that our

---

[5] The detailed configuration of the evaluation is explained in appendix [1].
[6] The Table 3 and Table 4 and the detailed analysis of schedulability are in appendix [1].

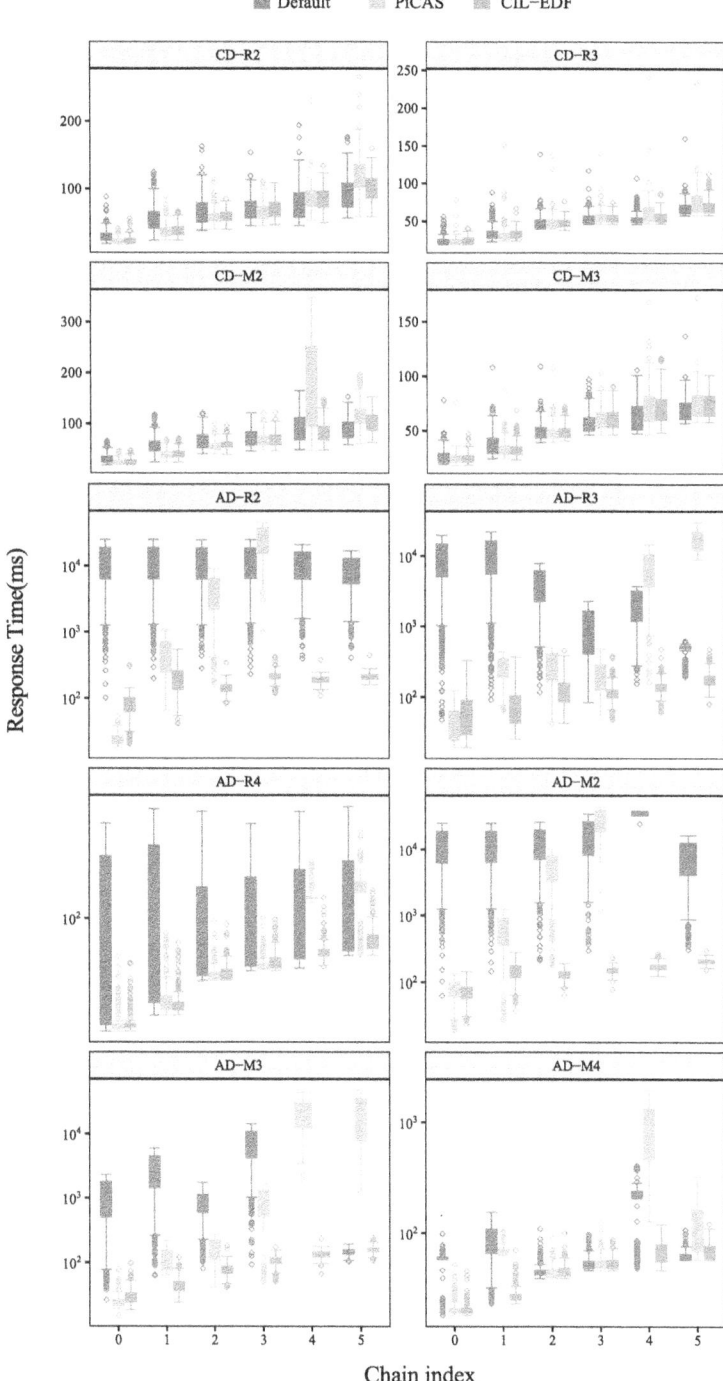

Fig. 5. Observed response time of chains.

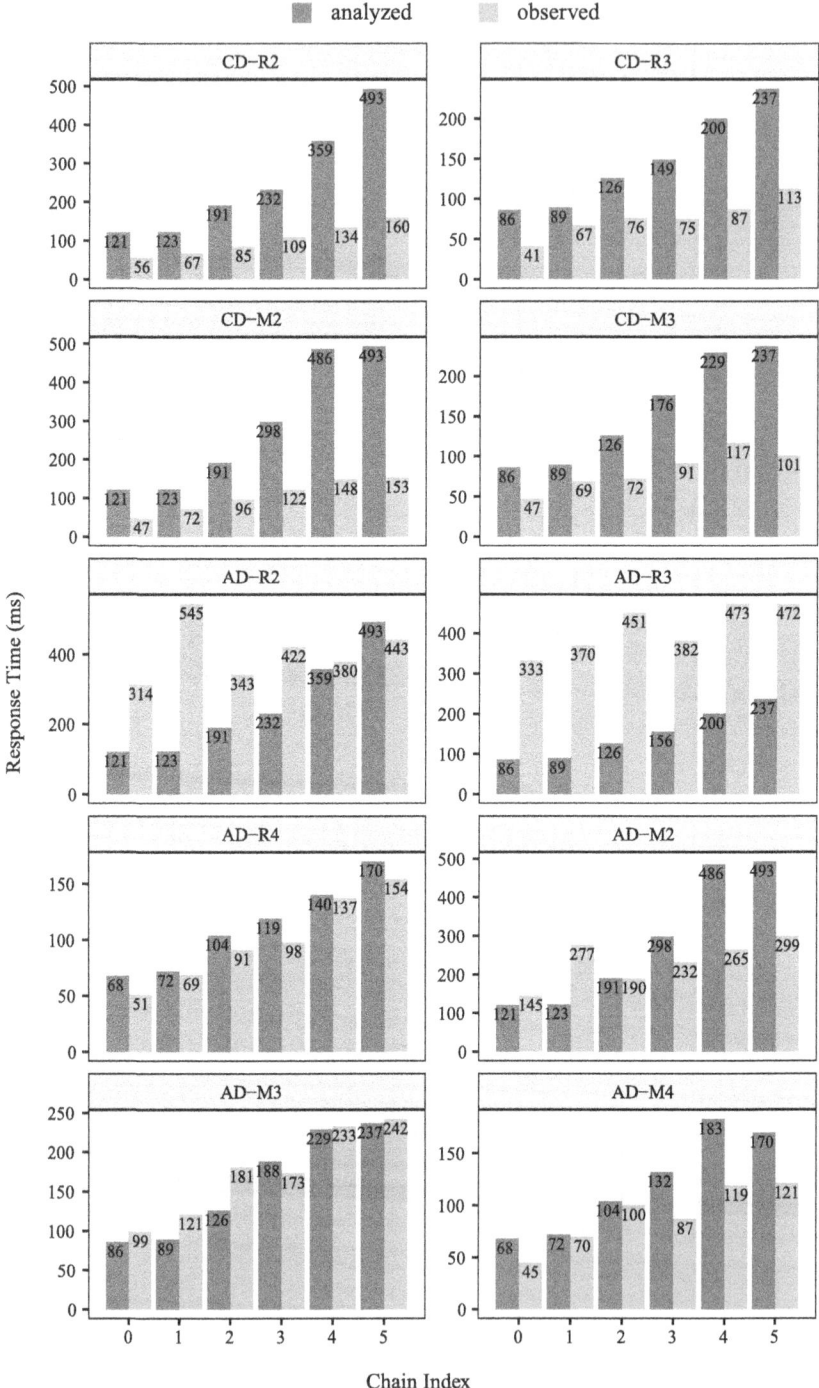

Fig. 6. Comparison of observed and analyzed WCRT for chains.

model oversight of non-schedulable chain instances leads to an underestimated workload. In cases where the number of threads is set to 2 or 3, numerous chain instances become non-schedulable due to preemption and waiting for execution, causing our model to fail in safely upper-bound the WCRT of chains. In conclusion, Our current proposed RTAM is more applicable to conditions where all chain instances are schedulable in the system.

7 Conclusion

In this paper, we proposed a CIL-EDF scheduling scheme for ROS2 multi-threaded executors to overcome the limitations of the existing scheduling schemes. We have redesigned the scheduling unit to equip executors with the capability to consider chain attributes in the scheduling of callback instances, changed multi-threaded executors architecture to enable prioritizing callback instances based on the deadline of chain instances as well as reduce runtime overhead, and introduced a fault correction mechanism for minimize the impact of priority inversion. We also proposed a RTAM for our proposed scheduler. Our model can analyze chains with both arbitrary and constrained deadlines, and take the effect of mutually-exclusive callback groups into account. We evaluated with case studies. The results demonstrate the superior performance of the CIL-EDF scheduling scheme in terms of WCRT and schedulability compare with the existing scheduling schemes of multi-threaded executors. And the analysis of RTAM results indicates that our current model is more applicable in conditions where all chain instances are schedulable in the system. As a next step, we will extend our RTAM to more common scenarios, which considers the workload caused by non-schedulable chain instances.

Acknowledgements. This work is supported by the Natural Science Foundation of China under Grant No. 91948303. We want to thank Haining Hu (Academy of Military Science) who provided useful help on drawing, Abdullah Al Arafat (University of Central Florida) who opened the source code of [3], and the anonymous reviewers for their helpful comments.

References

1. Appendix (online). https://github.com/Wuzhengda55/CIL-EDF-for-ROS2-multi-threaded-Executors/blob/main/Appendix.pdf
2. ROS-introduction. http://wiki.ros.org/ROS/Introduction. Accessed 20 Oct 2023
3. Arafat, A.A., Vaidhun, S., Wilson, K.M., Sun, J., Guo, Z.: Response time analysis for dynamic priority scheduling in ROS2. In: Proceedings of the 59th ACM/IEEE Design Automation Conference, pp. 301–306. ACM, New York (2022)
4. Blaß, T., Casini, D., Bozhko, S., Brandenburg, B.B.: A ROS 2 response-time analysis exploiting starvation freedom and execution-time variance. In: 2021 IEEE Real-Time Systems Symposium (RTSS), Dortmund, DE, pp. 41–53. IEEE (2021)

5. Casini, D., Blaß, T., Lütkebohle, I., Brandenburg, B.: Response-time analysis of ROS 2 processing chains under reservation-based scheduling. In: 31st Euromicro Conference on Real-Time Systems, pp. 1–23. Schloss Dagstuhl – Leibniz-Zentrum für Informatik, Dagstuhl, Germany (2019)
6. Choi, H., Xiang, Y., Kim, H.: PiCAS: new design of priority-driven chain-aware scheduling for ROS2. In: 2021 IEEE 27th Real-Time and Embedded Technology and Applications Symposium (RTAS), Nashville, TN, USA, pp. 251–263. IEEE (2021)
7. Guan, N., Yi, W.: General and efficient response time analysis for EDF scheduling. In: 2014 Design, Automation & Test in Europe Conference & Exhibition (DATE), Dresden, Germany, pp. 1–6. IEEE (2014)
8. Jiang, X., Ji, D., Guan, N., Li, R., Tang, Y., Wang, Y.: Real-time scheduling and analysis of processing chains on multi-threaded executor in ROS 2. In: 2022 IEEE Real-Time Systems Symposium (RTSS), Houston, TX, USA, pp. 27–39. IEEE (2022)
9. Macenski, S., Foote, T., Gerkey, B., Lalancette, C., Woodall, W.: Robot operating system 2: design, architecture, and uses in the wild. Sci. Robot. **7**(66), 60–74 (2022)
10. Saito, Y., Azumi, T., Kato, S., Nishio, N.: Priority and synchronization support for ROS. In: 2016 IEEE 4th International Conference on Cyber-Physical Systems, Networks, and Applications (CPSNA), Nagoya, Japan, pp. 77–82. IEEE (2016)
11. Saito, Y., Sato, F., Azumi, T., Kato, S., Nishio, N.: ROSCH: real-time scheduling framework for ROS. In: 2018 IEEE 24th International Conference on Embedded and Real-Time Computing Systems and Applications (RTCSA), Hakodate, Japan, pp. 52–58. IEEE (2018)
12. Shin, I., Lee, I.: Compositional real-time scheduling framework with periodic model. ACM Trans. Embedded Comput. Syst. (TECS) **7**(3), 1–39 (2008)
13. Sobhani, H., Choi, H., Kim, H.: Timing analysis and priority-driven enhancements of ROS 2 multi-threaded executors. In: 2023 IEEE 29th Real-Time and Embedded Technology and Applications Symposium (RTAS), San Antonio, TX, USA, pp. 106–118. IEEE (2023)
14. Suzuki, Y., Azumi, T., Kato, S., Nishio, N.: Real-time ROS extension on transparent CPU/GPU coordination mechanism. In: 2018 IEEE 21st International Symposium on Real-Time Distributed Computing (ISORC), Singapore, pp. 184–192. IEEE (2018)
15. Tang, Y., et al.: Response time analysis and priority assignment of processing chains on ROS2 executors. In: 2020 IEEE Real-Time Systems Symposium (RTSS), Houston, TX, USA, pp. 231–243. IEEE (2020)
16. Tang, Y., Guan, N., Jiang, X., Luo, X., Yi, W.: Real-time performance analysis of processing systems on ROS 2 executors. In: 2023 IEEE 29th Real-Time and Embedded Technology and Applications Symposium (RTAS), , San Antonio, TX, USA, pp. 80–92. IEEE (2023)
17. Teper, H., Günzel, M., Ueter, N., von der Brüggen, G., Chen, J.J.: End-to-end timing analysis in ROS2. In: 2022 IEEE Real-Time Systems Symposium (RTSS), Houston, TX, USA, pp. 53–65. IEEE (2022)
18. Wei, H., et al.: RT-ROS: a real-time ROS architecture on multi-core processors. Futur. Gener. Comput. Syst. **56**, 171–178 (2016)

Efficient Coupling Streaming AI and Ensemble Simulations on HPC Clusters

Jiazhi Jiang, Hongbin Zhang, Deyin Liu, Jiangsu Du, Xiaojiao Yao, Jinhui Wei, Pin Chen, Dan Huang[✉], and Yutong Lu

School of Computer Science and Engineering, Sun Yat-sen University, Guangzhou, China
{jiangjzh6,zhanghb55,weijh28}@mail2.sysu.edu.cn,
{liudy55,dujiangsu,yaoxj5,chenp85,huangd79,luyutong}@mail.sysu.edu.cn

Abstract. As scientific research grows more complex, a wide range of HPC-AI workflows have been proposed, in which machine learning model learns from interactions with ensemble simulations on HPC clusters. However, existing distributed frameworks and solutions fall short in facilitating this intensive integration, struggling with challenges like nontrivial application migration, heterogeneous task management and inefficient I/O operations. To address these challenges, we present RTAI, a distributed runtime system aimed at optimizing emerging HPC-AI workflows. Specifically, it consists of several key components: RTAI Packer is a flexible abstraction that parallelizes and constructs a dynamic dependency graph of the workflow. RTAI Orchestrator improves workflow efficiency and cluster-wide resource utilization by adaptively organizing resources and managing heterogeneous tasks. RTAI FileHub is a tailored ad-hoc file system that is employed for in-memory caching of dynamically generated files and enhancing I/O efficiency. Our experiments show that RTAI significantly improves the makespan, cluster utilization, scalability and usability for HPC-AI applications when compared to other candidate solutions like Ray and Radical-Pilot.

Keywords: HPC-AI · workflow · scheduling · online learning · ensemble

1 Introduction

As computational and experimental complexities increase, many scientists are turning to machine learning (ML) techniques to handle and analyze data from simulations. The integration of AI/ML models into conventional simulations enhances accuracy and offers potential for substantial performance gains. For example, Cosmoflow [9] utilizes deep learning to interpret cosmological simulations, providing insights into the universe's structure and evolution. Deep-DriveMD [4] significantly boosts molecular dynamics (MD) performance by

---

J. Jiang and H. Zhang—Contribute equally to this work.

merging simulation ensembles with ML on large-scale parallel computers. This approach is referred to as an **HPC-AI workflow**.

Figure 1 illustrates that the HPC-AI workflow often entails continuously producing streaming data from thousands of simulations for real-time deep learning (DL) model training. This workflow differs from traditional ones by enabling AI to direct the HPC phase, such as through DL model inferences for simulation adjustments or utilizing mutual APIs. This requires a more intricate interaction between HPC and AI, adding complexity and marking them as "new applications" that include a wide range of tasks across large-scale computing campaigns [6]. Moreover, it demands advanced, scalable workflows for enhancing DL models, as supporting these workflows on large-scale clusters calls for high performance and throughput. Yet, current systems, often designed for either HPC or AI, fall short of meeting the integrated needs of HPC-AI workflows, posing unique challenges that remain unaddressed.

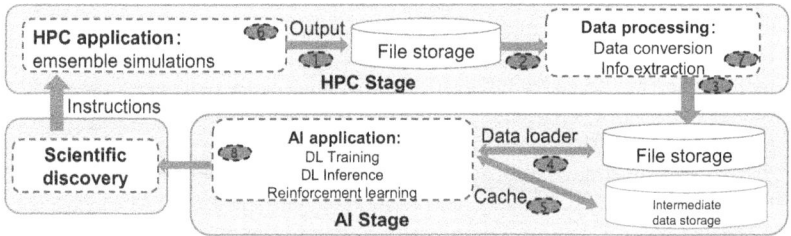

Fig. 1. Workflow of HPC-AI application.

Non-trivial Migration Works Required for Deploying and Scaling Applications on Distributed Frameworks. Manual conversion of HPC-AI applications using the parallelized API provided by the framework is not only laborious but also prone to errors. Many frameworks require significant changes to adapt existing workloads for distribution. Merlin [14] uses the Maestro [12] interface for workflow orchestration, but its YAML-based system, limited to shell syntax [3], poses restrictions. Additionally, the adoption of NoSQL databases like MongoDB and Redis for faster data operations necessitates modifications to the original application's data access methods. These requirements complicate the quick migration and deployment of applications.

Dilemma of Tightly Coupling HPC-AI Applications Within a Unified Framework While Effectively Managing Heterogeneous Tasks. Constructing HPC-AI workflows within a unified distributed framework allows for more nuanced interactions, but these workflows often involve varied tasks, such as MPI-based simulations, neural network operations, and I/O intensive data processing, as indicated by steps ❻ ❼ ❽ in Fig. 1. This diversity poses a challenge for distributed systems, as standard HPC and deep learning frameworks rely on homogeneous computation models and a uniform scheduler. This approach falls short in optimally scheduling a mix of simulation, ML training, and inference tasks for peak parallel efficiency.

Substantial Volume of Remote Data I/O on Backend Storage Cluster. Figure 1 shows that steps ❶ ❷ ❸ ❹ ❺ in HPC-AI workflow require extensive file and data handling. However, HPC clusters always have separate storage and computing systems, not optimized for managing large-scale project data. This often causes storage congestion in HPC clusters, with slow I/O speeds becoming critical bottleneck and negatively impacting workflow performance.

To overcome these challenges, we propose RTAI, a distributed runtime system with a comprehensive design tailored to the emerging HPC-AI workflow. It consists of several key system components: **RTAI Packer**, **RTAI Orchestrator** and **RTAI FileHub**. In summary, our contributions are as follows:

– We build a holistic system RTAI that distributes and parallels HPC-AI workflow on HPC clusters. It integrates multiple system techniques to jointly improve the both efficiency and usability of the proposed framework.
– RTAI Packer, a flexible Python abstraction, facilitates HPC-AI applications to be easily parallelized and scaled with minimal code changes. Moreover, the application's POSIX I/O calls are redirected to in-memory file system via interception library, optimizing I/O performance transparently to users.
– To optimize the management of heterogeneous tasks, the RTAI Orchestrator employs a two-tiered scheduling approach. The first tier organizes its allocated nodes into distinct resource bundles, with a bundle coordinator ensuring load balancing across these bundles. The second tier features an in-bundle scheduler within each bundle, dedicated to handling specific task types.
– RTAI FileHub, an interception-based in memory I/O system is integrated to reduce remote I/O and disruptions on the backend parallel file system. The RTAI FileHub is co-designed with distributed framework to eliminate potential architecture conflicts that arise from naive merging of in-memory IO module and cluster scheduler.

We evaluate RTAI experimentally and show that RTAI supports flexible executions across different stage of HPC-AI workflow compared to other candidate systems. RTAI scales DeepdriveMD application to 64 GPUs and outperforms the Ray and Radical-Pilot by up to 2.2× and 1.6x. Experiments conducted on separate modules indicate that RTAI FileHub effectively eliminates remote I/O congestion and improve I/O performance of HPC-AI workflows up to 1.5x to 5x. The RTAI Orchestrator can efficiently manage heterogeneous tasks and has significantly enhanced the resource utilization.

2 Background and Motivations

2.1 HPC-AI Workflow

Large-scale simulations use machine learning to optimize and guide thousands of varying instances, benefiting scientific applications [18]. DeepDriveMD [4] exemplifies an HPC-AI workflow, merging simulations with ML through stages of

Table 1. Comparison between RTAI and other existing popular systems.

Features	Data Staging		Pilot		Distributed ML	Traditional workflows	RTAI
	Rise	Stacker	Parsl	Radical	Ray		
Distributed Environment	✓	✓	✓	✓	✓	✓	✓
Task Heterogeneity Awareness	✗	✗	◐	◐	◐	✓	✓
Load Balance Across Diverse Task	✗	✗	✗	✗	✗	✗	✓
In memory I/O	✓	✓	✗	✗	✗	✗	✓
Non-intrusive migration for application	✗	✗	✓	✗	✓	✓	✓
Fine-grained interactive between stages	◐	◐	✓	✓	✓	✗	✓
General Used	✗	✗	✓	✓	✓	✗	✗

Note: ◐ denotes partially addresses the issue but does not fully resolve it.

exploration, aggregation, training, and inference, built on Radical-Pilot. Similarly, Colmena [18] and IMPECCABLE [15] showcase systems for experimental steering and drug discovery, respectively, leveraging quantum chemistry and MD simulations for design and adaptability. These HPC cluster workflows face challenges in coordinating complex simulation-learning tasks.

2.2 Related Work

We analyze the design space of potential solutions. They generally fall into the following categories.

Data Staging Frameworks. Data staging and in-situ workflows, like DataSpaces [5] and RISE [16], address scientific workflows' data overhead by integrating simulation, management, analysis, and visualization. DataSpaces offers efficient data exchange and redistribution, while RISE optimizes data availability and manages I/O contention through intelligent scheduling. These methods, however, introduce complex resource and task scheduling challenges in HPC-AI workflows.

Distributed Frameworks for ML. Ray [11] excels at scaling AI and Python apps but faces challenges with MPI-based HPC code due to its RPC framework. The need for process control in MPI conflicts with Ray's approach, leading to resource clashes and efficiency drops. While Ray supports task diversity, it struggles to handle the varied demands of HPC tasks, necessitating MPI code adaptation for effective scaling.

Traditional Workflow System. Traditional workflow systems often integrate data staging and distributed DL frameworks via file systems or message queues, isolating HPC and AI applications within separate systems with different distributed solutions and interfaces [8,19]. This approach limits dynamic task construction and sophisticated controls in HPC-AI workflows, thus restricting HPC and AI application interactions.

Pilot Frameworks. Pilot frameworks, exemplified by Radical-Pilot [10], aim to ease the management of tasks and resources in HPC clusters for parallel and distributed applications. HTDcr [7] is a job execution framework for high-throughput computing on supercomputers. Despite their utility, the dependence on pilot job management may challenge those new to the concept. While suitable for initial development, such frameworks may not fully address HPC-AI workflow requirements like adjusting workloads according to DL inferences, potentially causing increased queue times and reduced resource efficiency due to the absence of automatic task load balancing. Table 1 highlights RTAI's potential by integrating features from various systems: user-friendly programming from Ray and Parsl, in-memory data management, and efficient HPC-AI specific resource and task management. This integration requires a comprehensive design approach across HPC cluster components. RTAI's customization for HPC-AI workflows, however, positions it as a domain-specific rather than a general-purpose framework.

3 Overall Optimization Design

3.1 Design Principles and Goals

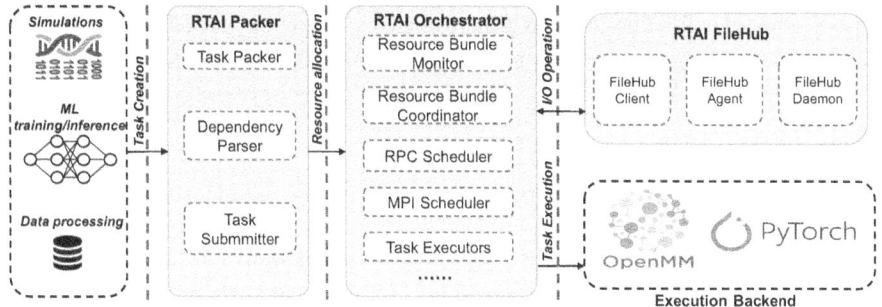

Fig. 2. Overall architecture of RTAI.

RTAI emphasizes user-friendliness by automating the integration of HPC/ML applications into distributed systems to minimize manual conversion errors. It also focuses on domain-specific solutions, optimizing for HPC-AI workflows in prevalent HPC cluster architectures with unique features like separate storage nodes. Its goals are to reduce the makespan of HPC-AI workloads and improve resource utilization across clusters.

3.2 System Architecture

Figure 2 shows RTAI's architecture, featuring three main components: **RTAI Packer** for parallelizing HPC-AI workflows with a flexible Python abstraction, automating task parsing and generation. **RTAI Orchestrator** optimizes task scheduling and resource management, improving HPC cluster resource utilization. **RTAI FileHub**, an interception-based in-memory I/O system, reduces I/O bottlenecks, supporting Posix interfaces. Each component includes modules tailored for specific functions.

- Task packer: provides a user-friendly interface for programming, along with code packaging and serialization.
- Dependency parser: constructs task graph execution and tracks task info.
- Task submitter: handles communication with the backend RTAI Orchestrator, task submission, and result retrieval.

Additionally, RTAI Orchestrator includes several modules:

- Resource bundle monitor: organizes nodes into resource bundles, monitoring their usage and load. Currently, the allocated resources are roughly divided into two bundles.
- Resource bundle coordinator: adjusts resource allocation adaptively for optimal load balancing based on each bundle's workload.
- In-bundle schedulers: implement tailored task scheduling within different resource bundles. Currently, there are two types: an MPI task scheduler for coarse-grained simulation tasks that follow the MPI paradigm, and an RPC task scheduler for fine-grained function tasks following the RPC paradigm.
- Task executors: executes applications on one or more target execution resources on HPC cluster.

Finally, RTAI FileHub contains three modules:

- Filehub client: captures file I/O system calls and subsequently forward these requests to filehub agent.
- Filehub agent: processes client requests, partitions data into stripes for storage, and transmits segmented data and metadata to the Filehub Daemon.
- Filehub daemon: receives metadata and data from the filehub agent and store them into either local memory or SSD.

4 Schemes for Usability

To enhance usability and reduce the migration burden of applications and workloads on large-scale HPC clusters, RTAI has made efforts in three key areas. Firstly, task packer module in RTAI Packer is designed to facilitate intuitive parallel and compositional programming in Python for HPC-AI workload. It provides a user-friendly programming interface, code packaging, and serialization capabilities. Secondly, dependency parser module in RTAI Packer is responsible for constructing and overseeing the task graph's execution and tracking relevant task information. Finally, to seamlessly integrate in-memory I/O systems without modifying I/O interfaces, RTAI Filehub ensures POSIX compatibility by intercepting and redirecting system calls.

Task Packer. RTAI, inspired by Parsl and Ray's API design, enables scaling of HPC-AI applications on HPC clusters efficiently with minimal code. It uses decorators to modify Python function behaviors for distributed computing. Specifically, RTAI supports two decorators: @rtai.submit_mpi for MPI-based and @rtai.submit_rpc for RPC-based applications, allowing customized function execution. The submit() method launches an RTAI task, returning a result object for accessing asynchronous outcomes. This object includes a rtai.wait() method for synchronous result waiting or exception handling.

Dependency Parser. Task dependencies are inferred from result object transfers, supporting synchronous and asynchronous HPC-AI workload executions [13]. A dependency parser, using an in-memory object manager inspired by Plasma [2], monitors these objects for result resolution or timeout. It tracks task information as key-value pairs, hashing task details for the key and storing task state and result stage as the value. Upon resolving all dependencies, a new thread is launched to submit the task to the RTAI Orchestrator via Cython.

Posix-Compatible I/O. Achieving POSIX-compatible I/O is primarily facilitated through the filehub client module. Filehub client is implemented as an embedded library to be preloaded in the application. Firstly, the **interceptor** captures and intercepts I/O calls made by applications, utilizing a system call interception library such as syscall_intercept. When an application initiates file I/O requests, these preloaded libraries intercept the I/O requests, as they have overridden the default I/O system call. Consequently, client module can process these requests based on their custom logic. In our implementation, the requests are forwarded to the filehub agent module mentioned in Sect. 6.

5 Schemes for Task Heterogeneity

RTAI Orchestrator is a core component of RTAI runtime service for HPC-AI tasks management and scheduling. It consists of several modules: resource bundle monitor, resource bundle coordinator, in-bundle schedulers, and task executors.

5.1 Architecture of RTAI Orchestrator

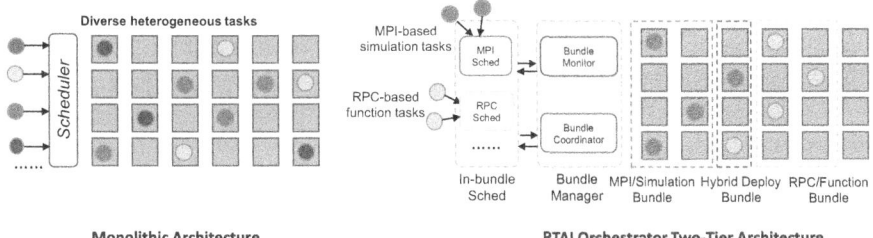

Fig. 3. RTAI scheduler architecture. Gray boxes represent the allocated cluster nodes. Circles represent the heterogeneous tasks. (Color figure online)

Two-Tier Scheduling. The RTAI Orchestrator, catering to the varied needs of HPC-AI workloads, features a dual-layer scheduling system as depicted in Fig. 3, moving away from traditional single-layer schedulers. At its heart, the resource bundle monitor serves as the main scheduler, organizing nodes into bundles and tracking their performance. Each bundle has its in-bundle scheduler for task allocation and execution, providing flexibility for different workload demands. This structure not only facilitates task-resource matching but also supports efficient task distribution across the HPC-AI workflow, maintaining a task queue for smooth operation.

Current Resource Bundles. RTAI identifies two main types of HPC-AI workloads: simulation tasks from the HPC phase, reliant on MPI for parallel execution, and AI-stage tasks using RPC for distribution and parallelization, as supported by Ray's work [11]. Given MPI's complexity and the non-modifiability of some codes, it's vital for RTAI's resource bundles to facilitate MPI task execution and scheduling. RTAI integrates RPC, based on the benefits outlined by Ray, for AI tasks within its dual in-bundle schedulers for HPC-AI workloads.

5.2 Load Balance Cross Bundles

HPC-AI workflows can select or terminate simulations based on AI inferences, with multiple workflows running within each resource bundle, leading to dynamic workload changes. To adapt to these shifts and prevent performance issues from fragmentation at higher loads, RTAI employs a reallocation mechanism across bundles and supports hybrid resource bundles, as shown in Fig. 3.

Resource Allocation for Different Bundles. Initially, the Bundle monitor allocates machines to resource bundles based on a user-configured JSON file, with the number of machines determined by the expected distribution and workload of HPC/AI tasks. In-bundle schedulers report changes in resource capacity or task queue lengths to the monitor each iteration. If there's a significant deviation from initial settings, the monitor reallocates machines between MPI/simulation and RPC/function bundles using a coarse-grained approach. For MPI/Simulation tasks, if the task queue exceeds threshold α, the monitor seeks machines in the hybrid bundle for rescheduling, as outlined in Algorithm 1. If the hybrid bundle is fully occupied, it searches the RPC/function bundle for low-utilization machines to move to the hybrid bundle. Reallocations and task transfers occur rarely, mainly when the hybrid bundle is not configured or fully occupied by a single workload type. Assuming the length of MPI bundle waiting task queue is MQ and the length of RPC waiting task queue is RQ, rescheduling between HPC and AI workloads happens only if the ratio MQ/RQ exceeds α, dynamically adjusted based on workload context. If the average execution time of MPI tasks increases, α decreases; otherwise, it increases.

Algorithm 1: Task Rescheduling via Bundle Coordinator

Input : OperationalType $opType$, Integer $nodeNum$
1 NodeStatusEnum = {Transferring, MPIProcessing, RPCProcessing};
2 TransferNodes ← EmptyList();
3 AvailableNodes ← EmptyList();
4 **for** $i \leftarrow 0$ **to** $nodeNum - 1$ **do**
5   fetchIdleNodeFromHybridBundle();
6   **if** $opType == ADD\_MPI$ **then**
7   NodeStatusEnum.MPIProcessing;
8   **else**
9   NodeStatusEnum.RPCProcessing;
10   AvailableNodes.add(node);
11 nodeNum = nodeNum - AvailableNodes.length();
12 **if** $nodeNum > 0$ **then**
13   **for** $i \leftarrow 0$ **to** $nodeNum - 1$ **do**
14   node ← **if** $opType == ADD\_MPI$ **then**
15   fetchRPCNodeFromHybridBundle();
16   **else**
17   fetchMPINodeFromHybridBundle();
18   TransferNodes.add(node);
19   **foreach** $node$ in TransferNodes **do**
20   node.status ← NodeStatusEnum.Transferring;
21   **if** $node.isAvailable$ **then**
22   AvailableNodes.add(node);
23   **else**
24   awaitTaskCompletion($node.id$);
25   AvailableNodes.add(node);
26   **foreach** $node$ in AvailableNodes **do**
27   node.status ← **if** $opType == ADD\_MPI$ **then**
28   NodeStatusEnum.MPIProcessing;
29   **else**
30   NodeStatusEnum.RPCProcessing;
31 reallocateTasksToNodes(AvailableNodes);

Task Scheduling Within Hybrid Bundle. The hybrid bundle acts as a dynamic buffer, flexibly supporting MPI-based simulation and RPC-based function tasks based on workload intensity. A bundle coordinator ensures resource balance by dynamically scaling resources between these tasks within the hybrid bundle, without deploying both task types on the same server to avoid kernel modifications for resource isolation. During high load periods for either task type, the coordinator dedicates servers in the hybrid bundle to the most burdened tasks, facilitating rescheduling as needed. This process, akin to Algorithm 1, involves node selection, clearance, and task rescheduling. If MPI simulations demand more resources, the coordinator uses the *fetchRPCNodeFromHybridBundle* function to select nodes with fewer RPC tasks for load balancing. These nodes are marked as *Transferring*, halting task assignment until they're clear and relabeled for MPI task processing, guiding the RTAI Orchestrator to reallocate tasks appropriately.

Task Transferred Strategies. When the hybrid bundle lacks idle machines, task transfer within or between bundles is necessary. There are three strategies: 1) terminating in-progress tasks and discarding results, causing resource waste;

2) waiting for tasks to complete before migration, preventing new assignments to the node; 3) transferring task context and results to another machine, needing a user code interface for saving/loading checkpoints. RTAI currently supports the first two strategies and plans to implement the third in future updates.

6 Schemes for Remote I/O Bottleneck

To systematically incorporate node-local memory into HPC-AI workflows, File-Hub enhances HPC-AI workflows by using node-local memory across compute nodes to mitigate I/O pressure, inspired by ad hoc file systems [17]. It separates request and result management into three components: filehub client, agent, and daemon, streamlining distributed execution as depicted in Fig. 4.

Nested Multi-process/Multi-thread Problem. Integrating a system call interception module with multi-threading into applications can enhance efficiency but may lead to unpredictability in distributed frameworks like Ray and RTAI, as they use "fork" to create child processes, duplicating the interception library. This can consume excessive CPU resources, with N executors and T threads per executor using $N * T$ CPU cores for I/O. RTAI FileHub addresses this by deploying a separate multi-thread handler as a local agent on each node, reducing the embedded library's replication in task executors, as illustrated in Fig. 4, directing I/O requests to this agent.

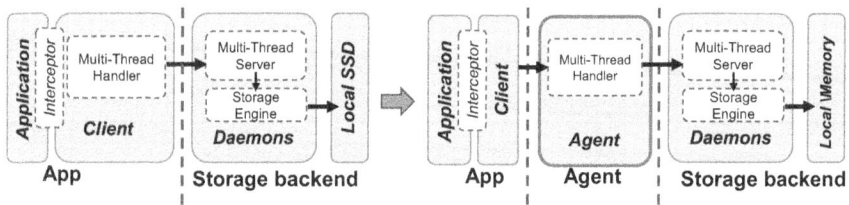

Fig. 4. Redesigned filehub with agent layer integration

Adaptive and Asynchronous I/O Handling. RTAI FileHub separates the filehub agent from the embedded I/O interception library to handle threads independently, preventing excessive CPU consumption. However, it still requires deploying an agent with multiple thread contexts on each machine to forward I/O requests. To avoid CPU contention between task executors and the filehub agent, it implements an adaptive I/O request handling mechanism. It monitors local CPU usage and adjusts thread usage accordingly. When CPU workload is high, it reduces threads and queues unprocessable requests; when CPU cores are available, it requests more resources to expedite processing.

Backend Storage Engine Optimization. The filehub daemon efficiently manages metadata and data, storing it in node-local memory or SSD storage. Multiple daemons are distributed across nodes, enhancing bandwidth performance.

We prioritize local memory for HPC-AI data due to its transient nature, using SSD for persistence or when memory is full. Persistence operations are asynchronous to minimize workload impact. We've optimized daemon numbers to balance efficiency and resource usage.

7 Experiments and Evaluation

7.1 Experiments Setup

Testbed. We conduct our experiments on an HPC cluster equipped with GPU nodes. Each GPU node has 4 NVIDIA V100 16 GB GPUs, 2 Intel Xeon Gold 6132 CPU @ 2.60 GHz with 14 cores and 256 GB memory. The cluster also features a separate storage backend, managed using Lustre version 2.12.2.

Workload and Application. DeepDriveMD [4] is an advanced computational workflow that integrates molecular dynamics (MD) simulations with deep learning techniques. Its primary goal is to identify and model intricate patterns and characteristics within the vast and high-dimensional datasets generated by MD simulations. We conduct an end-to-end comparative analysis of the frameworks Radical, Ray, and RTAI, using DeepDriveMD as a primary real-world workload.

Baselines. We consider the following two frameworks as baselines: (1) Ray [11]: an open-source distributed computing framework for building scalable and efficient applications. The Ray version used for evaluations in our experiment is 2.7. (2) Radical-Pilot [3]: a framework designed to facilitate the execution of large-scale scientific and data-intensive applications on distributed computing environments. The Radical-Pilot version used in our experiment is 1.33.

7.2 Real-Workload Evaluation

First, we evaluate our solution with real-world application (DeepDriveMD) running on the HPC cluster and compare it to deploy on the baseline frameworks, Ray and Radical-Pilot. We assess and analyze the completion time for a single iteration of DeepdriveMD on eight GPU nodes, encompassing a total of 32 GPUs and 224 CPU cores. The first test case launch 32 simulation instances and the second test case launch 64 simulation instances. Figure 5(a) illustrates the evaluation of two test cases for DeepDriveMD's makespan. RTAI outperformed Ray by approximately 2.2 times and was about 1.6 times faster than Radical-Pilot. The primary reason behind this performance difference is attributed to the RTAI FileHub, which enhances the I/O performance of the HPC-AI workflow by minimizing remote I/O operations and thus reducing the overall I/O time for the workload. Furthermore, when compared to frameworks like Ray, which primarily support the RPC parallel paradigm, RTAI excels in accommodating various parallel paradigms. This flexibility enhances the resource utilization of the cluster and reduces the task queuing wait time in HPC-AI workflows by implementing effective load balancing between bundles of tasks.

7.3 Evaluations on Scalability

We conducted a study involving 16 nodes (64 GPUs and 448 CPUs) to analyze both strong and weak scaling of RTAI and other frameworks. We evaluate scalability with DeepDriveMD workflow for the completion of one iteration. In strong scaling, we maintained a constant total number of simulation instances, while in weak scaling, we kept the number of simulation instances per GPU constant. In the weak scalability assessment, we consistently launch 4 simulations per node, with the count of simulation instances rising as the number of nodes increases. Meanwhile, for the strong scalability evaluation, 64 simulation tasks are initiated across all nodes. RTAI delivers outstanding performance in both weak and strong scaling evaluations. As depicted in Fig. 5(b) and 5(c), RTAI provides the best performance and scalability in all cases. While all frameworks exhibit similar trends, the scalability of Ray leaves much to be desired. Its suboptimal performance can be attributed to Ray's reliance on a monolithic scheduling architecture and it only supports the RPC parallel paradigm, which proves less adaptable when dealing with MPI-based parallel tasks. This becomes particularly pronounced when confronted with the complex and diverse nature of heterogeneous tasks inherent in HPC-AI applications. In contrast, RTAI employs a two-tier scheduling architecture, offering superior flexibility for effectively managing the scheduling and resource allocation of diverse task types. This ensures that diverse types of tasks within RTAI are effectively scheduled and parallelized.

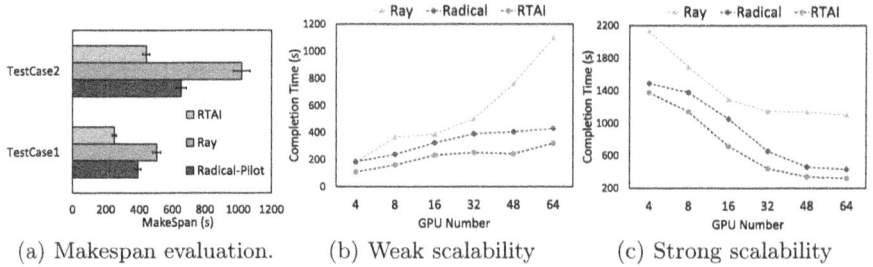

(a) Makespan evaluation.   (b) Weak scalability   (c) Strong scalability

Fig. 5. Comparison of the makespan, strong scalability and weak scalability of different frameworks for deploying HPC-AI workflow

7.4 Evaluations on Separate Modules

In this section, we conduct separate evaluations of the in-bundle RPC scheduler and bundle monitor modules within RTAI Orchestrator, as well as assess the performance of RTAI FileHub. These evaluations aim to validate whether each module has achieved its intended design objectives.

Resource Usage Enhancement with Resource Bundle Coordinator.
The resource bundle coordinator is designed to achieve load balancing between different resource bundles and improve the overall resource utilization of the

cluster. We conduct an ablation experiment to evaluate the effectiveness of the resource bundle coordinator in improving resource utilization. The experiment is conducted on 16 GPU nodes. When the resource bundle coordinator and the hybrid resource bundle are not enabled, RTAI consistently allocates 8 out of 16 nodes to the MPI resource bundle and the remaining 8 nodes to the RPC resource bundle. When the resource bundle coordinator and the hybrid resource bundle are enabled, RTAI allocates 8 nodes to the MPI/simulation resource bundle, 4 nodes to the hybrid resource bundle, and another 4 nodes to the RPC/function resource bundle. The resource bundle coordinator dynamically adjusts the resource allocation within the hybrid resource bundle based on the real-time workload demands of the tasks. We analyzed the average CPU and GPU utilization rates of nodes occupied by different types of tasks under two scenarios. The CPU/GPU utilization for nodes running MPI tasks is illustrated in Fig. 6(a), while that for nodes running RPC tasks is presented in Fig. 6(b).

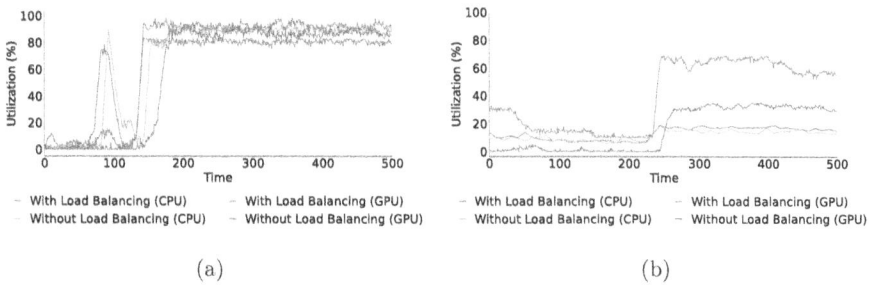

Fig. 6. Average CPU & GPU utilization for nodes running MPI (Figure a) and RPC (Figure b) tasks with and without load balance.

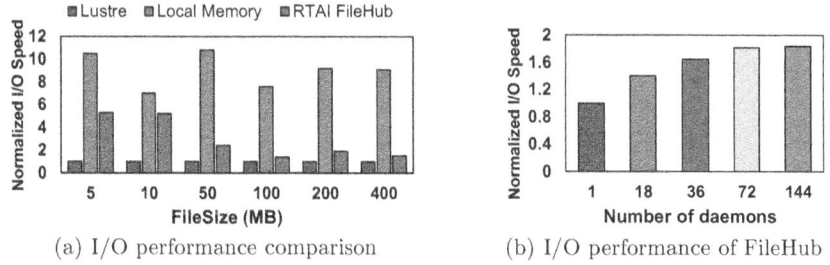

Fig. 7. a) I/O performance comparison between RTAI FileHub, Lustre and local memory. b) Relationship between I/O performance and the number of daemons.

From Fig. 6(a), it can be observed that MPI tasks consistently carry a substantial workload, with CPU/GPU utilization remaining high. Following the initialization phase (starting at 200 s in the figure), the resource bundle monitor detected that the resource utilization for the RPC resource bundle was relatively low. Consequently, it reallocated the resources originally assigned to RPC tasks to the MPI tasks within the hybrid resource bundle. As a result, it is evident that after load balancing, the CPU/GPU utilization on nodes running RPC tasks has significantly improved as shown in Fig. 6(b). The MPI tasks gained access to increased computing resources from the hybrid resource bundle, thereby significantly reducing in the task execution time.

Performance Improvement of I/O with FileHub. To evaluate the performance benefits of RTAI FileHub, we launched 32 OpenMM simulation instances, distributed across 8 nodes, with 4 instances per node. These instances are used to generate simulation data and perform DL training tasks. Figure 7(a) compared the total time required for writing data during the simulation phase and reading data during the training phase of our simulation program. We configured the size of simulation data generated by OpenMM to range from 5 MB to 400 MB. For local memory testing, each process on the nodes writes directly to local memory. In case of RTAI FileHub, we conduct data tests with 72 daemons enabled. Figure 7(b) conducted tests on RTAI FileHub with varying daemon quantities to evaluate how the number of daemons affects its I/O performance. We configured size of simulation data generated by OpenMM to be 50MB. As shown in Fig. 7(a) and 7(b), I/O performance of local memory is more than 7 times faster on average compared to writing to the remote Lustre file system. However, direct writing in local memory is not a feasible solution because data in local memory cannot be accessed across nodes. RTAI FileHub also employs in-memory I/O, but its performance is noticeably inferior to local memory I/O due to the overhead of interception and forwarding of system calls, along with the chunk-based data distribution across nodes for read and write operations. However, when compared to Lustre, it still exhibits a substantial improvement. When dealing with smaller simulated files, RTAI FileHub demonstrates a performance improvement of up to 5 times compared to Lustre. However, for larger simulated files, this advantage narrows to approximately 1.5 times faster than Lustre. This is because Lustre stores file metadata separately. When the files being read or written are relatively small, the time overhead of metadata operations becomes more significant. RTAI FileHub, on the other hand, does not have a separate metadata storage, so its advantages over Lustre become even more pronounced. As shown in Fig. 7(b), increasing the number of daemons leads to a significant improvement in RTAI FileHub's I/O performance at the beginning. However, once a certain number of daemons is reached, further increments in the daemon count no longer result in noticeable advancements in I/O performance.

We initiated over 200 simulation programs on the 8 nodes allocated to our HPC-AI workloads, writing HDF5 data to a remote storage cluster. Subsequently, we run IOR benchmark [1] on other unoccupied nodes to observe its interference on other workloads. As shown in Fig. 8(a), jobs executing concurrently within the same HPC cluster encountered interference in their I/O performance. IOR tests indicate a significant decrease in the read and write speeds of other jobs when they concurrently run with the HPC-AI workload. We conducted an evaluation of the interference caused by HPC-AI workloads on other users' jobs with RTAI FileHub, using the same experimental setup as depicted in Fig. 8(a). The experimental results are presented in Fig. 8(b). It can be seen that due to the reduced volume of remote I/O operations on the shared back-end storage, the I/O performance of other users' jobs is no longer negatively impacted by the presence of HPC-AI workloads.

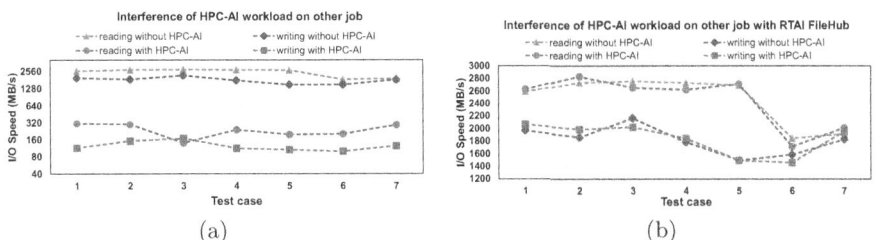

Fig. 8. Evaluations on RTAI FileHub. a) Interference of HPC-AI workflow on I/O of other workload. b) Interference of HPC-AI workflow with RTAI FileHub on I/O of other workload.

8 Conclusion

Driven by the unique characteristics of HPC-AI workflow, we introduce RTAI, designed for effectively scaling and parallelizing HPC-AI workloads on HPC clusters. It mainly consists of three components: RTAI Packer, RTAI Orchestrator and RTAI FileHub. RTAI Packer is designed to provide a flexible programming model and interface, alleviating the laborious work of application migration and parallelization for users. RTAI Orchestrator specializes in efficiently managing and scheduling inherently heterogeneous HPC-AI tasks, enhancing the resource utilization of clusters. RTAI FileHub employs in-memory I/O as a substitute for remote storage I/O to prevent congestion in remote storage clusters. Our experiments show that RTAI offers an effective solution to the challenges encountered by HPC-AI workflows on HPC clusters, providing a unified platform that combines flexibility, performance, and ease of use for the development of future HPC-AI workflow applications.

Acknowledgments. This research was supported by the National Key R&D Program of China 2021YFB0301300, and was also supported by NSFC 62332021, the Major Program of Guangdong Basic and Applied Research: 2019B030302002, Guangdong Province Special Support Program for Cultivating High-Level Talents: 2021TQ06X160, Pazhou Lab Research Project: PZL2023KF0001, and the Fundamental Research Funds for the Central Universities, Sun Yat-sen University (23xkjc016).

References

1. Ior benchmark. https://openbenchmarking.org/tests
2. Plasma. https://arrow.apache.org/blog/2017/08/08/plasma
3. Alsaadi, A., et al.: Radical-pilot and parsl: executing heterogeneous workflows on hpc platforms. In: 2022 IEEE/ACM Workshop on Workflows in Support of Large-Scale Science (WORKS), pp. 27–34. IEEE (2022)
4. Brace, A., et al.: Coupling streaming ai and hpc ensembles to achieve 100–1000× faster biomolecular simulations. In: 2022 IEEE International Parallel and Distributed Processing Symposium (IPDPS), pp. 806–816. IEEE (2022)
5. Docan, C., et al.: Dataspaces: an interaction and coordination framework for coupled simulation workflows. In: Proceedings of the 19th ACM International Symposium on High Performance Distributed Computing, pp. 25–36 (2010)
6. Jha, S.e.a.: Ai-coupled hpc workflows. arXiv preprint arXiv:2208.11745 (2022)
7. Jiang, J., et al.: Htdcr: a job execution framework for high-throughput computing on supercomputers. SCIENCE CHINA Inf. Sci. **67**(1), 112104 (2024)
8. Khaldi, M., et al.: Fault tolerance for a scientific workflow system in a cloud computing environment. Int. J. Comput. Appl. **42**(7), 705–714 (2020)
9. Mathuriya, A., et al.: Cosmoflow: using deep learning to learn the universe at scale. In: SC18: International Conference for High Performance Computing, Networking, Storage and Analysis, pp. 819–829. IEEE (2018)
10. Merzky, A., et al.: Design and performance characterization of radical-pilot on leadership-class platforms. IEEE Trans. Parallel Distrib. Syst. **33**(4), 818–829 (2021)
11. Moritz, P., et al.: Ray: a distributed framework for emerging {AI} applications. In: 13th USENIX Symposium on Operating Systems Design and Implementation (OSDI 18), pp. 561–577 (2018)
12. Natale, F.: Maestro workflow conductor. In: Lawrence Livermore National Laboratory (2018)
13. Pascuzzi, V.R., et al.: Asynchronous execution of heterogeneous tasks in ml-driven hpc workflows. In: Workshop on Job Scheduling Strategies for Parallel Processing, pp. 27–45. Springer (2023)
14. Peterson, J.L., et al.: Merlin: enabling machine learning-ready hpc ensembles. Technical report, Lawrence Livermore National Lab., Livermore, CA (United States) (2019)
15. Saadi, A.A., et al.: Impeccable: Integrated modeling pipeline for covid cure by assessing better leads. In: Proceedings of the 50th International Conference on Parallel Processing, pp. 1–12 (2021)
16. Subedi, P., et al.: Rise: Reducing i/o contention in staging-based extreme-scale in-situ workflows. In: 2021 IEEE International Conference on Cluster Computing, pp. 146–156. IEEE (2021)
17. Vef, M.A., et al.: Gekkofs-a temporary burst buffer file system for hpc applications. J. Comput. Sci. Technol. **35**, 72–91 (2020)
18. Ward, L., et al.: Colmena: scalable machine-learning-based steering of ensemble simulations for high performance computing. In: 2021 IEEE/ACM Workshop on Machine Learning in High Performance Computing Environments. IEEE (2021)
19. Wratten, L., et al.: Reproducible, scalable, and shareable analysis pipelines with bioinformatics workflow managers. Nat. Methods **18**(10), 1161–1168 (2021)

Context-Aware Runtime Type Prediction for Heterogeneous Microservices

Yibing Lin, Binbin Feng[(✉)], and Zhijun Ding[(✉)]

Department of Computer Science and Technology, Tongji University, Shanghai, China
{2151631,bining,dingzj}@tongji.edu.cn

Abstract. Serverless function is becoming increasingly popular as a new runtime type for application execution. However, it is not suitable for arbitrary microservices. Different components in microservice applications are often suitable to be deployed with different runtime types according to their own attributes and workload characteristics. However, the complex topology of microservice applications often leads to difficulty in determining the optimal runtime types of microservices, and the existing container-based microservice systems only support a single runtime type. Therefore, we propose a targeted heterogeneous runtime unified orchestration solution to address the above problems. First, we propose an execution need characterization model for microservice applications and introduce a microservice resource sensitivity type analysis method. Second, we propose a graph neural network-based approach for context-aware accurate prediction of heterogeneous microservice runtime types, which synthesizes the characteristics of each component and the correlation relationships between components to determine the optimal runtime type specific to each microservice. Third, we design and implement a unified orchestration system for heterogeneous microservice applications to support user-independent automated orchestration of serverful and serverless microservices. Finally, we validate the advantages of the system in terms of service performance and cost efficiency through experiments on real clusters.

Keywords: Cloud Computing · Heterogeneity · Serverless · Serverful · Graph Learning

1 Introduction

In recent years, cloud-native technologies have evolved, and microservice containerization has become the mainstream application development and deployment model. Serverless functions are becoming increasingly popular as a new runtime type for cloud development, and many cloud service vendors have introduced serverless functions, such as AWS Lambda [2].

Compared to traditional cloud computing, serverless functions are characterized by on-demand allocation, function-based granularity, and dynamic removal and creation. Developers realize their advantages and start trying to migrate their entire microservice applications to serverless computing platforms. However, the serverless function is not suitable for arbitrary microservices.

Providing temporary extensions to user deployments at the function level introduces many complexities to serverless systems, such as the problem of cold-start latency [4]. Cold-start latency can lead to reduced application performance and increased resource consumption. For serverful computing, maintaining a pool of free resources to alleviate this problem also leads to resource wastage.

For the differences in the dynamic creation of resources between serverful and serverless computing, two scenarios are considered: streaming load and discrete load. For streaming loads, the serverless deployment mode may need to repeatedly create and remove resources in a shorter time to handle continuously arriving requests, which increases resource consumption and waiting time and is unsuitable for microservices with strict latency requirements. For discrete loads, serverful deployment mode maintains idle resources when no requests arrive, which increases resource consumption. In summary, different components of microservice applications are often suitable for different deployment models based on their attributes and load characteristics.

The modularity and independent deployment of microservices provide prerequisites for heterogeneous runtime support of microservice systems. On this basis, determining the optimal runtime type for microservices with complex topologies is a challenging problem. Currently, existing orchestration systems that support containerized runtimes allow only a single runtime type, i.e., serverless or serverful. For each microservice in a microservice application, developers need to manually analyze it themselves or determine the optimal runtime type based on experts' experience with its characteristics, manually breaking the system boundaries and rewriting the application [1,9]. This process, which is separate from the process by which the system collects the application load logs, is technically demanding for developers, and the manual process introduces uncertainty in terms of efficiency and classification accuracy.

Aiming at the technical difficulties related to the selection of optimal runtime types for heterogeneous microservices and heterogeneous microservice runtime orchestration, we design an accurate analysis method for heterogeneous microservice runtime types and implement a unified system for heterogeneous runtime microservice application orchestration as follows:

– We propose a complex microservice application execution need modeling characterization approach to determine microservice-specific resource sensitivity types to guide runtime type analysis through automated analysis of microservice application topology and component-level log information.
– We propose a context-aware runtime type prediction method for heterogeneous microservices. It synthesizes each component in a microservice application, considering its attributes and load characteristics. It also analyzes the inter-component correlation relationships to make an end-to-end decision on the optimal runtime type specific to a microservice based on graph neural networks.

- We design and implement a unified orchestration system for heterogeneous runtime microservice applications, which supports automated orchestration and management of heterogeneous runtime types through modular design and interaction with open-source tools.
- Through experiments on real clusters, we verify the advantages of the system in terms of service performance and cost efficiency.

The remainder of the paper is organized as follows: Sect. 2 surveys related work, Sect. 3 describes the specific design of the algorithms, Sect. 4 outlines the system framework design, Sect. 5 presents experimental evaluations, and Sect. 6 concludes the paper.

2 Related Work

Regarding the heterogeneity of requirements for running microservice applications, the existing literature [10,12] concludes that no single resource provision can best satisfy all application requirements. However, these efforts do not consider different deployment models for different components in microservice applications. Savi et al. [13] only discussed scenarios where specific objects apply to serverless functions without considering the generic scenarios. Serverless functions do not fit into arbitrary microservices.

Regarding solving optimal runtime types for microservices, Raza et al. [10] proposed an economic model of deployment cost in VM and FaaS modes to classify different deployment modes by comparing the deployment cost to determine the threshold of the request rate. Son et al. [15] selected the FaaS deployment mode when meeting user performance requirements and achieving a specified average request rate. The above studies only considered the impact of the size of the request rate on the selection of hybrid deployment modes and did not take into account the different microservices' attributes and the status quo of load changes. In addition to this, Reuter et al. [11] simulated all the possible deployment scenarios from pure VMaaS to pure FaaS, including hybrid deployment scenarios, to determine the minimum sum-of-costs scenarios, which do not take into account enough of the changes in the load profile of microservices and are too high in overhead. Nday et al. [9] manually define active and inactive hours to correspond to the selection of different types, and the manual self-analysis process is highly inefficient and less accurate.

Regarding existing microservice systems, the studies by Gunasekaran et al. [6] and Raza et al. [10] support heterogeneous operations on VMs to some extent. However, with the development of cloud-native technologies, containers have become the mainstream runtime. Existing runtime orchestration systems that support containerized runtimes allow only a single runtime type, i.e., either a serverful or serverless mode. Burckhard et al. [5] proposed the Netherite, a new architecture for executing serverless workflows on elastic clusters; Yussupov et al. [16] designed a deployment system for serverless function workflows only. All of the above systems only support a single runtime type. In constructing microservice applications involving heterogeneous types, developers must manually break

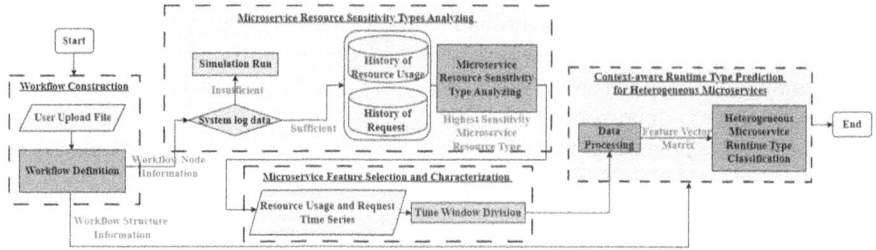

Fig. 1. The overall structure of the algorithm in this paper.

the system boundaries and complete the orchestration and management of the two runtimes, which is a very high threshold and low efficiency.

3 Method Description

The overall algorithm structure of this paper is shown in Fig. 1. Firstly, the workflow definition method is applied according to the user uploading files. Access the system log data through the workflow node information, simulate and run when the data is insufficient, get the resource usage and request time series. Then, the microservice resource sensitivity analysis method is applied to get the resource type with the highest sensitivity, take it and the request volume time series as the microservice features, and apply the time window division method to divide the time series. Data preprocessing is completed in runtime type prediction to form the feature vector matrix and synthesize workflow structure information for heterogeneous microservice runtime type classification.

3.1 Methodology for Modeling the Characterization of Execution Needs for Complex Microservice Applications

Based on the previous discussion, for the problem of heterogeneous execution needs of complex microservice applications, different deployment modes should be chosen accordingly. The current deployment of heterogeneous workflow applications requires users to manually rewrite the application to match the corresponding deployment mode [9,15]. Therefore, we propose to guide the user-independent orchestration of applications through a unified workflow microservice application definition, which includes the definition of workflow microservice application topology and individual components. We aim to automate the external rewriting of the application without intruding into the user's code to realize the orchestration and management of heterogeneous microservice applications.

Workflow Construction. The user-constructed workflow microservice application consists of the dependencies between each node and the microservices represented by each node. On the microservice application topology construction, we extend the workflow definition approach based on the already standardized Argo Workflow [3] workflow engine, where the user defines the structure of the microservice application as a directed acyclic graph (DAG) by specifying the dependencies of each node through the application configuration file written in the YAML language. The parallel and serial relationships between nodes are defined by keywords such as "–" and "-". The "template" defines the workflow microservice application component to which the node corresponds. On the microservice component node construction, the user defines the source code and container image configuration file. When the nodes are deployed with serverful mode through the k8s container orchestration tool, the container image configuration file Dockerfile is used to define the container build process and runtime environment, etc. By defining the workflow microservice application through the above files, deployment in serverless and serverful modes can be realized respectively, without manually rewriting the configuration files.

Methodology for Analyzing Microservice Resource Sensitivity Types. Microservice application execution needs are intricately linked to historical load data, reflecting running characteristics. A comprehensive analysis of historical resource consumption and request load is crucial for accurate load assessment. Two scenarios are considered: Firstly, if load judgment relies solely on microservice resource usage history, anomalies like cluster failures can lead to empty resource load data, inaccurately representing the actual load. Secondly, evaluating load based only on historical microservice call volumes may overlook the heterogeneous request load and resource usage patterns, leading to misinterpretations. Therefore, a balanced consideration of both resource and request load situations is essential for accurate load assessment.

Meanwhile, the diversity of microservice resource types will also bring too many factors that interfere with the judgment of historical load characteristics. Therefore, this paper proposes the microservice resource sensitivity type analysis method to determine the type of resource consumption that is subject to the most variations of request load fluctuations and take it as one of the characteristics reflecting the microservice load situation to guide the determination of microservice runtime types.

Specifically, first, the historical request load data of the microservice is obtained through the logging system. When faced with insufficient historical request load data, sufficient data is obtained by simulating and running for a period of time. The microservice resource sensitivity types are analyzed in terms of four aspects: CPU, I/O, memory, and network. Snapshots of the resource metrics collected by Prometheus are taken at a predefined frequency between the start time t_0 and the end time t_1 of the application, and the resource usage recorded in each snapshot is denoted as

$$U = \{U_i | U_i \in \{C_i, O_i, M_i, N_i\}\} \tag{1}$$

where C_i denotes CPU utilization, O_i denotes disk I/O utilization, M_i denotes memory utilization, and N_i denotes network bandwidth utilization.

Next, on the one hand, the magnitude of the resource consumption that is subject to changes in the request load is measured by calculating the slope of the resource consumption with respect to the change in the request volume.

Calculate the slope k of each resource type U_i about the request load r for n data points over a period of time θ.

$$k = \frac{n(\sum U_i r_i) - (\sum U_i)(\sum r_i)}{n(\sum U_i^2) - (\sum U_i)^2} \quad (2)$$

On the other hand, the fluctuating value of resource consumption is assessed by calculating the variance of resource consumption over a period of time. Calculate the variance of the change in the amount of each resource over time θ:

$$\sigma = \frac{\sum_{i=1}^{n}(U_i - \overline{U})^2}{n} \quad (3)$$

The slope and variance are obtained according to the formula (2) (3) to establish the formula for assessing the type of resource sensitivity:

$$S = w_1 k + w_2 \sigma \quad (4)$$

The evaluation scores for CPU, memory, disk, and network resource types are obtained using the formula in (4).

$$S_{max} = max(S_C, S_O, S_M, S_N) \quad (5)$$

The resource type that corresponds to the highest score of the indicated resource sensitivity type assessment obtained through the formula in (5) is judged to be the resource type with the highest microservice resource sensitivity.

Microservice Feature Selection and Characterization Method. Based on the discussion above, heterogeneous instance runtime types should consider whether the application load profile tends to be streaming or discrete, which closely relates to the microservice resource usage sequence and historical invocation volume sequence. Hence, the historical invocation time series $R = [R_1, R_2, ..., R_n]$ and resource usage time series $U = [U_1, U_2, ..., U_n]$ serve as microservice features.

System log histories are often lengthy, increasing computational costs for analysis. Therefore, we impose an upper limit of T on the time series length. When the time series length exceeds this limit, we apply a time window to extract subsequences of a specified length. We then compute statistical features and trends within each time window to better represent the original time series.

In selecting the time window size, begin by determining the lower limit of the time window size w_{min}, based on the upper limit of the time series length T and the length of the original historical time series data N, $w_{min} = N/T$. Of course, larger time window sizes can also be chosen, but as the window size increases, the sampled time series will lose detail about changes.

3.2 Context-Aware Runtime Type Prediction for Heterogeneous Microservices

Based on the previous discussion, the analysis of microservice load characterization affects the determination of the optimal runtime types for heterogeneous microservices. As for workflow microservice applications, individual components are often influenced by the characteristics of their upstream and downstream components in the workflow, which makes correlation relationships between load variations of microservice components. Considering the above, graph neural networks can effectively capture the complex relationships between nodes in the workflow structure and are applicable to this problem. Therefore, in this paper, we construct an accurate prediction method for heterogeneous microservice runtime types based on graph convolutional neural networks.

Heterogeneous Microservice Runtime Type Classification Model Construction. First, the microservice characteristic time series undergoes processing. Based on previous analysis, the impact of the load profile on serverless and serverful deployment models primarily stems from the load's streaming or discrete characterization. To mitigate the influence of load non-zero value fluctuations on assessment, collected historical data is converted into a binary time series. Here, x denotes the value of a single data point on the time series, and $x_{limit}, x_{limit} \in \{R_{limit}, U_{limit}\}$ denotes the threshold of x in terms of request volume and resource usage respectively.

$$x' = \begin{cases} 0, x < x_{limit} \\ 1, x \geq x_{limit} \end{cases} \quad (6)$$

The data within the time window is averaged to reflect the average load, and the number of times the load changes are recorded for the data within the time window reflects the degree of load dispersion within the window:

$$z_1 = \frac{x'_1 + x'_2 + ... + x'_n}{n} \quad (7)$$

$$z_2 = \sum_{i=2}^{n}(x'_i - x'_{i-1}) \quad (8)$$

According to Eqs. (7) (8), the historical call data and microservice load data time series are processed separately to obtain the time series R_1, R_2, U_1, U_2, consisting of multivariate time series of the feature vector matrix $X = [R_1, R_2, U_1, U_2]$ as the graph neural network individual node feature representation.

Next, establish the graph structure. Firstly, the correlation matrix D is established to calculate the similarity of each node feature using DTW [8] measure where D_{ij} denotes the (i,j) item of the correlation matrix.

$$D = \begin{bmatrix} dtw(X_1, X_1) & \cdots & dtw(X_N, X_1) \\ \vdots & \vdots & \vdots \\ dtw(X_1, X_N) & \cdots & dtw(X_N, X_N) \end{bmatrix} \quad (9)$$

In workflow microservice applications, the relationship between upstream and downstream nodes outlined in the workflow topology is crucial, directly impacting overall workflow effectiveness. Tasks within a workflow typically adhere to specific scheduling policies, resulting in similar load variations among neighboring nodes. Regarding resource competition, neighboring nodes may share computational and storage resources. Furthermore, task execution within the workflow may rely on predecessor node completion, and neighboring nodes may perform similar or related tasks, leading to similar node load impacts. Thus, focusing on the workflow's upstream and downstream node relationship is essential for understanding node load changes. Based on this analysis, when constructing the adjacency matrix, we introduce a scaling parameter to describe the workflow topology, adjust correlation matrix weights, and regulate the strength of node relationships based on time-series similarity. This allows for flexible topology modeling, as expressed by the following equation, where A_{ij} denotes the (i,j) item of the adjacency matrix, and the scaling parameter $\gamma \in [0, \infty)$.

$$A_{ij} = \gamma \frac{1}{e^{D_{ij}}} \tag{10}$$

In the process of constructing the adjacency matrix, we introduce the guidance of the workflow topology for the runtime type analysis of the upstream and downstream microservice components by the scaling parameter. Specifically, according to the workflow topology, the adjacent upstream and downstream nodes of workflows represented by the graph neural nodes apply the parameter γ_1, and the rest of the nodes apply the parameter γ_2. In the neural network, the node features should be more focused on the aggregation of the features of the neighboring workflow nodes, thus defining the relation $\gamma_1 > \gamma_2$.

Next, the first K neighbors of each node are sampled, and each row in the adjacency matrix is computed, keeping only the K terms with the largest weights and setting the other terms to zero, thus obtaining a sparse matrix. Finally, a normalization operation is performed on the adjacency matrix, and the graph structure is constructed based on the obtained adjacency matrix.

The neural network architecture diagram is shown in Fig. 2. During the construction of the graph neural network classification model, the problem of a large span of time series in historical data is faced. The residual network (ResNet) is beneficial to capture the long-time dependency of time series [14]. Therefore, in this paper, node feature extraction work is carried out by the residual network. The network consists of a series of residual data blocks. Each block consists of three one-dimensional convolutional layers followed by batch normalization and a ReLU activation function:

$$F_1 = ReLU(BN(Conv1d(X))) \tag{11}$$

$$F_2 = ReLU(BN(Conv1d(F_1))) \tag{12}$$

$$F_3 = ReLU(BN(Conv1d(F_2))) \tag{13}$$

$$F_{output} = ReLU(F_3 + X) \tag{14}$$

where Conv1d denotes one-dimensional convolution, BN denotes batch normalization, ReLU denotes the ReLU activation function, and F_{output} is the output of the residual network.

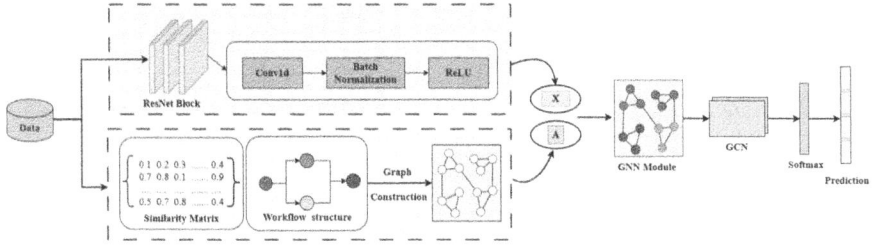

Fig. 2. Graph Neural Network Architecture.

The residual network processes the feature vector of the time series represented by each node, and the output of the residual network is used as the attribute information matrix $\widetilde{X} \in R^{N*M}$ of the graph, where N is the number of nodes, and M is the dimension of the feature vector. According to the attribute feature matrix and adjacency matrix, the final structure of the constructed graph is expressed as $G = (A, \widetilde{X})$, $A \in R^{N*N}$, $\widetilde{X} \in R^{N*M}$. Considering that there are usually some local features in the load time series, such as bursts, periodic fluctuations, etc., the convolutional layer can effectively capture these local features and, therefore, construct the graph convolutional neural network. Construct a two-layer GCN convolutional neural network. The GCN layer performs feature aggregation on neighboring nodes, where W is the trainable parameter and Z is the output of the GCN layer.

$$Z = A\widetilde{X}W \quad (15)$$

The classification is accomplished using ReLU and Softmax activation function:

$$Z = f(\widetilde{X}, A) = softmax(AReLU(A\widetilde{X}W^{(0)})W^{(1)}) \quad (16)$$

Finally, the cross entropy loss function is applied to the labeled nodes. The final output of the neural network is (p_1, p_2), which satisfies $p_1 + p_2 = 1$, denoted as the probability that the function node is deployed in serverful deployment mode and serverless deployment mode, respectively. When $p_1 > 0.5$, the microservice component favors the serverful deployment mode. When $p_2 > 0.5$, the microservice component favors serverless deployment mode.

4 System Design

The architecture of the heterogeneous runtime microservice application unified orchestration system is shown in Fig. 3, which is mainly divided into three modules: monitoring center, development center, and orchestration center.

The main component of the monitoring center is Prometheus, which is used to monitor the microservice applications in the Kubernetes cluster, collect the historical invocation and resource usage sequences of the microservice applications, and store the collected metrics data in a local time series database.

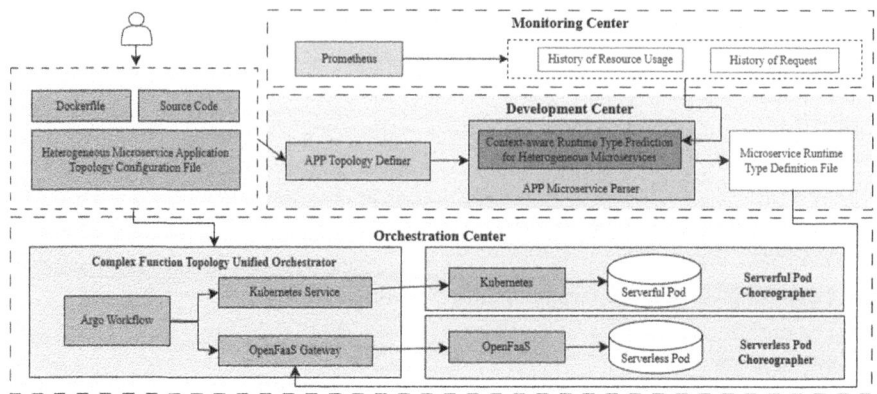

Fig. 3. System Overview.

The development center consists of an APP topology definer and APP microservice parser, which processes the heterogeneous microservice application topology configuration file, source code, and container image configuration file provided by the user, analyzes the resource sensitivity of each microservice by applying the microservice resource sensitivity type analysis method, and provides the results to the APP microservice parser, which obtains the corresponding monitoring data from the monitoring center, applies the heterogeneous microservice runtime type precision method to analyze the runtime types and generate the corresponding type definition files.

The orchestration center completes the unified construction of heterogeneous runtimes for microservice applications with complex topologies. On the deployment of a single microservice node, the serverless pod orchestrator and the serverful pod orchestrator obtain the microservice runtime type definition file and the APP topology definer configuration file from the development center, automatically complete the related user-imperceptible rewriting work, and complete the corresponding pods' creation on OpenFaaS and Kubernetes. Further, on microservice application construction, the Argo Workflow engine builds a complex topology unified orchestrator, invokes OpenFaaS Gateway and Kubernetes Service, connects serverless pods and serverful pods, and completes the workflow orchestration according to the microservice application profiles.

5 Evaluation

5.1 Experimental Setup

In this paper, we build a Kubernetes V1.27.0 cluster with one master node and two worker nodes, each with Linux Centos7 Kernel 3.10.0 64bit operating system, Xeon 2.1 GHz CPU (8 cores), and 16 GB RAM. OpenFaaS was deployed as serverless runtime support in a Kubernetes cluster. Prometheus and Grafana are

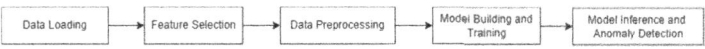

Fig. 4. Workflow structure for experimental objects.

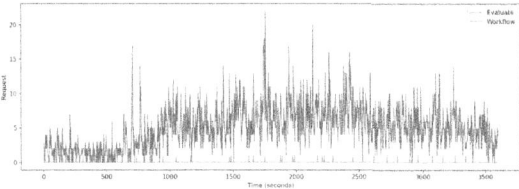

Fig. 5. Experimental workload trend over time.

installed as monitoring tools. Resource configuration of each function is determined by the resource needs of average request workloads.

We have selected a neural network workflow for neural network-based traffic anomaly detection [7] for our experiments, and the main workflow structure is shown in Fig. 4. Considering the practical situation, the first four steps of the workflow consist of an online incremental training process, which periodically performs model updating, and thus the load is relatively discrete; the last step is an online inference process of the model, which continuously performs traffic load anomaly detection, and thus the load is relatively continuous.

We constructed two copies of load data of one hour in length based on the Azure Function Trace 2019 real load dataset [14], which are the offline training flow load and the online inference load. As shown in Fig. 5, each load data is an array of integers of 1200, representing the number of requests for a single function instance every 3 s in an hour.

5.2 Comparative Experimentation and Evaluation of Heterogeneous Workflow Microservice Applications

In this set of experiments, we validate the load characteristics of the components of cloud-based applications using fully serverful mode deployment, fully serverless mode deployment, and hybrid mode deployment, respectively, to prove that the deployment using different computing modes is more advantageous in terms of performance-cost issues. The experimental results are shown in Fig. 6(a)(b).

From Fig. 6(a), it can be seen that the workflow performance of the hybrid deployment model and the serverful deployment model outperforms that of the serverless deployment model, and both the hybrid deployment model and the serverful deployment model satisfy the service level objective (4000 ms). In the serverless deployment model, the pod responds to requests with a cold-start delay, whereas in the serverful deployment model, the pod is always running and responds to requests in a timely manner. Therefore, the serverful deployment mode is better than the serverless deployment mode in terms of response time and requests per second (RPS). For the hybrid deployment mode, only the last

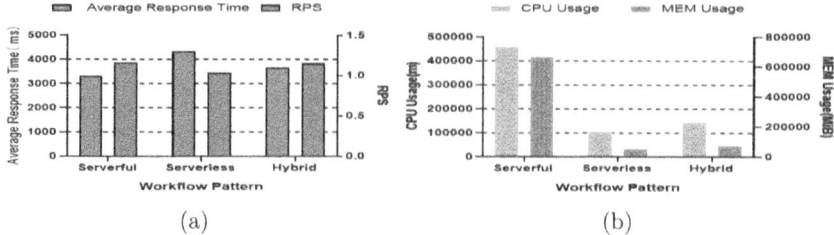

Fig. 6. (a): Comparison of application performance under different workflow deployment models. (b): Comparison of resource consumption under different workflow deployment models.

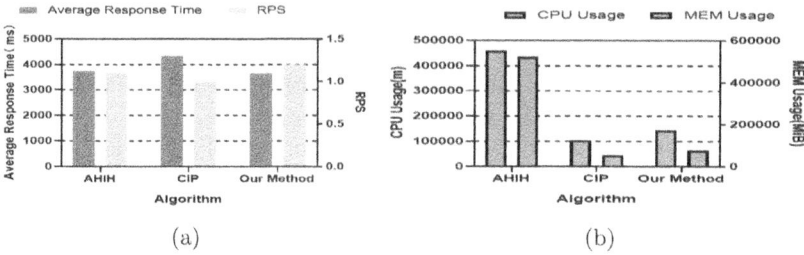

Fig. 7. (a): Comparison of workflow performance with different algorithms. (b): Comparison of workflow resource consumption under different algorithms.

workflow node with continuous request load is deployed with serverful mode, which can process the request in time, while the other nodes are deployed with a serverless deployment mode, and the performance of the application on the other nodes is lower than that of the serverless deployment mode due to the effect of the slight cold-start time but still meets the service level objective.

Figure 6(b) shows that in the serverful deployment mode, the CPU and memory (MEM) resource consumption is much higher than that in the serverless deployment mode and the hybrid deployment mode. In serverful deployment mode, all workflow pods are running, leading to a significant amount of idle resource consumption and a serious waste of resources.

Therefore in conclusion, in the case that both the hybrid deployment mode and the fully serverful deployment mode satisfy the service level objective, the hybrid deployment mode is less in terms of resource consumption. Hybrid deployment model is more advantageous in solving the performance-cost problem.

5.3 Comparative Experiments and Evaluation of Heterogeneous Microservice Runtime Type Precision Analysis Methods

To verify the superiority of our precise analysis method for heterogeneous microservice runtime types over recent approaches in addressing the performance-cost problem, we compare our algorithm with CIP [10] and AHIH [9] using the aforementioned experimental configurations. These methods differ in load analysis. CIP assesses deployment costs based on cost modeling and establishes request rate thresholds for categorized deployment models. AHIH categorizes active and inactive times to determine deployment modes based on load size. In contrast, our method accurately classifies deployment modes based on load fluctuation, distinguishing between streaming and discrete loads.

Figure 7(a) shows that the workflow deployment model under the CIP algorithm performs poorly and fails to meet the service level objective, while the AHIH algorithm and the algorithm in this paper meet the service level objective. Under the CIP algorithm, the load on the last node of the workflow is continuous, but the average load rate does not reach the load request rate threshold, so it is deployed in a serverless mode and performs poorly in application performance. The AHIH algorithm is similar to this paper's algorithm in terms of application performance, and both of them satisfy the service level objective.

From Fig. 7(b), it can be seen that compared with the AHIH algorithm, the algorithm in this paper consumes fewer resources and performs close to the workflow deployment mode under the CIP algorithm in terms of cost consumption. The AHIH algorithm defines the active time and inactive time by the size of the average request rate and adopts the serverful deployment mode in the active time, which has the case that the average request is high in some intervals but discrete, which results in a large amount of wasted idle resource consumption.

Therefore, in the case that both the AHIH algorithm and the workflow deployment model under this paper's algorithm satisfy the service level objective, the workflow deployment model under this paper's algorithm consumes fewer resources and is more advantageous in solving the performance-cost problem.

6 Conclusion

In this paper, we implement a complex microservice application execution need modeling characterization method and context-aware runtime type prediction method for heterogeneous microservices to solve the current problems of heterogeneous execution needs of complex microservice applications and the difficulty of determining the runtime types. Based on the above methods, this paper constructs a unified orchestration system for heterogeneous runtime microservice applications, which supports user-independent automated orchestration of heterogeneous runtime microservice applications. Finally, through experiments on real clusters, we demonstrate the advantages of the precise analysis method of microservice runtime types over other classification methods.

Acknowledgments. This work is partially supported by the National Key Research and Development Program of China under Grant 2022YFB4501704 and partially supported by the National Natural Science Foundation of China under Grant 62372330.

References

1. Albuquerque Jr, L.F., Ferraz, F.S., Oliveira, R., Galdino, S.: Function-as-a-service x platform-as-a-service: Towards a comparative study on faas and paas. In: ICSEA, pp. 206–212 (2017)
2. Amazon Web Services: Aws lambda (2024). https://aws.amazon.com/lambda/
3. Argo: Argo workflows (2024). https://argoproj.github.io/workflows/
4. Baldini, I., et al.: Serverless computing: Current trends and open problems. Research advances in cloud computing, pp. 1–20 (2017)
5. Burckhardt, S., Chandramouli, B., Gillum, C., Justo, D., Kallas, K., McMahon, C., Meiklejohn, C.S., Zhu, X.: Netherite: efficient execution of serverless workflows. Proc. VLDB Endowment **15**(8), 1591–1604 (2022)
6. Gunasekaran, J.R., Thinakaran, P., Kandemir, M.T., Urgaonkar, B., Kesidis, G., Das, C.: Spock: exploiting serverless functions for slo and cost aware resource procurement in public cloud. In: 2019 IEEE 12th International Conference on Cloud Computing (CLOUD), pp. 199–208. IEEE (2019)
7. KlausMichael0: Taffic_anomaly_detection_based_on_neural_network. https://github.com/KlausMichael0/Taffic_Anomaly_Detection_based_on_Neural_Network (2020)
8. Muda, L., Begam, M., Elamvazuthi, I.: Voice recognition algorithms using mel frequency cepstral coefficient (mfcc) and dynamic time warping (dtw) techniques. arXiv preprint arXiv:1003.4083 (2010)
9. Nday, B.A., Kusuma, G.P., Fredyan, R.: Serverless utilization in microservice e-learning platform. Procedia Comput. Sci. **216**, 204–212 (2023)
10. Raza, A., Zhang, Z., Akhtar, N., Isahagian, V., Matta, I.: Libra: an economical hybrid approach for cloud applications with strict slas. In: 2021 IEEE International Conference on Cloud Engineering (IC2E), pp. 136–146. IEEE (2021)
11. Reuter, A., Back, T., Andrikopoulos, V.: Cost efficiency under mixed serverless and serverful deployments. In: 2020 46th Euromicro Conference on Software Engineering and Advanced Applications (SEAA), pp. 242–245. IEEE (2020)
12. Rosario, V.M.D., Camacho, T.A.S., Napoli, O.O., Borin, E.: Fast and low-cost search for efficient cloud configurations for hpc workloads. arXiv preprint arXiv:2006.15481 (2020)
13. Savi, M., Banfi, A., Tundo, A., Ciavotta, M.: Serverless computing for nfv: Is it worth it? a performance comparison analysis. In: 2022 IEEE International Conference on Pervasive Computing and Communications Workshops and other Affiliated Events (PerCom Workshops), pp. 680–685. IEEE (2022)
14. Shahrad, M., Fonseca, R., Goiri, I., Chaudhry, G., Batum, P., Cooke, J., Laureano, E., Tresness, C., Russinovich, M., Bianchini, R.: Serverless in the wild: Characterizing and optimizing the serverless workload at a large cloud provider. In: 2020 USENIX annual technical conference (USENIX ATC 20), pp. 205–218 (2020)
15. Son, M., Mohanty, S., Gunasekaran, J.R., Jain, A., Kandemir, M.T., Kesidis, G., Urgaonkar, B.: Splice: an automated framework for cost-and performance-aware blending of cloud services. In: 2022 22nd IEEE International Symposium on Cluster, Cloud and Internet Computing (CCGrid), pp. 119–128. IEEE (2022)
16. Yussupov, V., Soldani, J., Breitenbücher, U., Leymann, F.: Standards-based modeling and deployment of serverless function orchestrations using bpmn and tosca. Softw. Practice Exp. **52**(6), 1454–1495 (2022)

Makespan Minimization for Scheduling on Heterogeneous Platforms with Precedence Constraints

Vincent Fagnon[iD], Giorgio Lucarelli[✉][iD], and Christophe Rapine[iD]

LCOMS, Université de Lorraine, Metz, France
{vincent.fagnon,giorgio.lucarelli,christophe.rapine}@univ-lorraine.fr

Abstract. Taking a good decision about the assignment of each job becomes crucial in the era of hybrid and heterogeneous computing systems, such as personal machines equipped with CPUs and GPUs, or HPC platforms composed of multiple generations of processors. In this study, we focus on the fundamental makespan minimization problem of scheduling jobs subject to precedence constraints on a platform composed of q different families of machines. Each family is constituted of identical parallel machines. The processing time of a job depends on the family where it is allocated. We propose an algorithm that guarantees an approximation ratio of $q+1+2\sqrt{q-1}$, which improves upon the existing upper bound of $q(q+1)$. In particular, this algorithm achieves a ratio of 5 in the special case of a machine composed only of CPUs and GPUs. This specific scenario with $q = 2$ families of machines has been widely studied by the scientific community in recent years. The best known lower and upper bounds known so far were 3 and 5.83, respectively.

Keywords: approximation algorithms · scheduling · precedence constraint · heterogeneous platforms · non-preemptive

1 Introduction

The enhanced heterogeneity of nowadays systems has as a consequence an increase of their complexity at different levels. In particular, choosing the appropriate machine type to allocate a job is a crucial step of scheduling algorithms. This decision does not only depend on the characteristics of the job but also on the actual load and its distribution on the different machines of the platform.

In this paper, we consider a platform composed of q types of machines. The machines of the same type are identical. In other words, the execution of a job takes the same time on any machine of the same type. However, no assumptions are made regarding the processing times of a job on any two different types of machines; for instance, a job may require less time on a CPU than on a GPU, while for another job a GPU is faster than a CPU. The jobs have to be executed non-preemptively, and their execution should respect some given precedence relations among them. The objective is to find a schedule of minimum makespan, that is, a schedule in which the machine that finishes last should complete its execution as early as possible.

Our goal is to provide algorithms with worst-case performance guarantees for this problem. Specifically, we are interested in the widely studied metric of approximation ratio: the worst-case ratio of the objective value of the solution obtained by our algorithm over the objective value of an optimal solution. In this direction, when dealing with the makespan minimization objective, it is known that two notions play an important role on analyzing the performance of an algorithm: the total *load* and the *critical path* [9]. The difficulty in heterogeneous scheduling is that these quantities depend on the chosen allocation for the jobs.

For this reason, most of the algorithms proposed in the literature are composed of two distinct phases: the allocation and the scheduling phases. In the first phase, a good allocation decision is to be taken for each job concerning the type of machines to use for its execution. This decision is based on an estimation of the final makespan, usually expressed in terms of lower bounds on the optimal solution. For instance, Kedad-Sidhoum et al. [11] proposed to use an integer linear program for the case where $q = 2$, corresponding to a platform composed of a set of identical CPUs and a set of identical GPUs. This integer linear program, as well as its natural generalization for q types of machines, are used in several papers (see for example [1,8]). The allocation decision is taken by rounding the optimal fractional solution of the corresponding linear relaxation. In the second phase, the scheduling algorithm should respect the allocation already decided and assign each job to a specific machine as well as to a specific time interval on this machine. The overlapping of the execution intervals of two different jobs assigned on the same machine is not allowed. The classical List Scheduling algorithm proposed by Graham is typically used in this phase.

Our Contribution. We propose to revisit the allocation phase applied in [1,8,11], by using the solution of the linear programming relaxation in a slightly different way. Instead of performing a rounding with respect to the fractional values returned by the linear program, we calculate an average processing time for each job based on these values. Then, this average processing time is used to discard the machine types which need significantly more time to execute the job. Finally, the allocation is decided among the remaining machine types without regarding the fractional values of the linear program, but only the contribution of the job to the load of each type. The basic ingredients of this idea can be also found in [6], where the platform is composed of q types of machines and each type is characterized by a speed. Hence, the execution time of a job is *related* to the allocated machine type, in contrast to our problem where it is *unrelated*.

Based on this method, we significantly improve the best known approximation ratio for our problem from a quadratic to a linear function with respect to the number q of different types of machines. Specifically, we move from the $q(q+1)$-approximation ratio proposed in [1] to a ratio $(q + 1 + 2\sqrt{q-1})$. In the case where $q = 2$, this result leads to a 5-approximation algorithm, improving upon the ratio of 5.83 shown in [8]. Note that closing the approximability gap for this special case is an interesting open question in scheduling community (see [14]), while the actual known lower bound is 3 [8]. Finally, we further refine our analysis for the special case of $q = 2$ in order to get better results, expressed as a function of the ratio of the number of machines of the two types.

2 Related Work

The scheduling problem of minimizing the makespan on q types of identical machines subject to precedence constraints generalizes the classical $P \mid prec \mid C_{\max}$ problem of scheduling on m identical machines, which corresponds to the case where $q = 1$. For the latter problem, the approximability question is closed since the approximation ratio of 2 achieved by the greedy List Scheduling algorithm [10] matches the known conditional lower bound based on a stronger version of the Unique Game Conjecture [2,16]. Moreover, our problem is a special case of the $R \mid prec \mid C_{\max}$ problem, where the platform is composed of m unrelated (completely heterogeneous) machines. For this general problem, it is known that executing each job to its faster machine leads to a simple $(m+1)$-approximation algorithm. However, no non-trivial approximation algorithms are known, except for some special cases concerning the precedence relations among the jobs (see for example [12]).

Chudak and Shmoys [6] presented an $O(\log m)$-approximation algorithm for the $Q \mid prec \mid C_{\max}$ problem where the platform is composed of m related machines. That is, the execution time of a job on a machine depends on the speed of this machine. The proposed algorithm creates $\log m$ groups of machines such that all machines belonging to the same group run at the same speed, by loosing a constant factor. Then, they deal with the resulting intermediate problem of scheduling on speed-related groups of identical machines. Shi Li [13] proposed an algorithm improving the approximation ratio for the problem to $O(\log m / \log \log m)$. Moreover, Bazzi and Norouzi-Fard proved that a constant factor approximation algorithm cannot exist assuming the hardness of an optimization problem on k-partite graphs [3]. In general, $Q \mid prec \mid C_{\max}$ is neither a special case nor a more general case comparing to our problem. However, the intermediate problem considered in [6] is a special case, since we do not consider speed relations among the types of the machines.

The problem of scheduling on q types of machines subject to precedence constraints has been studied in few contexts; see for example the intermediate problem in [6] for scheduling on q speed-related types of identical machines, and [15] for scheduling moldable jobs. For our problem of scheduling on q (unrelated) types of identical machines, it is known that widely popular heuristics like HEFT [17], cannot lead to constant factor approximation ratios [1]. Amaris et al. [1] proposed a $q(q+1)$-approximation algorithm.

In the case where $q = 2$, Kedad-Sidhoum et al. [11] have presented a 6-approximation algorithm based on the two-phases approach. In [8], this result that has been improved to $3 + 2\sqrt{2} = 5.83$, while a lower bound of 3 subject to a version of the Unique Game Conjecture has been also proposed. Eyraud-Dubois and Kumar [7] have proposed an adaptation of the List Scheduling algorithm, called HeteroPrio, in which the jobs are considered in the order of their acceleration factors. This algorithm achieves an approximation ratio of $2 + \frac{m_1}{m_2}$, where m_1 and m_2 are the numbers of the machines of the two types, assuming that $m_1 \geq m_2$. If the jobs arrive online in an order respecting the precedence relations, a $4\sqrt{m_1/m_2}$-approximation algorithm has been proposed in [1]. This result has been improved to $2\sqrt{m_1/m_2} + 1$ in [5], where a lower bound of $\sqrt{m_1/m_2}$ has been also provided. For a more detailed related work, see the survey in [4].

3 Notations and Preliminaries

We consider a set of n jobs $\mathcal{J}$ that have to be scheduled on a platform composed of q types of identical machines. Let $\mathcal{M}$ be the set of the different machine types of the platform and m_k be the number of machines of type $k \in \mathcal{M}$. By convention, we number the types of machines in non-increasing order of their sizes, i.e., $m_1 \geq m_2 \geq \ldots \geq m_q$. The execution of a job $j \in \mathcal{J}$ on any machine of type $k \in \mathcal{M}$ takes a time p_{jk}.

A Directed Acyclic Graph $G = (V, E)$ describes precedence relations among the jobs. More specifically, each vertex of this graph corresponds to a job, while an arc $(i, j) \in E$ imposes that the execution of the job j cannot start before the completion of the job i. By slightly abusing the notation, we write $V = \mathcal{J}$.

The objective is to find a non-preemptive schedule of the jobs to the platform which respects the imposed precedence constraints, such that the completion time of the latest job is minimized. That is, we search for a schedule of minimal makespan, $C_{\max}$.

We introduce here some additional notations which are used henceforth in this paper. An allocation of the jobs to the platform can be represented by a binary vector $x = \{x_{jk}\}$, where $x_{jk} = 1$ indicates that job $j \in \mathcal{J}$ is allocated on a machine of type $k \in \mathcal{M}$. Given such an allocation x, we define by

$$W_k(x) = \sum_{j \in \mathcal{J}} p_{jk} x_{jk}$$

the workload assigned to type k and by $W(x)$ the total workload corresponding to this allocation:

$$W(x) = \sum_{k \in \mathcal{M}} W_k(x) = \sum_{k \in \mathcal{M}} \sum_{j \in \mathcal{J}} p_{jk} x_{jk}$$

Graham [10] proposed two widely used lower bounds for the case where the platform is composed of parallel identical machines: the average load of the platform and the critical path of the precedence graph. These bounds can be naturally generalized for our problem. However, there are two important differences. First, we are interested in the average load per type of machines and not for the whole platform. Second, in the case of identical machines, the values of these lower bounds can be computed directly from the instance. In our problem, their values depend on the allocation. Hence, given an allocation x, we consider:

- the *average load* of each type $k \in \mathcal{M}$, defined as $\frac{W_k(x)}{m_k}$, and
- the *critical path*, $CP(x)$, of the precedence graph G, which corresponds to the longest path of G, that is the path for which the sum of processing times (based on the allocation x) of the jobs is maximum.

Using these notation, the bound of Graham can be generalized for heterogeneous platforms, see [1,6]. The makespan of any algorithm following the List Scheduling policy for a fixed allocation x verifies:

$$C_{max} \leq \sum_{k \in \mathcal{M}} \frac{W_k(x)}{m_k} + CP(x) \qquad (1)$$

4 The Algorithm

In this section, we present an approximation algorithm following the two-phases approach used in [1,6,8,11], which consists in deciding first the allocation of each job to a type of machines, and then a schedule of the jobs respecting the allocation. For the sake of completeness, we present all the ingredients of our algorithm, although most of them can be found in the previously mentioned works.

Phase 1: Allocation of the Jobs to the Types of Machine. The allocation phase is based on solving the following linear program (P):

$$\text{minimize } z$$

$$\frac{1}{m_k} \sum_{j \in \mathcal{J}} p_{jk} x_{jk} \leq z \qquad \forall k \in \mathcal{M} \qquad (2)$$

$$C_j \leq z \qquad \forall j \in \mathcal{J} \qquad (3)$$

$$C_i + \sum_{k \in \mathcal{M}} p_{jk} x_{jk} \leq C_j \qquad \forall (i,j) \in E \qquad (4)$$

$$\sum_{k \in \mathcal{M}} x_{jk} = 1 \qquad \forall j \in \mathcal{J} \qquad (5)$$

$$C_j \geq 0, \ x_{jk} \geq 0 \qquad \forall j \in \mathcal{J}, \forall k \in \mathcal{M} \qquad (6)$$

A solution of the LP is a fractional allocation to the types of machines. Specifically, the variable x_{jk} represents the fraction of job j allocated to machine type k. The variable C_j represents the longest path in the precedence graph between the root and the job j (for simplicity, we introduce a fictive job 0 with null processing time that precedes all the other jobs). More precisely, Constraint (4) enforces that a job j cannot be completed before the latest completion time of its predecessors plus its processing time in the allocation. Notice that a fractional allocation allows to distribute the processing of a job onto several platforms, but these processing cannot be performed in parallel. The objective of the LP is to minimize the variable z, which must be greater than the critical path of the graph (Constraint (4)) and the average load of any machine (Constraint (2)). Clearly, the optimal value of z provides a lower bound of the optimal schedule.

Restricting the Allocation to the Efficient Type of Machines. Let $\bar{x}$ be the (fractional) optimal solution of the linear program (P). We denote by $\bar{p}_j$ the *average processing time* of the job $j \in \mathcal{J}$ in this fractional allocation:

$$\bar{p}_j = \sum_{k \in \mathcal{M}} p_{jk} \bar{x}_{jk}$$

For each job j, we prohibit to allocate it on types where its processing time is too large relatively to $\bar{p}_j$. For a given parameter λ to be chosen, a type k is *eligible* if p_{jk} does not exceed $\bar{p}_j$ by a factor more than λ. Let $\mathcal{E}_j$ be the set of eligible types for job j:

$$\mathcal{E}_j = \{k \in \mathcal{M} \mid p_{jk} \leq \lambda \bar{p}_j\}$$

Notice that choosing $\lambda \geq 1$ guarantees that the set $\mathcal{E}_j$ is not empty, since it contains at least the fastest type of machine for the job.

Finding a Feasible Allocation on the Eligible Types. To find a feasible allocation restricted to the eligible types, we solve to optimality the following integer linear program (IP'). Its objective is to minimize the average load of the types of machine, under the constraint that each job is allocated to one of its eligible types.

$$\min f(x) = \sum_{k \in \mathcal{M}} \frac{W_k(x)}{m_k}$$

$$\sum_{k \in \mathcal{E}_j} x_{jk} = 1 \qquad \forall j \in \mathcal{J}$$

$$x_{jk} \in \{0, 1\} \qquad \forall j \in \mathcal{J}, k \in \mathcal{M}$$

As the objective function can be rewritten as $f(x) = \sum_{j \in \mathcal{J}} \sum_{k \in \mathcal{M}} \frac{p_{jk}}{m_k} x_{jk}$, the optimal solution x^a simply consists in assigning each job j to the eligible type minimizing the value p_{jk}/m_k (breaking ties arbitrarily). Then, we set:

$$x_{jk}^a = \begin{cases} 1 & \text{if } k = \arg\min_{\ell \in \mathcal{E}_j} \{\frac{p_{j\ell}}{m_\ell}\} \\ 0 & \text{otherwise} \end{cases}$$

Phase 2: Scheduling. Given the feasible allocation x^a obtained, a classical List Scheduling algorithm is applied respecting the allocation x^a for the jobs and the precedence constraints. Specifically, a job is considered to be *ready* if all of its predecessors are already completed. List Scheduling assigns in an iterative way a ready job to the earliest available machine respecting its allocation.

Algorithm 1 summarizes the above procedure. Note that the input of the algorithm is an instance of our problem as well as the parameter λ.

Algorithm 1.

Input: An instance of the problem $(\mathcal{J}, \mathcal{M}, G)$ and a parameter $\lambda \geq 1$.
Output: A non-preemptive schedule for the jobs in $\mathcal{J}$ on the platform $\mathcal{M}$ respecting the precedence constraints described by the graph G.

1: Find an optimal solution for the linear program (P). Let $\bar{x}$ and $\bar{z}$ be the fractional allocation and the objective value, respectively.
2: **for** each job $j \in \mathcal{J}$ **do**
3: $\quad \bar{p}_j \leftarrow \sum_{k \in \mathcal{M}} p_{jk} \bar{x}_{jk}$
4: $\quad \mathcal{E}_j \leftarrow \{\ell \in \mathcal{M} \mid p_{j\ell} \leq \lambda \bar{p}_j\}$
5: $\quad x^a_{jk} \leftarrow \begin{cases} 1 & \text{if } k = arg\,min_{\ell \in \mathcal{E}_j} \{\frac{p_{j\ell}}{m_\ell}\} \\ 0 & \text{otherwise} \end{cases}$
6: Use the List Scheduling algorithm in order to create a schedule, respecting the allocation $x^a = \{x^a_{jk}\}$.

5 Performance Guarantee of the Algorithm

In this section, we analyze the performance of the algorithm depending on the value of the parameter λ used to define the eligible types. Recall that the algorithm computes a feasible allocation x^a restricted to the eligible types of machine and then schedules the jobs using the List Scheduling algorithm. Hence, Eq. (1) ensures that the makespan $C^a_{\max}$ of the schedule delivered by the algorithm is bounded by the average load on the types plus the critical path:

$$C^a_{\max} \leq \sum_{k \in \mathcal{M}} \frac{W_k(x^a)}{m_k} + \text{CP}(x^a) \tag{7}$$

We bound the different terms of this inequality relatively to $\bar{z}$, the optimum objective value of the linear program (P), which is a lower bound of the optimum value. Recall that, for each job j, based on its average processing time $\bar{p}_j$ and the value of the parameter λ, we discard some types of machines to restrict the allocation to the eligible types. This step guarantees that the resulting critical path is bounded by $\lambda \bar{z}$:

Lemma 1. *For any allocation x restricted to the eligible types of machine of the jobs, we have:*

$$CP(x) \leq \lambda \ CP(\bar{x}) \leq \lambda \bar{z}$$

Proof. By definition, the machine k to which job i is assigned verifies $p_{jk} \leq \lambda \bar{p}_j$. Hence, the length of any path in the allocation x is at most multiplied by λ compared to the allocation $\bar{x}$. It results in particular that $\text{CP}(x) \leq \lambda \text{CP}(\bar{x})$. Constraint (4) of the LP ensures that $\bar{z}$ is greater than or equal to $\text{CP}(\bar{x})$, which allows to conclude. □

We say that a type is *discarded* for job j if it is not an eligible type. While Lemma 1 shows that restricting the allocations to the eligible types preserves the critical path, discarding some types may result in a dramatic unbalance of the loads. We show in the following that it is not the case.

Lemma 2. *For any job $j \in \mathcal{J}$, the fraction of j processed on the discarded types according to the allocation x is at most $1/\lambda$:*

$$\sum_{k \notin \mathcal{E}_j} \bar{x}_{jk} < \frac{1}{\lambda}$$

Proof. By definition, we have:

$$\bar{p}_j = \sum_{k \in \mathcal{M}} p_{jk} \bar{x}_{jk} = \sum_{k \in \mathcal{E}_j} p_{jk} \bar{x}_{jk} + \sum_{k \notin \mathcal{E}_j} p_{jk} \bar{x}_{jk} \geq \sum_{k \notin \mathcal{E}_j} p_{jk} \bar{x}_{jk}$$

As a type k is discarded for the job j only if $p_{jk} > \lambda \bar{p}_j$, we obtain directly:

$$\bar{p}_j > \sum_{k \notin \mathcal{E}_j} (\lambda \bar{p}_j) \bar{x}_{jk} = \left(\lambda \sum_{k \notin \mathcal{E}_j} \bar{x}_{jk} \right) \bar{p}_j$$

The result follows. □

We now exhibit a particular (fractional) allocation $\tilde{x}$ on the eligible types. The purpose of $\tilde{x}$ is to show that restricting an allocation to the eligible types do not prevent from obtaining a load balancing between the types almost as good as in allocation $\bar{x}$. Basically, we redistribute the work allocated on the discarded types in $\bar{x}$ towards the eligible types, in a proportional way with respect to the fraction of the job performed on each eligible type. Formally, we define

$$\tilde{x}_{jk} = \begin{cases} \frac{1}{\sum_{\ell \in \mathcal{E}_j} \bar{x}_{j\ell}} \bar{x}_{jk} & \text{if type } k \text{ is eligible} \\ 0 & \text{if type } k \text{ is discarded} \end{cases}$$

Clearly, $\tilde{x}$ defines a (fractional) allocation of the jobs, that is, for each job j the sum of its fractions $\tilde{x}_{jk}$ is equal to 1. Due to Lemma 2, we have for any value of $\lambda > 1$:

$$\tilde{x}_{jk} \leq \frac{\lambda}{\lambda - 1} \bar{x}_{jk} \quad \forall j \in \mathcal{J}, \; k \in \mathcal{M} \tag{8}$$

As a consequence, the work allocated to an eligible type of platform in $\tilde{x}$ cannot exceed the work allocated in $\bar{x}$ by more than a factor of $\lambda/(\lambda - 1)$, and hence the following lemma holds.

Lemma 3. *For any type k of machines, we have $W_k(\tilde{x}) \leq \frac{\lambda}{\lambda-1} W_k(\bar{x})$.*

One important thing to notice is that, if the work allocated to each platform can increase by at most a factor of $\lambda/(\lambda - 1)$ in the reallocation, the total work can only decrease. In other words, the reallocation from the discarded types does decrease the total workload, at the expense of increasing some individual workloads. We state this fact in the following lemma, where $W(x)$ denotes the total amount of work to process in an allocation x. This observation is crucial to our analysis since it allows us to improve upon the intermediate result given in [6].

Lemma 4. *We have $W(\tilde{x}) \leq W(\bar{x})$.*

Proof. Every fraction of work processed initially on a discarded machine in $\bar{x}$ is reallocated to an eligible machine in the allocation $\tilde{x}$. By definition, for any job $j \in \mathcal{J}$, its processing time on an eligible type is lower than its processing time on a discarded type. Hence its average processing time $\tilde{p}_j = \sum_{k \in \mathcal{M}} p_{jk} \tilde{x}_{jk}$ is lower than or equal to its average processing time $\bar{p}_j$ in $\bar{x}$. □

As a consequence, we have the following lemma bounding the average load of the types of machine in the feasible allocation x^a:

Lemma 5. *The average load in the feasible allocation x^a verifies*

$$\sum_{k \in \mathcal{M}} \frac{W_k(x^a)}{m_k} \leq \left((q-1)\frac{\lambda}{\lambda-1} + 1\right) \bar{z}$$

Proof. Due to Constraint (2) in linear program (P), for any type k of machines we have $W_k(\bar{x})/m_k \leq \bar{z}$. Hence, Lemma 3 asserts that for the fractional allocation $\tilde{x}$ we have

$$\frac{W_k(\tilde{x})}{m_k} \leq \frac{\lambda}{\lambda-1}\bar{z}$$

However, Lemma 4 implies that for at least one type of machines, say ℓ, the work has decreased in the reallocation, that is, $W_\ell(\tilde{x}) \leq W_\ell(\bar{x})$. It results that

$$f(\tilde{x}) = \sum_{k \in \mathcal{M}} \frac{W_k(\tilde{x})}{m_k} \leq (q-1)\frac{\lambda}{\lambda-1}\bar{z} + \bar{z}$$

To conclude the proof, notice that allocation $\tilde{x}$ is a feasible solution of the linear relaxation of (IP'). Clearly, (IP') has the same optimal value as its linear relaxation. Hence, by optimality of x^a, we have $f(x^a) \leq f(\tilde{x})$. The result follows. □

Putting together Lemma 1 and Lemma 5, bounding the critical path and the average load, respectively, Bound (7) on the makespan delivered by the algorithm can be rewritten as:

$$\frac{C_{\max}^a}{\bar{z}} \leq \left(\frac{q-1}{\lambda-1} + 1\right)\lambda + 1 \qquad (9)$$

Since $\bar{z}$ is a lower bound of the optimal makespan, we get a performance guarantee for the algorithm. This guarantee depends on the choice of the parameter λ. By derivation of the expression, the best compromise for λ is to chose

$$\lambda^a = \sqrt{q-1} + 1$$

We obtain the following theorem.

Theorem 1. *The algorithm achieves an approximation ratio of $q+1+2\sqrt{q-1}$.*

Corollary 1. *If the platform is composed of a set of identical CPUs and a set of identical GPUs ($q = 2$), the algorithm achieves an approximation ratio of 5.*

6 A Refined Analysis for Two Types

In this section, we present an in-depth analysis of Algorithm 1 in the case where we have only two types of machines. Recall that, based on the (fractional) optimal solution $\bar{x}$ of the linear program (P), the algorithm restricts the allocations to the eligible types. In the analysis of the algorithm, we have introduced a (fractional) allocation $\tilde{x}$ to show how the work discarded from a type can be reallocated to the eligible types. The key observation when we have only two types is that the load reallocated to a type is necessarily discarded from the other type.

So, we are interested in tracing the load exchanged through the two types. Let Δ_k^+ be the amount of workload reallocated to type k and let Δ_k^- be the amount of workload discarded from type k. Formally, we have

$$\Delta_k^+ = \sum_{j \in \mathcal{J}} p_{jk}(\tilde{x}_{jk} - \bar{x}_{jk})^+$$

$$\Delta_k^- = -\sum_{j \in \mathcal{J}} p_{jk}(\tilde{x}_{jk} - \bar{x}_{jk})^-$$

where u^+ denotes $\max\{0, u\}$ and u^- denotes $\min\{0, u\}$. Notice that both quantities are positive. By definition, for any type k, we have $W_k(\tilde{x}) = W_k(\bar{x}) + (\Delta_k^+ - \Delta_k^-)$. The following Lemma bounds both quantities relatively to the work allocated to type k in allocation $\bar{x}$.

Lemma 6. *For any type of machines $k \in \mathcal{M}$, we have:*

$$\Delta_k^+ \leq \frac{1}{\lambda - 1} W_k(\bar{x}) \quad \text{and} \quad \Delta_k^- \leq W_k(\bar{x})$$

Proof. By definition of Δ_k^+ and using Eq. (8), we have:

$$\Delta_k^+ = \sum_{j \in \mathcal{J}} p_{jk}(\tilde{x}_{jk} - \bar{x}_{jk})^+ \leq \sum_{j \in \mathcal{J}} p_{jk}\left(\frac{\lambda}{\lambda-1}\bar{x}_{jk} - \bar{x}_{jk}\right)^+ = \frac{1}{\lambda-1}W_k(\bar{x})$$

Moreover, as the discarded workload Δ_k^- for type k cannot exceed the workload $W_k(\bar{x})$ initially allocated to it, the second part of the lemma directly holds. □

Let us now focus on two types of machines. The following lemma relates the workload discarded from a type with the workload reallocated to the other type. Basically it states that for each unit of work reallocated to a type, at least λ units of work are discarded from the other type.

Lemma 7. *For a platform composed of two types of machines, we have:*

$$\lambda \Delta_2^+ \leq \Delta_1^- \quad \text{and} \quad \lambda \Delta_1^+ \leq \Delta_2^-$$

Proof. Consider a job $j \in \mathcal{J}$ for which only one type of machines is eligible, and let β be the fraction of the job to be discarded from the other type. Moreover, let a and b be the processing times of j on the reallocated type and on the discarded type, respectively. Hence, the amount of the discarded workload for j is βb, while the amount of the reallocated workload is βa. By the definition of $\bar{p}$ and the fact that we have only two types of machines, it holds that $b > \bar{p} > a$. In addition, by the definition of eligible types in Algorithm 1, we have that $b > \lambda \bar{p}$, and thus $\beta b > \beta \lambda a$. It proves that the amount of work discarded is greater than the amount of work reallocated by a factor λ. By summing up over all jobs with one eligible type, the lemma follows. $\square$

We denote by $\mu = m_1/m_2$ the ratio between the number of machines of the platforms. Recall, that $m_1 \geq m_2$, and thus we have $\mu \geq 1$. Assume that we choose λ such that $1 \leq \lambda \leq \mu$. We can bound the average load of all types in allocation $\tilde{x}$ as follows:

$$\begin{aligned} f(\tilde{x}) &= \frac{W_1(\tilde{x})}{m_1} + \frac{W_2(\tilde{x})}{m_2} = \frac{W_1(\bar{x}) + \Delta_1^+ - \Delta_1^-}{m_1} + \frac{W_2(\bar{x}) + \Delta_2^+ - \Delta_2^-}{m_2} \\ &\leq \frac{W_1(\bar{x})}{m_1} + \frac{W_2(\bar{x})}{m_2} + \frac{1}{m_1}\left(\frac{1}{\lambda}\Delta_2^- - \Delta_1^-\right) + \frac{1}{m_2}\left(\Delta_2^+ - \Delta_2^-\right) \\ &\leq f(\bar{x}) + \left(\frac{1}{\lambda\mu} - 1\right)\frac{\Delta_2^-}{m_2} + \frac{\Delta_2^+}{m_2} - \frac{\Delta_1^-}{m_1} \\ &\leq f(\bar{x}) + \frac{\Delta_2^+}{m_2} - \frac{\Delta_1^-}{m_1} \end{aligned} \qquad (10)$$

where the first inequality follows by Lemmas 4 and 7, while the last one is simply due to the fact that $1 \leq \mu\lambda$. In what follows, we explore two directions by expressing the last quantity in terms of Δ_2^+ or Δ_1^-.

Working with Δ_1^-

By using Lemma 7, we get

$$\frac{\Delta_2^+}{m_2} - \frac{\Delta_1^-}{m_1} \leq \frac{\Delta_1^-}{\lambda m_2} - \frac{\Delta_1^-}{m_1} = \left(\frac{\mu}{\lambda} - 1\right)\frac{\Delta_1^-}{m_1} \leq \left(\frac{\mu}{\lambda} - 1\right)\frac{W_1(\tilde{x})}{m_1}$$

where the last inequality holds by Lemma 6 and the fact that $\lambda \leq \mu$. Hence, by Eq. (10) we obtain

$$f(\tilde{x}) \leq \frac{W_1(\bar{x})}{m_1} + \frac{W_2(\bar{x})}{m_2} + \left(\frac{\mu}{\lambda} - 1\right)\frac{W_1(\tilde{x})}{m_1} \leq \frac{\mu}{\lambda}\frac{W_1(\tilde{x})}{m_1} + \frac{W_2(\tilde{x})}{m_2}$$

Using the last inequality, as well as Lemma 1 and the upper bound (7), we obtain the following performance guarantee:

$$\frac{f(x^a)}{\bar{z}} + \frac{CP(x^a)}{\bar{z}} \leq \frac{f(\tilde{x})}{\bar{z}} + \frac{\lambda CP(\bar{x})}{\bar{z}} \leq \frac{\mu}{\lambda} \frac{(m_1 \bar{z})}{\bar{z} m_1} + \frac{(m_2 \bar{z})}{\bar{z} m_2} + \lambda \frac{CP(\bar{x})}{\bar{z}} \leq \frac{\mu}{\lambda} + 1 + \lambda$$

By derivation of the expression, the best compromise for λ is to choose $\lambda^* = \sqrt{\mu} < \mu$. Then, the following theorem follows.

Theorem 2. *Algorithm 1 achieves an approximation ratio of $1 + 2\sqrt{\mu}$, when the platform is composed of two types of machines.*

Working with Δ_2^+

By using Lemma 7, we get

$$\frac{\Delta_2^+}{m_2} - \frac{\Delta_1^-}{m_1} \leq \frac{\Delta_2^+}{m_2} - \frac{\lambda \Delta_2^+}{m_1} = \frac{\Delta_2^+}{m_2}\left(1 - \frac{\lambda}{\mu}\right) \leq \frac{1}{m_2}\left(1 - \frac{\lambda}{\mu}\right)\frac{W_2(\bar{x})}{\lambda - 1}$$

where the last inequality holds by Lemma 6 and the fact that $\lambda \leq \mu$. Using the same arguments as for Theorem 2, we obtain a performance guarantee of

$$1 + 1 + \frac{\mu - \lambda}{\mu} \cdot \frac{1}{\lambda - 1} + \lambda$$

The best compromise is

$$\lambda^{**} = 1 + \sqrt{\frac{\mu - 1}{\mu}}$$

For this value λ^{**} the guarantee is equal to

$$2 + \frac{1}{\lambda - 1}\frac{\mu - \lambda}{\mu} + \lambda = 3 + \sqrt{\frac{\mu}{\mu - 1}} - \frac{1}{\mu}\sqrt{\frac{\mu}{\mu - 1}} - \frac{1}{\mu} + \sqrt{\frac{\mu - 1}{\mu}}$$

$$= 3 - \frac{1}{\mu} + 2\sqrt{\frac{\mu - 1}{\mu}}$$

However, we must have $\lambda^{**} \leq \mu$, which is true only if $\mu \geq \phi \simeq 1.62$. Notice that the guarantee is asymptotically equal to 5 when μ tends to $+\infty$.

Theorem 3. *For any $\mu > \phi$, Algorithm 1 achieves an approximation ratio of $3 - \frac{1}{\mu} + 2\sqrt{\frac{\mu-1}{\mu}}$, when the platform is composed of two types of machines.*

Figure 1 visualizes and compares the approximation ratios obtained in this section, as well as, the ratio of HeteroPrio [7]. All three ratios depend on the parameter $\mu = \frac{m_1}{m_2}$.

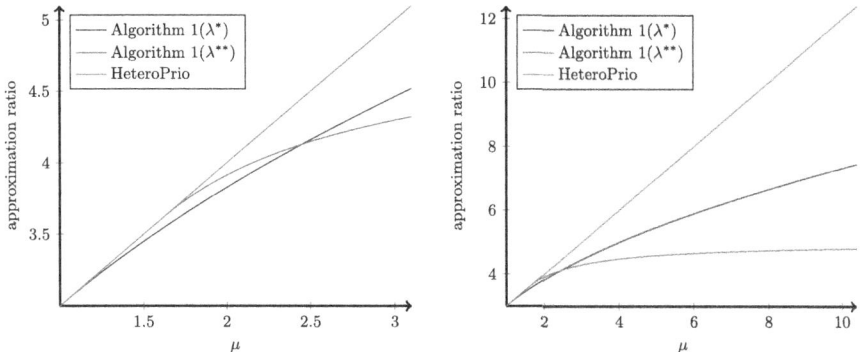

Fig. 1. Comparison of the approximation ratios of HeteroPrio [7], Algorithm 1(λ^*) and Algorithm 1(λ^{**}). On the left, we focus on the domain $[1,3]$ where the three lines intersect, while on the right we observe the asymptotic behavior of the three ratios. Note that Algorithm 1(λ^{**}) dominates the other algorithms for any value $\mu > 2.45$, but it does not work for small values of $\mu < \phi$. Moreover, Algorithm 1(λ^{**}) tends asymptotically to 5, without exceeding it.

7 Conclusions

We have presented new approximation ratios for the problem of scheduling on q types of identical machines subject to precedence constraints. In particular, we have improved the approximation ratio for scheduling on hybrid platforms from 5.83 to 5. It would be interesting to further improve this result in order to close the gap with the known lower bound of 3. For the case of arbitrary q, the gap is even larger, since the best known lower bound comes from the hybrid platforms. Finally, the linear program (P) is only used in order to compute an average processing time for each job guaranteeing a lower bound on the objective of our problem. So, another interesting direction is to obtain these average processing times without passing through the resolution of a linear program.

References

1. Amaris, M., Lucarelli, G., Mommessin, C., Trystram, D.: Generic algorithms for scheduling applications on heterogeneous platforms. Concurr. Comput. Pract. Exp. **31**(15) (2019). https://doi.org/10.1002/CPE.4647
2. Bansal, N., Khot, S.: Optimal long code test with one free bit. In: 50th Annual IEEE Symposium on Foundations of Computer Science, FOCS 2009, October 25–27, 2009, Atlanta, Georgia, USA. pp. 453–462. IEEE Computer Society (2009). https://doi.org/10.1109/FOCS.2009.23
3. Bazzi, A., Norouzi-Fard, A.: Towards tight lower bounds for scheduling problems. In: Bansal, N., Finocchi, I. (eds.) ESA 2015. LNCS, vol. 9294, pp. 118–129. Springer, Heidelberg (2015). https://doi.org/10.1007/978-3-662-48350-3_11
4. Beaumont, O., et al.: Scheduling on two types of resources: a survey. ACM Comput. Surv. **53**(3), 56:1–56:36 (2021). https://doi.org/10.1145/3387110

5. Canon, L., Marchal, L., Simon, B., Vivien, F.: Online scheduling of task graphs on heterogeneous platforms. IEEE Trans. Parallel Distributed Syst. **31**(3), 721–732 (2020). https://doi.org/10.1109/TPDS.2019.2942909
6. Chudak, F.A., Shmoys, D.B.: Approximation algorithms for precedence-constrained scheduling problems on parallel machines that run at different speeds. J. Algorithms **30**(2), 323–343 (1999). https://doi.org/10.1006/JAGM.1998.0987
7. Eyraud-Dubois, L., Kumar, S.: Analysis of a list scheduling algorithm for task graphs on two types of resources. In: 2020 IEEE International Parallel and Distributed Processing Symposium (IPDPS), New Orleans, LA, USA, May 18–22, 2020, pp. 1041–1050. IEEE (2020). https://doi.org/10.1109/IPDPS47924.2020.00110
8. Fagnon, V., Kacem, I., Lucarelli, G., Simon, B.: Scheduling on hybrid platforms: improved approximability window. In: Kohayakawa, Y., Miyazawa, F.K. (eds.) LATIN 2021. LNCS, vol. 12118, pp. 38–49. Springer, Cham (2020). https://doi.org/10.1007/978-3-030-61792-9_4
9. Graham, R.L.: Bounds for certain multiprocessing anomalies. Bell Syst. Technical J. **45**(9), 1563–1581 (1966)
10. Graham, R.L.: Bounds on multiprocessing timing anomalies. J. SIAM Appl. Math. **17**(2), 416–429 (1969)
11. Kedad-Sidhoum, S., Monna, F., Trystram, D.: Scheduling tasks with precedence constraints on hybrid multi-core machines. In: 2015 IEEE International Parallel and Distributed Processing Symposium Workshop (2015)
12. Kumar, V.S.A., Marathe, M.V., Parthasarathy, S., Srinivasan, A.: Scheduling on unrelated machines under tree-like precedence constraints. In: Chekuri, C., Jansen, K., Rolim, J.D.P., Trevisan, L. (eds.) APPROX/RANDOM -2005. LNCS, vol. 3624, pp. 146–157. Springer, Heidelberg (2005). https://doi.org/10.1007/11538462_13
13. Li, S.: Scheduling to minimize total weighted completion time via time-indexed linear programming relaxations. SIAM J. Comput. **49**(4) (2020). https://doi.org/10.1137/17M1156332
14. Megow, N., Shmoys, D.B., Svensson, O.: Scheduling (dagstuhl seminar 20081). Dagstuhl Reports **10**(2), 50–75 (2020). https://doi.org/10.4230/DAGREP.10.2.50
15. Perotin, L., Sun, H., Raghavan, P.: Multi-resource list scheduling of moldable parallel jobs under precedence constraints. In: Sun, X., Shende, S., Kalé, L.V., Chen, Y. (eds.) ICPP 2021: 50th International Conference on Parallel Processing, Lemont, IL, USA, August 9–12, 2021. pp. 23:1–23:10. ACM (2021). https://doi.org/10.1145/3472456.3472487
16. Svensson, O.: Hardness of precedence constrained scheduling on identical machines. SIAM J. Comput. **40**(5), 1258–1274 (2011). https://doi.org/10.1137/100810502
17. Topcuoglu, H., Hariri, S., Wu, M.: Performance-effective and low-complexity task scheduling for heterogeneous computing. IEEE Trans. Parallel Distributed Syst. **13**(3), 260–274 (2002). https://doi.org/10.1109/71.993206

Node Bundle Scheduling: An Ultra-low Latency Traffic Scheduling Algorithm for TAS-Based Time-Sensitive Networks

Qian Yang, Xuyan Jiang, Wei Quan[✉], Rulin Liu, and Zhigang Sun

College of Computer, National University of Defense Technology, Changsha, China
{yangqian_yq,jiangxuyan,w.quan,rl_liu,sunzhigang}@nudt.edu.cn

Abstract. Time Aware Shaper (TAS) and the corresponding traffic scheduling algorithms jointly ensure low-latency and low-jitter data transmission in Time-Sensitive Networking (TSN). However, existing TAS-based traffic scheduling algorithms suffer from either high scheduling failure rate or heavy computation overhead. Such limitations make the algorithms unable to satisfy some TSN applications with harsh scheduling requirements like ultra-low latency and frequent scenarios reconfiguration requirements, such as smart factories in industrial control. Therefore, more efficient traffic scheduling algorithms are required for the specific TSN applications.

To achieve this goal, a Node Bundle Scheduling (NBS) algorithm is proposed in this paper. NBS is based on a TAS traffic scheduling abstraction which greatly simplifies the scheduling problem under the premise of sacrificing a certain amount of bandwidth. To improve the scheduling success rate and optimize the scheduling efficiency, it considers resource allocation in both spatial and temporal dimensions. NBS is compared with typical and state-of-the-art algorithms under different industrial topologies. The results show that the scheduling success rate of NBS is 34.25% higher than that of Tabu Search under low transmission latency scenarios. Compared with the typical SMT solver, NBS can reduce the time overhead by over 99.9% in some complex scheduling scenarios, at a cost of extra 11.86% bandwidth consumption.

Keywords: Time-Sensitive Networking · Traffic Scheduling · Time Aware Shaper · Industrial Control

1 Introduction

Time-Sensitive Networking (TSN) has been proposed recently to meet the increasing demands for transmission latency determinism and reliability in many fields like industrial and automotive [18]. Time Aware Shaper (TAS) is a core mechanism to ensure low latency and low jitter transmission in TSN [9]. It accurately controls data transmission by output queue gating. The opening and closing of network output queues are controlled by pre-planned Gate Control Lists (GCLs) [3]. To generate the required GCLs for TAS, it is required to centrally schedule traffic with deterministic transmission requirements.

To solve the above TAS deterministic traffic scheduling problem, many scheduling algorithms have been proposed. Heuristic algorithms are commonly employed in existing solutions. Yao et al. [17] and Yan et al. [15] propose heuristic algorithms to realize efficient traffic scheduling. Such heuristic algorithms use prior experience to obtain an approximate optimal scheduling scheme, which could suffer from a low scheduling success rate as their primary optimization goal is minimizing time overhead. Another typical scheduling method is the Satisfiability Modulo Theories (SMT) solver. Craciunas et al. [2] and Oliver et al. [12] propose the SMT solver based scheduling strategies that ensure the certainty of end-to-end transmission latency and jitter. However, the SMT solver suffers from heavy computation overhead, such as requiring more than 40 h to schedule 50 flows in a medium-sized topology [12].

The commonly used algorithms mentioned above are not suitable for some special TSN application scenarios with harsh scheduling requirements like ultra-low latency and frequent scenarios reconfiguration requirements, such as smart factories in industrial control. The latency requirements for data transmission in industrial control systems range from 0.2 µs to 0.5 ms with 1 Gbps link speeds [10]. The ultra-low latency requirement makes scheduling more difficult, which could further increase the scheduling failure rate. Besides, smart factories adopt the "assembly-to-order" strategy, which requires more flexible and reconfigurable assembly systems. For efficient smart factories with configurations updated every three to four hours [16], frequent system reconfiguration requires that the traffic scheduling can not be time exhaustive.

In this paper, for TSN scenarios with extremely low latency and frequent scenario reconfiguration requirements, we propose an ultra-low latency traffic scheduling algorithm named Node Bundle Scheduling (NBS). NBS is based on a TAS scheduling abstraction that greatly simplifies the scheduling problem under the condition that a certain bandwidth consumption is acceptable. In addition, NBS introduces the concept of time slot occupancy to combine spatial-temporal allocation to improve both solving efficiency and scheduling success rate.

To comprehensively evaluate the effect of NBS, we conduct experiments in different industrial topologies. The results demonstrate that NBS achieves a 34.25% higher scheduling success rate compared with the state-of-the-art Tabu Search under conditions of low latency requirements. Furthermore, the results show that with an acceptable bandwidth utilization sacrifice of 11.86%, the efficiency of NBS is improved by over 99.9% compared with the typical SMT solver in some scenarios with complex topology and numerous flows.

In conclusion, the main contributions of this paper are:

- We propose a TAS scheduling abstraction, which specifies that the same flow is transmitted from source to destination in the same time slot. This abstraction greatly simplifies the search space and guarantees minimal latency.
- We propose an efficient traffic scheduling algorithm called NBS that adopts Slot-Occupancy-Balance (SOB) Path Planning in the spatial dimension and On-the-fly Policy-Guided (OPG) Slot Searching in the temporal dimension, which greatly improves the scheduling success rate and solving efficiency.

– We test NBS on the FPGA prototype system. The effectiveness of NBS and the correctness of the scheduling results are verified by confirming the consistency between the actual latency of flows and the theoretical expectations.

2 Motivation

2.1 Mechanism of Time Aware Shaper

TAS is one of the important deterministic mechanisms in TSN to ensure low-latency transmission requirements of periodic Time Sensitive (TS) flows. It protects the transmission of TS flows from other flows such as Rate Constrained (RC) flows or Best Effort (BE) flows. The core of TAS is the gating mechanism. As shown in Fig. 1, each output queue of a switch port has a control gate, which has only two states: open and closed. For instance, the Gate Control List status at time slot T07 is "01000000", indicating that only the gate of Queue 6 is open while the gates of other queues are closed. Only when the gate is open, the packet in this queue can be dispatched and sent. The opening and closing of the gate are controlled by the GCLs derived from TAS-based scheduling algorithm.

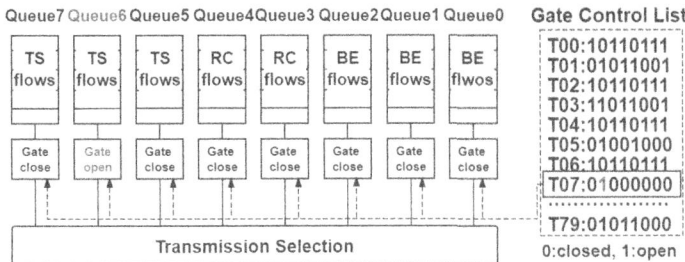

Fig. 1. The gate control mechanism of TAS.

2.2 Limitation of Target TAS Scheduling

For the target scenarios with extremely low latency and frequent network reconfiguration requirements, existing scheduling algorithms have certain limitations as follows.

Low Scheduling Success Rate Under Ultra-low Latency Requirements. Tabu Search is a commonly used heuristic scheduling algorithm for traffic scheduling [8,15]. It explores only a subset of the entire solution space, prioritizing shorter time cost while potentially sacrificing schedulability. Therefore, the scheduling success rate of Tabu Search may be limited in demanding scenarios with ultra-low latency requirements. The scheduling success rate represents the proportion of successfully scheduled flows among all flows that need to be scheduled. As the latency requirement decreases, the scheduling success rate tends to decrease as well. This observation is supported by the results shown in Fig. 2(a), where Tabu Search achieves a scheduling success rate of less than 50% in a network with 2000 flows when the latency requirement of each flow is under 500 μs.

Heavy Time Overhead in Complex Networks. The SMT solver is another typical method for traffic scheduling [2,12]. It involves enumerating all possible scheduling schemes and performing verification, resulting in heavy computation overhead. Therefore, it faces challenges in complex networks with frequent scenario reconfiguration requirements that require fast and efficient traffic scheduling. In a given complex network consisting of 35 nodes, the time overhead using the SMT solver under different flow numbers is shown in Fig. 2(b). It can be observed that the time overhead of the SMT solver increases nearly exponentially with the increase in the number of flows. For instance, scheduling with only 300 flows takes more than 1 h, and finding a scheduling scheme for more than 400 flows within 5 h is practically infeasible.

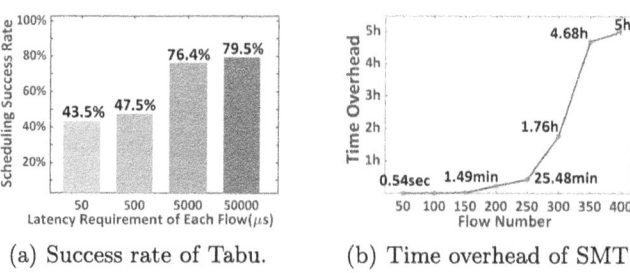

(a) Success rate of Tabu. (b) Time overhead of SMT.

Fig. 2. Limitations of existing algorithms.

2.3 Observation of TAS Scheduling

In order to explore a traffic scheduling algorithm suitable for the above application scenarios, we studied the traffic scheduling problem and made the following two observations.

Small Bandwidth Usage of TS Flows and High Capabilities of Switches. The TS flow typically occupies a small bandwidth, like the MIL-STD-1553B protocol in avionics with a bandwidth of merely 1Mbps [4]. With advancements in TSN, available bandwidth has significantly increased from hundreds of Mbps to hundreds of Gbps [7], providing hundreds or thousands of times more capacity than required for the TS flow. Considering the capability of packet processing, current TSN switches can achieve low latency at a few microseconds level [11]. Additionally, industrial network topologies typically have fewer than 7 hops [6]. The low processing latency per hop and small number of hops contribute to low end-to-end latency of flows without large queuing latency. Based on these two trends above, it is feasible to simplify the TAS scheduling problem, which can significantly reduce the scheduling complexity and minimize the end-to-end latency at the cost of sacrificing part of network bandwidth resources.

Strong Correlation of Spatial-temporal Scheduling. In some actual industrial topologies like ring and mesh [7], a flow may have multiple possible paths. However, current studies often assume that the flow paths are known and provide fixed routes as input to scheduling algorithms, neglecting the impact of routing decisions on scheduling [14]. Although this assumption simplifies the scheduling problem, it may lead to infeasible scheduling schemes for a practical and schedulable system [13]. To address this challenge, it is essential to consider both spatial and temporal allocation for each flow during the traffic scheduling process. This paper ensures that both routing and scheduling decisions are considered together, leading to more effective and feasible scheduling schemes.

3 Problem Statement

3.1 Scheduling Problem Abstraction

Based on observations of our target TAS scheduling problem, we build a TAS traffic scheduling abstraction and design a global resource view suitable for TAS-based TSN, as shown in Fig. 3. The global resource view is mainly composed of four modules:

- **Network Topology.** The number of switches, the number of end systems, the link bandwidth and the type of topology (linear, ring, mesh) determine the topology.
- **Flow Features.** TS flows are generated periodically and have deterministic transmission requirements. Features such as packet size and period are used to describe the flows.
- **Scheduling Algorithm.** It is divided into two main stages: path planning and time slot searching, to determine the optimal gating configuration. Path planning determines the path for each flow in advance. Time slot searching efficiently allocates the appropriate time slot for each data packet.
- **Configuration Information.** GCLs include the port number, the time slot sequence of each port and the gating status for each time slot.

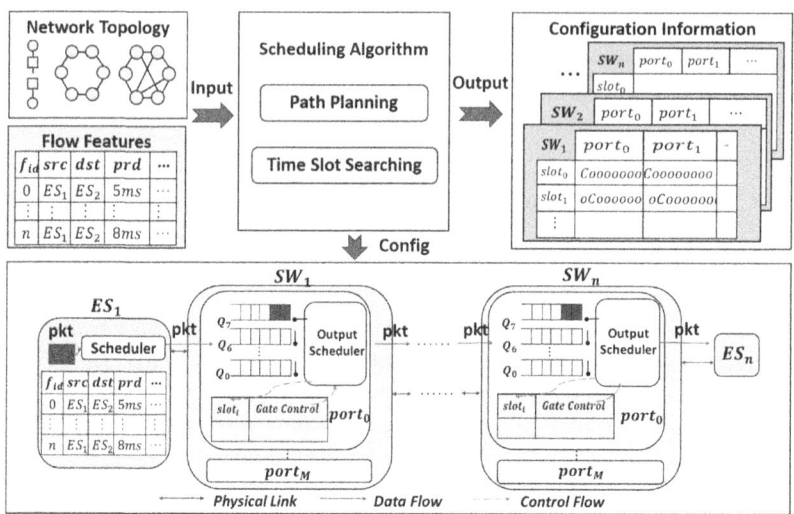

Fig. 3. A global resource view of TAS-based TSN.

3.2 Scheduling Problem Formalization

In this paper, the network topology is abstracted as an undirected graph $G = \{V, E\}$, where V represents the set of network nodes v_i (switches and end systems), and E represents the set of links connecting the nodes. A full-duplex physical link between nodes creates a logical link in both directions. If there is a physical link between v_i and v_j, then $(v_i, v_j), (v_j, v_i) \in E$, where the first vertex represents the source node and the second represents the destination node.

A six-tuple is used to characterize each TS flow, as shown in Eq. (1).

$$\forall f_i \in F, \forall i \in [0, n-1], f_i = \{f_i.prd, f_i.size, f_i.ddl, f_i.offset, f_i.src, f_i.dst\}, \quad (1)$$

where F represents the set of n TS flows in the network. $f_i.prd$ is defined as the minimum interval between two consecutive data packets. It is assumed that the flow sends only one packet in each period. $f_i.size$ and $f_i.ddl$ are the packet size and the maximum allowable latency for packet transmission separately. $f_i.offset$ refers to the sending time slot in the source node. $f_i.src$ and $f_i.dst$ are the source and destination nodes of the flow respectively.

D_{f_i} is used to represent the end-to-end latency of f_i. The optimization goal of this paper is to minimize the total end-to-end latency of all flows, i.e.,

$$minimize \sum_{i=0}^{n-1} D_{f_i}. \quad (2)$$

3.3 Core Constraints in NBS

Since the generation and transmission of TS flows are periodic, the allocation scheme needs to be examined to ensure satisfaction of the resource constraint within a scheduling period. In practical scenarios, flow periods vary across different applications. As shown in Eq. (3), the scheduling period is defined as the least common multiple (LCM) of the sending period of all flows.

$$P = LCM(f_0.prd, f_1.prd, \cdots, f_{n-1}.prd). \tag{3}$$

Additionally, since the time slot is the smallest scheduling unit, the time slot size $slot_{size}$ is usually assumed to be one of the common divisors (CD) of all flow sending periods [15]. The set of optional time slots is shown in Eq. (4).

$$slot_{size}\_set = CD(f_0.prd, f_1.prd, \cdots, f_{n-1}.prd). \tag{4}$$

Frame Sending Offset Constraint: The sending offset of data packets in the network is based on the time slot. As represented by Eq. (5), this constraint guarantees that the offset falls within the range of 0 to the number of time slots in a sending period of the flow, which effectively reduces the search space for each flow offset.

$$\forall f_i \in F, \forall i \in [0, n-1], 0 \leq f_i.\textit{offset} < \frac{f_i.prd}{slot_{size}}. \tag{5}$$

Time Slot Constraint: This constraint specifies the upper and lower bounds of the time slot. In this paper, the key constraint is that it restricts the transmission of the same flow in the same time slot from source to destination. As illustrated in Fig. 4, all nodes along the transmission paths of the same flow are treated as a bundle for time slot allocation instead of a hop-by-hop allocation adopted in state-of-the-art algorithms. This is the origin of the name NBS, and the rationale behind this is the small bandwidth usage of TS flows and the efficient capabilities of switches mentioned in Sect. 2.3.

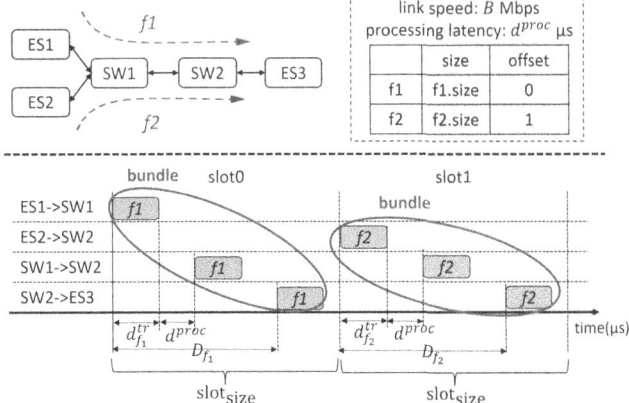

Fig. 4. Diagram of time slot constraint for node bundle scheduling.

Based on the above constraint, the size of the time slot is restricted to the least common divisors of all flow sending periods while ensuring it is not less than the maximum end-to-end latency of all flows, as shown in Eq. (6). This aims to ensure that the duration of the time slot is sufficient to guarantee the completion of transmission for all flows while ensuring an adequate number of time slots for allocation to minimize bandwidth waste.

$$\forall f_i \in F, \forall i \in [0, n-1],$$
$$slot_{size} = min\left(slot_{size}\_set \cap [max\{D_{f_0}, D_{f_1}, \cdots, D_{f_{n-1}}\}, +\infty)\right). \quad (6)$$

In general, the end-to-end latency consists of transmission latency, propagation latency, processing latency, and queuing latency. In this paper, the propagation latency is ignored due to the short transmission distance. Additionally, the above constraint specifies the immediate processing and forwarding of flows at each node, along with the exclusive occupancy of the same time slot along the entire transmission path, thereby eliminating the queuing delay. Therefore, the end-to-end latency D_{f_i} in this paper mainly consists of the sum of per-hop transmission latency $d_{f_i}^{tr}$ and processing latency d^{proc}, as shown in Eq. (7).

$$D_{f_i} = (d_{f_i}^{tr} + d^{proc}) \times \gamma_{f_i} \quad (7)$$

where γ_{f_i} is the number of switches on the transmission path of f_i.

End-to-end Latency Constraint: The end-to-end latency of each flow from source to destination is constrained to be no higher than its specified maximum latency, as shown in Eq. (8).

$$\forall f_i \in F, \forall i \in [0, n-1], D_{f_i} \leq f_i.ddl. \quad (8)$$

4 Algorithm Design

Based on the TAS scheduling abstraction, NBS is proposed for the above mentioned scheduling problem. It considers traffic scheduling in both temporal and spatial dimensions to improve the scheduling success rate. To reduce the complexity of the target scheduling problem, NBS uses a divide-and-conquer method to solve the temporal and spatial scheduling. However, different from most state-of-the-art TAS-based scheduling algorithms where the spatial-temporal traffic scheduling process is completely isolated, NBS considers the factors that will affect the success rate of temporal scheduling during spatial scheduling. Based on this factor, it is feasible to pre-determine a path for each flow that is a near-optimal path instead of trial iterating path by path, which is time-consuming.

NBS adopts SOB path planning for spatial traffic scheduling and OPG slot searching for temporal traffic scheduling. The temporal traffic scheduling which allocates suitable time slots to TS flows is equivalent to the knapsack problem, which is NP-hard [5]. To reduce the complexity of TAS traffic scheduling, NBS restricts the same flow to be transmitted in the same time slot from source to destination. Different from the hop-by-hop time slot allocation adopted in state-of-the-art algorithms, NBS allocates the same time slot to all nodes along a flow's transmission path. Due to the dramatic reduction of the search space, this algorithm can greatly reduce the scheduling complexity.

4.1 Slot-Occupancy-Balance Path Planning

Existing common path planning algorithms, such as the Shortest Path Algorithm (SPA), ensure the minimum route hops for each flow. However, blindly selecting the shortest path for all flows without considering resource allocation may lead to a premature bottleneck of traffic transmission on some paths. It is necessary to migrate the flows on the overloaded links to other links. The path lengths of some flows are sacrificed to balance more resources to carry more flows.

In our previous experiments, we found that the number of available time slots on each link is an important factor that affects the subsequent temporal traffic scheduling, i.e., as long as there is no available slot on one of the links along the transmission path of the flow, the flow is unscheduled. On this basis, this paper proposes a new concept of time slot occupancy and tries to reduce the highest time slot occupancy in the whole network as much as possible.

δ^l is used to represent the time slot occupancy of the l-th link, as shown in Eq. (9). It consists of the time slot occupancy of all flows on the l-th link, i.e., $\delta^l = \sum_{i=0}^{n-1} \delta^{l.f_i}$.

$$\delta^l = \frac{\sum_{i=0}^{n-1} N^l_{f_i.pkt}}{N^l_{slot}}, \qquad (9)$$

where N^l_{slot} is the number of time slots on the l-th link in a scheduling period and $N^l_{f_i.pkt}$ represents the number of data packets from i-th flow transmitted on the l-th link within one scheduling period.

SOB path planning is improved based on SPA. The core idea is to divert flows on the link with high time slot occupancy to other links, so as to reduce the maximum time slot occupation and balance the time slot resources of the entire network. The specific process of SOB path planning is shown in Algorithm 1. Initially, SPA is used to determine the paths for all flows (line 2). Then, the flow with the largest proportion on the link with the highest slot occupancy, denoted as f^*, is identified (line 5). This flow is assigned to an alternative path if it reduces the maximum link slot occupancy (lines 6–11). These steps are repeated until the maximum link slot occupancy cannot be further reduced, indicating the completion of path planning (line 12).

Algorithm 1: NBS Algorithm

Input: Network Topology G, Flow set F.
Output: $F.timeslot$.
1 $P = LCM(f_i.prd)$; $slot_{size} = compute\_slot(G, F)$;
2 $F.path_{init} \leftarrow shortest\_path(G, F)$;
3 **repeat**
4      $\delta^l_{before} \leftarrow compute\_occupancy(G, F, P, slot_{size})$;
5      $l^* \leftarrow \arg\max_l \delta^l_{before}$; $f^* \leftarrow \arg\max_{f_i} \delta^{l^* \cdot f_i}_{before}$;
6   **for** each path in $f^*.paths$ **do**
7         $f^*.path_{upd} \leftarrow \arg\min_{path}(\max \delta^l)$;
8   **if** $\max(\delta^l_{upd}) < \max(\delta^l_{before})$ **then**
9         $f^*.path_{final} \leftarrow f^*.path_{upd}$;
10   **else**
11        $f^*.path_{final} \leftarrow f^*.path_{before}$;
12 **until** $\max(\delta^l_{final}) = \max(\delta^l_{before})$;
13 $F = flow\_sort(F)$;
14 **while** F is not completely scheduled **do**
15   **for** each f_i in F **do**
16   **while** $f_i.offset < \frac{f_i.prd}{slot_{size}}$ **do**
17           $slot\_flag = True$;
18   **for** each instance in $[0, \frac{P}{f_i.prd} - 1]$ **do**
19   **for** each hop in $[0, Len(f_i.path) - 1]$ **do**
20   **if** slot is occupied **then**
21                    $slot\_flag = False$;
22   **break**;
23   **if** $slot\_flag$ **then**
24   the slot is allocated to f_i;
25   **break**;
26   **else**
27              $f_i.offset + +$;
28   **if** $f_i.offset \geq \frac{f_i.prd}{slot_{size}}$ **then**
29   **return** $unsat$;
30 **return** $F.timeslot$;

4.2 On-the-Fly Policy-Guided Slot Searching

To improve the scheduling success rate and computation efficiency, which are the main targets of NBS, the slot searching of NBS has the following two features.

Policy-Guided Searching. The time slot allocation order of the flows has a significant impact on the scheduling results. Normally, period and packet size of flows can influence the link bandwidth utilization. However, in our TAS scheduling abstraction, packet size will not influence the time slot scheduling results. Because each packet occupies an exclusive time slot regardless of the packet size according to Eq. (6), which will not affect the allocatable time slots. Considering the factor of flow period, flows with smaller period require more time slot resources that are relatively more difficult to be scheduled. Therefore, such flows should be given higher priority, and slot searching is conducted in ascending order of flow periods (line 13).

On-the-fly Searching. The core of NBS is to uniformly allocate available time slot resources to all nodes along the transmission path of the target flow. The allocation is achieved by the loop in Algorithm 1. When flows are not scheduled completely, each flow f_i is analyzed in turn (line 15). The slot searching starts from the 0-th slot under the condition that the time slot constraint is satisfied (lines 16). Once time slots for all hops of all packet instances in a scheduling period are found to be free, they are allocated to f_i (lines 18–25). If there are no available slots for f_i to be found in a scheduling period, it means that the allocation scheme cannot be obtained (lines 28–29). This uniform allocation makes the search process very fast, which we vividly call "on-the-fly searching".

5 Evaluation

5.1 Experimental Setup

To demonstrate the effectiveness and superiority of NBS, we conduct comparisons with heuristic algorithms (Naive Search and the state-of-the-art Tabu Search [8,15]) and the typical SMT solver (Frame-SMT [2] and Win-SMT [12]). These comparisons are carried out under different flow features and system settings of a TAS-based TSN system. Naive Search utilizes SPA and random time slot search without policy guidance. Frame-SMT enforces strict time constraints for sending packets within each fixed-size time slot. In contrast, Win-SMT regulates packet transmission by dynamically adjusting the number of sending windows, which is selected from {1, 2, 3} for observation.

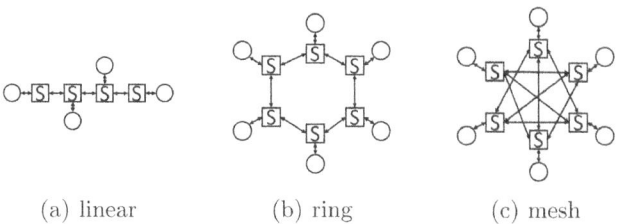

(a) linear (b) ring (c) mesh

Fig. 5. Network topology type.

TAS-Based TSN System Settings. This paper considers three common topologies in industrial control networks, as shown in Fig. 5. The network structure is denoted by (SW, ES), where SW represents the number of switches, and ES represents the number of end systems per switch. For each TAS-based TSN switch, the resource settings include link bandwidth, time slot size and processing latency. In this simulation, we set the link bandwidth to 1 Gbps. In our implemented FPGA prototype system, the processing latency for each TSN switch d^{proc} is measured to be nearly 2.12 μs.

Flow Features. In the absence of an open-source TSN flow set, we utilize the flow features outlined in IEC/IEEE 60802 standard [7] for industrial automation networks as a reference. In our experiment, all flows are randomly generated according to the guidelines of 60802 standard. The packet size for each flow is randomly selected between 64 bytes and 1518 bytes. Due to the diversity of TS flows, we consider multiple period combinations. The alternative set of periods includes P1 = {5, 7.5, 10, 20, 25, 50, 75, 100, 200, 250, 500}ms, P2 = {10, 20}ms, P3 = {10, 25, 50, 100}ms, P4 = {5, 10, 100, 200, 500, 1000}ms, and P5 = {200}ms.

5.2 Experimental Results

NBS vs Heuristic: The advantage of NBS over the heuristic algorithm is demonstrated in Fig. 6(a). In scenarios with very low latency requirements such as 50μs or 500μs, the scheduling success rate of NBS is average 48% higher than that of Naive Search and 34.25% higher than that of the state-of-the-art Tabu Search. This illustrates that the combination of SOB path planning and OPG slot searching performs better than other compared algorithms. As shown in Fig. 6(b), NBS reduces the maximum time slot occupancy by an average of 23.81% compared to Naive in different topologies.

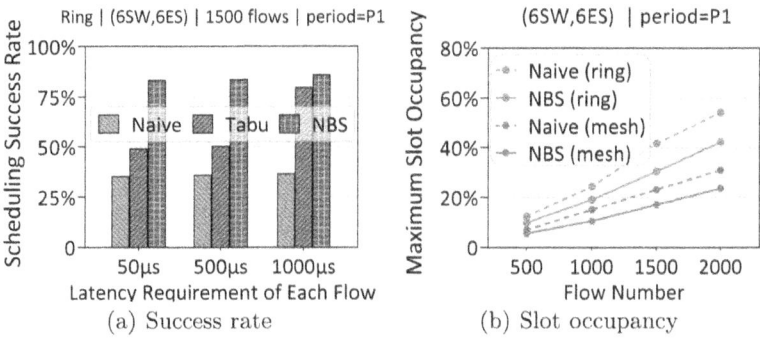

Fig. 6. Comparison of scheduling success rate and maximum time slot occupancy by NBS and heuristic algorithms in different topologies.

NBS vs SMT: End-to-end latency is an important indicator to evaluate the quality of a scheduling scheme. The quality of scheduling using NBS is evaluated under different topologies, which is shown in Fig. 7(a). Compared with Frame-SMT, NBS reduces the total latency of scheduling results by an average of 96.4%. This is because NBS restricts each data packet to use the same slot on each hop, which greatly reduces the transmission latency of flows.

In addition, to verify that NBS can effectively break the bottleneck of high time overhead, the time overhead of different algorithms (NBS, Frame-SMT,

Win-SMT) are compared. The search for the scheduling scheme will be stopped once the time limit of 3 h for scheduling is reached. Figure 7(b) shows that the time overhead of NBS is less than that of Frame-SMT as the flow number increases, which has stability when the flow period is diversified. Figure 7(c) demonstrates that SMT can even fail to find a solution in complex networks with strict time requirements such as within 3 h. By contrast, NBS has obvious advantages in scheduling time and solving ability. Compared with Frame-SMT, the time overhead of NBS is reduced by up to 99.9% in the network with highly complex topology and 400 flows.

Furthermore, the actual bandwidth sacrifice using NBS is analyzed. As shown in Fig. 7(d), in scenarios with relatively complex topology and a large number of flows, the maximum link bandwidth using NBS is reduced by an average of 11.86% compared with Frame-SMT, which is acceptable in exchange for ultra-low latency and extremely short scheduling time.

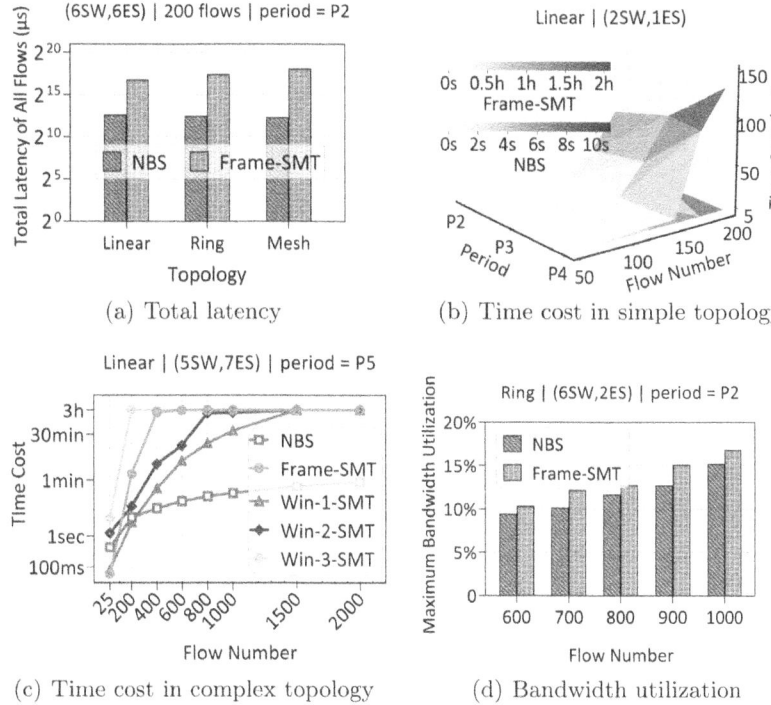

Fig. 7. Comparison of total latency, time cost and maximum bandwidth utilization metrics by NBS and SMT solvers.

Verification of NBS on FPGA Prototype System: To validate the feasibility and the correctness of NBS, we experiment on the open-source FPGA prototype [1] with a topology of (2SW, 1ES), as illustrated in Fig. 8. The FPGA based TSN switches and TSN tester are implemented with required TSN standards including 802.1AS, 802.1Qbv, etc. The tester acts as both the source node for sending flows and the destination node for receiving flows, under the control of the tester controller. The flows sent by the tester traverse switches SW0 and SW1 before returning to the tester. The controller configures the TSN switches with the obtained scheduling results from NBS. We consider three flows with different packet sizes: 128 bytes (flow0), 256 bytes (flow1) and 512 bytes (flow2).

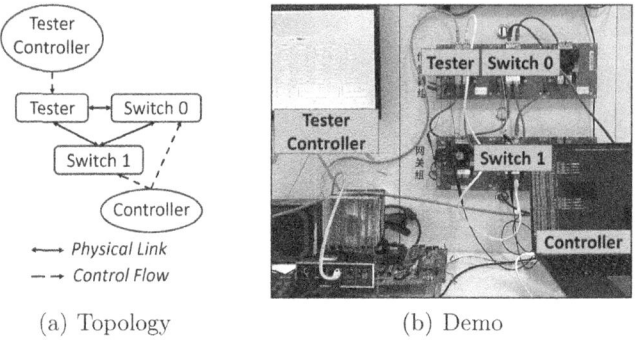

(a) Topology (b) Demo

Fig. 8. Experimental FPGA prototype system.

We employ NBS to schedule these three flows, then the scheduling results are configured for SW0 and SW1. We measure the actual end-to-end latency of the first 300 packets for each flow by recording the outgoing and incoming packet times at the tester. The theoretical end-to-end latency using the formula (7) is also calculated according to the measured switch processing latency. The result, depicted in Fig. 9, demonstrates that the maximum deviation between the actual and theoretical latencies does not exceed 1.09 µs. The latency difference is mainly caused by time synchronization deviation between two switches. These results provide strong evidence that NBS can effectively achieve latency performance that closely aligns with the theoretical expectations.

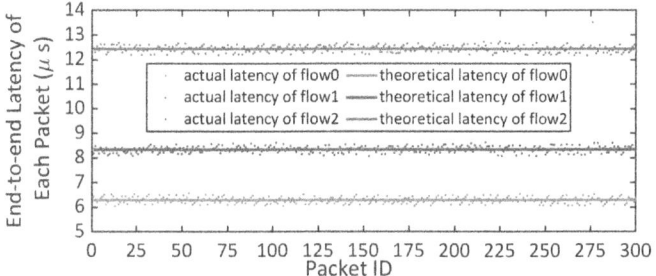

* Note that the theoretical latency here is not the upper bound of the latency, it is the fitted value of the actual end-to-end latency derived from the known parameter.

Fig. 9. Theoretical and actual end-to-end latency.

6 Conclusion

In this paper, we proposed a TAS based traffic scheduling abstraction that enables traffic to be transmitted in TSN with extremely low latency. The abstraction stipulates all nodes on the same path of each flow transmit within the same time slot. Based on the abstraction, a scheduling algorithm NBS for allocating resources from both temporal and spatial dimensions was proposed. It achieves path planning with balanced time slot occupation in the spatial dimension and on-the-fly slot searching under the guidance of the policy in the temporal dimension. To fully evaluate the effectiveness of NBS, we conducted simulations on typical industrial topologies and verified on the FPGA prototype system. The results verify the correctness and efficiency of the proposed algorithm.

Acknowledgments. This work is supported by National Natural Science Foundation of China under Grant No. U22B2005, and Hunan Provincial Innovation Foundation For Postgraduate under Grant No. CX20220013.

References

1. OpenTSN project. https://gitee.com/opentsn/open-tsn4.0
2. Craciunas, S.S., Oliver, R.S., Chmelík, M., Steiner, W.: Scheduling Real-Time Communication in IEEE 802.1Qbv Time Sensitive Networks. In: ACM RTNS (2016)
3. Fu, W., Quan, W., Yan, J., Sun, Z.: Fenglin-I: an open-source time-sensitive networking chip enabling agile customization. IEEE Trans. Comput. **72**, 140–153 (2023)
4. GmbH, A.: MIL-STD-1553 Tutorial (2022). https://www.aim-online.com/products-overview/tutorials/mil-std-1553-tutorial
5. Hellmanns, D., Glavackij, A., Falk, J., Hummen, R., Kehrer, S., Dürr, F.: Scaling TSN Scheduling for Factory Automation Networks. In: IEEE WFCS (2020)
6. Huang, Y., Wang, S., Zhang, X., Huang, T., Liu, Y.: Flexible cyclic queuing and forwarding for time-sensitive software-defined networks. IEEE Trans. Network Serv. Manag. **20**, 533–546 (2023)
7. IEEE: IEC/IEEE 60802 TSN Profile for Industrial Automation (2022). https://1.ieee802.org/tsn/iec-ieee-60802
8. Lin, M., Xu, Q., Lu, X., Zhang, J., Chen, C.: Control and transmission co-design for industrial CPS integrated with time-sensitive networking. In: IEEE SMC (2022)
9. Nasrallah, A., et al.: Performance Comparison of IEEE 802.1 TSN Time Aware Shaper (TAS) and Asynchronous Traffic Shaper (ATS). IEEE Access (2019)
10. Nasrallah, A., et al.: Ultra-Low Latency (ULL) networks: the IEEE TSN and IETF DetNet standards and related 5G ULL research. IEEE Commun. Surv. Tutor. (2019)
11. NXP Semiconductors: SJA1105PEL/QEL/REL/SEL Series Ethernet Switches (2024). https://www.nxp.com/products/interfaces/ethernet-/automotive-ethernet-switches/sja1105pel-qel-rel-sel-series-ethernet-switches:SJA1105PQRS
12. Serna Oliver, R., Craciunas, S.S., Steiner, W.: IEEE 802.1Qbv gate control list synthesis using array theory encoding. In: IEEE RTAS (2018)

13. Smirnov, F., Glaß, M., Reimann, F., Teich, J.: Optimizing message routing and scheduling in automotive mixed-criticality time-triggered networks. In: ACM/EDAC/IEEE DAC (2017)
14. Steiner, W.: An evaluation of SMT-based schedule synthesis for time-triggered multi-hop networks. In: IEEE RTSS (2010)
15. Yan, J., Quan, W., Jiang, X., Sun, Z.: Injection time planning: making CQF practical in time-sensitive networking. In: IEEE INFOCOM (2020)
16. Yang, Z., et al.: CaaS: enabling control-as-a-service for time-sensitive networking. In: IEEE INFOCOM (2023)
17. Yao, M., et al.: A unified flow scheduling method for time sensitive networks. Comput. Networks (2023)
18. Zhang, Y., Xu, Q., Xu, L., Chen, C., Guan, X.: Efficient flow scheduling for industrial time-sensitive networking: a divisibility theory-based method. IEEE Trans. Ind. Inform. (2022)

Towards High-performance Transactions via Hierarchical Blockchain Sharding

Haibo Tang[1,2], Huan Zhang[1,2], Zhenyu Zhang[1,2], Zhao Zhang[1,2(✉)], Cheqing Jin[1,2], and Aoying Zhou[1,2]

[1] East China Normal University, Shanghai, China
{haibtang,hzhang,zyzhang}@stu.ecnu.edu.cn,
{zhzhang,cqjin,ayzhou}@dase.ecnu.edu.cn
[2] Engineering Research Center of Blockchain Data Management, Ministry of Education, Shanghai, China

Abstract. Blockchain sharding, a promising approach to improve system performance, divides the network into several small parallel working shards. However, the performance of existing sharded blockchain systems may degrade seriously due to the existence of cross-shard transactions. To overcome such drawbacks, we propose a blockchain system called HieraChain to process transactions with robust cross-shard transactions tolerance, based on a novel hierarchical sharding architecture. The upper-layer shards order the cross-shard transactions and the participants process them asynchronously to pipeline the transactions ordering. Furthermore, HieraChain proposes an optimized locality-aware protocol to trade off the local access patterns and the induced remote access events. Extensive experimental results demonstrate that HieraChain outperforms the state-of-the-art approaches significantly in the presence of cross-shard transactions, achieving up to 3× and 2× higher throughput than Saguaro and SharPer under general workload respectively. Moreover, our locality-aware approach further reduces transaction latency by 68 % and 51% compared to our basic approach and traditional baselines, respectively.

Keywords: cross-shard transaction · hierarchical sharding · locality-awareness · blockchains

1 Introduction

Permissioned blockchain has been widely adopted to support massive collaboration, such as finance, supply chain, etc. With the rapid growth of participants and the emergent requirement of performance, how to process transactions efficiently becomes more and more critical. Sharding, a promising solution to enable concurrent transaction processing, divides the system into individual shards to enhance performance. Moreover, due to the existence of cross-shard transactions (abbr. CSTs), how to improve system throughput is challenging [10,16,22].

Most existing sharding techniques use flat architecture, where all shards are at the same level, and capable of communicating with any other shard [1,5–7,9,10,12,15,16,19–21]. The communication task includes voting messages for consensus, cross-shard transaction commit protocol, etc. Hence, even though the flat structure works well for a small-sized network, it is still insufficient for a large network that includes hundreds of shards due to massive crisscrossing inter-shard messages. The messages may be transmitted via wide-area network so that the latency is significant if the coordinator is far away from other shards.

To deal with this issue, the latest researches focus on organizing all shards hierarchically to lower the communication cost, i.e., Pyramid [8] and Saguaro [2]. In this architecture, all shards are organized as a tree, and the parent/ancient shard is responsible for coordinating the cross-shard transaction processing. Saguaro which works in edge computing scenarios uses the nearest upper-layer shard to coordinate the cross-shard transactions processing to reduce wide-are communication, while Pyramid allows the upper-layer shard to store the entire state of multiple lower-layer shards to avoid cross-shard transactions. However, existing hierarchical works still exhibit the following three drawbacks:

- **Inefficient cross-shard transaction processing.** Currently, there are two main ways to deal with cross-shard transactions, including a two-phase commit(2PC)-based approach [2,6,7,12] and flat consensus-based approach [1]. The former requires multiple round-trips of blocking communication between the coordinator and participant shards, which results in significantly reduced throughput, while the latter requires all nodes in the involved shards to run PBFT [4] which incurs high communication cost for a large network. Some works split cross-shard transactions into multiple intra-shard transactions that can be processed sequentially in different shards, but they only support the UTXO-based blockchains [20, 21].
- **Ignorance of remote access events.** Though the state data is distributed among all shards, it is meaningful to access the same set of states in one shard when processing transactions. In large-scale scenarios, shards are typically distributed in different locations. The states assigned to each shard could be involved in access patterns with both local and remote shards simultaneously, so that bringing some states into the same shard could cause remote access events by users around other shards. Hence, how to leverage local access patterns among shards in large-scale scenarios becomes critical.

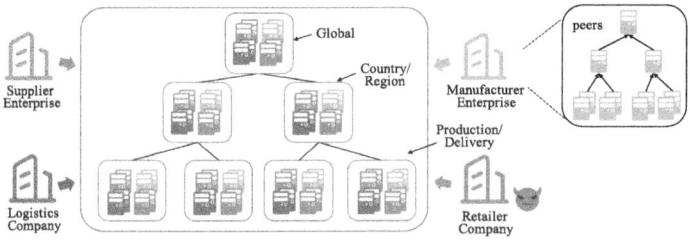

Fig. 1. An example of hierarchically sharded supply chain

- **Ignorance of collaboration between different roles.** In real-world scenarios, nodes with different roles usually collaborate each other to improve efficiency. Take the e-commerce supply chain as an example. Assume there are four kinds of organizations and each shard contains peers from different organizations. As shown in Fig. 1, the entire network comprises three layers with different authority levels. Each superior level plays a role in decision-making for the nearby shards to reduce coordination overhead, which means, the superior shard takes responsibility for executing certain tasks, such as achieving consensus on the cross-shard transactions from low-layer shards. Empowered by this collaboration model, it is feasible to improve efficiency.

In this paper, we build a novel hierarchically sharded blockchain system called *HieraChain*, to address such challenges. Each upper-layer shard in this architecture is able to order the cross-shard transactions for participants to reduce coordination overhead, the participants process them asynchronously to pipeline the processing of transactions. HieraChain employs a deterministic rule to guarantee data consistency for the case with more than two layers. Furthermore, HieraChain adopts a locality-aware transaction commit protocol to allow certain states to be updated in both local and remote shards to trade off the local access patterns and the induced remote access events.

The contributions are summarized below.

- **A novel sharding architecture.** We propose a sharded blockchain, called HieraChain, over hierarchical architecture which is adequate for a broader range of real-world scenarios since it inherits the advantage of scalability and robust cross-shard transaction tolerance.
- **Efficient cross-shard transaction processing.** HieraChain orders cross-shard transactions with participants' common ancestor's ordering service, and the participant shards process all transactions asynchronously to pipeline transaction ordering. Meanwhile, our extensive work can deal with multiple layers while ensuring data consistency.
- **Optimized locality-awareness.** We present an optimized locality-aware transaction commit protocol to leverage local access patterns. It allows both local and remote shards to take over the ownership of the transferred states and keep consistency to reduce the impact of remote access events.
- **Prototype implementation.** We implement a prototype blockchain system that integrates the above techniques and conducts evaluations. Extensive experimental results show that our proposed approaches outperform competing solutions, and the optimized locality-aware approach further enhances system performance under the workloads that exhibit locality.

The rest of this paper is organized as follows. Section 2 reviews related work. Section 3 discusses the design of HieraChain. Sections 4–6 present the key components of HieraChain. Section 7 evaluates the performance of HieraChain. Finally, Sect. 8 concludes the paper.

2 Related Work

The basic idea of sharding is to divide the entire system into multiple shards to process transactions in parallel. Existing works include three types: network sharding, transaction sharding, and complete sharding. Network sharding, divides the entire network into several subnetworks (called shards), where each shard works independently with its own consensus validators. Transaction sharding assigns the workload to different shards for higher throughput [14]. Complete sharding further divides the entire state into separate partitions to reduce storage overhead [1,6,12,20,21].

The major sharding solutions are based on flat structure [1,6,7,9,10,12,15, 16,19–21]. Elastico [14] is the pioneering work that adopts transaction sharding, where each shard validates the transactions in parallel and maintains a full copy of all states. Moreover, many other works adopt complete sharding, where each shard is assigned disjoint states, and focus on the security and efficiency of cross-shard transactions processing [1,6,12,20,21]. OmniLedger [12] and AHL [6] use classic two-phase commit (2PC) protocol to process CST, which involves multiple round-trips blocking communications across different shards. ByShard [7] proposed a distributed-2PC protocol to reduce the number of stages in 2PC. However, blocking communication between different shards still leads to significantly reduced throughput, especially for contended workloads. RapidChain [21] first decomposes a CST into several intra-shard transactions, and then processes them by input and output shard sequentially. Monoxide [20] presents eventual atomicity to improve the efficiency of CST processing. However, RapidChain and Monoxide only support UTXO-based blockchains. SharPer [1] presents a flat decentralized cross-shard consensus protocol without a third party, where all nodes in the involved shards run PBFT [4] to achieve the consensus.

Some work leverages local access patterns to reduce the number of CSTs. OptChain [15] groups both related and soon-related transactions into the same shards to reduce the number of CSTs. BrokerChain [10] models historical transactions as a graph, achieving workload balance with fewer CSTs through state-graph partition. TxAllo [22] formulates the transaction allocation problem and treats it as a community detection problem. These works assume all shards are in close proximity, the state transfer may cause remote access events with high latency by some users around other shards in the geo-distributed scenario. CST is similar to distributed transactions in distributed databases, some works also leverage access locality to reduce the number of distributed transactions [11,17].

Another kind of sharding solutions are based on non-flat structure. Pyramid [8] allows some shards to store the entire state of multiple other shards, rather than complete sharding, to process CSTs in an intra-shard manner. This approach sacrifices complete sharding and conducts a 2PC-based protocol to commit the state updates to the lower-layer shards. Saguaro [2] leverages the hierarchical structure of edge computing network to reduce wide-area communication cost. It proposes a 2PC-based protocol and an optimistic protocol to process CTS with low latency, but the optimistic protocol relies on the assumption that CTS has no conflict with intra-shard transactions. Hence, how to process CSTs efficiently remains an ongoing challenge.

3 Architecture

Security Assumption. In HieraChain, nodes follow the Byzantine failure model where Byzantine nodes may exhibit arbitrary malicious behavior. The number of malicious nodes in each shard is under a safe threshold, it cannot break the consensus protocol (assuming at most f malicious nodes in a shard, and $3f+1$ nodes in each shard). Each shard can not only receive the consensus result from the upper layer, but also evaluate the correctness of the received information.

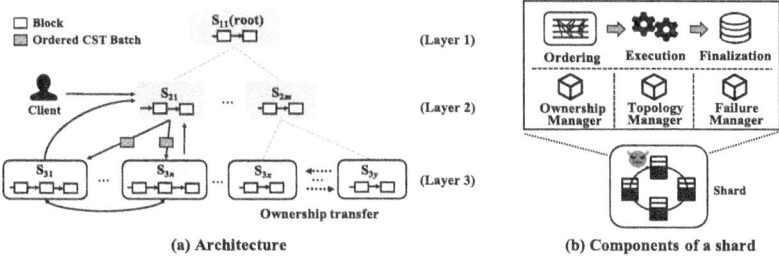

Fig. 2. Overview of HieraChain

Figure 2(a) depicts the architecture of HieraChain, where all shards are organized as a tree. There are two types of shards: *coordinator shard* and *leaf shard*. Each leaf shard stores the states assigned to it, while the rest non-leaf shards are *coordinators*. Each coordinator maintains the state ownership metadata of their children, and is responsible for serving the ordering of cross-shard transactions if it happens to be the nearest common ancestor (NCA) of all involved shards. For example, S_{21} is the NCA of S_{31} and S_{3n}, and S_{11} is the NCA of S_{3n} and S_{3x}. Furthermore, in each shard, one node is pre-elected as the forwarding node, responsible for forwarding the messages to other shards, and these messages are signed by at least $2f+1$ nodes within the shard. Note that the read and write sets of the transactions processed by HieraChain can be known in advance.

Each leaf shard, assigned to disjoint states, follows the *order-execute-finalize* (OEF) paradigm [3]. The ordering service is responsible for ordering transactions among nodes in a shard. Specifically, the ordering service of the coordinator shard is responsible for ordering CSTs for their children. The transactions are executed by the execution service, and the results are stored by the finalization service. The topology manager stores its parent shard (see Sect. 4 for details). The ownership manager stores ownership metadata and leverages local access patterns in workloads to enhance performance. Each leaf shard's ownership manager stores ownership metadata about the states assigned to it, and each coordinator shard stores the metadata of all children (see Sect. 5 for details). The failure manager is responsible for fault tolerance (see Sect. 6 for details).

4 Cross-Shard Transaction Processing

Cross-shard transaction processing still remains challenging, especially for hierarchical structure. In this section, we study how to process cross-shard transactions efficiently. For clarity, we start with the simple two-layer case in Sect. 4.1 and then extend to the case with multiple layers in Sect. 4.2.

4.1 Get Started: a Protocol for Two-Layer Situation

The hierarchical structure is encountered by two major challenges to deal with cross-shard transactions. First, how to process cross-shard transactions ordered by the NCA efficiently. Second, how to deal with potential data inconsistency among different participants, as the leaf shards may receive ordered CSTs from different upper-layer shards at the same time.

We propose a new protocol that allows intra-shard transactions and cross-shard transactions to be ordered in parallel by different shards, and guarantees cross-shard transactions executed deterministically among participants. Furthermore, each participant processes the received cross-shard transactions asynchronously to pipeline the cross-shard transactions ordering in NCA. It experiences three phases, including *prepare*, *prepared*, and *execution* phases.

- **Prepare phase.** Once receiving a CST m, NCA initiates the ordering task immediately. Then, NCA's forwarding node multicasts *prepare* messages (including the transactions and their order for each participant) to the respective participants, including $2f+1$ signatures from different nodes of NCA.
- **Prepared phase.** Upon receiving a valid *prepare* message from NCA, each participant achieves consensus about this message. Then, all nodes in the shard append the CST m and the order to the ledger with their ordering service, and execute these transactions deterministically.
- **Execution phase.** Participants execute CSTs based on the ordering result given by the NCA. Once starts to execute a CST, the participant sends read or write sets to other participants by its forwarding node in advance. This message includes $2f+1$ signatures from different nodes. When the CST is committed, the participant replies *commit* message to the NCA.

All participants process the received ordered cross-shard transactions and execute them asynchronously, i.e., the transactions are executed in a pipeline style. To reduce the communication overhead when transferring the read or write sets among the shards, the cross-shard transactions involving the same participants are adjacent in the ordering result, so that they can be sent in batch to amortize the communication cost.

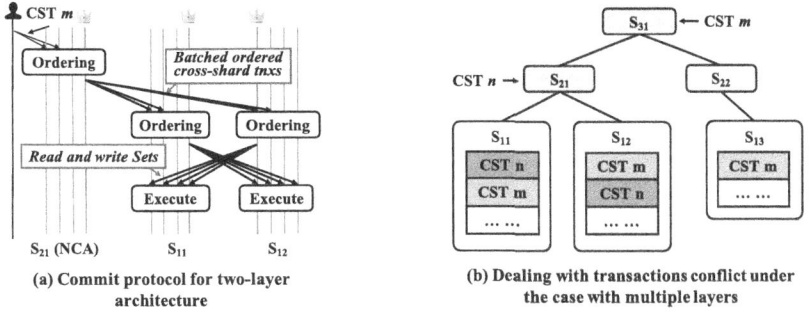

Fig. 3. Cross-shard transaction commit protocol

Example 1. Figure 3(a) presents an example of three shards organized in a binary-tree structure, where S_{21} is the parent (also the NCA) of S_{11} and S_{12}. When a leaf shard receives a CTS m, it forwards m to parent shards to find out the NCA recursively. When S_{21} receives m, which involves S_{11} and S_{12}, it first achieve consensus for this transaction and produces the batch id and sequence number in the batch. At the same time, the ordering service of S_{11} and S_{12} order the received transactions in parallel. Moreover, once S_{21} delivers the ordering result, S_{11} and S_{12} append the result to their ledgers. When start to execute m, S_{11} and S_{12} send read or write sets in advance. Once all the necessary read and write sets are ready, S_{11} and S_{12} execute and commit the updates.

Performance Analysis. Assume the number of nodes in each shard is M, and the network communication cost between shards is W, all the CSTs involve p participants ($p>1$). HieraChain orders CSTs in the coordinator shard and leaf shard serially, which incurs a network cost of $(p+1)M^2$. Moreover, the coordinator shard needs to deliver ordering results to participants, and each participant needs to send read or write sets messages to each other. This incurs a network cost of pW^2, i.e., $pW+p(p-1)W$. Hence, the total network cost of HieraChain is $(p+1)M^2 + pW$. The 2PC-based approaches [2,6,12], require two-round blocking communications between coordinator and participants, and the network cost is $(p+1)M^2+4(p-1)W$, which is larger than that of HieraChain ($3p-4>0$, ($p=2$, 3...)). Moreover, blocking communications in 2PC-based approaches is disastrous for performance, while HieraChain pipelines the transaction processing to achieve high performance. The consensus-based approach [1] engages all nodes of the participants in a three-phase all-to-all communication to achieve consensus, resulting in $(pM)^2(p-1)W$ network cost which is higher than HieraChain.

4.2 Extension to the Multiple-Layer Situation

To extend to a general case with multiple layers, it is crucial to ensure data consistency among different participants. As each leaf shard receives the ordered CST batches from different NCAs at the same time, the order of CST batches from different NCAs among participants may be different. This will cause data inconsistency if these batches have overlapping read or write sets.

To avoid data inconsistency, it's important to detect the divergence in advance. At first, we add additional information (the hash value of the CST batch) into the read and write sets messages, to identify which batch the read or write sets belong to. Then, if the participants find the received read or write sets message conflicts with the expected message, they process these messages based on the following rule.

Rule 1. Upon receiving a message about the conflicted read and write sets of an unexpected CST batch, the shard compares the shard ID of the message sender to generate an ordering result to process transactions consistently among participants. Finally, the conflicted CST batch from the smallest shard among the overlapping participants is picked up for processing first.

Example 2. Figure 3(b) shows an example in three-layer architecture, where S_{21} is the parent (also the NCA) of S_{11} and S_{12}, S_{22} is the parent of S_{13}, and S_{31} is the parent of S_{21} and S_{22}. Consider two CSTs, m crosses S_{11}, S_{12} and S_{13} (will be ordered by S_{31}), and n crosses S_{11} and S_{12} (will be ordered by S_{21}). However, since S_{11} and S_{12} process m and n in different order, the read and write sets have conflicts. According to the aforementioned rule, since S_{11} has the smaller shard ID ('11' < '12'), S_{12} turns to process CST n and resends its read and write sets to S_{11}. After n has been committed, S_{12} tries to execute m.

5 Locality-Aware Cross-Shard Transaction Processing

In this section, we start with the state ownership transfer protocol in Sect. 5.1 and then introduce transaction commit protocol to leverage locality access patterns in Sect. 5.2.

5.1 State Ownership Transfer

As mentioned before, the states assigned to each shard may be involved in access patterns with both local and remote shards simultaneously. Figure 4(a) illustrates an example, where each vertex represents a state, and each edge represents two states are commonly accessed in the same transactions, while the weight reflects the frequency of this event. States A and B are involved in the local access pattern across S_{11} and S_{12}. Although we can move the state B to S_{11} to reduce the number of CSTs, it induces some remote access events (i.e., the transaction that accesses B and E initiated by the users around S_{12} at the same time). Hence, there are two major challenges to leveraging local access patterns. First, which shard to transfer the states involved in local access patterns to. Second, how to reduce the impact of induced remote access events. Our idea is to transfer the states involved in local access patterns to the shard that incurs the least impact of remote access events. As the impact of the remote access event is related to the probability that the transferred states are accessed, and the hot

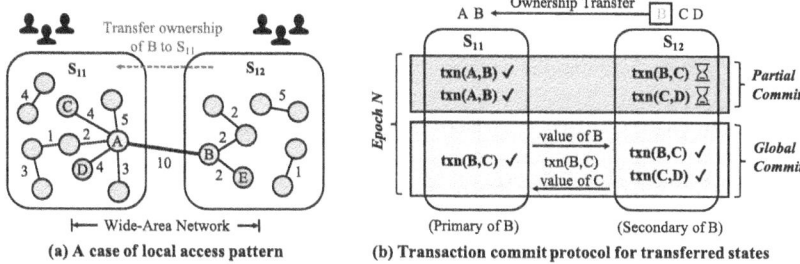

Fig. 4. Transaction commit protocol for the transferred states

degree of other states that are accessed with the transferred state at the same time, we define the local contention rate in Definition 1. Moreover, we allow the source shard to share the ownership of the transferred states with the target shard periodically, so that the users around the source shard can still access the transferred states from the nearby shard with low latency (such as users around S_{12} can still access B quickly in the example in Fig. 4(a)).

Definition 1 (Local contention rate). *Given a shard S_i, its local contention rate (LCR) to a certain state key is calculated as Eq. 1, where X denotes the set of recently accessed states of S_i, $P(key, x)$ denotes the probability that a transaction to be processed in S_i accesses key and x at the same time, and $Freq(x)$ refers to the access frequency of the state x.*

$$LCR(S_i, key) = \sum_{x \in (X \setminus key)} P(key, x) * Freq(x) \quad (1)$$

Definition 2 (State contention ratio). *Given two states A and B that are assigned to S_i and S_j respectively, the state contention ratio (SCR) of A and B is calculated as Eq. 2.*

$$SCR = \frac{LCR(S_i, A)}{LCR(S_j, B)} \quad (2)$$

Each leaf shard has an ownership directory, which contains two fields, including *key*, a unique identifier for a state, and *status*, the ownership status to the state *key* either *primary* or *secondary*. Note that *primary* means the shard takes over the ownership of state *key*, and each shard is the primary of its assigned states by default. *Secondary* means the shard will also take over the ownership of *key* periodically. Note that HieraChain allows at most two shards (one primary and one secondary) to take over the ownership of a state at the same time.

To sense the contention rate of other shards' states, we add the contention information into the read or write sets messages. Each shard computes SCR of two states that are involved in the local access pattern by dividing the local state's rate by that of another state from another shard. When the SCR is great, it means the contention rate is unbalanced and higher than the remote shard. Then, the ownership manager in shard sends an ownership transfer request.

5.2 Transaction Commit Protocol for the Transferred States

By now, the primary shard has taken over the ownership of the transferred states. To reduce the negative effects caused by remote access events in the secondary shard, we allow the secondary shard to access the transferred states as its local states in a specific phase periodically, where the primary and secondary update the transferred state deterministically. Specifically, We divide the full transaction execution timeline into a number of epochs, each epoch consisting of two phases:

- **Partial commit phase.** During the partial commit phase, only the primary shard of the transferred states is allowed to access the received states, while the remote accesses induced by the state ownership transfer in the secondary shard are held temporarily.
- **Global commit phase.** During the global commit phase, the primary sends the latest value of the received state to its secondary shard, and the secondary shard sends the holding transactions accessing the transferred state to its primary shard. Both shards execute these transactions deterministically and the transferred states achieve consistency.

Example 3. Figure 4(b) shows an example, where S_{11} is the primary of state A, and S_{12} is the primary of the states C and D. S_{11} and S_{12} are also the primary and secondary shards of state B respectively. Let $txn(k_1, k_2, ...)$ denote a transaction that accesses a number of states, $k_1, k_2, \cdots$. During the partial commit phase, as S_{11} is able to access state B, $txn(A, B)$ can be processed, $txn(B, C)$ is held unfortunately and $txn(C, D)$ is processed by S_{12}. During the global commit phase, S_{11} sends the latest value B to S_{12}, S_{12} sends the holding transactions accessing state B ($txn(B, C)$) to S_{11}. S_{11} and S_{12} execute $txn(B, C)$ deterministically, so that state B in S_{11} and S_{12} achieves consistency eventually.

The timing for the shift from the partial commit phase into the global commit phase for the partial and secondary shards is notified by the top shard periodically, e.g., every 0.2 s as in our evaluation. Once receiving the notification, each shard appends the instruction to its ledger and enters the global commit phase.

Performance Analysis. HieraChain incurs lower network costs in CST processing compared to traditional locality-awareness transaction processing protocols [2,10,11,15,22]. Assume the transferred state is accessed C times per unit time in its source shard, and the network cost for processing a CST is λ. Within an interval T, the traditional locality-aware approaches result in CT new CSTs, the network cost to process these transactions is $CT\lambda$. In HieraChain, the shard enters the secondary commit phase from the partial commit phase after each epoch (interval t), and each batch of Ct CSTs is processed at the same time, with network cost $(T/t)\lambda$.

6 Fault Tolerance

In the Byzantine environment, due to the existence of malicious nodes, HieraChain employs PBFT [4] consensus protocol to ensure the safety of each shard. Since the forwarding node is responsible for sending signed messages among shards, a malicious forwarding node may do simply ignore this message. To deal with this issue, the failure manager will report an exception detected by the timeout event. Specifically, there are three cases should be considered.

Ignore Prepared Message. The forwarding node of NCA doesn't send *prepared* messages to all the participants. In other words, the forwarding node only sends message to some (not all) participants, or sends to no participant. For the first case, it means we can find at least one shard, which only receives prepared message, but not the read and write sets messsage from certain participant when its timer expires. Then, this shard will multicast a *read and write sets query* message to them, requesting the read and write sets of certain CSTs. As the participant's nodes have not received *prepare* messages, they multicast a *prepare query* message to all nodes of NCA, urging the forwarding node to resend *prepare* message. If the participant still cannot receive *prepare* messages, the NCA's forwarding node is treated as a malicious node, and NCA will initiate consensus to change its forwarding node.

For the second case, the nodes in NCA haven't received any *commit* message from all participant shards if the timer expires. The NCA nodes multicast a *commit query* message to participant nodes, if at least $2f+1$ messages from different participant nodes report to the NCA that they haven't received *prepare* messages from the NCA, NCA will then initiate consensus to change its forwarding node. Other two cases the forwarding node **ignores read and write sets message** or **ignores commit message** can be resolved similarly, we will not present the details due to the space limit.

7 Performance Evaluation

7.1 Experimental Setting

Experimental Testbed. We implement HieraChain and four baselines on top of FISCO BCOS [13]. In our experiments, we deploy hundreds of nodes in total. Each shard that consists of four nodes (at most one malicious node) runs the PBFT [4] algorithm to ensure data consistency. Each node houses 16 GB RAM and Intel Xeon Gold 6330 processor with four cores clocked at 2.00 GHz. The average latency between any pair of nodes in different shards is 10 ms if they are located in the same area, or 50 ms otherwise. The leaf shards and their parent are located in the same area.

Workload. We use Smallbank benchmark [18] to simulate bank transfer operations, where 10,000 accounts are employed per shard with different percentages of CSTs. The access pattern to these accounts in general workload follows uniform distribution except for the workload used in locality-aware protocol evaluation.

Baselines. We evaluate the performance of HieraChain in comparison with the following representative approaches:

- **AHL** [6]. It adopts 2PC and two-phase locking (2PL) to guarantee the atomicity and isolation of cross-shard transaction processing.
- **Saguaro** [2]. It extends AHL to the hierarchical structure of edge computing networks to reduce the overhead of wide-area communication.
- **SharPer** [1]. It incorporates a decentralized flat protocol, where all nodes in the involved participants run PBFT to achieve consensus of a CST.
- **Zeus** [11]. It brings all states that are involved in local access patterns to the same shard to reduce the number of CSTs.

7.2 Overall Performance

We first evaluate the overall performance of HieraChain and baselines. We construct a network of 9 shards organized in a three-layer tree, where the root shard has two children, and each child has three leaf shards. We evaluate their performance on five workloads, each with different percentages of CSTs respectively. Moreover, we define the shards located in the same area as a cluster, we consider 5% of CSTs to be cross-cluster transactions to simulate the workloads in the geo-distributed scenarios. Figure 5 reports the throughput and latency of all approaches. HieraChain always achieves the highest throughput among all approaches. Especially, the throughput is 2x and 3x higher than SharPer and Saguaro under 100% CST percentage respectively, because that HieraChain reduces the expensive coordination cost of processing CSTs, and pipelines the CST processing. AHL exhibits the highest latency due to its multiple round-trips blocking communication and the limitation to support two more layers.

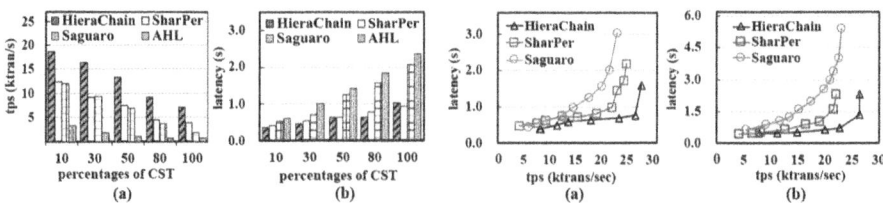

Fig. 5. Varying the percentage of CST **Fig. 6.** Varying transactions arrival rates

7.3 Varying Transaction Arrival Rates

We then measure the performance of all approaches under different transaction arrival rates. The experiments are conducted with different percentage of CSTs (10% and 30%), among which 5% transactions of these are cross-cluster transactions. The network is the same as that used in Sect. 7.2. Figure 6 reports the latency under different throughputs. As the transaction arrival rate increases, the latency of all approaches rise continually. When throughput is close to the peak, the latency rises rapidly. It is important to note that HieraChain has significantly higher maximal throughput than SharPer and Saguaro.

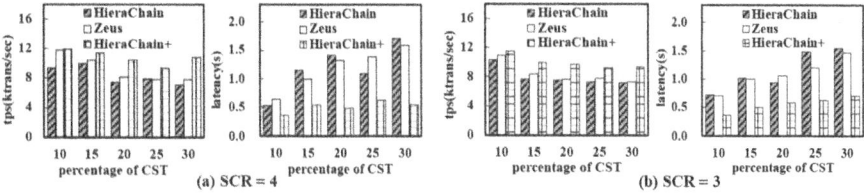

Fig. 7. Effect of the locality workloads.

7.4 Effect of the Locality Workloads

We measure the performance of our locality-aware transactions processing protocol (HieraChain+) in comparison with the general protocol (HieraChain) and representative locality-aware approach Zeus. The network consists of 4 shards which are organized in a two-layer tree, where the root shard has three children. To simulate the locality workloads, we figure all the CSTs follow local access patterns, the sum of the probability that a transaction in the secondary shard accesses the transferred states is 0.2, and the access pattern among other states in the shard follows a uniform distribution. We evaluate their performance with different percentage of CSTs and state contention ratio SCR. As shown in Fig. 7, HieraChain+ always achieves higher throughput with lower latency. The general approach (HieraChain) achieves the lowest throughput with high latency, as it cannot leverage any locality access patterns. Zeus achieves better performance than the general approach but falls short of HieraChain+, because Zeus causes new remote access events after transferring state ownership between shards.

7.5 Scalability

We evaluate the scalability of HieraChain in five kinds of networks, namely tiny (4 shards), small (9 shards), middle (13 shards), large (40 shards), and huge (60 shards). Shards are organized in a ternary tree (except for 9 shards). Four workloads with different percentages of CSTs are tested in all networks (80% and 100%), among which 5% transactions of these are cross-cluster transactions. As shown in Fig. 8(a-b), when the number of shards rises, the maximal throughput of HieraChain also increases. Specifically, the average throughput peak under different percentages of CSTs of the *huge* scale is about 1.4×, 4.0×, 6.7× and 13.7× greater than that of the *large*, *middle*, *small* and *tiny* scale network respectively. Moreover, Fig. 8(c) illustrates the throughput peak and corresponding lowest latency of each case, showing that HieraChain has an excellent property of linear scalability.

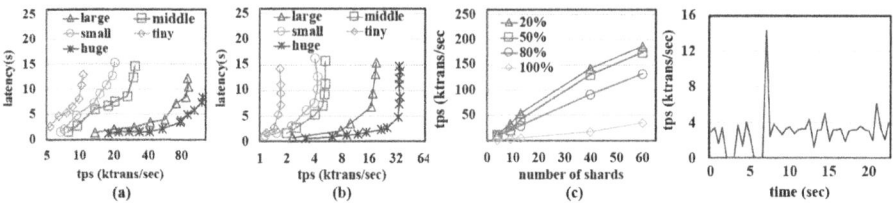

Fig. 8. Scalability

Fig. 9. Fault tolerance

7.6 Failure Tolerance

Finally, we conduct an experiment on three shards to evaluate the impact of forwarding node failure. As shown in Fig. 9, we terminate the forwarding node of the NCA and one participant after 2 and 5 s respectively, and observe the system's recovery. After the old forwarding node is killed, a new node will be elected among live nodes to forward requests. After a new forwarding node is elected in the participant, the system throughput quickly climbs to a peak as the system attempts to process transactions queued up during the crash.

8 Conclusion

This paper introduces HieraChain, a hierarchical sharding blockchain with high throughput. This novel hierarchical architecture inherits robust cross-shard transaction tolerance. We propose an efficient cross-shard transaction processing protocol via intensive pipelining, and extend it to support architecture with multiple layers. As data access locality is a key factor, we propose an optimized locality-aware transaction protocol to leverage local access patterns. Our evaluation shows that HieraChain can scale well under different percentages of cross-shard transactions, and achieve high throughput comparable to state-of-art flat and non-flat sharding systems.

Acknowledgments. This work was supported by National Key Research and Development Program of China (No. 2021YFB2700100), Shanghai "Science and Technology Innovation Action Plan" Project (No.23511100700) and Program of Shanghai Academic/Technology Research Leader (No. 23XD1401100).

References

1. Amiri, M.J., Agrawal, D., et al.: Sharper: sharding permissioned blockchains over network clusters. In: Proceedings of the 2021 International Conference on Management of Data, SIGMOD 2021, New York, pp. 76–88. Association for Computing Machinery (2021)
2. Amiri, M.J., Lai, Z., et al.: Saguaro: an edge computing-enabled hierarchical permissioned blockchain. In: 2023 IEEE 39th International Conference on Data Engineering (ICDE), pp. 259–272 (2023)

3. Androulaki, E., Barger, A., et al.: Hyperledger fabric: a distributed operating system for permissioned blockchains. In: 2018 ACM 13th International European Conference on Computer Systems (EuroSys), New York. Association for Computing Machinery (2018)
4. Castro, M., Liskov, B.: Practical byzantine fault tolerance. In: 1999 USENIX 3rd Symposium on Operating Systems Design and Implementation (OSDI), pp. 173–186 (1999)
5. Chen, Z., Zhuo, H., et al.: Schain: a scalable consortium blockchain exploiting intra- and inter-block concurrency. In: 2021 ACM 47th International Conference on Very Large Data Bases (VLDB), New York, pp. 2799–2802. Association for Computing Machinery (2021)
6. Dang, H., Dinh, T.T.A., et al.: Towards scaling blockchain systems via sharding. In: Proceedings of the 2019 International Conference on Management of Data, SIGMOD 2019, New York, pp. 123–140. Association for Computing Machinery (2019)
7. Hellings, J., Sadoghi, M.: ByShard: sharding in a byzantine environment. VLDB J. **32**(6), 1343–1367 (2023)
8. Hong, Z., Guo, S., et al.: Pyramid: a layered sharding blockchain system. In: 2021 IEEE International Conference on Computer Communications, INFOCOM 2021, pp. 1–10 (2021)
9. Huang, H., Huang, Z., et al.: Mvcom: scheduling most valuable committees for the large-scale sharded blockchain. In: 2021 IEEE 41th International Conference on Distributed Computing Systems (ICDCS), pp. 629–639 (2021)
10. Huang, H., Peng, X., et al.: Brokerchain: a cross-shard blockchain protocol for account/balance-based state sharding. In: 2022 IEEE 42th International Conference on Distributed Computing Systems (ICDCS), pp. 1968–1977 (2022)
11. Katsarakis, A., Ma, Y., et al.: Zeus: locality-aware distributed transactions. In: 2021 ACM 16th International European Conference on Computer Systems (EuroSys), New York, pp. 145–161. Association for Computing Machinery (2021)
12. Kokoris-Kogias, E., Jovanovic, P., et al.: Omniledger: a secure, scale-out, decentralized ledger via sharding. In: 2018 IEEE Symposium on Security and Privacy (SP), pp. 583–598 (2018)
13. Li, H., Chen, Y., et al.: Fisco-bcos: an enterprise-grade permissioned blockchain system with high-performance. In: Proceedings of the 2023 International Conference for High Performance Computing, Networking, Storage and Analysis, SC 2023, pp. 1–17 (2023)
14. Luu, L., Narayanan, V., et al.: A secure sharding protocol for open blockchains. In: Proceedings of the 2016 ACM SIGSAC Conference on Computer and Communications Security, CCS 2016, pp. 17–30 (2016)
15. Nguyen, L.N., Nguyen, T.D.T., et al.: Optchain: optimal transactions placement for scalable blockchain sharding. In: 2019 IEEE 39th International Conference on Distributed Computing Systems (ICDCS), pp. 525–535 (2019)
16. Qi, X., Chen, Z., et al.: Schain: Scalable concurrency over flexible permissioned blockchain. In: 2023 IEEE 39th International Conference on Data Engineering (ICDE), pp. 1901–1913 (2023)
17. Serafini, M., Taft, R., et al.: Clay: fine-grained adaptive partitioning for general database schemas. In: 2016 ACM 42th International Conference on Very Large Data Bases (VLDB), pp. 445–456 (2016)
18. Smallbank benchmark. http://hstore.cs.brown.edu/documentation/deployment/benchmarks/smallbank (2021)

19. Tao, Y., Li, B., et al.: On sharding open blockchains with smart contracts. In: 2020 IEEE 36th International Conference on Data Engineering (ICDE), pp. 1357–1368 (2020)
20. Wang, J., Wang, H.: Monoxide: scale out blockchains with asynchronous consensus zones. In: 2019 USENIX 16th Symposium on Networked Systems Design and Implementation, NSDI 2019, pp. 95–112 (2019)
21. Zamani, M., Movahedi, M., et al.: Rapidchain: scaling blockchain via full sharding. In: Proceedings of the 2018 ACM SIGSAC Conference on Computer and Communications Security, CCS 2018. pp. 931–948 (2018)
22. Zhang, Y., Pan, S., et al.: Txallo: dynamic transaction allocation in sharded blockchain systems. In: 2023 IEEE 39th International Conference on Data Engineering (ICDE), pp. 721–733 (2023)

Resource-Aware Heterogeneous Federated Learning with Specialized Local Models

Sixing Yu[1]([✉]), J. Pablo Muñoz[2]([✉]), and Ali Jannesari[1]([✉])

[1] Iowa State University, Ames, USA
yusx@iastate.edu, jannesar@iastate.edu
[2] Intel Labs, San Jose, USA
pablo.munoz@intel.com

Abstract. Federated Learning (FL) is extensively used to train AI/ML models in distributed and privacy-preserving settings. Participant edge devices in FL systems typically contain non-independent and identically distributed (Non-IID) private data and unevenly distributed computational resources. Preserving user data privacy while optimizing AI/ML models in a heterogeneous federated network requires us to address data and system/resource heterogeneity. To address these challenges, we propose Resource-aware Federated Learning (RaFL). RaFL allocates resource-aware specialized models to edge devices using Neural Architecture Search (NAS) and allows heterogeneous model architecture deployment by knowledge extraction and fusion. Combining NAS and FL enables on-demand customized model deployment for resource-diverse edge devices. Furthermore, we propose a multi-model architecture fusion scheme allowing the aggregation of the distributed learning results. Results demonstrate RaFL's superior resource efficiency compared to SoTA.

Keywords: Federated Learning · Resource Heterogeneous · AutoML

1 Introduction

Federated Learning (FL) has emerged as a privacy-aware decentralized AI/ML model training and optimizing paradigm, widely adopted by the technology industry, to leverage the massive data generated at the edge (e.g., mobile phones and IoT devices). FL involves local client nodes distributively training and optimizing AI models, with an aggregating server integrating the decentralized results without accessing users' private data.

However, FL introduces two key challenges: data heterogeneity and resource/system heterogeneity, making it difficult to scale. The private data collected on edge devices is non-independent and identically distributed (Non-IID), causing uncertainties and optimization failures when training with naïve decentralized methods [4]. Additionally, resource heterogeneity, where edge devices have different specifications and computational capacities, leads to inefficient resource utilization. Moreover, the expensive communication overhead produced by frequently sharing weights/gradients between edge clients and servers becomes a bottleneck for scaling up the network, especially in cross-device and model-centric FL settings involving possibly millions of edge devices, resulting in massive bandwidth consumption.

State-of-the-art (SoTA) FL baselines mainly focus on addressing data heterogeneity (i.e., non-IID data on edge devices), while ignoring system and resource heterogeneity among edge devices, which exhibit significant variations, particularly in cross-device FL settings. Simply deploying the same model architecture to every client leads to poor resource utilization, causing resource-hungry edge devices to consume precious energy supplies while underutilizing more capable edge devices. Although AutoML solutions, such as Neural Architecture Search (NAS) [1,20], have achieved success in generating high-performance neural architecture models for resource-heterogeneous environments, integrating NAS into existing FL solutions presents challenges, as it requires identical neural architecture among clients for aggregating decentralized training results. Recent efforts [8,27] dedicated to integrating NAS, network pruning, and weights dropout in FL rely on zero-padding model weights to enable multi-neural architectures, helping in model sparsity but offering limited contributions to model size reduction and communication efficiency.

To address both data and system heterogeneity, we propose Resource-aware Federated Learning (RaFL), a multi-architecture FL framework. RaFL leverages a weight-sharing supernet to efficiently specialize resource-aware models on edge devices, tailored to their specific resource constraints. This approach enables the deployment of diverse model architectures across edge-FL clients while maintaining the ability to aggregate and share knowledge. Central to RaFL is the use of a small-size **knowledge network** that cooperates with the resource-aware local model for neural knowledge sharing among clients. RaFL clients engage in deep mutual learning [30] to co-train their network pairs and diffuse knowledge into their knowledge networks. The RaFL server then aggregates the local knowledge from each client's knowledge network, effectively combining the decentralized training results and supporting multi-architecture FL. Given the availability of public data, RaFL provides the option of using ensemble distillation to improve the robustness of knowledge fusion. RaFL makes the following contributions:

- Mitigates resource/system heterogeneity by deploying resource-aware neural architectures, and maximizes resource utilization.
- Provides ensemble knowledge distillation and transfer learning algorithms specifically designed for federated learning, which aim to improve the robustness of knowledge fusion.
- Employs high-performing specialized neural architectures to accelerate inference at the edge.
- Reduces FL communication overhead by using a smaller interceding knowledge network.
- Provides alternative configurations to take advantage of transfer learning, and public data, making it scalable and applicable in real-world scenarios.

2 Related Works

Federated Learning. The pioneering FL research by [19] introduced FedAvg, which combined local stochastic gradient descent (SGD) model optimization with global model averaging. Recently, several variants of FedAvg have emerged. For example, FedProx [17] was proposed to address convergence issues associated with data and device heterogeneity, which was achieved by permitting the participation of "straggler" devices and introducing a proximal term in the local loss. FedNova [23] normalized and scaled local updates by modifying weights to mitigate gradient bias. SCAFFOLD [13] introduced gradient-based control variates to correct client drift and speed up convergence. These SoTA methods inherently assume uniformity in edge resource capacities by deploying architecturally identical models onto resource-heterogeneous edge devices. In contrast, heterogeneous edge computational capacities require the deployment of specialized client network architectures. As such, accounting for potential network architectural diversity is imperative.

Personalized FL. Personalized FL [3,5,6,12,29] has gained attention as a solution to the challenges posed by *statistical heterogeneity*, such as non-IID data distribution, varied sample sizes among clients, and imbalanced class distributions across local datasets. Uniform FL models can degrade overall performance, while personalized models increase robustness. Personalized FL allows edge clients to tune model weights to better fit local data, but these approaches still adopt the same model architecture at the client, failing to address the heterogeneity of computational capacities.

Knowledge Distillation in Federated Learning. Knowledge distillation (KD) has been adopted in FL as a means to address model heterogeneity [7,15,18,21,22]. For example, Fed-ensemble [22] integrates the prediction output of all client models; FedKD [24] proposes an adaptive mutual distillation framework to learn a student and a teacher model simultaneously on the client side; FedDF [18] distills the ensemble of client and teacher models to a server student model; [15], proposes the application of a public dataset as a medium of exchanging knowledge among customized client models; [28] proposes the use of KD to transfer knowledge between a global network and a student network rather than using a direct assignment. In contrast, our approach utilizes local deep mutual learning [30] coupled with an optional ensemble-based multi-model fusion in the cloud whenever public data is available. In the absence of public data, we perform global model aggregation. This makes our pipeline quite flexible and applicable in real-world scenarios.

3 Methodology

There are three main stages in RaFL: resource-aware model specialization, local knowledge fusion with deep mutual learning, and cloud knowledge aggregation (Fig. 1). RaFL performs an on-demand model architecture search from weight-sharing supernet [1] to tailor to the resource utilization requirements of edge

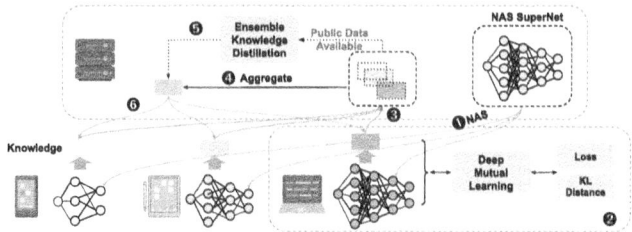

Fig. 1. During initialization, edge clients request for specialized resource-aware models from the weight-sharing supernet with neural architecture search (NAS). During local training, the local resource-aware model and knowledge network are co-trained together via deep mutual learning. The server fuses the neural knowledge from clients and performs optional ensemble learning if public data is present.

devices, unlike mainstream FL systems that deploy identical model architectures on all devices (❶ in Fig. 1). Local devices train their specialized model on local data and transfer the model's knowledge to a smaller knowledge network via deep mutual learning (❷). Edge clients then communicate their local knowledge to the cloud server (❸), which aggregates the received knowledge into a global knowledge network (❹). When public data is available, RaFL optionally provides ensemble distillation to further improve the robustness of the knowledge aggregation stage (❺). Finally, the RaFL server transfers the global knowledge to the edge devices (❻).

3.1 Resource-Aware Federated Learning Using Specialized Models

Mainstream FL solutions assume homogeneous resource capacities across clients, which is impractical in cross-device settings with varying computational resources. Simply deploying an identical model architecture leads to poor resource utilization. RaFL proposes a resource-aware federated neural architecture search to obtain resource-tailored models for heterogeneous edge devices.

We first deploy a weight-sharing super-network on the cloud. During FL initialization, clients query this supernet [1] to obtain resource-aware subnets matched to their computational constraints. The supernet is trained by minimizing a validation loss over a distribution of subnet architectures (Eq. 1).

$$\min_{\Theta} \sum_{arch_i} L_{val}(C(\Theta, arch_i)) \quad (1)$$

where Θ represents the super-network weights, $arch_i$ is a subnetwork configuration, and $C(\Theta, arch_i)$ samples the subnetwork weights from the super-network. Once trained, subnetworks can be efficiently derived without retraining the super-network.

In the NAS process, RaFL defines a search space $\mathcal{S}$ that encompasses the possible architectures for the specialized models. The search space is constrained by a set of resource requirements $\mathcal{R}$, which includes memory, computational power, and energy consumption limitations of the edge devices. The objective is to find an optimal architecture $arch^*$ that maximizes performance while satisfying the resource constraints:

$$arch^* = \arg \max_{arch \in S} P(arch) \quad \text{s.t.} \quad R(arch) \leq \mathcal{R} \tag{2}$$

where $P(arch)$ represents the performance metric of the architecture $arch$, and $R(arch)$ denotes the resource consumption of $arch$. RaFL employs a search strategy to efficiently explore the search space and extract the specialized models M_i from the supernet, tailored to the specific capabilities of each edge device i. This process ensures that the obtained models maximize resource utilization and performance in the federated learning setting.

3.2 Local Knowledge Fusion

Traditional FL methods deploy a uniform model across clients, enabling simple weight/gradient averaging for aggregation. However, in RaFL, where varying resource-aware architectures are used, weight averaging is infeasible. Instead, we propose communicating extracted knowledge from local models via deep mutual learning (DML) [30].

For the lth client C_l, we denote its resource-aware model as θ_l and a downloaded knowledge network as θ_l^k. C_l jointly optimizes θ_l and θ_l^k on its local data. For an input batch, we first computes the cross-entropy loss $L_c(\theta; B)$ (Eq. 3) for both networks independently.

$$L_c(\theta; B) = -\frac{1}{|B|} \sum_{x,y \in B} y^T \log(\sigma(\theta(x))) \tag{3}$$

It then measures the Kullback-Leibler (KL) divergence $D_{KL}(\theta_l || \theta_l^k; B)$ (Eq. 4) between the predicted distributions.

$$D_{KL}(\theta_l || \theta_l^k; B) = \frac{1}{|B|} \sum_{x,y \in B} \sigma(\theta_l(x)^T) \log(\frac{\sigma(\theta_l(x))}{\sigma(\theta_l^k)}) \tag{4}$$

The mutual learning loss (Eqs. 5 and 6) combines the cross-entropy loss and KL divergence, enabling learning from data while aligning the networks.

$$L_{\theta_l} = L_c(\theta_l; B) + D_{KL}(\theta_l^k || \theta_l; B) \tag{5}$$

$$L_{\theta_l^k} = L_c(\theta_l^k; B) + D_{KL}(\theta_l || \theta_l^k; B) \tag{6}$$

DML outperforms solo learning due to the dissimilarity between the participating models (θ_l and θ_l^k). Their varying architectures and the intermittent aggregation of θ_l^k enable learning different data representations, allowing them to capture each other's knowledge. Moreover, while the smaller θ_l^k reduces communication overhead, co-learning with the larger θ_l boosts its performance.

As clients communicate their θ_l^k networks, they share local knowledge and receive global knowledge. Successive DML steps further converge both θ_l and θ_l^k on the global data distribution. Overall, initializing clients with resource-specific NAS subnetworks paired with a smaller θ_l^k addresses device heterogeneity and reduces communication overhead.

3.3 Cloud Knowledge Aggregation and Ensemble Distillation

RaFL utilizes the knowledge network as a medium to support interoperability among multi-model FL clients. The function of the knowledge network is to exchange knowledge among Non-IID clients (Fig. 1 ❸ and ❻). RaFL provides two model fusion solutions, weight aggregating and ensemble knowledge distillation, to support comprehensive FL practical scenarios (Fig. 1 ❹ and ❺).

Assume θ^k is the global knowledge network, and θ_l^k as the lth client's knowledge network. We select a set of communication clients S in the current communication round. Once we receive the knowledge from edges, we aggregate the knowledge networks (Eq. 7).

$$\theta^k \leftarrow \frac{n_l}{N_S} \sum_{l \in S} \theta_l^k \qquad (7)$$

Here, N_S is the total data size in selected clients S, and n_l is the number of data samples in the lth client. When public data is available, RaFL provides an ensemble knowledge distillation option for boosting cloud aggregation. RaFL ensembles knowledge networks using the average logits strategy (Eq. 8) to produce a combined output on the public dataset. The outputted soft labels are then coupled with the unlabeled dataset to train the global knowledge network in tandem. The distillation loss is defined in Eq. 9.

$$\theta_{ens}(x) = Avg(\theta_l^k(x))_{l \in S} \qquad (8)$$

$$L_d = D_{KL}(\theta_{ens} || \theta^k; B) \qquad (9)$$

Notably, the knowledge network is a small-sized network derived from the NAS super-network. Our ablation study shows the trade-off between the size and the overall performance of the knowledge network, indicating no significant gain in increasing the size of the knowledge network.

4 Experiments

4.1 Experimental Setup

Datasets and models. We conducted experiments on datasets consistent with the baselines: CIFAR-10/100 [14], FEMNIST [2] under Non-IID benchmark settings [16]. The models we deployedwere sampled from MobileNetV2/V3 [10,11] or ResNet [9] super-networks [1]. To avoid confusion, we identify networks by their FLOPs, e.g., we identify ResNet-34 as ResNet with 76 MFLOPs.

Federated Learning Settings. We set up different numbers of clients from 30 to 3000 in our experimental FL environment, with 10% to 70% client participation rate in each round of communication. We simulated scaled, dynamic sporadic, and asynchronous FL scenarios. Clients are allocated to Non-IID local datasets following the benchmark's Non-IID settings [16].

NAS Settings. We initialize an weight-sharing supernet with architectures for ResNet, MobileNetV2, and MobileNetV3.

Baselines. We compare RaFL with state-of-the-art (SoTA) FL algorithms, including:

- Strong FL optimization methods, such as FedAvg [19], FedProx [17], FedNova [23], SCAFFOLD [13], SPATL [26].
- Knowledge distillation-based methods, such as FedDF [18].
- Neural architecture search in FL methods, such as FedNAS [8].

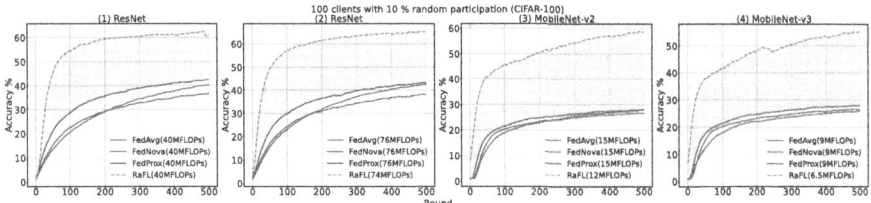

Fig. 2. Comparison of RaFL with SoTAs under **vanilla aggregation** setting.

4.2 Learning Efficiency

We explore the learning efficiency and optimization ability of RaFL by evaluating the training performance with respect to communication rounds and comparing it with FedAvg [19], FedNova [23], and FedProx [17]. We consider all possible practical situations ((a), (b), and (c) settings in below) for a fair and extensive comparison.

(a) Vanilla Aggregation. RaFL with vanilla aggregation (Fig. 1 step ❹ and Eq. 7) is used to aggregate local models in each communication round without requiring public data. Figure 2 shows the comparison results on training performance versus communication rounds under different model architectures and capacities. RaFL outperforms the baselines with a large margin and exhibits a stable optimization process while consuming fewer resources. For example, when optimizing MobileNet-v3, RaFL produces 28% higher accuracy than the baselines. Figure 4a illustrates that RaFL consistently outperforms the baselines across diverse settings and achieves higher convergence accuracy. RaFL effectively resists overfitting and shows better learning capacity (Fig. 5a).

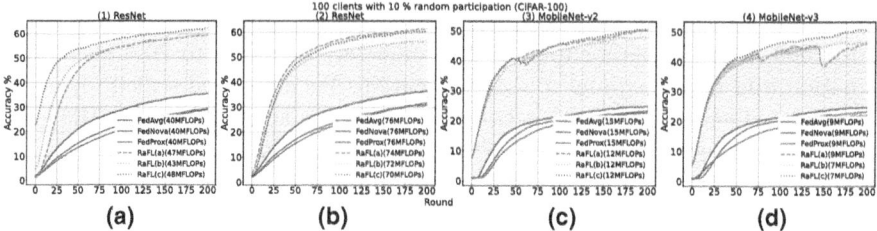

Fig. 3. Comparison of SoTAs with RaFL using (a) **vanilla aggregation**, (b) **ensemble distillation** and (c) **transfer learning** settings.

(b) Public Data with Ensemble and Knowledge Distillation. RaFL offers an ensemble distillation option to enhance server aggregation (steps ❹ and ❺). Figure 3 RaFL(b) shows that RaFL equipped with ensemble distillation outperforms strong baselines with significant margins. Ensemble distillation improves and stabilizes training in sporadic connected FL (Fig. 3 (4)). However, its effectiveness depends on the similarity of public and private client data distributions.

(c) Transfer Learning with NAS. RaFL takes advantage of transfer learning on its pre-trained NAS subnetworks when specialized networks are applied to

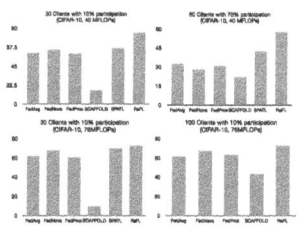

(a) Convergence accuracy overhead under various FL settings.

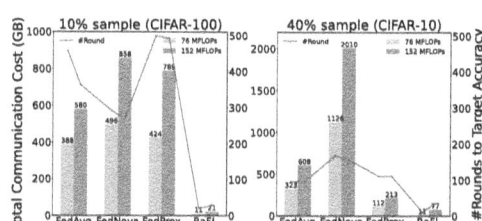

(b) Communication cost to achieve target accuracy.

Fig. 4. Performance comparison of RaFL and baselines.

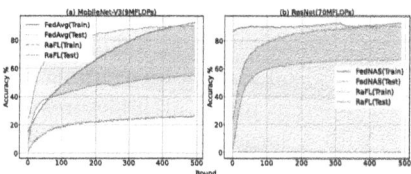

(a) Local training accuracy vs. test accuracy.

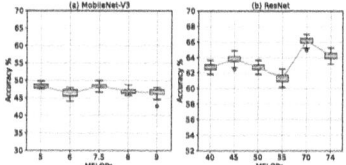

(b) RaFL under resource heterogeneous setting.

Fig. 5. Performance analysis of RaFL.

the Non-IID FL dataset. Figure 3 RaFL(c) shows that RaFL (c) benefits from pre-trained initial weights, resulting in high accuracy in the initial training stage and quick convergence during fine-tuning.

4.3 Communication Efficiency

RaFL exhibits significant superiority in communication efficiency compared to SoTAs, attributed to utilizing smaller knowledge networks for communication. We demonstrate RaFL's communication efficiency by optimizing models to reach target performance and achieve converged performance, considering the vanilla aggregation setting (Sect. 4.2.a).

Table 1. Communication cost to achieve target accuracy.

Method	Model Arc.	Resource Usage (MFLOPs)	Clients	Dataset	Target Accuracy	Communication Cost			
						Round/Client	Total	Δ Cost	Speed Up
FedAvg [19]	ResNet	40	100	CIFAR100	40%	0.85 GB	388 GB	0 GB	(1 $\times$)
		76				1.6 GB	580 GB	0 GB	(1 $\times$)
		40		CIFAR10	60%	3.4 GB	323 GB	0 GB	(1 $\times$)
		76				6.4 GB	608 GB	0 GB	(1 $\times$)
FedNova [23]	ResNet	40	100	CIFAR100	40%	1.7 GB	496 GB	+108 GB	(0.78 $\times$)
		76				3.2 GB	858 GB	+278 GB	(0.68 $\times$)
		40		CIFAR 10	60%	6.7 GB	1126 GB	+803 GB	(0.29 $\times$)
		76				12.8 GB	2010 GB	+1402 GB	(0.30 $\times$)
FedProx [17]	ResNet	40	100	CIFAR100	38%	0.85 GB	424 GB	+36 GB	(0.92 $\times$)
		76			40%	1.6 GB	789 GB	+209 GB	(0.74 $\times$)
		40		CIFAR 10	60%	3.4 GB	377 GB	+54 GB	(0.86 $\times$)
		76				6.4 GB	710 GB	+102 GB	(0.86 $\times$)
RaFL (Ours)	ResNet	28	100	CIFAR100	40%	0.66 GB	13.2 GB	−374.8 GB	(**29.4** $\times$)
		51				1.07 GB	31.0 GB	−549 GB	(**18.70** $\times$)
		28		CIFAR10	60%	2.2 GB	77 GB	−246 GB	(**4.19** $\times$)

Optimizing Model to Achieve Target Performance. Table 1 shows that RaFL consistently outperforms SoTAs in communication overhead under various configurations. For example, when using ResNet on CIFAR-100, RaFL reduces communication cost by up to 29.4$\times$ compared to FedAvg [19] while using significantly less computational resources. Figure 4b further demonstrates RaFL's superiority on larger model capacities (76 MFLOPs and 152 MFLOPs), requiring fewer communication rounds to achieve target performance.

RaFL's communication efficiency stems from two main factors: (1) high-performance neural architectures generated using Neural Architecture Search, enabling faster convergence, and (2) knowledge network communication, resulting in a reduced communication cost with up to 4$\times$ less bandwidth per round (Table 1).

Optimizing Model for Convergent Performance. Table 2 summarizes the results on CIFAR-100, showing that RaFL uses less communication cost while achieving significantly better model performance. For instance, RaFL reaches around 65% accuracy on ResNet-74MFLOPs, while the next best method, FedNova, converges at around 43% with a total cost 1200 GB higher.

Overall, RaFL results in a lower communication cost to achieve both target performance and overall convergence across a wide range of FL settings.

Table 2. Communication cost to model converge

Method	Model	datasets	Resource Usage (MFLOPs)	Clients	Round Cost	Total Cost	Converged Accuracy	Δ Accuracy
FedAvg [19]	ResNet	CIFAR-100	40 MFLOPs	100	0.85 GB	425GB	(40.00 ± 1.21)%	0%
			76 MFLOPs		1.6 GB	800 GB	(42.21 ± 0.80)%	0%
	MobileNet-V2		15 MFLOPs		280 MB	137 GB	(27.80 ± 0.80)%	0%
	MobileNet-V3		9 MFLOPs		230 MB	112 GB	(25.89 ± 0.87)%	0%
FedNova [23]	ResNet	CIFAR-100	40 MFLOPs	100	1.7 GB	850 GB	(42.29 ± 1.23)%	+2.29%
			76 MFLOPs		3.2 GB	1600 GB	(43.02 ± 0.76)%	+0.81%
	MobileNet-V2		15 MFLOPs		560 MB	273 GB	(27.98 ± 0.55)%	+0.18%
	MobileNet-V3		9 MFLOPs		225 MB	460 MB	(26.25 ± 0.82)%	+0.36%
FedProx [17]	ResNet	CIFAR-100	40 MFLOPs	100	0.85 GB	425 GB	(36.43 ± 1.10)%	-3.57%
			76 MFLOPs		1.6 GB	800 GB	(38.04 ± 1.59)%	-4.17%
	MobileNet-V2		15 MFLOPs		280 MB	137 GB	(26.65 ± 0.82)%	-1.15%
	MobileNet-V3		9 MFLOPs		230 MB	112 GB	(24.39 ± 0.52)%	-1.50%
RaFL (Ours)	ResNet	CIFAR-100	47 MFLOPs	100	0.66 GB	**340 GB**	**(62.01 ± 1.84)%**	**+22.01%**
			74 MFLOPs		0.80 GB	**400 GB**	**(65.28 ± 1.22)%**	**+23.07%**
	MobileNet-V2		12 MFLOPs		180 MB	**88 GB**	**(58.66 ± 1.40)%**	**+30.86%**
	MobileNet-V3		6.5 MFLOPs		140 MB	**68 GB**	**(50.49 ± 2.49)%**	**+24.6%**

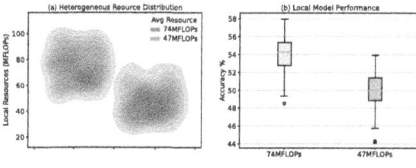

Fig. 6. Local model performance in resource heterogeneous FL.

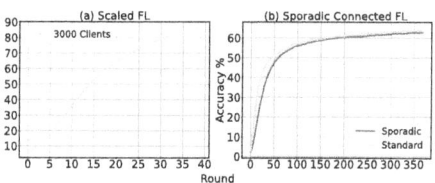

Fig. 7. Scaled and Sporadic Connected FL.

Additionally, the model deployed by RaFL requires fewer FLOPs at the edge and demonstrates lower resource consumption while achieving higher accuracy, enabling faster inference and better downstream task applications.

4.4 Resource-Aware System Heterogeneity

We investigated RaFL's ability to cope with resource heterogeneity by evaluating its resource utilization efficiency and learning efficiency under system heterogeneity.

Resource Utilization Comparison. Compared with uniform model deployment FL methods (such as FedAvg [19], FedNova [23], FedProx [17], SCAFFOLD [13]), Table 3 shows that RaFL demonstrates significant resource utilization efficiency and high accuracy overhead. At least 90% of the resources were utilized by RaFL across different resource constraints, with the highest utilization being 99%. In contrast, the single model deployment in the baselines would have their resource utilization limited by the clients with the lowest resource capacity.

Model Performance Under Different Resource Budget. Fig. 5b illustrates the impact of different resource budgets on model accuracy optimized by RaFL.

Table 3. Resource utilization efficiency

Method	Model	Total Resource	Utilized Resources	Resource Utilization	Accuracy
Uniformed Baselines	ResNet	5GFLOPs	2.75GFLOPs	55%	41%
		8GFLOPs	5.02GFLOPs	63%	43%
	MobileNet-V2	1.2GFLOPs	1.07GFLOPs	89%	29%
	MobileNet-V3	0.7GFLOPs	0.49MFLOPs	70%	27%
RaFL	ResNet	5GFLOPs	4.63GFLOPs	**93%**	**65%**
		8GFLOPs	7.26GFLOPs	**91%**	**67%**
	MobileNet-V2	1.2GFLOPs	1.15GFLOPs	**99%**	**60%**
	MobileNet-V3	0.7GFLOPs	0.64GFLOP	**91%**	**57%**

RaFL exhibits stable performance under various resource heterogeneity scenarios. Even with significant differences in preset resource overhead, RaFL maximizes learning efficiency and resource efficiency, producing stable final model performance. This adaptability and effectiveness highlight RaFL's ability to address diverse resource constraints while maintaining consistent performance across various systems.

Edge Performance Under System Heterogeneity. We set up two systems with different average resource constraints (74MFLOPs and 47MFLOPs). Figure 6 (a) shows the heterogeneous resource distributions within these systems. Despite the significant variance in local client resources, Fig. 6 (b) demonstrates that the models running at the edge exhibit similar performance. This can be attributed to the optimal architecture search performed by the neural architecture search under the provided resource constraints, emphasizing RaFL's effectiveness in addressing system heterogeneity and ensuring consistent performance across diverse edge devices.

4.5 Scaled and Sporadic FL

In practice, a typical FL system interacts with a large number of clients. The system is dynamic and asynchronous, meaning new clients may join and leave the network at any stage of FL training, and the number of participating clients may be large. Figure 7 shows RaFL's performance under scaled and sporadic FL settings. Large-scale federated learning is one of the biggest challenges in FL, as shown in Fig. 7 (a), we set up 3000 clients with distinct heterogeneous local data on FEMNIST, RaFL converges quickly and remains stable. Figure 7 (b) shows the sporadic FL in CIFAR-100. We implemented a client stream to simulate a sporadic FL setting. For each round of communication, we uniformly replace 10% of clients with new ones, to mimic 10% of clients losing connections and 10% of clients joining the current stage of training. RaFL achieves impressive results under sporadic FL and produces competitive model performance compared to the standard FL setting. This is despite the total clients flowing through the sporadic FL setting equalling 3500, which is 35× more than the standard setting.

The results highlight RaFL's robustness and adaptability in dynamic and large-scale federated learning scenarios.

4.6 Comparison with FL Approaches that Use Neural Architecture Search

Learning Efficiency Comparison. We compared RaFL to FedNAS [8], which deploys super-networks directly to edge devices and searches sub-networks locally for edge applications. Figure 5a(b) shows that FedNAS diverged due to overfitting in our experiment settings. We also analyzed DecNAS [25]. It is important to note that RaFL has a different objective compared to FedNAS [8] and DecNAS [25]. While FedNAS and DecNAS aim to optimize the NAS super-network via federated learning on user private data, RaFL focuses on efficiently deploying resource-aware specialized networks to heterogeneous clients to maximize resource utilization and achieve robust performance in dynamic and large-scale federated learning scenarios.

Distinguishing RaFL from Other NAS-Based Federated Learning Approaches. Other approaches may not yield efficient neural architectures. For instance, FedNAS performs neural architecture search at the beginning of the training, which may not result in high-performance architectures. Existing methods might not effectively tackle resource heterogeneity in edge devices. For example, FedNAS conducts neural architecture search directly on edge devices, which can be computationally demanding and unsuitable for resource-limited edge devices. Optimizing super-networks in FL environments can easily lead to divergence. These approaches might work when the number of clients is limited. However, when the number of clients in FL becomes large, it becomes almost impossible to converge the over-parameterized super-networks. In contrast, RaFL aims to efficiently deploy resource-aware specialized networks to heterogeneous clients to maximize resource utilization and achieve robust performance in dynamic and large-scale federated learning scenarios. RaFL ingeniously avoids the above limitations by dynamically deploying specialized high-performance networks to edge clients based on their local resource overhead, enabling efficient utilization of local resources and better downstream tasks.

4.7 Comparison with KD-Based FL

As shown in Table 4, utilizing knowledge distillation to aggregate local models may not enhance the learning efficiency of the FL system. The performance of knowledge distillation heavily relies on the similarity between public data and local data, making it unsuitable for all general FL environments. We compared RaFL with the knowledge distillation baseline FedDF [18] under various public data scenarios. RaFL is more robust; it initializes the global knowledge network by weighted averaging local knowledge networks using Eq. 7 and then optionally performs ensemble knowledge distillation. In cases where the public data significantly deviates from the overall local data distribution in FL, RaFL experiences fewer negative effects.

4.8 Extra Burdens of Knowledge Networks

To address concerns regarding the potential extra computational overhead introduced by incorporating knowledge networks and performing local deep mutual learning in the RaFL framework, we designed and conducted experiments using two distinct FL environments: Environment A: 12 MFLOPs MobileNet-V3 and an 8 MFLOPs MobileNet-V3 knowledge network deployed at each local client. Environment B: 20 MFLOPs MobileNet-V3 deployed at each local client, directly updating the model with the SGD algorithm without knowledge distillation. Both FL environments were trained for 500 rounds separately using the same nodes and the same type of GPU (NVIDIA V100). Results show that Environment B required 49 h and 19 min to complete training, while Environment A only took 48 h and 25 min. This indicates that incorporating knowledge networks and performing deep mutual learning did not add significant computational overhead to the edge.

Table 4. Comparison with FedDF under different public data.

Public Data	Method	Local Dataset	Clients	Participation	Accuracy
CINIC-10	FedDF	CIFAR-100	100	10%	diverge
	RaFL-(b)		100	10%	50.51
CIFAR-10	FedDF	CIFAR-10	30	40%	73.35
	RaFL-(b)		30	40%	72.49
TinyImageNet	FedDF	CIFAR-100	100	10%	diverge
	RaFL-(b)		100	10%	54.95

5 Conclusion

In this paper, we present RaFL, a resource-aware FL approach that seamlessly integrates AutoML solutions, such as NAS, into FL environments. By providing clients with specialized networks tailored to their individual resource constraints, RaFL offers a robust solution for achieving efficient learning and improved resource utilization. Experiments conducted on various heterogeneous FL environments demonstrate RaFL's practicality and efficacy in enabling heterogeneous FL with faster convergence and enhanced communication efficiency. The promising results obtained by RaFL highlight the potential of integrating AutoML solutions into FL environments to better accommodate the diverse resource constraints of edge devices, paving the way for wider applications in real-world situations. Moreover, RaFL exhibits effectiveness in addressing FL scenarios, showcasing its potential for easy extension to decentralized and distributed training frameworks.

Acknowledgment. This research was supported by the National Science Foundation under Grant number 2243775 and ISU Dean's Emerging Faculty Leaders Award (Grant Number: SG2703882). We also appreciate the provision of computational resources by Intel Labs for this project. Furthermore, we thank the ResearchIT team [1] at Iowa State University for their continuous and helpful assistance.([1] https://researchit.las.iastate.edu)

References

1. Cai, H., Gan, C., Wang, T., Zhang, Z., Han, S.: Once for all: train one network and specialize it for efficient deployment. In: Proceedings of International Conference on Learning Representations (ICLR) (2020)
2. Caldas, S., et al.: LEAF: a benchmark for federated settings. In: Proceedings of Advances in Neural Information Processing Systems (NeurIPS) (2019)
3. Dinh, C.T., Tran, N.H., Nguyen, T.D.: Personalized federated learning with moreau envelopes. arXiv preprint arXiv:2006.08848 (2021)
4. Kairouz, P., et al.: Advances and open problems in federated learning. Found. Trends® Mach. Learn. **14**(1-2), 1–210 (2021)
5. Fallah, A., Mokhtari, A., Ozdaglar, A.: Personalized federated learning: A meta-learning approach. In: Proceedings of Advances in Neural Information Processing Systems (NeurIPS) (2020)
6. Hanzely, F., Hanzely, S., Horváth, S., Richtárik, P.: Lower bounds and optimal algorithms for personalized federated learning. In: Proceedings of Advances in Neural Information Processing Systems (NeurIPS) (2020)
7. He, C., Annavaram, M., Avestimehr, S.: Group knowledge transfer: federated learning of large CNNs at the edge. In: Proceedings of Advances in Neural Information Processing Systems (NeurIPS) (2020)
8. He, C., Annavaram, M., Avestimehr, S.: Towards non-IID and invisible data with FEDNAS: federated deep learning via neural architecture search. arXiv preprint arXiv:2004.08546 (2020)
9. He, K., Zhang, X., Ren, S., Sun, J.: Deep residual learning for image recognition. In: Proceedings of Conference on Computer Vision and Pattern Recognition (CVPR) (2016)
10. Howard, A., et al.: Searching for MobileNetV3. In: Proceedings of International Conference on Computer Vision (ICCV) (2019)
11. Howard, A., Zhmoginov, A., Chen, L.-C., Sandler, M., Zhu, M.: Inverted residuals and linear bottlenecks: Mobile networks for classification, detection and segmentation. In: Proceedings of Conference on Computer Vision and Pattern Recognition (CVPR) (2018)
12. Huang, Y., et al.: Personalized cross-silo federated learning on non-IID data. In: Proceedings of AAAI Conference on Artificial Intelligence (AAAI) (2021)
13. Karimireddy, S.P., Kale, S., Mohri, M., Reddi, S.J., Stich, S.U., Suresh, A.T.: SCAFFOLD: stochastic controlled averaging for federated learning. In: Proceedings of International Conference on Machine Learning (ICML) (2020)
14. Krizhevsky, A., Hinton, G.: Learning multiple layers of features from tiny images. Master's thesis, Department of Computer Science, University of Toronto (2009)
15. Li, D., Wang, J.: FedMD: heterogenous federated learning via model distillation (2019)

16. Li, Q., Diao, Y., Chen, Q., He, B.: Federated learning on non-IID data silos: an experimental study. In: Proceedings of IEEE International Conference on Data Engineering (2022)
17. Li, T., Sahu, A.K., Zaheer, M., Sanjabi, M., Talwalkar, A., Smith, V.: Federated optimization in heterogeneous networks. In: Proceedings of Conference on Machine Learning and Systems (MLSys) (2020)
18. Lin, T., Kong, L., Stich, S.U., Jaggi, M.: Ensemble distillation for robust model fusion in federated learning. Adv. Neural. Inf. Process. Syst. **33**, 2351–2363 (2020)
19. McMahan, H.B., Moore, E., Ramage, D., Hampson, S., Arcas, B.A.: Communication-efficient learning of deep networks from decentralized data. In: Proceedings of International Conference on Artificial Intelligence and Statistics (AISTATS) (2017)
20. Munoz, J.P., Lyalyushkin, N., Akhauri, Y., Senina, A., Kozlov, A., Jain, N.: Enabling NAS with automated super-network generation. CoRR, abs/2112.10878 (2021)
21. Seo, H., Park, J., Oh, S., Bennis, M., Kim, S.-L.: Federated Knowledge Distillation. Machine Learning and Wireless Communications, p. 457 (2022)
22. Sui, D., Chen, Y., Zhao, J., Jia, Y., Xie, Y., Sun, W.: FedED: federated learning via ensemble distillation for medical relation extraction. In: Proceedings of Conference on Empirical Methods in Natural Language Processing (EMNLP) (2020)
23. Wang, J., Liu, Q., Liang, H., Joshi, G., Poor, H.V.: Tackling the objective inconsistency problem in heterogeneous federated optimization. In: Proceedings of Advances in Neural Information Processing Systems (NeurIPS) (2020)
24. Wu, C., Wu, F., Lyu, L., Huang, Y., Xie, X.: Communication-efficient federated learning via knowledge distillation (2022)
25. Xu, M., Zhao, Y., Bian, K., Huang, G., Mei, Q., Liu, X.: Federated neural architecture search. arXiv preprint arXiv:2002.06352 (2020)
26. Yu, S., et al.: SPATL: salient parameter aggregation and transfer learning for heterogeneous federated learning. In: Proceedings of the International Conference for High Performance Computing, Networking, Storage and Analysis (SC) (2022)
27. Yu, S., Nguyen, P., Anwar, A., Jannesari, A.: Adaptive dynamic pruning for non-IID federated learning. arXiv preprint arXiv:2106.06921 (2021)
28. Yu, T., Bagdasaryan, E., Shmatikov, V.: Salvaging federated learning by local adaptation. arXiv preprint arXiv:2002.04758 (2020)
29. Zhang, M., Sapra, K., Fidler, S., Yeung, S., Alvarez, J.M.: Personalized federated learning with first order model optimization. In: Proceedings of International Conference on Learning Representations (ICLR) (2021)
30. Zhang, Y., Xiang, T., Hospedales, T.M. Lu,, H.: Deep mutual learning. In: Proceedings of Conference on Computer Vision and Pattern Recognition (CVPR) (2018)

Author Index

A

Abbas, Qasim   III-88
Ahmed, Nesreen   I-121
Ait-Salaht, Farah   I-283
Alcaraz, Jordi   I-18
Anderson, Daniel   III-103
Angersbach, Richard   III-240
Araujo, Guido   III-167
Atoofian, Ehsan   II-196

B

Baboulin, Marc   III-31
Badia, Rosa M.   III-225
Bandet, Alexis   I-137
Bauinger, Christoph   I-33
Beaumont, Olivier   I-225
Bhattacharjee, Arijit   I-121
Binder, Walter   III-400
Blomer, Jakob   II-18
Blott, Michaela   II-121
Boddu, Sharon   III-134
Boehme, David   I-107
Boito, Francieli   I-137
Bombieri, Nicola   III-74
Bouzel, Rémi   I-225
Brunet, Elisabeth   I-77
Busato, Federico   III-74
Byna, Suren   II-182

C

Caday, Peter   I-47
Calderon-Mateos, Alejandro   II-62
Camarmas-Alonso, Diego   II-62
Canon, Louis-Claude   I-195
Carastan-Santos, Danilo   I-152
Carissimi, Alexandre   II-211
Carneiro, Tiago   III-386
Carretero, Jesus   II-62
Castelló, Adrián   II-377
Castro, Maria C. S.   III-298
Catalán, Sandra   II-377

César, Eduardo   I-18
Chen, Bin   III-196
Chen, Jiageng   III-212
Chen, Le   I-121
Chen, Pin   I-313
Chen, Yifan   III-342
Chen, YuAng   III-356
Chen, Zhe   I-269
Cheng, Yuanhu   II-77
Chitty-Venkata, Krishna Teja   II-317
Claver, José M.   III-327
Conejero, Javier   III-225
Costa, Jessé   III-167
Cruz, N.C.   III-270
Cui, Yangguang   II-408
Cui, Yongquan   II-274

D

Da Costa, Georges   I-152
Dai, Tuo   I-61
Dang, Haoran   II-346
de la Rosa, Miguel Sánchez   II-242
de Wolff, Ivo Gabe   III-103
Deng, Quan   II-77
Diamantopoulos, Georgios   III-255
Ding, Zhijun   I-329
Donfack, Simplice   III-31
Du, Jiangsu   I-313
Dugois, Anthony   I-195
Dutta, Akash   I-18

E

Eedi, Hemalatha   III-312
Elis, Bengisu   I-107
Ellis, Marquita   I-180
Emani, Murali   II-317
Engan, Kjersti   I-210
Escudero-Sahuquillo, Jesús   II-242
Esfahani, Mohsen Koohi   III-88
Eyraud-Dubois, Lionel   I-225

F

Fagnon, Vincent I-343
Fan, Dongrui II-91, II-302, II-346
Fan, Xiaokang III-371
Feng, Binbin I-329
Feng, Dan II-485
Feng, Guofeng III-182
Feng, Yixiao I-298
Fernandes, Luiz Gustavo III-400
Filipovič, Jiří I-18
Fiorin, Leandro II-167

G

Gao, Chaochen II-424
Gao, Yue I-269
Garcia, Pedro J. II-242
Garcia-Carballeira, Felix II-62
Garcia-Pineda, Miguel III-327
Gavin, Alex II-182
Ge, Zhen III-371
Giugno, Rosalba III-74
Gomez-Lopez, Gabriel II-242
Graillat, Stef III-17
Griebler, Dalvan III-400
Grosso, Paola I-210
Guo, Zhuoqiang III-182
Gutiérrez-Aguado, Juan III-327

H

Hafezan, Mohammad II-196
Hahnfeld, Jonas II-18
Han, Dengke II-91
Han, Jizhong II-424
Han, Yoonsang III-3
Harutyunyan, Suren I-18
Hasabnis, Niranjan I-121
He, Xiaowei II-77
He, Zhezhi II-107
Hegeman, Steef II-226
Helbecque, Guillaume III-386
Heldens, Stijn I-91
Henry, Greg I-47
Hiraga, Kohei II-439
Hou, Rui II-32
Howland, Sylvia II-317
Hu, Songlin II-424
Hu, Yuchong II-485
Hua, Zhengchang III-255
Huang, Chun III-371

Huang, Dan I-313
Huang, Jun II-454
Huang, Kejie II-137
Huang, Libo II-77
Huang, Tsung-Wei III-151
Huang, Zhuoyao III-255

I

Igual, Francisco D. II-377
Izri, Nora I-283

J

Jahadi, Reza II-196
Jannesari, Ali I-18, I-121, I-389
Jézéquel, Fabienne III-17
Jia, Jie III-342
Jia, Weile III-182
Jiang, Jiazhi I-313
Jiang, Li II-107
Jiang, Xuyan I-357
Jin, Cheqing I-373
Jin, Zhou III-182
Jing, Naifeng II-107

K

Kanwal, Neel I-210
Kao, Odej II-362
Kaya, Oguz III-31
Kayraklioglu, Engin III-386
Keller, Gabriele K. III-103
Kenter, Tobias II-121
Khan, Maleq III-134
Kindratenko, Volodymyr I-180
Kokkila-Schumacher, Sara I-180
Kollegger, Thorsten II-18
Korkmaz, Esragul I-225
Köstler, Harald III-240
Kothapalli, Kishore III-312
Kuckuk, Sebastian III-240

L

Laarman, Alfons II-226
Lagadec, Pierre-Axel II-242
Lan, Haocheng II-288
Lee, Eunji III-3
Li, Huawei II-259
Li, Liujia I-166
Li, Mingzhen III-182
Li, Pei III-212

Li, Ruixuan II-424
Li, Xiaowei II-3, II-259
Li, Xing II-107
Li, Yuhang II-408
Liang, Xiaoyao II-107
Liao, Jianxin II-454
Liao, Yunkun II-3, II-259
Lin, Dian-Lun III-151
Lin, Fang III-342
Lin, Hanyue II-259
Lin, Quanwei I-269
Lin, Yibing I-329
Lingas, Andrzej III-45
Liu, Dazheng III-283
Liu, Deyin I-313
Liu, Rulin I-357
Liu, Tao II-393
Liu, Tingkai I-180
Liu, Tong II-408
Liu, Wenhao I-269
Liu, Wenjuan III-283
Liu, Xin II-302
Liu, Yanke III-342
Liu, Yi III-342
Liu, Yuxue II-485
Liu, Zhibing II-424
Löff, Júnior III-400
Long, Sifan III-371
Lorenzon, Arthur II-211
Lu, Rongwei III-196
Lu, Songfeng II-274, II-332
Lu, Weijia II-408
Lu, Wenyan II-3, II-259
Lu, Yicheng I-180
Lu, Yutong I-313
Lu, Zhi II-274, II-332
Lucarelli, Giorgio I-343
Luo, Guojie I-61
Luo, Handong I-269
Luo, Jiajun III-196
Luo, Yingwei I-166
Lupión, M. III-270
Lurati, Milo I-91
Lv, Jiguang II-393
Lv, Mingtai I-298
Lyashevsky, Alexander I-47

M
Maltempi, Thiago III-167
Man, Dapeng II-393

Marchal, Loris I-195
Martínez, Héctor II-377
Mary, Theo III-17, III-31
Mei, Hengquan I-239
Melab, Nouredine III-386
Melo, Alba C. M. A. III-298
Meng, Dan II-32
Meyer, Marius II-121
Miguel, Joshua San III-151
Mikina, Filip I-254
Molina, Roméo III-17
Mongandampulath Akathoott, Anju I-3
Moon, Gordon Euhyun III-3
Mukunoki, Daichi III-17
Muñoz, J. Pablo I-389
Muñoz-Muñoz, Dario II-62

N
Naman, Pranjal II-470
Nasre, Rupesh I-3
Nassyr, Stepan II-47
Navaux, Philippe O. A. II-211
Nie, Hewang II-274, II-332
Ning, Wanyi II-454
Nissim, Roy III-59

O
O'Brien, Kenneth II-121
Ogras, Umit III-151
Oliveira, Fábio II-211
Oren, Gal I-121
Ortigosa, P.M. III-270
Overton, Ian III-88

P
Pallez, Guillaume I-137
Panetta, Jairo II-211
Pearce, Olga I-107
Peña-Ortiz, Raúl III-327
Peng, Lin III-371
Peng, Shaoliang III-283
Pereira, Marcio III-167
Peri, Sathya III-312
Petit, Eric I-47
Petrica, Lucian II-121
Pilla, Laercio I-225
Pleiter, Dirk II-47
Plessl, Christian II-121
Poquet, Millian I-152

Q

Qi, Qi II-454
Qian, Jiahong II-288
Qiu, Kun I-269
Quan, Wei I-357
Quiles, Francisco J. II-242
Quintana-Ortí, Enrique S. II-377

R

Ramezanikebrya, Hamidreza II-152
Rapine, Christophe I-343
Rebai, Maher I-283
Ren, Xiaoli III-283
Rigo, Sandro III-167
Rigon, Pedro II-211
Ripeanu, Matei II-152
Robeyns, Matthieu III-31
Rodríguez-Sánchez, Rafael II-377
Romero, F. III-270
Romero, L.F. III-270
Rong, Chunming I-210
Rzadca, Krzysztof I-254

S

Sahu, Subhajit III-312
Salcedo-Navarro, Andoni III-327
Sanchez, Keegan II-182
Sardinha, Alexandre II-211
Sastry, Varuni Katti II-317
Schulz, Martin I-107
Schussler, Brenda II-211
Schwartz, Oded III-59
Sclocco, Alessio I-91
Seletskiy, Aleksei III-103
Shanmugavelu, Sanjif II-317
Shen, Haibin II-137
Shen, Jingran III-255
Shen, Wenfeng II-408
Shi, Bizhao I-61
Sikora, Anna I-18
Silva, Fabricio A. B. III-298
Silva, Helena S. I. L. III-298
Silva, Pedro M. II-211
Silvano, Cristina II-167
Simmhan, Yogesh II-470
Song, Jiajun III-196
Song, Zhuoran II-107
Spiga, Filippo II-211
Spiizer, Yuval III-59

Stolf, Patricia I-152
Su, Teng II-288
Sui, Bingcai II-77
Sun, Guangzhong I-239
Sun, Guichu II-77
Sun, Haifeng II-454
Sun, Jingwei I-239
Sun, Ninghui III-182
Sun, Peng I-239
Sun, Zhigang I-357

T

Taboada, Hugo I-77
Tan, Guangming III-182
Tan, Hongbing II-77
Tang, Haibo I-373
Tang, Tao III-371
Tang, Xuehai II-424
Tao, Huili I-180
Tatebe, Osamu II-439
Tatu, Cristian Cătălin III-225
Theodoropoulos, Georgios III-255
Tian, Wenhong II-288
Trahay, François I-77
Trystram, Denis I-152
Tsigas, Philippas III-119
Tziritas, Nikos III-255

V

Van Kempen, Alexandre I-225
Van Lanker, Lucas I-77
van Werkhoven, Ben I-91
Vandierendonck, Hans III-88
Vázquez-Novoa, Fernando III-225
Vishwanath, Venkatram II-317
Vo, Vy I-121
von Geijer, Kåre III-119

W

Wang, Chuhui II-137
Wang, Hongyu III-182
Wang, Jingyu II-454
Wang, Lin II-485
Wang, Mu II-332
Wang, Xiaolin I-166
Wang, Xingbin II-32
Wang, Yan II-32
Wang, Yongwen II-77
Wang, Yuandou I-210

Author Index

Wang, Zhenlin I-166
Wang, Zhi III-196
Wei, Jinhui I-313
Wei, Xinming I-61
Wiesner, Philipp II-362
Wijs, Anton II-226
Wittkopp, Thorsten II-362
Wöltgens, Daan II-226
Wu, Jianping III-283
Wu, Jianyu I-166
Wu, Jingya II-3, II-259
Wu, Junjun II-274
Wu, Kesheng II-182
Wu, Meng II-91, II-302, II-346
Wu, Xing II-424
Wu, Zhengda I-298

X

Xiao, Jue II-274, II-332
Xiao, Liquan II-77
Xiao, Renzhi II-485
Xie, Shuzhao III-196
Xie, Yuanlun II-288
Xu, Shuchun II-393
Xue, Runzhen II-91

Y

Yan, Guihai II-3, II-259
Yan, Mingyu II-91, II-302, II-346
Yan, Wei II-302
Yang, Canqun III-371
Yang, Qian I-357
Yang, Sining I-298
Yang, Wu II-393
Yang, Ziheng I-269
Yao, Shixiong III-212
Yao, Xiaojiao I-313
Yao, Yiming I-166
Ye, Xiaochun II-91, II-302, II-346

Ye, Zewen II-137
Yi, Zepu II-274, II-332
Yu, Jeffery Xu III-356
Yu, Sixing I-389
Yviquel, Hervé III-167

Z

Zhan, Xiaodong II-393
Zhang, Bo I-298
Zhang, Hongbin I-313
Zhang, Huan I-373
Zhang, Jing II-77
Zhang, Nan III-255
Zhang, Qi I-269
Zhang, Weigang II-424
Zhang, Xuan II-107
Zhang, Xuechen II-182
Zhang, Yuxiang II-302
Zhang, Zhao I-373
Zhang, Zhenyu I-373
Zhao, Juan III-283
Zhao, Tong III-182
Zhao, Zhiming I-210
Zheng, Zhong II-77
Zhou, Aoying I-373
Zhou, Biyu II-424
Zhou, Diyu I-166
Zhou, Guangyao II-288
Zhou, Xianlong III-212
Zhou, Zechun I-239
Zhu, Liren I-166
Zhu, Mengde II-454
Zhu, Wenjun I-269
Zhu, Zhongbo I-180
Zhuang, Zirui II-454
Ziche, Filippo III-74
Zou, Sunan I-61
Zubair, Mohammad I-33
Zuk, Pawel I-254

SPRINGER NATURE

GPSR Compliance

The European Union's (EU) General Product Safety Regulation (GPSR) is a set of rules that requires consumer products to be safe and our obligations to ensure this.

If you have any concerns about our products, you can contact us on ProductSafety@springernature.com

In case Publisher is established outside the EU, the EU authorized representative is:

Springer Nature Customer Service Center GmbH
Europaplatz 3
69115 Heidelberg, Germany

The manufacturer's authorised representative in the EU is Springer Nature Customer Service Centre GmbH, Europaplatz 3, 69115 Heidelberg, Germany. If you have any concerns regarding our products, please contact ProductSafety@springernature.com

Printed and bound by CPI Group (UK) Ltd, Croydon, CR0 4YY

25/03/2026

02078187-0018